THE ECOLOGY OF A TROPICAL FOREST

SEASONAL RHYTHMS AND LONG-TERM CHANGES

EDITED BY
EGBERT G. LEIGH, JR.,
A. STANLEY RAND, AND
DONALD M. WINDSOR

SECOND EDITION

© 1982, 1996 by the Smithsonian Institution

Library of Congress Cataloging-in-Publication Data

The Ecology of a tropical forest : seasonal rhythms and long-term
changes / edited by Egbert G. Leigh, Jr., A. Stanley Rand, and
Donald M. Windsor.
        p.   cm.
A project of the Smithsonian Tropical Research Institute.
Includes bibliographical references (p.   ).
ISBN 1-56098-642-5 (alk. paper)
   1. Forest ecology—Panama—Barro Colorado Island.
2. Seasons—Panama—Barro Colorado Island.   3. Biological
rhythms—Panama—Barro Colorado Island.   4. Barro Colorado
Island (Panama).   I. Leigh, Egbert Giles.   II. Rand, A. Stanley
(Austin Stanley), 1932–   .   III. Windsor, Donald M.
IV. Smithsonian Tropical Research Institute.
QH108.P3E26   1996
574.5'2642'0972875—dc20   96-6889

British Library Cataloguing-in-Publication Data available

Manufactured in the United States of America
02 01 00 99 98 97 96   6 5 4 3 2 1

♾ The paper used in this publication meets the minimum requirements of the American National Standard for Permanence
of Paper for Printed Library Materials Z39.48-1984.

Front cover: Vegetation of Barro Colorado Island. Adapted from
drawing by Marshall Hasbrouck on page 73 of this book. Cover
design by Kathleen Sims.

Contents

Contributors

The contributors to this volume are listed below, in alphabetical order by last name, along with their most recent mailing addresses. Contributors' addresses at the time the research results were submitted for the first edition appear at the heads of the articles. The addresses of some authors (those marked with an asterisk*) could not be verified for the second edition.

Robin M. Andrews
Department of Biology
Virginia Polytechnic Institute and State University
Blacksburg, VA 24061, USA

Carol K. Augspurger
Department of Plant Biology
University of Illinois
Urbana, IL 61801, USA

Nicholas V. L. Brokaw
Manomet Bird Observatory
Box 1770
Manomet, MA 02345, USA

Milton Clark
Apartado 6-6048
El Dorado, Republic of Panama

Phyllis D. Coley
Department of Biology
University of Utah
Salt Lake City, UT 84112, USA

William E. Dietrich
Department of Geology and Geophysics
University of California
Berkeley, CA 94720, USA

Thomas Dunne
Department of Geology
University of Washington
Seattle, WA 98195, USA

Robin B. Foster
Smithsonian Tropical Research Institute
Apartado 2072
Balboa, Republic of Panama

Nigel Franks
School of Biological Sciences
University of Bath
Claverton Down
Bath BA2 7AY, UK

Jeffery W. Froehlich
Department of Anthropology
University of New Mexico
Albuquerque, NM 87131, USA

Nancy C. Garwood
Botany Department
The Natural History Museum
Cromwell Road
London SW7 5BD, UK

Jacalyn Giacalone
Great Ideas in Science Consortium
College of Science and Mathematics
Montclair State University
Upper Montclair, NJ 07043, USA

William E. Glanz
Department of Zoology
University of Maine
Orono, ME 04469, USA

Judy Gradwohl
Office of Environmental Awareness
International Center
Smithsonian Institution
Washington, DC 20560, USA

Russell Greenberg
Smithsonian Migratory Bird Center
National Zoological Park
Washington, DC 20008, USA

Lawrence R. Heaney
Field Museum of Natural History
Roosevelt Road at Lake Shore Drive
Chicago, IL 60605, USA

Henry F. Howe
Department of Biological Sciences
University of Illinois at Chicago Circle
Chicago, IL 60680, USA

James R. Karr
Institute for Environmental Studies
University of Washington
Seattle, WA 98195, USA

Egbert G. Leigh, Jr.
Smithsonian Tropical Research Institute
Apartado 2072
Balboa, Republic of Panama

Sally C. Levings
Post Office Box 97
Sopchoppy, FL 32358, USA

Katharine Milton
Department of Anthropology
University of California
Berkeley, CA 94720, USA

John R. Oppenheimer
Environmental Science Program
The College of Staten Island
Staten Island, NY 10314, USA

Francis E. Putz
Department of Botany
University of Florida
Gainesville, FL 32611, USA

A. Stanley Rand
Smithsonian Tropical Research Institute
Apartado 2072
Balboa, Republic of Panama

William M. Rand
Department of Community Health
Tufts University School of Medicine
136 Harrison Avenue
Boston, MA 02111, USA

R. Rudran
Research Building
National Zoological Park
Washington, DC 20008, USA

*James K. Russell
Department of Zoology
University of North Carolina
Chapel Hill, NC 27599, USA

Douglas W. Schemske
Department of Botany
University of Washington
Seattle, WA 98195, USA

Neal G. Smith
Smithsonian Tropical Research Institute
Apartado 2072
Balboa, Republic of Panama

Nicholas Smythe
Smithsonian Tropical Research Institute
Apartado 2072
Balboa, Republic of Panama

*Bernice Tannenbaum
Portland, Oregon, USA

*A. Tarak
Buenos Aires, Argentina

Richard W. Thorington, Jr.
Division of Mammals
National Museum of Natural History
Smithsonian Institution
Washington, DC 20560, USA

Catherine A. Toft
Department of Zoology
University of California
Davis, CA 95616, USA

Donald M. Windsor
Smithsonian Tropical Research Institute
Apartado 2072
Balboa, Republic of Panama

Henk Wolda
Smithsonian Tropical Research Institute
Apartado 2072
Balboa, Republic of Panama

Andrea Worthington
Department of Biology
Siena College
Loudonville, NY 12211, USA

Preface to the Second Edition

This second edition has an additional chapter, an epilogue describing research that is relevant to the book's themes and has been published since 1979, when manuscripts were submitted for the first edition. The rest of the book remains unchanged from the first edition, except for the correction of typographical errors and the updating of addresses in the list of contributors. The epilogue deals only with work done on Barro Colorado Island, to avoid repeating material from another book I am writing, which will set the biology of Barro Colorado in a wider context. Even with this limitation, I cannot help reflecting on studies of singular beauty and interest that otherwise go unmentioned in this volume.

Since the first edition of this volume was published, several works on related topics have appeared. John Terborgh (1983) described the ecology of the Parque Nacional Manú of Amazonian Peru. This park could be called our "sister station": Of all the major research sites in the tropics, its climate and flora are most like those of Barro Colorado. Moreover, the studies in the Manú, like those on Barro Colorado, have largely been motivated by the desire to understand the ecology of mammals, birds, and plants.

Two books have come from the Organization for Tropical Studies: *Costa Rican Natural History*, edited by Daniel Janzen (1983), and *La Selva*, edited by Lucinda McDade and others (1994). *Four Neotropical Forests*, edited by the late Alwyn Gentry (1990), provides further information on La Selva, Barro Colorado, the Manú, and the forest of central Amazonia north of Manaus. C. F. Jordan (1989) edited a book on the nutrient-starved forests of San Carlos de Rio Negro, which is in the catchment of a blackwater "river of hunger" (cf. Sponsel and Loya, 1991): a more succinct account of these forests is given by E. Medina and E. Cuevas (1989).

The preface to the first edition failed to mention P. Charles-Dominique's (1977) book on the ecology of nocturnal primates in Gabon, which gives some idea of the understanding French biologists (helped by Emmons, 1980) have obtained of the exceedingly interesting African rainforest near Makokou. Also unmentioned was a book on the nocturnal lemurs of the fascinating dry forest in western Madagascar (Charles-Dominique et al., 1980). Another work on Africa has just appeared: *Serengeti II,* edited by A. R. E. Sinclair and P. Arcese (1995). The Serengeti is not rainforest; nonetheless *Serengeti* by Sinclair and M. Norton-Griffiths (1979) is perhaps the best book on tropical ecosystems I know, founded as it is on a deep knowledge of the plants and vertebrates of the Serengeti and how they interact.

In 1990 a Spanish edition of *The Ecology of a Tropical Forest* appeared (Leigh, Rand, and Windsor, 1990). This was a new edition, not just a translation: five papers were revised and expanded, three new ones added, and one replaced, while supplements were added to two others. After it appeared, I learned of two other Spanish-language books, one on the cloud forest at Rancho Grande, Venezuela (Huber, 1986), and one on a plot in Cuba's Sierra del Rosario (Herrera et al., 1988).

How I wish there were comparable books to cite for tropical forest ecosystems in Africa, Asia, and Madagascar, not to mention other sites in the Neotropics! French researchers have done enough work in French Guiana and Gabon to fill good books on both sites. Many other tropical forests await books that will make their wonders known to a wider public: the Ituri forest of Zaire, which shelters the mysterious okapi (Hart and Hart, 1992) and a legendary people of the forest (Turnbull, 1961); the reserve of Analamazaotra in east-central Madagascar, which resounds each morning with the whistling whoops of the babacottos, Madagascar's largest living lemurs (Ganzhorn, 1988, 1989); and many a dipterocarp forest of Malesia, home of the fabled durian (Corner, 1954) and some extraordinary animals (Chivers, 1980; Leighton and Leighton, 1983). Tropical forests differ wonderfully from one another, so that the analysis of one without reference to others confers very limited understanding.

I am most grateful to Robert F. Stallard, S. Joseph Wright, E. Allen Herre, A. Stanley Rand, Stephen Hubbell, and Lucinda McDade for helpful and instructive comments on the epilogue added to this edition. I am also indebted to Michael Keller, Robert Stallard, John Barone, Richard Condit, Suzanne Loo de Lao, and John Nason for access to unpublished data and conclusions. Most of all, I thank the students of Barro Colorado for providing me with so rich a story; the responsibility of doing justice to it is sobering.

Egbert Giles Leigh, Jr.
Trinity Sunday, 1995

LITERATURE CITED

Charles-Dominique, P.
1977.   *Ecology and Behavior of Nocturnal Primates.* New York: Columbia University Press.

Charles-Dominique, P., H. M. Cooper, A. Hladik, C. M. Hladik, E. Pages, et al.
1980.   *Nocturnal Malagasy Primates.* New York: Academic Press.

Chivers, D. J. (ed.)
1980.   *Malayan Forest Primates.* New York: Plenum Press.

Corner, E. J. H.
1954.   The Evolution of Tropical Forest. Pages 34–46 in *Evolution as a Process,* edited by J. S. Huxley, A. C. Hardy, and E. B. Ford. London: Allen and Unwin.

Emmons, L. H.
1980.   Ecology and Resource Partitioning among Nine Species of African Rain Forest Squirrels. *Ecological Monographs,* 50:31–54.

Ganzhorn, J. U.
1988.   Food Partitioning among Malagasy Primates. *Oecologia,* 75:436–450.
1989.   Niche Separation of Seven Lemur Species in the Eastern Rainforest of Madagascar. *Oecologia,* 79:279–286.

Gentry, A. H. (ed.)
1990.   *Four Neotropical Rainforests.* New Haven: Yale University Press.

Hart, T. B., and J. A. Hart
1992.   Between Sun and Shadow. *Natural History,* 101 (11): 28–35.

Herrera, R. A., L. Menéndez, M. F. Rodriguez, and E. E. Garcia (eds.)
1988.   *Ecología de los bosques siempreverdes de la Sierra del Rosario, Cuba.* Montevideo, Uruguay: UNESCO-ROSTLAC.

Huber, O. (ed.)
1986.   *La selva nublada de Rancho Grande: Parque Nacional "Henri Pittier."* Caracas: Fondo Editorial, Acta Científica Venezolana.

Janzen, D. H. (ed.)
1983.   *Costa Rican Natural History.* Chicago: University of Chicago Press.

Jordan, C. F. (ed.)
1989.   *An Amazonian Rain Forest.* Paris: UNESCO; Carnforth, U.K.: Parthenon Publishing.

Leigh, E. G., Jr., A. S. Rand, and D. M. Windsor (eds.)
1990.   *Ecología de un bosque tropical: Ciclos estacionales y cambios de largo plazo.* Balboa, Panama: Smithsonian Tropical Research Institute.

Leighton, M., and D. R. Leighton
1983.   Vertebrate Responses to Fruiting Seasonality within a Bornean Rain Forest. Pages 181–196 in *Tropical Rain Forest: Ecology and Management,* edited by S. L. Sutton, T. C. Whitmore, and A. C. Chadwick. Oxford, U.K.: Blackwell Scientific Publications.

McDade, L. A., K. S. Bawa, H. A. Hespenheide, and G. S. Hartshorn
1994.   *La Selva: Ecology and Natural History of a Neotropical Rain Forest.* Chicago: University of Chicago Press.

Medina, E., and E. Cuevas
1989.   Patterns of Nutrient Accumulation and Release in Amazonian Forests of the Upper Rio Negro Basin. Pages 217–240 in *Mineral Nutrients in Tropical Forest and Savanna Ecosystems,* edited by J. Proctor. Oxford, U.K.: Blackwell Scientific Publications.

Sinclair, A. R. E., and P. Arcese (eds.)
1995.   *Serengeti II: Dynamics, Management, and Conservation of an Ecosystem.* Chicago: University of Chicago Press.

Sinclair, A. R. E., and M. Norton-Griffiths (eds.)
1979.   *Serengeti: Dynamics of an Ecosystem.* Chicago: University of Chicago Press.

Sponsel, L. E., and P. C. Loya
1991.   Rivers of Hunger? Indigenous Resource Management in the Oligotrophic Ecosystems of the Rio Negro, Venezuela. Pages 435–446 in *Tropical Forests, People and Food,* edited by C. M. Hladik, A. Hladik, O. F. Linares, H. Pagezy, A. Semple, and M. Hadley. Paris: UNESCO; Carnforth, U.K.: Parthenon Publishing.

Terborgh, J.
1983.   *Five New World Primates: A Study in Comparative Ecology.* Princeton: Princeton University Press.

Turnbull, C. M.
1961.   *The Forest People.* London: Chatto and Windus.

Preface to the First Edition

Many of the papers in this book were contributed by individuals who have worked in Barro Colorado Island as graduate students or postdoctoral fellows, and others were contributed by the scientific staff of the Smithsonian Tropical Research Institute. To all the authors, we are most grateful. Many of them put extraordinary effort into their papers; many showed a generosity seldom witnessed by symposium editors, in providing sufficient material for a rounded picture rather than safeguarding some of it for future papers.

This book would not have been written without the stimulus and assistance of the Smithsonian Institution's Environmental Sciences Program, which financed environmental monitoring on Barro Colorado Island and in other areas. The tropical monitoring program was organized by A. Stanley Rand, and he was its first coordinator, succeeded in 1979 by Donald M. Windsor. Few of the papers included here represent projects sponsored by the monitoring program. This program, however, provided the background data which sets all these papers in perspective, and thereby stimulated the writing of many of them. It also provided small but essential amounts of financial aid for a large number of these projects. Through Windsor, the program made possible many of the relevant computations and analyses of data, and it contributed to the purchase of a word processor on which the final drafts of all the papers and the earlier drafts of many were typed. Roberta Rubinoff and Windsor edited annual compilations of the data collected by the program, thereby greatly enhancing their accessibility.

We are also grateful to Nicholas Smythe, who was responsible for organizing and executing the monitoring program on Barro Colorado Island; to Miguel Estribí and Gary Stump, whose duties included collecting insects; keeping track of the varieties of fruiting figs; marking, weighing, and releasing the (often very annoyed) animals they found in their live-traps; checking instruments; and building a 138-foot tower; to Benjamin Morgan, who built the weir; and to Bonifacio de León, who so delights in this forest, who discovers the sloth and the silky anteater almost immediately upon request, and whose discerning eye we count upon for the phenology census.

A. Stanley Rand "commissioned" the book and put Egbert G. Leigh, Jr., in charge of the project. Leigh and Rand decided what papers to invite. Leigh edited the papers for organization, clarity of presentation, and scope, trying to fashion them, as much as possible, into a unified book, and he wrote the introductory material. Windsor and Rand edited the papers for accuracy of argument, and Windsor also assisted greatly with clarifying and reorganizing tables and figures.

The editors considered it no part of their business to eliminate contradictions between papers, even when they had an opinion as to who was "right"; it would suit our ignorance of tropical forest very ill indeed to attempt to promulgate a unified and harmonized body of dogma about it. Thus some of the papers contradict each other on specific points. More often than not, at least one of the authors involved in such a contradiction presents enough data to allow readers to form their own opinions.

The director of the Smithsonian Tropical Research Institute, Ira Rubinoff, and the acting director, Michael Robinson, encouraged the project and arranged for the preparation of final copy at a time when typing assistance was at a premium for the Institute as a whole.

We are very grateful to Arilla Kourany, who prepared the final draft of the book and earlier drafts of most of the papers, checked all the tables and figures, and discovered many errors and difficulties the editors overlooked. If, indeed, we have brought order out of chaos, she has had a great deal to do with it. Hazel Mackenzie and DeLoris Highsmith also assisted with the typing.

Egbert G. Leigh, Jr.
1982

Introduction

EGBERT G. LEIGH, JR.   Smithsonian Tropical Research Institute, Balboa, Republic of Panama

GENERAL REMARKS

This book is devoted to the ecology of Barro Colorado Island. Its primary emphasis is on interactions: the relationships between plants and the animals that eat them, pollinate their flowers, and disperse their seeds; the means by which different animals obtain food and avoid being eaten; and the mechanisms by which different animal populations are regulated. A primary tool for deciphering these interactions is to study the responses of different components of the forest community to seasonal changes in the physical environment, and the resultant changes in food supply and abundance of predators. This book is by no means a complete review of the work done on Barro Colorado, and it contains some chapters on work done off the island, but it attempts as representative a survey as our knowledge permits of those processes that play an important role in the ecological organization of the forest community there.

The two most complete previous studies of tropical forest ecosystems are *A Tropical Rain Forest*, Odum and Pigeon's (1970) study of the ecosystem at El Verde, Puerto Rico, and volume 30, part 2 (1978) of the *Malayan Nature Journal*, which contains reports from an unusually well-balanced International Biological Programme devoted to the dipterocarp forest and its animal community at Pasoh Reserve, Malaysia. Both these volumes emphasize forest production and nutrient budgets more than we do. The studies at Pasoh also have far more to say than we do about both the modes and the rates of decomposition of dead plant material, ranging from fallen leaves to fallen trees; indeed, the lack of knowledge about the manner, speed, and completeness of nutrient recycling is perhaps the most serious hole in the picture we will present of the ecology of Barro Colorado Island. On the other hand, this book will have far more to say than its predecessors about the various relations between the forest and its animals, especially its vertebrates. In this respect, our book will more nearly resemble the volume edited by Sinclair and Norton-Griffiths (1979) on the Serengeti ecosystem, with its emphasis on how climate and other physical factors affect the relation between the vegetation, its consumers, and their predators, and its explicit interest in the modes of regulation of vertebrate populations.

BACKGROUND

Barro Colorado is an island which was isolated from the surrounding mainland in 1914, after the Chagres River was dammed to form Gatun Lake, the central portion of the Panama Canal. Ninety minutes by train and boat from Panama City, Barro Colorado's accessibility, its protected location in Gatun Lake, and its comfortable, amply subsidized facilities have allowed it to become perhaps the best-studied 1500 ha. of tropical forest to be found anywhere in the world.

From 1916 onward, naturalists, students of animal behavior, and the occasional quantitative ecologist were already beginning to visit the island. Thanks to the efforts of Thomas Barbour, a biologist of independent means, and James Zetek, a local entomologist who was to run the field station at Barro Colorado for 33 years, the island was declared a reserve in 1923. In 1946, it was placed under the jurisdiction of the Smithsonian Institution. In 1957, Martin Moynihan, an ethologist, was appointed director: he began to build up mainland facilities and a scientific staff for what in 1966 was to become the Smithsonian Tropical Research Institute. Thanks to the new staff, increased interest from visitors, and an influx of graduate students and postdoctoral fellows financed by a timely Smithsonian educational program, the tempo of the research on Barro Colorado accelerated considerably in the 1960s.

Moynihan's appointments largely shaped the directions of research on Barro Colorado. He never tried to organize or finance team research, nor did he ever seek to direct the work of his appointees: instead, he expected them to work out their own ideas with no interference and a minimum of technical assistance. Yet the work of these appointees and their students provides a remarkably coherent picture of the ecology of this island. One of Moynihan's predoctoral fellows had a remarkable gift for showing others how easily one could identify tropical plants. He also elucidated some of the rhythms of flowering, fruiting, and leaf flush of the different plants on the island, showed how these contributed to a seasonal rhythm of the forest as a whole, and observed how interruption of this rhythm could devastate the animal community. Other predoctoral fellows, appointed at nearly the same time, began to study how the seasonal rhythms in supply of fruit and new leaves were reflected by seasonal changes in hunger, trappability, foraging and competitive behavior, and mortality of animals that depended on these items for food. Finally, Moynihan appointed a senior postdoctoral fellow, whose studies on how different animals, fungi, and microbes assist in breaking down dead plants into the nutrients that allow new life to rise from the ashes of the old, were interrupted by death from leukemia. These three themes—the rhythms of plant production; the effects of these rhythms on frugivores, folivores, and some of their predators; and the nature of the community supported by the decomposing litter of the forest floor—will occupy much of this book.

The interests of the scientific staff of the Smithsonian Tropical Research Institute have extended far beyond the island, and responsibilities unconnected with research are increasing. As a result, more and more of the research on Barro Colorado Island is being done by graduate students and postdoctoral fellows visiting for one or two years. They have the freedom to concentrate on their favored animals or plants for over a year, which allows them to learn how their organisms respond to the rhythms of the forest. These students are sufficiently numerous, and their backgrounds and interests are sufficiently diverse, that they largely educate each other. Much of this work has been financed by the Smithsonian Office of Academic Programs and by the National Science Foundation dissertation improvement program: without these two programs, our knowledge of the island would be far poorer.

If the reactions of animals to the seasonal rhythms of the forest are so informative, their reactions to yearly variations in these rhythms should be even more so. In 1971, A. Stanley Rand and Nicholas Smythe, financed by the Smithsonian Environmental Sciences Program, organized a monitoring program on Barro Colorado Island, keeping records of rainfall, wind, temperature, runoff, the times of leafing, fruiting and flowering in a few selected trees, the catches of insects at light-traps, and the catches of mammals in live-traps. At first, the program's primary goal was to test MacArthur's (1972) proposition that stabler environments support more diverse faunas, by comparing the effect of environmental variation on plant populations and their animal consumers in a tropical forest and on a tropical reef flat with its effects in a temperate forest and a neighboring brackish estuary. This goal, however, was too amorphous; we knew too little about the inner workings of these communities to decide which aspects of "environmental variation" were relevant and worth measuring. Moreover, too schematically comparative a program would have made it difficult to win the necessary knowledge; each community needed to be studied individually, on its own terms. So the environmental monitoring program on Barro Colorado became in theory what it had already been in fact: a program to learn how the forest community is organized from the responses of various of its members to changes in abundance of food or predators and to exigencies of the weather. The program was not without problems. Directed or coordinated research was new to Barro Colorado and accorded ill with its traditions of untrammelled independence. Moreover, before Donald Windsor put its data processing in order, the program nearly choked on the superabundance of its records. However, the skimpy financing of the program, which prevented us from collecting as much data as we would have liked, thereby forced us to think more carefully about what was most appropriate to measure and prevented us from accumulating too spectacular a surfeit of data. In the end, the background data provided by this monitoring program, and the specific studies it has financed to plug gaps in our knowledge, has contributed materially to the coherence of our understanding of the ecology of Barro Colorado Island.

In short, the Smithsonian's facilities, Moynihan's appointments, the financing provided for graduate students by the Smithsonian and the National Science Foundation, and the framework of background information and supplemental studies provided by the Smithsonian Environmental Sciences Program have all contributed decisively to the picture set forth in this book.

ARGUMENT

Barro Colorado Island has a dry season strong enough to affect every feature of its community. Although it receives an average of over 2500 mm of rain a year, in more than half the years of record less than 100 mm fell during the first 3 months. Although Barro Colorado's dry season does not come nearly as close as a northern winter to bringing the life of the forest to a stop, many of the canopy trees of Barro Colorado do lose their leaves during the dry season, fewer insects are flying then, there is less activity among the decomposers of the forest floor, and few birds and mammals are breeding then. Late in an especially severe dry season the forest of Barro Colorado can look as leafless, from a distance, as a northern forest in November.

Yet, unlike true "dry forest" such as that in Guanacaste in Costa Rica, the forest here is tall and green enough that many mistake it for genuine rain forest, the sort of forest where there is never a regular season when the average monthly rainfall falls short of 10 cm, the monthly "potential evapotranspiration" normal for lowland rain forest. The responses of the plants of Barro Colorado to its seasonal climate imposes alternation of feast and famine on folivores, frugivores, and their predators, thereby making relationships of interdependence more obvious than they might be in a less seasonal setting. Yet it appears that in rain forest these relationships are not really very different. Complex as it is, Barro Colorado provides a simplified model that may help us understand the ecology of rain forest.

First we will consider the physical environment. A whole host of factors, such as humidity, radiation, and the like, bear decisively on the behavior of various kinds of animals, and the distributions of different species of plants are affected to an unknown but presumably important degree by an equal variety of such factors. We know a great deal less of these relationships than we would like.

If we focus on seasonal rhythms, however, and how they vary from one year to another, then rainfall emerges as the physical variable whose fluctuation is most decisive to the life of the forest. As we shall see, its influence on plants is apparently mediated primarily through its influence on the moisture content of the soil. Dietrich, Windsor, and Dunne describe general features of the climate, such as rainfall, temperature, humidity, radiation, and wind speed, and of the physical structure of the soil, and they discuss the relation between the intensity of the rainfall in a given storm, the moisture content of the soil, the rate at which water runs off the catchment, and the modes by which it comes to do so. They use this information to draw up a "water budget" for the 10-ha. Lutz catchment near the laboratory clearing, relating rainfall to runoff and soil moisture content, month by month. Then Rand and Rand describe the spatial distribution of rainfall on Barro Colorado and show how the seasonal rhythm in rainfall has changed from year to year over the past half century.

Next, we turn to the general features of the organic environment. Foster and Brokaw describe the vegetation of the island, showing that its flora is typical of fertile, moderately seasonal habitats. They discuss the differences in regeneration from various types of disturbance, ranging from the fall of an individual canopy tree to a landslip or an agricultural clearing, and they use this information, and inferences from old aerial photographs, to reconstruct the recent history of the island's vegetation. Half of its forest seems to have been disturbed rather little during the last three or four centuries, while the other half is recovering from widespread disturbance that seems to have been connected with the building of the French canal late in the nineteenth century. Thorington et al. observe that a hectare of forest on Barro Colorado carries an average of 57 species of trees over 60 cm in circumference. What maintains this diversity? It does not seem to be a matter of each preferring a different microhabitat. It had been believed that the more common a tree, the more it suffered from herbivory, but Thorington et al. find that distributions of many species of trees are clumped, as if herbivores do not "discriminate against the clumps."

Putz and Milton find that the average life expectancy of trees over 60 cm in circumference is 60 ± 11 years (mean $\pm$ 95% confidence interval), and that such trees are longer-lived in more mature forest, perhaps because they are made of stronger wood. Brokaw finds that roughly one gap of area over 20 sq. m is opened in the canopy per hectare of forest per year by falling trees, and that the size of such gaps averages 65 sq. m in the younger forest of the island and 90 sq. m in the more mature forest. These gaps are decisive to the pace of regeneration in this forest because many seedlings will germinate only in gaps over 100 sq. m in area, and it appears that the saplings of many other species will mature only if a tree's fall exposes them to full sun. One might expect this forest's diversity to be maintained in part by a tendency of different species to settle in gaps of different sizes, but Brokaw finds a distinction only between "pioneers," which colonize treefall gaps well over 100 sq. m in area, and "persistents," typical species of the mature forest, which colonize smaller gaps. The precise factors which limit pioneers to larger gaps, but which permit them to attain at least temporary dominance there, are not known.

We then turn to our primary concern, the seasonal rhythm of the forest and its animals. Each species of plant in the forest seems to have its own "phenological rhythm," its own schedule of leaf flush, leaffall, flowering, and fruiting; often enough, members of the same species differ in this respect. Very little is known of the mechanisms responsible for these different schedules, or the consequences for a species of following a particular phenological rhythm or a particular spectrum of phenological rhythms. Yet, when we view the forest as a whole, certain overriding rhythms are obvious. A massive flush of new leaves and a crescendo of flowering follows the first rains. This is by no means as dramatic as the onset of a northern temperate spring, when an abundance of leaves and flowers bursts forth from the bare forest floor, and then the trees leaf out, assuming a variety of muted colors before becoming fully green. After all, no season on Barro Colorado is as harsh as a northern winter, nor is dry season, itself a time of abundant flowers, quite as harsh as the late rainy season, when fruit, flowers, and new leaves are all in shortest supply. Yet, the onset of the rainy season does usher in a time of fatness for the forest's insects, and the birds and bats that eat them, a time of awakening for the decomposers of the forest floor, and the time of greatest fruitfall and seedling growth. As May wears on into October and November, sunlight decreases, flowering slows down, fewer new leaves appear, less fruit is available, and the late rainy season shortage is upon us. The shortage eases just when the dry season approaches, but can return in full vigor before the next rainy season begins.

Leigh and Windsor discuss the timing and amount of the fall of leaves, fruit, flowers, and twigs to the forest floor, and estimates how much fruit and foliage vertebrates eat and how much foliage insects eat, in order to calculate the forest's net production of leaves and fruit. Like other moist and wet lowland tropical forests the world around, including mangrove swamps, the forest on Barro Colorado produces roughly 8 tons dry weight of leaves per year, twice as much and more as do most temperate forests, even those whose wood production matches that of any forest in the tropics. We do not know what governs the production of tropical forest: there is, for example, no obvious correlation between soil fertility and wood production in mature tropical forests.

Coley finds that herbivores, mostly insects, may consume a fifth or more of the leaf production on Barro Colorado. She shows that young leaves are eaten vastly more rapidly than old and that leaves of "pioneer" plants, which can germinate and grow only in full sunlight, are eaten far more rapidly than those of plants that can germinate and persist in the shade. The preference of insects for new leaves must explain, at least in part, why the rhythm of leaf flush entails a rhythm of insect abundance.

Foster finds that on Barro Colorado Island flowering peaks after the onset of the rainy season, but that many plants flower at other times, particularly in the dry season, as if responding to various degrees of drought. Some plants produce showy flowers, some produce inconspicuous ones; some flower in a wave of synchrony, while others put out their flowers little by little. Some attract hummingbirds to pollinate their flowers, others attract bats, one even attracts opossums; some attract a specific insect as pollinator, while others seem to settle for any insect they can get. The reasons for all this diversity are not known. More work has been devoted to this problem in Costa Rica than on Barro Colorado, but most of this work treats pollination as an end in itself, and does not inquire how the mode of pollination or the means employed to secure it influences the number or quality of the fruit the plant disperses.

The understory shrub *Hybanthus* is the only plant on Barro Colorado whose flowering rhythm and pollination ecology has been studied with full panoply of experiment, but this study is a model of its kind. Augspurger shows that, after a drought, a hard rain stimulates a wave of synchronous flowering. She finds that shrubs in a clump must flower together to attract their pollinators. For this species, the ultimate advantage of synchronous flowering seems to be that synchronous fruiting satiates the caterpillars that would otherwise destroy the fruit. After all, synchronous flowering should be a means for fruiting appropriately.

Foster describes how, on Barro Colorado, fruiting peaks near the beginning of the rains, from April through June, and again in mid rainy season, from August through October; there is a severe shortage of fruit between November and February. Garwood, however, finds only a single peak of seedling germination; most seeds dispersed in the middle of the rainy season or later remain dormant until the onset of the following rainy season.

Many trees depend on animals to disperse their fruit. The variety of ways different tropical trees attract dispersers has long been a byword, but the ecological meaning of these differences is only beginning to receive serious attention. Few topics remind us more effectively of our abysmal ignorance of tropical ecology. To know the consequences of attracting a particular disperser, one may first have to ask how well seeds germinate and seedlings survive in different sorts of sites, and how survival is affected by distance from conspecific seedlings and adults. If so, one must then ask, not only how efficiently the disperser removes seeds from the parent tree, but how likely it is to carry seeds to suitable sites and disperse them in an appropriate manner. This is not an easy program.

Howe reasons that one might expect some species to attract a variety of opportunists through spectacular displays of great numbers of fruit, each one of no great value, while others, presumably with larger seeds, might attract specialized dispersers, which trouble to seek out and return to sources of valuable food, by offering a limited number of seeds and a richer reward for dispersing each one. Howe finds that *Tetragastris* and *Virola* provide a good example of this dichotomy, but that many small-seeded plants offer rich rewards and thereby secure efficient dispersal.

Such differences in dispersal methods may play an integral role in maintaining the diversity of tropical forest. Mathematical theory suggests that these differences exploit a varying environment; if some years favor seeds dispersed by terrestrial rodents, while others favor seeds dispersed by toucans and so forth, then species dispersed by these different methods can co-exist merely by virtue of their different modes of dispersal. We are a long way from knowing how much of the diversity in tropical trees these differences account for, however.

Similarly, many animals depend on fruit for food. Most plants fruiting in the mid rainy season flower in response to the onset of the rains. Foster finds that if the preceding dry season is too short or too wet, many of these plants fail to flower, others flower but do not fruit, and famine stalks the forest. Nearly all the community, plant and animal, depends on the appropriate alternation of drought and rain.

Barro Colorado harbors a great variety of vertebrate frugivores, many of which have been studied. It appears that, just as Louis XIV reduced his nobility to the status of pensioners whose power and well-being depended on his bounty, so have the trees of this forest reduced their vertebrate frugivores to pensioners whose numbers are limited by the seasonal shortage in fruit supply. Several examples suggest this. Worthington has measured the production of those fruit which manakins, small birds of the forest understory, eat, and the numbers of these manakins, on an island just off Barro Colorado. She finds the number of manakins on that island is precisely adjusted to the rate of supply of suitable food during the season of shortage and that the manakins do not breed in the season when fruit is short. Smythe et al. have estimated the population densities of agoutis and pacas, terrestrial rodents which depend largely on fallen fruit for food, and they have measured the total weight per unit area of fruit falling to the forest floor, month by month. During the season of shortage, too little fruit falls to the forest floor to support these animals. The food habits of these animals, and of other terrestrial frugivores such as peccaries, are more clearly differentiated during the season of shortage, with peccaries concentrating more on roots, pacas on seedlings and other vegetation, and agoutis on seeds they buried during the season of plenty. Despite these alternate sources of food, these animals, like the squirrels discussed by Glanz et al. and the white-faced monkeys discussed by Oppenheimer, are hungriest and most easily trapped during the season of fruit shortage, which is also the time when their breeding rates are lowest and their death rates highest.

Howler monkeys depend for food on both new leaves, from which they derive protein, and fruit, from which they derive energy. Milton finds that after a long increase since the last yellow fever epidemic, the howler monkey population is stabilizing, controlled, like those of other frugivores, by seasonal shortages of suitable food. From fingerprints, Froehlich and Thorington trace relationships between different troops of howlers and infer how these troops have spread out over the past years. They find that other morphological features of these animals, as well as troop size, sex ratio, proportion of infants in the troop, etc., reflect the nutritional status of their troop, which in turn reflects the diversity of foods to which that troop has access: a curious example of the interplay between heredity and environment.

Relatively few vertebrates depend primarily on leaves for food: sloths and iguanas in the trees, tapir and deer and perhaps others on the ground. These animals are all either cryptic or elusive, and accordingly very difficult to study. The factors that govern what kinds of leaves they choose to eat are still mysterious: the ecology of these animals seems rather complicated, and they are only beginning to receive the attention they deserve. This book devotes no chapters to them, although Leigh discusses their role in the trophic balance of the forest in his chapter on litter production. Previously published information suggests that the sloth population is food-limited. The other vertebrate folivores may be, too; the disappearance from Barro Colorado of large predators such as pumas and jaguars has been attended by no such disorders as resulted from the absence of wolves from Isle Royale or as have been reported to accrue from the elimination of the pumas and wolves of the Kaibab Plateau. In contrast to temperate-zone forests, the forest of Barro Colorado seems able to control its vertebrates without assistance from predators.

We know far less about Barro Colorado's insects. Leafcutter ants alone may consume more foliage than all vertebrates combined, but they have received far less attention than sloths or howler monkeys, even though they are by far the best-known insect "herbivores" (strictly speaking, they eat a fungus which they grow on leaf fragments in underground caves). We have even less idea of the sizes of the insect populations nourished by nectar, pollen, rotting fruit, and the like, or the role such insects play in the diets of birds or bats. To be sure, information is accumulating on "foraging strategies" and "niche differentiation," a useful first step; but until we know something of their numbers and feeding rates in relation to food supply and mortality from predators, it will be hard to set this information in ecological context.

The abundance of flying insects follows a clear seasonal rhythm. Smythe finds that the total weight of insects of all kinds caught at light-traps, and the numbers of these insects over 5 mm long, is highest shortly after the beginning of the rains, but the number of very small insects varies little from season to season. Wolda finds that the total number of Homoptera caught at light-traps seems controlled largely by the availability of new leaves, although the times when different species fly is distributed irregularly over the year. In general, Homoptera populations on Barro Colorado fluctuate as much from year to year as most insect populations do in the north temperate zone.

Some insect populations fluctuate quite spectacularly. *Urania fulgens* is a day-flying moth whose caterpillars feed only on vines of the genus *Omphalea*. Smith finds that if a vine is defoliated several times over, it will put more poison in its leaves and *Urania* caterpillars can no longer eat them. *Urania* populations sometimes erupt, with spectacular numbers of these moths migrating through the neotropics, seemingly looking for vines whose leaves are still suitable for caterpillars to eat. Less spectacular insect outbreaks are by no means uncommon on Barro Colorado, but they often pass unnoticed because the plants affected are rarer than the species defoliated by gypsy moths or spruce budworms in the temperate zone.

On Barro Colorado Island, insectivorous bats breed in the season when flying insects are most abundant. This is also true for forest-dwelling birds, taken as a whole. Food supply, however, is not the only factor that governs when young birds are successfully produced. Gradwohl and Greenberg find that several antwrens of the forest understory produce most of their young in the middle of the rainy season, when food supply is already declining, apparently because snakes eat most clutches laid earlier.

One would think that since far more foliage, wood, etc., falls to the ground than is eaten in the trees, litter organisms play the dominant role in the life of the forest. They break down the constituents of dead plants, releasing mineral nutrients to fuel new growth. The timing and manner in which this happens must influence the proportion of the nutrients released, which are leached out or washed away, and thus the speed and efficiency of nutrient cycling, as well as the rhythm of growth. Very little, however, is known of such topics. Most of the primary consumers of litter are minute, as are many of their predators. Decaying litter thus supports a much less striking array of larger animals than do the living plants. Only in an age when romance counts less in a biologist's choice of what to study than the problems he can thereby solve, has the litter fauna begun to receive serious attention. Even so, the animals big or odd enough to arrest attention, like anteaters, frogs, lizards, and army ants and the

birds that follow them, are receiving more attention than the minute decomposers.

Levings and Windsor find that litter accumulates rapidly on the forest floor during the dry season and only begins to decompose after the rains come. At the onset of the rainy season, most groups of litter arthropods produce more young and their numbers increase. In some groups, numbers continue to increase throughout the rainy season, while in others, numbers decline as the litter thins out. The rainy season of 1977, which followed an unusually protracted dry season, was a particularly favorable one for litter arthropods.

A variety of animals feed largely on litter arthropods. Franks finds that army ants, *Eciton burchelli*, harvest a variety of litter insects, but that their population seems regulated primarily by the abundance of the larvae of two species of forest-floor ant. The numbers of *Eciton burchelli* seem to have changed little over the past 20 years. Toft, Rand, and Clark find that those frogs that eat litter arthropods as adults breed according to when habitat suitable for tadpoles is available, even though this causes the young frogs to emerge at a time when litter arthropods are relatively scarce. Andrews and Rand find that the numbers of the small lizard *Anolis limifrons*, which lives on litter arthropods, change greatly from year to year, but these changes seem correlated primarily with the length of the dry season, when it is apparently too dry for these lizards to breed. Only when these lizards are unusually numerous do the effects of food shortages become apparent. Russell, however, finds that coatis, which feed primarily on beetles and other larger insects of the leaf litter, time their annual breeding so that their young emerge from the nest at the time of maximum food abundance, and their breeding rate seems to change from year to year in response to food supply. It is perhaps no accident that the vertebrates with the lowest metabolism—the frogs—are the least food-limited, and the lizards slightly more so, while the coatis, like ant-following antbirds, with their high metabolism, are most obviously limited by the abundance of litter arthropods.

A number of species have disappeared from Barro Colorado Island since its isolation from the mainland in 1914, presumably because the island is too small to ensure that rarer or more specialized populations will not fluctuate to extinction. In a world where natural vegetation is increasingly confined to reserves, interest is growing in how much of the original biota can be preserved in a park of given size. The general principle seems to be that populations diversify until the advantages of increased specialization are balanced by the risks of extinction such specialization entails. MacArthur used such an argument to conclude that the greater diversity of tropical communities reflects the greater stability of tropical environments. The fluctuations of animal populations, and their causes, are therefore of some interest.

Earlier papers mention fluctuations of individual populations: the almost constant numbers of the army ant *Eciton burchelli* over the past 20 years; the sixfold fluctuation in numbers of the lizard *Anolis limifrons* over the past 8 years, primarily in response to weather conditions; the stabilizing numbers of the howler monkey *Alouatta palliata* protected by destruction of the intervening forest from the yellow fever epidemics which formerly spread up from Colombia; the tenfold increase in numbers of the squirrel *Sciurus granatensis* over the past decade, for which we do not know the cause. We can explain some of these fluctuations but not others. We know far too little of relationships within the community to judge how fluctuations in one population affect its competitors, predators, and food species.

More generally, it may be impossible to account in a coherent manner for the timing and amplitude of fluctuations in different populations on the basis of such knowledge as we are likely to obtain of their modes of regulation. However, one can at least begin to survey these fluctuations. Karr, Schemske, and Brokaw find that the relative numbers of the different kinds of birds they netted on a 4-ha. plot of mainland forest change from month to month and from year to year. In general, the numbers of those species that depend on patchy and variable sources of food vary most. The same is probably true for Barro Colorado, 11 km away. Glanz finds that the numbers of some of the mammals of Barro Colorado have changed greatly during the last decade. The causes of most of these changes are unknown.

LITERATURE CITED

MacArthur, R. H.
1982.   *Geographical Ecology.* New York: Harper and Row.

Odum, H. T., and R. Pigeon (editors)
1970.   *A Tropical Rain Forest.* Springfield, Va.: U.S. Atomic Energy Commission, Division of Technical Information.

Sinclair, A. R. E., and M. Norton-Griffiths (editors)
1979.   *Serengeti: Dynamics of an Ecosystem.* Chicago: University of Chicago Press.

THE PHYSICAL SETTING

Geology, Climate, and Hydrology of Barro Colorado Island

WILLIAM E. DIETRICH   Department of Geological Sciences and Quaternary Research Center, University of Washington, Seattle, Washington 98195

DONALD M. WINDSOR   Smithsonian Tropical Research Institute, Balboa, Republic of Panama

THOMAS DUNNE   Department of Geological Sciences and Quaternary Research Center, University of Washington, Seattle, Washington 98195

ABSTRACT

Barro Colorado Island is a 1500-ha. hill protruding 137 m above Gatun Lake. Its broad, flat top is underlain by dense basalt. From it radiate steep ridges and valleys cut into sedimentary rocks containing much volcanic debris. Soils mantling the island are generally less than 50 cm deep and are rich in clay; soils deeper than 1 m occur only on the flat hilltop. Soil properties appear to be greatly influenced by topography.

The climate of Barro Colorado is typical in many ways of the lowland moist tropics: in the open, the average annual temperature is 27°C, the average diurnal temperature range is 9°C, and potential evapotranspiration (Penman) is about 12 cm a month. Per year, 2600 mm of rain fall, 90% during a rainy season lasting from May through December. During the dry season, trade winds prevent convective storms, thereby dictating the seasonal rhythms of climate on this island.

A simple model predicts runoff and soil moisture content from rainfall, potential evapotranspiration, and fixed characteristics of the soil. At the beginning of the dry season, the ground contains about 40 cm of water available to plants. It appears that, early in the dry season, leaffall increases markedly when a third of this moisture is exhausted, while increases in soil moisture content stimulate flowering in many plants. This model may enable one to infer phenological rhythms of the forest in years past from rainfall records.

The permeability of many tropical soils, especially clays, decreases markedly below the fine root zone. Thus, especially if the soil is nearly saturated, runoff from a heavy rain can be forced to the surface as it travels downslope, forming saturation overland flow. Early in the rainy season, little of the rainfall reaching the soil runs off. Instead, the water replenishes the soil moisture depleted by evapotranspiration. Subsequent rainfall enters the soil and travels as a shallow subsurface flow and a deeper groundwater flow to drainage channels. This water reaches the channel slowly and causes stream flow to increase gradually. Later in the rainy season, rainfall saturates the soil in a progressively larger fraction of the catchment, leading to more and faster runoff from the hillslopes by saturation overland flow. We estimate that about 20% of the total runoff is by saturation overland flow.

Based on 2 years of suspended sediment measurement and 4 years of water discharge record, the Lutz Creek catchment appears to be eroding at the high rate of 598 t/sq. km/yr. or about 0.75mm/yr. Some of this sediment is derived from erosion of banks cut in landslide deposits, and some is probably generated by surface erosion by rain splash and overland flow.

INTRODUCTION

Between April and December, Barro Colorado Island experiences short, intense rainstorms. The soils swell, and in many places they become saturated and discharge water to small ravines dissecting the island. When the rainy season ends, water ceases to run in the ravines, and vegetation withdraws water from soils faster than the infrequent rains of the dry season replenish it. The soils slowly dry and break into broad, deep cracks. The stress on the forest depends on how dry the soil becomes, which depends in turn on the supply of water stored in the soil relative to the needs of the vegetation.

The depth and texture of the soil largely determine the total amount of water stored in the soil and available to plants. Growth of roots, uprooting of trees, burrowing by animals, and development of a plant cover greatly influence the balance between erosion and soil formation, and thereby govern the depth and texture of the soil and of the weathered bedrock below. The topography and the texture of the soil control the amount of water running off after rainstorms, and the modes by which runoff occurs, thereby influencing the degree and manner of erosion and, consequently, the further development of the topography.

Quantification of the physical and biological interactions outlined above will lead to a general model for predicting the spatial variation of soil properties and consequent soil moisture availability for plants. In this paper we describe the influence of the geology of Barro Colorado Island on soil development and topography. A section on climate is then presented to give basic data for a water budget constructed for the Lutz Creek catchment. A quantitative model of runoff production would improve our water budget model and, to move toward this goal, we have examined the runoff record from Lutz Creek and estimated the importance of different runoff processes. We complete our discussion with observations on rates of erosion on Barro Colorado Island.

THE GEOLOGICAL SETTING

Panama

The isthmus of Panama probably became a land bridge between 2 million and 3 million years ago (Marshall et al., 1979). This recent uplift partly explains its rugged topography. In central Panama, near the Panama Canal, rocks can be crudely classified as either dense, relatively impermeable volcanics, or as porous, chemically unstable sedimentary rocks and volcanic mud-flow deposits. Woodring (1958) has proposed a similar dichotomy. Weathering of the dense volcanics, which tends to be shallow, sometimes penetrating only a few centimeters into the rocks along fractures, yields soils rich in clay on gentle slopes and shallow, rocky soils on steep slopes. On the other hand, weathering tends to penetrate several meters into the more porous rocks and yields clay-rich soils on both steep and gentle slopes.

In a landscape with both dense volcanics and more porous rocks, erosion brings out the differences in their weathering. As rivers carve their way into hillslopes, the deeply weathered sedimentary rocks experience deep-seated landslides, and the fine texture of the soil formed on these rocks encourages overland flow and consequent erosion of the soil surface. In contrast, landslides on the dense basalts may involve just the soil mantle. On the steeper slopes, soils overlying basalts are of coarse texture and overland flow may be rare.

These differences lead to dramatic differences in topography. In central Panama, most major hills and many small ones are underlain by dense volcanics (see map in Woodring, 1957). These hills are isolated, conical or dome-shaped projections, dominating the lower hills formed in the sedimentary rocks. Some of these hills may have formed about volcanic dikes intruded vertically into the sedimentary rocks. However, much of the basalt was formed as lava flows over the sedimentary rocks (Woodring, 1957). As rivers cut through the layer of basalt mantling the uplifted landscape, they formed valleys in the sedimentary rocks underneath, making a mosaic of low valleys and basalt-capped heights. Once the basalt cap was breached, erosion of underlying sedimentary rocks could have steepened the slopes formed on basalt to the point that landslides occurred. Erosion by repeated landslides would cause slopes to retreat into the basalt mantle, removing the basalt entirely in many areas and leaving isolated basalt-capped hills such as Barro Colorado Island.

Barro Colorado Island

Barro Colorado Island (9°09′N, 79°51′W) is a hill capped by intrusive and extrusive basalt (Figures 1 and 2). It was partially submerged during the formation of Gatun Lake in 1914, forming an island of roughly 1500 ha. The hilltop is broad and flat, and ends abruptly in steep (20°–30°) slopes, which descend into the surrounding sedimentary formations. A chemically resistant unit composed of dense basalt gravel and sand similar in composition to that capping the hilltop underlies a diagonal section across the island, and also occurs on the northern hillslopes which

Figure 1. Topographic map of Barro Colorado Island. Trails are shown as dotted lines. Contours are given every 10 m, and elevations are given meters above mean sea level (map by Robin Foster, Stanley Rand, and Donald Windsor).

A = site of the "big trees" mentioned in the text.

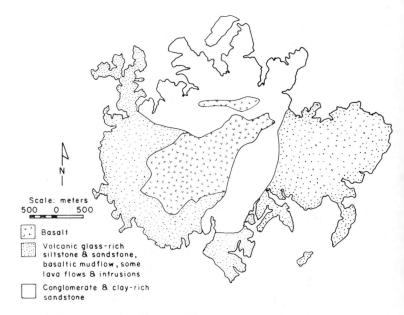

Figure 2. Simplified geologic map of Barro Colorado Island modified from Woodring (1958).

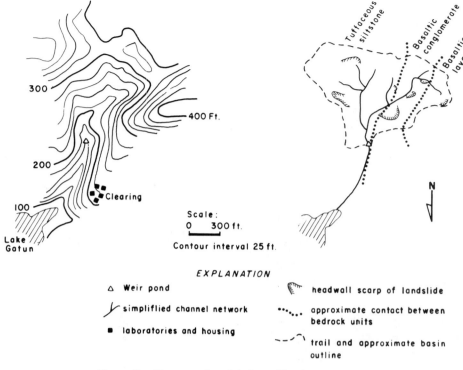

Figure 3. Topography of (left) and landslides in (right) the Lutz Creek catchment. Approximate base map by N. Smythe. Bedrock is shown as mapped by Woodring (1958). Outer trails mostly follow the drainage divide. Some basalt outcrops occur in the region underlain principally by tuffaceous siltstones.

descend into Gatun Lake (Figure 2). The other rocks on the island consist of a wide range of volcanic, glass-rich sandstones and siltstones, basaltic agglomerate (volcanic mudflow deposits), limestones, and sandstones rich in silt and clay.

Narrow ridges and deep ravines cut into the bedrock radiate in all directions from the basaltic hilltop, giving the island a crenated shoreline. On the short, steep hillslopes, numerous local steps in the topography suggest that landslides involving the underlying bedrock are common. Seven obvious landslide scars, with nearly vertical back walls 2–8 m high, have been found in Lutz Creek catchment (Figure 3). These scars affect about 5% of the 10-ha. basin. Some of the slides appear to have been active within the last 25 years. In December 1959, five days of nearly continuous rain activated several slides on Barro Colorado Island (Moynihan, 1960). The character of the vegetation on two of the slides in the catchment also indicates that they moved during this event (Robin Foster, personal communication). These two slides may also have been active before 1959; we do not know when the other slides occurred. Although they form pronounced topographic steps, landslide scars are not obvious on aerial photographs or by direct observation from the air because of the tall, dense forest.

The mantle of rock debris which drapes this topographically diverse landscape contains four distinct vertical zones (Figure 4) differing, sometimes radically, in mineralogy, strength, and permeability, and representing progressive stages of weathering. The lowermost zone is the original fresh bedrock. As the primary minerals of the bedrock oxidize and are leached by percolating water, the zone becomes weathered bedrock, which can be distinguished by the clouding and discoloration of minerals and matrix material. If the weathering process is given sufficient time, the bedrock takes on the appearance of soil, except that it is not physically disrupted and it retains a relict structure of the underlying rock. This zone is referred to as saprolite. The surface layer, which lacks the original rock structure, is the soil and is made by

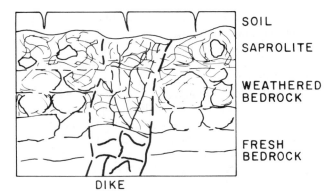

SOIL

SAPROLITE

WEATHERED BEDROCK

FRESH BEDROCK

DIKE

Figure 4. Four principal horizons resulting from rock weathering and soil formation. In this case, a basaltic lava flow intruded by a dike of more dense basalt has been extensively weathered to form a weathered bedrock zone where much of the original rock appearance and strength are preserved. Weathering causes isolation of roughly spherical regions of much less weathered rock called corestone. Continued weathering produces the saprolite which has a soil-like texture but retains the general structure and some of the original rock strength. The amount of corestone in the weathered material can be used to define the difference between saprolite and weathered rock (Deere and Patton, 1971). Disruption of the saprolite by physical mixing produces the soil.

physical disturbance or mixing of the underlying material. Not every area has all four zones. For example, if the rate of disruptive soil formation is high relative to rates of chemical weathering of the rock, the saprolite zone may be absent. Soils may tend to be coarse textured if they incorporate bedrock that is only partially weathered. The balance between local rates of downslope transport of soil and rates of soil formation determines the thickness and texture of the soil.

We have cursorily surveyed the soils of Barro Colorado by digging pits and coring soils at several locations on the island. Soil properties appear to vary systematically with the type of the underlying rock and with the topographic setting. On the broad, flat top of the island, which is underlain by dense basalt, erosion rates are very low. Root exposure is minimal and the soils, cracking red clays with a brown, organically enriched surface horizon less than 5 cm thick, are over a meter deep. In contrast, on the narrow, gently sloping (9°) ridges such as between Miller and Wheeler trails (Figure 1), which are also underlain by basalt, soils are yellow-brown, less than 50 cm thick, and end abruptly in boulder-sized chunks of fresh bedrock with thin weathering rinds. The soils are also rich in clay but contain occasional fresh gravel-sized rocks. Along parts of the narrow ridge between the

two main branches of Lutz Creek (Figure 3), basalt reaches the surface and soil is absent. On the steep side-slopes, where gradients can exceed 20°, the soil is of coarse texture, with much material of the size of fine gravel, and less than 50 cm thick. On 50° slopes, weathered basalt reaches the surface, and the soil forms a discontinuous cover trapped in places by the roots of trees.

Siltstones rich in volcanic glass underlie most of Lutz catchment and much of the island. Their soils are yellow-brown silty clays. The thicker soils show cracks up to 2 cm wide and at least 10 cm deep during the dry season. Typically, these soils have a surface horizon 5 cm thick, enriched with organic material. In general, these soils also tend to be thin, their thickness varying systematically with steepness of slope, as occurs elsewhere (Dietrich and Dunne, 1978). On narrow ridgetops with gradients of less than 5%, soils may be less than 20 cm thick. They are 30–50 cm thick on slopes of 20°–30°, but on steeper slopes of 40° the soils are only 10 cm thick. There appears to be saprolite below the soil even on the steeper slopes, perhaps because the parent siltstones are porous and susceptible to chemical weathering. The soils formed on the conglomerate (Figures 2, 3) have not been studied sufficiently to characterize, although our one sample appeared similar to the soils formed on siltstones. Knight (1975) reported a soil from at least three sites on the island whose properties suggested seasonal restriction in drainage. We did not have time to study this soil or map its distribution.

On Barro Colorado, plant roots are concentrated in the upper 10 to 20 cm of the soil (Figure 5, from Odum, 1970). Major roots may also penetrate deep into saprolite and extensively weathered bedrock, in areas where these layers are present. On recently fallen trees we have observed roots that extended 80 cm below the surface into the underlying saprolite. Roots are important hydrologically, not only because they increase the permeability of the soil, but also because when exposed they criss-cross the soil surface. These exposed roots act as small dams that retard overland flow and subtantially reduce its velocity and erosive capabilities. Rainsplash is an important erosive agent in the tropical forest (Ruxton, 1967; Tricart, 1972), and the ponding of water behind root dams decreases the frequency of impact of raindrops on the soil surface.

Barro Colorado has experienced varying degrees of human disturbance. Grinding stones (metates) found in the forest suggest that the hilltop was once subject to shifting agriculture (Enders, ms.; Foster and Brokaw, this volume). We have also found charred wood in the soils near the Armour trail #8, by the "big trees"

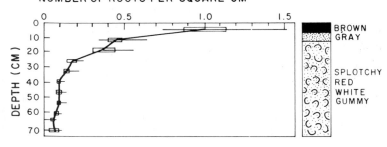

NUMBER OF ROOTS PER SQUARE CM

BROWN
GRAY

SPLOTCHY
RED
WHITE
GUMMY

Figure 5. Distribution of roots below soil surface and description of soil for a site which was probably located on the eastern side of the Lutz Creek catchment (from Odum, 1970).

(Figure 1). During the early phase of construction of the Panama Canal, the French cleared parts of the hilltop for a distillery, and perhaps also to grow sugarcane (Chapman, 1938). About half the island, including all of Lutz catchment, was subject to shifting agriculture at this time. However, an aerial photograph taken in 1929 suggests that second-growth forest was well established in these areas (Chapman, 1938). Foster and Brokaw (this volume) review the history of human disturbance more thoroughly.

The hydrologic impact of this disturbance is unclear. Our soil survey found no evidence that the short-lived plantation on the hilltop altered the properties of the soil, and we suggest differences in soil characteristics seem to reflect differences in rates of soil formation and erosion now prevailing under the forest cover. Disturbance has modified the island's vegetation, but it is not obvious that it has greatly modified the runoff process 50 to 100 years later.

CLIMATE

Data on various aspects of the climate of Barro Colorado Island have been taken since 1971 under the auspices of the Smithsonian Environmental Sciences Program (Smythe, 1974; Windsor, 1975, 1976, 1977). The Panama Canal Commission (formerly Panama Canal Company) has measured rainfall on the island with a tipping bucket gauge stationed atop the dining hall in the laboratory clearing for the past 50 years (Rand and Rand, this volume).

Water Demand

Solar radiation, air temperature, relative humidity, and wind speed are the primary factors governing the rate at which plants transpire water. As a result of the proximity of Barro Colorado Island to the equator,

the solar radiation entering the upper atmosphere above the island, varies by only 22% during the year, from about 895 cal/sq. cm/day in April to 731 in December (computed from Dunne and Leopold, 1978, p. 107, Table 4–2).

Clouds decrease the solar radiation that reaches the earth's surface and, on the isthmus of Panama, the variation in cloud cover between wet and dry season causes the monthly incoming solar radiation to vary by a factor of two (U.S. Army Tropic Test Center, 1979). Since 1976 the Radiation Biology Laboratory has monitored solar radiation reaching the forest canopy on Barro Colorado from atop a 42-m tower, extending 8 m above the forest canopy, near the weir at the base of the Lutz catchment. Earlier, radiation had been measured with an Eppley sensor atop a 27-m tower elsewhere in the Lutz catchment. Lightning and other electrical problems have plagued both solarimeters, resulting in reliable data for only 23 months of the 84 ending December 1979. Measured monthly solar radiation on Barro Colorado Island ranges from an average of 264 cal/sq. cm/day in June 1973 to 552 in February 1975 and correlates most closely with that at Flamenco Island, near the Pacific mouth of the Panama Canal. For those months where measurements are lacking on Barro Colorado, we estimated the incoming solar radiation (Q_s) for the island from the regression

$$Q_s \text{ (Barro Colorado)} = -156 \\ + 1.34 \, Q_s \text{ (Flamenco)}, \\ (N = 23, r^2 = 0.58)$$

Mean monthly temperatures vary only slightly through the year. The midpoint between the daily maximum and the daily minimum temperature averages about 27°C for the year in the laboratory clearing, ranging from a monthly average of about 26°C in December or January to about 28° in April. This midpoint averages about 25°C for the year in the forest near the weir, ranging from about 24°C in December or January to 26°C or 27°C in April. Average diurnal temperature range is 8°C or 9°C in the clearing and 6°C or 7°C in the forest.

Relative humidity remains high all year because of the proximity of Gatun Lake and the great oceanic bodies to the north and south, and also because of the abundance of water available for transpiration by plants. The monthly average relative humidity at midday, as measured by a sling psychrometer, normally varies from 62–68% in March or April to 80% or more by November in the laboratory clearing, and from 75–77% in March or April to 93% by November, in the forest near the weir (Table 1).

Average wind speed, as measured first from atop

the dining hall and then from 8 m above the forest canopy near the weir, varied from 3 km/hr. between June and November to 6–9 km/hr. at the height of the dry season between February and April (Table 1). These data confirm observations elsewhere (U.S. Army Tropic Test Center, 1979) that the mean wind speed is much lower in the mid-isthmus region of Panama than along the coasts. Despite the relatively high humidity, vegetation on the northeastern margin of the island, exposed to the dry-season tradewinds sweeping across the lake, shows signs of desiccation (Enders, ms.)

The amount of water evaporated from soil and plant surfaces and transpired by plants is termed evapotranspiration. Depending on the availability of water to plants, the evapotranspiration demand created by local meteorologic conditions may or may not be fulfilled. The evapotranspiration that occurs when water is freely available is termed potential evapotranspiration, and there are several methods to compute its magnitude from meteorological data. We have used the Penman (1948) procedure, which yields the evapotranspiration rate as a function of net radiation and the evaporating power of the air, which in turn depends on air temperature, humidity, and wind speed. The Penman formula can be written as

$$E_t = [E_a + (de_{sa}/dT)H/c] / [1 + (de_{sa}/dT)/c]$$

where evapotranspiration E_t is measured in cm/day, E_a is evaporation due to wind blowing across the evaporating surface, again in cm/day, de_{sa}/dT is the rate of change of saturation vapor pressure e_{sa}, in mb, with respect to temperature, T, in degrees Kelvin (273 + temperature Centigrade), calculated for the mean monthly temperature from an appropriate table (cf. Dunne and Leopold, 1978, p. 114), c is the psychometric constant, 0.66 mb per degree Kelvin, and H is net radiation, translated into the number of centimeters of water it can evaporate per day. $H = Q_n/\rho L$, where Q_n is net radiation in cal/sq. cm ground area/day, ρ is density of water (g/cu. cm), and L is latent heat of vaporization, about 590 cal/g.

Net radiation, Q_n, and evaporation by wind, E_a, are the two quantities whose measurement requires further discussion. We have used the radiation balance to compute the net radiation:

$$Q_n = Q_s (1 - \alpha) - Q_{lw}$$

where Q_s is solar radiation incident upon the forest canopy, α is albedo, the proportion of this solar radiation reflected back to the atmosphere, and Q_{lw} is net longwave radiation from the evaporating surface back to the atmosphere which, following Dunne and Leopold (1978, p. 109), we estimate from the empirical relation

$$Q_{lw} = \sigma T_2{}^4 (0.56 - 0.08 \sqrt{e_2}) (1 - aC)$$

Here, σ is the Stefan-Boltzmann constant, 1.17×10^{-7} cal/sq. cm/°K^4/day, T_2 is the air temperature 2 m above the evaporating surface, in degrees Kelvin; e_2 is the vapor pressure in millibars 2 m above the evaporating surface, a is a constant reflecting the type and height of clouds in the sky, and C is the mean proportion of the sky covered by clouds. Evaporation by wind, E_a, can be estimated from the empirical relationship (Penman, 1948),

$$E_a = (0.013 + 0.00016V_2) (e_{sa}(T) - e_2),$$

where V_2 is wind speed (km/day) 2 m above the evaporating surface, e_{sa} is vapor pressure at saturation at the mean temperature T, and e_2 is the average vapor pressure 2 m above the evaporating surface.

In summary, potential evapotranspiration E_t is

$$\frac{(.013 + .000016V_2)(e_{sa}(T) - e_2)}{1 + (de_{sa}/dT)/c}$$
$$+ \frac{Q_s(1 - \alpha) - \sigma T_2{}^4 (.56 - .08 \sqrt{e_2}) (1 - aC)}{\rho L[1 + c(dT/de_{sa})]}$$

Table 1 contains the climatic variables used to compute E_t on a monthly basis. We set V_2, the wind speed 2 m above the evaporating surface, equal to the monthly average wind speed measured on the canopy tower. We set the vapor pressure 2 m above the evaporating surface, e_2, equal to $e_{sa}(T)$ times (R.H.)/100, where R.H. is monthly average relative humidity (percent) in the laboratory clearing, which we take to be (100 + R.H. at noon)/2, and $e_{sa}(T)$ is the saturation vapor pressure at the mean monthly temperature T, which we take to be the midpoint between the average daily maximum and the average daily minimum in the laboratory clearing. We also assume $T = T_2$, the temperature 2 m above the evaporating surface. We set the albedo $\alpha = 0.18$, the value measured for a tropical hardwood forest in Kenya (Dunne and Leopold, 1978, p. 113); the "cloud-type constant" $a = 0.6$, the value appropriate for clouds at a medium height. The mean cloudiness was computed from an empirical expression given in Dunne and Leopold (1978, p. 106),

$$C = -0.332 + \sqrt{1.863 - 2.183Q_s/I_o},$$

where I_o is the solar radiation entering the upper atmosphere (computed from Dunne and Leopold, 1978, p. 107) and Q_s/I_o is the fraction of the month's solar radiation that penetrates the atmosphere to the forest canopy. We estimated the mean cloudiness C for each month of the year by averaging the values of C calculated from values of Q_s and I_o for that month in

Table 1. A monthly reconciliation of the water budget for the Lutz watershed including meteorological and hydrological variables

Month/year	Avg. daily temp. (C°)*	Wind-speed (km/day)*	Relative humidity (%)*	Atmos-pheric vapor pressure (mb)	Saturation vapor pressure (mb)	Penman's dimensionless parameter	Cloudi-ness (%)	Solar radiation external to the atmosphere (cal/sq.cm/day)	Avg. daily solar radiation at earth's surface (cal/sq.cm/day)	Net longwave radiation (cal/sq.cm/day)
Oct. 1976	26.6	70	75.5	31.1	35.4	3.15	0.59	830	387	69.8
Nov. 1976	26.6	70	80.7	32.0	35.5	3.16	0.54	770	391	68.6
Dec. 1976	27.3	103	80.0	33.2	36.9	3.27	0.42	730	432	70.3
Jan. 1977	26.6	158	69.4	30.1	35.5	3.17	0.43	755	443	84.9
Feb. 1977	27.1	147	73.4	31.6	36.4	3.24	0.47	820	458	75.3
Mar. 1977	27.4	166	67.3	31.1	37.2	3.29	0.52	870	452	74.6
Apr. 1977	27.6	158	70.1	32.0	37.7	3.33	0.49	895	487	72.5
May 1977	27.8	93	73.8	33.1	38.1	3.36	0.60	885	402	61.1
June 1977	26.5	70	84.2	32.5	35.3	3.15	0.71	870	308	56.2
July 1977	26.9	93	85.0	33.5	36.2	3.22	0.61	870	389	58.4
Aug. 1977	26.0	73	85.5	31.9	34.3	3.07	0.66	885	358	61.6
Sept. 1977	27.2	70	82.8	33.6	36.8	3.26	0.64	880	371	56.4
Oct. 1977	27.0	73	84.3	33.5	36.4	3.23	0.61	830	373	58.5
Nov. 1977	26.9	77	84.3	33.2	36.0	3.20	0.57	770	372	61.9
Dec. 1977	27.1	89	82.0	33.3	36.6	3.24	0.53	730	373	63.8
Jan. 1978	27.0	112	71.2	31.2	36.4	3.23	0.20	755	545	94.6
Feb. 1978	27.0	154	71.8	31.3	36.4	3.23	0.39	820	503	82.0
Mar. 1978	27.3	143	69.3	31.3	37.0	3.28	0.34	870	560	85.0
Apr. 1978	27.3	150	78.3	33.0	37.0	3.28	0.45	895	513	70.1
May 1978	27.0	98	82.8	33.2	36.3	3.23	0.55	885	442	63.2
June 1978	26.4	66	88.9	33.1	35.1	3.13	0.63	870	376	58.4
July 1978	27.1	93	85.9	33.9	36.5	3.24	0.58	870	412	58.3
Aug. 1978	26.4	70	86.9	32.7	35.0	3.13	0.56	885	434	64.1
Sept. 1978	26.7	70	82.5	32.5	35.6	3.17	0.52	880	456	67.4
Oct. 1978	26.2	70	85.9	32.2	34.6	3.10	0.51	830	440	69.3
Nov. 1978	26.7	73	83.5	32.8	35.7	3.18	0.49	770	421	68.3
Dec. 1978	27.3	89	80.3	33.3	36.9	3.27	0.42	730	432	70.0
Jan. 1979	27.1	129	65.6	30.3	36.6	3.25	0.36	755	478	89.0
Feb. 1979	27.4	146	69.4	31.5	37.2	3.30	0.30	820	549	86.7
Mar. 1979	27.6	160	61.5	30.5	37.7	3.33	0.43	870	510	84.1
Apr. 1979	27.8	141	77.8	33.9	38.1	3.36	0.51	895	470	62.7
May 1979	27.3	123	76.3	32.6	37.0	3.28	0.50	885	476	69.0
June 1979	26.8	117	88.6	33.8	35.9	3.19	0.55	870	431	60.0
July 1979	27.2	110	88.9	34.8	36.8	3.27	0.52	870	451	57.6
Aug. 1979	26.6	102	82.5	32.5	35.6	3.17	0.57	885	424	64.7
Sept. 1979	26.8	58	86.2	33.4	35.8	3.19	0.56	880	433	61.8
Oct. 1979	26.9	56	78.1	32.2	36.2	3.22	0.52	830	432	69.0
Nov. 1979	26.6	54	77.1	31.4	35.5	3.16	0.68	770	299	62.7
Dec. 1979	26.5	56	72.2	30.4	35.3	3.15	0.48	730	402	79.8
Jan. 1980	27.4	138	71.2	31.8	37.1	3.29	0.37	755	475	81.0
Feb. 1980	27.0	152	65.8	30.2	36.4	3.23	0.39	820	506	87.9
Mar. 1980	27.8	160	61.7	30.8	38.1	3.36	0.39	870	537	85.5

Observed variables are indicated by asterisks; other variables are derived from formulas.

Evaporation due to mass transfer (cm)	Thornthwaite's potential evapotranspiration (cm)	Penman's potential evapotranspiration (cm)	Rainfall (cm)*	Soil moisture (%)*	Runoff (cm)*	Actual evapotranspiration (AET) (cm)	Rainfall − AET (cm)	Available water capacity (cm)	Predicted soil moisture (%)	Predicted runoff (cm)
0.11	12.8	10.7	25.15	42.80	8.19	10.66	14.49	41.30	45.00	18.19
0.08	12.6	1C.3	21.60	42.40	9.22	10.33	11.27	41.30	45.00	11.27
0.11	13.9	12.2	3.30	36.10	0.04	12.22	−8.92	32.38	42.05	0.00
0.21	12.7	12.7	2.50	32.90	0.00	12.67	−10.17	22.21	38.26	0.00
0.18	13.7	12.1	5.80	35.30	0.01	12.06	−6.26	15.96	35.68	0.00
0.24	14.8	13.7	2.30	29.83	0.00	13.67	−11.37	4.59	30.39	0.00
0.22	15.8	14.3	1.50	28.49	0.00	1.50	−12.78	0.00	28.00	0.00
0.14	16.6	11.9	24.40	34.78	0.11	11.86	12.54	12.54	34.18	0.00
0.07	13.6	8.1	21.80	40.50	0.68	8.06	13.74	26.27	39.83	0.00
0.08	14.4	11.0	18.00	39.75	2.50	11.00	7.00	33.27	42.35	0.00
0.06	12.4	9.7	63.00	42.45	45.00	9.66	53.34	41.30	45.00	45.31
0.08	14.7	10.2	29.50	43.90	9.30	10.18	19.32	41.30	45.00	19.32
0.07	13.8	10.4	41.40	45.30	29.60	10.44	30.96	41.30	45.00	30.96
0.07	13.2	9.9	42.90	44.50	30.40	9.94	32.96	41.30	45.00	32.96
0.09	13.6	10.4	6.40	43.50	1.80	10.38	−3.98	37.32	43.72	0.00
0.16	13.5	15.3	0.76	36.01	0.21	15.32	−14.56	22.76	38.48	0.00
0.19	13.7	13.3	1.78	34.72	0.02	13.26	−11.48	11.28	33.61	0.00
0.20	14.6	16.5	4.83	30.70	0.01	4.83	−11.71	0.00	28.00	0.00
0.15	15.0	14.7	19.56	34.74	1.59	14.70	4.86	4.86	30.53	0.00
0.09	14.6	12.7	18.29	40.26	0.73	12.66	5.63	10.49	33.24	0.00
0.05	13.4	10.0	21.08	41.90	2.08	9.96	11.12	21.61	38.02	0.00
0.07	14.8	11.8	28.96	40.40	9.36	11.75	17.21	38.82	44.21	0.00
0.06	13.1	12.0	28.45	44.40	11.72	12.03	16.42	41.30	45.00	13.94
0.07	13.4	12.4	13.46	45.20	5.41	12.39	1.07	41.30	45.00	1.07
0.06	12.1	12.0	31.24	45.40	16.44	12.02	19.22	41.30	45.00	19.22
0.07	12.9	11.2	29.46	45.50	22.07	11.24	18.22	41.30	45.00	18.22
0.10	13.9	12.2	2.54	42.88	1.06	12.16	−9.62	31.68	41.80	0.00
0.21	13.8	13.7	0.51	32.27	0.31	13.72	−13.22	18.47	36.74	0.00
0.21	14.5	14.6	3.05	31.40	0.12	14.58	−11.54	6.93	31.55	0.00
0.28	15.4	15.5	0.76	29.20	0.00	0.76	−14.75	0.00	28.00	0.00
0.15	16.3	13.7	30.99	32.40	0.90	13.68	17.30	17.30	36.26	0.00
0.14	15.3	14.0	24.89	38.96	2.50	13.98	10.91	28.22	40.55	0.00
0.06	14.2	11.8	38.35	40.60	16.11	11.83	26.53	41.30	45.00	13.44
0.06	15.1	13.0	32.51	43.24	14.55	13.01	19.50	41.30	45.00	19.50
0.09	13.6	12.0	33.02	46.49	15.03	11.98	21.04	41.30	45.00	21.04
0.06	13.6	11.7	27.18	41.86	12.71	11.74	15.43	41.30	45.00	15.43
0.09	13.6	12.1	26.65	41.22	15.17	12.07	13.58	41.30	45.00	13.58
0.09	12.6	7.7	27.18	41.04	12.37	7.68	19.50	41.30	45.00	19.50
0.11	12.3	10.8	22.35	40.80	10.89	10.77	11.58	41.30	45.00	11.58
0.19	14.3	13.8	11.20	38.50	5.74	13.78	−2.58	38.72	44.18	0.00
0.23	13.7	13.9	4.83	36.54	0.89	13.87	−9.04	29.68	41.09	0.00
0.28	15.8	16.4	0.51	31.20	0.09	16.38	−15.87	13.81	34.74	0.00

successive years of our study (Table 1). These values differed by an average of two percentage points from the average portion of daylight hours with sunshine in each month of the year at Balboa Heights, as calculated from records of the Panama Canal Commission for the years 1908–65.

Monthly values of potential evapotranspiration computed by this procedure are given in Table 1. From 1977 through 1979, the average annual potential evapotranspiration was 146.4 cm, which works out to 12.2 cm/month (13.9 cm/month during the dry season, 11.4 cm/month during the rainy season). Solar radiation is the principal factor controlling evapotranspiration in general, but the lack of strong seasonal variation in magnitude of the other meteorologic variables on Barro Colorado Island causes the potential evapotranspiration to be a simple linear function of solar radiation ($r^2 = 0.94$, $n = 42$). Table 1 indicates that potential evapotranspiration ranges by a factor of less than two from wet to dry season, responding to changes in solar radiation caused largely by the seasonal variation in cloud cover.

The greatest source of error in the calculation of potential evapotranspiration is the estimate of solar radiation from the regression on values observed at Flamenco: this could introduce an error of 10% in our estimate of E_t. Although albedo probably varies seasonally, the error from assuming it constant through the year is much less than 10%. The value of the "cloud-type consonant" a can range from 0.3 to 0.9, introducing an uncertainty in E_t of $\pm$ 5%. Because the area is so humid, even large errors in estimates of windspeed are not likely to lead to great error in E_t.

We also calculated potential evapotranspiration by the less accurate Thornthwaite method, as described by Dunne and Leopold (1978), which requires data only on mean monthly air temperature. During our study, E_t as estimated by Thornwaite's method averaged 168.2 cm/year or 14 cm/month, and seasonal fluctuations were less than those estimated according to Penman's method. The general agreement between the values of E_t calculated by these two independent methods seems encouraging.

Water Supply

On Barro Colorado most rain occurs as storms fed by the upward movements of warm, moist air. The average duration of these storms is less than half an hour, and they rarely last over 3 hr. Such convective storms are unstable, and only a small part of the storm cloud may be producing rain, so rainfall may be very local. It may, however, be very intense for a few minutes. On Barro Colorado, 1.3 cm falls in 5 min. (representing a rate of 16 cm/hr.) about once a year, and 6.4 cm falls in an hour about once a year (Panama Canal Company, 1948).

Barro Colorado receives about 2600 mm of rain a year, 90% of which falls between 1 May and 31 December. During these months, rainstorms sweep southward over the isthmus, leaving over twice as much rain on the northern coast as on the southern. Mean monthly rainfall on Barro Colorado during the wet season is 31 cm. The prevention of convective storms by the trade winds is primarily responsible for the seasonality of climate on Barro Colorado Island.

Between mid-November and the end of December, the trade winds develop, disrupting the convection of moist air and causing dramatic decreases in rainfall (Table 1). The average monthly rainfall during the dry season is 5.1 cm. The trade winds usually last into April; in over half the years of record, less than 100 mm of rain falls between 1 January and 1 April, much less than the accumulated potential evapotranspiration demand on the plants. The rainy season usually begins between mid-April and mid-May. Rainfall may slacken for a month or more during the rainy season, sometimes causing understory plants to wilt, but in every calendar month from July through November of each of the 50 years for which we have rainfall records, rainfall exceeded the average potential evapotranspiration for that month. Rand and Rand (this volume) discuss the variation in rainfall, spatial and temporal, in more detail.

A WATER BUDGET FOR THE LUTZ CREEK CATCHMENT

Physical Setting and Field Methods

Lutz catchment is a 10-ha., roughly diamond-shaped basin with diverse topography (Figure 3). The eastern half of the catchment is underlain by siltstone rich in volcanic glass and consists of slopes about 50 m long, averaging 25°. A narrow ridge forms the drainage divide of the eastern half of the catchment. The south central part of the catchment, between the two main branches of the stream, slopes at less than 9° and is dissected by numerous channels. The hillslopes on the western half of the catchment are mostly underlain by basaltic conglomerates and agglomerates. Here, the slopes average 15°, and many are over 90 m long. Added to this large-scale variation of slope characteristics are the seven landslide scars (Figure 3), which introduce dramatic changes in local topography and soil drainage.

The three components of a catchment water budget are the input, storage, and outflow of water. Procedures for collecting meteorologic data are described above. Water outflow from the catchment is computed from a strip chart record of the water level in a pond approximately 8 m long, 6 m wide, and 1.5 m deep when full of water behind a 120° V-notch weir. In order to determine the seasonal storage of water as soil moisture, samples from the upper 5 cm of soil have been collected with a 2-cm diameter auger, and the sample weight was recorded before and after drying. Since 1975, five paired samples have been obtained at weekly intervals along a 10-m transect along the lower quarter of a 15° hillslope. This site is used as an index for the soils of the basin. The soils here are clay rich and about 50 cm deep over a saprolite of basaltic conglomerate. For an average soil-moisture content of 40% by weight, the dry bulk density of the soil based on seven samples is 0.8 g/cc, with a standard deviation of 0.2 g/cc. As the soil dries and cracks during the dry season, the dry bulk density sampled by this method increases, with the greatest increase probably occurring near the soil surface. We lack data on the seasonal variation of bulk density, on the vertical change in bulk density through the soil column at a particular time, and on the spatial distribution of soil bulk density within the catchment. Therefore the data from the transect can only serve as an approximate index.

If the volume of soil is not changed by adding water, the percentage volume of water in the soil (V) is

$$V = \frac{100\, X \rho_s}{(100 - X)\rho_w} \qquad (1)$$

where X is the measured percent by weight soil moisture, ρ_s is the bulk density of the dry soil, and ρ_w is the density of water. Note that 1g of soil will contain $(X/100)/\rho_w$ cu. cm of water and $(100 - X)/100\rho_s$ cu. cm of dry soil. V is the ratio of the volume of water to the volume of soil, times 100. In a dry soil, the total volume of the soil (V_s) multiplied by its bulk density (ρ_s) will equal the weight of the soil and this must be equal to the volume (V_{sp}) occupied by the specific weight of the minerals (ρ_m) in the soil:

$$V_s\rho_s = V_{sp}\rho_m$$

The volume of pore space (V_p) in a soil which the water will fill is then equal to the volume not occupied by the soil particles:

$$V_p = V_s - V_{sp}$$

For a unit volume of soil, a bulk density of 0.8 gm/cc and a mineral specific gravity of 2.5 gm/cc (typical of the clay minerals present on Barro Colorado Is-

land), the pore space is equal to 68% of the volume. The specific gravity of minerals in the soil range down to 2.0 gm/cc (a value more representative of expanding clays), and the corresponding pore space for a soil composed just of these minerals is 61%. Typically, during the wettest months the soils attain average monthly water contents near 45% by weight, which according to equation (1) is 65% by volume. This implies that the surface soil during these months is always close to saturation.

Soil Moisture and the Seasonal Rhythm of the Forest

The weekly rainfall amount and percentage by weight of water in the upper 5 cm of soil at the index site are plotted for four years of measurement in Figure 6. As the rains begin to decrease in frequency at the

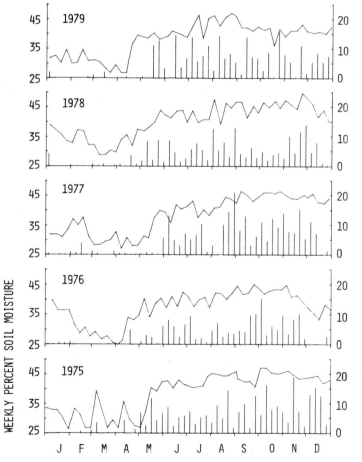

Figure 6. Weekly average percentage of soil moisture content by weight (curves) for 10 samples from five localities along a hillslope transect and weekly rainfall total from a plastic rain gauge in the clearing (vertical lines).

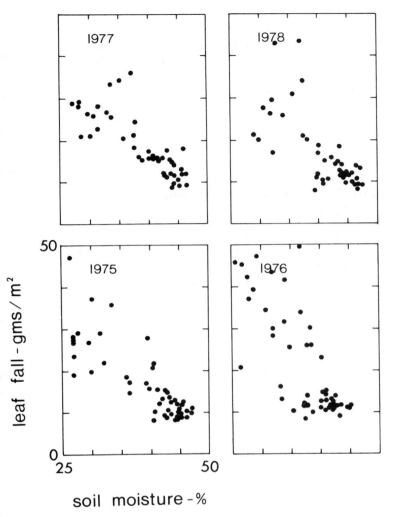

Figure 7. The relationship between total weekly leaffall collected in about 200 tubs in the Lutz Creek catchment and soil moisture content in the upper 5 cm of soil along a hillslope transect. In each year when soil moisture content dropped below 40% by weight, leaffall increased dramatically.

broad cracks in the soil, causing the soil moisture content to increase dramatically (Figure 6). By August, continued rainfall has increased the soil moisture content to a maximum of about 45% by weight.

Changes in moisture content of the soil time many biologic events in the forest. Augspurger (this volume) shows how a sudden change in soil moisture content, such as is brought on by a dry-season rain, after a sufficient period of drought, causes shrubs such as *Hybanthus* to flower in tight synchrony. The onset of the rainy season stimulates many species of trees to flower, the more so the more pronounced the preceding dry season (Foster, this volume). More generally, Lugo et al. (1978) have proposed that soil moisture availability controls the dry-matter production, leaffall rate, and physiognomy of the Guánica forest in Puerto Rico. Jackson (1978) supplies other references on the seasonality of leaffall in tropical forests.

Figure 7 shows weekly leaffall rates, measured in 0.083 sq. m plastic tubs at 200 sites around the catchment, plotted against contemporaneous soil moisture content at the transect described previously. The method of collecting and processing of samples is discussed in Leigh and Windsor (this volume). Each year of record, when the soil moisture content fell below 40% by weight or 52% by volume, the rate of litterfall increased dramatically. The total available water can be defined as the difference in water content between the monthly maximum of 45% by weight during the wet season and the monthly minimum of 27% by weight during the dry season. From equation (1) the total volume of water available is the maximum (65% by volume) minus the minimum (30%) or 35% by volume of the soil column. Thus, the consumption of water

end of November and in December, soil moisture content is decreased by plant uptake and subsurface drainage. During the driest months of January, February, and March, the occasional rainstorms that penetrate beyond the canopy cover infiltrate only a short distance into the soil and soil moisture content declines toward a minimum value of about 27% by weight. By late January, the clay-rich soils usually have broken into cracks up to 2 cm wide and 10 cm deep, although in the swales the higher water content delays the development of cracks. At the onset of the wet season in May, rainwater regularly penetrates through the forest canopy to the soil surface and runs down the

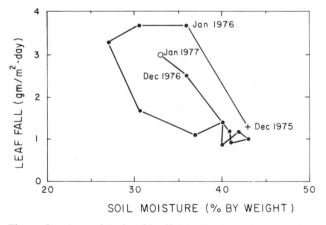

Figure 8. Annual cycle of leaffall in the Lutz Creek catchment as a function of average monthly percentage of soil moisture content by weight. Note difference between a wet December of 1975 and a December of 1976.

beyond the critical value of 52% by volume represents a 34% decrease in total available water.

The sequence of leaffalls in successive months reveal a characteristic pattern (Figure 8). If December is a dry month, significant leaffall will begin then, but the leaffall rate is usually greatest in January. As the soil moisture content continues to decline, the leaffall rate slowly diminishes. The onset of rains in April replenishes the soil water supply and as the wet season progresses the soil moisture content increases to a relatively constant value between 40% and 45% by weight. Correspondingly the rate of leaffall declines to about 1 gm/sq. m/day for the latter months of the wet season. This annual cycle is repeated when the soil moisture content is once again driven below about 40% by weight as the plants withdraw water which rainfall does not replace.

In Table 2, data on leaf-litter fall from 10 species of canopy trees indicate systematic differences between species in timing of first leaffall and of maximum leaf loss. Individuals of the same species may begin dropping leaves at very different times. Lacking data on soil moisture content at the site of each tree we cannot separate the effect of soil moisture content from the duration of the dry period on the timing of leaffall for individuals or species.

Many of the plants contributing to leaffall probably drop most of their leaves over a short time period once a threshold of soil moisture availability is crossed. This would create the sudden rise in leaffall rate and the decline in the rate as the remaining leaves to be shed are lost. Plants with the greatest sensitivity to soil mositure content or with the least amount of water available to them will lose leaves earliest in the dry season. Less sensitive plants, and those in wetter sites, will drop leaves later on. This spatial variation in soil moisture content, and the varying sensitivity of different species to water loss, maintains the loss of leaves depicted in Figures 7 and 8 at high rates during the dry season as the soil progressively loses water. The annual cycle of leaffall shown in Figure 8, then, expresses both the temporal and spatial variation in soil water availability and differences in the sensitivity of plants to water loss.

The Water Budget Model

Because soil moisture is so important to the biology of Barro Colorado Island, we have developed a simplistic model to predict the monthly average moisture content of the soil at the index site and monthly runoff from the Lutz Creek catchment. This model is a "water budget" based on a general water balance for a catchment which can be expressed as

$$P = I + OF + AET + \triangle SM + \triangle GWS + GWR$$

Precipitation (P) supplies water to the catchment. An amount I of this water returns to the atmosphere because it is *intercepted* by vegetation or other surface cover and evaporates before reaching the ground. An amount AET returns through *actual evapotranspiration* from the vegetation. Some of the rain that reaches the ground causes an increase $\triangle SM$ in soil moisture content, and an increase $\triangle GWS$ in groundwater storage. The water that is not evaporated or stored in the ground leaves the catchment as runoff, either as overland flow (OF) or as groundwater runoff (GWR). During periods without rain, water leaves the catchment as AET and GWR.

At the moment we cannot construct a complete, physically based, water budget including all the terms of the above equation, because we only know the moisture content of the top 5 cm of the soil, from one site in the basin, and we lack field data on several terms in the equation. Instead, we have assumed that once monthly rainfall declines below potential evapotranspiration, runoff ceases, all rainfall is consumed by evapotranspiration, and the water stored in the soil which can be used by plants (the available water capacity) is tapped. Continued water use by plants exhausts the available water capacity to the point where the only water available to plants is from precipitation. When rainfall rate once again exceeds water demand by plants, the soil will fill with water until the available water capacity is restored and continued rainfall will leave the basin as runoff. Actual evapotranspiration is assumed equal to potential evapotranspiration until the available water capacity is exhausted, at which time it equals just the precipitation.

We have not included interception (I) because we have no field measurements and no reliable means of predicting its magnitude precisely. On an annual basis it may reduce runoff by roughly 10% to 20% (Dunne, 1978). Interception is most important to the available water in the soil during the dry season, but because potential evapotranspiration is so much larger than precipitation the effect is probably small. Also the transition to the dry season is abrupt so that interception will not greatly effect the timing of leaffall.

Our model does not distinguish between the contribution to the total runoff measured at the weir by overland flow and that by groundwater runoff. Although overland flow (OF) seems to occur at varying amounts through the year we cannot yet predict its magnitude quantitatively. Overland flow may constitute an important loss during the beginning of the dry season when soil moisture is declining toward the threshold that induces leaffall. It also causes runoff

Table 2. The relation between changes in soil moisture and leaf litter fall to the timing of leaf drop in selected species of canopy trees

Day/Month/Year	Leaf litter dry weight	Average soil moisture	Median soil moisture	No. individuals of each species dropping "few" leaves										No. individuals of each species dropping "many" leaves									
				A	B	C	D	E	F	G	H	I	J	A	B	C	D	E	F	G	H	I	J
31 Oct. 1975	124	45	43	—	1	—	—	—	—	—	—	—	—	—	—	—	—	—	—	—	—	—	—
7 Nov. 1975	130	46	45	—	2	—	1	—	—	—	—	—	—	—	—	—	—	—	—	—	—	—	—
14 Nov. 1975	125	45	45	—	1	—	—	—	—	—	—	—	—	—	—	—	—	—	—	—	—	—	—
21 Nov. 1975	133	43	43	—	—	—	—	—	—	—	—	—	—	—	—	—	—	—	—	—	—	—	—
28 Nov. 1975	123			1	—	—	—	—	—	—	—	1	—	—	—	—	—	—	—	—	—	—	—
5 Dec 1975	132	44	43	1	1	—	—	—	—	—	—	—	—	—	—	—	—	—	—	—	—	—	—
12 Dec. 1975	158	45	46	—	1	—	—	—	1	—	—	2	—	—	—	—	—	—	—	—	—	—	—
18 Dec. 1975	151	42	42	2	1	—	—	—	5	—	—	3	—	—	—	—	—	—	1	—	—	—	—
24 Dec. 1975	171	43	42	1	1	—	—	4	1	—	1	2	1	—	—	—	—	1	—	—	—	—	1
30 Dec. 1975	478	43	42	5	2	2	—	2	1	—	—	2	2	—	—	—	—	4	—	—	2	2	—
9 Jan. 1976	522	40	40	5	2	3	2	2	1	2	—	2	—	1	—	3	—	3	1	—	—	1	1
16 Jan. 1976	434	36	36	3	2	1	2	—	2	2	—	1	—	3	1	5	—	2	1	2	—	2	2
23 Jan. 1976	403	36	36	3	3	1	1	—	1	1	—	1	2	3	—	4	1	2	2	3	—	—	1
29 Oct. 1976	84	45	46	—	—	—	—	—	—	—	—	—	—	—	—	—	—	—	—	—	—	—	—
5 Nov. 1976	101	41	41	—	—	—	—	—	—	—	—	—	—	—	—	—	—	—	—	—	—	—	—
12 Nov. 1976	131	41	40	1	—	—	—	—	—	—	—	—	—	—	—	—	—	—	—	—	—	—	—
18 Nov. 1976	153	41	42	1	—	—	—	1	—	—	—	2	—	—	—	—	—	—	—	—	—	—	—
26 Nov. 1976	301	37	37	1	—	—	—	1	—	—	—	4	—	—	—	—	—	—	—	—	—	—	—
3 Dec. 1976	336	35	35	2	—	—	—	3	—	—	—	3	—	—	—	—	—	—	—	—	—	1	—
10 Dec. 1976	299	33	33	2	3	1	—	—	1	—	1	1	1	—	—	—	5	—	—	—	3	—	—
17 Dec. 1976	282	38	38	5	2	4	—	1	1	1	—	—	1	1	—	—	1	4	—	—	—	3	—
23 Dec. 1976	253	37	37	4	1	2	1	—	1	2	1	—	—	2	1	3	1	3	1	1	—	2	1
30 Dec. 1976	377	32	33	3	2	—	2	—	1	1	—	2	1	2	1	4	—	3	1	2	2	—	1
7 Jan. 1977	360	32	31	1	2	1	—	—	2	2	—	1	2	4	1	4	1	2	2	2	1	1	2
14 Jan. 1977	343	33	32	1	1	—	—	—	2	2	—	1	1	5	2	3	—	2	1	1	1	1	3
21 Jan. 1977	245	34	33	1	1	—	—	—	1	1	—	—	—	4	2	—	—	1	2	2	—	1	4
4 Nov. 1977	115	45	46	2	—	—	—	—	—	—	—	2	—	—	—	—	—	—	—	—	—	—	—
11 Nov. 1977	118	44	42	1	—	—	—	—	—	—	—	2	—	—	—	—	—	—	—	—	—	—	—
17 Nov. 1977	129	44	44	1	—	—	—	1	—	—	—	2	1	—	—	—	—	—	—	—	—	1	—
24 Nov. 1977	122	44	44	—	—	1	1	1	—	—	1	1	1	—	—	—	—	1	—	—	—	1	—
1 Dec. 1977	146	44	43	2	—	—	2	2	—	—	1	—	—	—	—	—	—	—	—	—	—	2	—
8 Dec. 1977	154	46	46	2	1	2	1	3	—	—	—	2	—	—	—	—	1	1	—	—	—	1	—
15 Dec. 1977	204	43	41	3	—	3	—	3	—	—	—	4	1	—	—	—	2	2	—	—	—	1	—
21 Dec. 1977	333	42	42	4	—	2	—	2	—	—	—	3	—	—	—	2	1	4	—	—	—	2	—
29 Dec. 1977	334	44	43	5	1	1	—	1	1	1	1	2	—	1	—	4	1	5	—	—	—	2	1
5 Jan. 1978	432	39	39	4	3	1	—	—	2	2	—	1	—	2	—	3	1	6	1	—	1	3	1
12 Jan. 1978	258			2	5	—	1	—	2	2	—	—	—	4	—	3	1	2	—	2	1	4	1
19 Jan. 1978	341	36	36	1	4	—	—	—	—	2	—	1	—	5	1	2	1	1	2	2	1	3	1
26 Jan. 1978	434	34	33	1	2	—	—	—	2	1	1	—	2	5	3	—	1	—	1	2	1	3	1

For each week we tabulate the average and median soil moisture determined gravimetrically for two samples removed at each of five sites in the Lutz catchment; the total dry weight in g of leaves falling that week into 200 tubs with a total collecting area of 16.7 sq. m; and the number of individuals of selected species observed dropping "few" or "many" leaves that week. The phenology census includes six individuals each of *Spondias mombin* (A), *Spondias radlkoferi* (B), *Anacardium excelsum* (C), and *Pseudobombax septenatum* (D); five *Sterculia apetala* (E); four each of *Cavanillesia platanifolia* (F), *Sapium caudatum* (G), *Zuelania guidonia* (H), and *Apeiba membranacea* (I); and three *Virola surinamensis* (J).

DIETRICH ET AL.

Table 2. (continued)

Day/Month/Year	Leaf litter dry weight	Average soil moisture	Median soil moisture	No. individuals of each species dropping "few" leaves										No. individuals of each species dropping "many" leaves									
				A	B	C	D	E	F	G	H	I	J	A	B	C	D	E	F	G	H	I	J
1 Nov. 1978	100	47	47	—	—	—	—	—	—	—	—	—	—	—	—	—	—	—	—	—	—	—	—
8 Nov. 1978	106	46	46	—	1	—	—	—	—	—	—	1	—	—	—	—	—	—	—	—	—	—	—
16 Nov. 1978	121	44	45	—	—	—	—	—	—	—	—	—	—	—	—	—	—	—	—	—	—	—	—
24 Nov. 1978	118	50	45	—	—	—	2	—	—	—	—	1	—	—	—	—	1	—	—	—	—	—	1	—
1 Dec. 1978	186			1	4	—	1	5	—	1	—	—	1	—	—	—	2	—	—	—	—	3	—
6 Dec. 1978	260	46	46	5	3	4	1	5	—	1	—	1	1	—	—	—	2	1	—	—	—	2	—
14 Dec. 1978	388	42	41	6	4	5	1	4	—	1	—	1	—	—	—	—	2	2	—	—	—	1	—
21 Dec. 1978	461	44	44	6	5	2	1	2	1	3	1	2	1	—	—	4	1	4	—	—	—	—	—
28 Dec. 1978	428	40	40	5	3	1	1	—	1	2	1	1	2	1	2	4	1	6	1	1	1	—	—
5 Jan. 1979	511	32	32	4	2	—	1	—	2	3	1	—	1	2	3	2	2	6	1	1	—	1	—
11 Jan. 1979	381	33	32	—	2	2	—	—	2	1	—	—	—	6	3	—	3	1	—	3	—	1	—
18 Jan. 1979	347	30	31	—	1	—	—	—	2	1	—	—	3	6	4	—	3	1	—	2	—	1	1
25 Jan. 1979	264	35	35	—	1	—	—	—	1	—	—	1	1	5	4	—	1	—	1	3	—	1	3

to be generated before the water content in the soil for the entire basin is restored to available water capacity. Overland flow during the transition into and out of the dry season probably reduces recharge of soil moisture by less than 20%, however, and therefore it does not cause serious error in this model to exclude this process.

Although some groundwater runoff (GWR) leaves the catchment as subsurface stormflow quite soon after a storm, other groundwater runoff reflects the slow drainage of groundwater stored in the basin. We have not taken into account how much of the runoff resulting from a given storm may occur as slow drainage from groundwater storage after the end of the month when the storm occurred. This effect is probably small because of the small size and steep slopes of the basin and the resulting rapidity with which much of the groundwater leaves it. Further, if baseflow at the beginning of the dry season is an index of this delay in runoff generated by wet season rainstorms, the data in Figure 17 (see later) suggests that this runoff component is small.

An important influence on actual evapotranspiration (AET) which is not included in this model is the increased difficulty in removing available water from storage in the soil as the soil moisture becomes depleted. This effect will reduce the rate of soil moisture decline during the dry season but increase the water stress on the plant (which is defined as the difference between potential evapotranspiration and actual evapotranspiration) because actual evapotranspiration will decline with decreasing water content. Because we are comparing our results with data for the first 5 cm of soil at an index site and because we lack a precise means to account for this effect we have not included it in our model.

The two most difficult quantities to define in this simplified water budget are potential evapotranspiration and the available water capacity of the soil. The previous section on water demand describes the procedure used to compute the monthly rate of potential evapotranspiration in the Lutz Creek catchment. In theory, measurement of the depth of rooting of plants in the field will give the depth of soil from which water can be extracted. The available water capacity will be equal to the depth of the soil times the proportion of the volume of the soil profile occupied by water which can be used by the plants. Traditionally, the latter is calculated as the difference between the field capacity (the greatest soil water content held by a soil when it is freely drained) and the wilting point.

In this study site it was very difficult to define the rooting zone from which water could be removed because very few overturned trees were available for inspection. Further, trees will root into the saprolite and weathered bedrock and it could not be assumed that the depth of soil and depth of rooting for water uptake were equal. However, based on observation from three uprooted exposures, the depth of rooting can exceed 80 cm.

As an alternative, we used the rainfall and runoff data to try to estimate the water entering storage in the soil during the wet season. We calculated the net amount of water stored in the ground during each rainy season, extending from the first through the last month when rainfall minus runoff exceeded potential evapotranspiration, by subtracting the total runoff and total evapotranspiration for the season from the total rainfall. We find that the total net storage of water during the rainy season (and thus, presumably, the total amount of water the soil could hold) was 52.2 cm in 1977, 29.7 cm in 1978, and 48.9 cm in 1979, averaging 43.6 cm. This method shifts some of the error in the water budget introduced by calculation of potential evapotranspiration into the estimate of available water capacity. If V is the percentage of the soil's volume occupied by water, then the amount of water, G, stored in soil of depth D, is

$$G = DV/100 \qquad (2)$$

The available water capacity of the soil (AWC) is G_{max}, the soil's water content when saturated, less G_{min}, its water content when it releases no more moisture. Thus

$$AWC = D(V_{max} - V_{min})/100$$
$$= G_{max} - G_{min} \qquad (3)$$

We defined V_{max} and V_{min} using equation (1) and observations on the annual maximum and minimum monthly percent by weight soil moisture (45% and 27%, respectively). Further, we have estimated the available water capacity from the rainfall and runoff data to be 43.6 cm.

Solving for D, we have obtained a value of 122 cm for the total depth from which water is withdrawn by plants. This depth is greater than the minimum depth of 80 cm suggested by rootwad exposure of fallen trees and suggests that the tree roots penetrate well into the underlying saprolite and weathered bedrock. The depth may also be overestimated because of systematic underestimation of the magnitude of evapotranspiration, as is suggested by the Thornthwaite estimates (Table 1). Solving equation (1) for X in terms of V, and expressing $V = 100\,G/D$ from equation (2), we find that

$$X = 100 \left[\frac{\rho_s D}{G} + 1 \right]^{-1} \qquad (4)$$

To see how the percentage of soil moisture by weight (X) is related to the total moisture content of the soil, consider the case at the beginning of a dry season when evapotranspiration exceeds precipitation by 5 cm. If the soil moisture content by weight at the be-

ginning of the month was 45%, then, by equation (1), the moisture content by volume will be 65%, which by equation (2) is 79.3 cm of water if $D = 122$ cm. Then, at the end of the month, $G = 79.3$ cm $-$ 5 cm $= 74.3$ cm. According to equation (4), if the density of dry soil is 0.8 g/cu. m, the new soil moisture is 43.2% by weight.

A Water Budget for 1976 to 1980 in the Lutz Creek Catchment

In Table 1 we have presented the raw meteorological data used in the Penman method to compute potential evapotranspiration. The calculated water budget is shown in Figure 9. The calculation procedure began

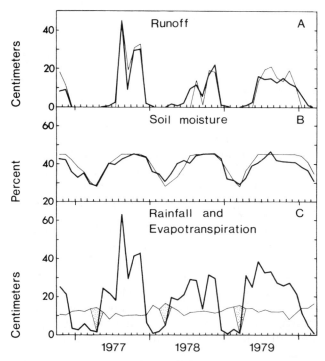

Figure 9. Part A: Predicted (light line) versus observed (heavy line) monthly runoff for the period of the water budget. Part B: Predicted (light line) versus observed (heavy line) monthly average soil moisture content by weight for the period of the water budget. Part C: Water budget for Lutz Creek catchment for October 1976 to March 1980. Monthly rates of rainfall (heavy line) and evapotranspiration (light line) are given in total depth of water over the entire catchment per month. Potential evapotranspiration varies little through the year. Because of the large water storage capacity in the soils and underlying weathered bedrock and saprolite and the relatively short dry season, for only one to two months of the year does this supply of water become exhausted by plant uptake and actual evapotranspiration equals just the rainfall.

for the month of October 1976, at which time it was assumed that available water capacity was 43.6 cm and soil moisture content was 45% by weight. At this time, precipitation greatly exceeded potential evapotranspiration demand and the difference between the two was the runoff. By December, however, precipitation dropped far below potential evapotranspiration, runoff ceased, and water was withdrawn from the soil reducing the soil moisture content. Measured runoff for December was only 0.05 cm. In March 1977 the available soil water was exhausted and the actual evapotranspiration fell to just the rainfall amount.

In May 1977, rain once again exceeded evapotranspiration demand, but runoff did not occur until 43.6 cm of excess rainfall had gone into storage in the soil, which occurred by July. Measured runoff for May and June were 0.1 and 0.7 cm, respectively. The same logic can be used to explain the remainder of the diagram. The region representing the difference between potential and actual evapotranspiration is called the soil moisture deficit and gives an indication of the severity of the dry season. The soil moisture deficit would be greater if the actual evapotranspiration were reduced as the water content diminished.

The goal in constructing the water budget was to devise a means for predicting the seasonal change in soil moisture content. Figure 9 shows the observed and predicted soil moisture for the period of the water budget. The form of the predicted soil moisture curve follows the assumptions of the model. Predicted soil moisture was assumed to range from a maximum of 45% by weight to a minimum of 27% on the basis of soil moisture measurements. Moisture content will decrease whenever precipitation falls below potential evapotranspiration until it reaches the imposed minimum. Although this procedure is a gross approximation, it gives a reasonable fit to the observed data collected from the topsoil at an index site. There are problems, however, such as the deviation between predicted and observed values of soil moisture in the last three months of 1979. These three numbers coincide with the advent of a new technician, and illustrate the uncertainties of interpreting monitoring data collected by a succession of different people.

Another test of the validity of the water budget model is to compare observed and predicted monthly runoff (Figure 9). In general, the predicted and observed runoff are similar. Deviation from the observed runoff is expected at the beginning of the wet season because runoff will occur before storage in the soil is completed and because some parts of the basin will become saturated sooner than indicated by the sample site along the transect. Storage in the basin as groundwater will delay the cessation of runoff beyond the predicted time and decrease the magnitude of

runoff in the wet season, but this effect could be expressed by use of a storage coefficient to modulate the timing of runoff from the basin. In general, the similarity between predicted and observed runoff rates appears to support the simple form this model has taken.

Construction of a quantitative model of runoff processes for individual storms would greatly improve the physical basis of our water budget model and its applicability to other tropical catchments. We have begun examining runoff processes in the Lutz Creek catchment and in the next section we will report some of our initial findings. Because the processes we will discuss are unfamiliar to most biologists, we will begin with a general review before passing to the specifics of Barro Colorado Island.

RUNOFF PROCESSES

Water striking a hillslope flows to drainage channels via several paths (Figure 10). The path it takes controls the magnitude and duration of runoff, the recharge of soil water for use by plants, the nutrient content of streamflow, and the intensity of surface erosion processes. Dunne (1978) explained these paths in detail and discussed the controls on the runoff contribution of each path.

If the soil surface has a low infiltration capacity relative to the intensity of the rainstorm, the excess rainwater runs overland to the channel (path 1). This process is called Horton overland flow after Robert Horton (1933), who first studied it formally and em-

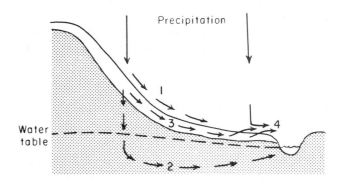

Figure 10. Possible paths of water moving downhill. Path 1 is Horton overland flow; path 2 is groundwater flow; path 3 is shallow subsurface stormflow; path 4 is saturation overland flow, composed of direct precipitation on the saturated area and infiltrated water that returns to the ground surface. The unshaded zone indicates highly permeable topsoil, and the shaded zone represents less permeable subsoil and bedrock (from Dunne and Leopold, 1978).

phasized its importance. Water that infiltrates the soil and bedrock may percolate vertically to the water table and travel to the channel as groundwater flow (path 2). If the infiltrating water encounters a relatively impermeable boundary, as often occurs at the transition from soil to bedrock, it will flow laterally to the channel as subsurface stormflow (path 3). Finally, if during a storm the soil becomes saturated with water, some of the subsurface flow will emerge at the surface and join the falling rain to form saturation overland flow (path 4). This occurs most commonly at the foot of the slopes, on hillsides with concave profiles and contours, or on slopes with shallow soils of low permeability.

The relative contribution of each path to the total runoff is controlled by the interaction of several factors, including climate, vegetation, geology, and land use. Within a catchment, spatial variation in topography and properties of the soil will lead to seasonal changes in the proportion of the basin contributing surface runoff. Recognition that spatial variation in rainfall intensity and soil permeability causes some areas to contribute more Horton overland flow than others, has led to the partial area concept (Betson, 1964; Yair et al., 1978). Similarly, recognition of the seasonal and spatial variation in the magnitude of saturation overland flow has led to the variable-source concept of runoff production (Hewlett and Hibbert, 1967; Dunne and Black, 1970). The data presented here confirm the importance of variable sources in the wet tropics.

A corollary to the variable-source concept is that soil moisture available for plant and animal use also will be seasonally and spatially variable. The temporal and spatial availability of soil moisture, which is predictable from soil properties and topography, influences the distribution of plants, their interspecific and intraspecific variation in growth rate, physiognomy and timing of reproduction, as we have mentioned above.

Runoff Processes in the Wet Tropics

The variable-source concept has recently stimulated quantitative studies of runoff production from hillslopes in the tropics. Nortcliff et al. (1979) monitored soil-water content at several sites along a steep, forested hillslope underlain by sandy, well-aggregated soils at Reserva Ducke near Manaus, Brazil. During their study, rainwater infiltrated the highly permeable soil of the hillside and traveled to the base of the slope near the floodplain, saturating the soil there and generating saturation overland flow. No overland flow was observed above the base of the slope.

In a tropical forest of North Queensland, Australia, Bonell and Gilmour (1978) set troughs into the soil at three levels to measure rates of surface and subsurface flow in a small, steep, forested catchment, and found that saturation overland flow was widespread on the slopes. The clayey soils at their study sites had very high permeabilities for the first 20 cm of depth, but below this depth permeability decreased dramatically. During a storm, this relatively impermeable boundary blocked infiltrating soil water, causing the topsoil to become saturated, and generating saturation overland flow over large areas of the catchment.

Leigh (1978a, b) has also measured overland flow from soil troughs in lowland dipterocarp forest in Malaya. These troughs were set in slopes of 4° to 14° mantled by clay-rich soils derived from shales. Leigh did not explain what caused the overland flow, which amounted to about 40% of the total runoff from the study site, but Leigh (1978b, p. 201) mentioned a "seepage depression" nearby, suggesting to us that saturation overland flow contributed to the runoff. Horton overland flow may also have been important, however; the distinction matters when one tries to model factors governing runoff or to design remedial measures for disturbed areas.

In sum, saturation overland flow is frequent in the tropics. The thickness of soil above an impeding horizon governs the area yielding such flow, and thus the contribution of saturation overland flow to total runoff. On the other hand, if the forest is destroyed and the soil rendered less permeable, Horton overland flow may dominate and accelerate soil erosion (Rougerie, 1960; Tricart, 1972; Roose, 1976; Lam, 1978; Daubenmire, 1972).

Influence of Geology on Runoff

Geology affects runoff primarily in two ways. First, the rates at which mountains build and stream channels are deepened control the general relief of the landscape from which rainwater must drain. Second, the types of the underlying rocks can greatly influence the depth and texture of the soil that forms, the availability of soil moisture during the dry season, and the path of runoff to drainage channels. Rocks which are easily penetrated by percolating waters will experience more accelerated leaching than denser rock and can be weathered more deeply. The texture of the soil derived from the weathered bedrock will depend in part on the degree of weathering of the rock, which reflects the permeability of the bedrock. Soil texture also depends in part on the inherent grain size of the parent rock, as Tricart (1972) has discussed more thoroughly. Rocks such as quartzitic sandstones will weather into a soil with a sandy texture and high permeability. Rocks composed of fine-textured minerals, volcanic glass, or minerals that weather relatively quickly, will break down into a soil rich in clays. Although the permeability of clay is low, it can be greatly increased by a dense network of roots, or by the presence of large, water-stable soil aggregates. Finally, in limestone bedrock, the lack of aluminosilicates prevents the formation of clay during weathering, resulting in very thin soils which can store very little water, thus leading to an extraordinarily xeric (drought-resistant) vegetation, as in the Guánica forest of Puerto Rico (Lugo et al., 1978).

The texture of the soil has pronounced effects on how runoff leaves a hillside. The principal difference between the style of runoff found by Nortcliff et al. (1979) at Manaus and that found by Bonell and Gilmour (1978) in North Queensland may be due to soil texture, which reflects differences in the underlying weathered rock. On the Manaus hillslope, the deep quartz-rich sandy soils and the saprolite derived from sandstone are quite permeable, and runoff from most of the hillslope is by subsurface flow to the base of the slope where a rising groundwater table contributes to saturation overland flow. In North Queensland, silica-poor and chemically unstable metamorphic rock has weathered to a clay-rich soil, which has a stratified permeability: very high in the first 20 cm, very low in the soil below this depth. This stratification, which leads to saturation overland flow, probably results from the growth of a dense network of roots in the upper 20 cm which greatly increases the permeability of the soil. In general, root systems of trees in the wet tropics are concentrated near the surface, although many species may have deeply penetrating taproots or sinker roots (Jenik, 1978). Thus the restriction of permeability to the top layer of soil observed in North Queensland may be a common feature of clay-rich soils in the wet tropics, and saturation overland flow correspondingly important there. Extremely high concentrations of roots near the soil surface are characteristic of soils formed from silica-rich bedrock, as at Reserva Ducke (Odum, 1970, Figure 28, p. H–34), but the high permeability of the sandy subsoil prevents overland flow except where the water table is near the surface.

Implications of the Mode of Runoff

The type, and the seasonal pattern, of runoff influences its nutrient content. The rate of chemical weathering on a hillslope depends in part on how long water remains in contact with the weatherable material (Dethier, 1977), which depends on the total volume of water moving past these minerals and the rate at which it does so. These in turn depend on how the runoff leaves the slope.

On hillslopes with soils that are nearly saturated before a rainstorm, saturation overland flow will only briefly be in contact with the soil. Therefore this flow should deliver dilute water to drainage channels containing just the leachate from the forest canopy and those few solutes it acquired from the flow returning to the surface. Nortcliff et al. (1979) suggested that streams in the Amazon Basin were so poor in nutrients because a large proportion of the runoff from storms is produced from saturated floodplains and the bases of adjacent slopes, and therefore has very little contact with the soil.

The concentration of ions in subsurface stormflow should vary with the season, as the predominant mode of runoff changes. At the beginning of the wet season the ground is covered with leaf litter and initial rains will percolate through the litter into the soil cracks, producing little or no runoff. Water in the soil will presumably be rich in ions leached from the litter, and more nutrients should be available to the plants than at any other time of year (Smythe, 1970). Leaf production is highest at this time (Leigh and Windsor, this volume; Leigh and Smythe, 1978). As the rains continue, they will accelerate the loss of nutrients to the streams by displacing soil water downslope as subsurface stormflow and by washing leaf litter downslope by saturation overland flow. As the rainy season progresses and the soil becomes more saturated, runoff will spend less time in contact with the soil and less and less leaf litter will remain on the ground, so the concentration of mineral nutrients in streams and groundwater should decrease progressively. Such a cycle in the availability of nutrients may have important consequences for plant productivity.

Different types of runoff also erode the surface of the catchment at very different rates. In regions without overland flow, soil moves downslope primarily by creep or by landsliding and, where vegetation is sparse, by rainsplash. Together, these processes typically erode the soil ten to a thousand times less rapidly than the rainsplash combined with sheetwash generated during Horton overland flow. We do not know how rapidly saturation overland flow can erode steep slopes with cohesive soils. Perhaps the cohesion of saturated clays intertwined with organic material effectively resists shearing by thin sheet flows, and a layer of water over the soil surface may greatly diminish rates of rainsplash, so that saturation overland flow leads to much lower rates of erosion than Horton overland flow. Regrettably, the mechanics of cohesive soil erosion are so poorly understood that we cannot make even simple calculations to test this hypothesis. However, saturation overland flow is important in the wet tropics generally and, in the next section, we suggest that saturation overland flow is an important contribution to runoff in the Lutz Creek catchment. We will conclude this chapter on runoff processes with a discussion of rates of erosion.

Runoff Processes in the Lutz Creek Catchment

Although we have observed overland flow during rainstorms, we have no direct measurement of its magnitude on the hillsides, nor could we distinguish whether the flow was saturation overland flow or Horton overland flow. However, observations on the soil moisture content and seasonal changes in peak runoff rates suggest that saturation overland flow is an important contributor to runoff in the Lutz Creek catchment. As we reported earlier, the moisture content by weight of the soils along the sampling transect reach a value of 45% during the wet season, which suggests that the soil is at or very close to saturation. Rain on

saturated soil will produce saturation overland flow which can travel rapidly on steep slopes to channels and produce high peak runoff rates.

The relative magnitude of the peak runoff in Lutz Creek for the same storm duration and peak rainfall intensity increases from less than 1% of the rainfall intensity in May up to 30–50% of the rainfall intensity in November (Figure 11). The substantial increase in runoff rate as the rainy season progresses is probably caused by an increasing contribution of saturation overland flow to the runoff peak. Early in the rainy season, the rainfall that penetrates the forest canopy to the soil surface runs down the cracks in the soil, increasing the soil moisture content but generating little runoff. Rain falling directly on the drainage channels and subsurface runoff from small parts of the catchment produce only a few low waves on the weir chart. As the rains continue, soil moisture content increases, cracks in the soil swell closed, and progressively less rainfall is needed to saturate the soil and produce saturation overland flow. For example, in June 1978 the soil water content was 42% by weight

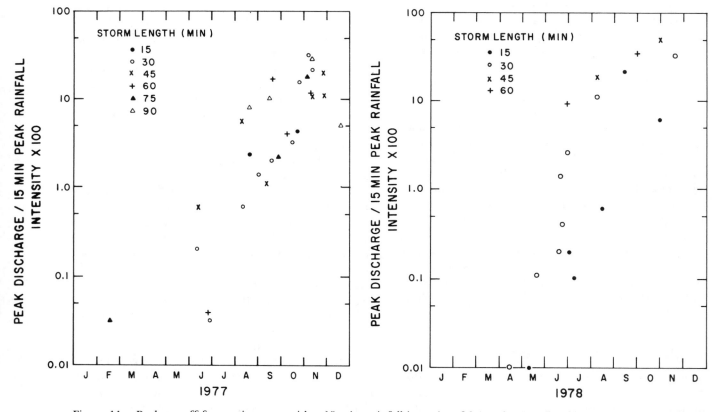

Figure 11.   Peak runoff from rainstorms with a 15-min. rainfall intensity of 3.1 and 4.1 cm/hr. for Lutz Creek in 1977 and 1978. The general relationship was the same for all 15-min. peak rainfall intensities and storm length. Generally the larger the storm for a given peak rainfall rate, the greater the runoff.

40

or 57% by volume. If the total pore space is 65% by volume, then in a 50-cm-deep soil column it will take 50 (0.65–0.57) or 4.0 cm of rainwater to saturate the soil, as compared with about 11.7 cm in April and nearly zero in November for the same year. Near the end of the wet season multiple-peaked flood hydrographs for a single large storm also appear, reflecting greatly increased sensitivity to oscillations in rainfall intensity.

The continued rapid increase in runoff rate during the latter part of the wet season must also reflect the fact that an increasing area of the watershed is approaching saturation. The thinnest, least porous soils with the shallowest rooting zones, and topographic depressions of swales where subsurface flow converges will saturate earliest. The central headwaters of the Lutz Creek basin has gentle topography broken by many shallow channels and we suggest that this region contributes saturation overland flow earliest in the wet season.

Three properties of the hydrographs recorded at the weir pond suggest that overland flow contributes significantly to the peak runoff from the catchment, although they cannot be used to distinguish Horton and saturation overland flow. First, the peak runoff rates can exceed 9 cm/hr. In Figure 12, the frequency density function of peak runoff rates indicates that about 10% of the flows in the two years 1977–78 exceeded 1.0 cm/hr. which is greater than the maximum peak discharge generated by subsurface stormflow alone from 10-ha. basins elsewhere (Dunne, 1978; Harr, 1977). Second, lag time between the peak rainfall intensity and peak runoff rate in the Lutz Creek catchment is very short, ranging from about 30 min. for small stormflows to as little as 3 min. for rarer, larger flows (Figure 13). Peak runoff generated by subsurface stormflow alone in basins of comparable size elsewhere has a lag time of greater than an hour (Dunne, 1978).

Finally, the recession limb of the hydrograph is very steep for the larger peak flows. If it is assumed that runoff after the peak flow is proportional to the water remaining in storage in the watershed, then the following expression can be derived (Chow, 1965, p. 14–9) for the recession limb

$$Q_t = Q_o K^t \qquad (5)$$

where Q_t is the discharge at any time t (hours) after the peak discharge, Q_o, and K is the recession constant. Rewritten for clarity the equation becomes

$$\ln K = \frac{(\ln Q_t - \ln Q_o)}{t}$$

K becomes the slope of the recession limb plotted

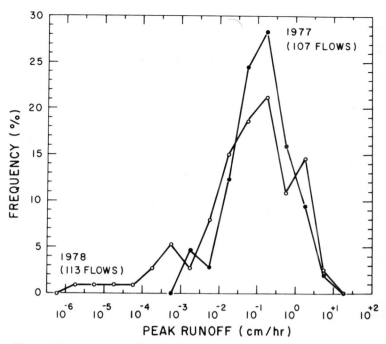

Figure 12. Frequency distribution of peak runoff for 1977 and 1978. The greater number of very small peak flows in 1978 may be an artifact of a more extensive examination of the 1978 runoff record.

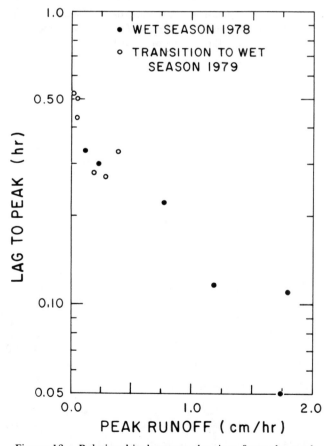

Figure 13. Relationship between the time from the peak rainfall intensity to the peak runoff rate (lag peak) and the magnitude of the peak runoff (data collected by Egbert Leigh).

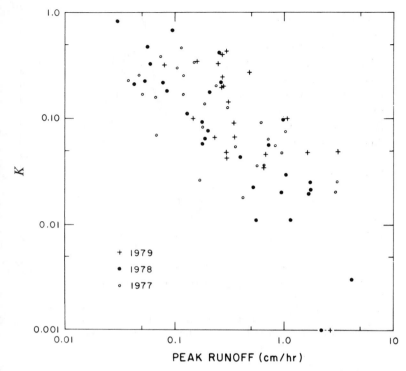

Figure 14. Relationship between the recession limb constant, K, for the first 3 to 23 min. after the peak runoff and peak runoff for three years of record.

on semilogarithmic paper; small values indicate steep recession limbs. Dunne (1978) found that runoff generated by overland flow typically had K values less than 0.5, whereas recession limbs resulting from subsurface stormflow had K values greater than about 0.8. In order to evaluate K for hydrographs from the study watershed, 79 storm hydrographs were digitized and the value of K for the first data point after the peak was computed and plotted on Figure 14. Although the time to the first data point ranged from 3 to 23 min., no improvement in the scatter of the data was achieved by grouping the points according to the time delay used. Also no clear effect of rainstorm length was detected. The data suggest that at peak runoff values of roughly 0.04 cm/hr. and less the recession limb will begin with K in excess of 0.5. Clearly the majority of the stormflows have very steep recession limbs, suggesting a significant contribution from overland flow.

Although it does not indicate the contribution of specific runoff processes, a measurement of the rapidity with which water leaves the basin can be obtained by dividing the flood hydrograph into rapid and slow runoff components. A widely accepted method of hydrograph separation, proposed by Hewlett and Hibbert (1967) involves drawing a line of constant slope of 0.0001968 cm/hr. per hour (0.55 1/sec.-sq. km-hr.) from the inception of storm runoff to the recession limb on the hydrograph and computing the volume of runoff above the line as "quickflow" and below the line as "delayed flow" (Figure 15). The background runoff rate above which the stormflow hydrograph is generated is commonly referred to as a baseflow. Baseflow was defined by joining points on the stream hydrograph at midday, or just before a flood event of that day if the flood occurred in the morning (Figure 15). The total daily runoff was added to

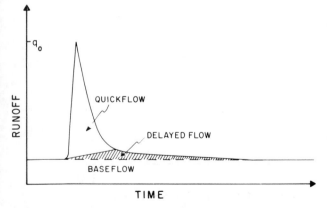

Figure 15. Schematic of a typical hydrograph for Lutz Creek. The sloping line separating quickflow from delayed flow can be defined using the Hewlett and Hibbert (1967) technique.

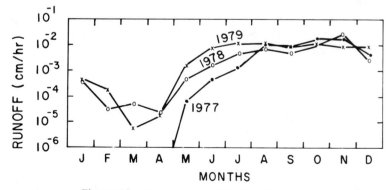

Figure 16. Average monthly baseflow from Lutz Creek catchment.

Table 3. Components of runoff (cm) from Lutz Creek catchment

Year	Rainfall	Runoff	Baseflow	Quickflow	Delayed flow
1977	259.2	123.7	45.0	33.5	45.2
1978	200.2	70.6	42.7	24.6	3.3
1979	259.6	100.7	53.2	37.5	10.0
Average annual percent of runoff			49.9	33.1	17.0

gether for each month to examine the monthly trend in baseflow (Figure 16) and to obtain the annual total baseflow (Table 3). Figure 16 illustrates that during the latter part of the wet season the baseflow for each month is approximately the same from year to year.

Table 3 summarizes the results of applying the separation technique to the runoff record for the three years 1977–79 and indicates that, on average, two-thirds of the runoff leaves the basin slowly after the rainstorm, with 50% of the total runoff occurring as baseflow. This suggests that subsurface runoff processes dominate the annual runoff from the Lutz Creek basin. The component of runoff that leaves as quickflow on an annual basis is about 33% of the total runoff, which is similar to that found in temperate regions dominated by variable-source runoff (Hewlett and Hibbert, 1967; Harr, 1977). For individual large stormflows, the quickflow component can exceed 70% of the total runoff. The three properties of the storm hydrograph described above suggest that the quickflow component is predominantly by an overland flow, which we propose is saturation overland flow. Our best estimate, based on a distinctive change in slope of the recession limb at 0.9 hr. after the peak, is that saturation overland flow contributes about 20% of the total runoff or about two-thirds of the quickflow. More quantitative conclusions can only be derived from direct measurement of runoff processes.

Rates of Erosion

Rainsplash pedestals, exposed tree roots, and large landslides suggest high rates of erosion in the Lutz Creek catchment. In order to quantify the total physical erosion rate, we began making measurements of suspended load in Lutz Creek in the wet season of 1978. We sample the suspended sediment with a handheld US DH–48 sampler (Guy and Norman, 1970) upstream of the weir pond during high flows. Below

the weir pond and during low flows we use a pint bottle instead. Samples were collected upstream and downstream of the weir in order to evaluate the trap efficiency of the pond and thereby compute the bedload transport from changes in sediment storage in the pond. The weir pond is excavated about three times a year, but difficulties in accurately recording the amount of sediment removed has prevented calculation of the bedload transport.

During storm runoff Lutz Creek turns a bright reddish brown and the results of sampling through a range of discharge during the wet seasons of 1978 and 1979 shown in Figure 17 suggest very high rates of suspended sediment transport. Some of the scatter in the relationship depicted in Figure 17 results from measurement error resulting from the samples being collected by six different people. However, most of the data are represented by measurements both above and below the weir pond, which tend to confirm differences in concentrations between the two years and suggest that the weir pond has a low trap efficiency. Part of the difference between 1978 and 1979 may be due to intentionally reduced use in 1979 of the footpaths which ring the Lutz Creek catchment. These footpaths may be relatively important contributors of sediment to the main channel at lower runoff rates when other parts of the watershed are not experi-

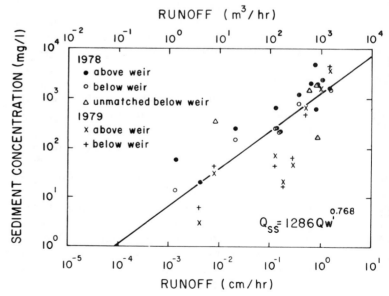

Figure 17. Concentration of suspended sediment in runoff from Lutz Creek. The best fit regression equation given in the figure is for the 21 data points above the weir and has an $r^2 = 0.64$. Q_{ss} is the sediment concentration in mg/l and q_w is the runoff in cm/hr.

encing significant overland flow.

The relationship found between water discharge and sediment concentration given in Figure 17 was used to compute annual suspended load discharge from the record of water discharge for the period 1976–79. During this time the computed average annual sediment discharge equalled 598 t/sq. km-yr. (equivalent to about 0.75 mm/yr. of soil erosion) which greatly exceeds values for mature forested watersheds elsewhere in the tropics (e.g., reference in Lam, 1978; Leigh, 1978a; Dietrich and Dunne, 1978). Enders (unpubl. manuscript) examined the rate of delta formation since 1929 into Fuertes Cove by Nemesia Creek with drains the northwest side of the island. He estimated that over a 36-year period a minimum of 21,650 cu. m of sediment was deposited in the flooded valley of Nemesia Creek which was derived from 354,830 sq. m of drainage area. Assuming the density of the deposit in the delta to be the same as in the soil, these numbers give an equivalent soil erosion rate of 1.69 mm/yr. Although his methods were very approximate, this result gives support to the high rates of erosion observed in the Lutz Creek basin. Unfortunately, the processes producing runoff at other study sites in the tropics have not been identified so that meaningful comparisons are difficult. In addition, there is another process contributing to suspended load of the Lutz Creek catchment, the magnitude of which has yet to be defined.

During storm runoff, chunks of weathered bedrock bordering the channel collapse into the stream and quickly break down to the size of suspended-load material. The lack of strength of weathered rocks is indicated by their weathered condition in the bank, the great ease with which rocks in gravel bars can be crushed by hand, and the scarcity of sediment in the channels. As of 1979, there was less than the equivalent of one year's sediment discharge stored behind roots and boulders in the stream. The supply of weathered bedrock is maintained in part by large landslides (Figure 3). The relative contribution of surface erosion associated with saturation overland flow and of landsliding to the total sediment discharge of Lutz Creek has yet to be resolved. A thorough examination of the processes contributing to saturation overland flow on the hillslopes combined with a program of erosion measurements from pins inserted into the soil surface and from troughs placed across the gradient of the hillslope would greatly enhance our ability to answer questions raised here.

CONCLUSION

The hydrology of the Lutz Creek watershed is strongly influenced by interaction between bedrock, soils, and forest organisms. Soil properties are determined by the rate of chemical weathering of the parent rock, which is largely subject to climatic controls and by the intensity of biologic disturbance which greatly affects rates of soil formation and soil erosion. The destruction of the residual physical properties of the parent material in saprolite and weathered bedrock which occurs during mixing to form a soil may be due largely to biologic activity. Burrowing insects (principally ants) and the growth of trees and tree throw may produce most of the thin mantle of soil in the Lutz Creek catchment.

The texture of the soil produced is dependent on the intensity of mixing and on the inheritable grain size of the weathered parent material. Most of the catchment is underlain by rocks rich in volcanic glasses: rocks which quickly decompose to clay. Soils formed from this material are clay-rich and as a result have low permeability unless colonized by a thick root mat. Without the benefit of vegetation cover and root penetration, these soils would experience severe erosion under Horton overland flow because of intensity of tropical rainstorms. Instead, the dense network of tree roots in the upper 20 cm of the soil greatly increases the permeability of the soils. However, they are concentrated only in this shallow layer which in places becomes saturated frequently during the wet season. Further, the roots withdraw vast quantities of water causing the soils to dry and break into broad deep cracks. In the early part of the wet season, most rain enters these soils and only a small amount of subsurface runoff is produced. Continued rain leads to saturation of the soil in the root zone and to development of saturation overland flow. The frequency and magnitude of saturation overland flow increases through the watershed as deeper, steeper, and more porous soils become nearly saturated.

The limitations of water storage in soil strongly affects the activity of trees on Barro Colorado Island. A pronounced leaffall occurs when evapotranspiration demand on the trees reduces the soil moisture content to a critical level. Spatial variation in available water capacity due to differences in bedrock, topography, and rates of soil formation and erosion may induce a systematic variation in species composition and productivity of trees. Several areas on Barro Colorado Island support stunted trees (E. Leigh, pers. comm.). A water-balance calculation for these sites based on a few field observations could test the importance of soil moisture limitations on the character of the forests.

We have developed a general picture of the hydrology of Barro Colorado Island from the interpretation of stream discharge records, which spatially average the runoff processes, and from meteorologic and pedologic data, which serve as indices only. It is now necessary to begin detailed hillslope measurements at a range of sites in the catchment to define quantitatively the runoff processes and their controls and to examine the spatial variation in physical controls of biologic activity.

ACKNOWLEDGMENTS

Egbert Leigh has contributed greatly to this paper. He collected some of the field data used here and supervised the collection of much of the rest. He encouraged the development of the paper and gave careful reviews of the manuscript. Most of the field data were collected by Gary Stump and Milton Clark for the Environmental Sciences Program. Mary Power made most of the sediment transport measurements in 1978, assisted in other aspects of field work, and helped in preparation of the manuscript. Robin Foster showed us one of the large landslides in the Lutz Creek catchment and David Janos assisted in examination of the soils. We thank Ben Morgan, who constructed the weir in the Lutz Creek catchment.

LITERATURE CITED

Augspurger, C. K.
1978.   Reproductive Consequences of Flowering Synchrony in *Hybanthus prunifolius* (Violaceae) and Other Shrub Species of Panama. Ph.D. dissertation, University of Michigan, Ann Arbor, Michigan.
1982.   A Cue for Synchronous Flowering. Pages 133–150 in *The Ecology of a Tropical Forest*, edited by Egbert G. Leigh, Jr., et al. Washington, D.C.: Smithsonian Institution Press.

Betson, R. P.
1964.   What is Watershed Runoff? *Journal of Geophysical Research*, 69:1541–1542.

Bonell, M., and D. A. Gilmour.
1978.   The Development of Overland Flow in a Tropical Rain Forest Catchment. *Journal of Hydrology*, 39:365–382.

Chapman, F. M.
1938.   *Life in an Air Castle*. New York: D. Appleton Company. 250 pp.

Chow, V. T.
1964.   Runoff. Pages 14–54 in *Handbook of Applied Hydrology*, edited by V. T. Chow. New York: McGraw-Hill.

Croat, T. B.
1978.   *Flora of Barro Colorado Island*. Stanford, Calif.: Stanford University Press. 943 pp.

Daubenmire, R.
1972.   Some Ecological Consequences of Converting Forest to Savanna in Northwestern Costa Rica. *Tropical Ecology*, 39: 31–51.

Deere, D. V., and F. D. Patton
1971.   Slope Stability in Residual Soils. Proceedings of the Fourth Panamerican Conference on Soil Mechanics and Foundation Engineering, Caracas, Venezuela.

Dethier, D. P.
1977.   Geochemistry of Williamson Creek, Snohomish County, Washington. Ph.D. dissertation, University of Washington, Seattle.

Dietrich, W. E., and T. Dunne
1978.   Sediment Budget for a Small Catchment in Mountainous Terrain. *Zeitschrift fur Geomorph. Suppl. Bld.*, 29:191–206.

Dunne, T.
1978.   Field Studies of Hillslope Flow Processes. Pages 227–293 in *Hillslope Hydrology*, edited by M. J. Kirkby. London: Wiley.

Dunne, T., and R. D. Black
1970.   Partial Area Contributions to Storm Runoff in a Small New England Watershed. *Water Reservoir Research*, 6:1296–1311.

Dunne, T., and L. B. Leopold
1978.   *Water in Environmental Planning*. San Francisco: Freeman. 818 pp.

Foster, R. B.
1982. The Seasonal Rhythm of Fruitfall on Barro Colorado Island. Pages 151–172 in *The Ecology of a Tropical Forest*, edited by Egbert G. Leigh, Jr., et al. Washington, D.C.: Smithsonian Institution Press.

Foster, R. B., and N. V. L. Brokaw
1982. Structure and History of the Vegetation of Barro Colorado Island. Pages 67–81 in *The Ecology of a Tropical Forest*, edited by Egbert G. Leigh, Jr., et al. Washington, D.C.: Smithsonian Institution Press.

Guy, H. P., and V. W. Norman
1973.   *Field Methods for Measurement of Fluvial Sediment*. Book 3, Ch. C2: Applications of Hydraulics. Reston, Va.: U.S. Geological Survey.

Harr, R. D.
1977.   Water Flux in Soil and Subsoil on a Steep Forested Slope. *Journal of Hydrology*, 33: 37–58.

Hewlett, J. D., and A. R. Hibbert
1967.   Factors Affecting the Response of Small Watersheds to Precipitation in Humid Areas. Pages 275–290 in *Forest Hydrology*, edited by W. E. Sopper and H. W. Lull. New York: Pergamon Press.

Horton, R. E.
1933.   The Role of Infiltration in the Hydrologic Cycle. *Trans. Am. Geophys. Union*, 14: 446–460.

Jackson, J. F.
1978.   Seasonality of Flowering and Leaf-Fall in a Brazilian Subtropical Lower Montane Moist Forest. *Biotropica*, 10: 38–42.

Jenik, J.
1978.   Roots and Root Systems in Tropical Trees: Morphologic and Ecologic Aspects. Pages 323–351 in *Tropical Trees as Living Systems*, edited by P. B. Tomlinson and M. H. Zimmerman. Cambridge: Cambridge University Press. 675 pp.

Knight, D.
1975.   A Phytosociological Analysis of Species-rich Tropical Forest, Barro Colorado Island, Panama. *Ecological Monographs*, 45: 259–284.

Lam, D.
1978.   Soil Erosion, Suspended Sediment and Solute Production in Three Hong Kong Catchments. *Journal of Tropical Geography*, 47:51–62.

Leigh, C. H.
1978.   Slope Hydrology and Denudation in the Pasoh Forest Reserve. I. Surface Wash: Experimental Techniques and Some Preliminary Results. *Malay. Nat. Journ.*, 30: 179–197.
1978.   Slope Hydrology and Denudation in the Pasoh Forest Reserve. II. Throughflow: Experimental Techniques and Some Preliminary Results. *Malay. Nat. Journ.*, 30: 199–210.

Leigh, E. G., and N. Smythe
1978.   Leaf Production, Leaf Consumption, and the Regulation of Folivory on Barro Colorado Island. Pages 33–50 in *The Ecology of Arboreal Folivores*, edited by G. G. Montgomery. Washington, D.C.: Smithsonian Institution Press.

Lugo, A. E., J. A. Gonzalez, B. Cintron, and K. Duggan
1978.   Structure, Productivity, and Transpiration of a Subtropical Dry Forest in Puerto Rico. *Biotropica*, 10: 278–291.

Marshall, L. G., R. F. Butler, R. E. Drake, G. H. Curtis, and R. H. Tedford
1979.   Calibration of the Great American Interchange. *Science*, 204: 272–279.

Moynihan, M. H.
1960.   Report on the Canal Zone Biological Area, 1960. Pages 172–176 in *Smithsonian Institution Report for 1960*. Washington, D.C.: Smithsonian Institution.

Nortcliff, S., J. B. Thornes, and M. J. Waylen
1979.   Tropical Forest Systems: A Hydrological Approach. *Acta Amazonica*, 4: 557–568.

Odum, H. T.
1970.   Rain Forest and Mineral Cycling Homeostasis. Pages H-1–H-52 in *A Tropical Rainforest*, edited by H. T. Odum and R. F. Pigeon. U.S. Atomic Energy Commission, Oak Ridge, Tenn.: Division of Technical Information.

Panama Canal Company
1948.   Design of Drainage Facilities. I.C.P. Memorandum 55. Balboa Heights, Canal Zone: Department of Operation and Maintenance, Special Engineering Division.

Penman, H. L.
1948.   Natural Evaporation from Open Water, Bare Soil and Grass. *Proceedings of the Royal Society, London, Series B*, 139: 120–145.

Rand, A. S., and W. M. Rand
1982.   Variation in Rainfall on Barro Colorado Island. Pages 47–59 in *The Ecology of a Tropical Forest*, edited by Egbert G. Leigh, Jr., et al. Washington, D.C.: Smithsonian Institution Press.

Roose, E. J.
1976.   Use of the Universal Soil Loss Equation to Predict Erosion in West Africa. Pages 60–74 in *Soil Erosion: Prediction and Control*, edited by G. R. Foster. Special Publication No. 21. Place: Soil Conservation Society of America.

Rougerie, G.
1960.   *Le façonnement actuel des modèles en Côte d'Ivoire forestière.* Mémoires de l'Institut Français d'Afrique Noire, no. 58. 542 pp.

Rubinoff, R. W.
1974.   1973 Environmental Monitoring and Baseline Data Compiled under the Smithsonian Institution Environmental Sciences Program, Tropical Studies. Unpublished report, Smithsonian Institution, Washington, D.C.

Ruxton, R. P.
1967.   Slope Wash Under Primary Rain Forest in Northern Papua. Pages 85–94 in *Landform Studies from Australia and New Guinea*, edited by J. A. Jennings and J. A. Mabbutt. Canberra: ANU Press.

Smythe, N.
1970.   Relationships Between Fruiting Seasons and Seed Dispersal Methods in a Neotropical Forest. *American Naturalist*, 104: 25–35.
1974.   Terrestrial Studies—Barro Colorado Island. Pages 1–115 *in* 1973 Environmental Monitoring and Baseline Data, compiled under the Smithsonian Institution Environmental Sciences Program, Tropical Studies, edited by R. W. Rubinoff. Unpublished report, Smithsonian Institution, Washington, D.C.

Tricart, J.
1972.   *Landforms of the Humid Tropics, Forests and Savannas: Geographies for Advanced Study.* London: Longmans. 306 pp.

Windsor, D.M.
1975.   1974 Environmental Monitoring and Baseline Data. Smithsonian Institution Environmental Sciences Program, Tropical Studies. Unpublished report, Smithsonian Institution, Washington, D.C.
1976.   1975 Environmental Monitoring and Baseline Data, Smithsonian Institution Environmental Sciences Program, Tropical Studies. Unpublished report, Smithsonian Institution, Washington, D.C.
1977.   1976 Environmental Monitoring and Baseline Data, Smithsonian Institution Environmental Sciences Program, Tropical Studies. Unpublished report, Smithsonian Institution, Washington, D.C.

U.S. Army Tropic Test Center
1979.   *Material Testing in the Tropics.* Report No. 790401, 6th ed.

Waldvoget, A.
1974.   The N_o Jump of Raindrop Spectra. *Journal of Atmospheric Science*, 31: 1067–1078.

Woodring, W. P.
1957.   Geology and Paleontology of Canal Zone and Adjoining Parts of Panama. Prof. Pap. 306–A. Reston, Va.: U.S. Geological Survey.
1958.   Geology of Barro Colorado Island, Canal Zone. Smithsonian Institution Miscellaneous Collections, Vol. 135, No. 3, Pub. No. 4304. Washington, D.C.: Smithsonian Institution.

Yair, A., D. Sharon, and H. Lavee.
1978.   An Instrumented Watershed for the Study of Partial Area Contribution of Runoff in the Arid Zone. *Zeit. fur Geomorph. Suppl. Bd.*, 29: 71–82.

Variation in Rainfall on Barro Colorado Island

A. STANLEY RAND Smithsonian Tropical Research Institute, Balboa, Republic of Panama

WILLIAM M. RAND Massachusetts Institute of Technology, Cambridge, Massachusetts 02139

ABSTRACT

Weekly rainfalls at various sites around the perimeter of Barro Colorado Island vary in both time and space. Weekly rainfall into gauges around the perimeter of the island are highly correlated but not identical. Variation among them is absolutely greatest during the wet season, relatively greatest during the dry season. The total annual rainfall on Barro Colorado Island is quite highly correlated with that at a site 5 mi. away, but in many years they are quite different. Annual rainfall on Barro Colorado is less closely correlated with that on the drier Pacific coast or the wetter Atlantic coast.

Rainfall on Barro Colorado Island comes largely in storms of short duration and is most likely during the early afternoon and least likely between midnight and dawn. Over the past 50 years, total annual rainfall on Barro Colorado has averaged 103 in. (2616 mm), ranging from 66 to 143 in. (1676–3632 mm). There is a significant downward trend of about one-third of an inch per year over this period. This trend occurs at other stations on Gatun Lake but not on either coast.

The year on Barro Colorado Island is dominated by wet and dry seasons which can be defined using soil moisture conditions predicted from observed rainfall. The dry season usually starts in late December, the rainy season at the end of April, but there is considerable variation in the precise timing. Most dry seasons have rainy periods; most wet seasons, dry spells.

Predictability of weekly rainfall was approached through harmonic and autoregressive models. The latter gives an R^2 of 0.41, the former an R^2 of 0.52; together they give an R^2 of 0.54. Rainfall is most predictable during the dry season and the first part of the wet season; it is least predictable during the transitions between the seasons.

INTRODUCTION

As in most of the tropics, the most conspicuous seasonal changes on Barro Colorado Island are associated with rainfall. Variations in rainfall affect the phenology of plants, and thereby the seasonal behavior of the animals that feed on them (Foster, this volume). It is therefore important to consider how rainfall varies, over space and over time. This chapter examines the rainfall at the laboratory clearing on Barro Colorado Island, comparing it with that on other parts of the island and other nearby areas and describing how it varies from day to day, from season to season, and from year to year.

SPATIAL VARIATION

Three years of weekly rainfall records were gathered from rain gauges calibrated in inches placed in the laboratory clearing and on supports in Gatun Lake around the perimeter of Barro Colorado Island (Figure 1). The weekly amounts of rain in these gauges

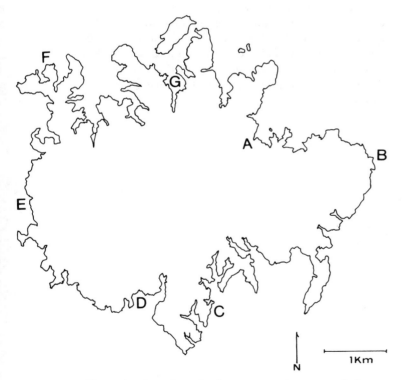

Figure 1. Location of rain gauge stations around the perimeter of Barro Colorado Island. Letters refer to the rain gauges mentioned in Table 1.

were highly correlated: correlations between different pairs of rain gauges ranged from 0.83 to 0.96 in 1972, 0.55 to 0.98 in 1974, and 0.70 to 0.95 in 1976. However, there was considerable variation in the amount of rain falling into different gauges during any given week. The greatest *absolute* variations occur during the rainy season, and if one corrects for the amount of rain by calculating a coefficient of variability it becomes apparent that the greatest *relative* variability occurs during the dry season, when rains are occasional, light, and apparently highly localized. Table 1 shows the seasonal totals; the greatest difference was in 1975 when station B recorded a total of 99 in. (2515 mm) of rain while station D, on the other side of the island, recorded 80 in. (2032 mm)—about 20% less. There is a generally prevailing wind from a northerly direction; one can see a suggestion that the gauges on the laboratory side of the island received more rain than those on the opposite side of the island. This hint is obscured by the stochastic variation between gauges presumably produced by unpredictable differences in local rainfall. The usually higher rainfall recorded from the laboratory gauge may be an artifact produced because the laboratory gauge (station A) was read daily, the other weekly.

On a broader scale, there is a strong gradient in rainfall across the isthmus of Panama (Figure 2); the Pacific side of the isthmus is usually drier (Balboa Heights, annual average 71 in. [1803 mm]) than is the Atlantic side (Cristobal, 129 in. [3277 mm]), and Barro Colorado Island (103 in. [2616 mm]) is usually intermediate. However, there is only a weak correlation ($n = 50$, $r = 0.45$) in annual rainfall between Atlantic and Pacific sites. Barro Colorado Island rainfall is more similar in amount and is more closely correlated with the wetter and physically closer Atlantic coast ($n = 49$, $r = 0.69$) than the drier Pacific coast ($n = 50$, $r = 0.32$). When Barro Colorado Island is compared with Monte Lirio, 5 mi. away, where total rainfall (107 in. [2718 mm]) averages about the same, there is a good correlation ($n = 41$, $r = 0.80$), although in many years there is considerable difference in the amount of rain at these two places.

In organisms whose biology is closely tied to the rains, local variation can be important because it means that different individuals that are only a kilometer or two apart may breed or produce fruit or new leaves at different times. For an animal, such as an euglossine bee or a fruit crow, that can easily move several kilometers, the local variability in rainfall provides a range of environmental conditions to select among. For a sedentary species such as a toad, it means that segments of a continuous population may be subjected to different conditions in the same year. Extinction and emigration following extremely successful breed-

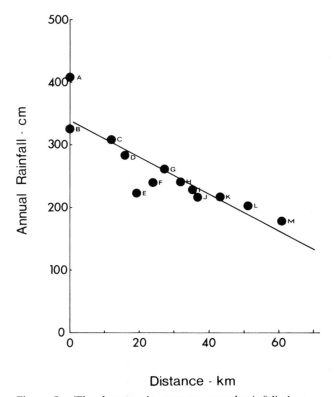

Figure 2. The decrease in average annual rainfall along a north-south transect of the isthmus of Panama.
A = Porto Bello, B = Cristobal, C = Gatun, D = Monte Lirio, E = Las Raices, F = Salamonica, G = Barro Colorado Island, H = Madden, I = Caño, J = Gamboa, K = Summit, L = Pedro Miguel, M = Balboa Heights.

Table 1. Circumferential rainfall totals (in inches)

Season	Rain gauge						
	A	B	C	D	E	F	G
1972 Dry season Wk. 1–12	10.82	9.14	8.95	8.20	9.47	7.64	8.35
1972 Wet season Wk. 13–26	240.20	237.97	209.82	195.90	218.07	203.44	208.18
1973 Dry season Wk. 1–12	7.52	4.27	4.31	5.33	4.89	5.47	5.37
1973 Wet season Wk. 13–26	216.85	191.60	200.62	178.58	182.29	190.70	192.42
1974 Dry season Wk. 1–12	9.83	4.92	6.27	8.19	10.21	11.48	12.73
1974 Wet season Wk. 13–26	240.14	217.24	205.59	220.22	238.02	228.20	243.23
1975 Dry season Wk. 1–12	34.47	33.73	32.77	29.31	32.84	32.44	29.44
1975 Wet season Wk. 13–26	193.75	182.75	187.91	172.16	155.35	163.45	181.18

ing, as far as they are primarily or secondarily dependent on rainfall, are more likely to be strictly local events than would be the case if the rainfall patterns were more widespread and nearby localities more closely correlated.

TEMPORAL PATTERNS

Diurnal Rhythms

Rainfall on Barro Colorado Island comes largely in thunderstorms of short duration and heavy rainfall. Long periods of continuous rain are rare; when they occur they may produce saturated soils and landslides.

Throughout the year rainfall is most likely during the early afternoon and least likely during the hours from midnight until dawn (Table 2). During the months with the most hours of rain, October and November, the chance of rain may be close to 50% just after midday, but is below 20% throughout the hours between midnight and noon.

This predictability of rainfall should be reflected in the behavior of plants and animals. Activities that are interfered with by rain, such as pollination of open flowers, should be programmed to occur in the morning or at night; those that are facilitated by rain or very wet conditions, such as sexual reproduction in ferns, should occur in the afternoon.

Seasonal Rhythms

The Panama Canal Commission (formerly the Panama Canal Company) has kept records of hourly rainfall on Barro Colorado Island since 1929. We have used these records, as weekly totals, through 1978. (See Table 3 for these 50 years of data.) In 1957 and 1962 there are gaps in the data because of collection problems.

Over the past fifty years, the annual rainfall on Barro Colorado Island has averaged just over 100 in. (2600 mm) a year. It has varied from a low of 66 in. in 1976 to a high of 143 in. in 1935, while for most of the years it has been between 80 in. (2032 mm) and 120 in. (3048 mm) (the standard deviation of annual rainfall is 16.6 in. [422 mm]). Moreover, there has been a significant ($p < 0.05$), downward trend of about a third of an inch per year (Figure 3). This does not

Table 2. Hourly distribution of rainfall

Month	A.M.												P.M.											
	1	2	3	4	5	6	7	8	9	10	11	12	1	2	3	4	5	6	7	8	9	10	11	12

Number of hours with rain 1974–78:

Month	1	2	3	4	5	6	7	8	9	10	11	12	1	2	3	4	5	6	7	8	9	10	11	12
Jan.	1	1	0	1	1	1	0	1	0	1	1	0	2	1	0	1	1	0	2	1	0	3	2	3
Feb.	0	1	1	0	0	1	0	0	1	5	4	3	2	4	0	0	0	1	2	3	0	0	1	1
Mar.	1	0	2	2	2	5	2	2	1	1	2	3	4	4	4	0	0	0	2	3	0	0	1	2
Apr.	1	1	2	3	1	0	2	2	4	1	4	8	8	6	7	5	2	2	1	1	0	0	1	1
May	4	3	2	1	2	3	2	2	1	4	10	12	12	23	24	18	8	5	6	4	4	5	4	0
June	7	5	3	3	4	3	2	7	1	4	10	12	13	15	20	20	11	12	9	11	6	3	3	7
July	1	2	9	7	6	6	5	8	5	6	5	14	17	12	14	11	13	11	4	10	6	2	7	3
Aug.	5	5	5	7	3	12	6	9	10	8	7	19	19	17	20	19	16	19	9	14	2	4	2	1
Sept.	1	2	1	2	5	5	4	2	4	7	7	10	21	25	25	22	21	15	9	6	4	6	2	1
Oct.	4	3	7	5	3	8	6	4	2	5	8	15	25	32	31	27	22	19	20	9	3	3	4	6
Nov.	9	9	8	10	10	10	7	9	4	9	15	19	20	11	18	23	20	11	12	8	8	12	7	12
Dec.	3	5	4	0	2	5	2	2	1	6	8	8	12	12	8	6	5	4	6	6	4	2	6	3

Percent probability of rain during a given hour and month:

Month	1	2	3	4	5	6	7	8	9	10	11	12	1	2	3	4	5	6	7	8	9	10	11	12
Jan.	2	2	0	2	2	2	0	2	0	2	2	0	3	2	0	2	2	0	3	2	0	5	3	5
Feb.	0	2	2	0	0	2	0	0	2	8	7	5	3	7	0	0	0	2	3	5	0	0	2	2
Mar.	2	0	3	3	3	8	3	3	2	2	3	5	7	7	7	0	0	0	3	5	0	0	2	3
Apr.	2	2	3	5	2	0	3	3	7	2	7	13	13	10	12	8	3	3	2	2	0	0	2	2
May	7	5	3	2	3	5	3	3	2	7	17	20	20	38	40	30	13	8	10	7	7	8	7	0
June	12	8	5	5	7	5	3	12	2	7	17	20	22	25	33	33	18	20	15	18	10	5	5	12
July	2	3	15	12	10	10	8	13	8	10	8	23	28	20	23	18	22	18	7	17	10	3	12	5
Aug.	8	8	8	12	5	20	10	15	17	13	12	32	32	28	33	32	27	32	15	23	3	7	3	2
Sept.	2	3	2	3	8	8	7	3	7	12	12	17	35	42	42	37	35	25	15	10	7	10	3	2
Oct.	7	5	12	8	5	13	10	7	3	8	13	25	42	53	52	45	37	32	33	15	5	5	7	10
Nov.	15	15	13	17	17	17	12	15	7	15	25	32	33	18	30	38	33	18	20	13	13	20	12	20
Dec.	5	8	7	0	3	8	3	3	2	10	13	13	20	20	13	10	8	7	10	10	7	3	10	5

occur at either Cristobal or Balboa Heights and so may not reflect a general trend, but it does occur at the five other stations on Gatun Lake (Gatun, Las Raices, Caño, Gamboa, and Monte Lirio). Overall, the total rainfall of any particular year is uncorrelated with the rainfall of the next or the last year.

Detailed analysis of the seasonal distribution of Central American rainfall and the meteorological causes underlying it can be found in Portig (1965, 1976). In outline, the seasonal rhythm of rainfall is dominated by the zenithal movement of the sun and associated movements in the trade wind belt. The sun is overhead at 9°10′N latitude on about 14 April and 30 August. Rainfall maxima occur about 10 weeks later, in June-July and in November. A long dry season occurs early in the year, and there is sometimes a short

dry season during August (Figure 4). Rainfall may also be influenced by "northers"—southward invasions of polar air—which may produce heavy and sometimes unseasonal rainfall in late wet and early dry seasons (Foster, this volume).

The times when wet and dry seasons start and stop are perhaps the most important aspect of the rainfall year on Barro Colorado Island. One way of defining these times is by considering the soil moisture. On Barro Colorado Island, this can be approximated by assuming that an inch (25.4 mm) of water evaporates each week, and that the soil can store 12 in. (305 mm) of rain, and that any overflow runs off. Dietrich et al. (this volume) calculated a weekly evaporation of 28 mm, and estimated that in Lutz ravine the soil could store 439 mm of rain. Using this, we can calculate the percent saturation of the soil for each week (Table 4) and can define four specific events of the year:

$T1$—the end of the wet period, when the soil first becomes permanently less than 100% saturated.

$T2$—the start of the dry period, when the soil first dries out completely, reaching its minimum moisture content of 27% by weight.

$T3$—the end of the dry period, when the soil moisture content first increases permanently above its minimum.

$T4$—the start of the wet period, when the soil first reaches 100% saturation.

Given these points, we can define the lengths of these periods:

$W/D = T2 - T1$: the length of the transition from wet to dry

$D = T3 - T2$: the length of the dry period

$D/W = T4 - T3$: the length of the transition from dry to wet

$W = T4 - T1'$: the length of the wet period, where the prime denotes the following $T1$.

In addition, we can define the wet season as lasting from $T3$ until the following $T1$ ($D/W + W$) and the dry period as lasting from $T1$ until $T3$ ($W/D + D$).

With these definitions we see (Table 5) that, on average, the dry season starts late in December, and that the wet season starts at about the end of April. The beginning and ending of both wet and dry seasons are independent of one another. An early or late start to the dry season does not presage either an early or a late end to it. An early start in one year predicts nothing about the next year.

Examining the length of the periods themselves (Table 6), we see that the drying out takes on average 15 weeks, that Barro Colorado Island is totally dry only 3 weeks (on average, ranging from 0 to 11 weeks), that the transition to saturation takes 7.5 weeks, and that the soil is saturated for almost half of the year. Thus, on average, the dry season lasts 18 weeks, and the wet season lasts 34 weeks.

Soil moisture shows less variance than rainfall over the year: it is essentially a moving average. There are still times, however, when the rainfall exceeds an inch a week during the dry season or is less than an inch a week during the wet season. These times are manifestations of the short-term storm activity which is superimposed on the dominant wet-dry annual cycle. Counting the number of times these "reversals" occur during each period gives Table 7. As expected, longer periods have more reversals. Most wet seasons and many dry seasons have at least one reversal.

In an earlier paper (Rand and Rand, 1979), we

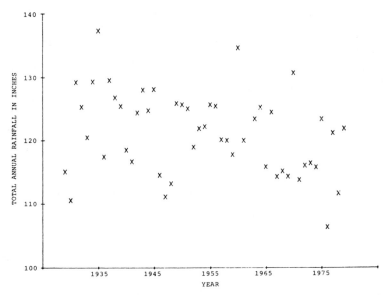

Figure 3.   Total annual rainfall on Barro Colorado Island, 1929–78.

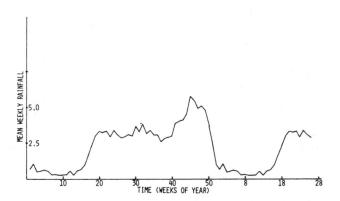

Figure 4.   Median weekly rainfall in the average year on Barro Colorado Island.

Table 3. Weekly rainfall on Barro Colorado Island, 1929–78 (tenths of inches)

Week no.	1929	1930	1931	1932	1933	1934	1935	1936	1937	1938	1939	1940	1941	1942	1943	1944	1945	1946	1947	1948	1949	1950	1951	1952	1953
1	3	1	7	1	9	13	3	0	6	16	0	17	5	1	4	2	1	3	0	5	1	1	2	0	7
2	0	10	1	0	14	1	3	0	5	1	0	0	4	1	0	0	1	1	0	5	5	0	7	1	27
3	0	6	0	3	0	0	2	2	9	2	4	4	4	0	4	11	1	0	0	3	0	0	8	1	3
4	0	3	3	12	1	0	8	6	3	3	0	16	9	9	12	4	26	0	4	6	1	0	5	0	4
5	1	1	3	1	1	0	3	2	1	6	0	16	9	19	1	9	1	3	2	1	0	0	3	23	6
6	0	0	3	2	0	2	46	0	0	3	0	2	6	10	0	5	6	0	11	0	0	4	18	2	3
7	0	2	1	0	0	0	1	0	2	0	0	1	9	2	4	0	0	1	9	0	0	8	13	0	0
8	1	4	1	0	0	5	7	1	0	1	0	16	6	2	10	0	0	0	0	2	0	6	4	0	0
9	0	0	5	1	1	0	5	0	1	14	1	1	7	0	16	3	0	0	1	0	0	0	0	2	0
10	25	1	2	1	2	0	2	2	1	0	3	5	0	17	0	1	1	1	2	0	3	0	0	2	
11	0	1	18	5	1	16	0	10	0	0	0	1	1	5	1	0	1	1	1	0	1	0	3	0	0
12	1	0	35	1	1	2	0	4	0	2	0	9	0	0	0	0	1	14	0	1	0	1	1	0	1
13	3	0	0	5	6	0	1	0	0	0	0	0	2	5	8	0	0	2	3	1	0	1	0	0	9
14	1	3	1	12	0	0	0	0	0	0	1	1	0	3	6	5	2	2	0	0	3	0	7	31	0
15	0	3	2	10	0	7	27	9	6	2	5	0	2	0	1	0	9	0	0	1	0	1	0	2	0
16	13	19	23	0	0	30	1	11	2	1	0	0	0	33	1	3	1	4	1	0	2	1	10	8	3
17	3	6	12	8	1	17	7	4	3	13	0	1	3	8	14	36	4	8	30	0	1	23	65	0	63
18	2	37	1	43	5	14	29	21	10	53	0	14	24	2	36	37	45	0	0	40	15	14	21	20	14
19	46	21	56	9	28	43	12	17	18	31	14	14	14	16	11	40	27	9	6	22	8	14	26	34	49
20	47	18	45	21	0	14	34	27	39	52	11	0	7	46	41	37	24	11	8	16	59	2	34	32	6
21	18	18	63	13	23	28	26	27	44	23	4	2	36	22	35	16	35	53	23	54	25	36	28	9	21
22	38	28	6	7	14	37	4	27	19	27	8	63	10	33	39	59	10	9	40	5	35	55	27	42	3
23	9	11	26	30	27	26	39	25	45	36	15	24	15	18	12	18	14	23	17	6	34	24	19	40	10
24	32	6	56	41	2	26	24	12	16	47	38	71	44	7	26	18	57	27	36	37	45	21	20	11	7
25	23	9	20	29	38	28	36	12	32	83	60	9	14	16	33	17	9	14	32	7	25	24	31	50	7
26	27	29	51	16	28	10	21	3	9	27	16	21	7	20	63	40	28	7	9	14	36	38	33	18	13
27	32	17	57	7	14	17	76	26	20	27	25	2	8	28	50	18	11	49	5	32	39	20	14	26	6
28	13	31	30	40	30	23	20	5	15	28	25	5	45	16	13	14	15	5	5	42	54	22	19	13	72
29	28	12	21	10	12	3	140	33	34	19	18	17	41	25	24	9	50	18	15	9	24	33	9	14	40
30	38	12	70	52	33	37	31	17	11	16	15	22	18	9	19	28	52	49	42	32	5	30	6	7	38
31	57	7	22	34	11	34	23	50	30	33	50	20	12	13	15	12	39	12	36	28	16	30	7	15	17
32	31	2	12	13	50	31	21	47	98	37	24	46	26	35	75	46	23	10	15	8	22	59	36	7	11
33	21	36	13	23	9	38	32	4	19	64	8	19	55	36	28	62	18	6	16	30	21	15	23	17	43
34	28	11	14	52	9	34	20	24	39	11	4	35	12	24	27	36	21	74	43	11	48	19	34	17	51
35	43	17	21	2	28	16	6	36	25	24	16	13	19	18	24	64	25	8	27	29	9	12	27	36	37
36	22	34	17	24	23	58	7	39	19	21	36	47	38	35	4	27	35	36	26	13	15	13	9	21	16
37	20	19	14	8	26	73	8	6	16	11	43	23	7	17	18	18	29	13	12	17	10	22	22	43	12
38	3	8	11	10	18	41	49	42	42	8	54	8	6	56	47	5	15	34	17	31	29	14	28	6	5
39	12	41	29	27	19	24	24	42	9	7	18	23	22	29	20	17	21	22	28	6	11	23	29	35	23
40	7	18	16	28	0	16	25	40	46	33	37	4	25	30	23	38	16	7	49	10	22	42	37	27	29
41	15	17	52	5	31	12	15	43	26	14	18	72	61	46	25	19	26	32	7	18	35	36	67	16	21
42	21	15	24	23	16	20	5	33	12	24	40	50	12	47	19	27	27	16	50	25	38	22	42	14	73
43	54	9	10	46	16	39	23	31	23	37	60	32	40	33	25	53	29	27	21	31	30	38	26	98	59
44	11	5	31	54	24	61	45	65	59	53	110	7	49	43	29	44	10	37	13	48	63	9	46	23	45
45	39	21	244	45	52	43	105	25	44	17	195	23	47	24	34	31	20	30	26	30	87	40	55	27	80
46	16	32	21	20	37	109	179	39	48	14	51	48	22	9	58	23	99	8	12	85	74	59	30	31	27
47	53	10	4	103	103	24	89	23	37	22	9	22	34	24	75	9	21	31	24	22	93	121	19	34	15
48	11	54	36	134	120	9	84	17	64	48	2	1	44	14	32	6	122	56	4	42	37	35	39	1	31
49	12	57	14	72	53	32	21	3	133	49	18	2	13	26	7	15	145	30	47	0	21	51	27	19	1
50	2	43	8	8	50	103	3	10	73	81	33	8	23	57	16	120	3	53	1	4	12	62	94	75	3
51	0	0	1	7	18	16	39	11	29	28	22	5	3	78	119	5	14	12	1	6	20	41	2	22	25
52	1	2	2	16	7	1	7	9	0	3	27	7	0	48	2	13	19	0	6	2	20	3	0	7	10
Total	878	765	1232	1134	1013	1234	1434	937	1240	1171	1137	865	918	1111	1202	1120	1204	865	779	831	1149	1144	1128	976	1049

Week no.	1954	1955	1956	1957	1958	1959	1960	1961	1962	1963	1964	1965	1966	1967	1968	1969	1970	1971	1972	1973	1974	1975	1976	1977	1978
1	0	3	23	5	10	0	7	1	11	56	2	1	2	0	0	2	0	21	23	0	2	0	1	1	0
2	11	54	6	1	18	0	0	2	3	24	0	5	17	1	0	6	112	5	28	16	0	0	2	1	2
3	0	27	3	0	14	3	9	0	2	0	0	22	8	0	1	6	5	15	10	5	0	1	3	4	1
4	2	1	15	0	0	1	11	7	0	0	0	1	0	3	0	3	1	0	0	0	0	0	3	4	0
5	7	6	8	1	57	0	2	2	3	1	0	1	6	1	0	1	2	2	2	1	1	0	0	15	0
6	1	2	16	0	1	2	0	2	2	6	0	0	1	0	2	1	18	1	9	4	0	2	0	1	3
7	1	1	0	1	13	0	8	0	4	13	0	0	0	1	1	1	2	2	1	3	1	2	0	5	1
8	2	0	4	3	2	0	0	0	0	12	3	1	0	3	7	0	6	3	4	0	0	0	0	2	3
9	4	1	1	0	3	0	1	0	0	0	0	0	4	3	9	4	0	0	0	1	17	9	0	0	0
10	0	0	0	0	0	0	10	3	0	0	0	2	0	0	0	3	5	5	4	0	1	9	0	0	4
11	1	0	0	0	1	0	4	0	0	0	2	1	0	2	21	0	3	6	2	0	0	0	1	5	1
12	0	0	14	0	25	1	29	1	—	16	0	0	0	2	6	0	5	11	0	1	0	1	1	4	0
13	0	9	8	0	0	1	2	11	—	0	0	0	0	1	8	2	2	0	1	0	1	0	0	0	14
14	0	1	1	0	13	0	74	7	—	0	0	3	0	1	0	1	9	1	0	0	0	0	0	0	4
15	2	2	11	0	1	5	61	0	—	0	5	5	0	3	2	0	32	0	12	4	1	17	19	1	6
16	8	1	2	0	19	0	42	29	—	8	1	0	12	22	0	5	1	0	21	6	1	0	0	2	33
17	20	0	13	0	14	5	0	12	9	28	41	0	15	17	1	41	0	0	16	0	3	6	5	3	30
18	31	31	14	0	39	43	21	1	4	29	0	5	8	5	10	7	7	51	11	8	0	26	13	2	12
19	4	26	26	12	22	13	29	27	55	15	29	40	29	25	60	23	16	101	19	31	3	13	7	1	6
20	8	3	77	12	14	7	21	38	27	59	31	3	19	3	25	39	94	56	18	19	10	44	9	37	35
21	29	17	42	25	43	14	35	10	40	11	54	6	13	7	14	28	42	10	19	33	14	27	18	37	18
22	54	54	7	16	14	16	53	15	23	20	55	48	14	36	12	5	32	8	33	27	20	16	30	19	9
23	34	21	29	9	36	24	17	20	50	17	67	14	40	30	14	1	22	14	37	30	20	35	28	14	7
24	24	50	3	21	17	31	35	26	20	15	20	15	42	15	30	24	28	13	29	62	41	9	6	26	21
25	46	15	27	12	19	12	30	16	3	7	15	31	33	43	16	16	11	22	36	19	36	23	26	20	31
26	4	33	9	18	11	15	5	33	8	8	79	24	18	37	42	19	14	22	6	29	21	27	38	26	23
27	36	11	34	2	21	18	54	20	33	15	23	8	13	22	12	27	13	23	13	19	9	24	6	41	14
28	38	26	34	39	9	18	32	27	25	15	43	3	18	27	15	43	57	19	3	31	18	11	8	8	50
29	4	16	47	44	12	14	21	4	28	22	69	20	15	14	16	4	20	23	25	29	60	25	10	8	13
30	65	40	46	24	39	37	7	18	46	33	19	35	39	13	21	48	43	18	8	8	20	21	10	1	32
31	20	26	50	49	26	27	9	32	3	112	22	21	28	16	35	3	8	33	1	26	53	14	38	40	17
32	20	43	29	69	51	15	20	73	76	28	2	30	28	30	13	25	36	7	2	9	24	36	2	57	45
33	55	27	33	55	24	10	4	26	37	7	30	16	39	47	27	1	26	20	26	6	9	22	13	103	16
34	21	12	13	22	11	4	24	56	12	50	26	32	38	6	36	26	39	20	43	0	21	56	19	29	12
35	40	29	13	27	29	45	14	31	21	42	27	19	13	26	50	5	34	29	32	0	19	6	16	38	26
36	23	28	48	38	10	42	15	15	48	20	35	27	20	35	17	4	15	38	14	12	16	31	13	11	13
37	16	26	18	10	32	33	37	14	—	16	8	59	20	3	16	28	14	18	62	22	30	36	46	33	16
38	23	3	26	42	7	39	26	34	—	5	49	20	29	21	10	30	3	21	16	8	16	9	38	31	7
39	32	27	11	30	53	22	16	50	—	31	20	4	30	5	25	25	19	13	38	78	36	47	35	36	15
40	11	17	10	49	3	7	38	53	—	18	30	10	25	11	14	71	27	36	62	22	16	25	15	42	20
41	9	4	41	39	53	28	60	25	—	15	54	50	49	53	42	21	22	11	13	37	71	66	19	32	8
42	71	106	67	35	30	20	47	27	—	45	30	7	15	22	79	10	32	4	6	27	26	35	22	52	41
43	19	29	43	32	45	16	44	66	13	23	13	36	21	11	45	22	8	10	33	7	58	30	35	35	26
44	35	16	29	—	29	33	6	8	35	71	54	14	100	44	10	10	33	37	41	31	11	29	16	44	37
45	32	33	31	—	9	55	15	17	22	59	22	60	45	26	22	23	23	34	6	35	20	15	41	51	59
46	15	53	23	—	22	23	67	17	41	38	87	48	27	51	31	39	65	20	27	120	46	78	29	35	21
47	100	39	41	—	22	7	50	36	35	21	17	33	59	30	12	51	42	12	14	29	46	23	7	43	23
48	12	57	28	—	34	6	66	35	45	31	23	70	41	25	40	19	113	25	4	30	66	8	0	10	4
49	36	24	1	5	2	200	106	34	14	4	23	22	63	35	6	42	65	6	4	7	9	77	1	1	5
50	29	11	35	13	13	5	81	6	33	6	2	3	18	14	8	16	14	0	0	13	3	36	0	5	9
51	5	66	26	20	10	4	4	10	22	5	0	26	34	5	2	28	17	0	67	3	0	50	11	16	0
52	1	21	2	3	1	31	0	8	2	14	1	1	11	9	0	6	14	3	3	5	1	10	1	0	0
Total	1057	1144	1138	Missing	1002	946	1368	1002	Missing	1087	1133	898	1114	859	881	860	1270	847	904	913	897	1087	661	1032	793

Table 4.   Soil moisture, 1929–78 (%)

Week no.	1929	1930	1931	1932	1933	1934	1935	1936	1937	1938	1939	1940	1941	1942	1943	1944	1945	1946	1947	1948	1949	1950	1951	1952	1953
1	0	69	82	76	99	100	87	88	90	97	85	100	71	78	94	86	91	94	83	76	68	92	87	76	95
2	0	68	75	67	100	92	81	80	86	89	77	91	67	70	86	78	83	86	74	71	64	84	85	68	100
3	0	65	66	61	91	84	74	73	85	82	72	86	61	61	80	79	76	78	66	65	55	75	83	60	94
4	0	59	60	63	84	76	72	69	79	76	64	91	61	60	82	73	89	69	60	61	47	67	79	52	88
5	0	51	54	55	76	67	66	62	71	73	55	96	60	67	74	72	81	63	54	53	39	59	72	62	85
6	0	43	47	49	68	60	97	54	63	67	47	89	57	68	66	68	77	55	54	45	31	54	79	55	79
7	0	36	40	40	59	52	89	45	56	58	39	81	56	61	61	59	69	47	53	37	22	53	82	47	71
8	0	30	32	32	51	48	87	37	48	50	30	86	52	55	60	51	61	38	45	29	14	49	77	39	62
9	0	22	27	24	43	40	83	29	40	54	22	79	50	46	65	45	52	30	37	21	6	41	68	32	54
10	12	14	20	16	36	31	76	22	32	46	16	75	42	52	57	38	45	22	30	13	0	35	60	24	47
11	4	7	27	12	29	37	67	22	24	37	8	67	34	48	49	29	37	14	22	4	0	27	53	15	39
12	0	0	48	4	21	30	59	17	15	30	0	66	25	39	41	21	29	17	14	0	0	19	45	7	31
13	0	0	40	0	18	21	51	9	7	22	0	57	19	35	39	12	21	10	8	0	0	11	37	0	30
14	0	0	32	2	9	13	43	0	0	14	0	49	10	30	36	8	13	4	0	0	0	3	34	18	22
15	0	0	25	2	1	10	57	0	0	7	0	41	3	21	28	0	12	0	0	0	0	0	26	11	13
16	2	7	36	0	0	27	49	0	0	0	0	33	0	40	20	0	5	0	0	0	0	0	25	9	7
17	0	3	38	0	0	32	47	0	0	2	0	25	0	39	24	22	0	0	16	0	0	11	71	1	52
18	0	26	31	27	0	35	62	9	0	39	0	28	11	32	46	44	29	0	8	25	4	14	81	9	55
19	30	36	70	27	15	63	64	15	6	56	3	31	14	37	47	70	43	0	5	34	2	17	94	29	89
20	61	42	99	36	7	67	84	29	31	92	4	22	11	68	73	93	55	0	3	39	44	10	100	48	86
21	68	49	100	38	18	83	97	43	60	100	0	16	34	77	95	98	76	36	14	76	56	32	100	47	95
22	91	64	96	36	21	100	92	57	67	100	0	61	33	97	100	100	76	36	39	72	77	71	100	74	89
23	90	64	100	52	35	100	100	70	97	100	4	73	38	100	100	100	80	46	45	69	97	83	100	99	89
24	100	61	100	78	29	100	100	72	100	100	27	100	66	97	100	100	100	61	68	91	100	92	100	100	86
25	100	60	100	94	52	100	100	74	100	100	70	99	69	100	100	100	98	64	86	88	100	100	100	100	84
26	100	76	100	99	67	99	100	68	99	100	75	100	67	100	100	100	100	62	85	92	100	100	100	100	87
27	100	83	100	97	71	100	100	81	100	100	88	93	65	100	100	100	100	95	81	100	100	100	100	100	83
28	100	100	100	100	88	100	100	77	100	100	100	88	95	100	100	100	100	91	76	100	100	100	100	100	100
29	100	100	100	100	90	94	100	96	100	100	100	94	100	100	100	98	100	97	81	98	100	100	98	100	100
30	100	100	100	100	100	100	100	100	100	100	100	100	100	99	100	100	100	100	100	100	96	100	95	97	100
31	100	97	100	100	100	100	100	100	100	100	100	100	100	100	100	100	100	100	100	100	100	92	100	100	100
32	100	90	100	100	100	100	100	100	100	100	100	100	100	100	100	100	100	100	99	100	98	100	100	97	100
33	100	100	100	100	98	100	100	95	100	100	98	100	100	100	100	100	100	96	100	100	100	100	100	100	100
34	100	100	100	100	97	100	100	100	100	100	92	100	100	100	100	100	100	100	100	100	100	100	100	100	100
35	100	100	100	93	100	100	96	100	100	100	97	100	100	100	100	100	100	97	100	100	99	100	100	100	100
36	100	100	100	100	100	100	93	100	100	100	100	100	100	94	100	100	100	100	100	100	100	100	98	100	100
37	100	100	100	98	100	100	91	96	100	100	100	100	97	100	100	100	100	100	100	100	99	100	100	100	100
38	93	98	100	98	100	100	100	100	100	98	100	98	93	100	100	95	100	100	100	100	100	100	100	96	96
39	95	100	100	100	100	100	100	100	98	95	100	100	100	100	100	100	100	100	96	100	100	100	100	100	100
40	93	100	100	100	91	100	100	100	100	100	100	94	100	100	100	100	100	97	100	96	100	100	100	100	100
41	97	100	100	95	100	100	100	100	100	100	100	100	100	100	100	100	100	97	100	100	100	100	100	100	100
42	100	100	100	100	100	100	95	100	100	100	100	100	100	100	100	100	100	100	100	100	100	100	100	100	100
43	100	99	99	100	100	100	100	100	100	100	100	100	100	100	100	100	100	100	100	100	100	100	100	100	100
44	100	95	100	100	100	100	100	100	100	100	97	100	100	100	100	100	100	100	100	100	99	100	100	100	100
45	100	100	100	100	100	100	100	100	100	100	100	100	100	100	100	100	100	100	100	100	100	100	100	100	100
46	100	100	100	100	100	100	100	100	100	100	100	100	100	100	100	100	100	100	100	100	100	100	100	100	100
47	100	100	94	100	100	100	100	100	100	100	98	100	100	100	100	99	100	100	100	100	100	100	100	100	100
48	100	100	100	100	100	99	100	100	100	100	91	92	100	100	100	95	100	100	95	100	100	100	100	92	100
49	100	100	100	100	100	100	100	93	100	100	98	85	100	100	97	99	100	100	100	91	100	100	100	99	92
50	92	100	98	97	100	100	94	93	100	100	100	83	100	100	100	100	93	100	92	86	100	100	100	100	86
51	84	91	90	95	100	100	100	93	100	100	100	79	94	100	100	95	97	100	84	82	100	100	93	100	99
52	77	85	83	100	97	92	97	93	91	94	100	76	85	100	93	98	100	91	80	75	100	94	84	97	99

+ = Rainfall data missing (assumption of no rainfall during weeks 12–16 gives the tabulated values).
* = Rainfall data missing (assumption of enough rainfall to keep soil saturated [> 1 inch] gives tabulated values).

Week no.	1954	1955	1956	1957	1958	1959	1960	1961	1962	1963	1964	1965	1966	1967	1968	1969	1970	1971	1972	1973	1974	1975	1976	1977	1978
1	90	81	100	88	94	79	97	78	95	100	83	68	85	91	86	72	88	100	84	85	83	68	92	58	76
2	91	100	96	80	100	71	89	71	89	100	75	64	91	83	77	69	100	95	99	90	74	60	85	50	69
3	82	100	91	72	100	65	88	63	82	91	66	74	89	75	70	65	95	100	99	86	66	52	79	45	61
4	75	91	95	63	91	57	89	60	74	83	58	66	81	69	61	60	88	91	91	77	57	44	73	40	53
5	72	88	93	55	100	48	82	54	68	75	49	59	77	61	53	52	81	84	84	70	50	35	65	44	44
6	65	81	99	47	92	41	74	47	62	71	41	50	70	53	46	44	88	76	83	65	41	28	56	37	39
7	57	74	90	40	95	33	73	39	56	74	33	42	61	45	38	36	81	69	76	59	33	22	48	33	31
8	50	65	85	34	88	24	64	30	48	75	26	34	53	39	36	28	78	63	71	50	25	13	39	26	25
9	45	58	77	26	82	16	56	22	39	67	18	26	48	33	35	22	70	55	62	43	31	12	31	17	17
10	37	49	69	18	74	7	56	16	31	58	9	19	39	25	26	16	65	51	57	34	23	11	22	9	11
11	29	41	60	9	66	0	51	8	23	50	3	11	31	18	36	8	59	47	50	26	15	3	15	5	4
12	20	32	64	1	79	0	67	0	15+	55	0	2	23	11	32	0	55	48	42	18	6	0	7	0	0
13	12	31	62	0	71	0	60	0	6+	47	0	0	14	3	30	0	48	40	34	10	0	0	0	0	3
14	4	23	54	0	74	0	100	0	0+	38	0	0	6	0	22	0	47	32	26	1	0	0	0	0	0
15	0	16	55	0	66	0	100	0	0+	30	0	0	0	0	15	0	66	24	28	0	0	5	7	0	0
16	0	9	48	0	74	0	100	15	0+	29	0	0	1	9	7	0	58	15	37	0	0	0	0	0	19
17	8	1	50	0	77	0	91	17	0+	43	25	0	5	16	0	26	50	7	42	0	0	0	0	0	36
18	26	18	54	0	100	27	100	9	0+	59	17	0	3	12	0	23	47	42	43	0	0	13	2	0	38
19	21	31	67	1	100	30	100	23	38+	63	33	25	19	24	41	34	52	100	50	17	0	16	0	0	34
20	18	25	100	3	100	28	100	47	52+	100	51	19	27	18	54	58	100	100	57	25	0	44	0	22	55
21	35	31	100	15	100	31	100	47	100	100	89	15	30	15	57	73	100	100	65	44	3	59	6	45	62
22	72	68	97	20	100	36	100	51	100	100	100	48	33	38	58	69	100	98	84	59	11	64	23	53	61
23	92	77	100	19	100	48	100	59	100	100	100	51	59	54	61	61	100	100	100	76	20	85	38	56	59
24	100	100	93	28	100	66	100	73	100	100	100	55	86	58	78	73	100	100	100	100	46	84	35	70	68
25	100	100	100	30	100	69	100	78	94	97	100	73	100	86	84	77	100	100	100	100	68	95	49	78	86
26	95	100	98	36	100	73	95	98	91	95	100	84	100	100	100	85	100	100	96	100	77	100	72	92	97
27	100	100	100	30	100	79	100	100	100	99	100	83	100	100	100	100	100	100	99	100	77	100	69	100	100
28	100	100	100	54	99	86	100	100	100	100	100	77	100	100	100	100	100	100	93	100	83	100	67	98	100
29	95	100	100	82	100	89	100	94	100	100	100	85	100	100	100	94	100	100	100	100	100	100	67	96	100
30	100	100	100	94	100	100	97	100	100	100	100	100	100	100	100	100	100	100	98	98	100	100	67	88	100
31	100	100	100	100	100	100	96	100	93	100	100	100	100	100	100	94	98	100	90	100	100	100	91	100	100
32	100	100	100	100	100	100	100	100	100	100	93	100	100	100	100	100	100	97	83	99	100	100	84	100	100
33	100	100	100	100	100	99	94	100	100	97	100	100	100	100	100	92	100	100	97	95	99	100	87	100	100
34	100	100	100	100	100	94	100	100	100	100	100	100	100	96	100	100	100	100	100	87	100	100	94	100	100
35	100	100	100	100	100	100	100	100	100	100	100	100	100	100	100	95	100	100	100	78	100	96	99	100	100
36	100	100	100	100	99	100	100	100	100	100	100	100	100	100	100	91	100	100	100	80	100	100	100	100	100
37	100	100	100	99	100	100	100	100	100*	100	98	100	100	93	100	100	100	100	100	90	100	100	100	100	100
38	100	94	100	100	97	100	100	100	100*	96	100	100	100	100	99	100	93	100	100	88	100	99	100	100	97
39	100	100	100	100	100	100	100	100	100*	100	100	94	100	96	100	100	100	100	100	100	100	100	100	100	100
40	100	100	100	100	94	97	100	100	100*	100	100	95	100	97	100	100	100	100	100	100	100	100	100	100	100
41	98	94	100	100	100	100	100	100	100*	100	100	100	100	100	100	100	100	100	100	100	100	100	100	100	98
42	100	100	100	100	100	100	100	100	100*	100	100	97	100	100	100	100	100	94	96	100	100	100	100	100	100
43	100	100	100	100	100	100	100	100	100	100	100	100	100	100	100	100	98	94	100	97	100	100	100	100	100
44	100	100	100	100*	100	100	96	97	100	100	100	100	100	100	99	100	100	100	100	100	100	100	100	100	100
45	100	100	100	100*	99	100	100	100	100	100	100	100	100	100	100	100	100	96	100	100	100	100	100	100	100
46	100	100	100	100*	100	100	100	100	100	100	100	100	100	100	100	100	100	100	100	100	100	100	100	100	100
47	100	100	100	100*	100	97	100	100	100	100	100	100	100	100	100	100	100	100	100	100	100	100	97	100	100
48	100	100	100	100*	100	93	100	100	100	100	100	100	100	100	100	100	100	100	94	100	100	98	88	100	94
49	100	100	92	95	93	100	100	100	100	94	100	100	100	100	96	100	100	96	89	97	99	100	81	92	90
50	100	100	100	97	96	95	100	96	100	91	92	94	100	100	95	100	100	88	81	99	93	100	72	88	89
51	95	100	100	100	96	90	94	96	100	86	84	100	100	95	88	100	100	79	100	94	84	100	73	93	81
52	87	100	92	94	88	100	86	94	92	90	76	92	100	94	79	96	100	73	94	89	77	100	66	84	72

Table 5. Times of starts and ends of wet and dry periods (weeks)

Middle of interval	Number of observations	Middle of interval	Number of observations
T1—Soil begins to lose water		T3—Soil begins to gain water	
−5	1	11	1
−4	1	12	2
−3	10	13	0
−2	7	14	1
−1	5	15	3
0	10	16	8
1	5	17	12
2	4	18	10
3	3	19	7
4	2	20	1
5	0	21	4
6	1	22	0
		23	1
$N = 49$; Mean $= -0.45$; SD $= 2.37$		$N = 50$; Mean $= 17.32$; SD $= 2.29$	
T2—Soil is dry		T4—Soil is saturated	
10	1	12	1
11	3	14	1
12	11	16	0
13	5	18	1
14	4	20	5
15	9	22	6
16	6	24	12
17	7	26	5
18	2	28	9
19	0	30	8
20	0	32	1
21	1	34	0
		36	1
$N = 49$; Mean $= 14.35$; SD $= 2.34$		$N = 50$; Mean $= 24.74$; SD $= 4.41$	

Table 6. Duration of wet and dry periods (weeks)

Middle of interval	Number of observations	Middle of interval	Number of observations
Soil losing water (T1 − T2)		Soil gaining water (T3 − T4)	
10	1	0	1
11	1	1	1
12	4	2	2
13	4	3	4
14	16	4	1
15	9	5	8
16	3	6	4
17	4	7	4
18	5	8	5
19	1	9	3
20	1	10	5
		11	7
		12	3
		13	1
		14	0
		15	1
Mean $= 14.80$; SD $= 2.10$		Mean $= 42$; SD $= 3.45$	
Soil dry (T2 − T3)		Soil wet (T3 − T1)	
0	17	12	1
1	4	16	0
2	6	20	5
3	2	24	12
4	5	28	17
5	3	32	11
6	5	36	2
7	2	40	0
8	4	44	1
9	0		
10	0		
11	1		
Mean $= 2.94$; SD $= 3.00$		Mean $= 26.86$; SD $= 5.20$	
Dry season (T1 − T3)		Wet season (T3 − T1)	
10	1	25	1
11	1	26	1
12	2	27	1
13	0	28	1
14	6	29	1
15	4	30	2
16	3	31	5
17	6	32	5
18	4	33	5
19	5	34	3
20	7	35	10
21	4	36	3
22	2	37	4
23	2	38	1
24	1	39	4
25	1	40	0
		41	2
		42	0
		43	1
Mean $= 17.74$; SD $= 3.44$		Mean $= 34.04$; SD $= 3.81$	

Table 7. Reversals in soil moisture during wet and dry periods

Middle of interval	Number of observations
Wet weeks during period while soil is losing water ($T1 - T2$)	
0	21
1	19
2	7
3	2
Mean = 0.79; SD = 0.84	
Wet weeks during period while soil is dry ($T2 - T3$)	
0	44
1	4
2	1
Mean = 0.12; SD = 0.39	
Dry weeks during period while soil is gaining water ($T3 - T4$)	
0	24
1	16
2	7
3	2
4	1
Mean = 0.80; SD = 0.97	
Dry weeks during period while soil is saturated ($T4 - T1$)	
0	2
1	7
2	14
3	15
4	7
5	4
6	1
Mean = 2.68; SD = 1.33	
Consecutive dry weeks	
0	18
1	4
2	9
3	3
4	4
5	3
6	4
7	1
8	3

Table 8. Autoregressive model for weekly rainfall

Model: $Y_t = a_0 + a_1 Y_{t-1} + a_2 Y_{t-2} + \cdots + E_t$

where Y_t is the cube root of the rainfall during week t.

Correlations:[1]	Y_t	$Y_t|Y_{t-1}$	$Y_t|Y_{t-1}Y_{t-2}$	$Y_t|Y_{t-1}Y_{t-2}Y_{t-3}$
Y_{t-1}	0.60			
Y_{t-2}	0.51	0.24		
Y_{t-3}	0.47	0.24	0.15	
Y_{t-4}	0.41	0.19	0.12	0.07
Y_{t-5}	0.34	0.13	0.06	0.01

Best estimate of model:

$$Y_t = 1.27 + 0.42\,Y_{t-1} + 0.17\,Y_{t-2} + 0.15\,Y_{t-3}$$

Standard error of estimate = 1.908

Stepwide R^2:

Variable entered	R^2
Y_{t-1}	0.36
Y_{t-2}	0.39
Y_{t-3}	0.41

[1]The correlation Y_t/Y_{t-1} with Y_{t-2} refers to the partial correlation of Y_t with Y_{t-2}, removing the effects of their common correlation with Y_{t-1}.

Table 9. Harmonic analysis model of weekly rainfall

Model: $Y_t = a_0 + \sum_k \left[a_k \sin\left(\frac{2\pi k}{52}t\right) + b_k \cos\left(\frac{2\pi k}{52}t\right) \right] + E_t$

Best estimate of model:

$$Y_t = 4.86 - 1.98 \sin\frac{2\pi}{52}t - 0.92 \cos\frac{2\pi}{52}t$$

$$- 1.08 \sin\frac{4\pi}{52}t + 0.52 \cos\frac{4\pi}{52}t$$

$$- 0.21 \sin\frac{8\pi}{52}t - 0.49 \cos\frac{8\pi}{52}t$$

Standard error of estimate = 1.718

Stepwise R^2:

Variable entered	R^2
1st harmonic	0.39
2nd harmonic	0.46
4th harmonic	0.52

Full model—Harmonics plus autoregression:

$$Y_t = 4.86 - 1.98 \sin\frac{2\pi}{52}t - 0.92 \cos\frac{2\pi}{52}t - 1.08 \sin\frac{4\pi}{52}t$$

$$+ 0.52 \cos\frac{4\pi}{52}t - 0.21 \sin\frac{8\pi}{52}t - 0.49 \cos\frac{8\pi}{52}t$$

$$+ 0.16 Y_{t-1}$$

Standard error of estimate = 1.69 $R^2 = 0.54$

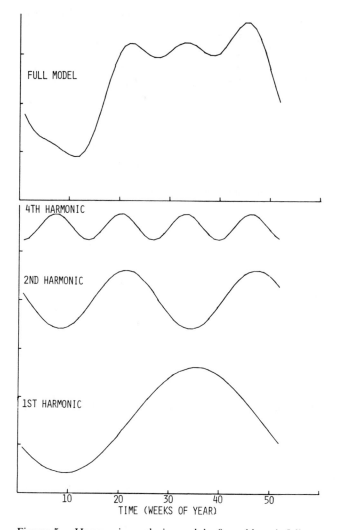

Figure 5. Harmonic analysis model of weekly rainfall on Barro Colorado Island.

attempted to investigate the predictability of rainfall on Barro Colorado Island by modeling it. We used weekly totals, and to correct for the skewed nature of the data we took the cube root of these weekly totals. The initial model was an autoregressive one (Table 8), where the rainfall in any given week is considered to be a constant plus another constant times the rainfall during the previous week (lag 1) plus another constant times the rainfall during the week prior to that (lag 2), etc. The first three lags are all that are useful in predicting weekly rainfall, and they give us an R^2 of 0.41. This says that knowledge of the rainfall of three consecutive weeks permits us to reduce our uncertainty about the amount of next week's rainfall

by about 40%. The degree to which rainfall can be predicted from preceding rainfall is interesting because this information is certainly available to animals and plants.

The periodicity of the data suggested that we use harmonic analysis to see how much of the variability it could explain. For this a series of sines and cosines was fitted to the data, using stepwise regression, and it was found (Table 9, Figure 5) that three terms (the first, second, and fourth harmonics) are all that are significant, and that they give an R^2 of 0.52. The three terms can be introduced as representing the annual, semiannual, and quarterly cycles.

The next step is to put the two models together,

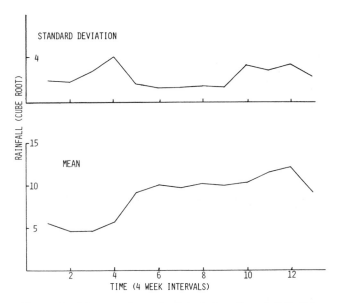

Figure 6. Means and standard deviations for rainfall of the average year on Barro Colorado Island (4-week totals).

CONCLUSIONS

In the preceding pages we have attempted to document the degree of spatial and temporal fluctuations in rainfall experienced by the tropical forest on Barro Colorado Island. The picture that emerges is one of small-scale unpredictable fluctuations imposed on a large-scale predictable pattern. The rainfall gradient from dry to wet across the isthmus provides the dominant spatial pattern, the alternation of wet and dry seasons, the dominant temporal patterning.

Local fluctuations obscure the transisthmian gradient as far as Barro Colorado Island is concerned. Temporal fluctuations make the precise prediction of the beginnning and end of wet and dry seasons and may meliorate or make more severe dry or wet seasons in specific years, but they do not obscure the dominant pattern of wet and dry season.

ACKNOWLEDGMENTS

We must acknowledge Nicholas Smythe and Bonifacio de León, who collected the data from the gauges around the perimeter of Barro Colorado Island; M. Hart of the Meteorological and Hydrographic Branch, who provided the Panama Canal rainfall data; and Donald Windsor, who advised on the analysis of the data.

LITERATURE CITED

Dietrich, W., D. M. Windsor, and T. Dunne
1982.   Geology, Climate, and Hydrology of Barro Colorado Island. Pages 21–46 in *The Ecology of a Tropical Forest*, edited by Egbert G. Leigh, Jr., et al. Washington, D.C.: Smithsonian Institution Press.

Foster, R. B.
1982.   Famine on Barro Colorado Island. Pages 201–212 in *The Ecology of a Tropical Forest*, edited by Egbert G. Leigh, Jr., et al. Washington, D.C.: Smithsonian Institution Press.

Portig, W. H.
1965.   Central American Rainfall. *Geographical Review* 55: 68–90.
1976.   The Climate of Central America. Pages 45–478 in *World Survey of Climatology, vol. 12: Climates of Central and South America*, edited by W. Schwerdtfeger. New York: Elsevier.

Rand, W. M., and A. S. Rand
1979.   The Rainfall on Barro Colorado Island, Panama. Pages 31–49 in *Actas del IV Symposium Internacional de Ecologia Tropical, Marzo 7–11, 1977*. vol. 1. Panama City: Impresora de la Nación, INAC.

first using harmonic analysis and then autoregression on the residuals. We find that the periodic terms explain much the same variability as did the autoregressive model, and that only the immediately preceding period contributes to further reduction of variability, giving a final R^2 of 0.54. This approach very nicely splits the predictability of the yearly rainfall into two types—long-term, based on what has happened over the last few years (the harmonic analysis part), and short-term, what has happened most recently (the autoregressive part). It suggests that a strategy of making definite long-range plans and deferring a final decision until the last possible moment would be as useful (in terms of probability of taking the correct action) as making vague long-range plans and updating more and more frequently as the decision time approached.

To ask if one part of the year is any different from any other part of the year in terms of predictability, we considered whether there are times of year when variance in rainfall is small. Figure 6 shows 4-week rainfall totals, and their variance (still using the cube root transformation to achieve normality). The figure shows that there are essentially two periods when rainfall is most predictable: during the dry period, when rainfall is low, and during the first half of the wet season, before the heavy rains of the late rainy season.

THE BIOTIC SETTING

Introduction: Why Are There So Many Kinds of Tropical Trees?

EGBERT G. LEIGH, JR.   Smithsonian Tropical Research Institute, Balboa, Republic of Panama

The number of species of trees in tropical forest is quite outside the experience of most visitors from the temperate zone. As Thorington et al. (this volume) will tell us, there are nearly 60 species of trees over 20 cm in diameter at breast height in a hectare of forest on Barro Colorado Island, whether the plot is in younger forest near the laboratory or in older forest on the other side of the island. This seems typical for lowland moist and wet tropical forest in the New World. Tropical forests in Malesia are more diverse. Richards (1952) found 98 species over 20 cm in diameter in 1.5 ha. of forest in Sarawak, and Paijmans (1970) found 90 such species in 0.8 ha. of forest in Papua New Guinea. By contrast, there are only 10 or 12 such species in a hectare of oak-hickory forest in southern Michigan, and 30 or 35 in the cove forest of the Great Smokies, the most diverse forest in the continental United States.

The tropics are also noted for diversity of animals. There are more kinds of birds, bats, and other wildlife in the tropics than in comparable settings in the temperate zone (here, I use diversity in the broad sense: the number of species and the Shannon-Weaver index represent different aspects of diversity). However, the diversity of tropical animals reflects either the stability of tropical environments, which permits production of some fruit and leaves the year around, or the diversity of tropical trees (Hutchinson, 1959).

Why are there so many kinds of trees in the tropics?

There are several competing explanations:

1. The species are in competitive equipoise, and diversity expresses the balance between speciation and extinction due to chance fluctuations in numbers (Hubbell, 1979). Specifically, Hubbell assumes that a community has K trees, that every so often a disturb-ance, to which each tree is equally liable, kills D of them, and that these D places are filled by replicates of D trees sampled (with replacement) at random from the K alive before the disturbance. Hubbell finds that, if this is the case, the distribution of the abundances of the different species will approach the log normal, the distribution of abundances most often observed in both tropical and temperate-zone forests.

2. These species coexist because different species occupy different habitats or stations in the forest. Thus some species live out their lives in the understory, while others cannot reproduce until they attain the canopy; some species are characteristic of valley bottoms, others of ridge tops. Ashton (1969, 1977) believes that he has obtained sufficient evidence that species segregate along environmental gradients to confirm the importance of such niche differentiation in maintaining the diversity of tropical forest.

3. Species may coexist by virtue of different response to gaps opened in the forest canopy by disturbances. Skellam (1951) showed how the recurrence of such disturbances could allow a "fugitive species," better at colonizing newly opened space, to coexist with a competitively superior "equilibrium species." A forest is subject to many scales of disturbance, ranging from the fall of an individual tree to the flattening of large areas by earthquakes or cyclones (Foster and Brokaw, this volume). It is not known how many species such a spectrum of disturbance can maintain, but Strong (1977) and Connell (1978) believe that the diversity of forest trees is correlated primarily with the frequency of such disturbance.

4. Species may coexist because their reproductive rates respond differently to environmental change. If the organisms involved are long-lived, environmental variation favors rare species because they gain far more

from a year favorable to reproduction than they lose in an unfavorable year. Chesson and Warner (1981) provide a theoretical example which they apply to coral reef fish, but which seems far more appropriate to tropical trees. Consider a community with K trees, and suppose that, in year t, $n_1(t)$ of these trees are of species 1 and $n_2(t) = K - n_1(t)$ are of species 2. Suppose, moreover, that at year's end a proportion d of each species dies, opening up Kd places, a proportion $n_1(t)b_1(t)/[n_1(t)b_1(t) + n_2(t)b_2(t)]$ of which are immediately reoccupied by species 1 and the remainder by species 2, where $b_1(t)$ and $b_2(t)$ are the number of seeds produced per parent in year t by species 1 and species 2. Then

$$n_1(t + 1) = n_1(t)(1 - d)$$
$$+ Kdb_1(t)n_1(t)/[n_1(t)b_1(t) + n_2(t)b_2(t)]$$

If $n_1(t)$ is very small and $n_2(t)$ is nearly K, $n_1(t + 1)$ is nearly

$$n_1(t)\{1 - d[1 - b_1(t)/b_2(t)]\}$$
$$\approx n_1(0) \prod_{i=0}^{t} \{1 - d[1 - b_1(i)/b_2(i)]\}$$

Suppose that, for example, the environment has a four-year cycle, where $b_1/b_2 = 5$ one year and $\frac{1}{5}$ the other three, while $d = \frac{1}{100}$. Then, if species 1 is rare,

$$n_1(t + 4) \approx n_1(t)(1 + 4/100)(1 - 4/500)^3$$

which exceeds $n_1(t)$. Thus, species 1 can increase when rare, even though it is favored far less often than its competitor, and environmental variation thus allows both to coexist. The same mechanism allows more than two species to coexist. More generally (see Chesson and Warner, 1981), if the average value of

$$\ln[1 - d_1(t) + d_2(t)b_1(t)/b_2(t)]$$

is positive, where d_1 and b_1 are death and reproductive rates of species 1 and d_2 and b_2 are the average death and reproductive rates of those other trees in the community not belonging to species 1, then species 1 will not die out. It is not clear, however, how many species can coexist by this means.

If, on the other hand, reproductive rates are constant, different patterns of mortality will not permit coexistence.

The incredible variety of ways by which different tropical plants are pollinated, their seeds dispersed, and their seedlings defended against herbivores, and the great variation in reproductive success of different species from year to year (see Foster, this volume) seem to confirm the importance of Chesson and Warner's mechanism; there seems, moreover, to be no such variety in the ways adult trees die.

Notice that Chesson and Warner's mechanism in-volves competition, since each species would benefit from the absence of the other, but it does not lead to spatial segregation.

5. A forest may contain many species of trees because insect pests do not allow any one of them to become too common (Gillett, 1962). Examples abound where the many seeds or seedlings under the crown of their parent tree are more heavily eaten than the few that are dispersed farther (Connell, 1978); the dangers of monoculture are a byword (Dethier, 1976), and the tropics seem a perfect heaven for insect pests.

How can we evaluate the relative importance of the different mechanisms? A crude test for generality is whether a mechanism can account for the vast difference in diversity between tropical and temperate-zone forests. This test seems to exclude the possibility that a tree's numbers are governed solely by the changes of sampling one generation from its predecessor; such chances should act everywhere alike. It seems to exclude the possibility that differentiation with respect to microhabitat and station in the forest accounts for all the forest's diversity, for the variety of microhabitats should not depend on distance from the equator, nor is the light gradient in a mature forest of northern hardwoods during the growing season very different from that in a tropical rain forest, nor is there any evidence that tropical trees have more specialized habitat preferences. Finally, it seems to exclude the possibility that diversity reflects degree of disturbance, for, once again, it is not clear that the timing of mortality, and the spatial arrangement of dying trees—how often trees die singly, and how often in clumps or whole stands—are closely correlated with latitude. However, these mechanisms may act in concert with others. Moreover, very distinguished people have different views of their importance.

Applying the same test, the coexistence of trees by virtue of different reproductive responses to a changing environment could in principle explain tree diversity because the relatively stable tropical climate, which permits some fruit and flowers to be produced all year round, accordingly permits a much greater variety of modes of reproduction, each with a different response to seasonal rhythms and longer-term changes. Similarly, the tropical climate permits insect pests to flourish all year long, which may well call forth a greater variety of plants, each with its peculiar mode of defense.

However, these arguments are controversial and incomplete. The proponents of chance, and of competitive niche differentiation, might argue that temperate-zone diversity has not yet recovered from the last glaciation or that, as Terborgh (1973) suggests, the far greater area of land with tropical climates permits these two processes to attain higher equilibrium diversity there. Proponents of competitive niche differentiation might also argue that the stabler tropical environment permits a finer subdivision of environmental gradients. The proponents of disturbance could argue that fire is a simplifying disturbance which is important in the temperate zone but occurs rarely in the tropics. One needs more precise tests for the importance of these different mechanisms, and such tests are not easily come by.

For example, one can devise a theoretical model accounting for tree diversity in terms of the random sampling (with replacement) of one generation's trees from those of the preceding generation, expressing diversity as the balance between the extinctions resulting from such sampling and a plausible speciation rate. To test the model adequately, however, one would have to know the rate at which tropical trees speciate and the spectrum of initial population sizes of these new species. This information is very difficult to obtain. At the moment, proponents of chance rely on verifying a distribution of species abundances derived from the model. Hubbell (1979), for example, shows that under certain seemingly reasonable auxiliary assumptions, species abundances are distributed according to the log normal, as is usually the case in natural communities. The issue is confused, however, because this distribution also results from a plausible model of competitive niche differentiation (Sugihara, 1980).

Again, one can construct a plausible model accounting for the diversity of forest trees from niche differentiation through competitive displacement. It is also easy to pick out a few fairly convincing examples of such "niche differentiation" (for example, overstory versus understory trees). However, we are far from showing that each species of tree is indeed peculiarly adapted to the microsites where it grows; we know too little of the ecological meaning of either the shapes or the physiology of different trees to even guess the answer to such a question. Too often, segregation of different species along an enviromental gradient is taken as evidence of competitive displacement. The intertidal ecologist (see Paine, 1974) knows many examples where such segregation reflects entirely different causes. Thus the zonation of intertidal organisms along an exposed rocky shore, with barnacles at the top, mussels in the middle, kelp below, and a subtidal pavement of coralline algae and other crusts below the kelp reflects, among other things, the presence of predatory starfish which prevent mussels from spreading downward and displacing the kelp (Paine, 1974) and the presence of seagulls, which prevent sea urchins from spreading upward from the subtidal and devouring the kelp (Paine and Vadas, 1969).

Although there is a clear distinction between "equilibrium" and "fugitive" tree species, both empirically (Brokaw, this volume) and theoretically (Skellam, 1951), it is not clear how many different species coexist, or even how many could conceivably coexist, by virtue of different responses to disturbance.

The theory that plant diversity is maintained by the tendency of seeds or seedlings of each species to be most heavily eaten when and where they are most common (Janzen, 1970; Connell, 1971) is very difficult to elaborate in testable form. To begin with, a simple model of tree crowns in a hexagonal lattice shows that one can arrange a community of only three species where no tree is adjacent to a consepecific (Hubbell, 1980). Another model suggests that discrimination against common plants which is too subtle to measure can maintain great diversity in the forest. Consider, for example, a community of 10^{10} canopy trees; at 30 such trees per hectare, this would be a region the size of Amazonia. Suppose that one new species arises, as a single individual, every century. Suppose also that the trees are distributed in a hexagonal lattice, so each tree has six neighbors, and that, three times every second, a tree chosen at random dies and is replaced by a replicate of another tree chosen at random from the community, save that a tree reduces the probability of a conspecific landing in an adjoining space by the factor $1 - k/6$. In this model, a tree's prospective lifetime is nearly a century. If $k = 1$, the community will contain over 22,000 species of canopy trees when at equilibrium; if $k = \frac{1}{10}$, it will contain over 7,300; and if $k = \frac{1}{100}$, it will contain over 2,400. The discrepancy between the two models is striking.

The difficulty with the first model is that it concerns a "rock-bottom equilibrium" in a world where extinction is possible but speciation is not. The difficulty with the second model is that in fact a tree is affected, not by the average density of conspecifics in the community as a whole, but by the average density of conspecifics in its neighborhood. The relevant measure of the effect of a tree species' numbers on its per capita growth rate is mean crowding (Lloyd, 1967), the average of the density of conspecifics neighboring each tree of the species. However, to calculate the change in mean crowding from generation to generation, we need to keep track of changes, not only in number of trees of this species, but in how they are arranged. Instead of one number, it now looks as if we must keep track of 10^{10}: the number (0 or 1) of trees of this species in each cell of the community (see Schaffer and Leigh, 1976). One hopes there will be a dodge, for it is important to know how much discrimination against the common species will support how much diversity, yet the difficulty of the problem as outlined here boggles the mind.

In any event, it is clear that the arrangement of trees in the forest is a matter of interest; the more clumped the distribution of each species, the less likely it is that excess herbivory on common species maintains diversity. Hence the concern to demonstrate that, on Barro Colorado Island (Thorington et al., this volume), as elsewhere (Hubbell, 1979), the distributions of individual tree species are clumped.

Fortunately, Chesson and Warner's theory of differential reproduction in a varying environment is more readily testable; the trick is to consider as species 2 all individuals in the community that do not belong to species 1. To test this theory, we need to know far more about how fruit crops vary from year to year, and the impact of this variation on the reproductive success of different species in successive years. Questions leading to such knowledge are already being asked, on Barro Colorado and elsewhere.

LITERATURE CITED

Ashton, P. S.
1969.   Speciation Among Tropical Forest Trees: Some Deductions in the Light of Recent Research. *Biological Journal of the Linnean Society*, 1:155–196.
1977.   A Contribution of Rain Forest Research to Evolutionary Theory. *Annals of the Missouri Botanical Garden*, 64: 694–705.

Brokaw, N. V. L.
1982.   Treefalls: frequency, timing and consequences. Pages 101-108 *The Ecology of a Tropical Forest*, edited by Egbert G. Leigh, Jr., et al. Washington, D.C.: Smithsonian Institution Press.

Chesson, P. L., and R. R. Warner
1981.   Environmental variability promotes coexistence in lottery competitive systems. *American Naturalist* 117:923–943).

Connell, J. H.
1971.   On the Role of Natural Enemies in Preventing Competitive Exclusion in Some Marine Animals and in Rain Forest Trees. Pages 298–312 in *Dynamics of Populations*, edited by P. J. den Boer and G. Gradwell. Wageningen: Centre for Agricultural Publication and Documentation.
1978.   Diversity in Tropical Rain Forests and Coral Reefs. *Science*, 199:1302–1310.

Dethier, V. G.
1976.   *Man's Plague? Insects and Agriculture*. Princeton, N.J.: Darwin Press.

Foster, R. B.
1982.   Famine on Barro Colorado Island. Pages 201-212 in *The Ecology of a Tropical Forest*, edited by Egbert G. Leigh, Jr., et al. Washington, D.C.: Smithsonian Institution Press.

Foster, R. B., and N. V. L. Brokaw
1982.   Structure and History of the Vegetation of Barro Colorado Island. Pages 67–81 in *The Ecology of a Tropical Forest*, edited by Egbert G. Leigh, Jr., et al. Washington, D.C.: Smithsonian Institution Press.

Gillett, J. B.
1962.   Pest Pressure, an Underestimated Factor in Evolution. *Systematic Association Publications*, 4: 37–46.

Hubbell, S. P.
1979.   Tree Dispersion, Abundance and Diversity in a Tropical Dry Forest. *Science*, 203: 1299–1309.
1980.   Seed predation and the coexistence of tree species in tropical forests. *Oikos*, 35:214–229.

Hutchinson, G. E.
1959.   Homage to Santa Rosalia, or, Why Are There So Many Kinds of Animals? *American Naturalist*, 93: 145–159.

Janzen, D. H.
1970.   Herbivores and the Number of Tree Species in Tropical Forests. *American Naturalist*, 104: 501–528.

Lloyd, M.
1967.   Mean Crowding. *Journal of Animal Ecology*, 36: 1–30.

Paijmans, J.
1970.   An Analysis of Four Tropical Rain Forest Sites in New Guinea. *Journal of Ecology*, 58: 77–101.

Paine, R. T.
1974.   Intertidal Community Structure. *Oecologia*, 15: 93–120.

Paine, R. T., and R. L. Vadas
1969.   The Effects of Grazing by Sea Urchins, *Strongylocentrotus* spp., on Benthic Algal Populations. *Limnology and Oceanography*, 14: 710–719.

Richards, P. W.
1952.   *The Tropical Rain Forest*. Cambridge: Cambridge University Press.

Schaffer, W. M., and E. G. Leigh, Jr.
1976.   The Prospective Role of Mathematical Theory in Plant Ecology. *Systematic Botany*, 1: 209–232.

Skellam, J. G.
1951.   Random Dispersal in Theoretical Populations. *Biometrika*, 38: 196–218.

Strong, D. R., Jr.
1977.   Epiphyte Loads, Treefalls, and Perennial Disruption: A Mechanism for Maintaining Higher Species Richness in the Tropics Without Animals. *Journal of Biogeography*, 4: 215–218.

Sugihara, G.
1980.   Minimal Community Structure: an Explanation of Species Abundance Patterns. *American Naturalist*, 116:770–787.

Terborgh, J. W.
1973.   On the Notion of Favorableness in Plant Ecology. *American Naturalist*, 107: 481–501.

Thorington, R. W., Jr., et al.
1982.   Distribution of trees on Barro Colorado Island: A five-hectare sample. Pages 83–94 in *The Ecology of a Tropical Forest*, edited by Egbert G. Leigh, Jr., et al. Washington, D.C.: Smithsonian Institution Press.

Structure and History of the Vegetation of Barro Colorado Island

ROBIN B. FOSTER   Department of Biology, University of Chicago, Chicago, Illinois 60637

NICHOLAS V. L. BROKAW   Department of Biology, University of Chicago, Chicago, Illinois 60637

ABSTRACT

Barro Colorado Island supports a semideciduous forest on clay soils derived from both basalt and sedimentary rocks. A large element of the island's flora is characteristic of fertile sites with dry seasons of intermediate intensity. The flora of the Panama Canal area has changed very little during the last 35,000 years, even though savannahs and sand deserts were much more widespread elsewhere in the tropics 18,000 years ago than they are now.

Half the island is covered by young forest a hundred or more years old; judging from the species composition, this forest is still growing back from old agricultural clearings. Most of the rest of the island is covered by older forest that has been subject to little disturbance over the past 200–400 years other than selective cutting of prized trees such as mahogany.

This area, however, was subject to shifting agriculture before the Spanish Conquest.

Both old and young forest have about 170 trees over 20 cm in diameter per hectare. Canopy trees in the "old forest" tend to be 30 to 40 m tall, while those in "young forest" are 10 m shorter. The young forest has fewer very large trees. The gaps opened in its canopy by falling trees accordingly tend to be smaller than in old forest, so the structure and appearance of the young forest tends to be more homogeneous. Although the structural differences between young and old forest are now rather subtle, they were much more obvious 50 years ago.

Since Barro Colorado became an island, old forest on western exposures has been much damaged, apparently by windstorms coming across the lake.

INTRODUCTION

In this chapter we will describe the vegetation and flora of Barro Colorado Island. We will contrast the younger forest of the northeastern part of the island with the more mature forest adjoining it on the south and west. We will discuss factors that disrupt the forest—individual treefalls, landslides, larger blowdowns, and agricultural clearings—and consider the mode of regeneration in each. We will then apply our knowledge of the effects of different types of disturbance to infer the history of old and young forest. Finally, we will consider how the vegetation has changed during the last 60 years.

Effects of Climate

The vegetation of Barro Colorado Island is semideciduous lowland forest, less obviously deciduous than that on the drier Pacific coast. There is a strong gradient in annual rainfall from the Pacific to the Atlantic side of the Panama Canal; Barro Colorado occupies an intermediate position on this gradient.

The higher elevations to the west of the Panama Canal create a rain shadow, making for the striking dichotomy between wet and dry forest characteristic of Costa Rica and other mountainous parts of Central and South America. However, large areas in the southwestern part of Panama and in the Bayano and Chucunaque basins east of the canal have rainfall regimes similar to those prevailing near the canal. Comparable climates also occur in many other areas of tropical forest which are not influenced by nearby mountain ranges, but which are sufficiently far from the equator to ensure a pronounced seasonality.

The semideciduousness of the forest is not simple. Only a small fraction of the tree species are even facultatively deciduous. A few species lose their leaves for several months every year; others are leafless for a few weeks or less in every year; while still others lose all or part of their leaves only in especially dry years. The relative abundance of these species determines how deciduous the forest is. While leaffall is largely a dry-season phenomenon, several species become deciduous even when the soil is saturated with water. Consequently, in some areas of forest the largest number of trees are leafless in June or July. It is worrying that deciduousness is given such a role in describing tropical forests when the presence and absence of just a few species, or the weather conditions of a given year, can so dramatically alter the appearance of vegetation.

The flora of Barro Colorado is composed of species characteristic of a wide array of climatic zones. These are catalogued in T. Croat's monumental *Flora of Barro Colorado Island* (1978). Some species and genera are typical of wetter forest; for example, *Cespedezia macrophylla* (Ochnaceae), *Drypetes standleyi* (Euphorbiaceae), *Vantanea occidentalis* (Humiriaceae), *Symphonia globulifera*, and most other species of Guttiferae. Others usually occur in dry forest, as do *Sterculia apetala* (Sterculiaceae), *Bombacopsis quinata* (Bombacaceae), *Enterolobium cyclocarpum* (Leguminosae), *Sloanea terniflora* (Elaeocarpaceae), and *Astronium graveolens* (Anacardiaceae). Still others have very broad climatic tolerance, as do *Ceiba pentandra* (Bombacaceae), *Spondias mombin* (Anacardiaceae), *Hura crepitans* (Euphorbiaceae), *Andira inermis* (Leguminosae), *Apeiba membranacea* (Tiliaceae), and *Luehea seemannii* (Tiliaceae). Finally, many species, including some of the most abundant, are largely restricted to intermediate climates which, like that of Barro Colorado, are neither wholly wet nor wholly dry. These include *Trichilia tuberculata* (Meliaceae), *Tetragastris panamensis* (Burseraceae), *Quararibea asterolepis* (Bombacaceae).

Pollen records for the last 35,000 years from what is now Gatun Lake (Bartlett and Barghoorn, 1973) indicate that lowland forest of the present type has continuously occupied the area near the Panama Canal, although the lower Chagres basin changed from mangrove to a freshwater swamp. Most of the taxa represented that were taken to imply drier or colder climates, such as *Ilex*, *Symplocos*, and the Ericaceae, are now known to occur on the wet lower slopes of the Caribbean side.

The intermediate character of the climate of Barro Colorado may be the most valuable feature of this site. Its widely representative flora, and its varying climate, allow one to observe species under stress, and thus to learn more about the selective forces that shape tropical communities and tropical species.

Effects of Soil

The flora contains mostly genera typical of richer tropical soils, including *Cedrela, Guarea,* and *Trichilia* in the Meliaceae, *Ficus* and other genera in the Moraceae, the characteristic emergent *Ceiba pentandra* (Bombacaceae), *Inga* (Leguminosae), *Piper* (Piperaceae), and many genera of the Bignoniaceae.

And indeed, judging by the nutrient content of the leaf litter (Bruce Haines, pers. comm.), the clay soils of Barro Colorado, derived from both igneous and sedimentary rocks, support a vegetation much richer in mineral nutrients than do most forest soils in Amazonia, Malaya, and Borneo. As is presumably the case on Barro Colorado, soils are much richer in much of Central America, the eastern foothills of the Andes, and volcanic areas of Africa and the East Indies, than in most of Amazonia or Malaysia (FAO soil map of the world).

FOSTER AND BROKAW

Figure 1. Profile of old forest exposed by the fall of a large tree near Armour trail, #13. The large tree at left is *Prioria copaifera*, that in the center is *Anacardium excelsum*, and that at right is *Quararibea asterolepis* (drawing by Daniel Glanz).

Figure 2. Profile of old forest seen across Shannon ravine from near the beginning of Shannon trail. The dark-trunked tree near the left is *Anacardium excelsum*; a *Quararibea asterolepis* is just to the right of and before it (drawing by Daniel Glanz).

Barro Colorado seems comparable in climate and richness of soil to the floodplain of Manu National Park, 12°S latitude, on the eastern rim of the Amazon basin in southeastern Peru. Seventy-five percent of the 335 genera so far collected in Manu Park also occur on Barro Colorado, and the two sites share at least 105 species in common. Both these forests have emergent *Ceiba pentandra*, conspicuous large *Dipteryx* (Leguminosae), *Hura crepitans*, *Brosimum alicastrum* (Moraceae), *Luehea*, and *Poulsenia armata* (Moraceae), an abundance of *Trichilia*, *Guarea*, *Quararibea*, and *Virola* (Myristicaceae), extensive stands of the large successional fig tree *Ficus insipida*, and a common understory shrub, *Rinorea* (Violaceae). Although Manu Park is 2,500 km from Barro Colorado and is on the other side of the equator, its flora seems to resemble Barro Colorado's at least as much as do those of forests on the two coasts of Panama, less than 50 km away;

these coastal forests, however, have not yet been studied in detail. There is no evidence so far that the different geological substrates on Barro Colorado give rise to forests of significantly different composition, structure, turnover rates, or productivity. Extensive sampling would be necessary to demonstrate these differences. However, the floristic composition of the island is obviously different from that on the mainland Cretaceous substrate a few kilometers to the northeast.

Distribution of Species on the Island

There are numerous examples of discontinuity in species distribution associated with the distribution of old versus young forest (see Knight, 1975; Croat, 1978). Similarly, there are characteristic ridge species such as *Cavanillesia platanifolia* (Bombacaceae), *Bombacopsis quinata* (Bombacaceae), and *Tabebuia guayacan* (Bignoniaceae), and ravine species such as *Macrocnemum* glabrescens (Rubiaceae), *Ocotea skutchii* (Lauraceae), and *Licania platypus* (Chrysobalanaceae); but there is considerable floristic overlap between ravines and ridges. Much of the east and west ends of the island consist of gradual slopes and plateaus, and differences in soil drainage may be more important here in restricting species distribution. Large thickets of the spiny terrestrial bromeliad *Aechmea magdalenae* and the terrestrial aroid *Dieffenbachia longispatha* are associated with poorly drained areas, but not exclusively so. Their inhibitory effect on other undergrowth may influence forest regeneration in these areas.

Patchy distribution seems to be the rule, but causal factors are usually not evident. On a large scale, the fan palm (*Cryosophila warscewicziana*) is widespread in the young forest on the eastern side of the island, but it is not on the northern peninsulas or in the young forest on the central plateau; the shrub *Psychotria capitata* (Rubiaceae) is found only in the far western and southcentral areas of the old forest, but is common in these areas. These distributions correspond roughly to geologic substrate pattern (Dietrich, et al., this volume) and are the only apparent examples linking plant distribution with the chemistry or structure of the soil. *Prioria copaifera* (Leguminosae) is common only on the southern half of the island, perhaps because of immigration from the former Gigante swamp forest nearby. At least one other swamp forest species, *Grias fendleri* (Lecythidaceae) is known only from the island's south shore.

Coussarea curvigemmia (Rubiaceae) and *Pseudobombax septenatum* (Bombacaceae) are associated in dense patches on former clearings in the young forest, such as Miller 3, Wheeler 6, Lake 2, Fairchild 4, Nemesia 3–4, perhaps indicating some common factor in the past treatment of these areas.

There are occasional dense aggregations of plants that are otherwise quite rare: there is a clump of *Terminalia chiriquiensis* (Combretaceae) southeast of Armour 7; *Anaxagorea panamensis* (Annonaceae) north of Zetek 6–7; *Myrcia fosteri* (Myrtaceae) between Wheeler 7 and Miller 1–2; *Hoffmannia eliasii* (Rubiaceae) in one ravine crossed by Wetmore trail; *Parathesis microcalyx* (Myrsinaceae) in a poorly drained area north of Zetek 3, as well as a spot on the edge of the south escarpment; and *Coccoloba acapulcense* (Polygonaceae) in two widely separated northside ravines and one spot on the edge of the north escarpment. It is not clear whether these clumps occur by chance (cf. Hubbell, 1979 or whether they reflect environmental factors unknown to us.

Forest Structure

With few small exceptions, the vegetation of Barro Colorado has been protected from all cutting since the island was declared a reserve in 1923. In 1930, half the island was young forest growing in areas that were obviously cleared in the presumably recent past, while the rest was covered by much older forest (Enders, 1935).

Stature The stature of the forest is not uniform. Bennett (1963) states that the upper stratum of the older forest averages 23 to 30 m in height (the lower figure probably refers to the average height of the bottoms of the crowns of canopy trees) while the upper stratum of the younger forest averages 18 to 24 m in height. Knight's (1963) profile diagrams show canopy trees in older forest mostly between 30 and 40 m tall, with occasional emergents approaching 50 m (Figures 1 and 2), and canopy trees in younger forest mostly between 20 and 30 m with occasional individuals approaching 40 m. Trees in ravines tend to be taller than on flats. The forest around the tower in Lutz Creek (Figures 3 and 4), a transition zone between old and young forest, is 34 m high. R. Foster measured 146 canopy-level *Tachigalia versicolor* (Leguminosae) trees in the older forest; they ranged from 20 to 47 m in height, averaging 33 m. If one includes the height of regeneration in treefall gaps, the average canopy height in older forest might be nearly as low as that in younger forest.

Density and Diversity There are roughly 1900 to 2000 stems greater than 2.5 cm in diameter at breast height (dbh) per hectare in older forest, and 2600 to 2700 in younger forest (Lang et al., 1971; Knight, 1975). There are approximately 170 trees greater than 20 cm dbh per hectare in maturing young forest, and 160 in older forest; in older forest, a bigger proportion of these trees are very large (Lang et al., 1971; Thorington et al., this volume; Putz and Milton, this volume).

In younger forest a hectare plot contains roughly 110 species represented by stems over 2.5 cm dbh (Lang et al., 1971). In both young and old forests, a hectare contains between 50 and 65 species of trees over 20 cm dbh (Thorington et al., this volume, Milton and Tarak in Milton, 1978).

NATURAL DISTURBANCE AND REGENERATION

Small-scale Disturbance

Falling branches and trees are forever creating gaps of different sizes in the forest canopy. Gaps smaller

Figure 3. View of forest canopy from 27 m up a tower near the weir in Lutz watershed. The emergent in the center is a young adult *Virola surinamensis* surrounded by *Ficus insipida* and *Ficus yoponensis*, and the liana *Uncaria tomentosa* (drawing by Lynn Siri Kimsey).

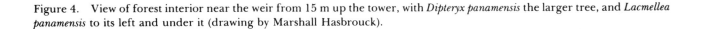

Figure 4. View of forest interior near the weir from 15 m up the tower, with *Dipteryx panamensis* the larger tree, and *Lacmellea panamensis* to its left and under it (drawing by Marshall Hasbrouck).

Vegetation of Barro Colorado Island

than 150 sq. m in area are settled primarily by "persistent species" whose saplings can survive in the shade for several years. Not even these species, however, seem to be able to grow up in the shade; they too need gaps. Judging from the fact that intermediate-sized individuals of persistent canopy species occur relatively rarely in the forest understory, and that shaded saplings grow very slowly, we conclude that saplings of these species probably require exposure to sunlight from the fall of a nearby canopy tree or branch in order to reach canopy height (see also Hartshorn, 1978). Such a sapling may persist through several openings and closings of gaps before attaining the canopy. These trees do not attain reproductive maturity until exposed to full sun.

The seedlings of other species, called "pioneers," will only grow in light gaps greater than 150m^2 and apparently require a continuous gap to reach maturity. Such "pioneers" include *Cecropia insignis* and *Cecropia obtusifolia* (Moraceae), *Zanthoxylum belizense* (Rutaceae), *Miconia argentea* (Melastomaceae), *Trema micrantha* (Ulmaceae), *Croton billbergianus* (Euphorbiaceae), *Hampea appendiculata* (Malvaceae), *Trichospermum mexicanum* (Tiliaceae), *Trattinnickia aspera* (Burseraceae), *Spondias mombin* and *Spondias radlkoferi* (Anacardiaceae), *Alchornea costaricensis* (Euphorbiaceae), and *Sapium caudatum* (Euphorbiaceae). These are probably the commonest, but the composition in each gap is a different subset. The first eight seem to be faster growing and shorter-lived than the others. Mature leaves of pioneer species are shorter-lived and far more heavily eaten by insect herbivores than those of persistent species (Coley, this volume). The total area of the large treefall gaps opened in the forest per unit time may thus govern the abundance of insect herbivores and their predators.

Brokaw (this volume) recorded the treefall gaps occurring within 10 m of 27 km of transect along the trails of Barro Colorado, half of which were in old forest. Between 1975 and 1978, one gap opened per hectare per year in both young and old forest, averaging 63 sq. m in the young forest and 88 sq. m in the old.

Gaps are apparently opening rapidly in exposed areas. In 12 ha. selected randomly from the central plateau that caps the island (R. Foster, unpublished data), an average of 161 sq. m of light gaps opened per hectare per year. Although 71% of the gaps were less than 100 sq. m in area, these accounted for only 19% of the area opened up.

The rate at which gaps form presumably varies greatly from year to year. Moreover, on a much longer time scale, the devastation wrought by large windstorms, landslides, and climatic changes may outweigh the effects of small-scale disturbance. However, the rate of fall of large trees that we have observed easily accounts for the abundance in the older forest of pioneer species whose juveniles rarely occur in the shaded understory.

Large-scale Disturbance

Landslides Late in the rainy season of 1959, after several days of continuous rain totaling 20 in. in one week, "lateral slumps" (Dietrich et al., this volume) completely denuded large areas on slopes in Lutz ravine, the east side of Drayton ridge, and in several other ravines (E. Willis, personal communication). The landslides of 1959 are the only well-known ones on Barro Colorado, but the ravines are full of evidence of earlier slides and more recent small slides. The only other year on record in which more than 20 in. of rain fell in a week was 1931, although one-week totals of 15 or more inches occurred in 1935 and 1939 (Rand and Rand, this volume). The escarpment north of Zetek 5–9 seems always to be suffering steep landslips. Since the trails of Barro Colorado do not follow ravines, most such landslips go unnoticed.

Wind Late in the rainy season of 1973, a few hectares of forest north of Zetek 23–24 were blown down, forming the "monster blowdown." The trees in this area nearly all fell northeastward, as if in a wave. Fingers of intact forest project into the blowdown, with *Tabebuia guayacan* and *Calophyllum longifolium* (Guttiferae), two trees with very strong wood, at their tips. These trees apparently protected the trees behind them from falling like dominoes. In July 1979, a violent storm crossed Frijoles Bay, causing individual trees to fall all over the island, and creating major blowdowns on each side of the laboratory clearing; as usual with such storms, the heavy damage was localized.

Although the blowdowns just mentioned are the best known, others have occurred before. In 1960 Bennett (1963) noticed a large area of blown-down forest near Drayton 4–5. From conversations with residents of the area in 1967, Knight (pers. comm.) ascertained that a large blowdown had occurred on the eastern half of Barbour trail. Other areas that have apparently been subjected to heavy wind damage include much of the edge of the island, the ridge slopes along Snyder-Molino 2–4, Drayton ridge, many of the exposed slopes below the escarpment, clockwise from Drayton to Pearson, and the area on the plateau bordering the stream between Conrad and the Zetek-Armour cutoff.

Table 1. Pioneer tree species found in young and old forests and persistent species found in old forest

Pioneer species more characteristic of young forest:

Annona spraguei	Apeiba tibourbou
Cecropia peltata	Coccoloba manzanillensis
Cordia alliodora	Didymopanax morototoni
Ficus insipida	Ficus yoponensis
Ochroma pyramidale	Pseudobombax septenatum
Scheelea zonensis	Terminalia amazonica
Trichospermum mexicanum	Triplaris cumingiana
Vochysia ferruginea	Zanthoxylum setulosum
Zuelania guidonia	

Pioneer species characteristic of both old and young forest:

Alchornea costaricensis	Alseis blackiana
Bombacopsis quinata	Apeiba membranacea
Casearia arborea	Cavanillesia platanifolia
Ceiba pentandra	Cecropia obtusifolia
Croton billbergianus	Gustavia superba
Hyronima laxiflora	Hura crepitans
Luehea seemannii	Jacaranda copaia
Spondias mombin	Miconia argentea
Tabebuia rosea	Spondias radlkoferi
	Trema micrantha
	Zanthoxylum panamensis

Pioneer species more characteristic of old forest:

Cecropia insignis	Hampea appendiculata
Pourouma guianensis	Oenocarpus panamanus
Trattinnickia aspera	Socratea durissima
	Zanthoxylum belizense

Persistent species characteristic of old forest as large adults:

Aspidosperma cruenta	Beilschmiedia pendula
Brosimum alicastrum	Calophyllum longifolium
Drypetes standleyi	Dipteryx panamensis
Guarea grandifolia[1]	Ficus tonduzii
Heisteria concinna	Guatteria dumetorum
Licania platypus	Hirtella triandra
Ocotea oblonga	Nectandra cissiflora
Pouteria fossicola	Ocotea skutchii
Pouteria unilocularis	Poulsenia armata
Protium tenuifolium	Prioria copaifera
Sloanea terniflora	Quararibea asterolepis
Terminalia chiriquensis	Symphonia globulifera
Trichilia tuberculata[2]	Tetragastris panamensis
Dicot hemiepiphytes	Virola surinamensis
	Strangler figs

[1]Guarea multiflora in Croat.
[2]Trichilia cipo in Croat.

Most blowdowns, other than those of July 1979, seem to have been caused by winds from the west. The lower ridges between Pearson and Standley trails are protected from westerlies by the Peña Blanca Peninsula and show relatively little disturbance. The ridges east of the high Drayton ridge are apparently protected by it, and seem less vulnerable than the ridges west of Drayton. The flat at the base of the escarpment on Zetek trail is another seemingly sheltered area. In general, ravines are less disturbed by windstorms than ridges or exposed slopes, but they are not immune.

A species of palm, Oenocarpus panamanus, though not immediately conspicuous after a large blowdown, quickly becomes abundant in the understory. This palm occasionally colonizes smaller gaps; but, wherever it is common, there is additional evidence of a former massive blowdown. On slopes, stilt palms, Socratea durissima, occur with Oenocarpus. These palms inhibit undergrowth to some degree. Groves of these palms appear to be sterile habitats, said to be avoided by arboreal animals (Enders, 1935).

Tachigalia By virtue of the semelparous life-history (Foster, 1977) of Tachigalia versicolor (Leguminosae), areas with high densities of this canopy tree can suffer considerable disturbance in a short time. When several nearby trees have their single reproductive event in the same year or within a few years of each other, the resultant mortality and treefalls create a devastated patch of forest similar in appearance to one hit by a windstorm. The 1975 and 1979 die-offs of Tachigalia have created such areas on the west side of Pena Blanca peninsula, on the peninsula opposite Termite House, and on lower slopes northwest of Barbour Point.

Shifting Agriculture Observations of agricultural clearings on the nearby mainland tell us something about the patterns of regrowth. The farmers leave occasional trees which, like Dipteryx or Ceiba, are difficult to cut, or which, like Scheelea, are useful; these trees may stand alone or in small patches. Unless the agriculture has been unusually intensive or prolonged, many of the original forest plants will continue to sprout from rootstalks. The forest boundary is usually sharp, except where the topography is steep or irregular, and lianas festoon the forest edge. However, the farmers can be expected to remove lianas from their fields, except for the basal sprouts. The regeneration from an abandoned field will usually have a uniform, high density of small stems, save for a few coppiced trees sprouting from old stumps, and an occasional relict tree. In contrast, regeneration in large blowdowns will be much more of a patchwork of many relict trees, tangles of large-diameter lianas, and sprouting from damaged plants of many different heights. The very heterogeneity in the regrowth from a blowdown in old forest may allow one to distinguish it from the more homogeneous regrowth from an abandoned field.

Moreover, some species, like *Oenocarpus panamanus,* will colonize blowdowns but rarely human clearings (Table 1). Other species will colonize human clearings but rarely blowdowns (Table 1). For example, *Ficus insipida,* which colonizes the natural levees of riverbends throughout the neotropics, does not often colonize blowdowns, but it will colonize the slopes and hills of abandoned human clearings.

An extensive study of mainland clearings may enable one to distinguish not only between regeneration from natural disturbance and regeneration from human clearing, but former pasture from former cropland, and between other variations in land use.

However, in ravines it may be more difficult to distinguish regrowth in human clearings from that of natural disturbance. In ravines, human clearing is likely to be irregular or unpredictable. Moreover, regrowth from landslides, like that from human clearing, may appear very uniform. Careful study of the topography may be needed to decide whether landslides contributed to a given disturbance.

The young forest to be seen on the train ride to Frijoles demonstrates how variable regeneration is from place to place. An idealized regeneration sequence of the canopy species in abandoned fields of the Panama Canal area is as follows. *Cecropia peltata, Cochlospermum vitifolium, Trema micrantha, Muntingia calabura* and *Ochroma pyramidale* shoot up rapidly in the first 5 years. They are later overtaken by *Cordia alliodora, Didymopanax morototoni,* and *Miconia argentea.* These are in turn overtaken by the long-persistent *Luehea seemannii, Terminalia amazonica, Ficus insipida, Anacardium excelsum, Spondias mombin, Spondias radlkoferi, Tabebuia rosea,* and many others of more limited and local importance. The interstices in the canopy are filled with small crowned *Zuelania guidonia, Triplaris cumingiana,* and *Gustavia superba.* On very thin soils or dry ridges, *Pseudobombax septenatum, Cavanillesia platanifolia, Bombacopsis quinata,* and *Bursera simaruba* are the more characteristic long-persistent successional species.

HISTORY OF THE VEGETATION

Old Forest

Current techniques do not allow us to decipher the detailed history of the old forest, but we may guess its approximate age. All of Barro Colorado Island has probably been subjected to shifting agriculture some time during the past 10,000 years, if not the last 500. In cores from Gatun Lake, maize pollen dates back to 7000 B.C. (Bartlett et al., 1969), and other indicators of cultivation, such as *Manihot esculenta* pollen, became common during the last 2000 years (Bartlett and Barghoorn, 1973). The agricultural population of Panama was high before the Spanish Conquest (Bennett, 1968); metate grindstones have been found along Armour, Conrad, and Wetmore trails in the old forest, and Dietrich et al. (this volume) have found charcoal in old forest soils.

The old forest may well have been cut as recently as several centuries ago. An enormous *Dipteryx panamensis* at Wheeler 16, near the top of the island, towers nearly 20 m above the 30-m canopy of the surrounding old forest. This species is noted for its slow growth and hard wood. As there is nothing unusual about the location of this giant, and as its crown is fully exposed to the strongest winds, it appears that the other *Dipteryx* in the old forest have not yet had opportunity to grow to their full height, which suggests that the rest of the old forest, as well, has not achieved its full stature. It is not clear whether increased stature can be achieved from continued growth of the same individuals or from collective increases over more than one generation.

Knight (1975) estimates that the old forest on Barro Colorado dates from not later than 1838. Since several species of trees have individuals in the old forest two to five times larger in diameter than any conspecifics in the younger forest, he concluded conservatively that the old forest was twice as old as the young; since he thought the young forest dated from 1900, in 1970 he concluded the old forest was about 140 years old. Knight (1975) also argues that the older forest is still in succession because so large a proportion of the canopy trees (40%) have few juveniles in the shaded understory, and because he finds little difference in structure and species composition between his young forest and old forest plots. We believe that he underestimates the age of the old forest for four reasons. (1) He underestimates the age of the young forest. (2) Falling trees open a sufficient number of gaps in the canopy of the old forest to account for the abundance of trees lacking saplings in the shaded understory. (3) His choice of old forest plots appears to be misleading. For example, we believe that his "old forest" plot at Donato 3.5 is only on the margin of the old forest. (4) He did not compare the species composition of trees with minimum size *greater* than 18 cm dbh, although the difference between old and young forest is likely to be greatest for large trees.

We believe that the young forest dates back to 1880 (see below). Since large trees of the older forest are often three to five times larger in diameter than their largest conspecifics in young forest, the old forest can be three or more times as old as the young forest, dating back at least to 1680. The diameter of the *Dip-*

teryx tree mentioned above has increased only 10–15% (20–30 cm) since Chapman measured it 50 years ago. This tree is therefore possibly 400–500 years old. Careful comparisons of the sizes of conspecific trees in old and young forest, and study of the relation between diameter and growth rate for trees of different species, is needed to verify this conclusion. Lacking such information, our guess is that the old forest is now (1980) mostly 300–400 years old, and surely more than 200 years old.

In the old forest area, shifting agriculture may have been mostly abandoned when the Spanish Conquest decimated native populations along the Chagres River through disease, enslavement, and slaughter between 1500 and 1600 (Bennett, 1968). The old forest has since been exposed to selective cutting, which presumably explains the absence from the island of *Swietenia macrophylla* (mahogany) and the rarity of *Cedrela odorata* (tropical cedar). Such cutting may have been particularly severe during the days of peak river transport and the building of the railroad in the mid-1800s. On the other hand, the old forest seems to have escaped serious disturbance over the last few hundred years, as we have seen; probably because it was far from the river and close to large dismal swamps. The forest on the other side of these swamps (Gigante) from Barro Colorado Island has also escaped serious disturbance until very recently.

Young Forest

As we have remarked, visiting scientists have generally assumed that the forest on the northeast half of Barro Colorado, with its lower stature, its greater abundance of smaller stems, and its lower frequency of formation of treefall gaps, is younger than that on the rest of the island, and represents regrowth from human clearing. Indeed, this view has usually been considered too obvious for serious attention, although Chapman (1938) did obtain some vague descriptions of the past history of the island from some older residents of the area.

The presence throughout the young forest of bottles and old crockery, shade trees such as *Enterolobium cyclocarpum*, and fruit trees such as *Mangifera indica*, *Byrsonima crassifolia*, and *Syzygium jambos*, reflect past human settlement. Knowledge of traditional agricultural methods in this region suggests that the area around these relicts was cleared for temporary crops or for pasture. The species composition of documented clearings abandoned on or near the island is quite similar to the composition of the young forest (Kenoyer, 1929; Knight, 1975), and much less so to the composition of regeneration from large areas of natural disturbance (pers. obs.).

Standley (1935), Kenoyer (1929), Chapman (1938), and Enders (1935) all consider the young forest to have been about 50 years old when they observed it in 1928–1932. This would imply that regeneration began about 1880, when the heavy river and railroad traffic along the Chagres River by gold seekers going to California had ceased and while the French were just beginning their canal. This date seems reasonable, but none of its proponents justified their choice. Since the early scientists believed tropical trees grow very rapidly, whereas this is often not the case, they were unlikely to overestimate the age of the forest. The area of the young forest is unlikely to have been all clear at once; more probably, it was an area of shifting agriculture, with some pasture (see Otis, 1867). Thus the young forest is probably a mosaic of different ages, some parts of which date back to 1800 or even earlier.

Some areas of young forest seem unusually scrubby, with a great density of stems in the understory, small tree crowns, and lower canopy, often no more than 20 m tall. The most obvious areas are the hill between Wheeler 6–8.5 and Miller 0–3, where there are a few French metal dump carts and an abundance of bottles lying about; the forest surrounding the tower clearing at the top of the island; and an abandoned cacao plantation on Peña Blanca Peninsula (Enders, 1973). This vegetation is more stunted than the forest now growing on Poacher's Peninsula, which was under cultivation in 1923.

The scrubby forest is rather like that of recently abandoned clearings, such as the area north of the dock. However, we do not know whether the scrubby forest is mostly younger than the rest of the young forest, or more exposed to damaging winds, or growing on poorer soil, or is regenerating from areas overgrazed or cultivated too many years in a row. Enders (1935) suggests that farmers abandoned the areas of scrubby forest as recently as 1900 to 1905, but it seems equally possible that these areas are as old as much of the rest of the young forest and are growing back more slowly. The apparently clandestine stills of Wheeler 6–8.5 (Chapman, 1938) and elsewhere may have been supplying alcohol to the crews working on the French locks at Bohio, a town near Orchid and deLesseps islands, rather than to crews working on the American canal.

Knight (1975) judged from counts of rings on *Cordia alliodora* that some forest along Barbour trail dated back only to 1900. However, such counts of tree rings often lead to underestimate, and we must wait for more thorough sampling and better ways of aging tropical trees before deciding the merits of his case.

Even now, a diligent search for early descriptions and illustrations may reveal much more about the age and the past history of the island's younger forest.

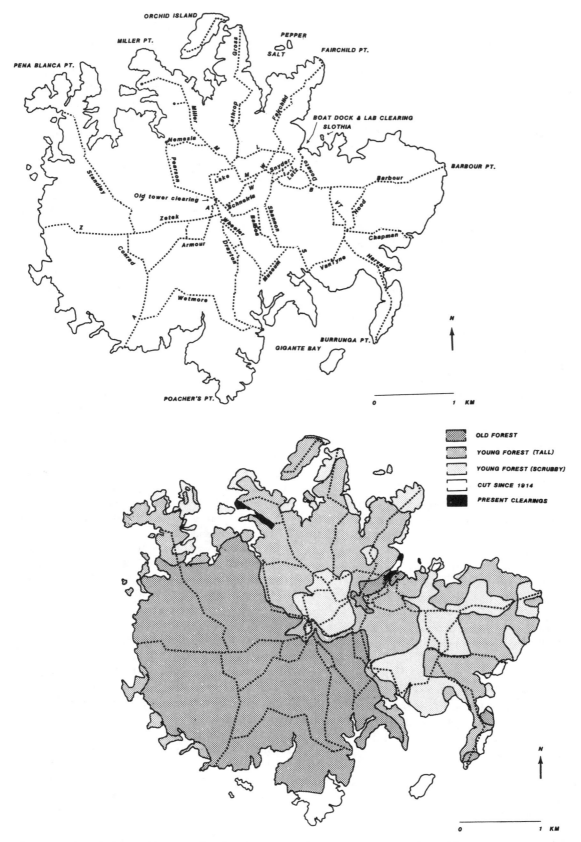

Figure 5. Part A: Map of Barro Colorado Island, showing trails and other points of interest. Part B: Vegetation map of Barro Colorado Island (maps by Robin Foster, Stanley Rand, and Donald Windsor).

FOSTER AND BROKAW

Probably, some photographs were made of this area during the construction of the canal. Otis's (1862) description and drawings of the sights from the train between Bohio Soldado and Frijoles are tantalizing but not sufficiently specific.

Recent Changes on the Island

Chapman's (1929) description of walking up Snyder-Molino and Wheeler trails in 1928 reads very much as if it were written today. Some of the specific trees he mentions are now gone, but the group of large trees at Snyder-Molino 4–5 he mentions lasted until 1975, and the open areas of Wheeler 5–6, the patches of palms at Snyder-Molino 3–4, and the *Pseudobombax* at Wheeler 6 are still there. Chapman recorded that, from Wheeler 8 to the summit at Wheeler 12, "the forest appears to be second growth"; it still does. He notes that near Wheeler 15, one encounters larger trees and less dense undergrowth, as one still does. The *Dipteryx* at Wheeler 16, the big *Ceiba* trees at Armour 7 and 9, and several other trees in his photos look much the same as they did 50 years ago.

However, there have been changes. Fifty years ago the boundary between young and old forest was much clearer than it is now. Kenoyer (1929) stated that "a sharp line of demarcation divides the island into two nearly equal portions, the primeval forest on the west and the second growth on the east." In two aerial photographs of the island taken in 1927, the canopy of the young forest is very different from that of the old. In the young forest, tree crowns were distinctly smaller, and the height of the canopy within a given patch of younger forest was much more uniform. No doubt the difference was less distinct in ravines and in areas where the young forest had grown nearly as tall as the older. On the whole, however, the structural differences between young and old forest were still obvious from the air in 1955, but they are far less obvious now that the young forest has grown and its canopy is being disrupted by falling trees.

Correspondingly, in 1928 one could see the canal from atop a 28-ft. tower in the summit clearing, but the forest soon outgrew that tower and a taller successor, and has grown 5 or 10 m in the last 50 years. Three or four agricultural clearings around the edge of Barro Colorado Island were abandoned when Thomas Barbour bought out the banana-growing settlers in 1923, or shortly before. Enders (1935) noted that one of these clearings was on the Burrunga Peninsula, and another on Poacher's Point; judging from aerial photographs, a third was south of the last hundred meters of Chapman trail.

Recently abandoned clearings include the plantation area north of Allee Creek and the dock, where cultivation stopped in 1937 (Enders, 1973), and clearing stopped in 1953 (Knight, 1975); and the "new plantation" on the peninsula between Slothia and Bat Cove, which was abandoned in 1933 after one year (Enders, 1973). At this time, clearings maintained on the island include the "laboratory clearing" surrounding the buildings of the field station, the "tower clearing" surrounding the summit shelter (there is no longer a tower in that clearing), the clearings around the range lights of Miller Peninsula, and small clearings surrounding the Panama Canal marker signs on the edge of the lake.

In our vegetation map (Figure 5), we have distinguished old forest and three types of young forest. Enders (1935) and Bennett (1963) distinguished young from old forest on their maps purely on the basis of structural characters, whereas we have also employed floristic criteria, such as the overwhelming predominance in young forest of pioneer species among the large canopy trees, and the predominance in old forest of characteristic persistent species (Table 1, bottom).

In the last 50 years, wind has greatly damaged the old forest. Even since our first observations in 1967, many large trees that contributed to a distinct border with young forest have blown down, creating heterogeneous patches of regeneration at the border with the young forest.

Enders (1935) considered the west rim of the island between the ends of Standley and Armour trails to be regeneration from human clearing, and commented that going upslope one then encountered a broad belt of "old forest with palms" (mostly *Oenocarpus*) before entering typical old forest. It appears that the "regeneration," with its small, short trees, is mostly old forest that has been repeatedly damaged by windstorms such as the one in 1973, and that the "old forest with palms" is subject to similar but less severe and less frequent wind damage. Since 1967 considerably more of the closed canopy in the old forest was blown down than has grown up to replace it. Much of what Enders called palm forest now looks more like second growth, and much of the old forest is coming to look more and more like palm forest. The changes are sufficiently obvious that one hesitates to initiate the enormous task of quantifying them.

Although extensive blowdowns are a normal if infrequent part of the life of tropical forest, the repeated blasting of the half-grown regeneration on the west side of the island appears to be a new situation. Perhaps the formation of Gatun Lake removed many topographic obstacles, reducing eddy turbulence to the west of the island and thereby increasing the speed and consequent turbulence of the wind as it slams into Barro Colorado. A recent unpublished meteorological report (Read, 1980) on the new Bayano reservoir in Panama shows that the only major climatic change in the area since formation of the lake is a dramatic increase in wind speeds. As the forest becomes damaged in exposed areas and along its edges, the trees downwind become increasingly vulnerable and the damage spreads. The forest will certainly grow back, but the inhibitory effect of the palms may make the process very slow. The continued selection against tall trees may lead to a generally shorter old forest. This may represent a long-delayed environmental impact of the building of the Panama Canal.

ACKNOWLEDGMENTS

We thank E. G. Leigh and A. H. Kourany for their many improvements and heavy pruning of the manuscript. We are grateful to Daniel Glanz, Lynn Siri Kimsey, and Marshall Hasbrouck for their fine drawings.

LITERATURE CITED

Bartlett, A. S., and E. S. Barghoorn
1973.   Phytogeographic History of the Isthmus of Panama During the Past 12,000 Years. Pages 203–99 in *Vegetation and Vegetational History of Northern Latin America*, edited by A. Graham. New York: Elsevier.

Bartlett, A. S., E. S. Barghoorn, and R. Berger
1969.   Fossil Maize from Panama. *Science*, 152:642–643.

Bennett, C. F.
1963.   A Phytophysiognomic Reconnaissance of Barro Colorado Island, Canal Zone. *Smithsonian Miscellaneous Collections*, 145:1–8.

Bennett, C. F.
1968.   Human Influences on the Zoogeography of Panama. *Ibero-Americana*, 51:1–112.

Brokaw, N. V. L.
1982.   Treefalls: Frequency, Timing, and Consequences. Pages 101–108 in *The Ecology of a Tropical Forest*, edited by Egbert G. Leigh, Jr., et al. Washington, D.C.: Smithsonian Institution Press.

Chapman, F. M.
1929.   *My Tropical Air Castle*. New York: Appleton. 417 pp.

Chapman, F. M.
1938.   *Life in an Air Castle*. New York: Appleton-Century. 250 pp.

Coley, P. D.
1982.   Rates of Herbivory on Different Tropical Trees. Pages 123–132 in *The Ecology of a Tropical Forest*, edited by Egbert G. Leigh, Jr., et al. Washington, D.C.: Smithsonian Institution Press.

Croat, T. B.
1978.   *Flora of Barro Colorado Island*. Stanford, Calif.: Stanford University Press. 943 pp.

Dietrich, W. E., D. M. Windsor, and T. Dunne
1982.   Geology, Climate and Hydrology of Barro Colorado Island. Pages 21–46 in *The Ecology of a Tropical Forest*, edited by Egbert G. Leigh, Jr., et al. Washington, D.C.: Smithsonian Institution Press.

Enders, R. K.
1935.   Mammalian Life Histories from Barro Colorado Island, Panama. *Bulletin of the Museum of Comparative Zoology*, 78:385–502.

Enders, R. K.
1973.   Unpublished manuscript on changes taking place on Barro Colorado Island over 40 years.

Foster, R. B.
1977.   *Tachigalia versicolor* is a suicidal neotropical tree. *Nature*, 268:624–626.

1980.   Heterogeneity and Disturbance in Tropical Vegetation. Pages 75–92 in *Conservation Biology*, edited by M. E. Soule and B. A. Wilcox. Sunderland, Mass. Sinauer Press. 395 pp.

Garwood, N. C., D. P. Janos, and N. Brokaw
1979.   Earthquake-caused Landslides: A Major Disturbance to Tropical Forests. *Science*, 205:997–999.

Gomez-Pompa, A., and C. Vasquez-Yanes
1976.   Estudios sobre sucesion secondaria en los tropicos calido-humedos: El ciclo de vida de las species secundarias. Pages 579–93 in *Regeneracion de Selvas*, edited by A. Gomez-Pompa et al. Mexico City: Compania Editorial Continental, S.A.

Food and Agriculture Organization of the United Nations
1970.   *Soil Map of the World*. Paris: UNESCO.

Hartshorn, G. S.
1978.   Treefalls and Tropical Forest Dynamics. Pages 617–38 in *Tropical Trees as Living Systems*, edited by P. B. Tomlinson and M. H. Zimmerman. Cambridge: Cambridge University Press.

Hubbell, S. P.
1979.   Tree Dispersion, Abundance, and Diversity in a Tropical Deciduous Forest. *Science*, 203:1299–1309.

Kenoyer, L. A.
1929.   General and Successional Ecology of the Lower Tropical Rain Forest at Barro Colorado Island, Panama. *Ecology*, 10:201–222.

Knight, D. H.
1963.   A Distance Method for Constructing Forest Profile Diagrams and Obtaining Structural Data. *Tropical Ecology*, 4:89–94.

Knight, D. H.
1975.   A Phytosociological Analysis of Species-rich Tropical Forest on Barro Colorado Island, Panama. *Ecological Monographs*, 45:259–284.

Lang, G. E., D. H. Knight, and D. A. Anderson
1971.   Sampling the Density of Tree Species with Quadrats in a Species-rich Tropical Forest. *Forest Science*, 17:395–400.

Milton, K.
1978.   Behavioral Adaptations to Leaf-eating by the Mantled Howler Monkey (*Alouatta palliata*). Pages 535–50 in *The Ecology of Arboreal Folivores*, edited by G. G. Mont-

gomery. Washington, D.C.: Smithsonian Institution Press.

Otis, F. N.
1867.   *History of the Panama Railroad.* New York: Harper and Brothers.

Putz, F. E., and K. Milton
1982.   Tree Mortality Rates on Barro Colorado Island. Pages 95–100 in *The Ecology of a Tropical Forest,* edited by Egbert G. Leigh, Jr., et al. Washington, D.C.: Smithsonian Institution Press.

Rand, A. S., and W. M. Rand
1982.   Variation in Rainfall over Barro Colorado Island. Pages 47–59 in *The Ecology of a Tropical Forest,* edited by Egbert G. Leigh, Jr., et al. Washington, D.C.: Smithsonian Institution Press.

Read, R. G.
1980.   Unpublished report presented at a symposium on the Natural History and Botany in Panama and Central America. University of Panama.

Standley, P. C.
1933.   The Flora of Barro Colorado Island, Panama. Contributions of the Arnold Arboretum of Harvard University, No. 5. Jamaica Plain, Mass.: Arnold Arboretum. 178 pp.

Thorington, R. W., Jr., B. Tannenbaum, A. Tarak, and R. Rudran
1982.   Distribution of Trees on Barro Colorado Island. Pages 83–94 in *The Ecology of a Tropical Forest,* edited by Egbert G. Leigh, Jr., et al. Washington, D.C.: Smithsonian Institution Press.

Tosi, J. A., Jr.
1971.   *Zonas de vida, en la Republica de Panama.* Rome: FAO. 89 pp. with map.

Distribution of Trees on Barro Colorado Island: A Five-Hectare Sample

RICHARD W. THORINGTON, JR. Division of Mammals, National Museum of Natural History, Smithsonian Institution, Washington, D.C. 20560

BERNICE TANNENBAUM National Park Service, Denver, Colorado

A. TARAK Buenos Aires, Argentina

R. RUDRAN Department of Zoological Research, National Zoological Park, Washington, D.C. 20008

ABSTRACT

We mapped the trees over 60 cm circumference in five 1-ha. plots of old secondary forest near the laboratory clearing, finding 856 trees representing 112 species. None of these species was significantly overdispersed, suggesting that the tendency of seeds, seedlings, or trees to be most heavily eaten where they are most common is not the dominant factor affecting the distribution of conspecific trees.

Of the 63 species common enough to test, 26 had more of their individuals in a single hectare than one would expect had they been distributed at random; that is to say, for these 26 species, the apportionment of individuals over the 5 ha. showed significant clumping. The distributions within hectares of smaller fractions of the species common enough to test were significantly clumped. This clumping affects the distributions of animals with small territories and seasonal changes in the places animals with larger home ranges look for food.

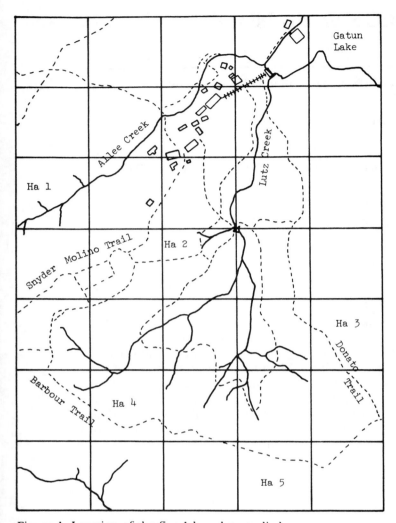

Figure 1. Location of the five 1-ha. plots studied.

INTRODUCTION

How many trees, and how many species of trees, are there in a hectare of forest on Barro Colorado Island? How are trees of a given species distributed? How might the distributions of different species of trees affect the island's vertebrates? To answer, we mapped, measured, and identified trees 60 cm or more in circumference at breast height in five 1-ha. plots in and near Lutz catchment, analyzing abundance, diversity, and distribution to learn whether distributions of individual species were clumped, and, if so, at what scale.

Tropical forests have long been known to contain an extraordinary number of species of plants. It has repeatedly been implied that the species were overdispersed. This has led to hypotheses to explain the overdispersion, such as Janzen's suggestion that seeds were most heavily eaten where were most aggregated (Janzen, 1970). Our observations caused us to question the hypothesis of overdispersion and led to the statistical tests resported in this paper.

We first examined the forest structure—sizes and numbers of trees—in our quadrats. Clumping of tree species could result from different agricultural histories and from the quadrats being in different stages of succession. To the extent that the forest is structurally homogeneous, the distribution of tree species is more likely to result from edaphic factors and biological factors like seed dispersal and predation. After examining the distribution patterns of the tree species, we return to the subject of forest structure, because it can be affected by tree clumping, as well as vice versa.

METHODS

All the trees included in this study were marked in February and March 1975 with numbered aluminum tags. The circumference of each was measured with a tape at the height of the tag, approximately 1.5 m above the ground. Buttresses were included in the measurement, although we avoided large buttresses and other protuberances as much as possible by measuring some trees 2 to 2.5 m above the ground. The trees were mapped with compass and tape, and the hectare boundaries were defined from these maps.

In this study we used trees with a circumference of 60 cm or more and all palms of the species *Astrocaryum standleyanum*. *Astrocaryum* smaller than 60 cm were not included in the analyses of tree size or diversity but were analyzed for clumping.

The trees were identified by vegetative characters. We were able to identify 851 of the 856 marked trees, although some of these were identified only to genus. Our identifications were made possible by the vegetative keys of Thomas Croat (1978) and Dennis Knight (1970), by the reference herbarium maintained on Barro Colorado Island, by the existence of a series of trees marked and identified by Robin Foster and Thomas Croat, and by the personal assistance of Robin Foster. Foster identified a number of trees, and it is because of his efforts that we list only five unknowns. Our identifications and our maps are available on Barro Colorado Island and in the 1974–75 progress report of the Smithsonian Institution's Environmental Sciences Program (Windsor, ed., 1975). The analyses are based on a corrected list of identifications, dated May 1978.

The 5 ha. examined were part of a 25-ha. study

area, 500 m on a side, centered on the Lutz catchment on Barro Colorado Island, Panama. They were regularly dispersed through this area according to the Knut Vik square as shown in Figure 1. Thus in the 5 × 5 matrix of hectares, we examined one hectare in each row and one in each column. It should be emphasized that this is not a random selection of hectares relative to the rows and columns. The hectares were numbered 1 to 5, from north to south. The center of hectare 1 is 50 m north and 250 m west of the weir in Lutz ravine, built by Benjamin B. Morgan in 1971.

Hectare 1 lies in the Allee catchment. It includes Allee Creek and its steep ravine. Hectare 2 lies in the Lutz catchment. It includes the western slope, a short section of the creek bed, and a small part of the 1959 landslide. Hectare 3 lies on the eastern ridge of the Lutz catchment and includes part of the next catchment to the east. Hectare 4 lies on the southern edge of the Lutz catchment and includes a bit of the next catchment to the south. Hectare 5 also straddles these two catchments but includes less of the Lutz catchment. The slopes of these hectares were measured by Putz (Putz and Milton, this volume). His data show that hectare 1 has the most steep slopes, hectare 2 includes the least terrain which is nearly level, and that hectares 3, 4, and 5 are very similar in their slopes. The species of trees occurring in each hectare are given in Table 1.

Our data on tree abundances were used by Milton (1977, 1978), but her figures are in error. She seems to have included trees that we marked outside the hectares or trees of small diameter tagged within some of the hectares.

In the analyses of clumping, probability levels were calculated from binomial and multinomial expansions, or from chi-square distributions where appropriate. In the analyses of the hectares and quarter hectares, the area was defined without reference to the location of the trees, and the frequency of occurrence of each species in the quadrat was tested for significance. For the hectare analyses, probabilities were calculated on the basis of the frequency of occurrence of each species in the 5-ha. sample. For the quarter-hectare analyses, they were based on the frequencies of occurrence in that hectare. In the analyses of sixteenth- and sixty-fourth-hectares, each tree was used as the center of a circle of the specified area and the frequency of occurrence of conspecific trees within this circle was tabulated. Binomial probabilities were based on the frequency of occurrence of each species within that one hectare, minus the one tree which defined the center of the circle.

The nested analyses of variance were conducted to test whether the variation in tree numbers found in

Table 1. Species and numbers of trees identified in each hectare

Species	Hectare					Total
	1	2	3	4	5	
Alchornea costaricensis	1	2	2	3	4	12
Alseis blackiana	12	14	5	22	2	55
Anacardium excelsum	1	11	12	0	0	24
Annona spraguei	1	0	1	0	2	4
Apeiba membranacea	5	3	1	4	1	14
Astrocaryum standleyanum	0	0	3	0	0	3
Astronium graveolens	1	0	0	1	1	3
Beilschmiedia pendula	2	0	0	0	0	2
Bombacopsis quinata	0	2	0	0	0	2
Bombacopsis sessilis	1	0	2	1	3	7
Brosimum alicastrum	4	0	0	0	0	4
Calophyllum longifolium	0	0	1	0	0	1
Casearia arborea	2	2	0	0	0	4
Casearia sylvestris	0	0	0	0	3	3
Cavanillesia platanifolia	1	0	0	1	1	3
Cecropia eximia	1	0	0	0	0	1
Cecropia longipes	0	1	0	0	0	1
Cecropia obtusifolia	1	2	0	0	0	3
Ceiba pentandra	0	0	0	1	0	1
Chrysophyllum panamense	1	1	0	1	0	3
Cordia alliodora	1	0	2	2	3	8
Cordia bicolor	1	1	0	0	0	2
Cordia lasiocalyx	1	0	1	1	0	3
Coussarea impetiolaris	0	0	0	1	0	1
Cupania latifolia	0	1	0	0	0	1
Cupania papillosa	1	2	1	3	1	8
Cupania sylvatica	0	1	0	0	0	1
Dendropanax arboreus	0	0	2	0	1	3
Dipteryx panamensis	1	0	0	1	0	2
Eugenia coloradensis	1	0	0	1	0	2
Ficus insipida	0	3	3	2	0	8
Ficus obtusifolia	1	0	0	1	0	2
Ficus tonduzii	2	0	1	0	1	4
Ficus trigonata	1	0	0	0	0	1
Ficus yoponensis	0	7	2	3	1	13
Genipa americana	0	1	0	0	1	2
Guapira standleyana	0	0	1	1	0	2
Guarea glabra	4	0	0	0	0	4
Guatteria amplifolia	0	1	0	0	0	1
Guatteria dumetorum	2	0	0	0	0	2
Gustavia superba	5	5	6	6	9	31
Hasseltia floribunda	1	0	0	3	3	7
Heisteria concinna	5	0	3	1	0	9
Hirtella americana	0	0	0	1	0	1
Hirtella triandra	2	0	0	1	0	3
Hyeronima laxiflora	1	16	5	5	1	28
Inga fagifolia	0	0	0	1	0	1
Inga goldmanii	0	1	0	0	1	2

Table 1. (continued)

Species	Hectare					Total
	1	*2*	*3*	*4*	*5*	
Inga marginata	0	0	0	1	0	1
Inga pezizifera	2	3	2	0	2	9
Inga quaternata	0	0	1	0	0	1
Inga umbellifera	0	0	0	0	1	1
Jacaranda copaia	2	2	0	1	0	5
Lacmellea panamensis	0	1	0	0	0	1
Lafoensia punicifolia	1	1	0	0	0	2
Licania platypus	2	0	0	0	0	2
Lindackeria laurina	1	0	0	0	0	1
Luehea seemanii	1	10	10	7	5	33
Macrocnemum glabrescens	3	18	12	6	16	55
Maguira costaricana	0	0	2	3	0	5
Miconia argentea	0	0	0	0	2	2
Nectandra	0	1	0	0	0	1
Nectandra latifolia	7	0	0	1	0	8
Ochroma pyramidale	0	1	0	0	0	1
Ocotea cernua	0	0	0	1	0	1
Ocotea oblonga	0	1	0	0	0	1
Ormosia coccinea	0	0	1	1	0	2
Platymiscium pinnatum	1	0	4	3	5	13
Platypodium elegans	1	1	3	3	5	13
Posoqueria latifolia	0	0	2	0	2	4
Poulsenia armata	31	7	2	2	0	42
Pouteria	1	0	0	1	0	2
Pouteria stipitata	1	0	0	0	0	1
Prioria copaifera	0	0	0	0	3	3
Protium costaricense	0	0	0	1	0	1
Protium panamense	4	1	2	3	1	11
Protium tenuifolium	5	3	1	1	0	10
Pseudobombax septenatum	0	5	0	1	0	6
Pterocarpus rohrii	1	7	0	11	0	19
Quararibea asterolepis	4	1	1	0	0	6

Table 1. (continued)

Species	Hectare					Total
	1	*2*	*3*	*4*	*5*	
Rheedia madruno	0	0	0	1	0	1
Sapium caudatum	1	1	4	2	0	8
Scheelea zonensis	1	0	5	3	20	29
Sloanea ternifolia	0	0	1	0	0	1
Spondias mombin	0	1	5	3	12	21
Spondias radlkoferi	3	4	8	10	17	42
Stemmadenia grandiflora	2	0	0	0	0	2
Sterculia apetala	0	0	0	1	1	2
Swartzia simplex	0	1	6	6	5	18
Symphonia globulifera	1	0	0	0	0	1
Tabebuia	1	1	8	4	9	23
Tabebuia rosea	2	0	1	1	4	8
Tachigalia versicolor	0	2	3	0	0	5
Terminalia amazonia	2	2	1	3	6	14
Terminalia chiriquensis	0	3	0	0	0	3
Tetragastris panamensis	3	0	0	0	0	3
Tetrathylacium johansenii	0	1	1	0	0	2
Trattinickia aspera	6	0	0	1	0	7
Trichilia cipo	4	0	2	1	0	7
Trichospermum mexicanum	0	3	0	0	0	3
Triplaris americana	0	0	1	2	1	4
Trophis racemosa	1	2	2	7	1	13
Unonopsis pittieri	0	1	0	0	0	1
Virola surinamensis	8	3	18	2	4	35
Virola sebifera	5	6	9	1	1	22
Vitex cooperi	0	0	1	0	0	1
Zanthoxylum	0	0	2	3	2	7
Zuelania guidonia	0	0	0	2	1	3
Unidentified	1	1	0	0	3	5
Total	173	172	175	168	168	856

one size of quadrat was greater than expected on the basis of the variation observed among the next smaller quadrats. Thus the variation among the sixteenth-hectares was used to test the variation among the quarter-hectares, and the variation among the quarter-hectares was used to test the variation among the hectares.

RESULTS

Tree abundance and tree sizes were analyzed first for nonrandomness, which might lead to clumping of species, as discussed in the introduction. The diversity data provide another measure of the differences among the hectares. Then we present our data on the dis-tribution of species among and within the hectares.

Tree Abundance

There were 856 trees of 60 cm girth or larger in the 5 ha. (Table 1). They were not randomly arranged among the hectares, quarter-hectares, or sixteenth-hectare quadrats. A chi-square analysis of the whole sample showed that the distribution among hectares was too even ($p < 0.01$), although their distribution among the 20 quarter-hectare and the 80 sixteenth-hectare quadrats did not depart from random. A separate analysis of each hectare showed that trees in hectare 4 were more clumped than expected among the quarter-hectare quadrats ($p < 0.01$), that trees

Table 2. Chi-square test of the random distribution of 856 trees

Hectare number	Sixteenth-hectare	Quarter-hectare
1	Too even ($p<0.01$)	—
2	—	—
3	Too clumped ($p<0.05$)	—
4	—	Too clumped ($p<0.01$)
5	—	—

Table 3. Nested analysis of variance in total number of trees (F values)

Hectare number	Quarter-hectare	Hectare
1	3.98	Not applicable
2	0.46	Not applicable
3	1.59	Not applicable
4	7.23*	Not applicable
5	0.63	Not applicable
All hectares	1.83	0.04*

* $p<0.01$ (two-tailed tests)

Table 4. Numbers of trees within each quarter-hectare, by size

Quarter hectares	Circumference of tree at breast height				
	0.6–0.89 m	0.9–1.19 m	1.2–1.79 m	1.8–2.39 m	2.4 + m
1A	21	8	7	4	1
1B	22	12	8	5	4
1C	21	6	2	5	4
1D	16	6	10	5	6
2A	23	4	12	4	2
2B	17	5	1	4	5
2C	25	7	1	0	6
2D	28	8	7	3	4
3A	18	8	10	5	5
3B	16	13	17	7	4
3C	20	5	10	4	1
3D	17	8	4	2	1
4A	12	12	4	1	4
4B	17	9	3	8	3
4C	20	5	5	1	3
4D	41	8	6	4	2
5A	19	7	13	5	1
5B	15	15	8	6	2
5C	9	12	10	2	3
5D	12	6	16	3	4

Quarter-hectares are labeled A = NW, B = NE, C = SW, D = SE.

were more evenly distributed than expected among the sixteenth-hectare quadrats of hectare 1 ($p < 0.01$), and that they were more clumped than expected among the sixteenth-hectare quadrats of hectare 3 ($p < 0.05$) (see Table 2).

A nested analysis of variance similarly indicated that there was less difference between the hectares than was expected on the basis of the differences between quarter hectares ($p < 0.01$). The differences in numbers of trees on different quarter-hectares were almost significant ($p \simeq 0.05$). Therefore this was examined for each hectare individually. The nested analysis of variance showed that there were significant differences between the quarter-hectares only in hectare 4 ($p < 0.01$) (Table 3).

Tree Sizes

A chi-square analysis showed that trees with circumference between 60 and 88 cm (Tables 4 and 5) were not randomly distributed among the five hectares ($p < 0.001$), nor among the sixteenth-hectare quadrats ($p < 0.01$). There were fewer small trees than ex-

pected in hectare 5, and small trees were unevenly distributed within hectare 4, both among the quarter-hectares ($p < 0.001$) and the sixteenth-hectares ($p < 0.01$).

Trees of larger size classes (0.9–1.2 m and greater than 1.8 m circumference) were randomly distributed among the 5 ha. Trees with circumferences 1.20–1.79 m were not randomly distributed ($p < 0.01$). There were more than expected in hectare 5 and fewer in hectare 4. The rank order was almost the opposite of the rank order for small trees.

Chi-square analyses suggested that within three hectares there were nonrandom distributions of larger trees ($p < 0.05$) among the quarter-hectare quadrats (Table 5). Nested analyses of variance were not significant in these cases, suggesting that the chi-square results were due to inhomogeneities among the sixteenth-hectare quadrats. This was examined for the four size classes of trees with circumferences greater than 90 cm, in each of the 5 ha. Only 1 of the 20 tests was significant ($p = 0.04$), and 2 others approached significance ($p \simeq 0.05$). These do serve to explain the chi-square analyses of the quarter-hectares, but they

Table 5. Randomness of distributions of trees of different sizes among quarter-hectares

Hectare number	All trees		Circumference of tree at breast height				
			0.6–0.89 m	0.9–1.19 m	1.2–1.79 m	1.8–2.39 m	2.4+ m
Test	χ^2	F	χ^2	χ^2	χ^2	χ^2	χ^2
1	2.14	3.98	1.10	3.00	5.15	0.16	3.40
2	2.19	0.46	2.78	1.67	9.00*	3.91	2.06
3	7.61	1.59	0.49	3.88	8.27*	2.89	4.64
4	12.14**	7.23**	12.73**	2.94	1.11	9.43*	0.67
5	1.48	0.63	3.98	5.40	3.13	2.50	2.00

* $p<0.05$
** $p<0.01$

Table 6. Species diversity in different plots

	Ha.1	Ha.2	Ha.3	Ha.4	Ha.5	All
Number of species	61	51	49	59	44	112
Number of trees	173	172	175	168	168	856
Brillouin's index (H)	3.15	3.07	3.13	3.21	2.91	3.81
H_{max}	3.61	3.48	3.46	3.57	3.38	4.47
$J = H/H_{max}$	0.87	0.88	0.90	0.90	0.86	0.85

do not demonstrate convincingly that there is clumping of larger trees among the sixteenth-hectare quadrats. Therefore we conclude that trees with circumferences greater than 90 cm are randomly distributed within hectares.

Diversity

The diversity of the 5 ha. was calculated and is presented in Table 6, based on our best estimates of the frequencies of occurrence of identified and unidentified trees. The first and fourth hectares have the largest number of species and the fifth has the fewest. Using Brillouin's diversity index, $H = (1/N) \log (N!/\Pi N_i!)$ for the reasons cited by Pielou (1976), we determined that the fifth hectare is least diverse, in keeping with the low number of species found therein, and that the fourth hectare is the most diverse. We also calculated the maximum diversity for the numbers of trees and species in each hectare and the evenness of apportionment of the individuals among the species ($J = H/H_{max}$). Hectares 3 and 4 have the highest evenness ratios. The diversity of all 5 ha. taken together is higher than that of any individual hectare, as expected, but the evenness ratio is lower.

Table 7. Trees with nonrandom distributions among hectares and among quarter-hectares

N	Species	Test of random distribution among hectares	Clumped in ha. number	Test of random distribution among quarter-hectares	Within hectare number
3	*Astrocaryum standleyanum*[1]	*	3	—	—
3	*Casearia sylvestris*	*	5	—	—
3	*Prioria copaifera*	*	5	—	—
3	*Terminalia chiriquensis*	*	2	—	—
3	*Tetragastris panamensis*	*	1	—	—
3	*Trichospermum mexicanum*	*	2	—	—
4	*Brosimum alicastrum*	**	1	—	—
4	*Guarea glabra*	**	1	—	—
6	*Pseudobombax septenatum*	**	2	—	—
7	*Trattinickia aspera*	**	1	—	—
8	*Nectandra latifolia*	***	1	**	1
9	*Heisteria concinna*	*	1	—	—
14	*Terminalia amazonica*	—	—	*	5
18	*Swartzia simplex*	*	3,4,5	—	—
19	*Pterocarpus rohrii*	**	2,4	*	2
21	*Spondias mombin*	***	5	—	—
22	*Virola sebifera*	*	1,2,3	—	—
24	*Anacardium excelsum*	***	2,3	**	2
28	*Hyeronima laxifolia*	***	2	—	—
29	*Scheelia zonensis*	***	5	—	—
31	*Tabebuia* spp.[2]	**	3,5	—	—
35	*Virola surinamensis*	**	3	***	3
42	*Poulsenia armata*	***	1	—	—
42	*Spondias radlkoferi*	**	5	—	—
55	*Alseis blackiana*	***	4	*	2,4
55	*Macrocnemum glabrescens*	***	2,5	*	2
60	*Astrocaryum standleyanum*[3]	***	3	—	—

* $p < 0.05$,   ** $p < 0.01$,   *** $p < 0.001$

[1] *Astrocaryum* with circumference $\geq$ 60 cm.

[2] *Tabebuia rosea* and *T. guayacan*.

[3] All mature *Astrocaryum*.

Clumping of Species among Hectares

The sample included 856 trees of 112 species, so the average number of trees per species was 7.64. For this discussion, we defined rare species as those occurring 4 or fewer times, average species as those occurring 5–15 times, and common species as those occurring more than 16 times (more than twice the average) in our sample.

For the 27 species that occurred only once in the total sample, there is obviously no way to determine whether or not each species is randomly distributed. Among the 18 species that occurred twice, 6 species occurred in the same hectare. This fits the hypothesis that they were randomly distributed ($p > 0.1$). Among the 14 species that occurred thrice, 6 had all three specimens in 1 ha. These species were not randomly distributed ($p = 0.04$), nor is it likely that 6 of 14 randomly distributed species would exhibit this pattern ($p < 0.001$). Seven species were represented in our sample by four specimens. Two of these were not randomly distributed ($p < 0.01$), each being found in only one of the hectares. It is unlikely that two of seven randomly distributed species would be so clumped ($p < 0.01$). Therefore we conclude that there was clumping of rare species in our sample. Nonrandom

Table 8. Nonrandom distributions in sixteenth-hectare circles

Species	Ha. 1		Ha. 2		Ha. 3		Ha. 4		Ha. 5	
	N	Clumping	N	Clumping	N	Clumping	N	Clumping	N	Clumping
Alseis blackiana	12	**(1)	14	*(3)**(2)	5	—	22	*(5)**(1)	2	—
Anacardium excelsum	1	—	11	**(3)	12	*(8)	0	—	0	—
Gustavia superba	5	—	5	—	6	*(2)	6	—	9	—
Hyeronima laxiflora	1	—	16	*(1)	5	—	5	—	1	—
Luehea seemanni	1	—	10	*(2)	10	—	7	—	5	—
Macrocnemum glabrescens	3	—	18	*(4)**(4)***(2)	12	*(1)	6	—	16	—
Nectandra latifolia	7	*(3)	0	—	0	—	1	—	0	—
Platymiscium pennatum	1	—	0	—	4	—	3	—	5	*(1)
Platypodium elegans	1	—	1	—	3	—	3	—	5	*(2)
Poulsenia armata	31	*(4)**(1)	7	—	2	—	2	—	0	—
Protium tenuifolium	5	*(1)	3	—	1	—	1	—	0	—
Sapium caudatum	1	—	1	—	4	—	2	*(2)	0	—
Swartzia simplex	0	—	1	—	6	*(3)	6	—	5	—
Terminalia amazonia	2	—	2	—	1	—	3	—	6	*(3)
Trattinickia aspera	6	*(3)	0	—	0	—	1	—	0	—
Virola surinamensis	8	—	3	—	18	**(4)***(2)	2	—	1	—
Virola sebifera	5	*(1)	6	—	9	—	1	—	1	—
Testable species	20		20		20		24		19	
Clumped species	30%		25%		25%		8%		16%	

N = number of trees in hectare.

* .01<*p*<.05   ** .001<*p*<.01   *** *p*<.001

A number in parentheses is the number of specimens which had an improbably large number of conspecifics in the surrounding sixteenth-hectare.

distributions (i.e., $p < 0.05$) are demonstrable for 8 of the 21 rare species that can be adequately tested.

There were 26 species of average abundance in our sample. Four of these were not randomly distributed. They occurred too frequently in one of the hectares. All the others had distributions among the hectares that appear to be random. No species was too evenly distributed among the hectares.

There were 16 common species. Fourteen of these were distributed nonrandomly among the 5 ha., being too common in one or two of the hectares or too rare in one of the hectares. No species was too evenly distributed among the hectares.

In total, 63 species could be tested individually for nonrandom distributions. Twenty-six (41%) of these were too clumped among the hectares to fit a random

distribution. No species was found to be overdispersed (Table 7).

Clumping of Species within Hectares

We examined the distribution of species within hectares at the level of the quarter-, sixteenth-, and sixty-fourth-hectare.

Among the 5 ha. there were 45 cases in which a species occurred twice in a hectare. In 17 cases they occurred within the same quarter-hectare, which is more frequently than expected ($p < 0.05$) for randomly distributed trees. There were 33 cases in which a species occurred thrice in a hectare, and in 5 of those cases all three occurred in the same quarter-

Table 9. Nonrandom distributions in sixty-fourth-hectare circles

Species	Ha. 1 N	Ha. 1 Clumping	Ha. 2 N	Ha. 2 Clumping	Ha. 3 N	Ha. 3 Clumping	Ha. 4 N	Ha. 4 Clumping	Ha. 5 N	Ha. 5 Clumping
Alseis blackiana	12	—	14	*(3)	5	—	22	*(1)**(2)	2	—
Anacardium excelsum	1	—	11	*(3)	12	*(3)***(1)	0	—	0	—
Cupania papillosa	1	—	2	*(2)	1	—	3	—	1	—
Hyeronima laxiflora	1	—	16	*(1)	5	—	5	—	1	—
Macrocnemum glabrescens	3	—	18	*(1)**(2)***(3)	12	*(1)	6	—	16	—
Nectandra latifolia	7	**(2)	0	—	0	—	1	—	0	—
Protium panamense	4	—	1	—	2	—	3	*(2)	1	—
Spondias mombin	0	—	1	—	5	—	3	—	12	*(1)
Spondias radlkoferi	3	*(2)	4	—	8	—	10	—	17	—
Terminalia amazonia	2	—	2	*(2)	1	—	3	—	6	**(3)
Trichospermum mexicanum	0	—	3	*(2)	0	—	0	—	0	—
Testable species	30		29		33		31		25	
Clumped species	6%		25%		6%		6%		8%	

N = number of trees in hectare.

* $.01 < p < .05$ ** $.001 < p < .01$ *** $p < .001$

A number in parentheses is the number of specimens which had an improbably large number of conspecifics in the surrounding sixty-fourth-hectare.

hectare. This barely fits the hypothesis that they were randomly distributed ($p = 0.052$). There were 45 cases in which a tree occurred 4 to 8 times in a hectare, and in only 3 of these was the distribution nonrandom among the quarter-hectares. Among the 25 cases in which a species was very common in a hectare, occurring from 9 to 31 times, there were 5 nonrandom distributions among the quarter-hectares. Therefore, among 60 cases in which nonrandom distribution might be detected, we found 8 cases (13%) of clumping among the quarter-hectares (Table 7).

The tests of clumping within sixteenth- and sixty-fourth-hectares were different from those conducted within hectares or quarter-hectares as described in the Methods section. It was possible to detect clumping within sixteenth-hectares only for species that occurred three or more times in a hectare, and within sixty-fourth-hectares for species that occurred twice or more. Since the same tree could be included in one or more "clumps," the degree of clumping was determined by species.

Among the sixteenth-hectares, we detected clumped distributions in 8% to 30% of the testable species of each hectare (Table 8). The weighted average in the 5 ha. was 20.4%. The distribution was decidedly nonrandom ($p < 0.01$) in 5.8% of the species. In the other 14.6%, clumping was not as dramatic ($0.05 > p > 0.01$), although it might be pervasive. For example, in hectare 3, 8 of 12 *Anacardium* were weakly clumped (i.e., $0.01 < p < 0.05$ of a random distribution).

Among the sixty-fourth-hectares, 6% to 25% of the testable trees in a hectare were clumped (Table 9). The weighted averages suggest that 10% ($p < 0.05$) or 3.3% ($p < 0.01$) of the species were not randomly distributed.

DISCUSSION

From the times of Wallace (1878) until recently (Janzen, 1970), it has been assumed and reported that species of trees are overdispersed in rain forests. Hubbell (1979) demonstrated that this is not so in a tropical deciduous (dry) forest in Costa Rica. Our study corroborates Hubbell's findings and demonstrates that species are clumped or randomly dispersed in the monsoon forest of Barro Colorado Island. We found that the highest percentage of species (41%) showed clumped distributions among the hectare plots and the lowest percentage (10%) at the smallest plot size (sixty-fourth-hectares). Thus the frequency of clumping appears to be directly proportional to scale. Also, for most species the significance level of the clumping is greater the larger the area examined in our study area. This seems to differ from the situation in the Costa Rican study, for Hubbell shows five graphs of Morisita's index of dispersion in which dispersion departs more and more from random at smaller quadrat sizes. The difference may reflect a greater large-scale heterogeneity in our study area than in Hubbell's since our quadrats were dispersed within two ravines and on their ridges.

The degree and scale of clumping of species may affect the structure of the forest. For example, the large number of small trees in hectare 2 reflects the concentration of *Macrocnemum* therein. Also, the greater than expected density of trees in one quarter of hectare 4 results from the unexpectedly large number of small trees in this quadrat, which in turn reflects the clumping of *Alseis* in this area. There are few large *Alseis* in the study plot. Similarly, the nonrandom distribution of trees in hectare 3 reflects a tight clumping of *Virola surinamensis* in one area, which contrasts with the low density of trees in a "blowdown area" elsewhere in the hectare. The too-even distribution of tree numbers among the sixteenth-hectares of hectare 1 was surprising to us in view of the heterogeneity of the area, which has Allee Creek running through it. However, we expected the distribution of trees to tend toward evenness because we suspect that trees grow better in a tropical forest the less they are shaded by their neighbors. This does not explain the unexpectedly similar number of trees in each of the hectares, however. We think this reflects the scale of topographic heterogeneity of the study area. It is as if each hectare contains approximately the same degree of heterogeneity, leading to an averaging effect, with respect to tree numbers.

There is a possible relationship between forest structure and diversity, because obviously there are more species of small forest trees than there are of large trees. In our study, the lowest diversity occurs in hectare 5, which has the fewest small trees, whereas the highest diversity is found in hectare 4, which has a large number of small trees. Unfortunately, our 5-ha. sample is not sufficient for testing whether this association is real or imagined.

These interrelated factors of dispersion of species, forest structure, and diversity of the forest affect the animals that live within it. For each species, the forest must appear to have a kaleidoscopically changing distribution of resources. As different trees flower, fruit, or put out new leaves, the pattern of resource distribution changes, and the animals change their use of the forest. These changes are accentuated by the clumped distributions of trees within the forest. These facts have been known to hunters and naturalists for millennia, if not longer, but their applicability to diverse tropical forests has not been widely appreciated. As in the temperate zones, the best way to locate animals in the tropics is to know what they are eating at any given season and to know the distribution of those foods in the forest. The phenomenal success of Handley and his colleagues at capturing bats on Barro Colorado is due to their locating appropriately fruiting trees during the day and then setting their nets there at night. In January, the best way to locate squirrels and agoutis on the island is to visit the fruiting *Dipteryx* trees. In April, one should visit the *Astrocaryum* trees, and in late June and early July, the fruiting *Scheelea* (see Glanz et al., this volume). Our data show how clumped are the distributions of these last two species and hence how locally concentrated are these major food sources at these times of year. A number of the species that are clumped are significant seasonal sources of food for howler monkeys, e.g., *Brosimum*, *Pseudobombax*, *Pterocarpus*, *Spondias*, *Anacardium*, and *Hyeronima*. We have observed troops of howlers to feed in these clumps of trees in our study area when they were producing appropriate food. Chivers (1969) documented major changes in foci of activity for howlers in the Lutz catchment. We suggest these are seasonal changes which correlate with the changing distribution of appropriate food trees. Since the different trees fruit or flush new leaves in fairly regular sequence through the year, and since the trees are long-lived and immobile, there should be a regular, seasonally changing, geographic pattern of resources for the animals. We noted such a pattern when we compared maps of the movements of howler monkeys in the Lutz ravine during 1972, 1973, and 1974 with one another and with the map prepared by Altmann (1955) based on his studies 20 years before. The animals visited the same trees (mostly figs) and in the same order, 20 years apart. We suspect that such conservatism on the part of the monkeys is dictated by the geographical and seasonal distribution of their resources.

The clumping of tree species not only affects the seasonal use of the forest by animals but it also determines the suitability of parts of the forest for survival and reproduction. For mammals the size of squirrels, which have home ranges on the order of 1 to 2 ha., or smaller animals with smaller home ranges, the observed scale of clumping means that adjoining areas may have very different resources. One home range may be quite inferior to another in terms of resources it provides. The red-tailed squirrel serves as an example of a species that faces this sort of environmental heterogeneity (Heaney and Thorington, 1978; Glanz et al., this volume). Females have exclusive home ranges and do not travel as widely as do the males, which have overlapping home ranges. Many males will forage in the same fruiting tree, having moved a considerable distance from the center of their ranges. This is one way of coping with the nonrandom distribution of food trees such as *Dipteryx*, *Scheelea*, and *Astrocaryum*. The females do not seem to travel so freely to resources at a distance from their dens. Accordingly, they are found primarily in areas that provide suitable resources within approximately 1 ha. There are areas, such as the second hectare of this study, where there are usually no resident female squirrels, although the adjoining hectare to the west may include parts of the ranges of several.

The situation is more complicated than suggested merely by the clumping of tree species. For frugivores, it is the clumping of the female trees of dioecious species which is important (e.g., *Spondias*). For herbivores, it is the distribution of trees with edible leaves. As shown by Glander (1978, in press), howler monkeys are not only selective of the species on which they feed but also of the individual trees. Some trees are highly palatable and others of the same species are not. The differences are correlated with the occurrence of specific plant secondary compounds in the leaves.

Therefore we must think of a home range being suitable for an animal only if it contains clumps of suitable species of plants comprising suitable individuals of these species. Diversity is important because at every time of year some food plant within the home range must be producing appropriate food. Thus it is not surprising that Froehlich and Thorington (this volume) found significant correlations between body weights of adult howler monkeys and a measure of floral diversity within their home range. The availability of food plants throughout the year in a part of the forest is probably correlated not only with an animal's weight but also with its ability to reproduce there and to raise its young. This should result in a net emigration from more suitable to less suitable home ranges and should affect the direction of gene flow within the mammalian population. In fact, Froehlich and Thorington (this volume) report such a situation for howler monkeys toward the periphery of Barro Colorado Island. We are therefore led to hypothesize that the heterogeneity of the forest affects not only the seasonally changing usage of it by animals but also indirectly affects the genetic structure of the animal populations that live there.

ACKNOWLEDGMENTS

This study was supported by the Smithsonian Institution's Environmental Sciences Program. We are grateful to the many botanists who helped us with identifications, especially to Robin Foster.

LITERATURE CITED

Altmann, S. A.
1959. Field observations on a howling monkey society. *Journal of Mammalogy*, 40:317–330.

Chivers, D. J.
1969. On the daily behavior and spacing of howling monkey groups. *Folia primatologica*, 10:48–102.

Croat, T. B.
1978. *Flora of Barro Colorado Island*. Stanford, Calif.: Stanford University Press. 943 pp.

Froehlich, J. W., and R. W. Thorington, Jr.
1982. The genetic structure and socioecology of howler monkeys *(Alouatta palliata)* on Barro Colorado Island. Pages 291–305 in *The Ecology of a Tropical Forest*, edited by Egbert G. Leigh, Jr., et al. Washington, D.C.: Smithsonian Institution Press.

Glander, K. E.
1978. Howling monkey feeding behavior and plant secondary compounds: A study of strategies. Pages 561–573 in *The Ecology of Arboreal Folivores*, edited by G. G. Montgomery. Washington, D.C.: Smithsonian Institution Press.
In press. Feeding patterns in mantled howler monkeys. In *Foraging Behavior*, edited by A. Kamil. New York: Garland Press.

Glanz, W. E., R. W. Thorington, Jr., J. Giacalone-Madden, and L. R. Heaney
1982. Seasonal food use and demographic trends in *Sciurus granatensis*. Pages 239–252 in *The Ecology of a Tropical Forest*, edited by Egbert G. Leigh, Jr., et al. Washington, D.C.: Smithsonian Institution Press.

Heaney, L. R., and R. W. Thorington, Jr.
1978. Ecology of Neotropical red-tailed squirrels, *Sciurus granatensis*, in the Panama Canal Zone. *Journal of Mammalogy*, 59:846–851.

Hubbell, S. P.
1979. Tree dispersion, abundance, and diversity in a tropical dry forest. *Science*, 203:1299–1309.

Janzen, D. H.
1970. Herbivores and the number of tree species in tropical forests. *American Naturalist*, 104:501–528.

Knight, D. H.
1970. *A Field Guide to the Trees of Barro Colorado Island, Panama Canal Zone*. Laramie, Wyo.: Department of Botany, University of Wyoming. 94 pp.

Milton, K.
1977. The foraging strategy of the howler monkey in the tropical forest of Barro Colorado Island, Panama. Ph.D. thesis, New York University. 257 pp.
1978. Behavioral adaptations to leaf-eating by the mantled

howler monkey (*Alouatta palliata*). Pages 535–549 in *The Ecology of Arboreal Folivores,* edited by G. G. Montgomery. Washington, D.C.: Smithsonian Institution Press.

Pielou, E. C.
1976.   *Mathematical Ecology.* New York: Wiley & Sons, Inc. 385 pp.

Putz, F. E., and K. Milton
1982.   Tree Mortality Rates on Barro Colorado Island. Pages 95–100 in *The Ecology of a Tropical Forest,* edited by Egbert G. Leigh, Jr., et al. Washington, D.C.: Smithsonian Institution Press.

Wallace, A. R.
1978.   *Tropical Nature and Other Essays.* London: Macmillan, p. 65, quoted by Hubbell (1979).

Windsor, D. M. (editor)
1975.   1974 Environmental Monitoring and Baseline Data. Tropical Studies. Unpublished report. Washington, D.C.: Smithsonian Institution. 409 pp.

Tree Mortality Rates on Barro Colorado Island

FRANCIS E. PUTZ   Department of Ecology and Systematics, Cornell University, Ithaca, New York 14850

KATHARINE MILTON   Department of Anthropology, University of California, Berkeley, California 94720

ABSTRACT

In two 1-ha. plots in old forest on Barro Colorado Island, 17 of 328 trees more than 60 cm in circumference at breast height died during a 5-year period, suggesting an expectancy of further life of 96.5 years. In five 1-ha. plots in young forest, 78 of 883 trees died during the same time period, suggesting an average expectancy of further life of 56.6 years. Of the tree deaths, 52% were due to snapped trunks, 17% were uprooted, 14% died standing, 8% snapped at ground level, and the mode of death could not be determined for 9%. Judging from measures of density, wood of young forest trees was weaker than wood of mature forest trees. Tree mortality rates were not closely related to the rate of formation or total area of treefall gaps in old and second-growth forest. Tree mortality rates on Barro Colorado Island were similar to those in mature forest on Bukit Lagong in Malaysia.

INTRODUCTION

What is the mortality rate of trees on Barro Colorado? How do these trees die? Do they die singly or in groups? Is the mortality rate the same in old second growth as in mature forest? Can mortality rates be estimated accurately from the rates at which gaps open in the canopy? How do mortality rates on Barro Colorado Island compare with those in Malaysian dipterocarp forest?

Our answers will be based largely on the mortality observed among marked trees in eight 1-ha. plots over a 5-year period.

METHODS

Study Sites

In February and March, 1975, Thorington et al. (this volume) mapped all trees more than 60 cm girth (cir-cumference at 1.5 m or above buttresses) on five per-manent 1-ha. plots in Lutz and Allee catchments and Milton and Tarak similarly mapped three 1-ha. plots on the central plateau (Figure 1).

The soil of all these plots is classified as Frijoles clay (Bennett, 1929; Knight, 1975). The plateau plots are on basalt, while the plots in Lutz and Allee catchments are on sedimentary rocks. Judging from the lists of indicator species proposed by Foster and Brokaw (this volume), plots K–2 and K–3 on the central plateau are in mature forest, undisturbed by human activity for over 200 years. Plot K–1 on the central plateau and the plots in Lutz catchment are in second-growth forest perhaps a hundred years old. Plot N0–W1 (plot 2 of Thorington et al., this volume) in Lutz catchment, just above the weir, is in a moderately steep area with thin soils, and is unusual in that part of the large landslide that occurred in 1959 (Dietrich et al., this volume) lies within its boundaries. Plot N1–W3 (plot 1 of Thorington et al., this volume) in Allee catchment

Table 1. Size class frequency of live (1975) and dead (1975–1980) trees in 1-ha. sample plots

	Young forest					
	S2–W2	N0–W1	S3–E0	S1–E1	K–1	Total
Girth (cm)						
60–90	90 (8)	94 (8)	56 (6)	71 (6)	94(10)	405(38)
90–120	34 (6)	24 (2)	40 (4)	35 (2)	35 (2)	168(16)
120–150	13 (1)	16 (1)	25 (0)	23 (2)	22 (4)	99 (8)
150–180	5 (2)	11 (1)	22 (4)	19 (1)	13 (0)	70 (8)
180–210	5 (0)	6 (0)	10 (3)	11 (0)	7 (1)	39 (4)
210–240	9 (0)	5 (0)	6 (0)	6 (0)	9 (1)	35 (1)
240–270	2 (0)	3 (0)	3 (0)	4 (0)	4 (1)	16 (1)
270–300	1 (0)	3 (0)	2 (0)	2 (0)	7 (0)	15 (0)
>300	9 (2)	11 (0)	5 (0)	5 (0)	6 (0)	36 (2)
Total deaths	19	12	17	11	19	78
Number of deaths per ha. per yr.	3.8	2.4	3.4	2.2	3.8	—
Total stems	168	173	169	176	197	883
Percent of deaths per yr.	2.3	1.4	2.0	1.3	1.9	1.7
Average life	44.2	72.1	49.7	80.0	51.8	56.6
Slope						
<15°	78	46	73	75	91	—
15–30°	20	45	23	25	9	—
30–45°	2	9	4	0	0	—

Slope figures represent the percentage of the area in 15 degree slope classes. The number of trees in each girth class is followed by the number of deaths in parentheses.

has a species composition intermediate between those of second-growth and mature forest; the terrain is very steep and the forest is shorter than most mature forest.

Techniques

In February 1980 these eight plots were resurveyed, recording which of the trees had died and describing the mode of death as opportunity allowed. Crude topographic maps were drawn for each plot, using a hand-held inclinometer: we report slopes in terms of the proportions of each plot in 15° classes.

RESULTS

Of the 1383 trees in our eight plots, 115 died in the 5 years intervening between the initial mapping and our survey, suggesting an expectation of further life (the inverse of the average proportion of trees dying

Steep terrain	Old forest		
N1–W3	K–2	K–3	Total
80 (8)	64 (2)	57 (3)	121 (5)
31 (2)	24 (3)	39 (2)	63 (5)
18 (6)	20 (2)	16 (1)	36 (3)
9 (0)	16 (2)	12 (1)	28 (3)
13 (1)	7 (0)	4 (0)	11 (0)
6 (2)	8 (1)	9 (0)	17 (1)
4 (0)	7 (0)	5 (0)	12 (0)
5 (0)	0 (0)	9 (0)	9 (0)
6 (1)	11 (0)	20 (0)	31 (0)
20	10	7	17
4.0	2.0	1.4	—
172	157	171	328
2.3	1.3	0.8	1.0
43.0	78.5	122.1	96.5
67	100	92	—
10	—	8	—
23	—	—	—

per year) of 60.1 years for trees over 60 cm girth. Life expectancies calculated for trees in the individual hectares range from 43 to 122 years (Table 1). The low expectancy of further life (43 years) observed in plot N1–W3 can be accounted for, at least in part, by the steepness of the terrain; 4 of the 20 trees that died appeared to have slid down the steep slides of the ravine, roots and all. The expectancy of further life in plot N0–W1 is 72 years, which seems high for second growth. Judging by the predominance of small trees in the southwestern part of the plot and the overall predominance of trees only 60–90 cm in girth, some of the area seems to be still recovering from the 1959 landslide. In plot S2–W2, expectancy of further life was low (44 years). This plot lies in the upper (southern) part of Lutz catchment on level ground and gentle slopes. Four of the 19 trees that died were involved in a small blowdown, 600 sq. m in area, in the southwest part of the plot. The resulting gap seems to be spreading; trees on its margins seem to be dying faster than their more protected neighbors.

Of the 115 trees dying in our eight plots, only 14 seem to have been involved in multiple treefalls. Fifty-two percent of these 115 trees died because their trunks snapped; 17% of them were uprooted; 14% died standing, 8% snapped off at ground level; the cause of death of the remaining 9% is unknown.

The average expectancy of further life was 56.6 years for trees in the five second-growth plots and 96.5 years for trees in the two mature plots ($\chi^2 = 4.41$, 1 d.f., $p < 0.05$). Judging from wood-density data in FAO (1971), trees listed by Foster and Brokaw (this volume) as characteristic of mature forest have denser wood [dry weight (g)/green volume (cu. cm); mean = 0.56, $N = 21$] than trees of second growth (mean = 0.40, $N = 10$). This difference is significant ($t = 2.36$, $p < 0.05$). Since wood strength is closely correlated with wood density (Forest Products Laboratory, 1974) mature forest trees may live longer because their wood is more durable.

These mortality rates do not appear to be closely correlated with the rates at which gaps open in the forest canopy. We find that in old and new forest, respectively, 1.7 and 3.1 trees over 60 cm girth die per hectare per year. Brokaw (this volume) finds that one gap over 20 sq. m in area opens in the forest canopy per hectare per year in both old and new forest. The average area of these gaps is 63 sq. m in the young forest and 88 sq. m in the old forest, and the average time between gaps is 159 years and 114 years. In contrast, the average mortality rates for trees more than 60 cm girth is 57 years in the young forest and 96 years in the old forest. The discrepancies between the rate of canopy gap formation and tree mortality rates are due, at least in part, to multiple treefalls and tree deaths not resulting in gaps. Although physiognomic similarities in lowland tropical forests the world around are often stressed (e.g., Leigh, 1975), one wonders whether differences in soils, topography, regime of disturbance, and/or species composition lead to differences in internal dynamics. Clearly larger sample sizes than ours are desirable to detect fine distinctions between mortality rates. Our data, however, permit comparison of mortality rates on Barro Colorado with those in three Malaysian forests (Table 2).

The expectancy of further life of trees on Barro Colorado over 60 cm in girth is much the same as for comparable trees of primary dipterocarp forests in Bukit Lagong and Sepilok Forest Reserves and longer than for trees in Sungei Menyala Forest Reserve. Low mortality on Bukit Lagong and high mortality in Sungei Menyala Forest Reserve continued through 1976 when the plots were last visited. It is hardly surprising that the big trees are rapidly dying off in Sungei Menyala Plots 103 and 105 since these plots "were laid down in small patches of high forest" (Wyatt-Smith, 1966) not far from what is now an oil palm plantation.

Lack of buffering doubtless jeopardized trees in these isolated stands. Sample Plot 102, also in Sungei Menyala Forest Reserve, likewise suffered a high mortality rate, but this is not a particularly isolated patch of high forest. This plot was established in 1947 in what was then described as mature to "overmature" forest. Much of the mortality observed can be attributed to the "windfall of single moribund giants" (Whitmore, 1975), i.e., the "overmature" trees. Whitmore (ibid.) also observed multiple treefalls on the periphery of existing canopy openings. The last five years have witnessed the same series of events in Plot S2–W2 on Barro Colorado Island, but while all this death and destruction were occurring in the plots, adjacent areas remained unscathed, evidence for a large stochastic component in forest dynamics.

Trees in the old forest plots on Barro Colorado Island and in Bukit Lagong and Sepilok Forest Reserves may have escaped damage simply because of the vicissitudes of treefall dynamics. At least for Bukit Lagong, however, this does not appear to be the case. Treefalls are relatively rare on Bukit Lagong, not only within the plot but also in the forest as a whole. Many

Table 2. Tree mortality from Malaysia and Barro Colorado Island

Site (Authority)	Average lifetime (years)	No. of trees	No. of deaths	Area (ha.)	Observation period (years)
Barro Colorado Island (this study)					
Old forest	96	328	17	2.0	5
Young forest	57	883	78	5.0	5
Bukit Lagong, Malaysia* (Wyatt–Smith, 1966)					
Primary forest	82	449	55	1.6	10
Disturbed site	79	95	12	0.4	10
Sungei Menyala, Malaysia* (Wyatt–Smith, 1966)					
SP 102					
Primary forest	58	334	69	1.6	12
Disturbed site	41	107	31	0.4	12
SP 103					
Primary forest	32	45	14	0.2	10
SP 105					
Primary forest	53	40	6	0.2	8
Sepilok, Sabah, Malaysia* (Nicholson, 1965)	101	505	30	1.8	6

* 61 cm girth is lower size limit for trees studied.

PUTZ AND MILTON

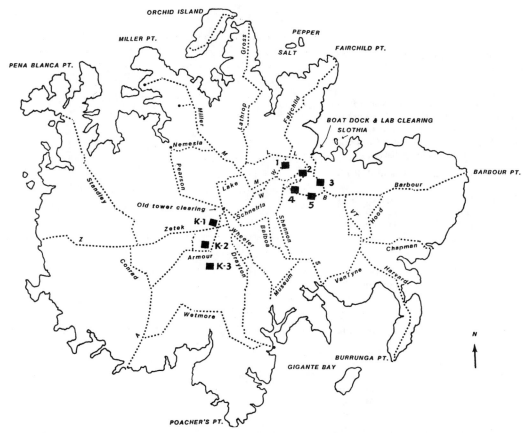

Figure 1. Location of permanent study plots. Plot one is N1-W3; Plot 2 is N0-W1; Plot 3 is S1-E1; Plot 4 is S2-W2; and Plot 5 is S3-E0.

people who have worked in both Malaysian diptero-carp and New World tropical forests are struck by the abundance of fallen trees and canopy openings in the latter. This may, however, reflect the much greater age of trees in the Malaysian forests. As we have seen, the mature forest trees on Barro Colorado apparently live longer than those of second growth. The same seems to be true in Malaysia (Table 2).

Death in the forest often comes in localized pulses. Trees in some parts of the forest seem more vulner-able to damage and death because of factors such as steep slopes and thin soils, but the condition of the stand and its species composition seem to play a role as well. It does not appear that entire forests develop and degenerate in concert, but in areas of one or a few hectares, brief epochs of high mortality seem to be followed by long, relatively quiescent, periods of recovery.

ACKNOWLEDGMENTS
We are grateful to Peter L. Marks and Gerald E. Lang for suggestions on the manuscript, and we thank the Smithsonian Tropical Research Institute for its fel-lowships.

LITERATURE CITED

Bennett, H. H.
1929.   Soil Reconnaissance of the Panama Canal Zone and Contiguous Territory. U.S. Department of Agricul-ture Technical Bulletin 94:1–46.

Brokaw, N. V.
1982.   Treefalls. Pages 101–108 in The Ecology of a Tropical Forest, edited by Egbert G. Leigh, Jr., et al. Washing-ton, D.C.: Smithsonian Institution Press.

Dietrich, W., D. Windsor, and T. Dunne
1982.   Geology, Climate, and Hydrology of Barro Colorado Island. Pages 21–46 in The Ecology of a Tropical Forest, edited by Egbert G. Leigh, Jr., et al. Washington, D.C.: Smithsonian Institution Press.

FAO
1971.   Inventariacion y demostraciones forestales, Panama. Propiedades y usos de ciento trece especies madera-bles de Panama. FC:SF/PAN 6, Informe tecnico 3.

Foster, R. B., and N. V. Brokaw
1982.   Structure and History of the Vegetation of Barro Col-orado Island. Pages 67–81 in The Ecology of a Tropical Forest, edited by Egbert G. Leigh, Jr., et al. Washing-ton, D.C.: Smithsonian Institution Press.

Knight, D. H.
1975.   A Phytosociological Analysis of Species-rich Tropical Forest on Barro Colorado Island, Panama. Ecological Monographs 45:259–284.

Leigh, E. G., Jr.
1975.   Structure and Climate in Tropical Rain Forest. *Annual Review of Ecology and Systematics,* 6:67–86.

Nicholson, D. I.
1965.   A Study of Virgin Forest near Sandakan, North Borneo. Pages 67–87 in *Symposium on Ecological Research in Humid Tropics Vegetation,* sponsored by the Government of Sarawak and the UNESCO Science Cooperation Office for Southeast Asia, Kuching, Sarawak.

Thorington, R. W. Jr., B. Tannenbaum, A. Tarak, and R. Rudran
1982.   Distribution of Trees on Barro Colorado Island. Pages 83–94 in *The Ecology of a Tropical Forest,* edited by Egbert G. Leigh, Jr., et al. Washington, D.C.: Smithsonian Institution Press.

U.S. Forest Products Laboratory
1974.   *Wood Handbook: Wood as an Engineering Material.* U.S. Department of Agriculture Agriculture Handbook 72, revised.

Whitmore, T. C.
1975.   *Tropical Rain Forests of the Far East.* Oxford: Clarendon Press.

Wyatt-Smith, J.
1966.   *Ecological Studies on Malayan Forest. I. Composition of and Dynamic Studies in Lowland Evergreen Rain Forest in Two 5-acre Plots in Bukit Lagong and Sungei Menyala Forest Reserve, 1947–59.* Research Pamphlet No. 52. Kepong, Malaya: Forest Research Institute, Forest Department.

Treefalls: Frequency, Timing, and Consequences

NICHOLAS V. L. BROKAW   Department of Biology, University of Chicago, Chicago, Illinois 60637

ABSTRACT

Three years of records indicate that on Barro Colorado Island trees fall most frequently during the middle of the wet season. This seasonal rhythm in treefalls may influence the timing of dispersal and/or germination of some tree species requiring a light gap for establishment. On the 28-ha. census plot, turnover rate (mean time between successive formation of gap area in any one spot in the forest) was 114 years for the old forest (300–400 years old) and 159 years for the young forest (about 100 years old) on Barro Colorado Island during the 3 years of the study. The data suggest that the number of gaps over 150 sq. m in area created by treefalls increases as the forest matures structurally. This trend has important consequences for the species composition of the forest, because, on Barro Colorado Island, pioneer trees are most successful in colonizing gaps over 150 sq. m in area. Hence, pioneer saplings are more common in the old than in the young forest, and it appears that suitable gaps are created often enough (roughly one per hectare every 5.3 years) in the old forest to support a high proportion of pioneers among Barro Colorado Island trees.

INTRODUCTION

Lowland tropical forest has been described as a mosaic of patches of different sizes and ages of regrowth originating as gaps created by falling trees (Richards, 1952; Baur, 1968; Whitmore, 1975; Oldeman, 1978). In these forests many canopy tree species depend, at one or all stages in their life histories, on growth in a gap to reach maturity (Richards, 1952; Baur, 1968; Whitmore, 1975; Hartshorn, 1978). For example, on Barro Colorado Island, Panama, the seeds of some tree species can germinate in the understory of closed forest, but their seedlings must subsequently be in a gap to ensure establishment (Garwood, 1979). Pioneers are trees whose saplings are found only in gaps. Their seedlings emerge in gaps of all sizes (Brokaw, 1980); however, their ensuing growth and survival on Barro Colorado Island is generally confined to gaps over 150 sq. m in area (Figure 1), most likely because of greater availability of light and/or reduced root competition in larger openings (Longman and Jenik, 1974; Whitmore, 1975; Hartshorn, 1978; Lee, 1978). The restriction of pioneer trees to large gaps has been noted in many tropical forests (Kramer, 1933; Richards, 1952; Schulz, 1960; Baur, 1968; Whitmore, 1975; Hartshorn, 1978; Acevedo and Marquis, 1979; Denslow, 1980). Another group of tree species can survive as suppressed saplings in closed forest until a gap (not necessarily large) forms above them, when growth apparently accelerates (Brown and Mathews, 1914; Richards, 1952; Jones, 1956; Whitmore, 1975).

Thus requirements for canopy opening vary among tropical forest tree species, and different degrees of canopy opening may lead to different species compositions at particular sites (Baur, 1968; Webb et al., 1972; Whitmore, 1974). Identifying patterns of dis-turbance in a community should help in understanding community composition as well as the distribution, abundance, and life history traits of component species (Levin and Paine, 1974; Pickett and Thompson, 1978; Paine, 1979). I undertook this study to answer the following questions: (1) Is there a seasonal pattern to treefall gap creation which might influence the timing of dispersal and/or germination of trees requiring a gap for initial establishment? (2) Are gaps over 150 sq. m in area created often enough on Barro Colorado Island to maintain a large proportion of pioneers in the forest? (3) Does the frequency of creation of gaps over 150 sq. m differ between the "young" and "old" forests on Barro Colorado Island (Foster and Brokaw, this volume), and, if so, is that difference reflected by contrasting abundances of regenerating pioneers?

METHODS

I defined a gap as a vertical "hole" in the forest extending through the canopy to within 2 m of the forest floor. Horizontal gap area was determined from a scale map drawn with coordinates of direction and distance to the gap edge recorded from a central point within it. Only openings of at least 20 sq. m were considered gaps.

The study area consisted of a strip 10 m wide along each side of 14 km of Barro Colorado Island trails. Trail sections used in the census passed through a representative sample of the topography and vegetation on Barro Colorado Island. I counted a gap as within the study area if more than half the base of the "gap-creating" tree (first tree to fall in the gap or that which knocked down others) was originally within the study area, regardless of where the actual opening lay.

The total area censused was 28 ha., including 13.4 ha. of "old" forest and 14.6 ha. of "young" forest. Foster and Brokaw (this volume) feel that it has been 300–400 years since the old forest has suffered large scale disturbance by man. The young forest, though not of uniform age, is about 100 years old (Foster and Brokaw, this volume). Structurally, the forests differ in that there are more very large trees in the old forest (Bennett, 1963; Foster and Brokaw, this volume), although the density of trees is greater in the young forest (Knight, 1975).

The study area was first censused in August 1975 to locate and mark all existing gaps. At the beginning of August 1976, I marked and measured all gaps formed in the study area since the first census. I repeated this census at the start of each succeeding month through November 1978. Falling limbs and vine tangles can create gaps as well as can falling trees. I termed all such disturbances treefalls. Treefalls occurring in

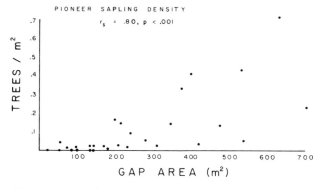

Figure 1. Maximum density of all saplings of potential canopy trees, 1 m tall or over, represented by pioneer individuals versus gap area, within two years after gap formation in 30 treefall gaps on Barro Colorado Island (Brokaw, 1980).

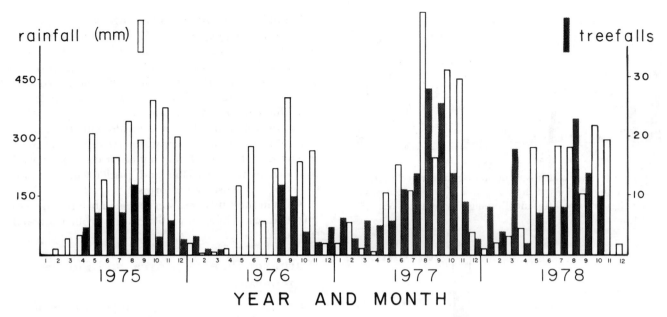

Figure 2. Monthly treefall totals from the study area and game wardens' records (April 1975 through March 1976) compared with monthly rainfall.

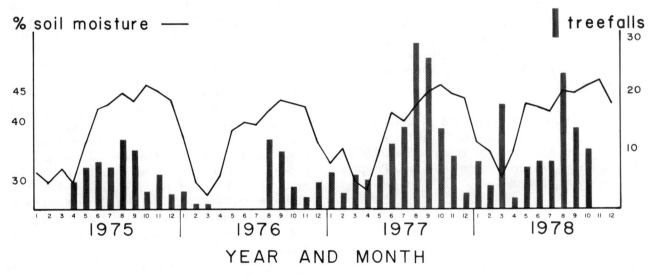

Figure 3. Monthly treefall totals from the study area and game wardens' records (April 1975 through March 1976) compared with mean monthly soil moisture.

the study area, but not creating openings conforming to the gap definition, and all treefalls immediately adjacent to the study area (visible from the trail) were tallied as well. All treefalls in and near the study area were used in the analysis of seasonality. I classified trees fallen in study area gaps as uprooted or broken off, measured their diameter at breast height (dbh, assumed to be 138 cm above ground), and determined which were gap-creating trees. At the time of the final census I counted the total number of individuals and species of pioneer saplings 1 m or more tall in the young and old sections of the study area (see list of common light-gap pioneer species, Foster and Brokaw, this volume).

I include in the seasonality results data from the game wardens' records of treefalls across Barro Colorado trails from April 1975 through March 1976. These data are not used in statistical evaluations. Rain-

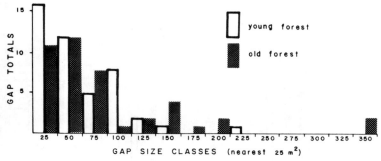

Figure 4. Size class distribution of gaps formed in the old and young sections of the study area. The distributions are not significantly different (Komolgorov-Smirnov test, $\chi^2 = 2.4$, d.f. $= 2$, $p < 0.5$).

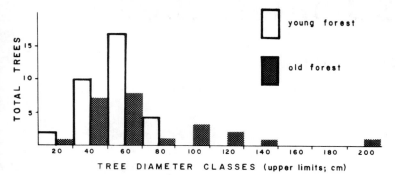

Figure 5. Diameter class distribution of gap-creating fallen trees in old and young sections of the study area. The distributions are not significantly different (Komolgorov-Smirnov test, $\chi^2 = 5.0$, d.f. $= 2$, $p < 0.1$).

fall data for Barro Colorado Island are from Panama Canal Company (now Panama Canal Commission) records (Rand and Rand, this volume). Soil moisture data are from the Environmental Sciences Program (Dietrich et al., this volume).

RESULTS

Seasonality of Treefalls

From 1975 through 1978, treefalls on Barro Colorado Island appear to have peaked around August and September of each year, with one subordinate peak in March 1978 (Figure 2). Despite the lack of complete monthly records from late 1975 through 1976 for my study area, the August and September 1976 totals of 12 and 10 treefalls probably represent a peak for that period, because only 40 treefalls occurred at the study area from August 1975 through July 1976. The temporal distribution of treefalls is significantly different from a uniform (Kolomorgorov-Smirnov test, $p < 0.001$) or random distribution (Runs test, $p < 0.005$).

Treefalls peak in August and September, at the middle of the wet seasons (Figure 2), three to four months after the beginning of the rains and the consequent steep increase in soil moisture (Figure 3). Treefalls per month were significantly correlated with both monthly rainfall ($r_s = 0.47$, $p < 0.02$) and mean monthly percent soil moisture ($r_s = 0.43$, $p < 0.05$). The treefall peaks do not coincide with the consistently high winds of the dry season (December to April; Dietrich et al., this volume) but occur during a period of perhaps more variable and gustier winds accompanying wet season rainstorms.

Gaps in the study area were created by broken trees in 36 cases, while only 16 resulted from uprooted trees.

Turnover Rate, Gap Area, and Pioneer Regeneration

Similar numbers of gaps opened per hectare in the young and old sections of the study area (Table 1). But turnover rate, the mean time between formation of gap area at any one point in the forest, based on current dynamics, was 114 years in the old forest section versus 159 years in the young forest section (computation and data in Table 1). The faster rate of the old forest was due to creation of several large gaps there (Figure 4).

For both sections combined, gap area is significantly correlated with dbh of gap-creating fallen trees ($r_s = 0.45$, $p < 0.001$). Frequency distributions of gap size (Figure 4) and dbh of gap-creating trees (Figure 5) suggest that large gaps, caused by larger trees, are more common in the old forest. However, neither frequency distributions nor median values of gap and gap-creating tree sizes are significantly different between old and young forests (Figures 4 and 5, Table 1). Means are also given in Table 1, but the data do not meet assumptions for tests on that parameter.

One gap over 150 sq. m was formed per hectare every 5.3 years in the old forest study area, but only one was formed per hectare per 50 years in the young forest section (based on eight gaps over 150 sq. m in the old forest versus one gap over 150 sq. m in the young forest during the study period). At the end of the census period there were 135 pioneer saplings, 1 m tall or over, representing 20 species in the old forest section, whereas there were 15 saplings of 4 species in the young forest section.

DISCUSSION

Seasonality of Treefalls

Seasonal peaks of treefalls are reported for several

Table 1. Parameters of gap formation and turnover rate in young and old sections of the study area

	Young forest	Old forest
Number of gaps formed	45	43
Gaps/ha.*	3.1	3.2
Sq. m gap/ha.*	198.5	277.5
Sq. m gap/ha. per yr.	62.7	87.6
(% ha. per yr.)	(0.63)	(0.88)
Turnover rate (yr.)**	159	114
Median gap area in sq. m	47	57
Range	232–22	342–26
Mean	64	86
Number of gap-creating trees	33	24
Median dbh in cm of gap-creating trees		
Range	70–9.2	200–20
Mean	45	67

Area of young forest = 14.6 ha.; area of old forest = 13.4 ha. Data are based on openings conforming to the gap definition and created during the 38-month study period. The differences between the median gap areas and the median diameter of causal trees in young and old forest are not significantly different ($p<0.15$, $p<0.13$; Mann–Whitney test).

* Computed by dividing the total number of gaps (for gaps/ha.) and total sq. m of gap (for sq. m gap/ha.), formed in the section during the study period, by the total ha. of the section.

** Computed by dividing the area of 1 ha. by sq. m gap/ha. per yr.

other forests in tropical and temperate locations: along creeks in French Guiana (Oldeman, 1972); at Los Tuxtlas, Veracruz, Mexico (Sarukhan, 1978); in the montane forest at Monteverde, Costa Rica (R. Lawton, pers. comm.); and in the Bialowieza Forest, Poland (Falinski, 1978). The first of these examples is attributed to seasonally wet soil and consequent loosening of roots; the latter three to seasonally high winds (associated with rain at Los Tuxtlas).

Heavy rain and gusty wind together probably contribute to the mid-wet-season peak of treefalls on Barro Colorado Island. Rain may encourage treefalls in three ways: (1) by loosening the hold of roots, (2) by increasing the weight limbs and trunks support, and (3) by reducing the ability of a tree to assume "streamlining" (Gloyne, 1968). During rain, every leaf on a tree (and associated vines and epiphytes) supports several drops of water, the bark and each crevice in it become saturated, and epiphytes on a tree store mois-

ture, all creating substantial "rainload" (Gloyne, 1968). Because so many more trees are broken off than uprooted, I suggest that rainload, rather than soil loosening, may be the more important effect of rain on the stability of trees on Barro Colorado Island.

Some ultimate reasons for treefalls are shallow rooting (Fowells, 1965) and fungal, insect, and other damage to stems and roots (Hubert, 1918; Stephens, 1956). Perhaps the damage accumulates all year long (periodic activity is also possible) until seasonal proximate causes, wind and water, provide the final impetus to bring damaged trees down. Those trees prone to fall go down during the first months of heavy rain and gusty wind and are mostly down before the latter part of the wet season. Hence treefalls peak by August and September, then decline despite the drenching rains of October and November. The high treefall total of March 1978 (Figure 2) may have resulted from the heavy rainfall in the last three days of that month (38.7 mm, including 25.4 mm in 1 hr.).

Treefalls and the Timing of Dispersal and Germination

One major peak of fruit dispersal by trees on Barro Colorado Island occurs at the annual dry-to-wet-season transition (Foster, this volume; Croat, 1978). This peak is followed by a peak of seedling emergence in the early part of the wet season among some tree species that can germinate under an intact canopy but must subsequently be in a light gap for initial establishment (Garwood, 1979).

These dispersal and seedling emergence patterns may be largely due to prior constraints on flowering and fruiting schedules, superior dispersal possibilities at the seasonal transition, or the advantage of seedling emergence at a time when favorable water relations are ensured for some months (Foster, 1973; Garwood, this volume). But for species requiring gap conditions for survival, a peak of treefalls at mid wet season could strengthen selection for dispersal and seedling emergence near the start of the wet season (Foster, 1973; Garwood, 1979). Emergence at that time maximizes the probability that a seedling will be in a new treefall gap within a few months. Similarly, Grime (1979) describes plant regeneration coordinated with seasonal disturbance in British grasslands. Another parallel situation may exist in the intertidal community where Paine (1979) observed that annual spore dispersal of a pioneer alga coincides with a seasonal peak of disturbance.

Seeds of many pioneer species may sustain dormancy until the microclimate of a light gap stimulates germination (Symington, 1933, in Richards, 1952; Keay, 1960; Baur, 1968; Bell, 1970; Guevara and

Gomez-Pompa, 1972; Webb et al., 1972; Hallé et al., 1978). The ability to remain dormant until disturbance is "detected" would exempt pioneers from selection, by a seasonal peak of treefalls, for a consistent seedling emergence schedule.

Turnover Rate, Gap Area, and Forest Composition

Methods of determining forest turnover rate differ among workers, and computed rates err because disturbance is such a patchy and erratic phenomenon. Furthermore, turnover rates derived from a few years' sample are problematic in light of relatively large-scale disturbances (Foster and Brokaw, this volume) and probable trends paralleling forest maturation (see below). Nonetheless, it is worth mentioning that the turnover rate calculated for the old forest (114 years) is slower than the 62 years computed by Foster for 12 ha. of Barro Colorado forest (Forest and Brokaw, this volume) and faster than the 250-year minimum estimate by Poore (1968) for a Malaysian forest. It is comparable to the 80 to 138 years for four plots in the lowland forest at La Selva in Costa Rica (Hartshorn, 1978) and the 100 years estimated for a tierra firme forest in Amazonia (Uhl and Murphy, 1980). My estimate for the Barro Colorado old forest is also similar to Runkle's (1978) average figure of 100 years for three old-growth deciduous forests in eastern North America.

The slower turnover rate of the young forest in this study results from the paucity of large gaps there. Although parameters of gap size were not significantly different between old and young forest sections (Table 1, Figure 4), it is well to keep in mind that, in evaluating the role of disturbance in forest dynamics, extremes may be more important than means (Pickett and Thompson, 1978; Whitmore, 1978). Gaps over 150 sq. m, which pioneer trees colonize successfully on Barro Colorado, were created more often in the old than young forest sections, and very large gaps (over 300 sq. m) are fairly common throughout the old forest. If the current formation rate of large gaps is maintained there, it seems ample to sustain numerous pioneer species in the Barro Colorado forest.

A greater frequency of large gaps may explain why mature individuals of the short-lived pioneers *Cecropia* spp. are more abundant in the old forest (Knight, 1975; Hartshorn, 1978). There they are found in conspicuous groups of tall canopy trees associated with other pioneers, and often at the site of large fallen boles (pers. observ.). Robertson et al. (1978) describe an apparently similar situation in adjacent old growth and secondary stands of floodplain forest in southern Illinois (USA). Gap-phase regeneration was the principal mode of regeneration in the old growth, where trees had reached large sizes, but was not observed in the secondary forest of smaller trees.

Thus, the creation of larger gaps and the acceleration of the turnover rate are seen as a consequence of forest maturation. At present, the young forest on Barro Colorado Island has relatively few large trees (Bennett, 1963; Foster and Brokaw, this volume) but a high density of stems (Knight, 1975), and thinning results in many small gaps filled in by bordering trees and formerly suppressed saplings. When the young forest matures to the current age of the old forest, its larger trees will then produce larger gaps, faster turnover, and regeneration space for pioneers. Jones (1945) describes this "breakup" accompanying maturation in several forests (also see Peet and Loucks, 1977).

According to one model of forest development, the old forest turnover rate may eventually slow down as large, long-lived secondary trees (present since an early large-scale colonization event) die out and are replaced by longer-lived primary species (Hallé et al., 1978). Alternatively, it is proposed that, because of extensive human disturbance, many primary tree species may be locally extinct in Central America, leaving the forest in a perpetual rapid cycle of short-lived secondary trees (P. S. Ashton, manuscript). Neither prediction is entirely warranted, since species with primary forest characteristics and long-lived secondary species are reproducing in the old forest (Knight, 1975; Brokaw, 1980).

The influence of natural disturbance on the structure and dynamics of biological communities has been emphasized recently (Pickett, 1976; Connell, 1978; Grime, 1979; Huston, 1979; White, 1979). An important aspect of disturbance is its predictability in time and space. For example, Sale (1977) attributes the high diversity of coral reef fish partly to the random or unpredictable occurrence of disturbance and colonization in their habitat. A similar effect may foster coexistence among trees on Barro Colorado, but within certain spatio-temporal scales, periodicity and trends in the magnitude of disturbance due to treefalls are somewhat predictable on Barro Colorado Island. This predictability has potentially significant consequences for plant phenology and community composition. First, the seasonal peak of treefalls may influence the timing of dispersal and/or germination of some species requiring a gap for initial establishment. Second, it appears that an increase in the number of large gaps accompanies forest maturation and promotes regeneration of pioneer trees.

ACKNOWLEDGMENTS

I greatly appreciated the ideas, interest, and encouragement of R. Foster, E. Leigh, A. S. Rand, and R. Lawton during this investigation. Comments on the manuscript by M. Acevedo, N. Garwood, D. Knight, E. Mallory, G. Montgomery, F. Putz, and D. Schemske were very helpful. I thank D. Windsor and P. Coley for various kinds of assistance. Funds were provided by Coulter Fellowships, Hutchinson Fellowships, and the Hinds Fund of the University of Chicago, and by the Environmental Sciences Program of the Smithsonian Tropical Research Institute (STRI). Maintenance of the nature preserve and field station on Barro Colorado Island by STRI made this study possible.

LITERATURE CITED

Acevedo, M., and R. Marquis
1979. A survey of the light gaps of the tropical rain forest at Llorona, Peninsula de Osa. Pages 290–303 in OTS Book 78.3. San Jose, Costa Rica: Organization for Tropical Studies.

Baur, G. N.
1968. *The Ecological Basis of Rain Forest Management.* Sydney, Australia: Forestry Commission, New South Wales. 499 pp.

Bell, C. R.
1970. Seed distribution and germination experiment. Pages D177–D182 in *A Tropical Rain Forest,* edited by H. Odum. Washington, D.C.: U.S. Atomic Energy Commission.

Bennett, C. F.
1963. A phytophysiognomic reconnaisance of Barro Colorado Island, Canal Zone. *Smithsonian Miscellaneous Collection* 145, No. 7.

Brokaw, N. V. L.
1980. Gap-phase Regeneration in a Tropical Forest. Ph.D. thesis, University of Chicago, Chicago, Illinois. 175 pp.

Brown, W. H., and D. W. Mathews
1914. Philippine dipterocarp forests. *Philippine Journal of Science,* 9 (Sect. A):413–561.

Connell, J. H.
1978. Diversity in Tropical Rain Forests and Coral Reefs. *Science,* 199:1302–1310.

Croat, T. B.
1978. *Flora of Barro Colorado Island.* Stanford, Calif.: Stanford University Press. 943 pp.

Denslow, J. S.
1980. Gap Partitioning Among Tropical Rain Forest Trees. *Biotropica,* Supplement 12:47–55.

Dietrich, W., D. M. Windsor, and T. Dunne
1982. Geology, Climate, and Hydrology of Barro Colorado Island. Pages 21–46 in *The Ecology of a Tropical Forest,* edited by Egbert G. Leigh, Jr., et al. Washington, D.C.: Smithsonian Institution Press.

Falinski, J. B.
1978. Uprooted trees, their distribution and influence in the primeval forest biotope. *Vegetatio,* 38:175–183.

Foster, R. B.
1973. Seasonality of fruit production and seed fall in a tropical forest ecosystem in Panama. Ph.D. thesis, Duke University, Durham, North Carolina. 155 pp.

1982. The Seasonal Rhythms in Fruitfall on Barro Colorado Island. Pages 151–172 in *The Ecology of a Tropical Forest,* edited by Egbert G. Leigh, Jr., et al. Washington, D.C.: Smithsonian Institution Press.

Foster, R. B., and N. V. L. Brokaw
1982. Structure and History of the Vegetation of Barro Colorado Island. Pages 67–81 in *The Ecology of a Tropical Forest,* edited by Egbert G. Leigh, Jr., et al. Washington, D.C.: Smithsonian Institution Press.

Fowells, H. A. (compiler)
1965. *Silvics of Forest Trees of the United States.* U.S. Department of Agriculture Forest Service, Agr. Handbook 271, 762 pp.

Garwood, N. C.
1979. Seedling Germination in a Seasonal Tropical Forest. Ph.D. thesis, University of Chicago.

1982. Seasonal Rhythms of Seed Germination in a Semideciduous Tropical Forest. Pages 173–185 in *The Ecology of a Tropical Forest,* edited by Egbert G. Leigh, Jr., et al. Washington, D.C.: Smithsonian Institution Press.

Gloyne, R. W.
1968. The structure of the wind and its relevance to forestry. *Forestry,* 41 (Supplement):7–19.

Grime, J. P.
1979. *Plant Strategies and Vegetation Processes.* Chichester, England: John Wiley and Sons. 222 pp.

Guevara, S. S., and A. Gomez-Pompa
1972. Seeds from surface soils in a tropical region of Veracruz, Mexico. *Journal of the Arnold Arboretum,* 53:312–335.

Hallé, F., R. A. A. Oldeman and P. B. Tomlinson
1978. *Tropical Trees and Forests: An Architectural Analysis.* Berlin: Springer-Verlag. 441 pp.

Hartshorn, G. S.
1978. Treefalls and tropical forest dynamics. Pages 617–683 in *Tropical Trees as Living Systems,* edited by P. B. Tomlinson and M. H. Zimmerman. Cambridge: Cambridge University Press.

Hubert, E. E.
1918. Fungi as contributory causes of windfall in the Northwest. *Journal of Forestry,* 16:696–714.

Huston, M.
1979. A General Hypothesis of Species Diversity. *American Naturalist,* 113:81–101.

Jones, E. W.
1945. The structure and reproduction of the virgin forest of the north temperate zone. *New Phytologist,* 44:130–148.

1956. Ecological studies on the rainforest of southern Nigeria. IV. The plateau forest of the Okumu Forest Preserve. *Journal of Ecology,* 43:564–594; 44:83–117.

Keay, R. W. J.
1960. Seeds in forest soils. *Nigerian Forestry Information Bulletin,* 4:1–4.

Knight, D. H.
1975. A phytosociological analysis of species-rich tropical forest on Barro Colorado Island, Panama. *Ecological Monographs,* 45:259–284.

Kramer, F.
1933. De natuurlijke verjonging in het Goenoeng-Ggedeh-complex. *Tectona,* 26:156–185.

Lee, R.
1978. *Forest Microclimatology.* New York: Columbia University Press. 276 pp.

Levin, S. A., and R. T. Paine
1974. Disturbance, patch formation, and community structure. *Proceedings of the National Academy of Science,* 71:2744–2747.

Longman, K. A., and J. Jenik
1974. *Tropical Forest and Its Environment.* London: Longman.

Oldeman, R. A. A.
1972. L'architecture de la végétation ripicole forestière des fleuves et criques guyanais. *Adansonia,* (N.S.) 12(2):253–265.
1978. Architecture and energy exchange of dicotyledenous trees in the forest. Pages 535–560 in *Tropical Trees as Living Systems,* edited by P. B. Tomlinson and M. H. Zimmerman. Cambridge: Cambridge University Press.

Paine, R. T.
1979. Disaster, catastrophe, and local persistence of the sea palm *Postelsia palmaeformis. Science,* 205:685–687.

Peet, R. K., and O. L. Loucks
1977. A gradient analysis of southern Wisconsin oak forests. *Ecology,* 58:485–499.

Pickett, S. T. A.
1976. Succession: an evolutionary interpretation. *American Naturalist,* 110:107–119.

Pickett, S. T. A., and J. N. Thompson
1978. Patch dynamics and the design of nature preserves. *Biol. Conserv.,* 13:27–37.

Poore, M. E. D.
1968. Studies in Malaysian rain forest. *Journal of Ecology,* 56:143–189.

Putz, F. E., P. D. Coley, K. Lu., A. M. Montalvo, and A. Aiello
Ms. Structural determinants and ecological consequences of mechanical damage and mortality of trees.

Rand, A. S.
1977. Number of Treefalls Per Month. Page 134 in *Environmental Monitoring and Baseline Data from the Isthmus of Panama, 1976, vol. IV,* edited by D. M. Windsor. Washington, D.C.: Smithsonian Institution.

Rand, A. S., and W. M. Rand.
1982. Variation in Rainfall over Barro Colorado Island. Pages 47–59 in *The Ecology of a Tropical Forest,* edited by Egbert G. Leigh, Jr., et al. Washington, D.C.: Smithsonian Institution Press.

Richards, P. W.
1952. *The Tropical Rain Forest.* Cambridge: Cambridge University Press, 450 pp.

Robertson, P. A., G. T. Weaver, and J. A. Cavanaugh
1978. Vegetation and tree species patterns near the northern terminus of the southern floodplain forest. *Ecological Monographs,* 48:249–267.

Runkle, J. R.
1978. Gap-phase dynamics in climax mesic forests. Ph.D. thesis, Cornell University, Ithaca, New York. 189 pp.

Sale, P. F.
1977. Maintenance of high diversity in coral reef fish communities. *American Naturalist,* 111:337–359.

Sarukhan, J.
1978. Studies on the demography of tropical trees. Pages 163–184 in *Tropical Trees as Living Systems,* edited by P. B. Tomlinson and M. H. Zimmerman. Cambridge: Cambridge University Press.

Schulz, J. P.
1960. Ecological studies on the rain forest in northern Surinam. *Verh. K. Ned. Akad. Wet., Afd. natuurk'd. Tweed Reeks,* 53:1–367.

Stephens, E. P.
1956. The uprooting of trees: a forest process. *Proceedings of the Soil Science Society of America,* 20:113–116.

Symington, C. F.
1933. The study of secondary growth on rain forest sites. *Malay Forester,* 2:107–117.

Uhl, C., and P. G. Murphy
1980. Composition, structure, and regeneration of a tierra firme forest in the Amazon Basin of Venezuela. *Tropical Ecology* (in press).

Webb, L. J., J. G. Tracey, and W. T. Williams
1972. Regeneration and pattern in the subtropical rain forest. *Journal of Ecology,* 60:675–696.

White, P. S.
1979. Pattern, process and natural disturbance in vegetation. *Botanical Review,* 45:229–299.

Whitmore, T. C.
1974. *Change with time and the role of cyclones in tropical rain forest on Kolombangara, Solomon Islands.* Institute paper 46, Oxford: Commonwealth Forestry Institute.
1975. *Tropical Rain Forests of the Far East.* Oxford: Clarendon Press. 282 pp.
1978. Gaps in the forest canopy. Pages 639–655 in *Tropical Trees as Living Systems,* edited by P. B. Tomlinson and M. H. Zimmerman. Cambridge: Cambridge University Press.

SEASONAL RHYTHMS
IN PLANTS

Forest Production and Regulation of Primary Consumers on Barro Colorado Island

EGBERT G. LEIGH, JR.   Smithsonian Tropical Research Institute, Balboa, Republic of Panama

DONALD M. WINDSOR   Smithsonian Tropical Research Institute, Balboa, Republic of Panama

ABSTRACT

On Barro Colorado Island, leaf flush peaks early in the rainy season. The number of deciduous trees bearing young leaves starts increasing in March, peaks in May and June, and is lowest from October to February. The seasonal rhythm of leaf flush is more complex in canopy evergreens, but minima tend to occur when few deciduous trees are leafing out, thus causing shortages of new leaves in the forest as a whole which may last several weeks.

About 6.5 tons dry weight of leaves fall to the ground per hectare per year, 7.3% of whose area consists of holes and gaps, representing a foliage consumption, presumably by insects, of 0.5 tons/ha./yr. Leafcutter ants probably eat another 0.3 tons/ha./yr., as do folivorous vertebrates; these leaves are presumably eaten whole and leave no identifiable traces in litter traps.

The numbers of leafcutter ants and vertebrate folivores are probably kept in check by the seasonal shortage of new leaves, while birds and other predators may help control the numbers of other folivorous insects.

Although individual trees produce over 500 g dry weight of fruit per square meter of crown in a good year, fruitfall in the forest as a whole is less than 100 g/sq. m/yr., or 1 ton/ha./yr. Although vertebrates only eat a third of this, frugivorous vertebrates are limited by seasonal shortage of fruit.

Litterfall on Barro Colorado Island is remarkably rich in mineral nutrients, especially phosphorus and nitrogen, apparently reflecting the fertility of the soil, which is derived from old volcanic deposits. If one compares figures for litterfall from different tropical forests, one finds that leaf production (like wood production) is unrelated to soil fertility, but fertile soil makes for higher fruit production and greater animal activity.

INTRODUCTION

In many seasonal forests, there is a period of leaf flush at the beginning of the favorable season, whether the favorable season is a time of sufficient warmth or of sufficient moisture. How pronounced is the rhythm of leaf flush on Barro Colorado Island, and how does this rhythm compare with those in less seasonal tropical forests? What role might this rhythm play in regulating folivore populations?

More generally, how much foliage do animals consume? How does this compare with fruit consumption?

Finally, how productive is the forest on Barro Colorado Island? What controls the various aspects of its production, and how might these controls affect the animal community?

METHODS

This paper is based primarily on records of phenology and litterfall taken under the auspices of the Smithsonian Environmental Sciences Program (ESP). To measure the seasonal rhythm of leaf production, Bonifacio de León, an experienced woodsman, has taken weekly records since August 1974 on nearly 400 trees in Lutz catchment and its neighborhood, recording for each tree (among other things) whether it is flushing many leaves, or few, or none. These records involve subjective judgments. How many new leaves must a tree put out to be scored as flushing many new leaves? How long does a leaf stay new? De León's judgments seem to have stabilized after the first year.

To measure forest production, from September 1971 through December 1979 ESP technicians have collected litter from 100 tubs, each with a collecting surface of $1/12$ sq. m, arranged around the loop trail within Lutz catchment. By January 1974, another 100 tubs had been added around the perimeter of the catchment. Litter was collected weekly, dried at 50° or 60°C for 2 weeks or more, separated into leaves, twigs, flowers, fruit, and remainder ("trash"), and weighed. On the central plateau of the island, Foster (this volume) measured litterfall into comparable tubs: some of this litter was analyzed for nutrient content. Healey and Swift (1977) also measured litterfall for 1 year, presumably using bigger collectors.

We will assess the rhythm of leaf flush in the forest canopy from records on 98 deciduous trees representing 26 species and 93 canopy evergreens representing 40 species. We will estimate annual leaf production as the annual fall of leaf litter, plus the annual consumption of foliage by herbivores. We estimate annual foliage consumption as follows: (1) We measure the proportion x of the area of fallen leaves which consists of holes and gaps (Leigh and Smythe, 1978), guessing, if necessary, the outline a leaf had when intact from the fragment in hand. We take the weight E of foliage eaten to be $Fx/(1 - x)$, where F is the total weight of leaf litterfall. (2) Following Leigh and Smythe (1978), we assume that vertebrates eat their leaves whole, and calculate their foliage consumption from their population sizes, their feeding rates, and the proportion of foliage in their diets. (3) We assume that leafcutter ants destroy whole leaves, and infer the rate at which they do so from estimates in the literature. (4) We assume that the total rate of leaf consumption is the sum of these three rates. This is an underestimate, since caterpillars, at least, sometimes defoliate whole plants (Wolda and Foster, 1978): however, leafcutter ants do seem to account for most defoliations encountered on the phenology census.

Next, we compare the weight of fruit falling to the forest floor with values of fruit production for selected trees and the aggregate rate of fruit consumption by vertebrates, as calculated from their numbers and metabolic rates in the manner of Leigh and Smythe (1978).

Finally, for a rough comparison of the relation of production to nutrient supply on Barro Colorado Island to those in other tropical forests, we compare the dry weight, and the nutrient content as given by Bruce Haines (personal communication), of different types of litter falling to the forest floor on Barro Colorado Island with corresponding figures for other sites taken from the literature.

RESULTS AND DISCUSSION

The Seasonal Rhythm of Leaf Flush

The trees of Barro Colorado Island leaf out according to many different rhythms, the causes of some of which are poorly known. Some *Ceiba pentandra* seem to replace all their leaves at irregular and unpredictable intervals; they sometimes keep their leaves until the next flush, and sometimes drop them a month or more beforehand. *Pseudobombax septenatum* all drop their leaves at the beginning of the new year and leaf out again at the beginning of May. *Spondias mombin* usually drop their leaves near the end of the year and leaf out again in early March, but some years they leaf out more synchronously than others, for no apparent reason. *Virola surinamensis* renew their leaves with the coming of the new year. *Anacardium excelsum* renew theirs 3 to 5 weeks after the beginning of dry season: they usually leaf out in the first or second week of January, although in 1976, when the rains ended a month early, they leafed out in the last week of December.

However, when one looks at the forest as a whole, there is a definite seasonal rhythm of leaf flush (Table 1). The number of deciduous trees bearing young leaves starts increasing in March, peaks in May and June, some time after the beginning of the rains, and then declines, bottoming out from October to early February. The seasonal rhythm is more complex in canopy evergreens. One can, however, detect a peak in September or early October, another peak at the beginning of the new year, and a third after the onset of the rains. In evergreens, periods of minimum leaf flush are brief and unpredictable, but they often coincide with times when there are very few new leaves in the forest. These shortages vary greatly in severity from year to year.

Far more trees were reported as simultaneously bearing new leaves in May and June of 1975 than in later years. To some extent, de León's standards changed. However, leaffall in the dry season of 1976, and presumably leaf production in 1975, were unusually high (Wolda, 1978). It is hard to distinguish these two factors.

A comparable census of the phenology of forest trees has been carried out in the rain forest at La Selva in Costa Rica (Frankie et al., 1974), although the trees there were checked every 2 weeks or every month rather than once a week as on Barro Colorado Island. La Selva receives 4000 mm of rain a year and no month of the year has an average rainfall less than 150 mm. The average rainfall for every month of the year thus exceeds the amount the forest can use in a month (Dietrich et al., this volume), although February and/or March are quite dry in some years. Their census included 93 species of overstory trees. The seasons of leaf flush were published for 54 of these, 8 other species were said to leaf at unspecified but discrete times of year, 26 were said to put out new leaves continuously through the year, and the behavior of the remaining 5 was undetermined. There is a striking seasonality of leaf flush among the species recorded (Table 2a), more striking even than among the deciduous trees of Barro Colorado Island, even though the two forests share many species in common, and even though only 26 of the censused species of overstory tree at La Selva had seasons of leaflessness or obvious leaf drop. At La Selva, however, leaf flush peaks in early dry season, rather than after the resumption of heavier rains. As on Barro Colorado, there is a secondary peak of leaf flush in September.

Comparable rhythms of leaf flush occur in the evergreen forest of Gabon (Table 2b: data from Hladik, 1978), and in the rain forests of Sarawak (Fogden, 1972) and Malaya (Whitmore, 1975; Ng, 1974), even though dry months are very rare in Sarawak and very unpredictable in Malaya (Medway, 1972).

The Regulation of Folivores by Seasonal Shortage of New Leaves

Vertebrate folivores seem limited by the seasonal shortage of new leaves. For example, a sloth's digestion is slow, and sloths may sometimes be hard put to find foods they can digest rapidly enough to maintain themselves. Montgomery and Sunquist (1978) have compared the rates at which sloths digest different foods, and find that sloths tend to feed from trees whose leaves they digest more rapidly. Moreover, sloths digest new leaves more rapidly than old. A disproportionate number of sloths die late in the rainy season, from October through early December; there are few new leaves then, as we have seen, and the few hours of sun and abundant rain typical of this time of year (Dietrich et al., this volume) may make it difficult for the sloths to maintain a body temperature high enough to facilitate digestion (Montgomery and Sunquist, 1978). Although we have no data at all, it seems reasonable to suppose that the same is true for iguanas, at least young ones: iguana hatching is timed to occur at the beginning of the rains, when new leaves are most abundant (Burghardt et al., 1977). Howling monkeys depend on an adequate supply of new leaves (Milton, 1979); on Barro Colorado more howlers die and fewer are born late in the rainy season than at other times of year (Milton, this volume).

Insect herbivory is restricted to some extent by predators. Holmes et al. (1979) found that excluding birds from understory saplings in a New Hampshire woodland increased the number of caterpillars on their foliage by half. As we shall see, birds prey relatively more heavily on insects in the tropics. However, insects are most abundant during the season of leaf flush (Wolda, 1978; Fogden, 1972), suggesting that their numbers are affected, at least in part, by the availability of suitable food.

Herbivory and Leaf Production

We assume leaf production is leaf litterfall plus leaf consumption, and we consider three sources of leaf consumption: the consumption by (a) vertebrates, and (b) leafcutter ants, which are assumed to eat their leaves whole, and (c) the consumption represented by holes and gaps in fallen leaves.

a. The principal vertebrate folivores of Barro Colorado Island are sloths, howling monkeys, and iguanas (Leigh and Smythe, 1978). The metabolism of animals of the first two species has been measured in the wild using the doubly-labeled water technique (Nagy and Montgomery, 1980; Nagy and Milton, 1979). Three-toed sloths, *Bradypus variegatus*, eat 15 g dry weight of food per kg body weight per day (Nagy and

Table 1. Number of species of trees with new leaves, week by week, and number of species of deciduous and of evergreen trees flushing new leaves in successive weeks

Week	1974–1975					1975–1976					1976–1977				
	Deciduous		Rain	Evergreen		Deciduous		Rain	Evergreen		Deciduous		Rain	Evergreen	
33	½	2	4	0	0	4	8	67	7	12	2	4	41	7	8
34 Aug.	½	½	45	0	0	2	6	60	7	8	2	7	40	7	11
35 Sept.	½	½	39	1	0	1	6	111	4	10	2	5	54	4	11
36	0	2	6	1	0	2	5	18	3	13	0	6	40	3	12
37	4	3	194	16	3	3	3	92	8	6	½	4	105	2	13
38 Sept.	2	2	146	12	2	2	3	96	9	12	½	4	108	5	6
39 Oct.	—	—	15	—	—	½	7	43	11	4	0	3	131	4	6
40	2	3	105	13	2	½	6	61	10	6	0	2	31	1	12
41	1	1	31	13	1	1	5	90	9	9	0	2	47	0	8
42	½	3	45	12	1	3	2	153	9	8	0	2	52	0	9
43 Oct.	0	0	45	9	2	2	3	40	7	7	0	2	99	0	9
44 Nov.	½	2	33	8	1	2	3	90	6	13	0	2	95	0	10
45	½	2	50	8	5	½	3	67	6	9	0	1	116	1	11
46	7	3	123	18	3	1	3	65	4	7	0	1	50	0	10
47 Nov.	½	2	155	6	5	2	2	192	4	6	½	0	14	0	6
48 Dec.	½	2	323	4	3	1	3	37	5	9	½	0	1	1	6
49	½	2	69	5	3	2	4	49	5	8	0	0	3	2	7
50	3	1	37	9	4	½	3	178	2	12	0	0	0	1	10
51	½	2	8	6	½	½	2	27	2	6	0	½	26	6	8
52 Dec.	½	0	0	14	3	0	2	56	4	5	½	0	3	6	7
1 Jan.	1	3	2	17	5	½	2	5	3	8	½	0	0	9	6
2	2	0	0	15	7	1	½	5	8	9	½	0	4	6	6
3	0	½	3	11	4	1	1	10	10	9	½	½	12	5	7
4 Jan.	2	1	0	18	5	1	½	15	7	9	0	2	10	0	6
5 Feb.	2	½	0	13	8	½	½	1	4	10	0	1	41	0	5
6	1	2	3	11	4	2	1	0	5	10	2	2	3	½	6
7	1	2	2	4	4	1	½	0	4	8	1	3	16	2	5
8 Feb.	3	3	2	11	9	1	1	0	3	11	3	1	1	2	5
9 Mar.	7	½	8	16	4	0	4	8	1	8	3	2	30	2	2
10	8	2	42	20	8	3	2	0	3	8	4	2	0	3	5
11	9	1	1	20	10	2	4	5	4	15	3	2	10	2	6
12 Mar.	13	2	0	20	8	5	3	3	6	9	3	4	0	4	4
13 Apr.	12	3	0	20	5	5	2	0	3	8	4	4	7	3	9
14	10	3	0	14	9	5	2	0	3	15	4	4	0	2	7
15	13	3	43	21	5	6	1	0	3	10	2	7	7	1	9
16 Apr.	13	5	1	20	6	8	6	0	7	11	4	7	0	3	7
17 May	14	3	0	15	9	9	6	10	9	13	6	7	0	6	2
18	17	3	9	17	10	8	4	24	7	13	5	4	4	4	3
19	17	3	70	29	3	11	5	19	6	11	4	4	2	3	5
20	19	2	41	26	6	8	5	27	7	9	5	2	73	2	6
21 May	21	2	121	30	3	6	7	45	5	9	9	2	60	7	9
22 June	19	4	69	28	8	3	8	81	6	9	6	9	48	8	19
23	21	3	23	31	½	3	9	79	6	8	7	11	64	10	14
24	18	6	3	29	5	4	9	16	6	10	4	11	48	4	18

For each category, the left-hand column counts those flushing a large number of new leaves, and the right-hand column counts those flushing fewer new leaves. Each number counts only half the species, only half of whose individuals are flushing in that category that week.

Table 1. (continued)

Week	1974–1975					1975–1976					1976–1977				
	Deciduous		Rain	Evergreen		Deciduous		Rain	Evergreen		Deciduous		Rain	Evergreen	
25 June	20	4	48	31	3	6	6	68	5	14	1	9	53	3	16
26 July	18	2	58	29	5	5	8	97	4	11	2	8	71	5	10
27	13	8	81	19	12	4	8	20	6	11	3	8	112	4	14
28	11	9	17	17	15	3	8	22	3	15	3	5	22	4	10
29	7	8	25	17	9	3	6	7	2	13	1	8	10	2	10
30 July	4	5	87	12	7	3	4	42	3	12	1	5	4	½	8
31 Aug.	3	7	63	8	6	3	6	95	5	12	½	5	70	3	7
32	3	4	93	5	12	3	7	2	7	9	½	5	147	2	10

Montgomery, 1980). Assuming that a two-toed sloth, *Choloepus hoffmanni*, eats two-thirds as much foliage per unit body weight as a three-toed sloth and supposing that, excluding dependent young, there are $18.1/0.7 = 25.8$ kg of three-toed sloths and $3.5/0.7 = 5.0$ kg of two-toed sloths per hectare on Barro Colorado, roughly 10 animals per hectare all told, (Montgomery and Sunquist, 1975), we find that these sloths eat 160 kg dry weight of foliage per hectare per year. Howling monkeys, *Alouatta palliatta*, eat 53.5 g dry weight of food per kilogram body weight per day (Nagy and Milton, 1979), roughly half of which is leaves (Hladik and Hladik, 1969). Excluding infants, there are 4.2 kg of howlers per hectare (Nagy and Milton, 1979), so the 1200 howlers of Barro Colorado eat 41 kg dry weight of leaves per hectare per year. We know much less about iguanas, but there are probably only a very few thousand adult iguanas on Barro Colorado and, since they are reptiles and are presumably blessed with lower metabolic rates, they presumably eat less than mammals of comparable weight (Leigh and Smythe, 1978). It seems safe to assume that on Barro Colorado, vertebrate folivores eat less than 300 kg dry weight of leaves per hectare per year.

b. A week-long study showed that during the rainy season, a colony of leafcutter ants in lowland forest on the Osa peninsula of Costa Rica was removing leaves at an annual rate of 424 kg dry weight per hectare (Lugo et al., 1973). Both the season and the specific conditions during the week of study were favorable: this figure is high. Haines (1978) reported that during the dry season, leafcutter ants in a 42-year-old forest near Barro Colorado were consuming leaves at an annual rate of 98 kg per hectare. He believes that this estimate is low, because leafcutter ants eat more leaves in the rainy season. It seems

Table 2a. Number of seasonally flushing species at La Selva, Costa Rica, putting out new leaves in successive months, in relation to rainfall (Frankie et al., 1974)

	Jan.	Feb.	Mar.	Apr.	May	June	July	Aug.	Sept.	Oct.	Nov.	Dec.
Monthly rainfall (mm; 9-yr. average)	233	160	158	220	313	427	440	360	325	338	449	431
Number of species in flush	5	21	14	10	10	9	4	3	8	0	1	0

Table 2b. Seasonal rhythm in number of trees in flush at Ipassa, Gabon (Hladik, 1978), from a census of 300 individuals

	Aug.	Sept.	Oct.	Nov.	Dec.	Jan.	Feb.	Mar.	Apr.	May	June	July
Monthly rainfall	0	180	150	250	85	100	80	210	200	240	30	5
Number of trees in flush	3	18	72	62	58	49	56	54	73	48	40	28

Table 3. Annual leaffall, in kg dry weight per hectare; total area of these leaves, including holes and gaps, in m² per m² of ground; percentage of leaf area consisting of holes and gaps; and total weight of the missing leaf matter

Year of record	Leaffall		Foliage consumed	
	Weight	Area	Percent	Weight
1 Dec. 1973–30 Nov. 1974	6060	8.0	10.3	700
1 Dec. 1974–30 Nov. 1975	5550	7.0	7.0	420
1 Jan. 1976–31 Dec. 1976	6700	6.8	5.3	375
1 Jan. 1977–31 Dec. 1977	6070	7.2	6.4	415

Data are based on the fall into 100 tubs set around the inner loop trail of Lutz catchment.

reasonable to suppose that the leafcutter ants of Lutz catchment consume a few hundred, perhaps 300, kg dry weight of leaves per hectare per year.

c. Between 1974 and 1977, an average of 7.3 sq. m of leaves fell per square meter of ground per year in Lutz catchment, 7.3% of the area of which consisted of holes and gaps. The dry weight of this missing matter averaged 480 kg per hectare per year (Table 3): we assume this is the weight of foliage consumed by the herbivores in forming these holes and gaps.

This is an overestimate: herbivores prefer young leaves, and the holes they make grow with the leaves (Coley, this volume). One can check to see if the error of the estimate is very great by calculating how much insect matter birds eat, and comparing the amount of foliage required to grow these insects with our estimate of insect consumption. Willis (1980) has estimated the numbers and weights of different kinds of birds on Barro Colorado Island, and one can estimate how much dry matter a bird consumes from its weight (Holmes and Sturges, 1975). Excluding woodpeckers, barkgleaners, and feeders on litter arthropods, we estimate that the birds of Barro Colorado eat roughly 24 kg dry weight of insects per hectare per year. As it takes 10 kg of foliage to raise 1 kg of insects, it would take 240 kg of foliage per hectare per year to fatten the insects these birds eat. If these birds eat primarily *folivorous* insects, the match between leaf consumption by insects and insect consumption by birds is remarkably close.

Using similar methods on data of Fogden (1970) and Karr (1971, 1976), we estimate that birds eat 27 kg dry weight of folivorous insects per hectare per year in lowland mixed dipterocarp forest in Sarawak, 34 kg in lowland forest 15 km from Barro Colorado, and 49 kg in forest on the lower slopes of Mt. Nimba,

Liberia. Although such birds apparently eat comparable quantities of insect matter in tropical forests the world around, they apparently eat far less in temperate forests: in the deciduous forest at Hubbard Brook, New Hampshire, they eat only 5 kg dry weight of insects per hectare per year (data from Holmes and Sturges, 1975).

It appears that, all told, herbivores on Barro Colorado consume a ton or more of foliage per hectare per year, or over 15% of the forest's foliage production. This is a very rough estimate, not least because it neglects the effects of sapfeeders and the like which leave little trace of their activities (cf. Windsor, 1978). Coley (this volume) believes that the amount herbivores eat may be even higher.

Tentatively, we conclude that the forest of Barro Colorado produces an average of 8 or more tons dry weight of leaves per hectare per year. Is this typical of lowland tropical forests in general? The similarity in rates of leaf litterfall, and in consumption of food by insectivorous birds, for such forests would lead one to think so (Table 4; see also Leigh, 1975; Leigh and Smythe, 1978).

Fruit Production and Consumption

Litter traps on Barro Colorado rarely catch as much as 100 g dry weight of falling fruit per square meter per year, and often catch much less. However, fruitfall is very patchy and irregular, and the traps of the Environmental Sciences Program, which are quite sufficient to measure leaffall, may be insufficient, perhaps through poor arrangement, to measure fruit. Smyth's (1970a, b) extensive sample of fruitfall in Allee catchment caught 90 g dry weight of fruit per square meter of collecting surface per year, as did Foster's traps (Foster, this volume) on the plateau during the year he sampled most extensively.

The fruit bats of Barro Colorado Island, including among others about 4000 *Artibeus jamaicensis* weighing nearly 50 g apiece, and, at least at some times of year, an equal number of *Artibeus lituratus* weighing 70 g apiece (C. Handley, personal communication), both of which eat roughly their weight in fruit every night (Morrison, 1978, 1980), together account for less than 5 g dry weight of fruit per square meter of ground per year. Frugivorous birds, including 600 parrots and 900 toucans averaging over 400 g apiece, 50 guans weighing 1 kg apiece, and 300 pigeons weighing 150 g apiece (Willis, 1980), also eat less than 5 g dry weight of fruit per square meter, as estimated by the techniques of Holmes and Sturges (1975). Howler monkeys eat a bit more fruit than the frugivorous birds (Nagy and Milton, 1979). Calculating the feeding rate of squirrels from their size and numbers, as Smythe

Table 4. Litterfall in tropical forests around the world

	Year	Leaves	Fruit	Flowers	Twigs	Trash	Total
Barro Colorado Island, Panama							
Plateau (Foster, this volume)	1969/70	578	93	—	—	—	1089
Plateau (Foster, this volume)	1970/71	643	65	—	—	—	1215
Plateau (Healey & Swift 1977)	1971	740	328	—	301	—	1340
Lutz catchment (ESP)	1972[1]	749	112	37	169	134	1200
Lutz catchment (ESP)	1973[2]	689	48	30	174	155	1096
Lutz catchment (ESP)	1974[3]	635	55	15	144	185	1034
Lutz catchment (ESP)	1975[3]	536	19	11	105	182	853
Lutz catchment (ESP)	1976[3]	688	32	11	110	173	1014
Lutz catchment (ESP)	1977[3]	622	16	12	124	172	946
Lutz catchment (ESP)	1978[3]	572	30	12	147	167	928
Lutz catchment (ESP)	1979[3]	638	25	16	136	178	994
Belem, Brazil (Klinge 1974, 1975)							
Mocambo (tierra firme)	1969/71	780	(80)		130	—	1000
Seasonally flooded, riverine	1969/71	750	(60)		140	—	1070
Blackwater swamp forest	1969	670	(40)		70	—	860
Banco, Ivory Coast (Bernhard 1970)							
Plateau	1966/67	820	(98)		220	—	—
Plateau	1967/68	920	(122)		296	—	—
Thalweg	1966/67	790	(39)		140	—	—
Thalweg	1967/68	730	(94)		78	—	—
Yapo, Ivory Coast (Bernhard 1970)							
Plateau	1967/68	660	(132)		121	—	—
Plateau	1968/69	760	(78)		168	—	—
Thalweg	1967/68	570	(66)		188	—	—
Thalweg	1968/69	680	(41)		265	—	—
Kade, Ghana							
Secondary forest (John 1973)	—	740	(39)		97	88	970
Ipassa, Gabon							
Mature evergreen forest (Hladik 1978)	—	650	(51)		459	243	1390
Pasoh, Malaya (Soepadmo 1972, 1973, 1974)							
Mixed dipterocarps	1971	680	—		—	—	920
Mixed dipterocarps	1972	740	—		—	—	1021
Mixed dipterocarps	1973	530	(33)		124	53	740

[1] fall into 100 tubs   [2] fall into 150 tubs   [3] fall into 200 tubs

Fall of leaves, twigs, flowers, fruit, and miscellaneous trash, in grams dry weight per square meter per year, in different lowland tropical forests. Figures in parentheses are the combined fall of flowers and fruits.

et al. (this volume) do for agoutis and pacas, we estimate squirrels eat 2 g dry weight of fruit per square meter per year. Two-toed sloths may eat 1 g dry weight of fruit per square meter per year (Nagy and Montgomery, 1980). In general, it seems that arboreal vertebrates do not eat more than 20 g dry weight of fruit per square meter per year.

In Lutz catchment, pacas and agoutis eat roughly 12 g dry weight or so of fruit per square meter per year (Smythe et al., this volume), and spiny rats may account for another 2 g. It is unlikely that other animals eat so much: the terrestrial frugivores of Lutz catchment probably do not eat much over 15 g of fruit per square meter per year, although agoutis may spoil or bury much that they do not eat. The remaining fruit, perhaps as much as 80 g per square meter per year, must feed a vast and busy community of insects of which we know nothing.

Taking Smythe's figure for fruitfall, 90 g dry weight per square meter per year, and adding the consumption by arboreal frugivores, it appears that the forest of Barro Colorado Island produces over 100 g dry weight of fruit per square meter per year, or over a ton per hectare.

Trees such as *Tetragastris panamensis, Spondias mombin,* and *Trichilia tuberculata* can produce 500 g dry weight or more of fruit per square meter of crown per year (Howe, 1980; Hladik and Hladik, 1969; Leighton, personal communication), while trees such as *Ficus insipida, Dipteryx panamensis, Virola surinamensis, Scheelea zonensis,* and *Miconia argentea* produce roughly 200 g dry weight of fruit per square meter of crown per year (Morrison, 1978; W. Glanz, personal communication; Howe and Vande Kerckhove, 1981; Hladik and Hladik, 1969). These figures are much higher than one would expect from the fall of fruit into litter tubs. As in other tropical forests, most species of trees on Barro Colorado attract animals to disperse their fruit (Table 5); one cannot blame low fruitfall on the prevalence of wind-dispersed trees. It is true, however, that fruit production has so far been measured only for a few species of conspicuous importance to animals, and investigators have often chosen to study crop size in "bumper years," as in *Tetragastris* and *Trichilia,* or chosen mature individuals at the peak of production. If one includes nonreproductive trees growing up in light gaps, and trees in "off years," etc., one may find that average fruit production is much closer to recorded fruitfall. Arboreal frugivores do consume most of the fruits of many animal-dispersed trees (Howe and Vande Kerckhove, 1979; Howe, this volume). Since these frugivores probably do not account for more than 20 g dry weight of fruit per square meter of forest per year, such productive trees must not make up a large proportion of the canopy.

Although the forest makes far more fruit per year than vertebrate frugivores can eat, these frugivore populations are limited, as we shall see, by seasonal fruit shortage. This shortage is sufficiently severe that the canopy fruit bats of Barro Colorado Island, which feed mostly on figs (Morrison, 1978; Bonaccorso, 1979), time breeding as if to avoid lactating, not in the season of fig shortage, but at the season when fruit of all kinds is in shortest supply, probably because competition for figs is most intense then.

Forest Production and Nutrient Return

As we have already noticed, the forest in Lutz catchment produces roughly 7.5 tons dry weight of leaves per hectare per year, of which 6.5 tons fall to the ground as litter, and roughly a ton of fruit per hectare per year. Twigs decompose in part before they drop (Edwards, 1977), so twigfall is one-half twig production. Thus, judging from the fall of twigs in the litter, the forest of Lutz catchment produces 2.5 tons of twigs per hectare per year. The unclassifiable material, or "trash," in the litter probably includes much of the matter "consumed" by animals; the digestion of many folivorous invertebrates is inefficient, so much of the foliage they eat appears in the traps as frass (Kira, 1978).

Wood production on Barro Colorado has yet to be measured. Both the densities and the death rates of trees of different sizes on Barro Colorado (Putz and Milton, this volume) are similar to those elsewhere in the wet tropics (Leigh and Smythe, 1978), suggesting that, at least in the mature forest of Barro Colorado Island, wood production is similar to that in other tropical forests, a few tons per hectare per year.

The litter of Barro Colorado Island is particularly rich in nutrients, especially phosphorus (Table 6), implying a rather fertile soil (Grubb, 1977). Soil fertility bears little relation to leaf production; the weight of leaf litter falling per unit area of ground is very much the same in lowland tropical forests the world around, despite very great differences in the content of mineral nutrient (Table 6); leaf production seems governed largely by climate (Leigh and Smythe, 1978). In climax forest, wood production is also unrelated to soil fertility. However, fruit production does appear higher on Barro Colorado than at other, less fertile, sites (Table 7). Soil fertility can also have an enormous effect on animal activity (Janzen, 1974): forests starved of nutrients support few animals, while Barro Colorado is full of animals eating, playing, resting, squabbling, and foraging.

Table 5. Fruit dispersal in different tropical forests

Means of dispersal	Species dispersed in Barro Colorado, Panama		Species dispersed in La Selva, Costa Rica		Species dispersed in Tai, Ivory coast
	Overstory	Understory	Overstory	Understory	Overstory
Birds	28	58	42	63	7
Bats	10	10	6	5	1
Primates	7	2	8	2	4
Terrestrial mammals	4	6	9	5	2
Elephants	0	0	0	0	19
Wind	24	0	12	1	14
Mechanical (explosive)	1	6	2	3	8
Unknown	3	6	14	14	16

Numbers of species of overstory and understory woody plants on phenology censuses at Barro Colorado Island, Panama, and La Selva, Costa Rica, dispersed by different means, according to data and guesses supplied by Robin Foster, and numbers of canopy species dispersed by different agents on a transect in evergreen forest in the Tai Reserve, Ivory Coast (Alexandre, 1978).

Table 6. Amounts of different elements, and of dry matter, in kg per hectare per year, contained in total litterfall and leaf litterfall of various lowland tropical forests

Country	Site		Date		N	P	K	Ca	Mg	Dry matter	Authority
Panama	Barro Colorado	Plateau	1969/70	Total	195	15.3	47	212	26	9870	B. Haines (personal com-
				Leaves	104	7.0	29	121	17	5830	munication)
Costa Rica	La Selva		1971	Total	135	6.0	20	59	16	9150	D. W. Cole (personal com-
											munication)
Brazil	Manaus		1963	Total	106	2.3	13	18	14	7900	Klinge and Rodrigues
				Leaves	86	1.9	12	14	12	6400	(1968)
Ivory Coast	Banco	Plateau	1966/67	Total	170	8.0	28	61	51	12675	Bernhard-Reversat (1975)
				Leaves	135	6.0	20	49	40	8766	
		Thalweg	1966/67	Total	158	14.0	81	85	36	9508	
				Leaves	142	12.5	72	75	32	7888	
Ivory Coast	Yapo	Plateau	1967/68	Total	113	4.0	26	105	23	8719	Bernhard-Reversat (1975)
				Leaves	89	3.2	18	85	19	6357	
Ghana	Kade		1958	Total	199	7.3	68	206	45	10530	Nye (in Lim 1978)
Malaysia	Pasoh		1972	Total	119	3.2	37	82	21	10259	Lim (1978)
				Leaves	90	2.3	29	54	16	7405	
			1973	Total	81	2.3	26	57	16	7488	
				Leaves	59	1.6	19	37	12	5391	

Table 7. Annual fruitfall at different localities (g dry weight per sq. m)

Country	Site	Date	Total trap area (sq. m)	Fruitfall	Authority
Panama	Barro·Colorado Island (Allee catchment)	1967	170	90	Smythe et al. (this volume)
Ivory Coast	Banco (Plateau and thalweg)	1966/67	80	69*	Bernhard (1970)
Ivory Coast	Banco (Plateau and thalweg)	1967/68	80	108*	Bernhard (1970)
Gabon	Ipassa	1972/73	40	51*	A. Hladik (personal communication)
Malaysia	Pasoh Reserve	1972	50	35*	Lim (1978)
Malaysia	Pasoh Reserve	1973	50	34*	Lim (1978)

* Includes flowers

ACKNOWLEDGMENTS

We are grateful to the Environmental Sciences Program of the Smithsonian Institution for its financial support, and to Gerald Chen, Bonifacio de Leon, and Gary Stump for their help in collecting the data.

LITERATURE CITED

Alexandre, D. Y.
1978.   La role disséminateur des éléphants en forêt de Tai, Cote d'Ivoire. *La Terre et la Vie,* 32:47–62.

Bernhard, F.
1970.   Etude de la litière et de sa contribution au cycle des éléments mineraux en forêt ombrophile de Cote d'Ivoire. *Oecologia Plantarum,* 5:247–266.

Bernhard-Reversat, F.
1975.   Recherches sur l'écosystème de la forêt subéquatoriale de basse Cote-d'Ivoire IV. Les cycles des macroéléments. *La Terre et La Vie,* 29:229–254.

Bonaccorso, F. J.
1979.   Foraging and Reproductive Ecology in a Panamanian Bat Community. *Bulletin of the Florida State Museum, Biological Sciences,* 24:359–408.

Burghardt, G. M., H. W. Greene, and A. S. Rand
1977.   Social Behavior in Hatchling Green Iguanas: Life at a Reptile Rookery. *Science,* 195:689–691.

Coley, P. D.
1982.   Rates of Herbivory on Different Tropical Trees. Pages 123–132 in *The Ecology of a Tropical Forest,* edited by Egbert G. Leigh, Jr., et al. Washington, D.C.: Smithsonian Institution Press.

Dietrich, W. E., D. M. Windsor, and T. Dunne
1982.   Geology, Climate, and Hydrology of Barro Colorado Island. Pages 21–46 in *The Ecology of a Tropical Forest,* edited by Egbert G. Leigh, Jr., et al. Washington, D.C.: Smithsonian Institution Press.

Edwards, P. J.
1977.   Studies of Mineral Cycling in a Montane Rain Forest in New Guinea. II. The Production and Disappearance of Litter. *Journal of Ecology,* 65:971–992.

Fogden, M. P. L.
1970.   Some Aspects of the Ecology of Bird Populations in Sarawak. D. Phil. thesis. Edward Grey Institute of Field Ornithology, Oxford.
1972.   The Seasonality and Population of Equatorial Forest Birds in Sarawak. *Ibis,* 114:307–342.

Foster, R. B.
1982.   The Seasonal Rhythm in Fruitfall on Barro Colorado Island. Pages 151-172 in *The Ecology of a Tropical Forest,* edited by Egbert G. Leigh, Jr., et al. Washington, D.C.: Smithsonian Institution Press.

Frankie, G. W., H. G. Baker, and P. A. Opler
1974.   Comparative Phenological Studies of Trees in Tropical Wet and Dry Forest in the Lowlands of Costa Rica. *Journal of Ecology,* 62:881–919.

Grubb, P. J.
1977.   Control of Forest Growth and Distribution on Wet Tropical Mountains, with Special Reference to Mineral Nutrition. *Annual Review of Ecology and Systematics,* 8:83–107.

Haines, B. L.
1978.   Element and Energy Flows Through Colonies of the Leaf-cutting Ant, *Atta colombica,* in Panama. *Biotropica,* 10:270–277.

Healey, I. N., and M. J. Swift
1977.   A One-year Study of Litter Decomposition in the Barro Colorado Island Forest. Abstract, IV International Symposium on Tropical Ecology, Panama.

Hladik, A.
1978.   Phenology of Leaf Production in Rain Forest of Gabon: Distribution and Composition of Food for Folivores. Pages 51–71 in *The Ecology of Arboreal Folivores,* edited by G. G. Montgomery. Washington, D.C.: Smithsonian Institution Press.

Hladik, A., and C. M. Hladik
1969.   Rapports trophiques entre végétation et primates dans la foret de Barro Colorado (Panama). *La Terre et la Vie,* 26:149–215.

Holmes, R. T., J. C. Schultz, and P. Nothnagle
1979.   Bird Predation on Forest Insects: An Exclosure Experiment. *Science,* 206:462–463.

Holmes, R. T., and F. W. Sturges
1975.   Bird Community Dynamics and Energetics in a Northern Hardwoods Ecosystem. *Journal of Animal Ecology*, 44:175–200.

Howe, H. F.
1980.   Monkey Dispersal and Waste of a Neotropical Fruit. *Ecology*, 61:944–959.
1982.   Fruit Production and Animal Activity in Two Tropical Trees. Pages 189-199 in *The Ecology of a Tropical Forest*, edited by Egbert G. Leigh, Jr., et al. Washington, D.C.: Smithsonian Institution Press.

Howe, H. F., and G. A. Vande Kerckhove
1979.   Fecundity and Seed Dispersal of a Tropical Tree. *Ecology*, 60:180–189.
1981.   Removal of Wild Nutmeg (*Virola surinamensis*) crops by Birds. *Ecology*, 62:1093–1106.

Janzen, D. H.
1974.   Tropical Blackwater Rivers, Animals, and Mast Fruiting in the Dipterocarpaceae. *Biotropica*, 6:69–103.

John, D. M.
1973.   Accumulation and Decay of Litter and Net Production of Forest in Tropical West Africa. *Oikos*, 24:430–435.

Karr, J. R.
1971.   Structure of Avian Communities in Selected Panama and Illinois Habitats. *Ecological Monographs*, 41:207–233.
1976.   Within and Between-habitat Avian Diversity in African and Neotropical Lowland Habitats. *Ecological Monographs*, 46:457–481.

Kira, T.
1978.   Community Architecture and Organic Matter Dynamics in Tropical Lowland Rain Forests of Southeast Asia with Special Reference to Pasoh Forest, West Malaysia. Pages 561–590 in *Tropical Trees as Living Systems*, edited by P. B. Tomlinson and M. H. Zimmermann. Cambridge: Cambridge University Press.

Klinge, H.
1974.   Litter Production on Tropical Ecosystem. IBP Synthesis Meeting, Kuala Lumpur, 12–18 August. Mimeographed report.
1975.   Fine Litter Production and Nutrient Return to the Soil in Three Forest Stands of Eastern Amazonia. Abstract, III Congress of Tropical Ecology, Kinshasa, Zaire, April.

Klinge, H., and W. Rodrigues
1968.   Litter Production in an Area of Amazonian Terra Firme Forest. II. Mineral Nutrient Content of the Litter. *Amazoniana*, 1:303–310.

Leigh, E. G., Jr.
1975.   Structure and Climate in Tropical Rain Forest. *Annual Review of Ecology and Systematics*, 6:67–86.

Leigh, E. G., Jr., and N. Smythe
1978.   Leaf Production, Leaf Consumption, and the Regulation of Folivory on Barro Colorado Island. Pages 33–50 in *The Ecology of Arboreal Folivores*, edited by G. G. Montgomery. Washington, D.C.: Smithsonian Institution Press.

Lim, M. T.
1978.   Litterfall and Mineral Nutrient Content of Litter in Pasoh Forest Reserve. *Malayan Nature Journal*, 30:375–380.

Lugo, A. E., E. G. Farnworth, D. Pool, P. Jerez, and G. Kaufman
1973.   The Impact of the Leafcutter Ant *Atta colombica* on the Energy Flow of a Tropical Wet Forest. *Ecology*, 54:1292–1301.

Medway, Lord
1972.   Phenology of a Tropical Rain Forest in Malaya. *Biological Journal of the Linnean Society*, 4:117–146.

Milton, K.
1979.   Factors Influencing Leaf Choice by Howler Monkeys: A Test of Some Hypotheses of Food Selection by Generalist Herbivores. *American Naturalist*, 114:362–378.
1982.   Dietary Quality and Demographic Regulation in a Howler Monkey Population. Pages 273-289 in *The Ecology of a Tropical Forest*, edited by Egbert G. Leigh, et al. Washington, D.C.: Smithsonian Institution Press.

Montgomery, G. G., and M. E. Sunquist
1975.   Impact of Sloths on Neotropical Forest Energy Flow and Nutrient Cycling. Pages 69–98 in *Tropical Ecological Systems*, edited by F. B. Golley and E. Medina. New York: Springer-Verlag.
1978.   Habitat Selection and Use by Two-toed and Three-toed Sloths. Pages 329–359 in *The Ecology of Arboreal Folivores*, edited by G. G. Montgomery. Washington, D.C.: Smithsonian Institution Press.

Morrison, D. W.
1978.   Foraging Ecology and Energetics of the Frugivorous Bat *Artibeus jamaicensis*. *Ecology*, 59:716–723.
1980.   Foraging and Day-roosting Dynamics of Canopy Fruit Bats in Panama. *Journal of Mammalogy*, 61:20–29.

Nagy, K. A., and K. Milton
1979.   Energy Metabolism and Food Consumption by Wild Howler Monkeys (*Aloutta palliata*). *Ecology*, 60:475–480.

Nagy, K. A., and G. G. Montgomery
1980.   Field Metabolic Rate, Water Flux and Food Consumption in Three-toed Sloths (*Bradypus variegatus*). *Journal of Mammalogy*, 61:465–472.

Ng, F. S. P.
1974.   The Life of Leaves in a Humid Tropic Environment with Special Reference to Malaysian Trees. IBP Synthesis Meeting, Kuala Lumpur, 12–18 August. Mimeographed Report.

Putz, F. E., and K. Milton
1982.   Tree Mortality Rates on Barro Colorado Island. Pages 95–100 *The Ecology of a Tropical Forest*, edited by Egbert G. Leigh, Jr., et al. Washington, D.C.: Smithsonian Institution Press.

Smythe, N.
1970a.   Ecology and Behavior of the Agouti (*Dasyprocta punctata*) and Related Species on Barro Colorado Island, Panama. Ph.D. thesis, University of Maryland, College Park.
1970b.   Relation Between Fruiting Seasons and Seed Dispersal in A Neotropical Forest. *American Naturalist*, 104:25–35.

Smythe, N., W. E. Glanz, and E. G. Leigh, Jr.
1982.   Population Regulation in Some Terrestrial Frugi-
        vores. Pages 227–238 in *The Ecology of a Tropical Forest,*
        edited by Egbert G. Leigh, Jr., et al. Washington, D.C.:
        Smithsonian Institution Press.

Soepadmo, E.
1972.   Report on the Malaysian International Biological Pro-
        gramme, 1970/71. Mimeographed.
1973.   Annual Report on the Malaysian International Bio-
        logical Programme, 1972. Mimeographed.
1974.   Annual Report on the Malaysian International Bio-
        logical Programme, 1973. Mimeographed.

Whitmore, T. C.
1975.   *Tropical Rain Forests of the Far East.* Oxford: Oxford
        University Press.

Willis, E. O.
1980.   Ecological Roles of Migratory and Resident Birds on
        Barro Colorado Island, Panama. Pages 205–225 in
        Migrant Birds in the Neotropics, edited by A. Keast and
        E. S. Morton. Washington, D.C.: Smithsonian Insti-
        tution Press.

Windsor, D. M.
1978.   The Feeding Activities of Tropical Insect Herbivores
        on Some Deciduous Forest Legumes. Pages 101–113
        in *The Ecology of Arboreal Folivores,* edited by G. G.
        Montgomery. Washington, D.C.: Smithsonian Insti-
        tution Press.

Wolda, H.
1978.   Seasonal Fluctuations in Rainfall, Food and Abun-
        dance of Tropical Insects. *Journal of Animal Ecology,*
        47:369–381.

Wolda, H., and R. Foster.
1978.   *Zunacetha annulata* (Lepidoptera, Dioptidae), An Out-
        break Insect in a Neotropical Forest. *Geo-Eco-Trop,*
        1:443–454.

Rates of Herbivory on Different Tropical Trees

PHYLLIS D. COLEY   Committee on Evolutionary Biology, University of Chicago, Chicago, Illinois 60637

ABSTRACT

Rates of herbivory on marked young and mature leaves from saplings of 21 canopy tree species were measured in the wet and dry seasons. Species were classified into two life history groups: persistent species which are found throughout the shaded understory, and pioneer species which only become established in light gaps created by fallen trees. Mature leaves of slow-growing persistent species were eaten by insects at an average annual rate of 21%, whereas rapidly growing pioneer species were grazed 4 times faster in the dry season and 10 times faster in the wet. In general, young leaves suffered higher rates of damage than mature leaves, with rates being an order of magnitude higher for persistent species. The higher variance between plants and low variance between leaves on the same plant in grazing damage for young persistent leaves suggests that their synchronous emergence at the beginning of the rains might satiate herbivores. There is no evidence that the patchy occurrence of pioneer plants only in light gaps leads to spatial escape from herbivores.

INTRODUCTION

How does grazing damage differ from season to season and from one species of tree to another? How much more rapidly are young leaves eaten than old ones? Are leaves of colonizing species eaten more than those of mature forest trees? This information will help us understand how different trees cope with herbivory and will shed light on the seasonal rhythms in the abundance and behavior of herbivores.

METHODS

The Data

I selected saplings of 21 species of canopy trees in order to measure rates of leaf consumption: 8 species of pioneers, which are fast-growing and shade-intolerant, and whose saplings only occur in sunny openings, and 13 species of persistents, which can germinate in the shade and either grow or persist suppressed in the understory until a gap opens in the canopy above (Foster and Brokaw, this volume). I selected these species according to their abundance as adults in the forest canopy on Barro Colorado and as saplings in clearings opened there by the fall of canopy trees.

I selected plants between 0.5 and 2 m tall, whose leaves were within reach, in treefall gaps less than three years old. Such light gaps are important centers of forest regeneration (Aubreville, 1971; Bray, 1956; Hartshorn, 1978; Jones, 1945; Schulz, 1960; Brokaw, this volume). I marked one set of 206 plants in the wet season, May and June of 1977, and another set of 143 plants in the dry season, February and March of 1979. I tagged an average of eight leaves per plant, including some leaves just emerging from the bud and a few of the mature leaves. I measured the total area of each tagged leaf and the total area of holes and damaged surfaces by placing a clear plastic grid (400 squares per square inch) over the leaf and counting the squares over the relevant areas. I measured damaged areas and total leaf area when tagging the leaves and again at a later time, 25 days later in the dry season, and every 14 days for up to three months in the rainy season.

The majority of the damaged areas I considered were caused by leaf consumption by insects. These were either holes, mines, galls, or scraped surfaces. However, I also included necrotic areas which may have been caused by microbial or fungal infection or by tissue death resulting from grazing. Herbivores chewed some leaves off at the petiole even though portions of the leaf blade remained, and the plants dropped other leaves, presumably because they were excessively damaged. There were a few cases of mammal grazing, easily distinguished by teeth marks: these were excluded from the analysis.

The Analysis

For each leaf, I calculated consumption rate as the percentage of area eaten per day, that is, the change during the sampling period in the percentage of the leaf's area devoted to holes, divided by the number of days of observation. Holes of known area punched in 105 young leaves grew with the leaves, so that the proportion of leaf area taken up by the holes did not change significantly as the leaves expanded ($r^2 = 0.88$). Expressing consumption as a rate and not as a single measure of standing crop also corrects for differences in leaf lifetimes.

Grazing damage is clumped, varying from leaf to leaf on the same plant and from plant to plant in the same species. I measured the first by the variance in the rate of damage to different tagged leaves on the same plant, averaged for the species. I measured the second by an intraclass correlation coefficient, r_I, which estimates the proportion of the total variance in leaf damage attributable to differences in the average damage per plant, where the damage x_{ij} to leaf j on plant i is now measured as ln (1000 times percent damage per day, plus 1). Assuming N leaves in all, distributed over c plants, where plant i has n_i leaves,

$$r_I = \frac{\frac{1}{c-1}\sum_i n_i(\bar{x}_i - \bar{x})^2 - \frac{1}{N-c}\sum_{ij}(x_{ij} - \bar{x}_i)^2}{\frac{1}{c-1}\sum_i n_i(\bar{x}_i - \bar{x})^2 + \frac{1}{c}\sum_{ij}(x_{ij} - \bar{x}_i)^2}$$

where $\bar{x}_i$ is the average damage per leaf on plant i, and $\bar{x}$ is the average damage per leaf for the species as a whole (Snedecor and Cochran, 1967). The interpretation of r_I as the proportion of the variance due to differences between plants assumes that "errors" about the means of different plants are drawn from the same distribution. In the 21 instances where each marked plant had at least two tagged leaves, at least one of which was damaged, I checked this assumption with Bartlett's test for homogeneity of variance (Snedecor and Cochran, 1967).

RESULTS AND DISCUSSION

Leaf Age and Herbivory

Young leaves of both pioneer and persistent species are eaten significantly more than mature leaves (Tables

1 and 2). For persistents this represents a tenfold difference in consumption rates.

Both vertebrate and invertebrate herbivores usually prefer young leaves (Reichle et al., 1973; Kennedy and Booth, 1951; Milton, 1979; Rockwood and Glander, 1979; Feeny, 1970), though there are some exceptions (Claridge and Wilson, 1978; Rhoades, 1977a,b). The higher nitrogen and water contents of young leaves (Dixon, 1970; Milton, 1979; Oelberg, 1956) can increase growth rates of insects (House, 1967; Reese and Beck, 1978; Scriber, 1977; Slansky and Feeny, 1977) and may be one reason for this preference. Some herbivores may prefer young leaves because they are less tough (Grime et al., 1968; Feeny, 1970; Tanton, 1962) and less fibrous (Milton, 1979). Feeny (1976) and Rhoades and Cates (1976) have suggested that young leaves contain lower concentrations of compounds such as tannins which bind with proteins and inhibit digestion, but in three-quarters of the species I studied, tannin concentrations were higher in young leaves (Coley, 1981). Similar results were found for desert shrubs (Rhoades, 1977a,b) and for tropical trees (Milton, 1979). Increased grazing rates on young leaves do not mean that phenolic secondary

Table 1. Wet- and dry-season grazing on young and mature leaves of pioneer and persistent tree species *(continued on next page)*

| | Persistent species | | | | | |
	Simarouba amara	Prioria copaifera	Virola sebifera	Tetragastris panamensis	Trichilia cipo	Poulsenia armata
Wet-season grazing						
Mature leaves:						
Mean (%/day)	0.003	0.002	0.002	0.005	0.003	0.004
Standard deviation	0.010	0.004	0.004	0.013	0.008	0.005
Number of leaves	46	20	31	27	50	25
Coefficients (r_I)	0.32	0.52	0.28	−0.05	−0.01	−0.14
Young leaves:						
Mean (%/day)	0.026	0.014	0.108	1.454	0.522	0.027
Standard deviation	0.066	0.029	0.294	2.435	1.609	0.091
Number of leaves	30	19	24	30	63	33
Coefficients (r_I)	0.18	−0.08 +	0.82	0.52	0.01	−0.05
Dry-season grazing						
Mature leaves:						
Mean (%/day)	0.000	0.003	0.003	0.001	0.008	0.007
Standard deviation	0.002	0.015	0.006	0.004	0.064	0.028
Number of leaves	39	30	23	25	131	23
Coefficients (r_I)	−0.04	−0.14	−0.13	−0.01	0.10	−0.02
Young leaves:						
Mean %/day)	1.567	0.581	0.416	0.881	0.606	0.000
Standard deviation	2.352	1.101	1.152	1.617	1.079	—
Number of leaves	32	10	12	34	76	1
Coefficients (r_I)	0.94	0.90	0.60	0.58*	0.92	—
Annual grazing						
Mature leaves (%)	1	1	1	1	2	2

Grazing rates are the percent leaf area eaten per day. An (*) indicates intraclass correlation coefficients (r_I) with inhomogeneous variances ($p<0.05$, Bartlett's test), a (+) indicates no significant difference, and cases where it was not possible to test are unmarked. Species are ranked by annual grazing rates which were extrapolations based on an 8-month wet season. Plant names follow Croat (1978).

Table 1. (continued)

	Persistent species						
	Tachigalia versicolor	Protium tenuifolium	Hirtella triandra	Zanthoxylum panamense	Quararibea asterolepis	Cupania sylvatica	Alseis blackiana
Wet-season grazing							
Mature leaves:							
Mean (%/day)	0.005	0.008	0.042	0.136	0.114	0.311	0.136
Standard deviation	0.014	0.026	0.111	0.632	0.234	1.029	0.480
Number of leaves	36	32	19	49	6	23	15
Coefficients (r_I)	0.23	0.23	0.04	-0.11	$0.25+$	0.07	0.68
Young leaves:							
Mean (%/day)	0.775	0.928	0.120	0.701	0.316	1.151	0.096
Standard deviation	1.913	2.045	0.201	1.895	0.464	2.588	0.152
Number of leaves	51	54	21	46	16	20	32
Coefficients (r_I)	0.50	0.40	0.60*	0.01	$0.72+$	$0.36+$	$0.33+$
Dry-season grazing							
Mature leaves:							
Mean (%/day)	0.010	0.028	0.019	0.008	0.124	0.026	0.496
Standard deviation	0.019	0.136	0.047	0.026	0.641	0.173	1.327
Number of leaves	35	31	25	42	33	54	27
Coefficients (r_I)	0.13	0.59	-0.01	0.10	0.33	$-0.03*$	$0.13+$
Young leaves:							
Mean (%/day)	0.667	1.078	1.278	1.009	0.730	1.786	0.227
Standard deviation	1.332	1.894	2.298	2.048	1.413	2.465	0.634
Number of leaves	66	16	8	20	17	8	11
Coefficients (r_I)	0.52*	0.65	$0.37+$	0.92	—	1.00	$-0.15+$
Annual grazing							
Mature leaves (%)	2	5	13	34	43	79	93

compounds are ineffective as grazing deterrents, but simply that they are not sufficient to counter the desirable attributes of young leaves.

The amount of damage tends to vary more among young leaves of a pioneer individual than among its old leaves (Table 3). This implies that young leaves may be less frequently discovered by herbivores, but that when they are, they are eaten more. Leaves are young for only a short period during which they undergo many physical and chemical changes. The time when a herbivore discovers a particular leaf may therefore be critical, because if the leaf is found to be at a palatable stage, it is heavily eaten. The variability between individual pioneer plants (r_I), however, is not significantly greater for young leaves than for old (Table 3). Young pioneer leaves appear to emerge continuously throughout the year, and there are generally a few young leaves of staggered ages on each plant. As a class, young leaves should therefore be as obvious to herbivores as mature leaves.

As with pioneer species, grazing rates on persistents varied more from one young leaf to another than from one mature leaf to another (Table 3). Young leaves are young only briefly, yet they suffer rates of damage an order of magnitude greater than those on mature leaves. Their high palatability and their speed of maturation would both contribute to a high variance in grazing on young leaves. Unlike pioneer spe-

	Pioneer species							
	Zanthoxylum belizense	Miconia argentea	Alchornea costaricensis	Spondias radlkoferi	Luehea seemannii	Cecropia insignis	Trema micrantha	Cecropia obtusifolia
Wet-season grazing								
Mature leaves:								
Mean (%/day)	0.081	0.189	0.210	0.186	0.456	0.783	1.071	2.267
Standard deviation	0.340	0.354	0.646	0.747	1.255	1.522	1.334	2.584
Number of leaves	24	30	42	88	31	78	30	12
Coefficients (r_l)	−0.06	0.58	0.24+	0.07*	−0.03	0.02	0.17	0.85
Young leaves:								
Mean (%/day)	0.624	0.509	0.818	1.492	1.108	0.111	0.053	1.299
Standard deviation	1.787	1.302	1.760	2.810	1.543	0.466	0.165	1.861
Number of leaves	36	34	44	69	36	68	40	19
Coefficients (r_l)	0.18	0.49	0.15	0.24*	0.22*	0.18	0.14	0.16*
Dry-season grazing								
Mature leaves:								
Mean (%/day)	0.006	0.058	0.026	0.193	0.062	0.019	0.147	1.383
Standard deviation	0.011	0.058	0.055	0.805	0.100	0.061	0.446	1.801
Number of leaves	31	18	14	25	20	41	25	9
Coefficients (r_l)	0.19	−0.02+	0.79	0.16	−0.16+	0.34	0.07	0.74
Young leaves:								
Mean (%/day)	0.038	0.241	2.887	1.687	0.095	0.034	0.330	0.217
Standard deviation	0.129	0.331	2.652	1.801	0.164	0.089	1.187	0.430
Number of leaves	29	14	2	26	3	18	16	13
Coefficients (r_l)	0.59	0.62+	—	0.72	−0.80	−0.22	0.44	0.11+
Annual grazing								
Mature leaves (%)	20	53	54	69	119	193	279	721

cies, persistents have a significantly higher variance between plants for grazing on young leaves (Table 3). All individuals of a persistent species flush young leaves synchronously at the beginning of the rains, perhaps satiating herbivores both locally around individual plants and in the forest at large (Janzen, 1971, 1974; Lloyd and Dybas, 1966; McKey, 1974). The high variation among plants also suggests that grazing damage may be due to specialists, which depend on the chance of finding foliage of a particular species or group of species, or to sedentary generalists (which would cause severe damage on some plants and not on others), rather than mobile generalists (which cannot eat too much of one kind of foliage without risking overdose of some secondary compound).

Plant Life History and Herbivory

Mature leaves of pioneer species are eaten 3–10 times more rapidly than mature leaves of persistent species (Tables 1 and 2). Pioneer species have significantly higher between-leaf variances in damage rates, but the distribution of damage between plants is equally clumped for pioneers and persistents (Table 3).

The lower rates of leaf consumption and the more even rates of damage on mature leaves of persistent species as compared with pioneers (Tables 2 and 3) may reflect features of their growth and dispersal.

Table 2. Grazing rates in relation to season, leaf ages, and life history patterns (% leaf area eaten/day)

Leaf group	Wet season				Dry season				Annual rates[2]
	Mean[1]	Std. error	No. of plants	No. of leaves	Mean[1]	Std. error	No. of plants	No. of leaves	
Young pioneer	0.731 a	0.187	91	346	0.521 d	0.368	51	183	
Mature pioneer	0.499 ab	0.167	88	335	0.135 de	0.167	44	121	190.4%
Young persistent	0.539 c	0.134	102	439	0.829 f	0.142	46	311	
Mature persistent	0.048 abc	0.026	105	379	0.043 def	0.038	84	518	21.3%

[1] Values followed by the same letter are significantly different, $p < 0.05$ for d and $p < 0.01$ for a, b, c, e, and f. Significance levels were determined by a 2-way nested analysis of variance considering leaves as replicates on a transformation of the data: ln $(1000 \times$ rate $+ 1)$.
[2] Annual rates are the average of the mean rates for each species presented in Table 1.

Table 3. Variability in grazing rates as measured by the variance in damage between plants and between leaves on the same plant

Leaf group	Leaf variance[1]		Plant variance (r_1)[2]	
	Wet	Dry	Wet	Dry
1. Young pioneer	6.43	5.53	0.180	0.207
2. Mature pioneer	5.21	2.62	0.230	0.264
3. Young persistent	3.98	3.40	0.366	0.624
4. Mature persistent	1.97	1.78	0.179	0.077
Contrasts[3]				
1 vs. 2	nsd	+	nsd	nsd
3 vs. 4	+ +	+ +	+	+ + +
1 vs. 3	+	nsd	nsd	nsd
2 vs. 4	+ + +	nsd	nsd	nsd

[1] Leaf variances are the between leaf variance in grazing rate for each plant averaged for each species and then for each of the four leaf groups. Calculations were on the transformed data: ln $(1000 \times$ rate $+ 1)$.
[2] Plant variances are the averages of the intraclass correlation coefficients computed for each species and presented in Table 1.
[3] Contrasts are between leaf groups within seasons. A Mann-Whitney U test was used for contrasting 1 vs. 3 and 2 vs. 4, and a paired sign test for contrasting 1 vs. 2 and 3 vs. 4, $+$ $p < 0.05$, $+ +$ $p < 0.025$ and $+ + +$ $p < 0.005$ (Siegal 1956).

Table 4. Seasonal abundance of young leaves on saplings of 8 pioneer and 13 persistent species

	Number of plants		Percentage of plants	
	Dry	Wet	Dry	Wet
Pioneer species				
Old leaves	117	8	32	1
New leaves	250	813	68	99
Persistent species				
Old leaves	339	297	71	33
New leaves	135	601	29	67
Total				
Old leaves	456	305	54	18
New leaves	385	1414	46	82

Values are the number and percentages of plants with mature and young leaves (New) and those with only mature leaves (Old). (All chi-square tests comparing seasonal distribution of new leaves are significant, $p < 0.005$).

Persistent species are dispersed throughout the understory and may therefore be easily found by herbivores. They grow slowly and perhaps cannot afford to replace leaves very often, so it is important for them to defend their leaves effectively against herbivores. In my study, persistent species did have higher concentrations of phenolic compounds in the leaves than did pioneers (Coley, 1981). In contrast, pioneer species rely on germination in newly formed light gaps followed by fast growth in order to reach the canopy. They appear to channel their energy into rapid growth rather than expensive defenses. Since pioneer saplings occur only in light gaps, their distribution in the forest is more clumped than saplings of persistent species.

The higher rates of leaf damage sustained by mature leaves of pioneers (Tables 1 and 2) agrees with the prediction that, because they are short lived and fast growing, they need less defense from herbivores than persistents. Damage varies from one mature leaf to another in pioneers (Table 3) as if these leaves were primarily eaten by specialist herbivores which, once on a leaf, stay and devour large portions of it, unembarrassed by the secondary compounds it contains. In contrast, the low variance between mature leaves of persistents (Table 3) suggests damage by more mobile generalist herbivores which feed for one time and then leave the leaf, perhaps to avoid risking an overdose of some secondary compound. This is in accord with extrapolations from current theories of interactions between plants and herbivores (Feeny, 1976; Rhoades and Cates, 1976). These theories also predict that pioneers are less "apparent" to herbivores, primarily escaping discovery because they occur in clumps, only in gaps. This does not seem to be true, since the r_I estimate of the proportion of variability attributed to between plant differences is not significantly different between pioneer and persistents (Table 3).

Young leaves of pioneers and persistents are eaten at the same relatively high rates (Tables 1 and 2), but the distribution of damage among leaves and among plants differs. Pioneers have a high variance between leaves on the same plant (Table 3). This may be because the average time a given leaf remains young is shorter for pioneers (38 days) than for persistents (56 days), and because there are several young leaves of staggered ages on pioneer plants at one time. Only some of these young leaves, however, will be an appropriate food resource for a herbivore. Since persistent plants produce a flush of young leaves all of the same age, they are equally palatable and have the same chance of being eaten. This would also cause the major source of variation to be between plants and not between leaves on the same plant. A higher intraclass correlation coefficient for young persistent leaves, though not quite significant, supports this (Table 3).

Seasonal Variation: Grazing on Mature Leaves

Grazing on mature leaves is greater in the wet season for just over half of the species studied (Table 1). Averaging over all species, grazing on mature leaves is 2.3 times higher in the wet season with the differences being most marked for pioneers ($p < 0.025$, paired t-test for species averages of herbivory on mature leaves). Insect abundance and activity are probably the main factors responsible for the elevated levels of herbivory in the early wet season (Smythe, this volume; Wolda, 1978).

Seasonal Variation: Grazing on Young Leaves

Almost twice as many plants in the light gaps I studied had young leaves in the wet season as in the dry season (Table 4). For both pioneer and persistent species these differences in the seasonal distribution of young leaves was significant (chi-square, $p < 0.005$). The differences for persistent species are more dramatic, with most plants waiting until the rains to put out a flush of new leaves. A similar rhythm of leaf production is found in canopy trees on Barro Colorado Island (Leigh and Smythe, 1978).

The amount and distribution of grazing damage on young pioneer leaves shows little seasonal variation (Table 2 and 3). Though there are fewer plants with young leaves in the dry season (Table 4), the difference is not as dramatic as with persistents, and the reduction in the number of young leaves may be balanced by the reduction in herbivores (Smythe, this volume; Wolda, 1978).

Patterns of grazing on young persistent leaves are quite different than on the other leaf groups. They are the only group that has higher rates of herbivore damage (Table 2) in the dry season and fewer leaves with no damage. The variability between leaves on a plant does not change seasonally, but the variability between plants is slightly higher in the dry season. The seasonal distribution of young persistent leaves (Table 4) may have a strong influence on the vulnerability of those leaves to herbivores. The synchronous emergence of young leaves at the beginning of the rains is probably effective in satiating herbivores and causes the lower rates of damage. Clumping of damage among plants (r_I, Table 3) is higher in the dry season, perhaps because of reduced movements of herbivores and increased grazing pressure on the young leaves that are present.

Annual Rates of Herbivory

I obtained estimates of the annual loss of leaf area by extrapolating from the grazing rates on mature leaves measured in this study (Tables 1 and 2). I averaged rates of leaf consumption for all my study species, but because species were not sampled in proportion to their abundance, this may not provide an accurate measure of herbivory in the forest as a whole. Herbivore pressure may also be quite different in the canopy. The annual rates would be higher if damage to young leaves were included, but I cannot measure this damage because I do not know how long leaves of different species remain young. Because these data were collected in order to determine loss of functional leaf area to the plant, they include necrotic areas and are not necessarily the amount of leaf area passing to herbivores.

The annual rate of leaf loss for mature leaves of persistent species is 21% of the leaf area (Table 2). This is high, but within the range of estimates for other forests: 20–60% for eucalyptus forests (Burden and Chilvers, 1974; Fox and Macauley, 1977; Misra, 1968; Springett, 1978), 5–10% for temperate forests (Bray, 1964, Fünke, 1973; Kaczmarek, 1967; Nielsen, 1978; Reichle and Crossley, 1967; Reichle et al., 1973; Woodwell and Whittaker, 1968) and 7–9% for tropical forests (Leigh and Smythe, 1978; Odum and Ruiz-Reyes, 1970). The average annual rate for mature leaves from pioneers is 190%. This estimate seems large, but fits with the observation that many pioneer saplings keep an individual leaf for only a few months. Leaf life on adult trees may be much longer.

There are several possible reasons why I found higher annual rates of herbivory than other researchers. They judged grazing from holes in either fallen leaves or in live leaves at the end of the growing season. I included necrotic areas in damage estimates which might not be noticeable on a dried fallen leaf. In addition, these measures of standing crop ignore leaves that were totally eaten, had been chewed off at the petiole, or had been dropped due to excessive blade damage. These forms of damage contribute significantly to a plant's loss of leaves. Of the 1353 mature leaves that were marked and measured in this study, 36 or 2.7% were completely eaten. This small percentage of wholly eaten leaves contributes substantially to the average grazing rates. Removing these leaves from the analysis, the annual rate becomes 13.2% for persistents and 116.3% for pioneers. The contributions of wholly eaten leaves to the annual rate of leaf loss is approximately 38%. Previous studies of herbivory may therefore considerably underestimate both the amount of damaged leaf area and the amount of tissue passing to herbivores.

LITERATURE CITED

Aubreville, A.
1971. Regeneration Patterns in the Closed Forest of Ivory Coast. Pages 41–55 in *World Vegetation Types*, edited by S. R. Eyre. New York: Columbia University Press.

Bray, J. R.
1956. Gap Phase Replacement in a Maple-Basswood Forest. *Ecology*, 37:598–600.
1964. Primary Consumption in Three Forest Canopies. *Ecology*, 45:165–167.

Brokaw, N. V. L.
1982. Treefalls: Frequency, Timing, and Consequences. Pages 101-108 in *The Ecology of a Tropical Forest*, edited by Egbert G. Leigh, Jr., et al. Washington, D.C.: Smithsonian Institution Press.

Burden, J. J., and G. A. Chilvers
1974. Leaf Parasites on Altitudinal Populations of *Eucalyptus pauciflora*. *Australian Journal of Botany*, 22:265–269.

Claridge, M. F., and M. R. Wilson
1978. Seasonal Changes and Alternation of Food Plant Preference in Some Mesophyll-feeding Leafhoppers. *Oecology*, 37:247–255.

Coley, P. D.
1981. Ecological and Evolutionary Responses of Tropical Trees to Herbivory: A Quantitative Analysis of Grazing Damage, Plant Defenses, and Growth Rates. Ph.D. thesis, University of Chicago, 151 pp.

Croat, T. B.
1978. *Flora of Barro Colorado Island*. Stanford, Calif.: Stanford University Press. 943 pp.

Dixon, A. F. G.
1970. Quality and Availability of Food for a Sycamore Aphid Population. Pages 271–87 in *Animal Populations in Relation to their Food Resources*, edited by A. Watson. British Ecological Society Symposium, No. 10.

Feeny, P. P.
1970. Seasonal Changes in Oak Leaf Tannins and Nutrients as a Cause of Spring Feeding by Winter Moth Caterpillars. *Ecology*, 51:565–581.
1976. Plant Apparency and Chemical Defense. Pages 1–40 in *Biochemical Interactions Between Plants and Insects*, vol. 10, edited by J. Wallace and R. Mansell. New York: Plenum.

Foster, R. B., and N. V. L. Brokaw
1982. Structure and History of the Vegetation of Barro Colorado Island. Pages 67–81 in *The Ecology of a Tropical Forest*, edited by Egbert G. Leigh, Jr., et al. Washington, D.C.: Smithsonian Institution Press.

Fox, L. R., and B. S. Macauley
1977. Insect Grazing on *Eucalyptus* in Response to Variation in Leaf Tannins and Nitrogen. *Oecologia*, 29:145–162.

Fünke, W.
1973. Rolle der Tiere in Wald-Ekosystemen des solling. Pages 143–64 in *Okosystemforschung*, edited by H. Ellenberg. Berlin: Springer.

Grime, J. P., S. F. MacPherson-Stewart, and R. S. Dearman
1968. An Investigation of Leaf Palatability using the Snail *Cepea nemoralis*. *Journal of Ecology*, 56:405–420.

Hartshorn, G. S.
1978.   Tree Falls and Tropical Forest Dynamics. Pages 617–638 in *Tropical Trees as Living Systems*, edited by P. B. Tomlinson and M. H. Zimmerman. Cambridge: Cambridge University Press.

House, H. L.
1967.   The Role of Nutritional Factors in Food Selection and Preference as Related to Larval Nutrition of an Insect, *Pseudosarcophaga affinis* (Diptera, Sarcophagidae) on Synthetic Diets. *Canadian Entomologist*, 99:1312–1321.

Janzen, D. H.
1971.   Escape of *Cassia grandis*. L. Beans from Predators in Time and Space. *Ecology*, 52:964–979.
1974.   Tropical Blackwater Rivers, Animals and Mast Fruiting by the Dipterocarpaceae. *Biotropica*, 6:69–103.

Jones, E. W.
1945.   The Structure and Reproduction of the Virgin Forest of the North Temperate Zone. *New Phytologist*, 44:130–148.

Kaczmarek, W.
1967.   Elements of Organization in the Energy Flow of Forest Ecosystems. Pages 663–672 in *Secondary Productivity of Terrestrial Ecosystems*, II, edited by K. Petrusewicz. Warsaw: Polish Academy of Sciences.

Kennedy, J. S., and C. O. Booth
1951.   Host Alterations in *Aphis fabae* Scop. I. Feeding Preferences and Fecundity in Relation to the Age and Kind of Leaves. *Annals of Applied Biology*, 38:25–64.

Leigh, E. G., Jr., and N. Smythe
1978.   Leaf Production, Leaf Consumption and the Regulation of Folivory on Barro Colorado Island. Pages 33–50 in *The Ecology of Arboreal Folivores*, edited by G. G. Montgomery. Washington, D.C.: Smithsonian Institution Press.

Lloyd, M., and H. S. Dybas
1966.   The Periodical Cicada Problem. I. Population Ecology. *Evolution*, 20:133–149.

McKey, D.
1974.   Adaptive Patterns in Alkaloid Physiology. *American Naturalist*, 108:305–320.

Milton, K.
1979.   Factors Influencing Leaf Choice by Howler Monkeys: A Test of Some Hypotheses of Food Selection by Generalist Herbivores. *American Naturalist*, 114:362–378.

Misra, R.
1968.   Energy Transfer Along Terrestrial Food Chains. *Tropical Ecology*, 9:105–118.

Nielson, B. O.
1978.   Above Ground Food Resources and Herbivory in a Beech Forest Ecosystem. *Oikos*, 31:273–279.

Odum, H. T., and J. Ruiz-Reyes
1970.   Holes in Leaves and the Grazing Control Mechanism. Pages 1–69 in *A Tropical Rain Forest*, edited by H. T. Odum. Washington, D.C.: Division of Technological Information, U.S. Atomic Energy Commission.

Oelberg, K.
1956.   Factors Affecting the Nutritive Value of Range Forage. *Journal of Range Management*, 9:220–225.

Reese, J. C., and S. D. Beck
1978.   Interrelationships and Nutritional Indices and Dietary Moisture in the Black Cutworm (*Agrotis ipsilon*) Digestive Efficiency, *Journal of Insect Physiology*, 24:473–479.

Reichle, D. E., and D. A. Crossley
1967.   Investigations of Heterotrophic Productivity in Forest Insect Communities. Pages 563–587 in *Secondary Productivity of Terrestrial Ecosystems*, edited by K. Petrusewicz. Warsaw: Panstwowe Wydawnietwo Naukowe.

Reichle, D. E., R. A. Goldstein, R. I. Van Hook, Jr., and G. J. Dodson
1973.   Analysis of Insect Consumption in a Forest Canopy. *Ecology*, 54:1076–1084.

Rhoades, D. F.
1977a.   Integrated Anti-herbivore, Antidesiccant, and Ultraviolet Screening Properties of Creosote Bush Resin. *Biochemical Systematics and Ecology*, 5:281–290.
1977b.   The Anti-herbivore Defense of *Larrea*. Pages 135–175 in *The Biology and Chemistry of the Creosotebush in New World Deserts*, edited by R. J. Mabry, J. Hunziker, and D. R. DiFeo, Jr. Stroudsburg, Pa.: Dowden, Hutchinson and Ross.

Rhoades, D. F., and R. G. Cates
1976.   Toward a General Theory of Plant Anti-herbivore Chemistry. Pages 169–213 in *Biochemical Interactions between Plants and Insects*, vol. 10, edited by J. Wallace and R. Mansell. New York: Plenum.

Rockwood, L. L., and K. E. Glander
1979.   Howling Monkeys and Leaf-cutting Ants: Comparative Foraging in a Tropical Deciduous Forest. *Biotropica*, 11:1–10.

Schulz, J. P.
1960.   Ecological Studies on the Rain Forest in Northern Suriname. *Verh. K. Ned. Akad. Wet. Afd. natuurkd Tweede. Reeks*, 53:1–367.

Scriber, J. M.
1977.   Limiting Effects of Low Leaf-water Content on the Nitrogen Utilization, Energy Budget and Larval Growth of *Hyalophora cecropia* (Lepidoptera:Saturniidae), *Oecologia*, 28:269–287.

Siegel, S.
1956.   *Nonparametric Statistics*. New York: McGraw-Hill. 312 pp.

Slansky, F., and P. P. Feeny
1977.   Maximization of the rate of nitrogen accumulation by larvae of the Cabbage Butterfly on wild and cultivated food plants. *Ecological Monographs*, 47:209–299.

Smythe, N.
1982.   The Seasonal Abundance of Night-flying Insects in a Neotropical Forest. Pages 309–318 in *The Ecology of a Tropical Forest*, edited by Egbert G. Leigh, Jr., et al. Washington, D.C.: Smithsonian Institution Press.

Snedecor, G. W., and W. G. Cochran
1967.   *Statistical Methods*. Ames: Iowa State University Press. 593 pp.

Springett, B. P.
1978.   On the Ecological Role of Insects in Australian Eucalypt Forests. *Australian Journal of Ecology*, 3:129–139.

Tanton, M. T.
1962.   The Effect of Leaf "Toughness" on the Feeding of
         the Larvae of the Mustard Beetle *Phaedon cochleariae*.
         Entomologia Experimentalis et Applicata, 5:74–78.

Woodwell, G., and R. H. Whittaker
1968.   Primary Production in Terrestrial Ecosystems. *American Zoologist*, 8:19–30.

Wolda, H.
1978.   Seasonal Fluctuations in Rainfall, Food and Abundance of Tropical Insects. *Journal of Animal Ecology*, 47:369–381.

A Cue for Synchronous Flowering

CAROL K. AUGSPURGER   Department of Botany, University of Illinois, Urbana, Illinois 61801

ABSTRACT

Hybanthus prunifolius is a shrub that occurs commonly in clumps in the forest understory of Barro Colorado Island. These shrubs flower in synchrony in the dry season, a few days after the first rain of 12 mm or more that is preceded by drought of sufficient duration and severity; a few flowers also appear in response to other dry-season rains. One can cause a *Hybanthus* shrub to flower by watering the soil around its roots after a period of sufficient drought, and one can prevent a shrub from flowering by watering it with sufficient frequency from the end of rainy season onward.

If a single shrub is stimulated to flower out of synchrony, it attracts few pollinators; but, if a whole clump is stimulated to flower in synchrony, it attracts its customary pollinator, apparently down from the canopy, and achieves normal fruit set. Synchronous flowering leads to synchronous fruiting, and fruiting in synchrony appears to satiate the granivorous caterpillars that would otherwise destroy the seeds of *Hybanthus* before they are dispersed. Flowering in response to a dry-season rain causes the *Hybanthus* population to flower and fruit in tight synchrony during most years, but it also can result in the plants fruiting early enough that seeds and seedlings are destroyed by drought before the dry season ends.

Several other species of shrubs and trees flower synchronously in response to dry-season rains; whether they derive the same advantages as *Hybanthus* by doing so is not known.

INTRODUCTION

Hybanthus prunifolius (Violaceae) (Figure 1) is a shrub that grows in dense clumps in the forest understory of Barro Colorado Island. These shrubs tend to flower in synchrony with one another; a week or so after a heavy dry-season rain, one may find the arching branches of each shrub hung with white flowers. Synchronized flowering aids the individual plant in attracting pollinators; the synchronized fruiting that follows satiates the insect larvae that would otherwise eat many of the developing seeds (Augspurger, 1981). What mechanism does an individual shrub use to flower in synchrony with others? How reliable is the mechanism by which this synchrony is achieved? What are its disadvantages?

A variety of other species flower synchronously in the dry season. One of the most familiar is *Tabebuia guayacan,* a species of canopy tree that has several waves of flowering each dry season. One day, one will see its crowns, full of bright yellow flowers, scattered over the hillsides of the island and surrounding areas, and before a week has passed all the flowers will have fallen. Do these other species achieve synchrony by the same means as *Hybanthus,* and do they derive the same advantages thereby?

To answer, I will describe observations and experiments designed to reveal the mechanism of synchrony in *Hybanthus prunifolius,* comment on the reliability with which synchrony is achieved, and discuss the risks associated with the mechanism. Finally, I will consider the extent to which findings from *Hybanthus* might apply to other species.

METHODS

The Study Organism

Hybanthus prunifolius is a shrub, usually about 2 m tall and rarely over 5 m, whose principal branches are arcs, whose horizontal tips support wide flat sprays of foliage (Troll's model, Hallé et al., 1978). On Barro Colorado Island, these shrubs may occur in clumps of more than a hundred individuals, with one to eight individuals per 10 sq. m. Leaves of these plants are sometimes attacked en masse by caterpillars of the dioptid moth *Zunacetha annulata,* with up to four defoliations in a summer (Wolda and Foster, 1978). The major seed predator of *Hybanthus* is a microlepidopteran larva (Cosmoptericidae, Chrysopeleiinae); a minor seed predator is a dipteran larva (Lonchaeidae, *Silba* sp.).

Hybanthus prunifolius attracts only one major effective pollinator, the social bee *Melipona interrupta* (Ap-

idae). Although many kinds of smaller bees, moths, and hummingbirds visit the flowers, they are ineffective pollinators (Augspurger, 1980). *Melipona interrupta* is thought to feed primarily in canopy trees such as *Tabebuia guayacan* (S. Hubbell, pers. communication), and quickly recruits a large number of foragers to an attractive plant. These bees overlook isolated small *Hybanthus,* however full of flowers they may be. Although a large *Hybanthus* individual flowering in temporal isolation sometimes attracts some bees, flowering in synchrony with the conspecifics in one's clump is the only way an individual can ensure high pollination success. It appears that the display of a clump of *Hybanthus* is nearly as spectacular as that of a canopy tree in full flower and thus attracts pollinating bees down from the canopy.

Although a *Hybanthus* stigma does not normally receive pollen from the same flower, up to 90% of pollinated flowers may be fertilized by pollen from the same plant: these plants are self-compatible. The remaining 10% are fertilized mostly by pollen from other individuals in the same clump (Augspurger, 1980).

The Mechanism of Synchrony in *Hybanthus*

All individuals in the forest may flower together in full bloom: this is a major response. Occasionally, however, a *Hybanthus* individual or a small clump puts out only a few flowers, or only a few scattered individuals burst into full bloom: these are minor responses. In one area there will usually be only one major response per year, but the same plant may participate in several minor responses. Rains may induce additional buds to form in the dry season, but I think it more likely that all buds are formed in the preceding rainy season and differ in their sensitivity to dry-season rains.

I correlated major and minor responses with rainfall records to learn under what circumstances a rain can induce flowering, and how much rain is needed to do so. To confirm experimentally that rain evoked flowering, I sprinkled 42 plants, each on a different day, from 25 January to 26 March 1976. Each sprinkling was usually for 7 hours, long enough to saturate dry soil at root depths, increasing its moisture content by up to 10%, from 26% to 36% by weight. I recorded the time to first and to peak flowering, where the day of peak flowering is that on which the most flowers opened. To see if shorter periods of watering are equally effective, I watered four individuals for 5 minutes apiece and four individuals for 10 minutes apiece; each of the four were watered on a different day (25,27,31 January and 8 March). To see how rain

Figure 1. *Hybanthus prunifolius* (drawing by Arlee Montalvo).

5 dm

4 cm

evoked flowering, I also watered only the roots of eight shrubs, while watering all parts of others, and compared the results.

The Timing of Flowering of *Hybanthus*

Since a dry-season rain can induce flowering while rains late in the wet season never do so, I designed some experiments to discover how late in the dry season rain need occur in order to evoke flowering. The dry season of 1976 began on 28 December 1975. For the 42 shrubs sprinkled from 25 January to 26 March, I determined the date at which I was first successful in experimentally evoking flowering. In addition, as a more precisely controlled experiment, eight individuals which had failed to respond to sprinkling prior to 11 February were watered a second time. The individual watered on 27 January was sprinkled again on 26 February, and seven others of the plants watered between 25 January and 11 February were watered again between 3 and 16 March.

Since a rain induces flowering only if it occurs sufficiently late in the dry season, it appears that, as in coffee (Alvim, 1960, 1973; Magalhaes and Angelocci, 1976), either bud dormancy must be broken by drought stress of a certain threshold before watering can evoke flowering, or else a rain can evoke flowering only

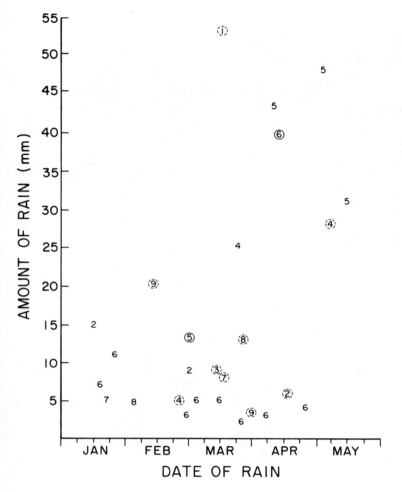

Figure 2.   Amount and date of probable rain triggering a flowering response in *Hybanthus prunifolius* for 9 years (1 = 1968, 2 = 1969, 3 = 1970, 4 = 1971, 5 = 1975, 6 = 1976, 7 = 1977, 8 = 1978, 9 = 1979). A circle represents known major responses actually measured in 1975 and 1976. Observations are complete only for 1975 and 1976. A broken circle represents suspected major responses based on incomplete observations. Since rainfall was measured in only one location and was not always uniform in amount across the entire island, the amount of rain listed as triggering flowering cannot be accurate. For example, the 20-mm rain of mid-February 1979 led to a major response on some parts of the island only, while the 3-mm light rain in late March 1979 correlated with a major response in other parts. It is unlikely that 3 mm was actually the quantity experienced by flowering plants as that amount is insufficient to penetrate the soil at root depths.

under certain daylengths. To check this, I watered 20 plants at frequent intervals during the dry season of 1976 in an attempt to prevent drought stress, and recorded whether watering could still induce them to flower at the same times as plants not previously watered. First, I watered them for 10 minutes every other day between 15 January and 19 February, except for a 3-day hiatus due to pump failure on 12 February. Since this sprinkling regime did not prevent decline in soil moisture content, I then began to water these plants for 4 hours every third day. The transition to the 4-hour sprinkling regime was made between 19 February and 27 February, on different days for different plants. From 27 February through 17 March each plant was watered for 4 hours every third day.

RESULTS

The Mechanism of Synchrony in *Hybanthus*

Flowering can occur from mid January to late May (Figure 2), and multiple flowering responses occur at different times in one dry season. Therefore, it seems unlikely that day length plays a role in controlling timing of flowering in *Hybanthus*.

It is more likely that flowering is related to the pattern of rainfall. The correlative evidence is based on rainfall records from the laboratory clearing and flowering records from the whole island. Since the rainfall from a given storm differs from place to place across the island (Rand and Rand, this volume), I cannot be certain how much rain a particular *Hybanthus* receives. Moreover, the particular rain evoking flowering cannot always be identified, because one rain may follow another in the period before flowers appear.

Still, several generalizations seem apparent. *Hybanthus* never flowers unless it has rained 4 to 9 days before the very first flower appears in the forest (Table 1). The mean number of days from rain to onset of flowering was 11 days in the major response in 1975 ($n = 70$ individuals); it was 8 days in 1976 (Table 2); it was 8 days for individuals responding to experimental watering ($n = 23$). The mean number of days from rain until the peak day of flowering for an individual was 13 days in the major response in 1975; it was 9 days in 1976 (Table 2).

Not all rains have equal effect. There is no record of a major response to a rain occurring earlier in the year than February 11. Major responses rarely occur to rains of less than 5 mm. Before the major response, rains of between 2 and 12 mm often evoke minor responses. In January, even heavy rains evoke at most minor responses. After the major response, heavy rains can evoke additional minor responses (Figure 2).

Several other generalizations apply for rains that occur when the plants are capable of a major response.

1. The heavier the rain, the shorter the time elapsed before *Hybanthus* flowers (Figure 3, Table 2).

2. The duration of flowering and total number of flowers per individual does not differ significantly in major responses to light versus heavy rains (Figure 3, Table 2).

3. Larger numbers of individuals flower in response to heavier rains (Figure 4). For rains greater than 12 or 13 mm, nearly every individual in the forest responds (Figure 2).

4. A heavier rain leads to a greater synchrony of both initial and peak day of flowering (Figure 3, Table 2). After a light rain, individuals near a stream may flower sooner than individuals on the island's central plateau. Finally, a rain barely sufficient to evoke a major response yields longer and less synchronous flowering than a heavier rain, both within a clump and among different clumps (Table 2).

After the first 8 weeks or so of dry season, I can routinely evoke flowering in forest *Hybanthus* by sprinkling these shrubs with water. As little as 5 minutes of sprinkling per quadrat can suffice, provided sprinkling occurs late enough in the dry season. Five and 10 minutes of sprinkling per quadrat evoked responses only after the 8 March waterings and not after the three attempts in January. Sprinkling for 5 minutes increases the weight due to moisture content by 5% in soil at root levels. The effects of sprinkling closely resemble those of rain. The flower buds, which are formed in the preceding wet season, begin development immediately after sprinkling. The first open flower appears 8–9 days after sprinkling ($n = 23$). The number of flowers per plant, the number of days a plant flowers, and the time elapsed from wetting to initial and peak response days for sprinkled individuals is indistinguishable from the corresponding characteristics of individuals flowering in response to a 40 mm rain on 10 April 1976.

Although I normally sprinkled the entire shrub, I can evoke normal flowering by watering only the ground surrounding the base of the shrub. It appears that a change in soil moisture evokes the response. This accords with the fact that very light rains, which do not affect the moisture content of the soil surrounding the roots, cannot evoke flowering.

The Timing of Flowering in *Hybanthus*

The probability of a plant's flowering in response to watering increased as the dry season progressed. The dry season began 28 December 1975. No response occurred in 11 individuals watered before 4 February 1976. A very minor response occurred in 2 of 5 individuals watered between 4 and 11 February. A minor response occurred in all 6 individuals watered between 12 and 26 February. A major response (full flowering) occurred in 18 of 20 individuals watered for the first time between 27 February and 26 March. The 2 nonresponsive individuals were watered 20 and 22 March. Plants adjacent to these nonresponsive individuals were watered on 24 and 26 March and bloomed normally.

To see if the nonresponsive plants would respond to a watering later in the dry season, I watered 8 of the 14 nonresponsive individuals again, 4–6 weeks after the first time. The individual first watered on 27 January and watered again on 26 February showed a minor response after the second watering. Seven other plants, first watered between 25 January and 11 February, showed a full response when watered again between 3 and 16 March.

One can prevent *Hybanthus* from normal flowering in response to sprinkling by watering them continuously during the dry season. Of the 20 individuals I was watering "continuously" between 15 January and 17 March, 7 plants showed one minor response to the sudden increase in soil moisture brought about by the switch to 4-hour sprinkling from 19–27 February. Three of these 7 plants had a second minor response to their second 4-hour sprinkling, while 2 of these 7 plants had a major response to their second 4-hour sprinkling. The remaining 13 plants did not respond at all through 17 March. By contrast, of 20 plants watered for the first time between 27 February and 26 March, 18 responded fully.

The heterogeneous response in the continuously watered plants may reflect differences in the rates at which soil surrounding their roots dried out, as well as differences in sensitivity to drought or to changes in soil moisture content. I did determine that during the period before 19 February, when the plants were being watered only for 10 minutes every other day, the soil under different plants dried out at different rates. During the 10-minute sprinkling regime and the period of pump failure the plants which later showed minor responses may have nearly reached their required level of drought. Their minor response suggests sufficient drought had not quite been achieved.

It thus appears that normally the soil must dry out to a certain degree to break bud dormancy before rain can cause *Hybanthus* to flower. This accords with the observation that major responses in *Hybanthus* between 1968 and 1971, and between 1975 and 1979, were all evoked by rains preceded by droughts of 4 to 8 weeks. For example, in 1976 there were scattered

Table 1. Major and minor flowering periods and possible rain cues in dry seasons, 1975 and 1976

Year and species	Flowering period		
	1	*2*	*3*

1975

Hybanthus prunifolius — MAJOR

	1	2	3
No. of individuals	70	18	4
Flower period	7–16 March	15–22 April	9–12 May
Peak day	13 March	19 April	10 May
Mean time lag	11 days	—	—
Possible cues	* 7– 8.4 mm	* 6–43.2	14– 8.8
	* 6– 4.9	—	* 7–47.6
	3–12.3	—	6–20.5
	1–23.4	—	—
	—	—	—
	—	—	—
	—	—	—
	—	—	—

Rinorea sylvatica — MAJOR

	1	2	3
Flower period	6–17 March	14–21 April	—
Possible cues	* 6– 8.4	* 5–43.2	—
	* 5– 4.9	—	—
	2–12.3	—	—

Turnera panamensis — MAJOR (period 3)

	1	2	3
Flower period	11–17 March	16–21 April	8–15 May
Peak day	—	—	10 May
Possible cues	11– 8.4	* 7–43.2	13– 8.8
	10– 4.9	—	* 6–47.6
	* 7–12.3	—	5–20.5
	* 5–23.4	—	—
	—	—	—
	—	—	—
	—	—	—

Randia armata — MAJOR (period 3)

	1	2	3
No. of individuals	1	1	44
Flower period	24–30 March	30 Apr.–5 May	18–27 May
Peak day	—	—	20 May
Possible cues	24– 8.4	* 21–43.2	23– 8.8
	23– 4.9	5– 8.8	*16–47.6
	*20–12.3	—	15–20.5
	*18–23.4	—	5–31.4
	—	—	4– 5.0

Maximum number of tagged individuals observed occurs under the major heading. Flower period includes the first and last flower observed on any individual in the forest. Peak day represents the day with the maximum number of individuals in flower (and maximum number of flowers). Mean time lag equals number of days from probable cue to onset of flowering (averaged for all individuals). Possible cues lists the number of days from a rain to the first observed flower, followed by the amount of each rain; only rains greater than 2 mm are listed).

   * = probable cue, arrived at by identifying the most common time lag for all flowering periods available for a species.

4	5	6	7	8	9
1	—	—	—	—	—
21–? May	—	—	—	—	—
—	—	—	—	—	—
—	—	—	—	—	—
* 8–31.4	—	—	—	—	—
7– 5.0	—	—	—	—	—
6– 3.0	—	—	—	—	—
5–13.6	—	—	—	—	—
4–13.6	—	—	—	—	—
3– 9.2	—	—	—	—	—
2–41.6	—	—	—	—	—
1–43.0	—	—	—	—	—
—	—	—	—	—	—
—	—	—	—	—	—
—	—	—	—	—	—
—	—	—	—	—	—
20–? May	—	—	—	—	—
—	—	—	—	—	—
* 7–31.4	—	—	—	—	—
6– 5.0	—	—	—	—	—
5– 3.0	—	—	—	—	—
4–13.6	—	—	—	—	—
3–13.6	—	—	—	—	—
2– 9.2	—	—	—	—	—
1–41.6	—	—	—	—	—
5	—	—	—	—	—
29 May–4 June	—	—	—	—	—
—	—	—	—	—	—
26–47.6	—	—	—	—	—
25–20.5	—	—	—	—	—
*16–31.4	—	—	—	—	—
15– 5.0	—	—	—	—	—
14– 3.0	—	—	—	—	—

Table 1. (continued)

Year and species	Flowering period		
	1	*2*	*3*

1975

Randia armata

	1	2	3
Possible cues (continued)	—	—	3– 3.0
	—	—	2–13.6
	—	—	1–13.6
	—	—	—
	—	—	—
	—	—	—
	—	—	—
	—	—	—
	—	—	—

Tabebuia guayacan

	1	2	3
Flower period	29–? Jan.	14–19 Feb.	23–27 Feb.
Possible cues	*13– 2.3	* 9– 2.0	18– 2.0
	—	—	* 9– 1.6
	—	—	* 8– 2.0
	—	—	—

Petrea aspera

	1	MAJOR 2	3
Flower period	?6–? Feb.	13–24 March	18–27 Apr.
Possible cues	2– 1.3	13– 8.4	* 9–43.2
	1– 2.0	12– 4.9	—
	—	* 9–12.3	—
	—	7–23.4	—

1976

Hybanthus prunifolius

	1	2	3
No. of individuals	1	1	10
Flower period	25–27 Jan.	1–3 Feb.	1–13 Mar.
Peak day	—	—	4 Mar.
Mean time lag	—	—	6 days
Possible cues	20– 4.6 mm	13– 6.6	* 4– 1.2
	16– 5.2	* 9– 3.2	* 3– 1.6
	* 8– 6.6	* 8– 7.6	—
	3– 3.2	7– 2.8	—

Rinorea sylvatica

	1	MAJOR 2	3
No. of individuals	27	40	1
Flower period	21 Jan.–6 Feb.	13–23 Apr.	26 Apr.–6 May
Peak day	24–25 Jan.	15–16 Apr.	—
Mean time lag	5 days	4 days	—
Possible cues	16– 4.6	9– 1.0	16–40.0
	12– 5.2	8– 1.6	* 4– 2.6
	* 4– 6.6	* 3–40.0	* 3– 1.8

Flowering period

4	5	6	7	8	9
13–13.6	—	—	—	—	—
12–13.6	—	—	—	—	—
11– 9.2	—	—	—	—	—
10–41.6	—	—	—	—	—
9–43.0	—	—	—	—	—
6– 8.2	—	—	—	—	—
4–19.8	—	—	—	—	—
2–14.2	—	—	—	—	—
1–15.8	—	—	—	—	—

MAJOR

7–16 March	16–22 April	4–11 May	11–? May	—	—
* 7– 8.4	* 7–43.2	* 9– 8.8	16– 8.8	—	—
6– 4.9	—	2–47.6	* 9–47.6	—	—
3–12.3	—	1–20.5	8–20.5	—	—
1–23.4	—	—	—	—	—

11–? May	—	—	—	—	—
16– 8.8	—	—	—	—	—
* 9–47.6	—	—	—	—	—
8–20.5	—	—	—	—	—
—	—	—	—	—	—

				MAJOR	
10	5	1	5	all	1
9–14 Mar.	22–24 Mar.	28 Mar.–1 Apr.	10–19 Apr.	16–23 Apr.	3–8 May
11 Mar.	23 Mar.	29 Mar.	14 Apr.	19 Apr.	5 May
9 days	9 days	—	7 days	8 days	—
12– 1.2	21– 1.9	27– 1.9	18– 2.0	12– 1.0	12– 2.6
11– 1.6	20– 3.4	26– 3.4	* 6– 1.0	11– 1.6	11– 1.8
* 8– 1.9	* 9– 5.2	15– 5.2	* 5– 1.6	* 6–40.0	* 7– 3.6
* 7– 3.4	—	* 5– 2.0	—	—	5– 3.6
—	—	—	—	—	4– 3.2

—	—	—	—	—	—
—	—	—	—	—	—
—	—	—	—	—	—
—	—	—	—	—	—
—	—	—	—	—	—
—	—	—	—	—	—
—	—	—	—	—	—

Table 1. (continued)

Year and species	Flowering period		
	1	*2*	*3*
1976			
Turnera panamensis			
No. of individuals	13	2	28
Flower period	5–13 Mar.	19–27 Mar.	9–17 Apr.
Peak day	—	—	12–13 Apr.
Mean time lag	7 days	6 days	7– 8 days
Possible cues	* 8– 1.2	18– 1.9	17– 2.0
	* 7– 1.6	17– 3.4	* 5– 1.0
	4– 1.9	* 6– 5.2	* 4– 1.6
	3– 3.4	—	—
	—	—	—
	—	—	—
	—	—	—
Randia armata	MAJOR		
Flower period	28 Apr.–29 May	12–21 May	—
Peak day	2 May	15 May	—
Possible cues	24– 1.0	21– 2.6	11– 1.9
	23– 1.6	20– 1.8	10– 3.4
	*18–40.0	16– 3.6	7–14.0
	6– 2.6	14– 3.6	6–13.0
	5– 1.8	13– 3.2	5– 2.0

Flowering period

4	5	6	7	8	9
MAJOR					
44	3	1	1	—	—
14–26 Apr.	1–8 May	10–15 May	25–28 May	—	—
18 Apr.	—	—	—	—	—
6 days	5 days	—	—	—	—
10– 1.0	10– 2.6	9– 1.9	20–14.0	—	—
9– 1.6	9– 1.8	8– 3.4	19–13.0	—	—
* 4–40.0	* 5– 3.6	* 5–14.0	18– 2.0	—	—
—	3– 3.6	4–13.0	15– 4.0	—	—
—	2– 3.2	3– 2.0	* 6–23.4	—	—
—	—	—	5– 4.4	—	—
—	—	—	2–33.2	—	—
—	—	—	—	—	—
—	—	—	—	—	—
—	—	—	—	—	—
—	—	—	—	—	—
—	—	—	—	—	—
—	—	—	—	—	—
—	—	—	—	—	—

Table 2. Differences in major flowering responses after light (1975) and heavy (1976) rain cues

	Major, 1975	*Major, 1976*	
Probable rain cue			
Date	28 Feb., 1 Mar.	10 Apr.	
Amount	8.4 mm + 4.9 mm	40.0 mm	
Flowering period			
Date	7–16 Mar.	16–23 Apr.	
Number of days	10 days	8 days	
Number of tagged individuals	70	70	
Number of sites	4	4	
Mean days from rain to first flower	11	8	
Mean days from rain to peak no. flowers	13	9	
Mean days in flower	3.7	3.5	n.s.
Mean number of flowers (SD)	178 (143)	194 (173)	n.s.
Population synchrony of initiation day (= 1 SD)*	1.36	0.69	
Population synchrony of peak flowering day (= 1 SD)*	1.14	0.52	

* Synchrony is not calculated for the entire forest irrespective of site differences. Rather it is derived by standardizing days for each site and then fusing at the forest level. First each individual is assigned an initiation day and peak day relative to the mean value at their site. Then the synchrony value is calculated by determining one standard deviation of these relative values around the standardized mean.

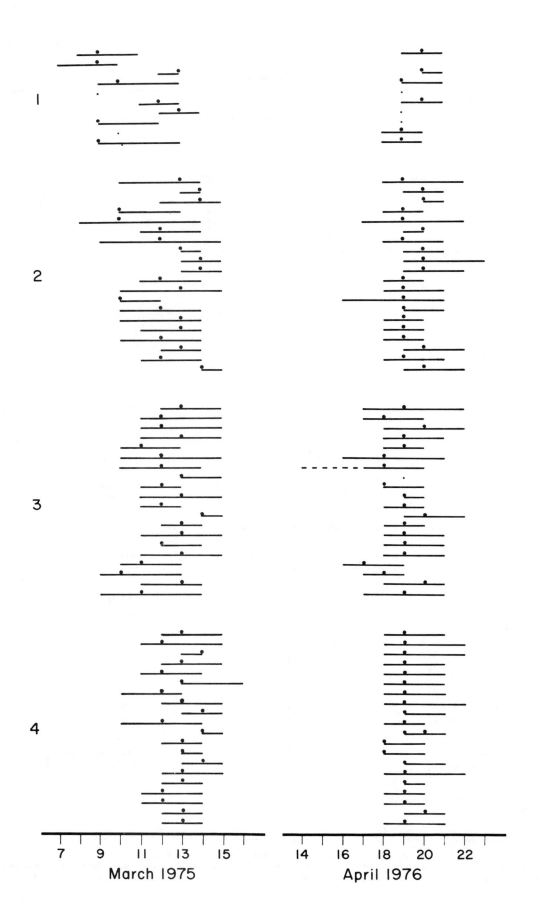

1

2

3

4

7   9   11   13   15

March 1975

14   16   18   20   22

April 1976

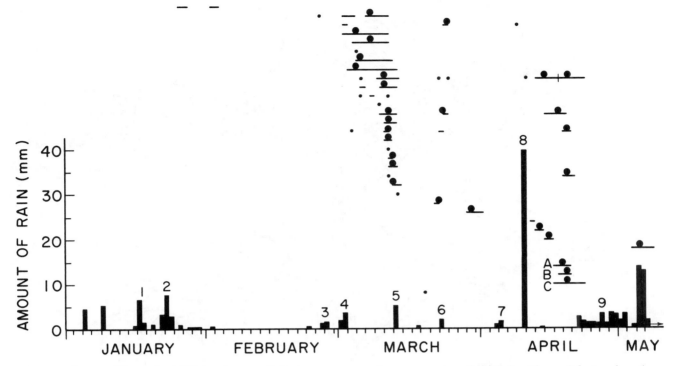

Figure 4. Dates of flowering of *Hybanthus prunifolius* in response to dry season rains of 1976. See Figure 3 for explanation of lines and dots. Numbers over rains correspond to numbered flowering periods in Table 1 (1–7, 9 = minor and 8 = major responses. The major response to rain 8 occurred throughout the forest (A = range of initiation days in forest, n = 93 individuals; B = range of peak flowering days in forest; C = length of response in forest. Major response, after rain 8, was closely observed only for the 93 individuals summarized in A, B, and C, above. Another 32 plants, whose minor responses are marked individually, were watched during the rest of the dry season, but not right after rain 8.

light rains in the second half of January, including one of 12 mm on 24 January, but no rain thereafter until very light rains the end of February (Figure 4). The first experimental full response was induced by watering on 27 February, 5 weeks after the last moderate rain.

Besides regulating the time during the dry season that *Hybanthus* flowers, drought also serves to increase synchrony of flowering. Drought results in buds accumulating and arresting at a comparable stage in all plants. Then when a rain occurs the rest of their development is completed nearly synchronously.

Figure 3. Dates of flowering for the same individuals of *Hybanthus prunifolius* after a light rain (1975) and a heavy rain (1976). See Table 2 for a summary of major differences between years. Each line equals length of flowering period for an individual. Large dot above line equals day of peak flower number for that individual. Lines on same level indicate same individual.

DISCUSSION

Other "Rain Flowers"

Judging from phenological data, several other species on Barro Colorado Island flower in response to dry-season rains, notably *Rinorea sylvatica* (Violaceae, Figure 5), *Turnera panamensis* (Turneraceae), *Tabebuia guayacan* (Bignoniaceae), *Randia armata* (Rubiaceae), and possibly *Petrea aspera* (Verbenaceae, Figure 6). This last species may also flower in the rainy season. Like *Hybanthus*, in each of these species individuals flower briefly, in synchrony, a fairly consistent number of days after a rain. None of these species will flower unless it has rained recently beforehand (Table 1, Figure 6).

As with *Hybanthus*, correlative data do not always permit us to tell which rain stimulated a particular flowering response, or just how much rain was necessary to do so. However, it appears that, like *Hybanthus*, these species usually have one major response and several minor responses each dry season. Until the major response has occurred, the level of response

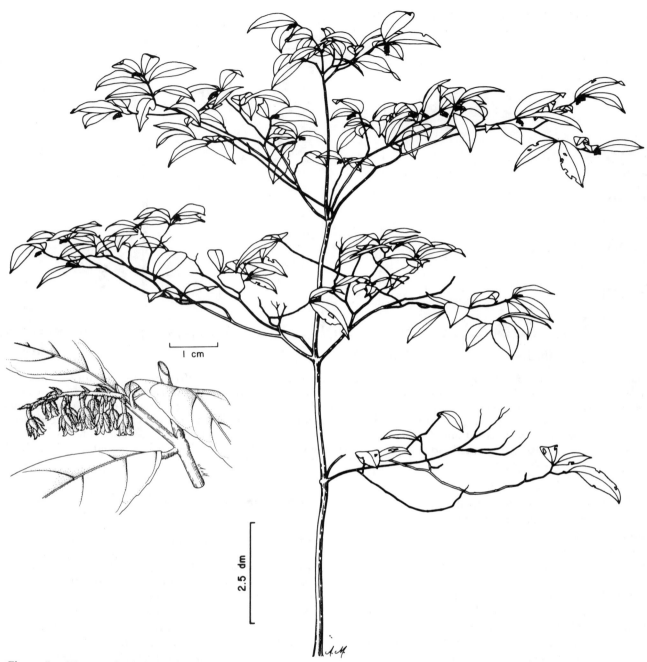

Figure 5. *Rinorea sylvatica* (drawing by Arlee Montalvo).

depends on the size of the rain, while after the major response heavy rains can evoke additional minor responses (Table 1, Figure 6). Since *Rinorea, Turnera,* and *Randia,* like *Hybanthus,* can flower at very different times in different dry seasons, photoperiod does not appear to play a major role in the timing of flowering; the decisive cue appears to be a rain of sufficient magnitude. Presumably, the rain must be pre-

ceded by a sufficiently intense drought, but I have not tested this proposition experimentally for any plant other than *Hybanthus.*

These species differ in the amount and timing of rain needed to evoke flowering (Figure 6). For example, *Tabebuia guayacan* flowers earlier, and in response to less rain, than do the other species. *Tabebuia guayacan* is leafless during the dry season, and once the leaves are lost (whether in response to drought or to other cues), a rain may evoke flowering. Since very light rains suffice, the stimulus for flowering may be wetting of plant parts above ground rather than increase in soil moisture.

These species may also differ in when and how often they form dormant flower buds. I have direct observations on the buds of *Hybanthus* and *Rinorea;* the rest I must infer from when the plants flower.

Hybanthus appears to form all its flower buds in the preceding wet season; after sufficient drought, the first major rain evokes flowering. *Rinorea* does roughly the same, but it develops its buds in several stages. First, small buds form, whose development is arrested in the middle of the wet season. Late in the wet season, they begin to grow again until, by the beginning of the dry season, they are nearly as big as the completed flowers. Light dry-season rains may stimulate further growth, until a large enough rain following a sufficient drought evokes flowering. In 1976, for example, a January rain elicited a minor flowering response and further growth of existing buds. When the major response finally occurred, in April, the buds were so well developed that peak flowering, with very high synchrony, was achieved just 5 days after the rain (Figure 7).

The major responses of *Randia* and *Turnera* are sometimes later than those of the other species (Table 1, Figure 6). Once the dry season begins, *Randia* may require two major rains before flowering, one to induce new or additional flower buds and/or to enlarge buds formed in the preceding rainy season, the second to trigger flowering in the now well-developed buds. A few individuals, however, will flower in response to the first rain. *Randia* may also require heavier rain before flowering. *Turnera* behaves similarly, although it may respond to somewhat different intensities of drought and rain (Figure 6). Individual plants, and individual flowers, vary greatly in their responses to rains (Figure 8); in 1976, one individual showed one major and six minor responses. Here, too, dry-season rains may induce new buds to form as well as stimulating growth in buds already formed.

These species differ in the size of dormant buds and of open flowers. These differences, in turn, lead to differences in the time it takes for flowers to develop in response to a rain. In general, the smaller the flower, and the larger the dormant bud relative to the open flower, the more quickly and synchronously the plants flower in response to rain.

Elsewhere in the tropics, early tropical biologists noticed that individuals with "rain flowers" produce dormant buds (Rutgers and Went, 1915; Seifriz, 1923) and then flower for a brief time in a highly synchro-

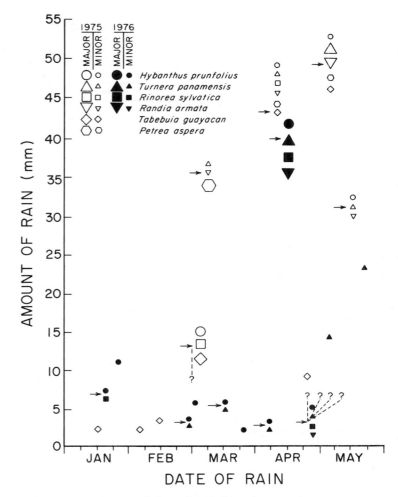

Figure 6.   Amount and date of probable rain cues triggering major and minor flowering responses in 1975 and 1976 for six species. An arrow indicates exact amount of rain when several species respond to the same rain. A question mark indicates consecutive rains making it difficult to determine the identity of the specific rain cue.

nous ("gregarious") population response a consistent number of days after a rain (Mueller, 1882; Schimper, 1903; Spruce, 1908; Coster, 1926; Holttum, 1935). Janzen (1967) and Opler et al. (1976) have noticed that in the more seasonal parts of Costa Rica, such as Guanacaste, many species flower in a brief synchronous period after a dry-season rain. Rain flowers have also been noticed in the Far East and in West Africa. One of these, the pigeon orchid, *Dendrobium crumenatum,* has been shown to flower in response to the temperature drop, often of 5°C or more, associated with a major storm (Holttum, 1949, 1954). In other cases, rainfall and a drop in temperature act jointly in evoking flowering. Buds of *Zephyranthes rosea* do

Benefits and Risks of Synchronous Flowering

As I have mentioned, *Hybanthus* must flower in synchrony to attract its pollinators. In *Hybanthus* flowering in synchrony, in turn, results in synchrony of fruit and seed development, which satiates the insect larvae that would otherwise destroy many of its seeds. Given these two advantages of synchrony (as well as the untested advantage of increasing outcrossing potential), there can hardly be a less ambiguous cue for synchronous flowering than a heavy rain following a long drought. This cue has an additional advantage in some years; when the rain-evoking flowering occurs at or shortly before the beginning of the wet season, plants will be dispersing their seeds soon after the wet season begins, when soil nutrients are quite abundant, and when the seedlings can get a good start before the next drought.

There are, however, three associated risks, related to the variability in amount and timing of the rain. First, minor responses occur because of variability in the amount of drought and rain and in individuals' sensitivity to drought and rain. Reproductive success, measured soon after pollination and at dispersal, is significantly lower for *Hybanthus* individuals flowering only in minor responses compared with those in major responses (Augspurger, 1981). Second, when the rain evoking a major response is light and is not soon followed by additional rains, fruit development is stunted and delayed by the stress of the ensuing drought. In 1975 this lowered the reproductive success of slower responding individuals in the major response following the rain of 28 February (Augspurger, 1978). Finally, variability in the timing of the flowering cue affects the conditions to which the dispersed seeds are subjected. Seeds of *Hybanthus* are quite vulnerable to the inconsistent, fluctuating soil moisture of the dry season. Consequently germination success and seedling establishment are both greatly reduced in some years (Augspurger, 1979).

Two other species on Barro Colorado with rain flowers have lower fruit set than *Hybanthus* (Augspurger, 1978). *Turnera*, which is self-incompatible, and *Rinorea* attract a variety of visitors and pollinators, among which no single species predominates, as does *Melipona interrupta* at *Hybanthus*. It is not clear that synchrony increases pollination success as greatly for these plants. Whether synchronous fruiting satiates their seed predators has yet to be tested.

ACKNOWLEDGMENTS

The research was completed with support from a Smithsonian Institution Predoctoral Fellowship and a

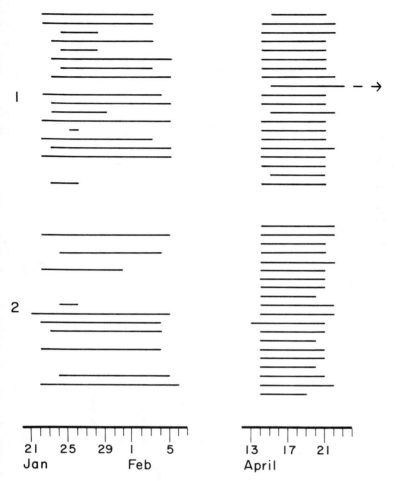

Figure 7. Dates of flowering of individuals of *Rinorea sylvatica* at two sites in 1976 ($n = 40$). Note one major and one minor response. See Figure 2 for explanation of lines.

not elongate in response either to an increase in water at a constant high temperature or to a decrease in temperature without water (Kerling, 1941). The temperature must be lowered in the presence of water to be effective.

A great many other species on Barro Colorado flower in response to amounts of rain which do not usually occur before the rainy season begins in earnest. In the exceptional year when extremely heavy rains occur in the dry season, many of these species may flower but they fail to fruit (Foster, this volume). However, they do not flower in the brief synchronous bursts one associates with "rain flowers" so they do not enter further into this story.

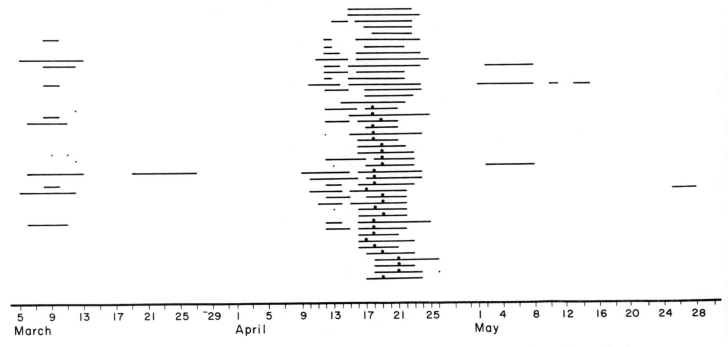

Figure 8. Dates of flowering of individuals of *Turnera panamensis* in 1976 (*n* = 44). Note one major and several minor responses. See Figure 2 for explanation of lines and dots.

University of Michigan Predoctoral Fellowship. Robin Foster's observations and interest in rain flowers stimulated the research itself. Field assistance from Tania Béliz, Paula Amann, and support from many Barro Colorado Island residents was indispensable.

LITERATURE CITED

Alvim, P.
1960.   Moisture stress as a requirement for flowering of coffee. *Science*, 132:354.
1973.   Factors affecting flowering of coffee. Pages 193–202 in *Genes, Enzymes, and Populations*, edited by A. M. Srb. London: Plenum Press.

Augspurger, C. K.
1978.   Reproductive consequences of flowering synchrony in *Hybanthus prunifolius* (Violaceae) and other shrub species of Panama. Ph.D. thesis, University of Michigan.
1979.   Irregular rain cues and the germination and seedling survival of a Panamanian shrub (*Hybanthus prunifolius*). *Oecologia*, 44:53–59.
1980.   Mass-flowering of a tropical shrub (*Hybanthus prunifolius*): influence on pollinator attraction and movement. *Evolution*, 34:475–488.
1981.   Reproductive synchrony of a tropical shrub: experimental studies on effects of pollinators and seed predators on *Hybanthus prunifolius* (Violaceae). *Ecology*, 62:775–789.

Coster, C.
1926.   Periodische Bluteerscheinungen in den Tropen. *Ann. Jaard. Bot. Buitenz.*, 35:125–162.

Foster, R. B.
1982.   The Seasonal Rhythms in Fruitfall on Barro Colorado Island. Pages 151–172 in *The Ecology of a Tropical Forest*, edited by Egbert G. Leigh, Jr., et al. Washington, D.C.: Smithsonian Institution Press.

Halle, F., R. A. A. Oldeman, and P. B. Tomlinson
1978.   *Tropical Trees and Forests: An Architectural Analysis*. Berlin: Springer-Verlag.

Holttum, R. E.
1935.   The flowering of Tembusu trees (*Fagraea fragrans*) in Singapore, 1928–35. *Gard. Bull. Singapore*, 8:73–78.
1949.   Gregarious flowering of the terrestrial orchid *Bromheadia finlaysoniana*. *Gard. Bull. Singapore*, 12:295–302.
1954.   *Plant Life in Malaya*. London: Longman Group Ltd.

Janzen, D. H.
1967.   Synchronization of sexual reproduction of trees within the dry season in Central America. *Evolution*, 21:620–637.

Kerling, L. C. P.
1941.   The gregarious flowering of *Zephyranthes rosea* Lindl. *Ann. Bot. Gdn. Buitenz.*, 51:1–42.

Magalhaes, A. C., and L. R. Angelocci
1976.   Sudden alterations in water balance associated with flower bud opening in coffee plants. *J. Hort. Sci.*, 51:419–423.

Mueller, F.
1882.   Bemerkungen zu Hildebrand's Abhandlung uber die Lebensdauer and Vegetationsweise der Pflanzen. *Engler's Jahrbucher,* 2:391–394.

Opler, P. A., G. W. Frankie, and H. G. Baker
1976.   Rainfall as a factor in the release, timing, and synchronization of anthesis by tropical trees and shrubs. *J. Biogeog.,* 3:231–236.

Rand, A. S., and W. M. Rand
1982.   Variation in Rainfall on Barro Colorado Island. Pages 47–59 in *The Ecology of a Tropical Forest,* edited by Egbert G. Leigh, Jr., et al. Washington, D.C.: Smithsonian Institution Press.

Rutgers, A. L., and F. A. Went
1915.   Periodische Erscheinungen bei den Bluten des *Dendrobium crumenatum* Lindl. *Ann. Jard. Bot. Buitenz.,* 29:129–160.

Schimper, A. F. W.
1903.   *Plant-geography upon a Physiological Basis.* Oxford: Clarendon Press.

Seifriz, W.
1923.   The gregarious flowering of the orchid *Dendrobium crumenatum. Amer. J. Bot.,* 10:32–37.

Spruce, R.
1908.   *Notes of a Botanist on the Amazon and Andes.* vol. 1. London: Johnson Repr.

Wolda, H., and R. B. Foster
1978.   *Zunacetha annulata* (Lepidoptera, Dioptidae), an outbreak insect in a neotropical forest. *Geo-Eco-Trop,* 2:443–454.

The Seasonal Rhythm of Fruitfall on Barro Colorado Island

ROBIN B. FOSTER   Department of Biology, University of Chicago, Chicago, Illinois 60637

ABSTRACT

The average number of species per hectare dropping significant amounts of fruit and seed peaks between March and June, and again in September and October; there is a mild depression in July and August, and a severe one from November through February. The forest's fruiting rhythm is dominated by canopy trees. Lianas (which are mostly wind-dispersed) fruit primarily between March and May, when the largest number of canopy trees are without leaves; understory trees and shrubs tend to fruit in November and December, when competition for animal dispersers is minimal. Wind-dispersed plants ripen fruit between March and May, presumably taking advantage of the season of leaflessness, while animal-dispersed plants contribute to both peaks. Larger-seeded plants tend to drop fruit in September and October. There is only one peak season of seed germination, at the beginning of the rainy season in May and June; the seeds of most plants dropping fruit late in the rainy season or in the dry season do not germinate until the beginning of the following rainy season. Flowering also peaks near the beginning of rainy season, coincident with a peak of insect abundance, when pollinators are presumably most numerous. Most species fruiting in September and October flower in response to the onset of the rainy season, as do a significant minority of the species that fruit between March and June. The time of fruiting appears to represent a compromise between the desirability of seeds germinating fairly early in the rainy season and the desirability of flowering early in the rainy season. Other selective forces are apparently of less consequence.

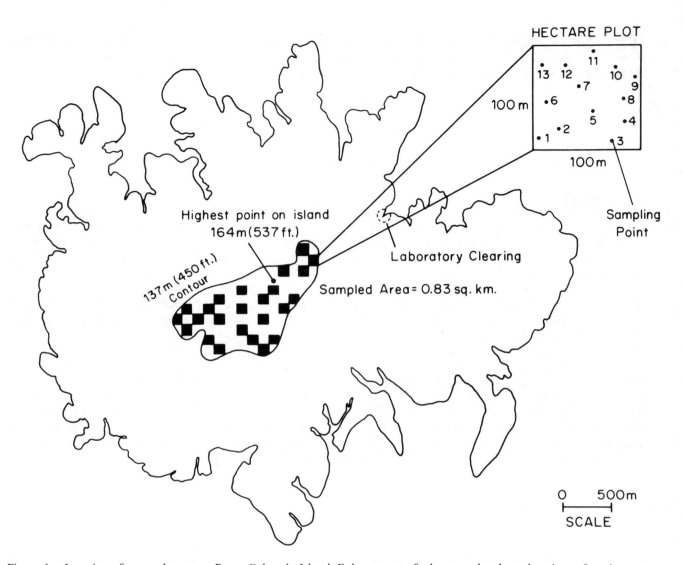

Figure 1.   Location of research area on Barro Colorado Island. Enlargement of a hectare plot shows locations of seed traps.

INTRODUCTION

How does fruiting activity in the forest on Barro Colorado Island vary with the season of the year? Are the rhythms different for different classes of plants? What factors might explain the timing and amplitude of these fluctuations?

To answer, I will assess the fruiting rhythm from samples of the seed rain onto randomly chosen points on the forest floor, rather than from studies of the phenology of individual trees. This allows a relatively unbiased and easily quantified sample of the rhythm of the vegetation as a whole, including lianas, and avoids the need for subjective judgments about when different fruits are ripe. I will compare fruiting rhythms in various classes of woody plants, such as trees and

lianas, in order to infer some of the factors that might affect these rhythms.

METHODS

Study Area

My study area consisted of that portion of the island above the 137 m contour (Figure 1), an area with relatively uniform topography and parent material. This area includes the plateau that caps the island, and some of the more gradual slopes of the surrounding escarpment. Two-thirds of the study area is covered by relatively mature forest, and one-third by younger forest; all of it rests on igneous rock. Except for one small swampy area in the center, pools of water do not form even after long, heavy rains.

Design of Seed Traps

I sampled the rain of seeds and flowers with circular green polyethylene utility tubs, 19 cm deep, with a collecting surface of $1/12$ sq. m. A piece of nylon netting with a mesh of 0.5 mm was set into each tub so as to catch anything falling into the tub, and I made drainage holes in the sides of the tubs. During heavy rains the tubs would fill up to the level of the drainage holes, but the netting acted as a sieve to prevent seeds being lost in the outflow from the tubs.

Placing the Seed Traps

I subdivided the study area into 83 one-hectare plots (Figure 1), and chose 24 of these at random, subject to the condition that no two plots shared an edge. Within one plot, I placed 13 seed traps at points whose coordinates were chosen at random, subject to the condition that each point be over 20 m from any previously chosen point. I then arranged the traps in the same way in all the other plots. I thus used 24×13, or 312, traps for the entire study.

Collection of Data

I emptied all 312 traps weekly from August 1969 to August 1970. The following year, I continued a reduced sample of 5 tubs per plot (120 in all) each fortnight to August 1971 (Foster, this volume). In Appendix 1, at the end of the text, I also include information on a few additional species from the second year.

I removed leaves and large debris and examined the samples with a dissecting microscope, recording for each trap the number of apparently viable (full) seeds of each species present. Names are from Croat (1978) except where noted. I deposited sets of voucher specimens of most species in the herbaria of the University of Panama and Duke University. Within a few genera or small groups of species, I could not consistently distinguish seeds of different species, and treated the group as a single species, as noted in Appendix 1.

I also recorded many of the species dropping flowers into the traps each week, and every week or two, from March 1969 to July 1970, I walked the trails, noting which species I saw in flower. When this was insufficient or obviously inappropriate to the seeds falling into the traps, I interpolated data from other years to fit the observed seed rain. For most species

it was possible to determine the half month in which flowering peaked.

Analysis

Each week, I recorded the total number of species dropping seeds into one or more traps. Then, in each 1-ha. plot, I measured for each species i the percentage P_i of traps containing at least one seed of that species, and the total number x_i of seeds of that species falling per square meter of trap in the plot. I then calculated the total number of species dropping one or more seeds into traps in that plot, the sum of the P_i for all these species (the "summed relative frequencies" of seedfall) and the sum of all the x_i (the total number of seeds falling per square meter of trap in that plot). Finally, I calculated the mean and standard deviation of these quantities over all 24 plots, and repeated the analysis for subsets of these species with a particular life form, mode of dispersal, or range of seed weight.

The numbers for each plot involve data pooled from 13 samples, and we have no reason to expect these numbers to be normally distributed about the mean for all 24 plots, so the standard deviations provide only a rough indication of the variability among plots in a given week. Although the variation among the plots is quite great, the seasonal trends in different plots may be quite consistent.

Accuracy of the Method

Error may arise because seeds somehow circumvent the traps, or because animals add, remove, or damage seeds. Observations, and experiments with known quantities of fruit in the traps, gave no indication that the samples were seriously affected (Foster, 1973). Such misrepresentations as did occur would be more likely to reduce the total number of seeds counted than the number of species represented.

When considered plot by plot, the samples emphasize species that are more abundant. The distance between traps was not always sufficient to avoid catching seeds from the same tree, especially if the tree was large. To this extent, the samples emphasize species that contribute more to canopy coverage as well as those that are numerically more common. The samples therefore permit one to assess the rhythm of the vegetation as a whole rather than a sum of the behaviors of different members of the flora, without regard to the relative abundance of species. With few exceptions, such as *Hura crepitans* and *Gustavia superba*, all the abundant or otherwise important species in the area were represented in the samples.

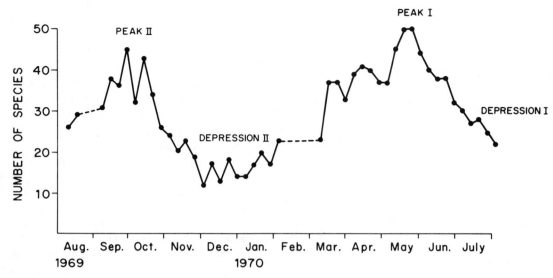

Figure 2.   Total number of species over all plots each week, having at least one seed in a trap. Dashed portions of line represent sampling intervals of longer than 1 week, the data from which could not be used for this and some of the other analyses.

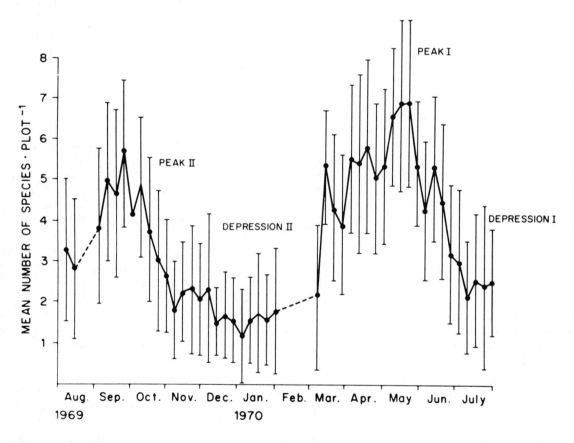

Figure 3.   Mean number of species represented per plot for 24 plots. Vertical lines represent one standard deviation above and below the mean.

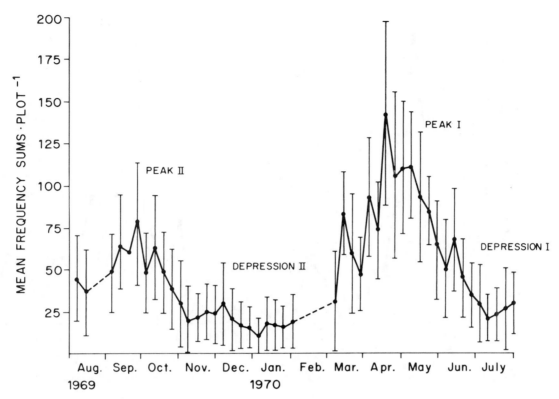

Figure 4. Mean frequency sums per plot for 24 plots. Sums are obtained from the relative frequencies (out of 13 traps per plot) of trap "hits" for each species.

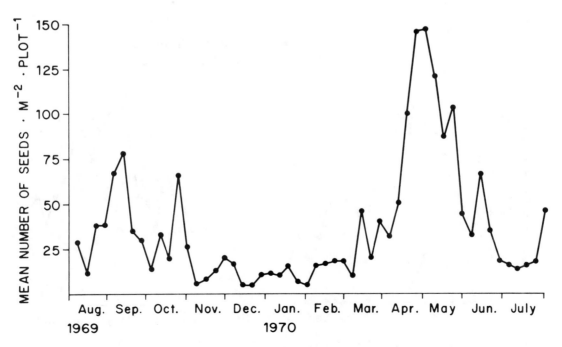

Figure 5. Mean number of seeds per square meter per plot for 24 plots. These data are strongly influenced by a few species.

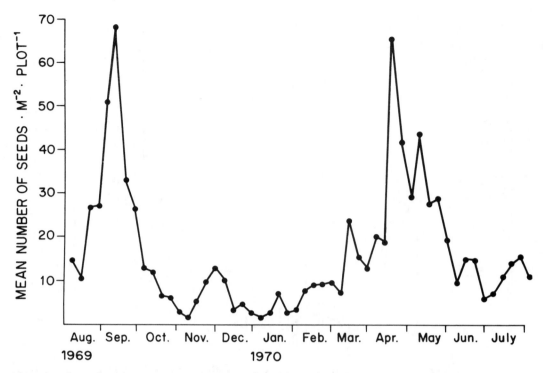

Figure 6. Mean number of seeds per square meter per plot without those from species of *Cecropia* and *Ficus*.

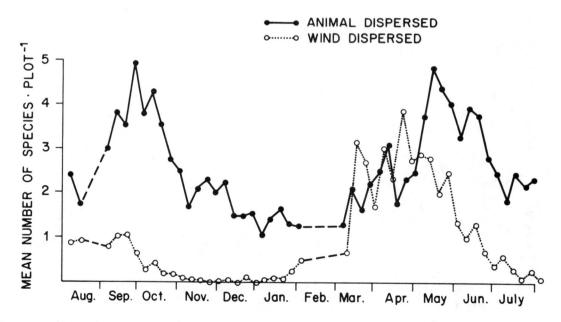

Figure 7. Comparison of the seasonality of animal-dispersed and wind-dispersed seed.

Those species that produce abundant small seeds and disperse them far are overrepresented. For example, Cecropia insignis, Luehea seemannii, Jacaranda copaia, Alseis blackiana, and Ficus insipida all appear in over half the traps when in peak fruit, while other species with equally many adults, or contributing equally to canopy coverage, drop seeds into far fewer traps. Thus, to some extent, species are weighted according to their colonizing ability. This emphasis is heaviest for relative frequency sums or the total number of seeds per plot, far less heavy for the average number of species dropping seed per plot, and least for the number of species dropping seeds into at least one trap somewhere in the study area.

RESULTS

Overall Pattern

Between August 1969 and August 1970, I find two main peaks when seed dissemination is significantly greater than during the rest of the year: a broad fruiting peak from March to June followed by a shallow depression in July and August, and a narrower peak in September and October followed by a prolonged low from November to February (Figures 2–5). This is true no matter what method of analysis is used. Relative frequency sums and the total number of seeds dropped per square meter of trap show a much higher peak in the spring than in the autumn. However, if one excludes seeds of Ficus and Cecropia, which are overrepresented in the samples, the remaining seeds show two peaks of nearly equal height (Figure 6). Hladik and Hladik (1969) had earlier noticed two peaks in the availability of animal-dispersed fruits on Barro Colorado, and Croat (1975) has mentioned this rhythm since. The qualitative observations I have made on Barro Colorado from 1971 to 1980 concur with this pattern, although the amplitudes vary significantly between years (Foster, this volume), and the calendar time of peaks can shift by a month or more.

The amplitude of fluctuation in fruiting depends on the measure used. The number of species dropping seeds into at least one tub (Figure 2) fluctuates least, with a fivefold difference between the highest and the lowest weeks, while the total number of seeds falling per square meter (Figure 5) fluctuates most, with a thirtyfold difference. Some of these measures appear more useful than others. The mean number of seeds falling per square meter (Figure 5) overemphasizes plants dropping abundant, small seeds, consequently giving the data a high variance. The sums of the relative frequencies (percentages) of the traps hit by seeds of the different species (Figure 4) overemphasizes plants that drop abundant, widely dispersed seeds. The total number of species dropping seeds into at least one trap (Figure 2) overemphasizes the occasional seed dropping well out of synchrony with the rest of its population. This can happen because an individual, a branch, or a single fruit may be out of synchrony with its fellows, or, more likely, because a seed gets stuck in its pod or stranded in the canopy. For example, Jacaranda copaia had essentially finished fruiting by the middle of October, but one or two Jacaranda seeds per week were still falling into the traps in April. The mean number of species per plot dropping fruit (Figure 3), however, represents a species once for each plot where its seeds were trapped, and thus emphasizes the more common species without giving undue weight to the total number of seeds per plant or their average dispersal distance. Although it too has distortions, this index best reflects the behavior of the vegetation and accordingly best measures the availability of fruit to animals: I shall use it for other comparisons.

Fruiting Rhythm in Relation to Dispersal Type

The difference between the rhythms of animal- and wind-dispersed seeds is most striking (Figure 7). There is a clear peak in wind-dispersed seeds during the transition from dry to rainy season, only a slight increase in September and October, and wind-dispersed seeds are almost completely absent late in the rainy season. The rhythm in the fall of animal-dispersed seeds, however, is clearly bimodal. Moreover, animal-dispersed seeds falling between March and June tend to fall after the rainy season starts, and nearly all the fruit falling between September and January is dispersed by animals. The breadth in the peak of the fruiting rhythm among wind-dispersed species is not significantly different from that in either peak among animal-dispersed species. There are too few species dispersed by other means, such as explosion, to warrant generalization.

Seasonality of Flowering

Those species dropping seed into the traps show a broad community peak of flowering lasting from late in the dry season through the first half of the rainy season. Those species whose fruiting peaked between July and February mostly flowered just after the beginning of the rainy season. Species fruiting between March and June had flowering times distributed over much more of the year, with a peak in the latter half

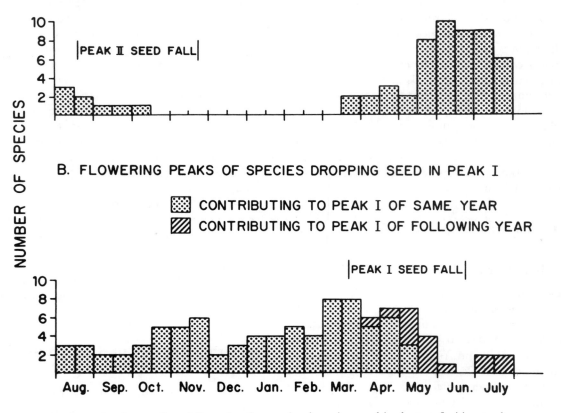

A. FLOWERING PEAKS OF SPECIES DROPPING SEED IN PEAK II

|PEAK II SEED FALL|

B. FLOWERING PEAKS OF SPECIES DROPPING SEED IN PEAK I

CONTRIBUTING TO PEAK I OF SAME YEAR
CONTRIBUTING TO PEAK I OF FOLLOWING YEAR

|PEAK I SEED FALL|

NUMBER OF SPECIES

Aug. Sep. Oct. Nov. Dec. Jan. Feb. Mar. Apr. May Jun. July

Figure 8.   Seasonality of flowering for species dropping seed in the two fruiting peaks.

of the dry season (Figure 8). Many of the species fruiting between March and June, however, flowered early in the preceding rainy season and took almost a year to mature their fruit; these included *Alseis blackiana, Apeiba membranacea, Apeiba tibourbou, Genipa americana, Guarea guidonia, Macfadyena unguis-cati, Ocotea skutchii, Pithecoctenium crucigerum, Platymiscium pinnatum, Prionostemma aspera, Strychnos panamensis, Tabernaemontana arborea,* and *Tocoyena pittieri.*

Fruiting Rhythm in Relation to Life Form

Although there are probably as many species of lianas and understory plants *in the forest* as there are trees, canopy trees are larger, produce more seeds, and perhaps disperse them farther; they accordingly dominate the fruiting rhythm in this forest (Table 1 and Figure 9).

The understory plants have two fruiting peaks of nearly equal size, but the second peak is in November and December, when fruiting among trees is near its minimum (Figure 9). The fruiting rhythm in lianas is

somewhat like that in trees, but the first peak is more pronounced and earlier because nearly 60% of the lianas are wind-dispersed (Table 1 and Figure 7).

The traps caught few seeds of epiphytes and hemi-epiphytes, perhaps because most such seeds land on other branches, or are too small (Figure 9). Hemi-epiphytes and epiphytes fruit mainly in the rainy season, with their primary peak in May and June. Most unidentified seeds may have been from epiphytes, as these were not well known.

Figs   The fruiting rhythms of the various species of *Ficus* have nothing in common but a weak depression from November to April (Figure 10). Individual species may show characteristic lows at another time of year; for example, *Ficus yoponensis* and *Ficus insipida* produce few fruit between July and October (Morrison, 1978). Compared with other plants, however, figs are strikingly unsynchronized. Occasionally, several individuals of a species will fruit concurrently with a precision that raises doubts about the importance of chance. But, considering all species together, the

Table 1. Life-form spectrum and dispersal type of all species caught in seed traps over a 2-year period

Dispersal type	Life form						Total[1]
	Canopy trees	*Understory*	*Lianas*	*Hemiepiphytes*	*Epiphytes*	*Unknown*	
Animal	71 (34%)	58 (28%)	33 (16%)	13 (6%)	4 (2%)	27 (13%)	206 (72%)
Wind	22 (31%)	0	45 (64%)	1 (1%)	0	2 (3%)	70 (25%)
Explosive	0	5	0	0	0	0	5 (2%)
Other	1	2	0	0	0	1	4 (1%)
Total	94 (33%)	65 (22%)	80 (28%)	14 (5%)	4 (1%)	30 (11%)	285

[1] Row totals are expressed as percentage of total of all dispersal types.

Numbers of species and percentages of the row total are given for each life-form class.

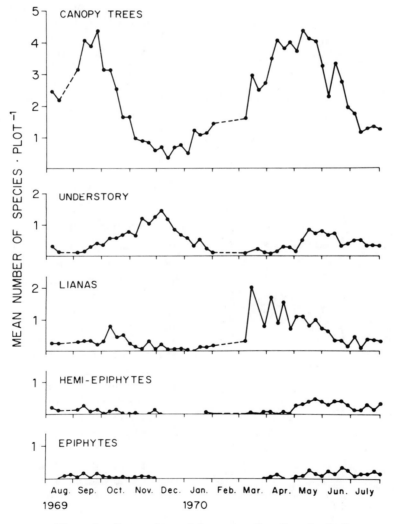

Figure 9. Comparison of the seasonality of seed rain for different life forms. The measurements are done as in Figure 3.

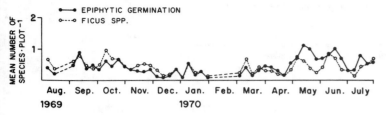

Figure 10. Seasonality of species that germinate epiphytically (solid line, dark circles) and all *Ficus* species (dashed line, open circles).

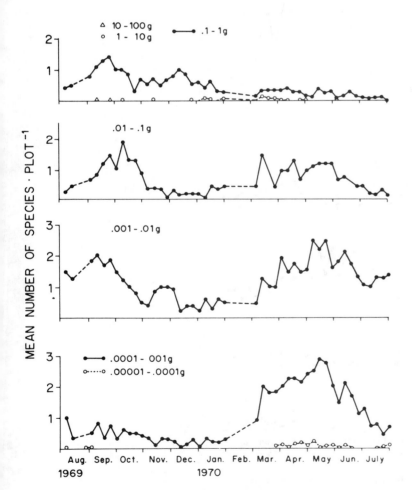

Figure 11. Comparison of the seasonality of different seed weight classes. The heavier seed classes are at the top.

fruiting peaks that occur irregularly throughout the year are probably not predictable.

The species of *Ficus* contribute most of the "noise" in the seasonal pattern. Fig trees "grow their own pollinators"; except for the time spent flying from one tree to another, the wasps which pollinate fig trees spend their entire lives in fig fruits (Corner, 1940; Ramirez, 1970; Janzen, 1979). With their unique, "built-in" pollination system, figs should be less affected by environmental change.

Fruiting Rhythm in Relation to Seed Weight

The traps did not sample very large (1–100 g) or very small (less than 0.1 mg) seeds sufficiently to reveal seasonal rhythms. Personal observation of large-seeded species leads me to conclude that the fall of very large seeds is no more seasonal than the fall of smaller ones (see Smythe, 1970, for a contrasting view). Medium to large seeds weighing from 0.1 to 1 g tend to fall from September through December, and small seeds weighing from 0.1 to 1 mg tend to fall from March through June (Figure 11). The fall of seeds weighing 1–100 mg, which represents the fruit falling from most of the species sampled (Table 2), has a clearly bimodal rhythm.

DISCUSSION

Factors Affecting the Season of Fruitfall

To what extent is the season when a plant drops fruit governed by when conditions are most favorable for seed germination, and to what extent is it governed by some other exigency, such as the availability of dispersers or the need to flower when pollinators are most available?

The Season of Seed Germination Although there are two peak seasons of fruitfall, the number of seeds germinating per month on Barro Colorado has only a single peak, shortly after the beginning of the rainy season (Garwood, this volume). Most of the seeds falling from March through June germinate immediately or as soon as the rains come, but a high proportion of the seeds falling from September through February remain dormant until the advent of the following rainy season. Heavier seeds may fall more often in the late rainy season because larger seeds or seedlings can cope better with drought (cf. Baker, 1972).

In light gaps, seedlings germinating at the start of the rainy season have a distinct advantage over those

Table 2. Seed-weight spectrum of all species caught in seed traps over a 2-year period, separated according to ecological category

Ecological category	Weight class[1]							Total
	1	2	3	4	5	6	7	
Dispersal type								
Animal	1 (1%)	7 (3%)	55 (27%)	78 (38%)	47 (23%)	15 (7%)	3 (1%)	206
Wind	0	0	7 (10%)	38 (54%)	16 (23%)	7 (10%)	2 (3%)	70
Explosive	0	0	0	3	1	1	0	5
Other	2	0	0	2	0	0	0	4
Total	3 (1%)	7 (2%)	62 (22%)	121 (42%)	64 (22%)	23 (8%)	5 (2%)	285
Life form								
Canopy trees	2 (2%)	5 (5%)	31 (33%)	28 (30%)	18 (19%)	8 (9%)	2 (2%)	94
Understory	0	1 (2%)	13 (21%)	29 (46%)	15 (24%)	4 (6%)	1 (2%)	63
Lianas	1 (1%)	1 (1%)	15 (19%)	46 (58%)	14 (18%)	1 (1%)	2 (3%)	80
Hemiepiphytes	0	0	0	6	5	3	0	14
Epiphytes	0	0	0	0	4	0	0	4
Unknown	0	0	3	12	8	7	0	30
Germination position								
Epiphytic	0	0	0	1	10	4	0	15
Ground	3	7	59	109	46	13	5	242
Unknown	0	0	3	11	8	6	0	28
Ficus spp.	0	0	0	1	3	1	0	5
Cecropia spp.	0	0	0	0	0	4	0	4

[1] Weight classes determined from oven-dry weight of seed: (1) 10–100 g, (2) 1–10 g, (3) 0.1–1 g, (4) 0.01–0.1 g, (5) 0.001–0.01 g, (6) 0.0001–0.001 g, (7) 0.00001–0.0001 g.

Numbers of species and percentages of the row total are given for each weight class. Percentages are omitted for those categories with only a small number of species.

germinating later; it seems advantageous to germinate as early in the rainy season as possible, apart from the risk of responding to a false start (Garwood, this volume). The season when a plant drops fruit is thus strongly but not invariably governed by when conditions for seed germination are most favorable.

The Availability of Dispersal Agents There would not be enough animals in the forest to disperse the fruit if all animal-dispersed species dropped fruit at the beginning of the rainy season; the competition for dispersers would be overwhelming. Presumably, some species would be pressured to ripen fruit at other times of the year.

There is a second peak in the fall of animal-dispersed fruits in September and October, just when the influx of birds migrating from the north temperate zone peaks (Karr, 1976); there is no corresponding peak period of influx in the spring from birds returning to North America. Thompson and Willson (1979) report that, in the temperate zone, many plants time the ripening of their fruit to take advantage of migrating birds; the same may sometimes happen in the tropics as well.

On Barro Colorado Island, understory species, including trees, shrubs and treelets, fruit in November and December, during the shortage of canopy fruit (Figure 12). This is also true for the understory trees (Frankie et al., 1974), but not for the understory shrubs and treelets (Opler et al., 1980), in the rain forest at La Selva, Costa Rica. Fruiting in November and December could exploit animals as dispersal agents which are hungry during the normal late rainy-season depression in fruiting. At least the understory plants may thereby avoid competing with canopy trees for dispersers (Frankie et al., 1974). On Barro Colorado,

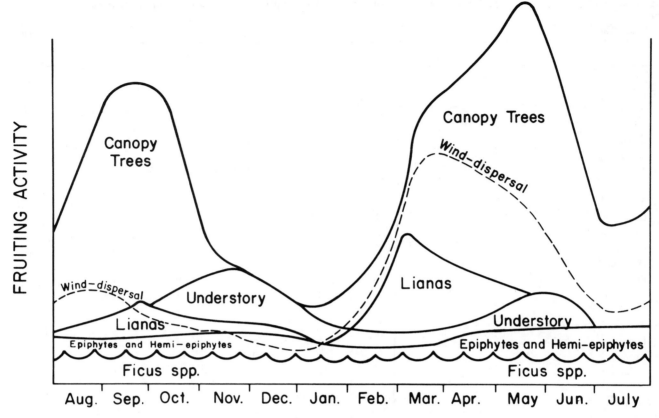

Figure 12. Schematic diagram of the seasonality of fruiting activity in a "normal" year. The diagram is derived from earlier figures and "activity" is intended to represent the proportion of the forest vegetation that is fruiting.

monkeys and canopy birds come conspicuously lower in the understory to feed during November and December. Selection may favor species with low energy budgets ripening their fruit during the famine season.

Although some heavy-seeded canopy trees such as *Platypodium* may rely on dry-season trade winds to disperse their seeds, as Janzen (1967), Smythe (1970), and Daubenmire (1972) suggest, most wind-dispersed species do not appear dependent on them. Nearly half the wind-dispersed fruits and seeds are released after the rains begin, when trade winds are much diminished. Trade winds are not really necessary for dispersal. In the rainy season, mornings are often bright and clear, with very strong winds building up before an afternoon thunderstorm. On a clear September morning with a moderate breeze, *Jacaranda copaia* trees can fill the air above the canopy with millions of seeds. Even the heavy winged fruit of *Pterocarpus rohrii* is dispersed in September.

Many wind-dispersed species fruit when the greatest number of forest trees is leafless, which occurs in the last month of the dry season and the first month of the rainy season. A wind-dispersed species may also disperse seeds when its own trees have fewest leaves, a circumstance that may be governed by factors other than dispersal.

Canopy species with explosive fruits, such as *Hura crepitans* and *Bauhinia reflexa*, also ripen their fruits when the maximum number of trees is leafless.

The Importance of Flowering Season The time intervening between flowering and the ripening of fruit is not directly related to the size of the seed or fruit produced and can presumably be adjusted through selection to suit the other needs of the plant. *Alseis blackiana* and *Gustavia superba* both flower early in the rainy season, but *Alseis* takes nearly a year to ripen its tiny fruits, while *Gustavia* grows its huge fruits in 1 or 2 months.

However, the season of flowering is related to the season of fruit dispersal. Most species dropping fruit in September and October flower early in the rainy season, apparently in response to the onset of the rains, as they flower earlier in those years when the rains start earlier. The flowering times of species dropping fruit between March and June are much more scattered through more of the year, although there is an increase from mid-February to mid-April. What could explain such a concentration of species' flowering in the early rainy season?

The season in which a species flowers affects the availability of potential pollinators, and the synchrony of flowering among its individuals. In Costa Rica, the numbers and diversity of small pollinating insects apparently increases early in the rainy season (Janzen and Schoener, 1968; Janzen, 1973). Such pollinators presumably also contribute to the early rainy-season peak in abundance of night-flying insects recorded by Smythe (this volume) on Barro Colorado. The proportion of species in flower on Barro Colorado which have small flowers changes little from season to season, but this means a large *number* of small-flowered species are flowering early in the rainy season, when insects abound. On the other hand, bat-pollinated plants such as *Ceiba pentandra, Bombacopsis sessilis, Bombacopsis quinata, Pseudobombax septenatum, Mabea occidentalis,* and *Lafoensia punicifolia,* and hummingbird-pollinated plants such as *Quassia amara, Passiflora vitifolia, Erythrina costaricana, Cavanillesia platanifolia,* and *Aphelandra sinclairiana* flower between October and March, presumably a time when more vertebrates than small insects are available as pollinators.

A species flowering early in the rainy season flowers more synchronously than a species flowering at another time of year (unpublished data of Foster, Windsor, Rand, Augspurger). The most conspicuous exceptions are shrubs such as *Hybanthus,* which flower in response to a dry-season rain, a cue which can be simultaneously detected over a large part of the island. And indeed, most species flowering early in the rainy season do seem to be flowering in response to the onset of the rains, a cue simultaneously detectable over a wide area, and one would accordingly expect them to flower in relative synchrony. If, on the other hand, a species flowers in response to the decline in soil moisture following the onset of dry season, one would expect the synchrony among its individuals to be less, since soils in different microhabitats dry out at different rates.

Greater synchrony is not intrinsically superior to less, but the synchrony of flowering and fruiting can influence the types of pollinators and dispersers it would be most desirable to attract. Synchronous flowering is more likely to preoccupy the attention of opportunist pollinators (Augspurger, this volume), and synchronous fruiting may satiate granivores which would otherwise destroy the fruit crop, as in *Hybanthus* (Augspurger, this volume), or attract the attention of opportunist frugivores (Howe, this volume). Asynchronous flowering and fruiting may predispose plants to reward pollinators and dispersers richly enough to attract a limited class of specialists which will return again and again to seek out the resource, as does *Virola surinamensis* with the rich aril surrounding its large seeds.

There is thus good reason to expect considerable selection on plants to use rainfall as a cue and for much flowering to be concentrated at the start of the rainy season. What is less clear is why the fruiting of these species should be so heavily concentrated in two months. On the short end, is it the physiological difficulty of developing fruit so fast or the abundance of seed predators and pathogens in July and August that select for a greater interval? On the long end is it the increased cost of maintaining and protecting fruit on the tree for long periods that selects for a shorter interval? These questions may eventually be testable.

CONCLUDING REMARKS

There seems to be strong selection both for flowering and for seed germination early in the rainy season. Many species do both, some by developing their fruits rapidly after flowering, some by taking a year to develop their fruits, and others with dormant seeds which only germinate at the onset of the following rainy season. There are very few species that neither flower nor germinate seeds at that time.

The timing of fruit ripening must resolve the conflict inherent in the simultaneous selection for flowering and germinating seeds early in the rainy season. The observed rhythm of fruiting may be additionally shaped by the availability of dispersal agents, environmental stresses on maternal physiology, and fluctuations in predators and pathogens. These ideas require considerably more information and testing. It would be quite instructive to study the phenological behavior of Barro Colorado species in different habitats within their distribution range. Whatever the selective forces or coincidence that brought it about, the fruit and seed resources during the year are an unstable resource for the Barro Colorado fauna.

ACKNOWLEDGMENTS

I thank especially W. D. Billings, A. S. Rand, and E. G. Leigh for their enormous assistance of all kinds. Many other staff and students at the Smithsonian and Duke University also contributed to this effort. Financial assistance came from the Smithsonian Institution, National Science Foundation, Botany Department of Duke University, and Department of Biology at the University of Chicago. E. G. Leigh and A. H. Kourany helped prepare the manuscript.

LITERATURE CITED

Augspurger, C. K.
1978.   Reproductive consequences of flowering synchrony in *Hybanthus prunifolius* (Violaceae) and other shrub species of Panama. Ph.D. thesis, University of Michigan, Ann Arbor.
1982.   A Cue for Synchronous Flowering. Pages 133–150 in *The Ecology of a Tropical Forest*, edited by Egbert G. Leigh, Jr., et al. Washington, D.C.: Smithsonian Institution Press.

Baker, H. G.
1972.   Seed weight in relation to environmental conditions in California. *Ecology*, 53:997–1010.

Corner, E. J. H.
1940.   *Wayside Trees of Malaya*. Singapore: Government Printer.

Croat, T. B.
1975.   Phenological behavior of habit and habitat classes on Barro Colorado Island (Panama Canal Zone). *Biotropica*, 7:270–277.
1978.   *Flora of Barro Colorado Island*. Stanford, Calif.: Stanford University Press.

Daubenmire, R.
1972.   Phenology and other characteristics of tropical semideciduous forest in northwestern Costa Rica. *Journal of Ecology*, 60:147–170.

Foster, R. B.
1973.   Seasonality of fruit production and seed fall in a tropical forest ecosystem in Panama. Ph.D. dissertation, Duke University, Durham, North Carolina.
1982.   Famine on Barro Colorado Island. Pages 201–212 in *The Ecology of a Tropical Forest*, edited by Egbert G. Leigh, Jr., et al. Washington, D.C.: Smithsonian Institution Press.

Frankie, G. W., H. G. Baker, and P. A. Opler
1974.   Comparative phenological studies of trees in tropical wet and dry forests in the lowlands of Costa Rica. *Journal of Ecology*, 62:881–919.

Garwood, N. C.
1982.   Seasonal Rhythm of Seed Germination in a Semideciduous Tropical Forest. Pages 173–185 in *The Ecology of a Tropical Forest*, edited by Egbert G. Leigh, Jr., et al. Washington, D.C.: Smithsonian Institution Press.

Hladik, A., and C. M. Hladik
1969.   Rapports trophiques entre vegetation et primates dans la forêt de Barro Colorado (Panama). *La Terre et la Vie*, 23:25–117.

Howe, H. F.
1982.   Fruit Production and Animal Activity in Two Tropical Trees. Pages 189–199 in *The Ecology of a Tropical Forest*, edited by Egbert G. Leigh, Jr., et al. Washington, D.C.: Smithsonian Institution Press.

Janzen, D. H.
1967.   Synchronization of sexual reproduction of trees within the dry season in Central America. *Evolution*, 23:620–637.
1973.   Sweep samples of tropical foliage insects: effects of season, vegetation types, elevation, time of day, and insularity. *Ecology*, 54:687–708.
1979.   How to be a fig. *Annual Review of Ecology and Systematics*, 10:13–51.

Janzen, D. H., and T. W. Schoener
1968.   Differences in insect abundance and diversity between wetter and drier sites during a tropical dry season. *Ecology*, 49:96–110.

Karr, J. R.
1976.   On the relative abundance of migrants from the north temperate zone in tropical habitats. *Wilson Bulletin*, 88:433–458.

Opler, P. A., G. W. Frankie, and H. G. Baker
1976.   Rainfall as a factor in the release, timing and synchronization of anthesis by tropical trees and shrubs. *Journal of Biogeography*, 3:231–236.
1980.   Comparative phenological studies of treelet and shrub species in tropical wet and dry forests in the lowlands of Costa Rica. *Journal of Ecology*, 68:167–188.

Ramirez B., W.
1970.   Taxonomic and biological studies of neotropical fig wasps (Hymenoptera: Agaonidae). *University of Kansas Science Bulletin*, 49:1–44.

Smythe, N.
1970.   Relationships between fruiting seasons and seed dispersal methods in a neotropical forest. *American Naturalist*, 104:25–35.
1982.   The Seasonal Abundance of Night-flying Insects in a Neotropical Forest. Pages 309–318 in *The Ecology of a Tropical Forest*, edited by Egbert G. Leigh, Jr., et al. Washington, D.C.: Smithsonian Institution Press.

Thompson, J. N., and M. F. Willson
1979.   Evolution of temperate fruit/bird interactions: phenological strategies. *Evolution*, 33:973–982.

Appendix 1. Flowering and seed rain phenology of individual species in the sample   *(continued on next page)*

Species	Peak flowering	Seed rain	Life form[1]	Dispersal[2]	Seed weight class[3]
Acanthaceae					
Mendoncia gracilis	—	Oct., Nov./Dec., Jan.	L	A	4
Mendoncia littoralis	—	May/Nov.	L	A	3
Anacardiaceae					
Anacardium excelsum	Late Feb.	Apr.	C	A	3
Spondias mombin	Late Apr.	Aug., Sept.	C	A	4
Spondias radlkoferi	Early May	Oct., Nov.	C	A	4
Annonaceae					
Annona spraguei	Late May	Sept., Oct.	—	A	4
Desmopsis panamensis	Oct.–Mar.	Jan.–July	U	A	3
Guatteria dumetorum	All year?	Feb.–Aug.	C	A	4
Unonopsis pittieri	Early Aug.	Mar.–June	U	A	2
Apocynaceae					
Lacmellea panamensis	—	Dec.	C	A	3
Odontadenia macrantha	Late May	Jan.	L	W	3
Prestonia sp.	—	Oct.	L	W	4
Tabernaemontana arborea	Early Apr.	Apr., May	C	A	3
Araceae					
Anthurium spp.[4]	—	Mar.–Sept.	E	A	5
Monstera dubia	Late June	July, *Aug.*, Sept.	H	A	4
Philodendron sp. 1[4]	—	Apr./June	H	A	4
Philodendron sp. 2[4]	—	May	H	A	4
Philodendron sp. 3[4]	—	Sept.	H	A	4
Philodendron sp. 4[4]	—	Sept., Oct.	H	A	4
Araliaceae					
Dendropanax arboreus	Early Aug.	Sept., Oct.	C	A	5
Dendropanax stenodontus	Early July	Sept., Oct.	U	A	4
Didymopanax morototoni	Late Oct.	Jan., Feb.	C	A	4
Asclepiadaceae					
Unidentified	—	Feb.	L	W	4
Bignoniaceae					
Amphilophium paniculatum	Late Oct.	Feb., *Mar.*, Apr.	L	W	4
Arrabidaea candicans	Late Sept.	Feb., *Mar.*–May	L	W	5
Arrabidaea patelliferum	Late Sept.	Mar., Apr.	L	W	4
Arrabidaea verrucosa	Early July/early Nov.	Sept., Oct./Feb., Mar.	L	W	4
Callichlamys latifolia	Early Nov.	Mar., Apr.	L	W	4

[1] Life form categories: C = canopy tree; U = understory tree or shrub; L = liana; H = hemiepiphyte; E = epiphyte.

[2] Dispersal categories: A = animal dispersed; W = wind dispersed; E = explosive mechanism; O = other means of dispersal.

[3] Seed weight categories: (1) = 10–100 g; (2) = 1–10 g; (3) = 0.1–1 g; (4) = 0.01–0.1 g; (5) = 1–10 mg; (6) = 0.1–1 mg; (7) = 0.01–0.1 mg.

[4] Seed of more than one species may be represented.

[5] *Guarea glabra* in Croat.

[6] *Trichilia cipo* in Croat.

[7] *Cynodendron panamense* in Croat.

Species	Peak flowering	Seed rain	Life form[1]	Dispersal[2]	Seed weight class[3]
Ceratophytum tetragonolobum	—	Jan.	L	W	4
Cydista aequinoctialis	Early July	Feb., *Mar.*	L	W	4
Jacaranda copaia	Early Mar.	July, *Aug.*, Sept.	C	W	5
Macfadyena unguis-cati	Late May	Feb., *Mar.*, Apr.	L	W	4
Martinella obovata	—	Apr.–June	L	W	4
Paragonia pyramidata	Late Mar.	July–Sept.	L	W	4
Phryganocydia corymbosa	June–Nov.	Feb.–June	L	W	4
Pithecoctenium crucigerum	Late May	Jan.–May	L	W	4
Stizophyllum riparium	—	Dec.	L	W	5
Tabebuia guayacan	Feb.–May	May	C	W	4
Tabebuia rosea	Feb.–May	Apr.–June	C	W	4
Unidentified	—	Jan.	L	W	4
Bombacaceae					
Ceiba pentandra	Early Jan.	Feb.–Apr.	C	W	4
Ochroma pyramidale	Late Jan.	May–July	C	W	5
Quararibea asterolepis	Late June	Aug., Sept., Oct.	C	A	3
Boraginaceae					
Cordia alliodora	Early Mar.	Apr., May, June	C	W	5
Cordia bicolor	Late Mar.	May, June, July	C	A	4
Cordia lasiocalyx	Early Mar.	Apr., May	U	A	4
Bromeliaceae					
Aechmea setigera	Jan.–Apr.	Apr.–July	E	A	5
Aechmea tillandsioides	Late Nov.	June	E	A	5
Burseraceae					
Protium tenuifolium	Early June	Aug.–Sept.	C	A	4
Tetragastris panamensis	Early July	Jan., *Feb.*–May	C	A	3
Trattinnickia aspera	Late July	Jan., Feb./May, June	C	A	4
Cactaceae					
Epiphyllum phyllanthus[4]	—	Apr.–Nov.	E	A	5
Capparidaceae					
Capparis frondosa	Jan., Feb./July–Sept.	May/Dec.	U	A	3
Combretaceae					
Combretum decandrum	Early Apr.	Apr., May	L	W	5
Combretum laxum	Early Nov.	Feb., Mar., Apr.	L	W	4
Terminalia amazonica	Late Feb.	Apr.–June	C	W	5
Terminalia chiriquensis	Late Oct./early Oct.	Jan., Feb./Mar.	C	W	5
Compositae					
Mikania leiostachya	Late Feb.	Feb., *Mar.*–May	L	W	6
Wulffia baccata	Late July	Oct.	L	A	5
Unidentified sp. 2	—	Aug.	—	W	6
Unidentified sp. 3	—	Feb.	—	W	6
Connaraceae					
Connarus panamensis	—	Aug.	L	A	3
Connarus turczaninowii	—	July	L	A	3
Rourea glabra	Early Jan.	Mar.	L	A	3

Species	Peak flowering	Seed rain	Life form[1]	Dispersal[2]	Seed weight class[3]
Convolvulaceae					
Maripa panamensis	Late Mar.	May–July	L	A	3
Cucurbitaceae					
Unidentified sp. 1	—	Mar.	L	A	4
Unidentified sp. 2	—	June	L	A	4
Dilleniaceae					
Davilla multiflora	Late Feb.	Apr., *May*, June	L	A	4
Doliocarpus dentatus	Late Feb.	Apr., May	L	A	4
Doliocarpus major	Early July	Sept., *Oct.*, Nov.	L	A	4
Doliocarpus olivaceus	Late May	Sept., Oct.	L	A	3
Tetracera portobellensis	Early Nov.	Feb.	L	A	4
Tetracera volubilis	Early Aug.	Feb.–Apr.	L	A	4
Elaeocarpaceae					
Sloanea terniflora	Late Aug.	Nov., Dec./Jan.–May	C	A	4
Euphorbiaceae					
Acalypha diversifolia	Late Apr.	May, June	U	E	6
Acalypha macrostachya	Early Apr.	May, June	U	E	5
Alchornea costaricensis	Late Apr.	June	C	A	4
Croton billbergianus	Early June	Aug., Sept.	U	E	4
Drypetes standleyi	Late May	Sept.	C	A	3
Hyeronima laxiflora	Late Oct., late Apr.	Nov., *Dec.*, Jan./May, *June*, July	C	A	5
Margaritaria nobilis	Early June	Sept.	U	A	5
Sapium caudatum	Late June	Aug., *Sept.*–Nov.	C	A	4
Flacourtiaceae					
Casearia arborea	Early Aug.	Aug., *Sept.*, Oct.	C	A	5
Casearia guianensis	Late Apr.	May	U	A	5
Casearia sylvestris	Early Oct.	Nov., Dec.	U	A	5
Hasseltia floribunda	Early Mar.	May, June	U	A	4
Laetia thamnia	Late Feb.	Feb., Mar./June/Nov.	C	A	5
Lindackeria laurina	Late Sept.	Jan., Feb.	C	A	4
Xylosma oligandrum	Late June	Sept.	U	A	4
Zuelania guidonia	Early Mar.	Apr.	C	A	4
Gnetaceae					
Gnetum leyboldii	Early Mar.	June	L	A	2
Guttiferae					
Clusia odorata	—	May–Sept.	H	A	5
Havetiopsis flexilis	Early Mar.	May, June	H	A	6
Rheedia edulis	Early Mar.	May	U	A	4
Hippocrateaceae					
Anthodon panamense	Early Jan./late July	Feb./Aug.–Oct.	L	W	4
Hippocratea volubilis	July, Aug./Oct./Dec.	Jan., Feb./Mar., Apr./June	L	W	4
Prionostemma aspera	Early Apr.	Feb., Mar.	L	W	3
Lauraceae					
Beilschmiedia pendula	Late Dec.	Apr.–June	C	A	2
Nectandra globosa	Late Mar.	June	C	A	3

Species	Peak flowering	Seed rain	Life form[1]	Dispersal[2]	Seed weight class[3]
Ocotea cernua	Early Mar.	Apr.	U	A	3
Ocotea oblonga	Early Aug.	Mar.	C	A	2
Ocotea skutchii	Early Apr.	May, *June*, July	C	A	2
Leguminosae					
Dipteryx panamensis	Early July	Jan., Feb.	C	A	2
Entada monostachya	Early July	Sept.	L	O	1
Inga sp. 1[4]	—	Jan., Feb.	—	A	3
Inga sp. 2[4]	—	Sept., Oct.	—	A	3
Inga sp. 3[4]	—	Feb.	—	A	3
Inga sp. 4[4]	—	Mar.	—	A	3
Inga sp. 5[4]	—	May	—	A	3
Inga sp. 6[4]	—	June	—	A	3
Lonchocarpus velutinus	Late Feb.	Apr.–June	C	W	4
Machaerium milleflorum	Late Mar.	Apr., May	L	W	4
Machaerium seemannii	Early Sept.	Mar.	L	W	3
Ormosia macrocalyx	—	June	C	A	3
Platymiscium pinnatum	Early May	Feb.–Apr.	C	W	3
Platypodium elegans	Late Apr.	Dec., Jan.	C	W	3
Prioria copaifera	Late Oct.	Apr.	C	O	1
Pterocarpus rohrii	Late May	Aug., *Sept.*, Oct.	C	W	3
Rhynchosia pyramidalis	—	Sept.	L	A	4
Swartzia simplex ssp. *grandiflora*	Early May	Nov.	U	A	3
Swartzia simplex ssp. *ochnacea*	Late June	Jan., Feb.	U	A	3
Tachigalia versicolor	Late Apr.	Feb.–Apr.	C	W	3
Unidentified	—	Feb.	—	O	4
Loganiaceae					
Strychnos panamensis	Early June	Mar.	L	A	3
Lythraceae					
Lafoensia punicifolia	Late Oct.	Apr.	C	W	4
Malpighiaceae					
Heteropteris laurifolia	Late Apr.	May, June	L	W	4
Hiraea faginea	Early June	July	L	W	4
Hiraea sp.[4]	—	Aug.	L	W	4
Malpighia romeroana	Late Sept.	Apr.	U	A	4
Mascagnia nervosa	Late Jan.	Feb., *Mar.*, Apr.–July	L	W	5
Stigmaphyllon lindenianum	Late Mar.	Apr.–June	L	W	4
Tetrapteris seemannii	Late Aug.	Mar.–May	L	W	4
Unidentified	—	Sept.	—	—	4
Malvaceae					
Hampea appendiculata	Early Oct.	Dec.	—	A	4
Marantaceae					
Calathea marantifolia	June–Oct.	Dec.	U	A	4
Marcgraviaceae					
Marcgravia nepenthoides	Early Nov.	Apr.	H	A	7
Souroubea sympetala	Late Jan.	Mar.–June	H	A	5

Species	Peak flowering	Seed rain	Life form[1]	Dispersal[2]	Seed weight class[3]
Melastomaceae					
Miconia argentea	Early Mar.	Mar., Apr.–June	C	A	7
Mouriri myrtilloides	Nov./Jan.–Mar.	Jan.–Apr./July–Sept.	U	A	4
Topobea praecox	Late June	June, *July*	H	A	5
Unidentified sp. 1[4]	—	May, June	U	A	6
Unidentified sp. 2[4]	—	Aug., Sept.	U	A	7
Unidentified sp. 3[4]	—	July, Aug.	U	A	6
Unidentified sp. 4[4]	—	Aug.	U	A	6
Meliaceae					
Cedrela odorata	June?	Sept.–Nov.	C	W	4
Guarea guidonia[5]	Early June	Feb., *Mar.*	U	A	3
Trichilia tuberculata[6]	Late June	Aug., *Sept.*–Nov.	C	A	3
Menispermaceae					
Unidentified	—	Sept.	L	A	5
Monimiaceae					
Siparuna pauciflora	Late Feb.	Sept., Oct.	U	A	4
Moraceae					
Brosimum alicastrum	—	Scattered	C	A	3
Cecropia insignis	Early Feb.	Mar.–*May*–July	C	A	6
Cecropia longipes	Late June	July, Aug.	C	A	6
Cecropia obtusifolia	Feb.–July	Feb.–Aug.	C	A	6
Cecropia peltata	Feb.–Nov.	Sept.–Oct.	C	A	6
Coussapoa panamensis	Early Apr.	Apr., *May*, June	H	A	5
Ficus costaricana[4]	—	Scattered	C	A	6
Ficus insipida[4]	—	Scattered	C	A	5
Ficus obtusifolia[4]	—	Scattered	C	A	5
Ficus paraensis	—	Scattered	H	A	5
Ficus tonduzii	—	Scattered	U	A	4
Olmedia aspera	Early June	Aug.–Nov.	U	A	4
Poulsenia armata	Apr./May/Nov.	May/June/Dec.	C	A	4
Sorocea affinis	Early Aug.	*Oct.*, Nov.	U	A	4
Myristicaceae					
Virola sebifera	Early June	Oct.–Dec.	C	A	3
Virola surinamensis	Early Oct.	Mar., Apr.	C	A	2
Myrsinaceae					
Ardisia pellucida	Early Dec.	Jan.	U	A	4
Stylogyne standleyi	Early Jan.	May	U	A	4
Myrtaceae					
Eugenia coloradensis	Late Jan.	Aug.–Oct.	C	A	3
Eugenia oerstediana	Early Jan.	Feb.	U	A	4
Myrica fosteri	Late June	Aug., Sept., Oct.	U	A	4
Psidium anglohondurense	Late Aug.	Sept., Oct.	U	A	3
Unidentified	—	Sept.	U	A	3
Nyctaginaceae					
Guapira standleyanum	Early Apr.	June	C	A	4
Pisonia aculeata	Late Feb.	Mar.	L	O	4

Species	Peak flowering	Seed rain	Life form[1]	Dispersal[2]	Seed weight class[3]
Ochnaceae					
Cespedezia macrophylla	Early Mar.	Apr., *May*	C	W	6
Olacaceae					
Heisteria concinna	Early Dec.	Mar.	U	A	3
Palmae					
Bactris sp.	—	Oct.	U	A	3
Desmoncus ithmius	Late Sept./late Feb.	Jan./July	L	A	3
Oenocarpus panamanus	Sept.–Feb.	Feb.–Aug.	C	A	3
Scheelea zonensis	—	Sept.	C	A	1
Socratea durissima	—	Oct./Jan./Mar., Apr.	C	A	3
Passifloraceae					
Passiflora ambigua	—	Mar.–May	L	A	4
Passiflora auriculata	—	May–July	L	A	5
Passiflora nitida	—	Mar., Apr.	L	A	4
Piperaceae					
Piper cordulatum	Early Feb.	May, *June*, July	U	A	5
Piper reticulatum	Early May	May–July	U	A	5
Piper sp.[4]	—	Feb.	U	A	5
Polygonaceae					
Coccoloba coronata	Late July	Feb.	U	A	4
Coccoloba parimensis	Late May	Sept.–Nov.	L	A	4
Triplaris cumingiana	Late Mar.	Apr., May	C	W	4
Rhamnaceae					
Gouania adenophora	Late July	Sept., Oct.	L	W	5
Gouania lupuloides	Late Jan.	Apr.	L	W	5
Rhizophoraceae					
Cassipourea elliptica	Late Aug.	Sept., Oct.	U	A	4
Rubiaceae					
Alibertia edulis	Early June	Dec., Jan.	U	A	4
Alseis blackiana	Early May	Feb.–*Apr.*, May	C	W	6
Amaioua corymbosa	Late July	May	U	A	5
Chomelia psilocarpa	—	Aug.	L	A	3
Cosmibuena skinneri	—	June	H	W	6
Coussarea curvigemmia	Late June	Dec., Jan.	U	A	5
Faramea occidentalis	Early June	Nov., *Dec.*, Jan.	U	A	3
Genipa americana	Late June	Feb., Mar./June	C	A	3
Macrocnemum glabrescens	Late Jan.	May, June	C	W	7
Palicourea guianensis	Late May	Oct., Nov.	U	A	4
Pentagonia macrophylla	Early July	Sept., Oct.	U	A	5
Posoqueria latifolia	Late June	Oct., Nov.	U	A	3
Psychotria deflexa	Late July	Oct.–Dec.	U	A	5
Psychotria furcata	Late June	Nov.–Feb.	U	A	4
Psychotria horizontalis	Late May	Sept.–Dec.	U	A	5
Psychotria marginata	Early Dec./early May	May–July/Sept., Oct.	U	A	5

Species	Peak flowering	Seed rain	Life form[1]	Dispersal[2]	Seed weight class[3]
Randia armata	Early May	June–Nov.	U	A	4
Tocoyena pittieri	Apr., May, June	June	C	A	3
Uncaria tomentosa	Late Apr.	July–Oct.	L	W	7
Rutaceae					
Zanthoxylum belizense	Early Sept.	*Jan., Feb.*–Apr.	C	A	5
Zanthoxylum panamense	Early June	*Sept., Oct.*, Nov.	C	A	4
Zanthoxylum procerum	Early Apr.	Sept.	C	A	5
Sapindaceae					
Cupania latifolia	Late June	Sept.	C	A	3
Cupania rufescens	Early Mar.	May	C	A	3
Cupania sylvatica	Early May	June	U	A	3
Paullinia glomerulosa	Early Aug.	Jan.	L	A	3
Paullinia pinnata	Early Aug.	Mar., Apr.	L	A	4
Paullinia turbacensis	Late Jan.	Mar.	L	A	3
Serjania atrolineata	Early Mar.	Mar., *Apr.*, May	L	A	4
Serjania cornigera	Late Dec.	Apr.	L	W	4
Serjania mexicana	Early Mar.	Mar., Apr., May	L	W	4
Serjania paucidentata	Early Mar.	Apr.	L	W	4
Serjania racemosa	—	Mar.	L	W	4
Serjania trachygona	Late Feb.	May	L	W	4
Serjania sp. 1	Late July	Sept., Oct.	L	W	4
Serjania sp. 2	—	May, June	L	W	4
Thinouia myriantha	Late Feb.	Mar., *Apr.*, May	L	W	4
Sapotaceae					
Chrysophyllum panamense[7]	Late Aug.	Jan., *Feb.*, Mar.	C	A	4
Pouteria unilocularis	Late May	July, *Aug.*, Sept.	C	A	3
Simaroubaceae					
Picramnia latifolia	Late Feb.	May–July	U	A	4
Simarouba amara	Early Mar.	May	C	A	4
Smilacaceae					
Smilax spp.[4]	—	Dec./Jan./Apr.	L	A	4
Solanaceae					
Markea panamensis	Jan.–June	Mar.–Aug.	H	A	6
Solanum argenteum	Early Apr.	Apr., May	U	A	5
Solanum hayesii	Early Dec.	Apr.–July	U	A	5
Solanum lanciifolium	Late Mar.	Apr., *May*–Aug.	L	A	5
Solanum sp.	—	June	U	A	5
Staphyleaceae					
Turpinia occidentalis	Late June	Aug.–Oct.	C	A	4
Sterculiaceae					
Guazuma ulmifolia	Late Oct.	Feb., Mar., Apr.	C	A	5
Sterculia apetala	Early Feb.	Jan., Feb.	C	A	3

Species	Peak flowering	Seed rain	Life form[1]	Dispersal[2]	Seed weight class[3]
Tiliaceae					
Apeiba membrancea	Apr.–Oct.	Feb.–Apr.	C	A	4
Apeiba tibourbou	Apr.–Jan.	Feb.–July	C	A	5
Heliocarpus popayanensis	Late Jan.	Mar., Apr.	C	W	6
Luehea seemannii	Early Feb.	Mar., *Apr.*–June	C	W	5
Ulmaceae					
Trema micrantha	Late June	June–Oct.	C	A	5
Verbenaceae					
Petrea volubilis	Late Mar.	Apr.	L	W	5
Violaceae					
Hybanthus prunifolius	Jan.–Mar.	Feb.–Apr.	U	E	4
Rinorea sylvatica	Jan.–Apr.	Feb., Mar.	U	E	4
Vitaceae					
Cissus sp.	—	Nov., Dec.	L	A	4
Vitis tiliifolia	—	June–Aug.	L	A	5
Zingiberaceae					
Costus sp.	—	Nov.	U	A	4
Renealmia cernua	Early July	Sept.–Dec.	U	A	4

Seasonal Rhythm of Seed Germination in a Semideciduous Tropical Forest

NANCY C. GARWOOD   Loyola University of Chicago, 6525 North Sheridan Road, Chicago, Illinois 60626

ABSTRACT

Although, considering the forest as a whole, there are two peak seasons of seed dispersal on Barro Colorado Island, there is only one peak season of seed germination, the early rainy season. In 1975, the median time of germination in trailside plots a meter wide and totaling 2 km in length, fell before June for 26% of the 187 dicot species observed, and occurred during June for 36%, while in 1976, when the rains started earlier, median germination time fell before June for 35% of the 182 dicot species observed and occurred during June for another 30%.

Germination experiments with 157 species in a greenhouse showed that most seeds dispersed during the dry season and half the seeds dispersed late in the rainy season were dormant, only germinating at the beginning of the following rainy season.

Seedling emergence in five light gaps opened by the fall of canopy trees peaked in the first fortnight of the 1976 rainy season. There were lesser peaks in June and, in some gaps, around September. From 21% to 65% of the seedlings germinating at various times in the rainy season died within two weeks of germination, the proportion being highest for those that germinated earliest. However, seedlings grew faster and survived the following dry season better, the earlier in the rainy season they had emerged.

Seedling emergence in shaded understory plots peaked 6 weeks later than in light gaps. Dry season mortality was higher among the shaded seedlings, and mortality rate, both in the 1976 rainy season and in the following dry season, was unrelated to time of emergence.

INTRODUCTION

The earliest stages of a plant's life are in many ways the most critical. The period between seed germination and initial establishment is often a time of high mortality (Harper and White, 1974; Cook, 1979). Early events can determine the final size and subsequent reproductive output (Harper, 1977) of the survivors. If germination can be timed to coincide with conditions more favorable for seedling establishment and growth, early mortality could be reduced, increasing reproductive success.

The timing of germination affects both the likelihood of suffering environmental stresses such as drought, and the prospects of competition from pre-existing seedlings. In many communities the relation of germination time to physical factors such as rainfall or temperature has been studied for one or more species, usually herbaceous, but ecological studies of the germination of woody perennials, particularly tropical species, are scarce (Angevine and Chabot, 1979). Two community-level studies have focused on the physiological mechanisms controlling time of germination in the winter annuals of the Mojave Desert (Went, 1948; Juhren et al., 1956) and plants of the cedar glades of Tennessee (e.g., Baskin and Baskin, 1971a,b,c, 1972, 1973, 1975, 1976).

Timing of germination with respect to other individuals, which concerns the variation between and within species, has received less study. Controlled intraspecific studies have shown that the order of emergence is extremely important: individuals emerging earlier are larger and suffer less mortality (Ross and Harper, 1972; Wanjura et al., 1969). Delays in emergence of only 5–9 days can cause a 50–70% reduction in size (Black and Wilkinson, 1963). In controlled interspecific studies, inferior competitors can become dominant if the emergence of the superior competitor is delayed three weeks (Sagar, 1959, cited in Ross and Harper, 1972). Such controlled studies do not consider the unpredictability of the environment. In intraspecific field studies, Baskin and Baskin (1972) found that earlier emerging individuals had higher mortality but greater fecundity, although Cook (1979) found lower mortality, larger size, and earlier reproduction in those seedlings that emerge earlier.

The relation of germination time to seasonal changes in either the physical environment or in the abundance of other seedlings has been little studied in the tropics, although seasonal constraints on seed germination have been invoked to explain the seasonality of fruiting. Seed germination early in the rainy season in seasonal tropical forests has often been predicted (Fournier and Salas, 1966; Smythe, 1970; Daubenmire, 1972; Foster, 1973; and Frankie et al., 1974).

Newly germinated seedlings are abundant in the early rainy season in at least some African and Panamanian forests (Taylor, 1960; Foster, 1973). The most common selective factor invoked for early seed germination was the advantage of having a long first growing season, which presumably reduced drought-related mortality during the dry season, although the release of nutrients from the litter at the beginning of the rainy season (Smythe, 1970) and the seasonality of formation of new light-gaps (Foster, 1973) have also been suggested. No one has remarked on the competitive advantage that may be gained by early emergence, although it should be important in habitats where seedling competition is intense, such as in light-gaps.

Seeds can germinate at favorable times either by remaining dormant until conditions are right or by ripening and dropping at the appropriate season. Most reports stress that tropical seeds usually germinate rapidly (Richards, 1952; Longman and Jenik, 1974; Whitmore, 1975; Ng, 1978), although enforced dormancy is common in secondary species (Vázquez-Yánes, 1974, 1976a,b). This suggests that in most tropical species the timing of germination is determined by the time of seed dispersal. The community peaks in seed dispersal found in many tropical forests (Koelmeyer, 1960; Daubenmire, 1972; Foster, 1973, this volume; Frankie et al., 1974) also suggest that timing of seed dispersal is the usual means of achieving germination at a favorable time, such as the beginning of a rainy season.

However, studies comparing many tropical species show a wide range of germination times (Ng, 1973, 1975, 1977; Taylor, 1960; Koebernik, 1971): many species require more than 4 weeks to germinate. Dormancy has occasionally been reported in other tropical species (Quarterman, 1970; Longman and Jenik, 1974; Whitmore, 1975; Hartshorn, 1978). Dormancy has been associated with avoidance of seasonal drought in five species (Enti, 1968; Hladik and Hladik, 1969; Frankie et al., 1974). Aiyar (1932) noted that seeds of many species in the monsoonal forests of India were dormant until the wettest and cloudiest part of the year was over.

On Barro Colorado Island, Panama, the site of this study, there are two peaks of seed dispersal, one at the beginning of the rainy season, as in other seasonal tropical forests, and a second later in the rainy season (Foster, 1973). Does this result in two peak seasons of germination, or are the seeds dispersed late in one rainy season dormant until the beginning of the next? What selective factors maintain this pattern of germination? To answer the first question, one must ask when most seeds germinate, how synchronous is germination in different species, and how commonly dormancy occurs, which can be done through periodic censuses of germinating seedlings, and by measuring the time different species require for germination under greenhouse conditions. The selective factors affecting time of germination that are maintaining the pattern found were examined by monitoring the growth and mortality of biweekly cohorts of seedlings throughout the year in both shaded understory and light-gap habitats. Previous studies of seedling survivorship of tropical species (Barnard, 1956; Wyatt-Smith, 1958; Nicholson, 1965; Connell, 1970; Fox, 1972, cited in Whitmore, 1975; Fox, 1973; Liew and Wong, 1973; Hartshorn, 1975; Van Valen, 1975; Sarukhán, 1978) have focused only on the proportions of seedlings dying per year.

METHODS

Field Census of Germination

Every 2 weeks from April 1975 to February 1977, all emerging seedlings with expanded cotyledons or first leaves greater than 0.25 sq. cm were removed from 20 nonadjacent trailside transects, each 1 × 100 m, located along a 4.5 km loop of infrequently used trails that passed through old and young forest on Barro Colorado Island. Only dicot seedlings were included in the analysis. Seedlings were sorted to morphological species; of more than 58,000 seedlings collected in 2 years, only 2% could not be assigned to a morphological species.

Seed Germination in the Greenhouse

Freshly fallen seeds of 157 species were collected in the forest; fleshy parts were removed if necessary. Seeds were planted in peat pots on the surface of well-drained Barro Colorado Island soil; pots were placed on a screen-topped bench in an open-air, screened enclosure located in the laboratory clearing of Barro Colorado Island. An additional layer of insect screening was placed approximately 30 cm above the bench top over the pots to reduce the intensity of direct sunlight. Observations were made approximately every 2 days from March 1976 to July 1977 and between July-September 1978. I watered seeds daily when necessary.

Mortality and Growth in Light-gap and Shaded Understory Habitats

Five recently created light-gaps, with no young seedlings present, were chosen in March-April of 1976.

Areas that were to include the study plots were cleared of all saplings and of all the large branches of the fallen trees, leaving the main trunk. Shaded understory sites were chosen adjacent to the light-gap sites, but far enough away that increased light levels were not perceptible; understory sites were not cleared. Sites were designated by their location along two trails, Zetek (Z) and Armour (A): Z11, Z1, Z2, A4, and A5. At each understory and light-gap site, eight 0.25 sq. m plots were randomly distributed among treatment plots. Only the results from the control plots will be discussed.

After 7 weeks, it was obvious that *Hybanthus prunifolius* dominated the understory plots. Therefore, four 1 sq. m transects were located near the understory sites and all seedlings except *H. prunifolius* monitored.

Biweekly censuses began on 7 May 1976, after the first rains, and continued until April 1977, the end of the dry season. Additional censuses were made in August 1977 and April and July 1978. At each census, emerging seedlings were identified and banded with numbered plastic bands; if seedlings were too small to be banded, they were marked with colored toothpicks and banded and identified if they grew larger. Cohorts of seedlings are consecutively numbered using the midpoint of the 2-week-long period in which they emerged. Total leaf area and height of all banded seedlings were measured every month from June 1976 to April 1977, except February.

Two points regarding this procedure should be kept in mind. First, all saplings were removed before seedlings emerged in the light-gaps. Therefore, competition between seedlings in these light-gaps is intense, but there are no interactions between seedlings and neighboring saplings. Second, these light-gaps opened either in the preceding dry season or late in the preceding rainy season: I have not studied the effect of the season when the gap formed on the regeneration therein.

Further details concerning methods are given by Garwood (1979).

RESULTS

Field Census of Germination

The number of seedlings of all species emerging throughout the year is shown in Figure 1. (Rate of emergence is the number of seedlings/collection period, corrected for differences in length of the collection period.) In both years, seedlings began to emerge in early May, just after the first rains of the rainy season. Numbers peaked in early and late June in 1975 and 1976, respectively, and numbers of

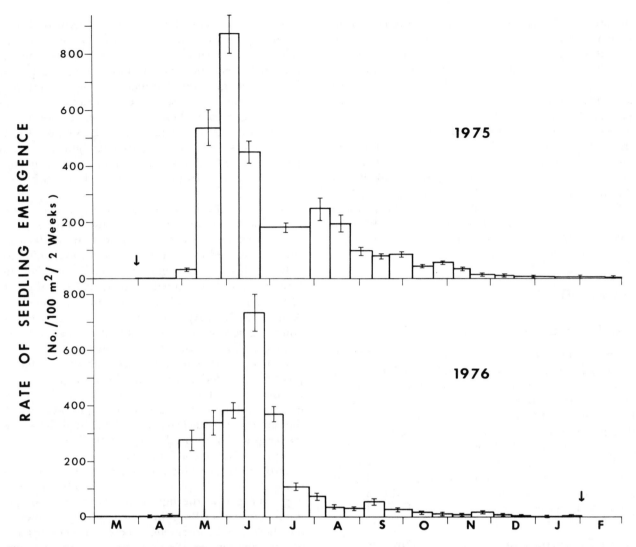

Figure 1. Mean (± *SE*) rate of seedling emergence (*N* = 20 transects). The arrows denote the beginning and end of the study.

emerging seedlings were significantly skewed to the right in both years. The average number of species emerging per collection period showed a similar pattern; the maximum average number of species germinated in early June, and the number germinating decreased steadily thereafter.

The median time of emergence of each species in the study was determined by pooling individuals from all 20 transects. The median time of emergence of the largest number of species is in early June and the distribution of germination times is significantly skewed to the right in both years (Figure 2). In 1975, the median germination time of 26% of the species occurred before the end of May, 62% before the end of June, and 73% before the end of July; for 1976,

the corresponding figures are 35%, 65%, and 76% respectively. A second peak in total number of seedlings or number of species was not seen in either year at or after the late rainy season peak in fruit production in late August-September. Although 75% of species emerge in the first three months of the rainy season, the peak in germination occurred approximately a month after the beginning of the rainy season, and 25% of the species do not germinate until its last 5 months.

The patterns of emergence of four common species are shown in Figure 3 to illustrate that synchrony within and between species varies enormously. Comparative studies of the patterns of emergence between species will be a rich area for further exploration.

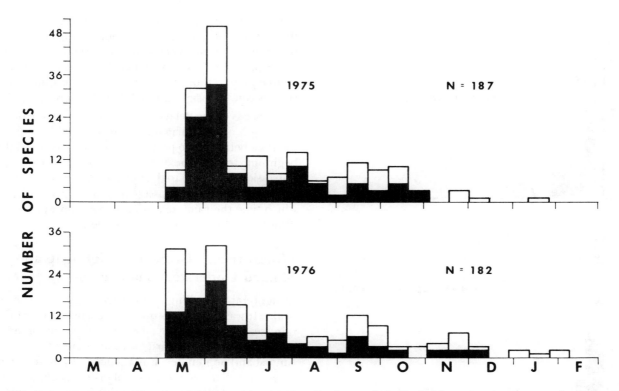

Figure 2. Number of species whose medians fall in each collection period. Shaded bars are common species ($N \geq 10$), unshaded bars are rare species ($N < 10$), and N is sample size per species.

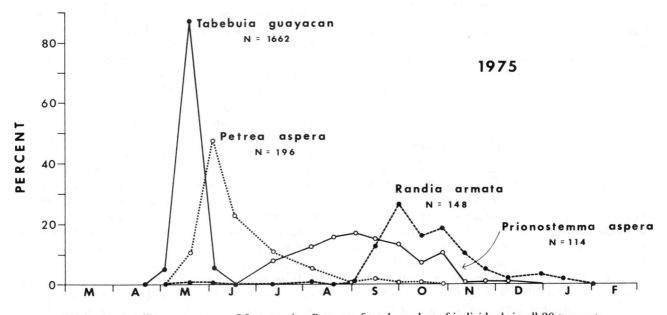

Figure 3. Seedling emergence of four species. Percent of total number of individuals in all 20 transects.

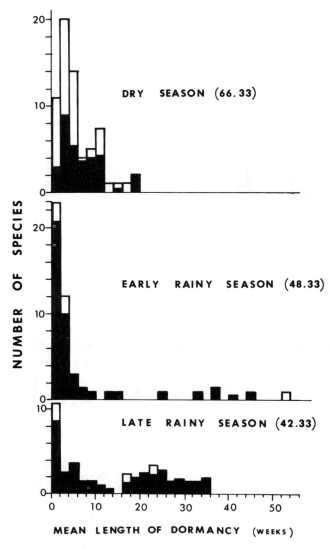

Figure 4. Mean length of innate dormancy of species whose seeds are dispersed in three seasons. Black bars are animal-dispersed species; open bars are wind-dispersed species. Total number of species in parentheses.

Seed Germination in the Greenhouse

The mean length of dormancy differed significantly for seeds dropped at different seasons (Figure 4). Rainy season species can be divided into two groups. "Rapid-rainy" species have an average period of dormancy less than 16 weeks; many of these germinate in less than 2 weeks. "Delayed-rainy" species have seeds that remain dormant an average of more than 16 weeks. Twelve percent of the species dispersed in the early rainy season, but 50% of those dispersed in the late rainy season showed dormancy lasting over 16 weeks.

Only 5% of the species whose seeds are dispersed in the dry season showed dormancy lasting that long, but most of these species had a dormant period of between 2 and 16 weeks, rather than germinating immediately like those in the rapid-rainy group; these species can be assigned to a "slow-dry" group.

For seeds of the delayed-rainy and slow-dry groups, the length of the dormant period is roughly equal to the time between the period of seed dispersal and the beginning of the next rainy season (Figure 5). A regression line fitted to the dormancy periods of seeds of these two groups crosses the axis in mid-May, by which time the rainy season has nearly always started (Rand and Rand, 1979; this volume).

Mortality and Growth in Light-gap and Shaded Understory Habitats

In light-gaps, seedling emergence occurred in three peaks. It was greatest in the first census period of the rainy season in early May; there was a second, broader peak in June and a third peak at some sites in late August and September. Emergence was low after October, and changes in total numbers of seedlings (Figure 6) reflect changes in mortality. There was only a slight decrease in numbers during the dry season, except in the densest site, Z2. Most mortality occurred in the early rainy season, accompanied by a rapid turnover of individuals. In the understory, the peak in emergence occurred approximately 6 weeks later than in the light-gaps. In the 0.25 sq. m plots, all sites except Z2 had peaks of emergence in late June-early July, caused primarily by a peak in *Hybanthus prunifolius*. Only in site Z1 was there a peak in the first week, which was caused by *Ceiba pentandra*, a light-gap species that quickly died in the shaded understory. In the 1 sq. m transects, all sites except A4 also had a peak in June-July or slightly later, and site Z2 had a pronounced peak in late September and a small peak in January, as did A5.

The total numbers of seedlings in the shaded understory are shown in Figure 7; since emergence was low from September on, except in Z2, changes in numbers after August reflect mortality. The rapid decline in numbers in the 0.25 sq. m plots are caused primarily by the mortality of *Hybanthus prunifolius*. The individuals in the transects had more variable behavior; numbers generally remained high during the rainy season, but declined rapidly at the beginning of the dry season, which is especially clear in sites Z11, Z2, and Z1.

In order to analyze mortality, individuals from all sites were pooled together. Of individuals surviving until the end of the rainy season, mortality by the end

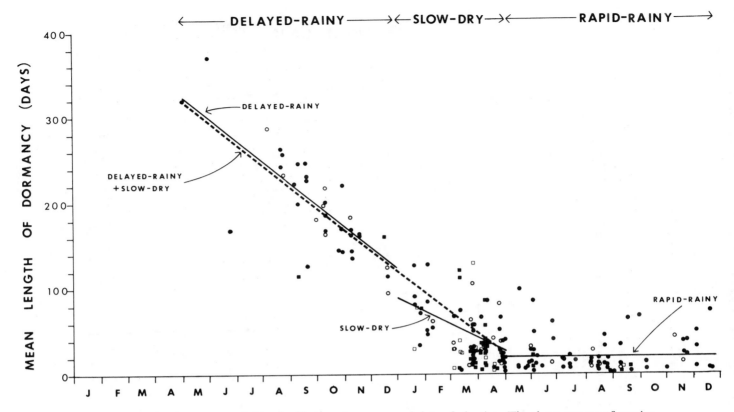

Figure 5. The relationship between mean length of innate dormancy and date of planting. The three groups of species—delayed-rainy, slow-dry, and rapid-rainy—are described in the text. Germination of all species occurs in the second rainy season, May-December. Circles = animal-dispersed species; squares = wind-dispersed species. Solid = the larger or only sample of a species; open = the smaller sample of a species with more than one planting.

of the dry season was greater in the shaded understory (58%) than in the light-gaps (30%). In light-gaps, mortality of early emerging cohorts was low in the dry season, but that of later emerging cohorts was very high. For example, only 3% of the surviving individuals of the first cohort died in the dry season, while 6% to 24% of the individuals in cohorts 3–13 (approximately mid-August), and more than 60% of later cohorts, died then. In the understory, mortality of all cohorts was high during the dry season, ranging from 25% to 75%, and was not related to week of emergence. In both light-gaps and the shaded understory, mortality was highest for seedlings less than 2 weeks old. In light-gaps, 65% of the seedlings in the first cohort, and 21% to 43% of the seedlings in later cohorts, died within the first 2 weeks of germination. The high mortality of the first cohort was associated with a drought, such as often occurs near the beginning of the rainy season. In the understory, 12% to 67% of the seedlings died within 2 weeks of germination, but mortality was not related to time of emergence.

If one measures growth by the change in the logarithm of 1 + total leaf area, one finds that the growth in leaf area differed significantly for seedlings of different ages at the same site, and the mean leaf area of the earliest emerging cohort was significantly larger than the means of all later cohorts combined (Figure 8).

In site Z2, which had the largest number of seedlings, growth rate, as measured by the regression of log (leaf area + 1) on log (age) was significantly higher for cohorts emerging earlier.

Growth in the understory sites did not show any differences between cohorts (Figure 9).

DISCUSSION

There is a single peak in seedling emergence on Barro Colorado: approximately 75% of the species emerge in the first 3 months of the rainy season. I predicted that, if a pattern of early germination was found, that seed dormancy would be common in species that disperse seeds late in the rainy season. And indeed, half

LIGHT-GAPS

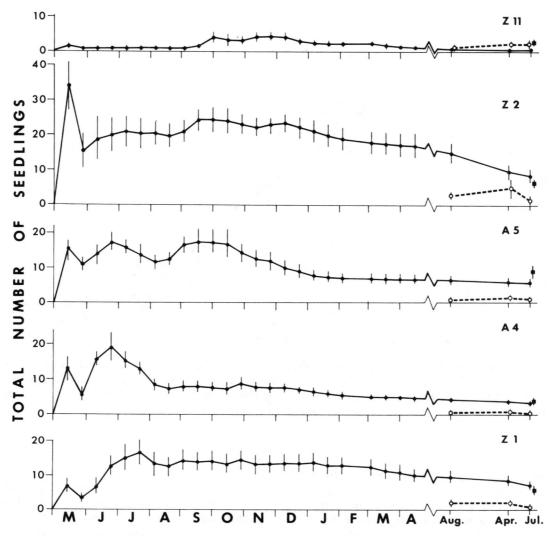

Figure 6.   Total number of seedlings of all ages in light-gap sites. Mean (± *SE*) number of seedlings of all ages in eight 0.25-sq. m plots at five sites in May-April 1976–1977, August 1977, and April and July 1978. The number of seedlings emerging in the second year is shown by the dashed line; the number emerging in the third year is shown by the solid black box.

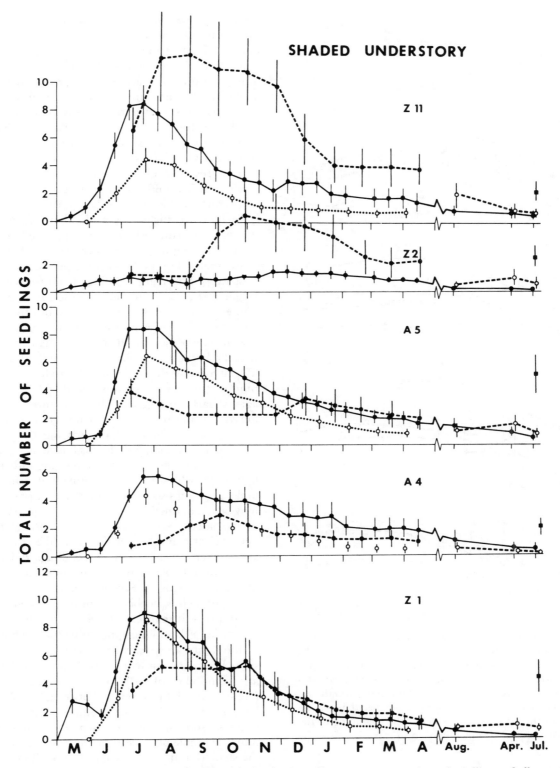

Figure 7. Total number of seedlings of all ages in understory sites. Mean (± SE) number of seedlings of all ages in eight 0.25-sq. m plots or four 1-sq. m transects. All species shown by the solid line and only *H. prunifolius* shown by the dotted line with open circles in the 0.25-sq. m plots; all species except *H. prunifolius* shown by the dashed line with solid circles in the 1-m transects, in May-April 1976–1977, and April and July 1978. The number of seedlings emerging in the 0.25-sq. m in the second year is shown by the dashed line with open circles; the number emerging in the third year is shown by the solid black box.

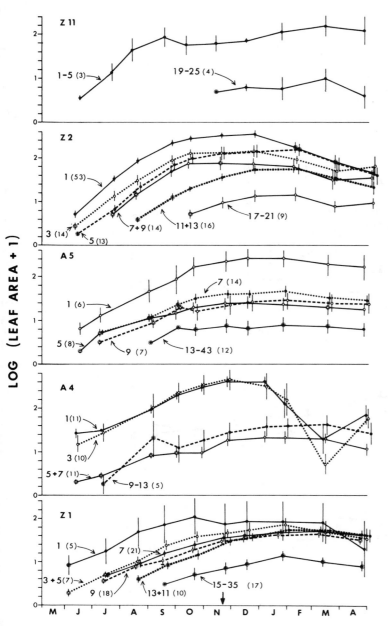

Figure 8. Seasonal changes in leaf area of cohorts of seedlings in light-gap sites. Mean (± *SE*) log (leaf area + 1). The sample sizes of cohorts are given in parentheses after each cohort number; an open circle around a point indicates that the sample size is lower than that given in parentheses. The heavy arrow at the bottom in November denotes the last rain of the rainy season, which is the beginning of the dry season. Leaf area is measured in sq. cm.

of the species that disperse seeds late in the rainy season have seeds that are dormant until the beginning of the next rainy season. The length of the dormant period decreases as the beginning of the next rainy season approaches. For species that are dispersed in the late rainy season, this suggests that dormancy is not simply a mechanism to avoid germinating late in the rainy season, but also a mechanism to prevent germination during unpredictable rains during the dry season. Many of the species dispersed in the dry season are also dormant, but for shorter periods, which would also prevent germination during unpredictable heavy rains during the dry season.

Factors favoring early germination in light-gap habitats appear to differ from those in shaded understory habitats. In light-gaps, the greatest number of seedlings emerged in the first census period, just after the first rains. Surviving seedlings from this cohort had larger leaf areas at the end of the rainy season and higher growth rates than seedlings of other cohorts. They also had lower mortality during the dry season, presumably because of their larger size. However, they had the highest mortality during the first 2 weeks of life, suggesting that the unpredictability of the beginning of the rainy season is a strong factor selecting against early emergence. The competitive advantages derived from early emergence must outweigh the disadvantages of a high risk of early mortality.

If early emerging individuals has such a great competitive advantage over later emerging individuals in light-gaps, why do so many individuals emerge later in the growing season? Variation in time of emergence may be maintained by factors other than competition. First, spatial heterogeneity could maintain late emergence; later emerging seedlings could be successful in areas where early emerging seedlings did not germinate or did not survive the unpredictable beginning of the rainy season. Second, chance events, such as falling branches, herbivores, or disease could remove or suppress the earlier emerging individuals and create space for later emerging individuals. Third, many of the light-gap species with high growth rates have short life spans and could create gaps in the canopy after a number of years; later emerging individuals might establish but remain suppressed until a second light-gap forms. Fourth, conditions in light-gaps later in the season, although less than ideal, might provide more favorable places for seedling establishment than the shaded understory, where few seedlings survived their first year.

In the understory, seed germination occurs later than in light-gaps, but still early in the rainy season. Earlier emerging seedlings did not have greater leaf areas or lower mortality in the dry season; there does not appear to be a direct competitive advantage to

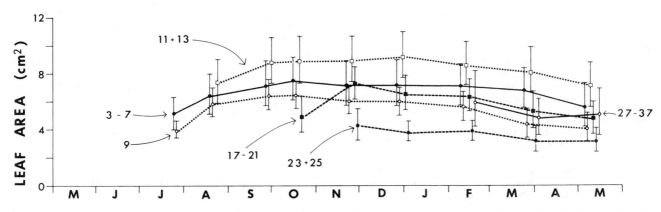

Figure 9. Seasonal changes in leaf area of cohorts of seedlings in shaded understory sites. Individuals in all sites combined. Mean (± *SE*) leaf area, not log (leaf area + 1) as in Figure 8. Other notation as in Figure 8.

early emergence in the shaded understory.

Most of the individuals germinating in the shaded understory did not survive until the beginning of the next rainy season, which suggests that they cannot establish in the shaded understory but must be in or near a light-gap to become established. Except for *Hybanthus prunifolius*, the number of seedlings in the shaded understory remains high through the rainy season, which includes the time on Barro Colorado Island when light-gaps are most frequently formed (Brokaw, this volume). The earlier a seedling emerges, the higher is the probability that it will be present before a light-gap is formed at that site (Foster, 1973). Seedlings that emerged before a gap occurred would have a competitive advantage over seedlings emerging after gap formation.

The delay in emergence in the understory, compared with light-gaps, could be related to several factors. First, delayed emergence avoids the unpredictable beginning of the rainy season, although the probability that the rainy season has not yet begun is already low in late May, about a month before the peak in seedling emergence. Second, the abundance of a thick layer of litter in the early rainy season might be a disadvantage to seedling emergence, especially for smaller species. Third, many species use the beginning of the rainy season as a cue to flower (Foster, 1973; Augspurger, this volume); the delay in emergence could reflect the time necessary after flowering to mature and disperse seeds, not the existence of factors directly selecting against early seedling emergence.

LITERATURE CITED

Aiyar, T. V. V.
1932. The Sholas of Palghat Division. Part II. *Indian Forester*, 58:473–486.

Angevine, M. W., and B. G. Chabot
1979. Seed Germination Syndromes in Higher Plants. Pages 188–206 in *Topics in Plant Population Biology*, edited by O. T. Solbrig, S. Jain, G. B. Johnson, and P. H. Raven. New York: Columbia University Press.

Augspurger, Carol K.
1982. A Cue for Synchronous Flowering. Pages 133–150 in *The Ecology of a Tropical Forest*, edited by Egbert G. Leigh, Jr., et al. Washington, D.C.: Smithsonian Institution Press.

Barnard, R. C.
1956. Recruitment, Survival, and Growth of Timber Tree Seedlings in Natural Tropical Rain Forest. *Malayan Forester*, 19:156–161.

Baskin, J. M., and C. C. Baskin
1971a. Germination Ecology and Adaptation to Habitat in *Leavenworthia* spp. (Cruciferae). *American Midland Naturalist*, 85:22–35.
1971b. Germination ecology of *Phacelia dubia* var. *dubia* in Tennessee glades. *American Journal of Botany*, 58:98–104.
1971c. Germination of *Cyperus inflexus* Muhl. *Botanical Gazette*, 132:3–9.
1972. Ecological life cycle and physiology ecology of germination of *Arabidopsis thalianai*. *Canadian Journal of Botany*, 50:353–360.
1973. Delayed Germination in Seeds of *Phacelia dubia* var. *dubia*. *Canadian Journal of Botany*, 51:2481–2486.
1975. Seed Dormancy in *Isanthus brachiatus* (Labiatae). *American Journal of Botany*, 62:623–627.
1976. Effects of Photoperiod on Germination of *Cyperus inflexus* seeds. *Botanical Gazette*, 137:269–273.

Black, J. N., and G. N. Wilkinson
1963.   The Role of Time of Emergence in Determining the Growth of Individual Plants in Swards of Subterranean Clover (*Trifolium subterraneum* L.). *Australian Journal of Agricultural Research*, 14:628–638.

Brokaw, N.
1982.   Treefalls: Frequency, Timing, and Consequences. Pages 101–108 in *The Ecology of a Tropical Forest*, edited by Egbert G. Leigh, Jr., et al. Washington, D.C.: Smithsonian Institution Press.

Connell, J.
1970.   On the Role of Natural Enemies in Preventing Competitive Exclusion in Some Marine Animals and Rain Forest Trees. Pages 298–312 in *Dynamics of Populations*, edited by P. J. den Boer and G. R. Gradwell. Wageningen, Netherlands: Center for Agricultural Publishing and Documentation.

Cook, R. E.
1979.   Patterns of Juvenile Mortality and Recruitment in Plants. Pages 207–231 in *Topics in Plant Population Biology*, edited by O. T. Solbrig, S. Jain, G. B. Johnson, P. H. Raven. New York: Columbia University Press.

Daubenmire, R.
1972.   Phenology and Other Characteristics of Tropical Semideciduous Forest in North-western Costa Rica. *Journal of Ecology*, 60:147–170.

Enti, A. A.
1968.   Distribution and Ecology of *Hildegardia barteri* (Mast.) Kosterm. *Bulletin de l'Institute Francaise de l'Afrique Noir*, (Series A) 30:881–885.

Fournier, L. A., and S. Salas.
1966.   Algunas observaciones sobre la dinamica de la floración en el bosque tropical humedo de Villa Colón. *Revista de Biologica Tropical*, 14:75–85.

Foster, R. B.
1973.   Seasonality of Fruit Production and Seed Fall in a Tropical Forest Ecosystem. Ph.D. thesis, Duke University. 155 p.

Fox, J. E. D.
1972.   The Natural Vegetation of Sabah and Natural Regeneration of the Dipterocarp Forests. Ph.D. thesis, University of Wales.
1973.   Dipterocarp Seedling Behavior in Sabah. *Malayan Forester*, 36:205–214.

Frankie, G. W., H. G. Baker, and P. A. Opler.
1974.   Comparative Phenological Studies of Trees in Tropical Wet and Dry Forests in the Lowlands of Costa Rica. *Journal of Ecology*, 62:881–913.

Harper, J. L.
1977.   *Population Biology of Plants*. London: Academic Press.

Harper, J. L., and J. White
1974.   The Demography of Plants. *Annual Review of Ecology and Systematics*, 5:419–463.

Hartshorn, G. S.
1975.   A Matrix Model of Tree Population Dynamics. Pages 41–51 in *Tropical Ecological Systems: Trends in Terrestrial and Aquatic Research*, edited by F. B. Golley and E. Medina. New York: Springer-Verlag.

1978.   Treefalls and Tropical Forest Dynamics. Pages 617–638 in *Tropical Trees as Living Systems*, edited by P. B. Tomlinson and M. H. Zimmerman. Cambridge: Cambridge University Press.

Hladik, A., and C. M. Hladik
1969.   Rapports trophiques entre végétation et primates dans la forêt de Barro Colorado (Panama). *La Terre et la Vie*, 23:25–117.

Juhren, M., F. W. Went, and E. Phillips.
1956.   Ecology of Desert Plants. IV. Combined Field and Laboratory Work on Germination of Annuals in the Joshua Tree National Monument, California. *Ecology*, 37:318–330.

Koebernik, J.
1971.   Germination of Palm Seed. *Principes*, 15:134–137.

Koelmeyer, K. O.
1959,   The Periodicity of Leaf Change and Flowering in the
1960.   Principal Forest Communities of Ceylon. *Ceylon Forester*, 4:157–189, 308–364.

Liew, T. C., and F. O. Wong
1973.   Density, Recruitment, Mortality and Growth of Dipterocarp Seedlings in Virgin and Logged-over Forests in Sabah. *Malaysian Forester*, 36:3–15.

Longman, K. A.
1969.   The Dormancy and Survival of Plants in the Humid Tropics. *Society for Experimental Biology Symposia*, 23:471–488.

Longman, K. A., and J. Jenik.
1974.   *Tropical Forest and Its Environment*. London: Longman Group.

Ng, F. S. P.
1973.   Germination of Fresh Seeds of Malaysian Trees. *Malaysian Forester*, 36:54–65.
1975.   Germination of Fresh Seeds of Malaysian Trees. II. *Malaysian Forester*, 38:171–176.
1977.   Germination of Fresh Seeds of Malaysian Trees. III. *Malaysian Forester*, 40:160–163.
1978.   Strategies of Establishment in Malaysian Forest Trees. Pages 129–162 in *Tropical Trees as Living Systems*, edited by T. B. Tomlinson and M .H. Zimmerman. Cambridge: Cambridge University Press.

Nicholson, D. I.
1965.   A Review of Natural Regeneration in the Dipterocarp Forests of Sabah. *Malaysian Forester*, 28:4–25.

Quarterman, E.
1970.   Germination of Seeds of Certain Tropical Species. Pages D173–175. in *A Tropical Rain Forest*, edited by H. T. Odum and R. F. Pigeon. Oak Ridge, Tenn.: U.S. Atomic Energy Commission.

Rand, W., and A. S. Rand
1979.   The Rainfall of Barro Colorado Island, Panama. Pages 31–49 in *Actas del IV Simposium Internacional de Ecologia Tropical, 7–11 Marzo 1977*. Panama City: Impresora de la Nacíon, INAC.
1982.   Variation in Rainfall on Barro Colorado Island. Pages 47–59 in *The Ecology of a Tropical Forest*, edited by Egbert G. Leigh, Jr., et al. Washington, D.C.: Smithsonian Institution Press.

Richards, P. W.
1952.   *The Tropical Rain Forest*. Cambridge: Cambridge University Press.

Ross, M. A., and J. L. Harper
1972.   Occupation of Biological Space During Seedling Establishment. *Journal of Ecology*, 60:77–88.

Sagar, G. R.
1959.   The Biology of Some Sympatric Species of Grassland. Ph.D. thesis, University of Oxford.

Sarukhán, J.
1978.   Studies on the Demography of Tropical Trees. Pages 163–184 in *Tropical Trees as Living Systems*, edited by P. B. Tomlinson and M. H. Zimmerman. Cambridge: Cambridge University Press.

Smythe, N.
1970.   Relationships Between Fruiting Seasons and Seed Dispersal Methods in a Neotropical Forest. *American Naturalist*, 104:25–35.

Taylor, C. J.
1960.   *Synecology and Silviculture in Ghana*. Edinburgh: Nelson.

Van Valen, L.
1975.   Life, Death and Energy of a Tree. *Biotropica*, 7:260–269.

Vásquez-Yanes, C.
1974.   Studies on the Germination of Seeds of *Ochroma lagopus* Swartz. *Turrialba*, 24:176–179.

1976a.   Seed Dormancy and Germination in Secondary Vegetation Tropical Plants: The Role of Light. *Comparative Physiological Ecology*, 1:30–34.

1976b.   Estudios sobre la ecofisiología de la germinación en una zona cálido-humedo de México. Pages 279–387 in *Investigaciones sobre la Regeneración de Selvas Altas en Veracruz, México*, edited by A. Gomez-Pompa, C. Vazquez-Yanes, S. del Amo Rodríquez, and A. Butanda Cervera. Mexico City: Compania Editorial Continental.

Wanjura, D. F., E. B. Hudspeth, Jr., and J. D. Bilbo, Jr.
1969.   Emergence Time Seed Quality, and Planting Depth Effects on Yield and Survival of Cotton. *Agronomy Journal*, 61:63.

Went, F. W.
1948.   Ecology of desert plants. I. Observations on germination in the Joshua Tree National Monument, California. *Ecology*, 29:242–253.

Whitmore, T. C.
1975.   *Tropical Rain Forests of the Far East*. Oxford: Clarendon Press.

Wyatt-Smith, J.
1958.   Seedling/sapling survival of three common economic tree species in Malaya. *Malaysian Forester*, 21:185–192.

FRUGIVORES

Fruit Production and Animal Activity in Two Tropical Trees

HENRY F. HOWE   Program in Evolutionary Ecology and Behavior, Department of Zoology, University of Iowa, Iowa City, Iowa 52242

ABSTRACT

Tetragastris panamensis and *Virola surinamensis* are two species of tropical tree with arillate fruits. In 1978, *Tetragastris* produced roughly the same total weight of fruit per tree as did *Virola* in 1979, but *Tetragastris* seeds are a tenth as large as those of *Virola*, and ten times more numerous. *Tetragastris* arils are sweeter, but less nutritious, than *Virola* arils.

Tetragastris fruit attracted twice as many species of visitors in 1978 as did *Virola* in 1979. The number of species visiting individual *Tetragastris* trees increased significantly with increased total fruit crop, but this was not true for *Virola*. Fruiting of individual *Tetragastris* attracts opportunist dispersers by spectacular displays of superabundant but mediocre fruit, while *Virola* attracts specialist dispersers willing to seek out small quantities of the fruit they particularly favor.

The proportion of seeds removed from under different *Tetragastris* trees ranged from 1% to 56%, av-eraging 23%, and was highest for trees with fruit crops of intermediate size. Dispersal of *Virola* was more efficient; the proportion of seeds removed from under different plants ranged from 13% to 91%, averaging 62%, and this proportion was correlated with seed size rather than size of the fruit crop. Animals preferred smaller-seeded, more easily handled fruit. *Tetragastris* seeds were dispersed largely by mammals, which tended to defecate many seeds in a single clump, so that dispersal was not only inefficient but wasteful, but *Virola* seeds were dispersed primarily by birds that regurgitated them one by one, scattering them more effectively. *Tetragastris* and *Virola* thus offer a contrast between a tree offering relatively "cheap" rewards for dispersal and attracting opportunist, indifferent, wasteful dispersers, and a tree offering a richer reward designed to attract efficient and interested specialists.

INTRODUCTION

Many tropical trees bear fleshy fruits adapted to attract dispersal agents, and many tropical animals eat fruit and either disperse or destroy seeds. Some trees produce many fruits with an abundance of small seeds; others produce fewer fruits, with larger seeds. How does the character of the fruit affect the prospects of dispersal? To answer, I will compare two tropical trees, *Tetragastris panamensis* (Engl.) O. Kuntze (Burseraceae) and *Virola surinamensis* (Rol.) Warb. (Myristicaceae), the production and dispersal of whose fruit I have studied in detail (Howe, 1980; Howe and Vande Kerckhove, 1980, 1981). I will relate the number, size, and quality of fruit they produce to the numbers and variety of consumers these fruit attract and the proportion of their seeds that are dispersed, and then consider these results in the context of other studies of fruit dispersal.

How might a plant best arrange for animals to disperse its seeds? Snow (1971) suggested that, within a population, selection favors those plants that produce the largest numbers of fruit, thereby attracting the largest number and variety of dispersal agents. McKey (1975) suggested that there was more than one way

to arrange for dispersal by animals: some plants may benefit from a variety of dispersers, while others would profit more from dispersal by a few reliable specialists. Species producing small seeds should invest little in rewards for dispersers, relying rather on a spectacular superabundance of fruit to attract a variety of opportunists, while species producing large seeds should provide rich and nutritious rewards to attract specialists which care to locate and return to particularly valuable sources of food. McKey implicitly assumed an unlimited supply of opportunists and a limitation on the number of specialists. Howe and Estabrook (1977) explored the logic of McKey's dichotomy, arguing that an unlimited supply of opportunists might favor those plants with the most spectacular arrays of superabundant fruit, while restriction of the number of specialists should lead to limited fruit production and selection on a plant to attract more dispersers through the quality rather than the quantity of its fruit.

Although they are not closely related, *Tetragastris* and *Virola* appear to represent the dichotomy implied by McKey (1975) and Howe and Estabrook (1977) (Figure 1). *Tetragastris* fruits are dehiscent capsules that expose one to six aromatic seeds with white arils against a dark purple core. The strong resinous smell, the dramatic color contrast, and the presentation of seeds both day and night suggest a generalized dispersal system (van der Pijl, 1972). Each arillate seed, the unit of dispersal, is approximately 2 cm long. The aril tastes sweet, and indeed consists largely of sugar. *Virola* capsules contain a single arillate seed, also about 2 cm long, but much more nearly spherical. The aril is scentless, brilliant red, bitter to the taste, and extremely fatty. Such characteristics, along with dehiscence early in the morning, suggest dispersal by birds (van der Pijl, 1972). As one would expect, the largest *Tetragastris* are roughly ten times more fecund than the largest *Virola*.

If these plants do represent McKey's dichotomy fairly, then we would expect that, since *Tetragastris* arils are less nutritious than those of *Virola*, (1) a smaller proportion of seeds will be dispersed from *Tetragastris* than from *Virola*; while, since *Tetragastris* is "playing to a larger gallery," (2) its trees will attract a much more numerous and diverse assemblage of dispersers than will *Virola*. Moreover, if there is a superabundance of opportunists ready to be attracted to the most spectacular display, but only a limited number of specialists, we would expect that (3) *Tetragastris* fruiting is more sharply peaked, while *Virola* fruiting is spread more evenly through the season, and (4) a comparable increase in crop size would yield greater increase in the number of species visiting *Tetragastris* than in the number visiting *Virola*. However, because no verte-

Figure 1. Compound fruit of *Tetragastris panamensis* (left) and single-seeded fruit of *Virola surinamensis* (right). *Tetragastris* seeds are white, standing out against a purple red core. *Virola* seeds are tan, surrounded by brilliant red arils. Both are approximately 2 cm long.

brate can live by sugar alone, while entrained specialists will presumably rely more on a single and perhaps sufficient source of food the more ample the supply, (5) the proportion of seeds dispersed should not decrease with increasing size of *Tetragastris* crop, because there are always more opportunists to draw from, while in *Virola* the proportion dispersed should be highest for intermediate crops because too large a crop would encourage frugivores to "camp out" on the resource, regurgitating seeds in place.

There is a limit to what can be learned from comparing two species. Any comparison of very different trees will yield differences. The differences may, however, turn out as predicted for entirely the "wrong" reasons, or other factors which we have not studied may confuse the outcome. Such a comparison may be a necessary first step toward understanding the factors affecting dispersal, but there is much more to do.

METHODS

The Trees

Tetragastris panamensis occurs from Belize to Peru and Brazil; *Virola surinamensis* occurs from Costa Rica and Panama to the Guianas and Brazil, with disjunct populations in the lesser Antilles (Croat, 1978). On Barro Colorado Island, both species are common in the mature forest, which is thought to be a few hundred years old (Foster and Brokaw, this volume). Most *Tetragastris* fruit appears between January and June. Flowering seems to be more synchronous, and fruit crops heavier, the later the preceding rainy season begins. In the last 14 years, *Tetragastris* did not fruit at all if the preceding rainy season began earlier than 15 April, while they produced a bumper crop in 1978 following a rainy season which began on 17 May 1977 (Foster, this volume). *Virola* trees mostly fruit between March and September. They seem to flower in response to the onset of drought, and they sometimes flower in response to droughts during rainy season. Since soils in different places dry out at different rates, while a heavy rain wets them all simultaneously, one might expect flowering and fruiting to be more spread out in *Virola* than in *Tetragastris* (Foster, this volume).

Procedures: General

I will only outline my methods here: they are detailed in Howe (1980) and Howe and Vande Kerckhove (1981). Between 11 March and 1 July 1978, I studied fruit production and frugivore visitation at 19 *Tetra-*

gastris trees near Wheeler trail #20. They ranged from 11 to 60 cm (33 ± 7 cm, mean ± 95% confidence interval) in diameter at breast height (dbh), and from 10 to 38 m (21 ± 4 m) in height. Between 21 May and 7 September 1979, I studied fruit and frugivores at 22 *Virola* trees in Lutz catchment and on surrounding ridges. These were thought to be in patches of forest a hundred or more years old surrounded by secondary forest 20 to 30 m tall (Foster, personal communication). Nineteen of these *Virola* ranged from 19 to 80 cm (51 ± 13 cm) in dbh, and from 14 to 34 m (26 ± 2 m) in height. I excluded one *Virola* from most analyses because a windstorm overturned it during my study, and four others because they were still dropping fruit when my study ended.

Fruit Crops

The study of fallen fruit can help answer the following questions.

1. How many fruits does a *Tetragastris* tree make, how much do these fruits weigh, and how much reward, in energy and nutrient, do they offer their disperser? How does this compare with *Virola*?

2. Is the season of fruitfall more sharply peaked in *Tetragastris* than in *Virola*?

3. Are a larger proportion of the seeds removed from under the parent tree in *Virola* than in *Tetragastris*?

4. How does the proportion of seeds removed from the parent vary with crop size in *Tetragastris* and in *Virola*?

To answer, I sampled the number and weight of fruit produced by sample trees of both species, making weekly collections from 1-sq. m traps under their crowns (Figure 2). Under each sample tree I randomly placed 4 to 20 such traps, covering, in most cases, 6%–15% of the area under the crown and up to 30% of the area under the crown of a very small tree.

For each *Tetragastris* tree, I estimated the number of seeds per square meter of crown dropped or eaten each week from the number of core locules appearing in the traps that week. White (1974) lists the average dry weight of a *Tetragastris* seed and of its aril. I weighed 30 capsules that had been oven-dried for 4 days at 65° C. Each capsule consisted of a core and fragments of the outer coat that covers each locule.

I calculated the proportion x of seeds that were dropped under the parent tree rather than removed elsewhere by dividing the number of seeds in the traps under a tree by the number of core locules there. The proportion removed from under the parent tree is

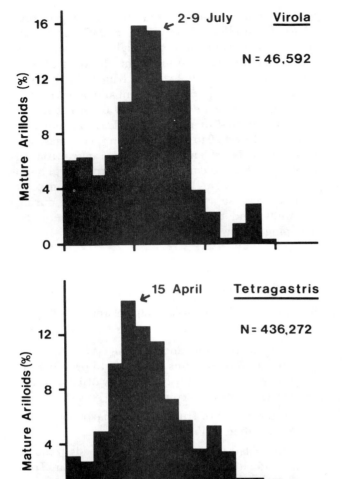

Figure 2. Weekly production of 19 *Tetragastris* trees and 15 *Virola* trees, expressed as a percent of the total seed crop (upper right hand corner of each histogram).

For each *Virola* tree, I estimated the number of fruits dropped or eaten each week from the number of capsules appearing in the traps. I took dry weights of capsules, arils, and seeds, and for each tree I had a composite sample of 15 arils, which I freeze-dried at Barro Colorado, and had commercially analyzed at Colorado State University for lipid, carbohydrate, protein, and tannin content (Howe and Vande Kerckhove, 1981).

I calculate the proportion of seeds dropped under the parent tree by dividing the number of fallen seeds by the number of fallen capsules. I also recorded the proportions of seeds in the trap which were regurgitated or destroyed or which had dropped with aril intact, thereby enabling me to calculate, among other things, the proportion of the tree's seeds that had had their arils eaten.

Dispersers

By periodically visiting trees to count the frugivores in their crowns and by watching specific trees for long periods of time to estimate feeding rates and rates of seed drop for the various frugivores, we can learn the following.

1. How many species visit *Tetragastris*, as compared with *Virola*, and how many of these visitors disperse seeds.

2. What proportion of the seeds is removed, and what proportion is destroyed or wasted, by different visitors.

3. How the diversity of visitors increases with crop size in *Tetragastris* as compared to *Virola*.

During the *Tetragastris* study, I counted the animals at each of my 19 trees once between 6:30 A.M. and 8:30 A.M., a second time between 11:00 A.M. and 1:00 P.M., and a third time between 3:30 P.M. and 5:30 P.M. 2 days a week. The 14 weeks of the study yielded 28 × 3 × 19 or 1596 tree scans.

To check for nocturnal frugivores, on 10 separate nights during May and June 1978, I searched 30 trees with an electric lamp and binoculars at the time of peak activity for such animals, between 7:00 P.M. and 10:00 P.M., and I recorded presence or absence of animals in each tree.

To evaluate feeding rates of different frugivores and the average duration of their visits to the trees, I watched each of ten *Tetragastris* trees for two 10-hour periods apiece.

During the *Virola* study, I made four randomly timed circuits of the 19 sample trees, counting the animals therein, three times a week. The 15 weeks of the study yielded 15 × 4 × 3 × 19 or 3420 separate

1 − x. Not all of these can be counted as dispersed, however, for if many are deposited in a single pile of feces, only one of those can grow to any extent. I calculated the proportion *y* of arils eaten as the proportion 1 − x of seeds removed from under the parent plus one-half the proportion of the tree's seeds that fell into the traps from opened fruits. I could not tell how many seeds fell or were dropped from their capsules with their arils intact, for arils disappeared from these seeds rather quickly after they had fallen into the traps.

tree scans. To check for presence or absence of nocturnal foragers, I inspected these trees on 14 different nights with light and binoculars.

To evaluate feeding rates and average duration of visits for the various frugivores, Vande Kerckhove and I watched eight *Virola* trees for eight 5-hour spells apiece, from 6:00 A.M. to 11:00 A.M. The schedule differs from the *Tetragastris* study because animals visited *Tetragastris* all day, but came to *Virola* mainly in the early morning.

To calculate the number of seeds eaten by each species, I multiplied the total number of visits observed for each visitor during the watches times the mean number of seeds eaten per visit. The percentage of seeds eaten by each species consists of the number estimated eaten by each species divided by the number estimated eaten by all species, multiplied by 100. To calculate the number of seeds dispersed by a species of bird, I multiplied the number of seeds eaten by birds of this species by the proportion of these seeds that were not spit out or regurgitated while the birds were still in the parent tree. Mammals often defecate several seeds in one "fecal clump," which are so close together that no more than one of the resultant seedlings can mature. Thus, to calculate the number of seeds dispersed by a mammal species, I divide the number of seeds eaten that are not spit out or regurgitated in the parent trees by an average number of seeds per fecal clump. The percentage contributed by a species to dispersal is the number of seeds it disperses, divided by the total number of seeds handled by any species, multiplied by 100.

RESULTS AND DISCUSSION

Comparison of the Fruit Crops

In *Tetragastris,* the total number of seeds produced during the season ranged from 165 to 99,000 (22,951 ± 13,213; mean ± 95% confidence interval) in 19 different sample trees, while for *Virola* the number ranged from 214 to 10,412 (2991 ± 1332; n = 17).

The average dry weights of *Tetragastris* capsules, arils, and seeds are 1.9, 0.4, and 0.2 g, respectively, compared with 2.0, 0.8, and 2.0 g in *Virola*. Since most *Tetragastris* capsules contain five seeds, there is 0.4 g dry weight of capsule, and a total of 1.0 dry weight of fruit parts of all kinds, per *Tetragastris* seed, compared with 4.8 g dry weight of fruit per seed in *Virola*. *Tetragastris* produced an average of 20,884g dry weight of fruit per tree in 1978, of which 13,480 g (64%) consisted of seeds and arils, while *Virola* produced 16,749 g dry weight of fruit per tree in 1979, of which 10,757 g (also 64%) consisted of seeds and arils (Tables

Table 1. Number of fruit parts dropped or removed from the vicinity of average *Tetragastris* and *Virola* trees

Species	N	Mean capsules dropped (± CI)	Mean seeds dropped (± CI)	Mean seeds removed (± CI)
Tetragastris	19	4590 ± 2642[1]	15,886 ± 8748[3]	6581 ± 4546
Virola	17	2991 ± 1331[2]	1031 ± 486	1960 ± 941

[1] Usually five seeds/capsule.

[2] One seed per capsule.

[3] Includes intact seeds, arillate seeds, and arillate seeds in mature but unopened fruit.

Table 2. Weight (in grams) of fruit debris dropped by average *Tetragastris* and *Virola* trees under and away from parent trees

Species	Dropped under parent tree			Dropped away from parent tree	
	Capsules	Seeds	Arils	Seeds	Arils
Tetragastris	8721	3177	3177	1316	4493[1]
Virola	5982	2062	511	3920	4274[1]

[1] Consumed and presumably digested by animals. Analysis assumes that arils were eaten off of half the seeds dropped under the parent tree.

Table 3. Nutritional content of *Tetragastris* and *Virola* arils (in percent of total dry weight)

Species	N	Protein (%)	Lipid (%)	Usable carbohydrate (%)	Kcal/gm
Tetragastris	7[1]	1.2[1]	3.6[1]	56.5[2]	4.1[1]
Virola	10	3.3	53.2	5.6	7.0

[1] From White (1974).

[2] From K. Milton, pers. comm.

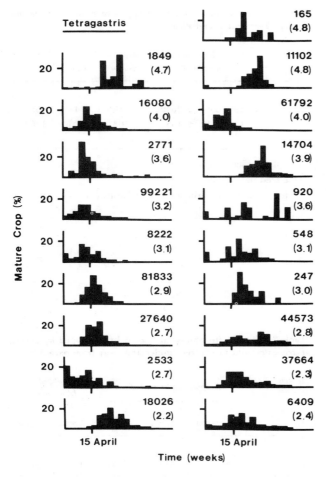

Figure 3. Individual fruiting phenologies of *Tetragastris* trees in weekly intervals. Crop sizes are given in the upper right corner of each histogram; kurtosis values are in parentheses.

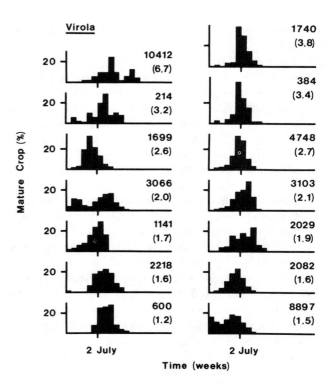

Figure 4. Individual fruiting phenologies of *Virola* trees in weekly intervals. Crop sizes are given in the upper right corner of each histogram; kurtosis values are in parentheses.

1 and 2). A third of the *Tetragastris* seeds left the vicinity of the parent; two-thirds of the *Virola* seeds did (Table 2).

The energy content of *Virola* capsules, arils, and seeds average 4.2, 7.0, and 7.5 kcal/g dry weight: the energy content of *Tetragastris* seeds and capsules are likely to be similar to those in *Virola* (E. Leigh, pers. comm.). Plugging in these figures, we find that during the appropriate seasons, *Virola* and *Tetragastris* dropped an average of 103,484 and 101,773 kcal per season (calculations are from Table 2). In *Virola,* 29% of the energy invested in fruit was accounted for by arils of seeds actually dispersed; the seeds actually dispersed accounted for 28% of the total energy expended. In *Tetragastris,* 18% of the total energy in fruit is accounted for by arils of seeds removed from trees; the seeds removed accounted for 10% of the budget. *Virola* puts more into dispersal, and obtains a higher energetic gain, than *Tetragastris*. *Virola* arils contain

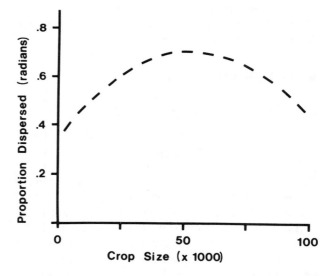

Figure 5. Interpretive summary of a weak curvilinear relationship between the proportion of crop removed and crop size at *Tetragastris* ($r^2 = 0.30, p = 0.07$). The first order term is significant at $p < 0.05$, the second at $p = 0.06$. Proportions are expressed in radians of the angular transformation. A comparable test with *Virola* is not significant ($p > 0.5$). Original analyses are in Howe (1980) and Howe and Vande Kerckhove (1981).

nearly 3 times as much protein and 15 times as much lipid as *Tetragastris* arils, per unit dry weight (Table 3).

In short, the total reproductive investments of our *Tetragastris* trees were rather similar to those of our *Virola*, yet *Tetragastris* made eight times as many seeds, each weighing a tenth as much as a *Virola* seed. As McKey (1975) predicted, the aril offered in reward for dispersing *Virola* is much richer and more nutritious than that in *Tetragastris*.

Phenology

To learn whether fruiting is spread more evenly through the season in *Virola* than in *Tetragastris*, I compared fruiting curves for individual plants sampled through their entire period of fruit drop (Figures 3, 4). I calculated measures of kurtosis for each tree (Sokal and Rolf, 1969). All exceed 1.0, and so all the curves must be considered "peaked." In the *Virola*, values of kurtosis ranged from 1.2 to an aberrant 6.7, with a mean of 2.6 ± 0.7. In general, fruiting curves showed sharper peaks in *Tetragastris* than in *Virola* ($U = 60$, $n_1 = 14$, $n_2 = 19$, $p < 0.01$). Such a comparison suffers from the statistical difficulty that both populations were sampled over a maximum of 15 weeks; hence all values are higher than they would have been with more sampling points. The problem is not severe because individuals of both species have fruiting periods of about the same length, roughly 12 to 15 weeks.

As expected, the more nutritious fruit is offered more evenly through the season, as if to attract specialists that rely on it. This may be true in most seasons, since *Tetragastris* flowers in response to the onset of rainy season, which is usually a more synchronous signal than the onset of drought, which is thought to stimulate flowering *Virola* (Foster, this volume).

Removal of Seeds from the Vicinity of Parent Trees

The proportion of seeds removed from the different *Tetragastris* trees I sampled ranged from 1% to 56% (23 ± 7%), while the proportion of seeds removed from different *Virola* ranged from 13% to 91% (62 ± 9%). As expected, the species of tree offering the richer reward gets more of its seeds removed.

The Effect of Crop Size on the Proportion of Seeds Removed

In *Tetragastris*, the relation between crop size X (in thousands of seeds) and the proportion Y of seeds removed from under the parent plant is

$$\arcsin Y^{1/2} = 0.3349 + 0.0134X - 0.0001X^2$$

where $\arcsin Y^{1/2}$ is expressed in radians (2π radians $= 360°$) (Figure 5). The term in X is significant at $p < 0.05$, and the term in X^2 is significant at $p = 0.06$; for the whole, $r^2 = 0.30$, $p = 0.07$. There is no such relationship in *Virola* between crop size and the proportion of seeds dispersed; a similar curvilinear regression yields $p > 0.5$.

It appears that, since *Tetragastris* fruit is less nutritious, a small crop easily escapes the attention of frugivores, while *Virola* fruit is valuable enough to be worth seeking even from a small crop. Variation in the proportion of *Virola* seeds removed from different trees is governed primarily by seed size: the greater the average dry weight of a tree's seeds, the smaller the proportion dispersed ($r^2 = 0.59$: Howe and Vande Kerckhove, 1980). It is as if, in contrast to *Tetragastris*, the *Virola* are competing for a limited supply of dispersers through the attractiveness of individual fruits: the greater attractiveness of small-seeded, easily handled fruit, however, seems to be counterbalanced by other advantages of large seeds.

The Numbers of Species Visiting and Dispersing *Tetragastris* and *Virola*

Despite their abundance, proximity, and comparably conspicuous fruits, *Tetragastris* and *Virola* attract different animals to eat their fruit. Diurnal watches of tree crowns revealed 8 species eating *Virola* fruit, of which 7 were dispersers, and 14 species eating *Tetragastris* fruit, of which 11 were dispersers (Table 4). I never saw any additional species eating *Virola* fruit in the tree, while I walked through the forest, censusing at night, although I saw howler monkeys sleeping in *Virola* trees on occasion, and I sometimes saw agoutis (*Dasyprocta punctata*) and coatis eating seeds or arils found on the ground. In contrast, I saw 12 other species eating fruit in *Tetragastris* crowns at one time or another (Howe, 1980). Of these, spider monkeys probably were important dispersal agents for *Tetragastris* near the laboratory clearing, although they rarely traveled as far as the study trees. At night, kinkajous (*Potos flavus*) were infrequent but regular visitors at *Tetragastris*, and they dispersed some seeds, although probably far fewer than did monkeys or perhaps even coatis. Moreover, the kinkajous were rather small, and tended to drop feces containing *Tetragastris* seeds under the crown. Rare nocturnal visitors to *Tetragastris* included opossums (*Didelphus marsupialis*) and olingos (*Bassaricyon gabbii*).

As predicted, *Tetragastris* attracts more species of visitors than *Virola*, 23 as opposed to 8, although the difference is less if we confine ourselves to diurnal

Table 4. Relative proportions of seeds eaten by different fugivores at *Tetragastris* and *Virola* trees

Common name	Binomial	Tetragastris system			Virola system		
		Obs. (N)	Seeds per visit ($\bar{x}$)	Contrib. (%)	Obs. (N)	Seeds per visit ($\bar{x}$)	Contrib. (%)
Howler monkey	*Alouatta palliata*	70	80.5	66	—	—	—
White-faced monkey	*Cebus capucinus*	18	97.9	20	—	—	—
Spider monkey	*Ateles geoffroyi*	—	—	—	29	1.3	7
Coatimundi	*Nasua narica*	4	226.8	11	—	—	—
Black-crested guan	*Penelope purpurascens*	2	—	—	10	5.1	10
Slaty-tailed trogon	*Trogon massena*	12	3.0	< 1	81	0.7	11
Black-throated trogon	*Trogon rufus*	2	1.0	< 1	—	—	—
Rufous motmot	*Baryphthengus martii*	—	—	—	97	0.9	17
Collared aracari	*Pteroglossus torquatus*	16	2.8	< 1	16	0.3	1
Keel-billed toucan	*Ramphastos sulfuratus*	26	2.6	1	112	0.5	11
Chestnut-mandibled toucan	*Ramphastos swainsonii*	4	3.8	< 1	119	1.8	42
Masked tityra	*Tityra semifasciata*	16	1.0	< 1	40	0.0	0
Fruit crow	*Querula purpurata*	88	1.2	1	—	—	—

Frequencies and mean number of seeds eaten per visit are derived from 200 hours of observation at *Tetragastris* and 320 hours at *Virola*.

observations. *Tetragastris* fruit seems to appeal equally to a great many animals; the frequency with which I saw the three different species of diurnal monkey eating *Tetragastris* fruit, for example, was indistinguishable from their relative abundance on the island (Howe, 1980). This was not true for *Virola;* I saw no howler monkey eat *Virola* fruit, and spider monkeys carefully tasted or smelled each aril before eating, as if the fruit were nearly distasteful enough to discourage the attentions of these wasteful animals as well.

Crop Size and Frugivore Diversity

In 1978, the total number Y of species seen in a given *Tetragastris* crown on at least one of the diurnal censuses was related to the total number X of thousands of seeds that tree produced by the regression

$$Y = 0.08X + 2.03$$
$$(r^2 = 0.53, p < 0.0005; \text{Howe, 1980})$$

In contrast, there is no significant correlation between the total number of species censused in a *Virola* tree's crown and that tree's fruit crop ($p = 0.15$). It is as if species visiting *Virola*, unlike those visiting *Tetragastris*, were interested enough in its fruit to seek out even small crops.

The Contribution of Different Species to Seed Removal and Waste

Calculations on this subject are rough, but it appears that three species of mammals account for 97% of the *Tetragastris* seeds eaten, while the different frugivores contribute more evenly to the consumption of *Virola* fruits (Table 4). Of more interest are the effects of different species on seed dispersal and waste at the two trees (Table 5). Of *Tetragastris* handled by animals, less than 11% are dispersed; 89% of those seeds handled are either dropped under the trees (23%) or are doomed to intense seedling competition in fecal clumps from which a maximum of one seedling can emerge as a healthy juvenile (66% are presumed killed). Of seeds handled by animals, mammals disperse 8% and "waste" 88%, while birds disperse 3% and waste less than 1%. Although they are conspicuous visitors at *Tetragastris*, birds appear to influence dispersal far less than mammals do. The opposite is true of the *Virola* assemblage. Spider monkeys are conspicuous visitors, but waste more seeds than they disperse and take fewer seeds than their size would lead one to anticipate. Birds waste few seeds, and disperse more nearly equivalent proportions of seeds than was the case with frugivores at *Tetragastris*. Overall, about 15% of the *Virola* seeds handled by animals are wasted, while approximately 85% are potentially dispersed. The essential difference is that dispersers at *Tetragastris* are far more wasteful; *Virola* attracts far more *suitable* species to eat and disseminate its fruits.

CONCLUSIONS

The dichotomy between dispersal of fruits of limited nutritional value and of those with both a high energetic reward and a diverse nutritional value holds reasonably well for *Tetragastris* and *Virola*. No animal can live on sugar alone, and *Tetragastris* is dispersed by a wide variety of animals that use its fruits for carbohydrate and find other nutrients in other foods. The known assemblage of dispersers includes 23 birds and mammals, of which the howler monkey contributes most to dispersal by virtue of its sheer abundance on Barro Colorado Island. There is no hint of specialization. As expected, waste of such "cheap" fruits is enormous. Two-thirds of the crop falls or is dropped underneath the parent trees, and only a small fraction of those seeds removed from the trees stand any appreciable chance of establishment in bouquets of seedlings that emerge from mammal droppings. By contrast, seven highly frugivorous birds and one frugivorous monkey remove nearly two-thirds of the fat- and protein-rich *Virola* fruits and scatter the seeds in the forest. These fruits are so worthwhile that birds seek out crops of all sizes. Discrimination reflects differences in fruit size and quality rather than abundance. The essential difference between these two systems is that the mammals eating *Tetragastris* waste most of the seeds that they handle; birds taking *Virola* and a few *Tetragastris* seeds are far more likely to disperse seeds that they handle.

The "low investment/high investment" framework has been a useful guide to research, but it does not account for all of the empirical findings. A complete revision of the framework would be premature; our ignorance of the relevant natural history is profound. But difficulties must be noted.

One must ask, for instance, why a variety of "opportunists" do not find and exploit *Virola*. A partial answer may reside in the efficiency with which specialists find and deplete small crops of nutritious fruits (also see Howe and Vande Kerckhove, 1979). A second possibility, yet untested, is that the plant defends its crop against exploitation by wasteful foragers. *Virola* arils are bitter; this naturalist can eat some but not others. The active compounds are probably tannins, which occur in concentrations of up to 0.35% dry weight of the arils (6.0% in the protective capsules). Spider monkeys usually smell and reject as many fresh fruits as they eat, suggesting active avoidance of an unpalatable substance. Future observations may show that some foragers, such as obligately frugivorous birds, detoxify *Virola* arils better than those mammals common in the forest. The subject of frugivore discouragement may have to be included in any reevaluation of McKey's (1975) thinking.

Whatever the dispersal agents, it is clear that richness of the aril, rather than seed size, accounts for most variation in the dispersal efficiency of known systems. As examples, it is clear that *Tetragastris* and *Virola surinamensis* have markedly different dispersal efficiencies, even though arils and enclosed seeds—the units of dispersal—are of roughly similar size. One might compare the energetic reward obtained by a hypothetical toucan that can eat four *Tetragastris* seeds, or four *Virola surinamensis* seeds, at once; it would ingest 3.3 kcal from the former and 22.4 kcal from the latter. Such a toucan could eat 15 seeds of the smaller *Virola sebifera*, ingesting 12.4 kcal. As in *Virola surinamensis*, animals remove a high proportion, 75%, of the seeds of *Virola sebifera* (Howe, 1981). Similarly, all the seeds of *Stemmadenia donnell-smithii*, each fruit of which contains an average of 132 small seeds embedded in an oily pulp, are removed as they become available (McDiarmid et al., 1977).

Table 5. Relative contributions to dispersal and waste of arillate seeds handled by frugivores visiting *Tetragastris* and *Virola* trees

Species	Tetragastris system[1]		Virola system[2]	
	Wasted (%)	Dispersed (%)	Wasted (%)	Dispersed (%)
Howler monkey	59	6	—	—
White-faced monkey	19	1	—	—
Spider monkey	—	—	9	3
Coatimundi	10	<1	—	—
Black-crested guan	—	—	0	9
Slaty-tailed trogon	0	<<1	<1	10
Black-throated trogon	0	<<1	—	—
Rufous motmot	—	—	2	14
Collared aracari	<1	<<1	0	1
Chestnut-mandibled toucan	0	<<1	2	35
Keel-billed toucan	<1	<<1	2	8
Masked tityra	0	<<1	5	<1
Fruit crow	0	1	—	—
Red-eyed vireo	0	0	—	—

Calculations of "waste" include seeds dropped under tree crowns as well as those facing inevitable mortality in fecal clumps (see text).

[1] From Howe (1980; Tables 3 and 4).
[2] From Howe and Vande Kerckhove (1981).

A third point is that although some "opportunistic generalists" appear to act as they "should," others show unexpected specialization on fruit. A variety of resident and migrant birds visit *Guarea glabra*, a small tree with arillate seeds in overabundance (Howe and De Steven, 1979). Such migrants appear to visit *Guarea* in an opportunistic fashion, much as predicted (cf. McKey, 1975). However, Greenberg (1981) finds two North American warblers (*Dendroica castanea* and *D. pensylvanica*) visit Panamanian *Lindackeria* trees far out of proportion to the relative abundance of the birds in the forest. Despite the fact that this plant produces small fruits in overabundance, it appears to be a "warbler tree" that attracts birds normally thought to be generalists. Such unexpected specialization clearly lies outside of the framework underlying *Tetragastris* and *Virola* studies. Other anomalies will undoubtedly appear as field work proceeds.

In short, McKey's (1975) "strategic dichotomy" is useful, but not sufficient. Aril richness does influence the composition of visitor assemblages and the efficiency of dispersal, but seed size is not closely correlated with aril richness. Future work should emphasize variation in both nutritional and toxin content within and between species of fruiting trees. Differences in visitor constancy and perhaps specialization by frugivores and fruiting trees will be understood only in light of a greatly expanded knowledge of relevant natural history.

Have *Tetragastris* and *Virola* coevolved with their dispersal agents? Some dispersal agents account for more seed removal than others at both *Tetragastris* and *Virola*, but interactions between animals and plants appear to be either quite general or to reflect relationships between broad taxonomic categories, not species pairs. Monkey visitation to *Tetragastris* reflects relative abundance of the various primate species, not specialization by the howler monkey (Howe, 1980). Intrinsic to the reproduction of this plant is an erratic fruiting behavior, with crops of individuals varying dramatically from year to year. Birds are likely to be important dispersal agents in lean years when crops are insufficient to support monkey troops that have far higher energy requirements than smaller frugivores (Howe, 1980). Perhaps an easily digestible sugary fruit, a distinctive bicolored display, and presentation both day and night constitute a generalized dispersal syndrome that "keeps options open" for a plant that must rely on different sorts of dispersal agents in different years. *Virola*, as a genus, may prove to be "toucan trees." The only hint of specialization is the small assemblage visiting *Virola surinamensis*—a situation that might be abetted by chemical defense of fruits against wasteful mammals. On Barro Colo-

rado, the majority of fruits of both *Virola surinamensis* and *V. sebifera* are fruits taken by various toucans and aracaris; the same is true of *Virola koschnyii* in Costa Rica (Howe, pers. observation). There is little chance that obligate mutualisms between *Virola* trees and particular birds have evolved, since the trees occur in forests with different toucan and aracari species throughout Central and South America. It may be that the different birds in the Ramphastidae place rather similar selective pressures on the plants, and that the various *Virola* species present similar digestive and behavioral challenges to the birds. It should also be noted that relationships that appear quite specific in a short-term study may be inconsistent in geographical space and ephemeral on an evolutionary time scale (Howe, 1977; Howe and Vande Kerckhove, 1979). Genera or families of birds, mammals, and plants are far more likely to interact consistently in time and space. "Coevolution," where it occurs, will probably reflect compatible habits between a group of related frugivores and a group of related plants, rather than obligate dependence between pairs of species.

ACKNOWLEDGMENTS

G. A. Vande Kerckhove contributed an integral portion of the data collection for the *Virola surinamensis* study; much of the material here has been distilled from our joint manuscripts. Egbert Leigh contributed greatly to the revision of the manuscript. Field work was supported by the Smithsonian Tropical Institute, the University of Iowa, and BSRG PS07035–13 of the National Institute of Health.

LITERATURE CITED

Croat, T. B.
1978.   *Flora of Barro Colorado Island.* Stanford: Stanford University Press.

Foster, R. B.
1982.   The Seasonal Rhythm of Fruitfall on Barro Colorado Island. Pages 151-172 in *The Ecology of a Tropical Forest*, edited by Egbert G. Leigh, Jr., et al. Washington, D.C.: Smithsonian Institution Press.

Foster, R. B., and N. V. L. Brokaw
1982.   Structure and History of the Vegetation of Barro Colorado Island. Pages 67–81 in *The Ecology of a Tropical Forest*, edited by Egbert G. Leigh, Jr., et al. Washington, D.C.: Smithsonian Institution Press.

Greenberg, R.
1981.   Frugivory in some migrant tropical forest wood warblers. *Biotropica*, 13: 215–222.

Howe, H. F.
1977.   Bird activity and seed dispersal of a tropical wet forest tree. *Ecology*, 58: 539–550.

1980. Monkey dispersal and waste of a neotropical fruit. *Ecology*, 61: 944–959.

1981. Birds and the dispersal of a neotropical nutmeg, *Virola sebifera*. *Auk*, 98: 88–98.

Howe, H. F., and D. De Steven
1979. Fruit production, migrant bird visitation, and seed dispersal of *Guarea glabra* in Panama. *Oecologia*, 39: 185–196.

Howe, H. F., and G. F. Estabrook
1977. On intraspecific competition for avian dispersers in tropical trees. *American Naturalist*, 111: 817–832.

Howe, H. F., and G. A. Vande Kerckhove
1979. Fecundity and seed dispersal of a tropical tree. *Ecology*, 60: 180–189.

1980. Nutmeg dispersal by tropical birds. *Science*, 210: 925–927.

1981. Removal of wild nutmeg (*Virola surinamensis*) crops by birds. *Ecology*, 62: 1093–1106.

McDiarmid, R. W., R. E. Ricklefs, and M. S. Foster
1977. Dispersal of *Stemmadenia donnell-smithii* (Apocynaceae) by birds. *Biotropica*, 9: 9–25.

McKey, D.
1975. The ecology of coevolving seed dispersal systems. Pages 159–191 in *Coevolution of Animals and Plants*, edited by L. E. Gilbert and P. Raven. Austin: University of Texas Press.

Snow, D.
1971. Evolutionary aspects of fruit-eating by birds. *Ibis*, 113: 194–202.

Sokal, R. R., and F. J. Rohlf
1969. *Biometry*. Freeman: San Francisco.

van der Pijl, L.
1972. *Principles of dispersal in higher plants*. New York: Springer-Verlag.

White, S. C.
1974. Ecological aspects of growth and nutrition in tropical fruit-eating birds. Ph.D. dissertation, University of Pennsylvania.

Famine on Barro Colorado Island

ROBIN B. FOSTER   Department of Biology, University of Chicago, Chicago, Illinois 60637

ABSTRACT

Between July 1969 and July 1970, as in most years, there were two peaks in abundance of falling fruit on Barro Colorado Island, one in September and October, and one between March and June. In the following year, the September-October peak was missing. The total weight of fruit falling per hectare between August 1970 and February 1971 was only a third of that during the corresponding period a year earlier, and many species that normally fruit during the second half of the rainy season, including a number whose fruit is very important to animals, failed to fruit in 1970. As a result, there was a prolonged famine lasting from July 1970 to April 1971. Animals foraged longer, fed on novel foods, some with obvious mechanical defenses, and died in unusual numbers.

Nearly all the plants that failed to fruit between September 1970 and February 1971 flower in response to the onset of the rainy season. They probably require a prolonged drought followed by a sharp, lasting increase in soil moisture content, as a stimulus to complete the development of their flowers. The dry season of 1970 was very wet, so there may not have been sufficient drought to allow the plants to flower in response to the onset of the following rainy season. In 1931 and 1958, similarly short, wet dry seasons were followed by similar fruit failures in the second half of the rainy season, again accompanied by signs of famine in the animal community. More generally, an index of "the weakness of the dry season," compounded of the total amount of rain between 1 January and 1 April and the start of the following rainy season, distinguishes as accurately as my data permit between years of severe famine and years of mild famine or of relative plenty.

The rhythm of a large part of the plant community seems to depend on dry seasons of the length and severity currently prevailing on the island. Excessive rain out of season is far more disruptive to the forest community than any other aberration of climate so far observed here.

INTRODUCTION

This paper considers how fruit production in the forest on Barro Colorado Island differs from year to year, what might cause these differences, and how these differences affect the island's mammal populations. Two years of quantitative data on fruitfall have brought some phenomena to my notice that would not be revealed either by purely qualitative observation of the community as a whole or by detailed studies of one or a few species. In concert with other data, the information on fruitfall may reveal much about how tropical communities are organized or regulated.

I will compare fruitfall from August 1969 through July 1970 with that in the following year at three levels: the total dry weight of fruitfall, compared with that of other forms of litter; an index of fruiting activity in the community as a whole; and the behavior of individual species. I will use my own observations from 1967 through 1979 and data from other sources to categorize the availability of fruit, and the resultant hunger stress among the mammals, in different years. Fruit availability is apparently related to the length and severity of the preceding dry season, which accordingly provides a convenient means of predicting years of severe fruit shortage and consequent famine.

METHODS

For two years, I sampled the rain of seeds and litter falling to the forest floor, using plastic litter traps with openings 1/12 sq. m in area arranged in each of 24 one-ha. plots scattered over 83 ha. of forest, mostly mature, on the plateau atop the island. I have discussed the sampling procedure in more detail elsewhere (Foster, this volume).

From August 1969 through 12 August 1970, I used 13 traps per plot and collected samples weekly; in the following year, I used 5 traps per plot and collected samples every fortnight. To compare the species composition of the seed rain in these two years, I considered only the seeds falling into those 120 traps that were used both years, lumping the data from the first year fortnight by fortnight, as in the second, and calculated the number of species dropping seeds into each of my 24 one-ha. plots each fortnight. I took the average of these numbers as a general index for that fortnight's fruiting activity. This index gives greater representation to species with greater abundance or coverage, without giving undue weight to species with huge quantities of tiny seed. The seed rain sample does not adequately represent low shrubs and epiphytes, species with seeds weighing over 10 g apiece, or species with seeds weighing 0.0001 g or less.

After studying the composition of the seed rain, I pooled the collections for each week or fortnight from all 24 ha. and separated the litter into leaves, fruit (including defecated seeds), and other material, such as bark, twigs, flowers, and other debris, removing logs and branches over 2.5 cm in diameter. I then dried the litter over light bulbs for a week, weighed it, and calculated the average weight of litter of each category falling per square meter of collecting surface per week (see Haines and Foster, 1977).

LITTERFALL

The dry weight of fruit falling between August 1970 and January 1971 was 63% lower than the fruitfall over the corresponding 6-month period a year earlier, while the dry weight of fruit falling between February and July was much the same in both years (Table 1). These data suggest a major fruit failure in the 6 months starting August 1970. Moreover, this failure was not reflected in the forest's vegetative production; indeed, the forest's vegetative production was higher during the second year, as if the energy saved by not fruiting were put to other use.

SEED RAIN

Between August 1969 and July 1970 there were clearly two periods when more plants shed seeds than at other times of the year (Foster, this volume). In the second year, however, the September-October peak was missing (Figure 1). The second year's pattern is not normal. Hladik and Hladik (1969) had noticed earlier that there were two peaks per year in the availability of fruit eaten by monkeys. Moreover, the species responsible for the fruiting peak of September and October 1969, but which failed to fruit in 1970, also fruited abundantly in 1967, 1968, 1971, 1973–77, and 1979.

Of the 154 species sampled during these two years

Table 1. Litterfall on the plateau of Barro Colorado Island in successive half-years, in g dry weight per sq. m

	August through January			February through July		
	Leaves	Fruit	Total litter	Leaves	Fruit	Total litter
1969–70	275	50.1	558	303	42.9	531
1970–71	285	18.7	588	358	45.9	627

which drop most of their seed between July and February, 85 (55%) did not appear in the traps between July 1970 and February 1971 (Table 2), while only 14 (9%) failed to appear the first year between July 1969 and February 1970. Only 63 of these 154 species were adequately represented in at least one year so that absence from the traps during the other was evidence of a nearly complete fruit failure—not chance omission. Of this adequately sampled subset (Table 2), 27 failed to fruit during the second year, 12 had greatly reduced fruit crops during the second year, and 24 fruited normally during both years.

Some of the species that failed to fruit during the second year apparently only fruit in alternate years, as do *Pterocarpus rohrii, Platypodium elegans,* and perhaps *Faramea occidentale.* Other species may have failed to fruit because their resources had been depleted by a large fruit crop in the preceding year. However, this does not explain the magnitude of the fruit failure.

Eighteen of the 39 species with little or no fruit during the second year normally flower during the first 2 months of the rainy season, and another 12 flower at some other period during the rainy season. In 1970 most of these 30 species either failed to flower, had only a few individuals in flower, or produced only a few flowers per individual. Most individuals in several of these species, including *Dipteryx panamensis, Trichilia tuberculata,* and *Tetragastris panamensis,* put out an additional set of leaves at the time they normally flower, but a few individuals of these species that were growing along the lake flowered and fruited normally.

Other species, such as *Tabernaemontana arborea* (Apocynaceae), began flowering much earlier than usual and continued intermittently for several months rather than flowering in one synchronous burst as they had in 1969. Asynchronous flowering could have reduced opportunities for outcrossing, and flowering out of season could cause the plants to miss their pollinators, thus reducing the fruit crop.

By contrast, 15 of the 24 species that fruited successfully between July and February of both years regularly flower, at least in part, during the dry season. In 1970 most species that usually flower in the dry season, unlike most of those that flower at the beginning of the rainy season, flowered normally.

No doubt every species, indeed every individual or sometimes even every branchlet, requires a different set of stimuli to initiate flower buds and to govern the stages of their development. However, many tropical species appear to use the moistening of the soil at the beginning of the rainy season as a cue to initiate flowering (Augspurger, this volume). Figure 2 indicates that 1970 hardly had a dry season. After a short dry spell at the end of December 1969 and during the first week of January 1970, during which the leaf litter

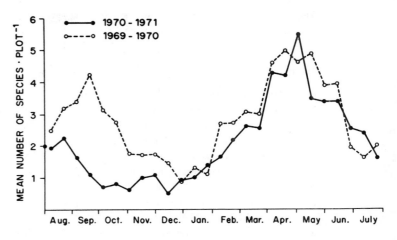

Figure 1. A comparison of community seed rain between two years. The data are from 24 one-ha. plots with five seed traps per plot, taken at 2-week intervals.

began to become crisp and the soil surface began to crack, there was a deluge of rain. Thereafter, from February through April, rain was so frequent and sunshine so rare that the forest never dried out again to the extent that it had during the first week of January. It appears that, in 1970, many species that normally flower in May, June, or July never formed reproductive buds, perhaps because the drought preceding the rainy season was too short or too weak, perhaps because there was insufficient time for a cue such as the increasing day length to cause differentiation of bud primordia prior to bud expansion as leafy shoots.

Tetragastris panamensis may provide an example of the second mechanism. These trees flower in June, July, or August of the rainy season preceding the year they fruit. Between 1969 and 1980 they failed to fruit only in 1971, 1973, and 1979. Although the dry season of 1978 was severe, in all three years the rainy season started early, the first soil-saturating rains occurring before 15 April. In 1975 and 1978 the fruit crops were extraordinarily large; 1974 and 1977 were the only two years during this period when the rainy season started later than 13 May. In the other years, fruit crops were of intermediate size, and the preceding rainy seasons started between 15 April and 13 May. It appears that increasing day length, or some other factor, initiates reproductive buds in most of the *Tetragastris* only after 15 April, and that the advent of the rainy season releases the buds, regardless of what proportion of them is yet differentiated for reproduction.

Those species that flowered as usual during the dry season of 1970, in January, February, or March, pre-

Table 2. Behavior of species that normally fruit between 1 July and 1 March on Barro Colorado Island

Failed to fruit: 1970–71

e	*Alibertia edulis* (Rubiaceae)	d	*Jacaranda copaia* (Bignoniaceae)
?	*Brosimum alicastrum* (Moraceae)	e	*Myrcia fosteri* (Myrtaceae)
w	*Casearia sylvestris* (Flacourtiaceae)	e	*Platypodium elegans* (Leguminosae)
w	*Chrysophyllum cainito* (Sapotaceae)	e	*Posoqueria latifolia* (Rubiaceae)
w	*Chrysophyllum panamense* (Sapotaceae)	e	*Pouteria unilocularis* (Sapotaceae)
	(*Cynodendron panamense* in Croat)	e	*Protium tenuifolium* (Burseraceae)
e	*Coccoloba parimensis* (Polygonaceae)	w	*Psidium anglohondourense* (Myrtaceae)
e	*Dipteryx panamensis* (Leguminosae)	e	*Pterocarpus rohrii* (Leguminosae)
w	*Doliocarpus major* (Dilleniaceae)	e	*Socratea durissima* (Palmae)
e	*Doliocarpus olivaceus* (Dilleniaceae)	w	*Sorocea affinis* (Moraceae)
e	*Eugenia coloradensis* (Myrtaceae)	w	*Tetragastris panamensis* (Burseraceae)
w	*Eugenia oerstediana* (Myrtaceae)	e	*Trichilia tuberculata* (Meliaceae)
e	*Faramea occidentale* (Rubiaceae)		(*Trichilia cipo* in Croat)
e	*Guarea guidonia* (Meliaceae)	w	*Zanthoxylum belizense* (Rutaceae)
	(*Guarea glabra* in Croat)	e	*Zanthoxylum panamense* (Rutaceae)

Poor fruit crop: 1970–71

e	*Casearia arborea* (Flacourtiaceae)	ew	*Lindackeria laurina* (Flacourtiaceae)
	Cissus spp. (Vitaceae)	dw	*Mouriri myrtilloides* (Melastomaceae)
w	*Dendropanax arboreus* (Araliaceae)	d	*Paragonia pyramidata* (Bignoniaceae)
e	*Dendropanax stenodontus* (Araliaceae)	ew	*Psychotria* spp. (Rubiaceae)
w	*Didymopanax morototoni* (Araliaceae)	e	*Sapium caudatum* (Euphorbiaceae)
w	*Hampea appendiculata* (Malvaceae)	?	Unknown sp. 3

Successful fruit crop: 1970–71

e	*Annona spraguei* (Annonaceae)	w	*Guazuma ulmifolia* (Sterculiaceae)
dw	*Apeiba membranacea* (Tiliaceae)	dw	*Hyeronima laxiflora* (Euphorbiaceae)
d	*Cecropia obtusifolia* (Moraceae)	e	*Quararibea asterolepis* (Bombacaceae)
e	*Coussarea curvigemmia* (Rubiaceae)	e	*Randia armata* (Rubiaceae)
dw	*Desmopsis panamensis* (Annonaceae)	?	*Serjania* sp. 1 (Sapindaceae)
d	*Epiphyllum phyllanthus* (Cactaceae)	d	*Spondias mombin* (Anacardiaceae)
dw	*Ficus costaricana* (Moraceae)	d	*Spondias radlkoferi* (Anacardiaceae)
dw	*Ficus inspida* (Moraceae)	d	*Sterculia apetala* (Sterculiaceae)
dw	*Ficus obtusifolia* (Moraceae)	ew	*Topobaea praecox* (Melastomaceae)
dw	*Ficus paraensis* (Moraceae)	w	*Trattinnickia aspera* (Burseraceae)
dw	*Ficus yoponensis* (Moraceae)	e	*Trema micrantha* (Ulmaceae)
dw	*Guatteria dumetorum* (Annonaceae)	dw	*Uncaria tomentosa* (Rubiaceae)

Only those species with abundant representation in fruit traps are included. Normal flowering conditions are indicated as follows: e = early in wet season, w = mid or late wet season, d = dry conditions, dw = both dry and wet conditions.

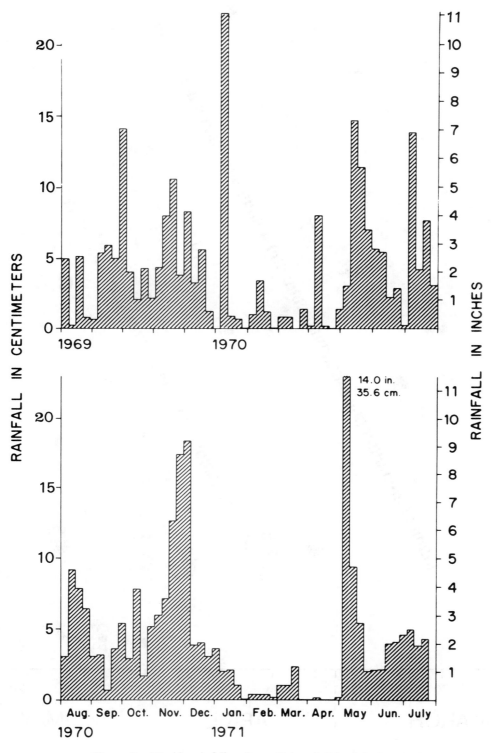

Figure 2.   Weekly rainfall on Barro Colorado Island during the two years of the study. The heavy rains that fell in January 1970 were followed by additional rain throughout the "dry season." In 1971, though rains continued into January, they were followed by a distinct dry period.

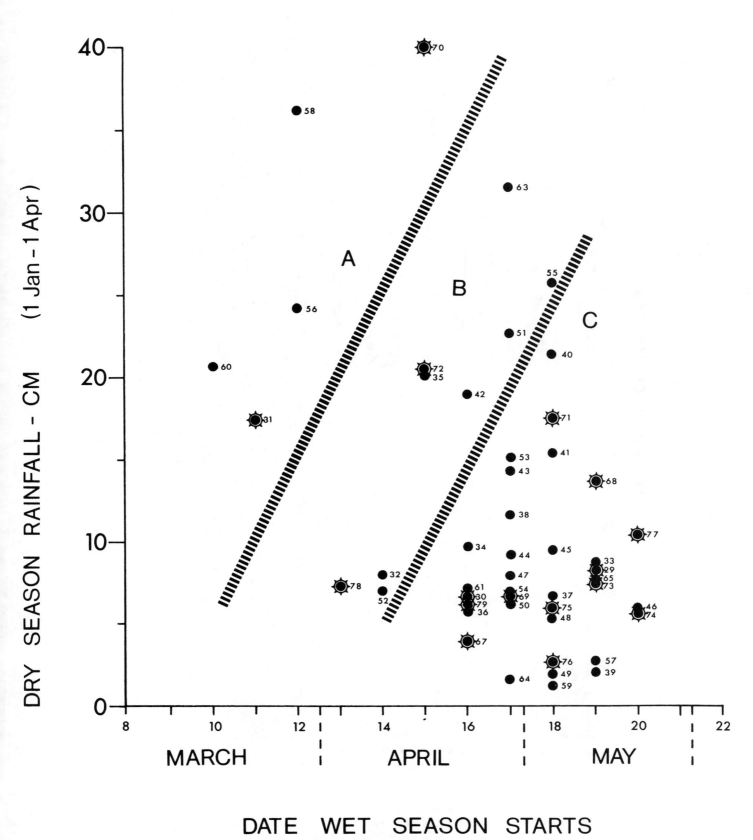

Figure 3. "Weakness" of the dry season, 1929–79. Increasing weakness from lower right to upper left. Solid black spots indicate years; spots with spiked edges indicate those 16 years in which observations of the author (1967–79) and of Enders and Chapman (1929–32) distinguished (A) severe famine years, (B) minor famine years, and (C) less severe or "good" years.

sumably depend on cues such as day length, which do not depend on the length of severity of the dry season, to initiate both the formation and the expansion of their reproductive buds. Some species, such as *Gustavia superba* and *Jacaranda copaia*, which normally flower during the dry season, failed to flower in 1970, suggesting that they rely on cumulative drought to initiate flowering.

RESPONSE OF THE ANIMAL COMMUNITY

Students of mammals on Barro Colorado almost invariably observe that the latter part of the rainy season is a time of hunger stress for most animals (Smythe, 1970, 1978; Milton, 1978). At this time the animals eat a wider range of food and go farther to find it, and many invade the laboratory clearing. This period of hunger stress is the time when the fewest species of ripe fruit are available (either per hectare or on the island as a whole), suggesting that, for frugivores and omnivores, the late rainy season is a time of low fruit availability and increased competition for what fruit is available.

Decreased plant reproduction leads to a decrease in the number of insects that feed on flowers, fruit, and seeds. Although no quantitative data are available, however crude, the abundance of insect-infested fruit and seeds suggests that this relatively energy-rich food source supports a large portion of the forest's insects.

Other groups of invertebrates, such as those involved in litter decomposition, also tend to decrease at this time of year, quite independently of fruit availability. As a group, foliage feeders presumably decrease, thanks to the shortage of new leaves at this season (Wolda, 1978). Yet, this may be a favorable season for carnivores, thanks to the increased vulnerability of their prey. In general, though, there is a recognized period of hunger stress late in the rainy season, and during parts of the dry season, when little fruit is available and many other resources are also in short supply.

In 1970, the fruit shortage lasted much longer. Less than half the maximum number of species were bearing fruit during the 8 months from July 1970 to nearly the end of March 1971. Moreover, the shortage of fruit in November and December of 1970 was much more extreme than during the corresponding period of the year before.

Twenty-four of the 27 species that normally fruit in the second half of the year but that failed to do so in 1970 are attractive to, and dispersed by, birds and mammals. Between July and March, the trees whose fruit is most important to animals include *Dipteryx panamensis*, *Trichilia tuberculata*, *Chrysophyllum cainito*, *Chrysophyllum panamense*, *Pouteria unilocularis*, *Brosimum alicastrum*, *Tetragastris panamensis*, *Faramea occidentale*, *Coussarea curvigemmia*, *Quararibea asterolepis*, *Spondias mombin*, and *Spondias radlkoferi*. All but the last four of these failed to fruit between July 1970 and March 1971. Other important food trees, *Gustavia superba* and *Beilschmiedia pendula*, failed to fruit just before this period, and still others, *Astrocaryum standleyanum*, *Calophyllum longifolium*, and *Oenocarpus panamanus*, failed to fruit between March and July 1971. The failure of these last was partially offset by an extraordinarily large fruit crop in *Symphonia globulifera* and in *Ocotea skutchii*.

The important fig species in my study area, *Ficus costaricana*, *F. insipida*, *F. yoponensis*, *F. obtusifolia*, and *F. paraensis*, all fruited at low frequency between early September and late December 1970. Fig fruiting peaked in January and February, and in April 1971.

Meanwhile, leaffall peaked in the second week of January 1970, but little leaf litter accumulated on the ground, since it decomposed so rapidly in the wet weather. By the end of June, most of the soil was bare of leaf litter and its attendant arthropods.

Beginning in July, the mammals showed signs of hunger stress which, generally speaking, intensified until January 1971. Coatis, agoutis, and collared peccaries visited the laboratory clearing in growing and unusually large numbers, their attention centered on a breadbox left outside the kitchen to induce the tapirs to stay on the laboratory side of the island. Tapirs visited regularly, in contrast to their previous regimen of intermittent visits. For the first time in many years, several pacas ventured in at night for bread, as did a kinkajou and an olingo, which had been released from captivity some years earlier but not seen again until this period. The kinkajou appeared starving and very ill when it first came. The spider monkeys, which normally visit the laboratory clearing at least once every day, now launched an all-out assault on food resources inside the buildings, learning for the first time to open doors and make quick forays to the dining room table, where they sought bread and bananas, ignoring the meat, potatoes, and canned fruit cocktail, and brushing aside the startled biologists at their dinner. In years after 1970, monkey raids and tapir visits occurred far more regularly.

In the forest, animals may not have starved to death en masse, but evidence of famine abounded. Mammal activity in the forest was far more obvious, as they continued to search for food at midday and during heavy rains. White-faced monkeys, spider monkeys, and coatis, normally diurnal, were often seen foraging after dark. Peccaries appeared especially emaciated.

Dead animals were found increasingly often until late November and December, when one could find at least one dead animal every 300 m along trails well away from the laboratory clearing. The most abundant carcasses were those of coatis, agoutis, peccaries, howler monkeys, opossums, armadillos, and porcupines; there were only occasional dead two-toed sloths, three-toed sloths, white-faced monkeys, and pacas. At times it was difficult to avoid the stench: neither the turkey vultures nor the black vultures seemed able to keep up with the abundance of carcasses. Ocelot tracks were frequent on the trails. Fruit-eating parrots, parakeets, and toucans were not seen at all on the island during this time, and large numbers were seen migrating east toward Colombia (N. G. Smith, personal communication).

Animals ate more different kinds of things, damaging vegetative parts of plants in the process. Every year when fruit is short, one sees some damage to the vegetative structures of plants, but during the famine it occurred on a scale not seen for at least several years. Forty-eight of the 50 *Hyeronima laxiflora* trunks that I checked for damage were girdled at the base, often severely. Judging from the surrounding tracks, and one direct observation, collared peccaries were gnawing the bark. Few of these trees showed signs of previous damage. Several individuals of the smaller trees, *Tetrathylacium johansenii* and *Eugenia oerstediana*, were also severely girdled during that famine. Enders (1935) mentioned that collared peccaries sometimes gnawed at the bases of trees.

In general, monocotyledons seemed to suffer the most, or the most conspicuous, damage. Palms, particularly *Geonoma* and *Bactris*, often had their leaves stripped back and their terminal buds eaten, resulting in death of those trunks. Individuals growing in clumps, as *Bactris* often do, suffered heavily, while isolated individuals were often overlooked. The *Bactris* stems are covered with long sharp spines, but the spines did not save them during the famine. In several areas, patches of thorny terrestrial bromeliads (*Aechmea magdalenae*) were heavily damaged, the center of each rosette being destroyed. Epiphytic bromeliads were ripped up in great numbers, apparently by monkeys searching for the bromeliad fauna. The terminal shoots and leaves of all *Dieffenbachia* species were damaged despite the presence of calcium oxalate crystals, which can inflict considerable discomfort when they are ingested. In general, mechanical or chemical deterrents, which may normally provide effective protection, failed to do so during the famine.

The signs of starvation abated noticeably in January and February 1971, apparently in response to a greatly increased supply of figs, but signs of hunger stress

Table 3. Fruit failure and famine years on Barro Colorado Island

Year	Rainfall (in.) in first 13 weeks of year	Starting week of wet season (calendar year)
1929	3.34	19
1930	2.52	16
1931**	7.05	11
1932*	3.18	14
1933	3.47	19
1934	3.96	16
1935*	8.06	15
1936	2.40	16
1937	2.74	18
1938	4.76	17
1939	0.85	19
1940	8.58	18
1941	6.18	18
1942*	7.60	16
1943	5.78	17
1944	3.69	17
1945	3.85	18
1946	2.38	20
1947	3.19	17
1948	2.17	18
1949	0.79	18
1950	2.48	17

Fruit failures were observed by the author in 1970, 1972, and 1978; they are known from the literature in 1931 and 1958; and they are inferred for other years based on dry-season rainfall and the starting week of the rainy season (from Figure 3). Famine and fruit failure usually begin in the second half of the designated year and extend into the first half of the following year. * = minor famine year. ** = extreme famine year. ? = missing data.

continued until June 1971, when the next rainy season was in progress.

COMPARISONS WITH OTHER YEARS

Enders (1935) was the first to recognize a general failure of the fruit crop and its effect on the island's mammals. He believed that extraordinarily heavy rains in November 1931, when 60 cm fell in 4 days, interfered with flowering and fruit development in species whose fruit was due to ripen in the dry season of 1932. In addition to the general shortage of fruit, however, he noticed that *Dipteryx panamensis*, which flowers in July, and the two species of *Chrysophyllum*, which flower in August and September, failed to bear fruit during that dry season.

Table 3. (continued)

Year	Rainfall (in.) in first 13 weeks of year	Starting week of wet season (calendar year)
1951*	9.07	17
1952*	2.83	14
1953	6.11	17
1954	2.69	17
1955*	10.36	18
1956**	9.76	12
1957	1.09	19
1958**	14.51	12
1959	0.56	18
1960*	8.32	10
1961	2.84	16
1962	?	?
1963*	12.66	17
1964	0.67	17
1965	3.20	19
1966	3.70	16
1967	1.64	16
1968	5.52	19
1969	2.65	17
1970**	16.03	15
1971	7.05	18
1972*	8.17	15
1973	3.09	19
1974	2.28	20
1975	2.36	18
1976	1.09	18
1977	4.16	20
1978*	2.87	13
1979	2.50	16

The accounts of Enders (1935, 1973) and Chapman (1938) of the famine of late 1931 and early 1932 sound remarkably similar to my observations during the famine of 1970–71. By early December 1931, a band of white-lipped peccaries (now extinct on the island) had moved into the laboratory clearing. Collared peccaries, coatis, agoutis, pacas, opossums (both *Didelphis* and *Marmosa*), kinkajous, Geoffrey's tamarins, and night monkeys were also in and around the clearing in unusual numbers. The animals stripped the fruit, not yet ripe, from a plantation which was then cultivated near the laboratory clearing. It was extraordinarily easy to catch small mammals with baited traps. Collared peccaries, which normally ignore the fruit of *Apeiba membranacea*, ate large quantities of it in early 1932. White-lipped peccaries photographed in the forest during this famine were emaciated (Chapman, 1938).

Enders attributes the sudden end of the famine to the ripening of figs at the end of March 1932. In 1971, famine was also alleviated, at least temporarily, by the increased supply of figs in January. While a famine is caused by the failure of several important species to fruit, its severity could depend largely on the timing of fig crops.

I use the biological observations for 1929–32 and 1967–79 to decide which of these were famine years, and inspect rainfall data for Barro Colorado Island from the Panama Canal Hydrographics (Rand and Rand, this volume), to see what features of rainfall correlate best with famine years. The "weakness of the dry season" seems to give the best fit. This weakness involves two aspects: (1) the total rainfall for the first 13 weeks of the year, 1 January–1 April, normally the height of the dry season; and (2) how early the rainy season starts. I define the rainy season to start on the first week after the ninth week of the calendar year in which $2.5\,n$ cm of rain falls ($n \geq 1$), followed by at least 2 cm total in the next 2 weeks, and fewer than n consecutive weeks with less than 2 cm of rain apiece thereafter. This definition is complex because it must exclude mid and late dry-season rains and early rainy season droughts. By this definition, a few weeks of drought may not constitute part of the dry season if rains immediately preceding them are exceptionally heavy. It is apparently more sensitive than the soil moisture definition used in Rand and Rand (this volume).

These are provisional indicators, which seem to fit what data are available. To learn what actually causes different plants to flower and fruit, or to fail to do so, we need to study changes in soil moisture at different depths, water tension in the plants, and the like. Unfortunately, most plants are less amenable to field experiments than the *Hybanthus* discussed by Augspurger (this volume).

Plotting first the 16 years for which something is known of fruit supply on a graph with the week the rainy season begins as x axis and dry season rainfall as y axis, one finds that the two exceptionally bad years, 1931 and 1970, fall above the line $x = 9 + 0.2y$; two less disastrously bad years, 1972 and 1978, fall between that line and the line $x = 13 + 0.2y$; and the other, more favorable years all fall below the second line (Figure 3). I then applied these criteria to the other years between 1929 and 1979 (Table 3).

The predictability of these criteria was tested using data from Kaufmann (1962), who studied the ecology of coatis on Barro Colorado for two years beginning July 1958. Table 3 suggests that 1957 and 1959 were good or average years, and 1958 was an extreme famine year. A weak dry season should cause famine late in the following rainy season, and also early in the dry season of the following year. In early 1959, several important coati foods, *Dipteryx*, the two species of *Chrysophyllum*, and *Astrocaryum*, all failed to fruit. Some figs were available nearly all through the famine, and the coatis were able to feed on the succulent, white, leaf bases of *Aechmea magdalenae* and the fruit of *Cecropia*, *Miconia argentea*, *Scheelea*, *Spondias*, and a few minor species including *Apeiba membranacea*. Late in the rainy season, *Coussarea* was the only fruit available. The parallel with 1970 is striking. The very wet dry season of 1958 presumably hastened the decomposition of leaf litter, which later on must have drastically reduced the availability of litter arthropods, the primary food of coatis. The population size of coatis decreased by 50% in the 8 months from September 1958 to May 1959. In the spring following the famine, none of Kaufmann's study animals bore young.

In the contrasting rainy season of 1959, *Coussarea* was the only species noted as failing to fruit, and in early 1960 there were large crops of *Dipteryx*, *Chrysophyllum*, and *Astrocaryum*. The adult coatis all produced litters that spring. Kaufmann (1962) also states that *Dipteryx* only fruited in quantity every other year, as if the weak dry seasons of 1956 and 1960, as well as that of 1958, had prevented fruiting. However, *Dipteryx* fruited in quantity after *every* dry season from 1974 through 1977, none of which was weak.

Enders (1973) provides other anecdotal information relating to the effect on mammals of weak dry seasons. Of his 16 different visits to Barro Colorado Island between 1929 and 1969, only one, the visit of 1931–32, followed a weak dry season, and that was also the only time he witnessed obvious famine. Moreover, he mentions that the numbers of collared peccaries, tayras, white-faced monkeys, and ocelots all peaked in 1955, which is the last year in a series of 24 years without an extremely weak dry season, the longest such interval in our 50-year record. The other mammals whose changes in numbers he mentions either show a continuing increase, such as pacas and agoutis, a continuing decrease, such as pumas and Geoffrey's tamarins, or have been subject to periodic epizootics not related to the occurrence of weak dry seasons, as were howler monkeys and sloths.

Weak dry seasons may also have other effects. Major outbreaks of the moth *Zunacetha annulata* (Dioptidae), described in more detail by Wolda and Foster (1978), occurred on the common understory shrub *Hybanthus prunifolius* in 1971, 1973, and 1979, in each case, following a year with a weak dry season. The largest outbreak was in 1971, following the year with the weakest dry season.

IMPORTANCE OF VARIATION IN DRY-SEASON CLIMATES TO PLANT POPULATIONS

The varying intensity of successive dry seasons may explain how species coexist on Barro Colorado whose ranges, as given by Croat (1978), suggest very different tolerances of drought. Species producing many seeds in years with weak dry seasons, such as *Symphonia globulifera*, may gain a temporary advantage in colonizing treefall gaps which occur after such years. Garwood (1979) finds significant differences in how the survivorship of different species of seedlings changes from year to year, which are apparently related to differences in rainfall pattern near the beginning of the rainy season. Similarly, climatic variation presumably alters growth rates of, and herbivore or disease damage to, different species in different ways, thereby constantly shifting the relative success of different species in attaining the canopy (cf. Grubb, 1977).

There are a variety of reasons why a given individual might flower only every other year. The timing of the last few weak dry seasons, however, may explain why nearly all the individuals of *Cavanillesia platanifolia*, *Platypodium elegans*, and *Pterocarpus rohrii* have only flowered in synchrony on odd-numbered years since 1966. There are exceptions, particularly among smaller trees and those in ravines and along the edge of the lake; although this is not well documented, the number of exceptions varies from year to year. Since years in which plants do not fruit or even flower may allow more resources to be stored for reproduction in the following year, the chance occurrence of the last several weak dry seasons in even-numbered years may have entrained these species to flower in synchrony in odd-numbered years.

If the above explanation is correct, then a single very weak dry season during an odd-numbered year may shift the flowering rhythm back one year, and an exceptionally good even-numbered year, or a moderately weak dry season in an odd-numbered year, may split one or more of these three species into two populations which flower in different years. Each species may therefore suffer a complicated series of shifts in the pattern of gene flow over a period of several decades.

There are several other species whose fruit production varies greatly from year to year, sometimes skipping several years, which might be entrained into a population-wide rhythm by an extreme year. These include *Faramea occidentale*, *Coussarea curvigemmia*, *Beilschmiedia pendula*, *Ocotea skutchii*, *Ormosia* spp., *Vatairea* sp., *Aspidosperma* spp., *Licania* spp., *Astronium graveolens*, and *Andira inermis*. Some of these may be entrained by very favorable years, and some, such as *Coussarea curvigemmia* or *Ocotea skutchii,* may be favored by very wet dry seasons.

CAUSES OF DRY-SEASON RAINS

The timing and duration of the dry season may be the most important climatic factor affecting the presence, distribution, and behavior of different species on Barro Colorado Island. Seasonal rhythms of the forest community are most frequently disrupted by dry-season rains; no one has yet been so impressed by the consequences of climatic perturbations at other times of year.

Dry-season rains usually result from outbreaks of polar air which move as fronts, called nortes or northers, south and southeastward across the Gulf of Mexico and the Caribbean (Portig, 1976). In Panama, these rains are not usually heavy or prolonged unless the front stalls over the isthmus. The amount of rain in Panama is thus not always related to the severity of the polar outbreak in North America.

The Western Hemisphere polar outbreaks, nortes, and their South American equivalents, the friagem, which push into tropical regions, are far better developed than such phenomena anywhere in the Old World except perhaps for Indochina, largely because the American cordillera blocks the prevailing westerly winds of the mid-latitudes. Perhaps the occasional very deep penetration of the friagem into the southwest portion of the Amazon basin, or the occasional penetration of the Siberian winter air mass into Indochina, also disrupt fruiting rhythms, as nortes do on Barro Colorado. In other areas of the seasonal tropics, different kinds of climatic disturbance may also lead to unusually heavy or prolonged dry-season rains, and may cause similar disruption in fruiting rhythms.

CONCLUSIONS

It may no longer be necessary to emphasize that tropical forests vary in many ways from year to year, but the nature of this variation, and its consequences, ecological and evolutionary, deserve continuing scrutiny. It is satisfying as a first step to be capable of predicting times of famine several months in advance.

In retrospect, the chance that led me to study fruit production between 1969 and 1971 could not have been more propitious. On Barro Colorado, fruiting rhythms are seriously disrupted once every 10 years, on the average, and mildly disrupted once every 5 years or so. These years stand out because of the obvious mortality or lowered reproductive output of many important mammals. For many other species these years are obviously not detrimental and may even be beneficial.

Since every year has a famine *season,* the organisms that cannot tolerate it must already have been screened out or had their populations reduced. Others have presumably developed specific reproductive, behavioral or structural adaptations to cope with the famine *seasons.* On the other hand, from the standpoint of most animals, famine *years* are unpredictable. Although a famine year would probably have a far more drastic effect were not the animals already adapted to a famine season, its unpredictability can still cause significant losses in population among species with otherwise fairly stable numbers.

The unpredictability of dry-season rains in any tropical forest need not necessarily cause unpredictability in the abundance of food; the unpredictability reflects the overall response of the plant community to those rains. A significant proportion of the Barro Colorado Island plant community apparently depends on rainfall or changes in soil moisture during or just after the dry season as cues for flowering or initiating flower buds. Moreover, these species contribute disproportionately to the nutrition of animals late in the rainy season and early in the dry season. The large number of food species fruiting between August and March, which cannot flower properly without a normal dry season, makes the animal community quite vulnerable to dry-season rains, despite the great diversity of the forest.

Despite the failure of many species to fruit after very wet dry seasons, each species is affected differently by minor fluctuations in the weather and by other perturbations. The diversity in seed type, modes of pollination and dispersal, and the like should cause the reproductive rates of different species to respond very differently to changes in the environment, which is probably a factor of major importance in allowing so many species of plants to coexist in such close proximity. So far we can readily observe fruit failures, but not the varying degrees of success; and the effects of extreme years, but not of more subtle differences between years. Even the investigation of these extreme years is only just beginning to progress beyond the anecdotal stage. True, extremes deserve attention; many species, and perhaps much of the community's organization, depend on them. But the stage is set for extreme years by what goes on in the interval, and extremes may affect many species only in proportion to how often they occur.

ACKNOWLEDGMENTS

W. D. Billings generously provided the necessary encouragement and advice for following up this unexpected opportunity. A. S. Rand and E. G. Leigh provided many important comments and criticisms, in addition to their continuing encouragement. A. H. Kourany and E. G. Leigh helped considerably with the manuscript. I was assisted at various times in the field by several people, notably Peter Johnson, Karen Gilbert, and Helen Kennedy. This work was also aided in part by the Botany Department and Computation Center of Duke University, a National Science Foundation Traineeship, a Smithsonian Research Fellowship, the Smithsonian Environmental Sciences Program, and the Department of Biology, University of Chicago. I thank them all.

LITERATURE CITED

Augspurger, C. K.
1982.   A Cue for Synchronous Flowering. Pages 133-150 in *The Ecology of a Tropical Forest*, edited by Egbert G. Leigh, Jr., et al. Washington, D.C.: Smithsonian Institution Press.

Chapman, F. M.
1938.   *Life in an Air Castle*. New York: D. Appleton & Co., Inc.

Enders, R. K.
1935.   Mammalian life histories from Barro Colorado Island, Panama. *Bulletin of the Museum of Comparative Zoology* (Harvard College), 78:385–502.
1973.   Unpublished manuscript on changes taking place on Barro Colorado Island over 40 years.

Foster, R. B.
1982.   Seasonal Rhythms in Fruitfall on Barro Colorado Island. Pages 151-172 in *The Ecology of a Tropical Forest*, edited by Egbert G. Leigh, Jr., et al. Washington, D.C.: Smithsonian Institution Press.

Garwood, N. C.
1979.   Seed Germination in a Seasonal Tropical Forest in Panama. Ph.D. thesis, University of Chicago, Chicago, Illinois.

Grubb, P. J.
1977.   The maintenance of species-richness in plant communities: the importance of the regeneration niche. *Biological Reviews*, 52:107–145.

Haines, B. L., and R. B. Foster
1977.   Energy flow through litter in a Panamanian forest. *Journal of Ecology*, 65:147–155.

Hladik, A., and C. M. Hladik
1969.   Rapports trophiques entre végétation et primates dans la forêt de Barro Colorado (Panama). *La Terre et la Vie*, 23: 25–117.

Howe, H. F.
1980.   Monkey dispersal and waste of a neotropical fruit. *Ecology*, 61:944–959.

Janzen, D. H.
1978.   Seeding patterns of tropical trees. Pages 83–128 in *Tropical Trees as Living Systems*, edited by P. B. Tomlinson and M. H. Zimmermann. Cambridge: Cambridge University Press.

Kauffmann, J. H.
1962.   Ecology and social behavior of the coati, *Nasua narica*, on Barro Colorado Island, Panama. *University of California Publications in Zoology*, 60:95–222.

Portig, W. H.
1976.   The climate of Central America. Pages 405–478 in *Climates of Central and South America*, edited by W. Schwerdtfegor. Amsterdam: Elsevier Scientific Publishing Company.

Rand, A. S., and W. M. Rand
1982.   Variation in Rainfall over Barro Colorado Island. Pages 47–59 in *The Ecology of a Tropical Forest*, edited by Egbert G. Leigh, Jr., et al. Washington, D.C.: Smithsonian Institution Press.

Smythe, N.
1970.   Relationship between fruiting seasons and seed dispersal methods in a neotropical forest. *American Naturalist*, 104: 25–35.
1978.   The Natural History of the Central American Agouti (*Dasyprocta punctata*). *Smithsonian Contributions to Zoology*, 257: 1–52.

Wolda, H., and R. Foster
1978.   *Zunacetha annulata* (Lepidoptera: Dioptidae), an outbreak insect in a neotropical forest. *Geo-Eco-Trop*, 2:443–454.

Population Sizes and Breeding Rhythms of Two Species of Manakins in Relation to Food Supply

ANDREA WORTHINGTON   Department of Zoology, University of Washington, Seattle, Washington 98195

ABSTRACT

The breeding rhythms and population sizes of two species of manakins on Orchid Island in Gatun Lake, Panama, were studied in relation to seasonal changes in food supply from November 1978 to November 1979. These two species, golden-collared manakins and red-capped manakins, were common in the forest understory and fed almost entirely on fruit. The production of ripe fruit per fortnight was determined for 21 different species of plants known to be fed upon by manakins. In the year of the study, the number of species in fruit changed little from season to season, but there was a long-lasting peak in fruit production from mid-December to mid-March, early in the dry season, and a sharp peak in May and June, early in the rainy season. Production of ripe fruit was uni-formly low throughout the last half of the rainy season, from August to December.

During the dry season, manakins feed on highly clumped foods, large fruit crops in scattered tall trees, while in the rainy season they feed on widely dispersed understory plants with small fruit crops. Late in the rainy season, the energy available from fruit just matched the minimum energy requirements of the manakin population, as estimated from standard metabolic curves. The manakins began to breed when the fruit supply increased suddenly in mid-December, and continued to do so until fruit production fell to a level just matching their minimum energy requirements, suggesting that predictable food shortage limits breeding to well-defined seasons.

INTRODUCTION

Two species of manakins (Pipridae), the red-capped manakin, *Pipra mentalis ignifera* Bangs, and the golden-collared manakin, *Manacus vitellinus vitellinus* (Gould), are common in the understory of second-growth forest on Barro Colorado Island and in surrounding areas. These small birds depend for their livelihood on a continuous source of fruit. Snow (1962a,b) found that the staggered fruiting seasons of understory plants, particularly those of the genus *Miconia*, provided an abundant food supply for the manakins of Trinidad all year long. Although unseasonable weather was once recorded to disrupt fruiting schedules in Guanacaste, Costa Rica, forcing manakins to eat unripe fruit (Foster, 1977), McDiarmid et al. (1977) and Foster (1977) make no mention of recurring seasonal shortage of manakin food; rather, they believe that abundant food is normally available to manakins all through the year. On the other hand, many animal populations on Barro Colorado that have been studied seem limited by a seasonal shortage of food (Willis, 1967, 1972, 1973; Smythe, 1970; Leigh and Smythe, 1978; many papers in this volume). Do the manakins here suffer similar food shortages?

Several questions arise. What are the energy and food requirements of the manakin populations? Does the abundance of fruit in the forest always meet these requirements? To answer, I studied manakin populations on Orchid Island, calculating their feeding rate from standard curves relating metabolism to body weight and comparing this with the seasonal rhythm of production of suitable fruits on Orchid Island.

Participants

The golden-collared manakin, *Manacus vitellinus v.* (Gould), is widely distributed in second-growth forest throughout its range from Panama to Columbia (Wetmore, 1972). It inhabits the low understory, preferring to stay less than 6 m from the ground, though it will fly directly up into the canopy of a tall fruiting tree, returning immediately to the understory after feeding for a brief moment at those heights. Golden-collared manakins prefer to take fruits by perching close to an infructescence and reaching or jumping for an item. Courtship displays begin in mid-December and last into August (Chapman, 1935; Willis and Eisenmann, 1979). Males congregate at traditional courting sites in groups of three to eight; the same sites reported by Chapman in 1935 around the Barro Colorado Island clearing are still in use today. Each male has a court, a small circle of ground cleared of leaves and debris where he performs the strenuous courtship display (Chapman, 1935; Snow, 1962a). With

calls, jumps, and mechanically produced pops and whirrs, the male attracts a female and dances with her. During the breeding season, the males never venture further than 50 m from their courts. The female alone has responsibility for nest-building, incubation, and care of the young. Nests with eggs have been found from February to August (Willis and Eisenmann, 1979). Nest success is very low and a female may attempt to nest up to three times in a season (Snow, 1962a). The birds are solitary when feeding, but females with young may join associations of antwrens (*Myrmotherula* spp.), probably for protection against predators (Willis, 1972). Male golden-collared manakins are larger than females (18.4 g and 16.9 g, respectively; Table 1).

The red-capped manakin, *Pipra mentalis ignifera* Bangs, is a smaller bird (14.4 g for both sexes), ranging from southeastern Mexico to Ecuador (Ridgely, 1976). It generally occupies more mature forest, although it is also common in second growth. Red-capped manakins range higher in the understory than golden-collared manakins (up to 10 m) and also will forage in tall fruiting trees but immediately return to lower levels. Red-capped manakins hover-glean fruit, fluttering out to seize at item and returning to a nearby perch. From December to August, groups of males gather 5 to 10 m above the ground and occupy individual display perches, horizontal branches clear of leaves and vertical stems. Skutch (1949) describes in detail the display that involves mechanically produced sounds and fast-flying acrobatics centered on the display perch. The same lek sites are used year after year. As is true for the golden-collared manakin, females alone build nests, incubate, and attend the young. Nests with eggs appear as early as February and newly fledged young have been seen as late as August (Willis and Eisenmann, 1979). Their nests are built higher in the understory than those of the golden-collared manakin but suffer the same degree of predation (Skutch, 1949; Snow, 1962b). Males without lek sites forage and travel together, as do females with young. Red-capped manakins have frequently been observed to move briefly with antwren associations, though not necessarily to search for insects (pers. obs.; Greenberg and Gradwohl, pers. comm.).

Karr's mist-netting study (1971) suggested these two species are nonoverlapping in habitat; the golden-collared manakin occupies second-growth (1.5 birds/ha.) and the red-capped manakin mature forest (4 birds/ha.). Willis (1980) estimates there are 1000 red-capped manakins on Barro Colorado Island and only 150 golden-collared manakins; the latter are found only in the few disturbed areas of the island, the laboratory clearing, and lake shore. However, in all the areas occupied by golden-collared manakins on Barro Col-

Table 1. Density, average weight, and energetic demands of the manakins of Orchid Island

	Density/ ha.	Mean weight (g)	BMR[1] (kcal/day)	DEE[2] (kcal/day)	EE/ ha.-fortnight	Caloric consumption[3]/ ha.-fortnight
Red-capped manakins	3.72	14.4 ± 2.3[4] (n = 64)	5.28	15.97	831.7	1109.0
Golden-collared manakins, female[5]	1.80	16.9 ± 2.1 (n = 38)	5.93	17.88	450.6	600.8
Golden-collared manakins, male	0.83	18.4 ± 2.0 (n = 32)	6.31	18.98	220.5	294.0
Total for manakin population	6.35	—			1503.0	2004.0

[1] Basal metabolic rate (Aschoff and Pohl, 1970).

[2] Daily existence energy (King, 1975).

[3] 4/3 × EE/ha.-fortnight based on 75% assimilation efficiency (see text).

[4] Weight ± 2 × SD.

[5] Juvenile males with female plumage are included in this weight class.

orado Island and surrounding islands, one finds red-capped manakins. Red-capped manakins freely enter and inhabit second-growth as well as mature forest. On Orchid Island the distribution of the two species of manakins is uniform.

The two species differ in their life histories (height preference, habitat preference, courtship behavior, weight, fruit harvesting method) but differ very little in their food habits, the main concern of this study. During the breeding season, the activities of the two *sexes* are very different, as I have already described, but these differences should not affect my calculations of energy requirements during the season of food shortage, when the behavior of the two sexes is far more similar.

METHODS

This study of manakins and bird-dispersed fruits was conducted on Orchid Island, 150 m north of Barro Colorado Island, in Gatun Lake, Panama, from November 1978 to December 1979. The 18-ha. island is essentially a narrow ridge (900 m long) with one broad side presented to the northeast trade winds of the dry season. The forest is maintained as second growth by the constant disturbance of treefalls.

Densities of manakins on Orchid Island were estimated from mark-recapture data and the relative re-sighting of marked and unmarked birds (Lincoln index). A total of 31 red-capped manakins and 36 golden-collared manakins have been banded on Orchid Island. Mist-netting efforts averaged 476 net-hours per month.

All netted manakins were weighed, examined for molt, held for collection of feces, and banded before being released. I estimated the manakins' caloric demands from standard weight formulas (see King, 1975, for review).

The diet of manakins was assembled from direct observations of feeding (n = 110) and from examination of feces and regurgitated seeds collected from mist-netted birds and under favored perches on male display courts (n = 63 collections). Mist-netted birds were held in a container for half an hour. Judging from the time it took captive birds to pass beads that they had ingested inside *Miconia* fruits, gut-passage time was 18 minutes ± 2.7 minutes (mean ± standard deviation, n = 7), so the birds would produce feces if they had fed just before capture.

In order to estimate how much food was available for manakins on Orchid Island, at fortnightly intervals from 15 November 1978 to 15 November 1979, I censused 21 plant species known to be manakin food (10 individuals each) for flower and fruit, counting total fruit crops and noting fruit disappearance. To calculate the amount of food available on a given time,

I multiplied the number of adult plants per hectare by the proportion bearing fruits, the average number of fruits available for consumption per fruiting tree, and the average weight of pulp per fruit. For most species I extrapolated the number of adult plants per hectare from the numbers of four mapped tracts whose area totaled 6136 sq. m; for those eight species not on the mapped area, I counted all the individuals I could find on the 18-ha. Orchid Island. Density was estimated for a total of 21 species. I extrapolated the proportion of adult plants bearing fruit that fortnight from the proportion of the 10 censused plants then bearing fruit.

I could count the entire standing crop of fruit for 14 species of shrubs and treelets. For seven other species, of larger trees or canopy vines (*Coccoloba manzanillensis, Cupania sylvatica, Didymopanax morototoni, Doliocarpus major, Lindackaria laurina, Miconia argentea, Tetracera volubilis*), it was impossible to count fruits directly. Therefore I counted the number of infructescences and, with subsamples, estimated the mean number of fruits per infructescence for each species.

I estimated the number of fruits of a given species available for consumption during a fortnight by counting the number of fruit, mature and immature, on plants of this species in one census, the number of these which were still on plants at the next census, and subtracting the latter from the former. Except for *Ouratea lucens* and *Psychotria marginata*, plants of the species censused developed all their fruit before ripening any of it, so one could measure the amount of fruit made available during a given fortnight from the decline in total fruit crop that fortnight. *Ouratea* and *Psychotria* differ in that the same plant can have flowers, immature fruit, and ripe fruit. For these I counted the amount of fruit made available each fortnight as the number of fruit of full size in the preceding census that had disappeared since.

Finally, I measured the fresh and dry weight of edible matter—skin, pulp, or aril, but not seeds, capsule wall, or stalks—on 25 fruits per species.

I calculated the amount of food available per fortnight for the 21 species. The summation of all species with fruit available for consumption in a census period is expressed as total grams dry weight of edible pulp per hectare-fortnight. There is an average of 4.5 kcal/g dry weight of fruit pulp (White, 1974).

Manakin Populations and Energy Demands

To calculate the aggregate feeding rates of the manakin population, one must count the manakins, weigh them, determine their caloric needs and, from this estimate, calculate the feeding rate of a manakin of a given weight.

My count of golden-collared manakins starts with the fact that by April 1979 I had marked all 12 adult males then present. Another six manakins, presumably in their second year of life, assumed adult plumage by September 1979, at which point at least nine of the older males were still alive. Therefore the total male population was 15. Snow (1962a) reports a one-to-one sex ratio for adults of the white-bearded manakin, *Manacus manacus*, in Trinidad. In addition, he calculated that each female produces one young per year. It is reasonable to apply this estimate to the birds on Orchid Island, as the breeding seasons last for the same length of time (7 months). Based solely on the known male population, I estimated that there are 3 times 15 or 45 golden-collared manakins on Orchid Island. I derived another count by noting that in the course of the study I marked 19 golden-collared manakins, females and young males which were not known to have assumed male plumage by time of writing. As 55% of the birds in female plumage that I observed between June and November were marked, I assume that there were 19/0.55 = 35 such birds in all. The total population estimate, adding the male birds, is 50 golden-collared manakins, or 1.8 female-plumaged birds and 0.83 adult males per hectare on Orchid Island.

Marked red-capped manakins are difficult to resight and to recapture. The estimate of population size is therefore a crude one. Observations of unmarked birds and, indeed, the visibility of red-capped manakins in general, increase dramatically from July to October, presumably from the influx of dispersing young birds. Between July and October 1979, I saw 7 birds of the 31 I had marked by that date and 8 birds that were clearly unmarked, suggesting that there were 67 red-capped manakins on Orchid Island, or 3.7 per hectare. Karr (1971) found four per hectare in a nearby mainland area.

I calculated a manakin's daily energy expenditure (DEE) from the formula (King, 1975):

$$DEE \; (kcal/day) = 317.7 \; weight(kg)^{0.752}$$

This estimate is based on energy demands of active but caged birds (Kendeigh, 1970; King, 1975) and must be viewed as an absolute minimum for a free-living bird.

To convert the density of manakins into their caloric demand per hectare per fortnight, I multiplied DEE by the number of days per fortnight, 14, times the number of manakins per hectare (Table 1). Because of significant weight differences female golden-collared, male golden-collared, and red-capped manakins were each calculated separately. The fortnightly energy expenditure was summed for all weight classes.

The assimilation efficiency of manakins is not known. Estimates of assimilation efficiencies of 49 to 81% have been reported for some frugivores (Walsburg, 1975; Moss, 1973; Pullianinen et al., 1968), but cannot be applied to manakins since either the birds digested seeds or nondigested seeds were included in the fecal material resulting in an underestimate of assimilation of usable fruit pulp. Estimates of assimilation efficiencies for seed-eating sparrows range from 67 to 90% (Siebert, 1949; Kontogiannis, 1968; Martin, 1968). I have assumed an assimilation efficiency of 75% to calculate the caloric consumption required to meet the estimated energy expenditure of these birds (Figure 1, Table 1).

Diet

Manakins are capable of eating all colorful soft fruits or arillate seeds with seeds less then 17 mm long. They swallow the fruits whole, regurgitating large seeds and passing smaller ones with their feces. This is not to say manakins do not have food preferences. My feeding observations and fecal specimens show that, in the year starting 15 November 1978, the manakins around Barro Colorado Island ate fruit from at least 62 species, of which 47 are found on Orchid Island (Table 3). These 47 include 2 species of epiphytes, 4 vines, 22 herbs and shrubs less than 5 m tall, 7 understory trees less than 10 m tall, 8 canopy trees, and 4 unidentified species. I monitored fruit production in 21 of these species, those which were the most important, and easily measured, sources of food.

Calculating the overlap between the diets of the two species of manakins from Table 3, using Morisita's index

$$2\sum_{i=1}^{n} (x_i y_i) \Big/ \sum_{i=1}^{n} (x_i^2 + y_i^2)$$

where, for each species i of plant which I saw fed upon by at least one manakin, x_i is the number of feeding records for red-capped manakins and y_i the number for golden-collared, I find an overlap of 0.87. This is very high (cf. Zaret and Rand, 1971). Probably all species of fruits on Orchid Island available to one manakin are available to the other.

Between August and November 1979, manakins were observed to feed on 22 species of fruit, of which 10 censused species accounted for 69 of the 89 records. During this season of fruit shortage, the censused plant species accounted for 78% of the fruit manakins ate.

Manakins eat little else besides fruit. Insect fragments do appear in feces, so the degree to which insects contribute to the caloric intake of manakins must be taken into account. I began microscopic examination of the feces on 5 July 1979. I collected 59 samples from under the perches of lekking males and 10 from mist-netted females. To quantify the intake of fruits and insects, I tried to reconstruct the number of fruits and insects that each fecal sample represented, calculate the dry weight of fruits and insects and transform dry weight into a kilocalorie contribution for each food type. For each fecal sample, the number of seeds of each species was used to calculate the minimum dry weight of fruits required to account for the number of seeds. The insect fragments were reconstructed into a maximum number of arthropods and then into dry weight of arthropods in the following way. I could categorize the fragments into three classes: spiders (3 to 9 mm in length, based on leg segments), flying ants and termites (e.g., *Camponotus* sp. or *Nasutitermes* spp.), and others. In each category I tried to reconstruct the number of arthropods in the fecal specimen, based on the number of different kinds of fragments and distinguishing parts such as wings and heads; a maximum number of arthropods in each class was determined. Dry weights of appropriate sized spiders (3–9 mm, $\bar{x} = 0.0025$ g, $s = 0.0019$, $n = 29$); termite alates (*Nasutitermes* spp., $\bar{x} = 0.0042$, $s = 0.0003$, $n = 370$; Thorne, pers. comm.); and small cockroaches (10–20 mm, $\bar{x} = 0.0119$, $s = 0.0097$, $n = 24$; Franks, pers. comm.) were applied to each class. I assumed that there are 4.5 kcal/g dry weight of fruits (White, 1974) and that, as in termite reproductives, there are 6.8 kcal/g dry weight of insects (Wiegert, 1970). I then calculated the proportion of kilocalories represented by insects in each fecal sample.

Ten of 33 fecal samples collected from red-capped manakins from July to October contained insect fragments. Of these 10, the proportion of kilocalories contributed by insects was 0.285 ± 0.028. (An arcsine transformation was used to calculate the means of the proportions since all proportions were less than 0.30.) Multiplying the proportion of fecal samples with insects (10/33) by the proportion of kilocalories contributed by insects in each sample (0.285), I estimated that 8.6% of the adult red-capped manakin's total caloric intake came from insect consumption. For the same period, 10 of 31 fecal samples collected from golden-collared manakins contained insect fragments. Of these 10, the proportion of kilocalories contributed by insects was 0.154 ± 0.015. Again I multiplied the proportion of fecal samples with insects (10/31) by proportion of kilocalories contributed by insects in fecal samples with insects (0.154); 5.0% of the golden-collared manakin's caloric intake was derived from insects. The proportion of feces with insect parts was much the same for both sexes.

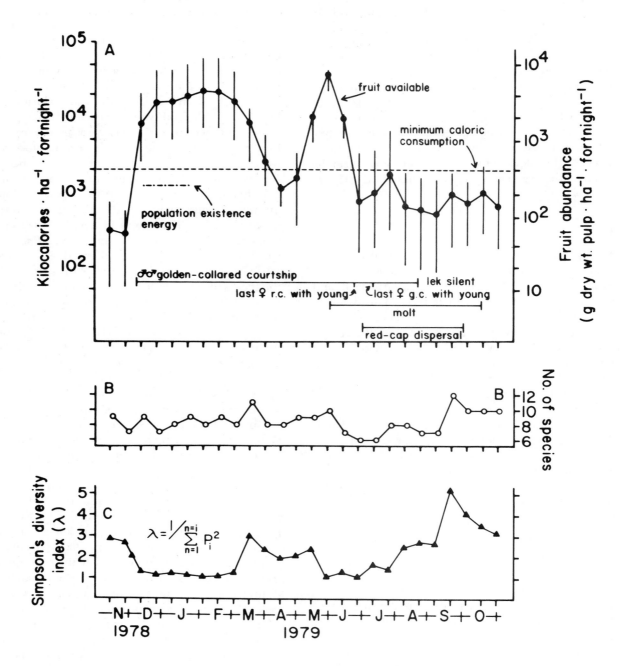

Figure 1. Seasonal abundance and diversity of manakin-favored fruits on Orchid Island, Panama. Part A: Energy available from fruit compared with caloric consumption of the manakin population per fortnight in Orchid Island. Energy available (left *y* axis) at fortnightly intervals (solid line) derived from fruit abundance (right *y* axis) (see text). 95% confidence intervals derived from the square root of the summation of the square of each species minimum or maximum abundance, calculated from log-transformed data. Calculations of minimum caloric consumptions and population existence energy are found in Table 1. Time intervals of seasonal activities of manakins are given below. g.c. = golden-collared manakin; r.c. = red-capped manakin. Part B: Number of species contributing to each fortnight's abundance. Part C: Simpson's diversity index (*lambda*) applied to the proportion (p_i) of grams dry weight of fruit contributed by each species in a fortnight. Indicated below are the months within which the fortnight samples fell.

Unfortunately, the same careful inspection was not applied to fecal specimens collected in the dry season and early in the rainy season. It is my impression, however, that manakins, especially female-plummaged birds, take more insects early in the rainy season, when both fruit and insects are abundant. In general, manakins feed their young both fruits and insects. Skutch (1949) and Lill (1974) report that manakins feed their young about 50% fruits and 50% insect matter. Outside of the requirements for growth of young, it appears that fruit is the major source of energy for red-capped (91.4%) and golden-collared (95.0%) manakins. From August through November 1979, censused fruits accounted for roughly 0.78 × 95%, or 73% of the calories consumed by these manakins.

Fruit Availability

The number of species in fruit changes little from season to season, but manakin foods show two major peaks in abundance, a long-lasting peak from mid-December to mid-March, early in the dry season, and a sharp peak in May and June, early in the rainy season (Table 2, Figure 1). Fruit abundance is uniformly lower throughout the last half of the rainy season (August-December). The drop in fruit abundance in April corresponds to the peak flowering time of those species which contribute to the May peak.

Only one species, *Didymopanax morototoni*, contributes significantly to the peak in the early dry season. One can see this from Simpson's diversity index, *Lambda* = $1/\Sigma p_i^2$, where p_i is the proportion of that fortnight's total dry weight of fruit contributed by species i (Figure 1,c). *Lambda* can be thought of as the number of species contributing fruit that fortnight were they all equally abundant and, in effect, counts the number of species dominating fruit production that fortnight. The dominant fruit trees of the dry season attract many frugivorous birds and are not exclusive food sources for manakins.

A high diversity of species contributes to the fruiting peak at the beginning of the rains except during one fortnight period, 30 May to 13 June. During this one fortnight, the contribution of all other species is eclipsed by the sudden ripening of *Coccoloba manzanillensis*. The trees participating in this fruiting peak are attractive to many species of frugivorous birds.

In the late rainy season, diversity is high even though the abundance of fruit is relatively low. The majority of understory shrubs (1 to 4 m) fruit during this time (Croat, 1969, 1978; Foster, this volume), and the fruit crop of any one species of understory plant is small. Manakins enjoy exclusive use of species producing fruit in the late rainy season until the arrival of migrants, most notably the migrant thrushes (veery, Swainson's thrush, and wood thrush) in October.

Food Shortage

The patterns of energy availability can be contrasted now with manakin requirements and their season of breeding. Assuming that there are 4.5 kcal/g dry weight of fruit (White, 1974), and supposing that during the late rainy season the manakins obtained 73% of their calories from fruit of censused plants, it appears that the manakins required 1463 kcal, or 325 g dry weight, of food per hectare per fortnight from the censused plants (Figure 1, a). At this season, the food supply barely meets the manakin's energy requirements.

Do seasonal rhythms in the activities of manakins corroborate the apparent shortage? The onset of breeding in golden-collared manakins was marked in staccato by the return of court-owners to the leks on 7 December 1979. The last observation of a female golden-collared manakin accompanying fledged and begging young was 9 July 1979. By 1 August, activity at the leks was much reduced; absence from the courts was confirmed by the lack of droppings there. The last day I heard a female red-capped manakin give the call used to gather young was 23 June 1979. The beginning and end of the males' courting season could not be pin-pointed, as I only discovered the red-capped manakin lek at Orchid Island on 8 July 1979, at which time I could see only one of the four adult male red-capped manakins I had marked by that time. Clearly the onset of breeding corresponds with the time when the fruit supply on Orchid Island increases beyond the minimum manakins require (Figure 1, a). Breeding ends when the fruit supply drops below this calculated minimum.

Molt is energetically costly and proceeds rapidly in both species of manakins. Snow and Snow (1964) report a complete replacement of the primary wing feathers in 80 days for *Manacus* and 96 days for *Pipra*. The greater the number of primary feathers changing, the quicker the molt. Snow and Snow (1964) report that, in the manakins of Trinidad, two to three primary wing feathers are changing at once; I found the same replacement pattern on Orchid Island manakins. I have records of six male golden-collared manakins and two male red-capped manakins that went completely from juvenile to adult plumage over the period of mid-June to late September. Three of the eight individual red-capped manakins examined in October were undergoing molt, but no molting golden-collared manakins were caught. Molt tends to overlap with breeding in the New World tropics in order that

Table 2. Fortnightly abundance of 21 species of fruit (g dry weight pulp per ha.)

Dates 1978–79	Aa 3	Ab 4	Ca 4	Cm 10	Cs 10	Dm 15	Dmv vine	Ep 8	Ga 8	Hl 10	Hv 2	La 8	Ll 15	Ma 12	Ol 4
15 Nov.	0.39	—	2.6	—	—	—	—	—	26	0.1	2.7	—	—	—	—
28 Nov.	0.39	—	2.6	—	—	—	—	—	34	—	2.3	—	—	—	—
12 Dec.	0.43	—	1.5	—	—	1584	—	—	50	—	1.6	—	148	—	—
27 Dec.	0.57	—	1.0	—	—	3168	—	—	27	—	1.1	—	219	—	—
10 Jan.	0.25	—	0.9	—	—	3168	—	—	34	—	0.5	—	177	—	131
20 Jan.	0.25	—	0.5	—	—	3900	—	—	47	—	0.1	—	22	—	196
4 Feb.	0.18	—	0.7	—	—	4632	—	—	45	—	—	—	—	—	132
16 Feb.	0.14	—	1.0	—	—	4546	—	—	84	—	—	—	—	84	39
2 Mar.	—	—	2.2	—	—	3110	—	—	74	—	—	—	—	261	13
14 Mar.	—	—	2.6	—	405	880	—	—	55	0.7	—	1.5	—	403	80
31 Mar.	—	—	2.1	—	3	—	—	185	2	—	—	0.2	—	319	62
15 Apr.	—	—	0.8	—	—	—	—	4	—	0.1	—	1.8	—	168	75
30 Apr.	—	—	0.6	—	231	—	—	26	11	—	0.1	5.7	—	25	36
18 May	—	0.17	0.8	1536	484	—	—	162	11	—	0.5	360.0	—	—	—
30 May	0.14	0.03	0.8	7856	24	—	—	58	9	—	1.0	289.0	—	—	—
13 June	—	—	0.9	1871	—	—	—	—	20	0.8	1.3	26.0	—	—	—
27 June	—	0.05	0.8	—	—	—	—	—	2	2.1	2.3	—	—	—	—
11 July	0.14	—	1.0	—	—	—	—	—	24	27.2	2.7	—	—	—	—
25 July	0.14	2.60	1.7	—	—	—	—	—	31	22.1	4.2	—	—	—	—
9 Aug.	0.14	4.10	2.6	—	—	—	—	—	35	9.9	4.1	—	—	—	—
24 Aug.	—	4.10	3.7	—	—	—	—	—	35	9.2	3.9	—	—	—	—
5 Sept.	—	4.10	2.5	—	—	—	—	—	36	5.1	3.6	—	—	—	—
19 Sept.	0.57	16.90	1.4	—	—	—	36	22	49	0.6	3.3	—	—	—	—
3 Oct.	0.72	18.90	0.6	—	—	—	36	—	67	—	3.0	—	—	—	—
17 Oct.	1.07	2.60	2.1	—	—	—	36	—	112	—	3.9	—	—	—	—
1 Nov.	0.32	0.02	2.6	—	—	—	36	7	20	—	3.4	—	—	—	—

Aa = *Annona acuminata*
Ab = *Ardisia bartletti*
Ca = *Coccoloba acuminata*
Cm = *Coccoloba manzanillensis*
Cs = *Cupania sylvatica*
Dm = *Didymopanax morototoni*

Dmv = *Doliocarpus major*
Ep = *Erythroxylon panamense*
Ga = *Guatteria amplifolia*
Hl = *Heisteria longipes*
Hv = *Heliconia vaginalis*
La = *Lacistema aggregatum*

Ll = *Lindackeria laurina*
Ma = *Miconia argentea*
Ol = *Ouratea lucens*
Pe = *Palicourea elliptica*
Pd = *Psychotria deflexa*
Ph = *Psychotria horizontalis*

both are completed before the lean season (Snow and Snow, 1964; Foster, 1974) but, in this case, a few individuals were found molting well into the lean period (Figure 1, a).

DISCUSSION

Although the number of species bearing manakin-favored fruits on Orchid Island changes little from season to season, the amount of fruit available varies greatly. My data suggest that the seasonal decrease in fruit abundance causes the manakins to stop breeding.

When fruit is abundant and predictable in space, manakins spend little time and energy foraging. Adult male long-tailed manakins, white-bearded manakins, and golden-headed manakins spend 8%, 10%, and 11%, respectively, of their daylight hours feeding (Foster, 1977; Snow, 1962a, b) or, in total, an adult male spends about an hour a day feeding. My observations on Orchid Island parallel this; a golden-collared manakin would be absent from the lek less than a minute during a foraging trip. From June to July, there is a distinct transition from a concentration of fruits in tall trees to the dispersion of fruits on small

Species (number = height in m)						Total	N
Pe 2	Pd 1	Ph 3	Pm 3	Qa 8	Tv vine		
—	0.5	6.1	32	0.5	—	71	9
—	—	4.7	17	1.8	—	63	7
—	—	1.6	6	0.9	—	1794	9
—	—	—	—	3.1	—	3420	7
—	—	—	—	18.5	—	3532	8
—	—	0.5	—	42.6	—	4210	9
—	—	0.2	—	19.3	—	4830	7
—	—	0.1	—	38.2	5.8	4798	9
—	—	0.1	—	25.9	5.8	3491	8
—	—	0.1	—	1.2	5.8	1835	11
—	—	—	—	3.3	—	577	8
—	—	—	3	2.0	—	255	8
—	—	—	3	—	—	338	9
—	—	—	12	—	—	2566	9
—	—	—	79	—	—	8317	10
—	—	—	223	—	—	2143	7
—	—	—	162	—	—	169	6
—	—	—	171	—	—	226	6
—	—	6.8	321	—	—	390	8
—	—	6.8	85	—	—	148	8
—	—	6.8	74	—	—	137	7
—	—	6.8	66	—	—	123	7
3.1	7.8	7.4	62	—	—	211	12
3.0	13.4	4.5	17	—	—	164	10
0.1	12.5	19.7	85	—	—	275	10
—	0.6	6.1	71	—	—	146	10

Pm = *Psychotria marginata*
Qa = *Quassia amara*
Tv = *Tetracera volubilis*

trees with small fruit crops. The manakins must travel farther and search longer to gather energy from a more dispersed resource. Courtship is abandoned altogether by late wet season. Breeding activity therefore must be responsive to changes in foraging efficiency. The situation on Orchid Island contrasts strikingly with the situation in the Armina valley in Trinidad, where male courtship is suspended only during brief unpredictable food shortages and when the males leave the display area to molt (Snow, 1962a, b; Lill, 1974a, b). However, the situation seems quite typical of Barro Colorado Island, where fruiting

rhythms are similar (Smythe, 1970; Leck, 1972; Croat, 1967, 1979; Foster, this volume). The shortage of fruit may in fact be more drastic in the mature forest of Barro Colorado Island.

More generally, food availability in the tropics does vary enough to limit the breeding of most tropical birds to well-defined seasons (Moreau, 1936, 1950; Skutch, 1950; Davis, 1953; Marchant, 1959; Miller, 1959, 1963; Snow and Snow, 1964; Fogden, 1972). My data strongly suggest that the initiation of breeding in manakins is associated with a tremendous rise in kilocalories of fruit available in the forest. Morton (1973) reports that in Panama *Vireo flavoviridis* (yellow-green vireo), *Turdus grayi* (clay-colored robin), and *Elaenia chiriquensis* (tyrannid flycatcher) initiate breeding only when fruit of *Miconia argentea* and *Miconia rubiginosa* become plentiful. He found that local differences in fruit availability could cause the onset of breeding in the clay-colored robin to differ locally by 2 to 4 weeks.

Ward (1969a, b), Fogden (1972), and Jones and Ward (1976) suggest that tropical birds will come into breeding condition whenever their protein level is sufficiently high to afford the costly production of eggs. Tropical birds therefore must be sensitive to changes in protein availability, hence insect food abundance. It follows that an alternative or confounding hypothesis is that manakins in Panama initiate breeding with a sudden availability of protein.

Manakins could (1) consume insects, (2) select protein-rich fruit, (3) efficiently extract proteins from fruit, or (4) consume fruit in large enough quantities to meet the protein demands of breeding. The high rate of gut-passage time suggests the latter two processes, at least, may be operating. Smythe (this volume) demonstrates there is a predictable though minor peak in nocturnal insect numbers from December to January due to the migration of Coleoptera and a minor emergence of Hymenoptera. Manakins may be able to take advantage of this seasonal abundance of insect foods. Careful observation of feeding behavior, examination of fecal specimens, and nutritional analysis of early dry-season fruits will reveal which cue, fruit abundance or insect abundance, initiates breeding in the two species of manakin.

The fruiting rhythms on Orchid Island are consistent with phenology sequences reported for other years on the neighboring Barro Colorado Island (Smythe, 1970; Croat, 1969; Foster, this volume). Variations in these sequences will affect the onset and duration of the manakin breeding season. In Trinidad, the breeding season of the white-bearded manakin (*Manacus manacus*) may be as short as 4 months or as long as 8 months (Snow and Snow, 1964). The

Table 3. Monthly feeding observations of manakins on plant species found on Orchid Island, Panama

Plant species	Dec.	Jan.	Feb.	Mar.	Apr.	May	June	July
Alibertia edulis	—	—	—	—	—	—	—	—
Annona acuminata**	—	R#	—	—	—	—	—	—
Anthurium clavigerum	—	—	—	—	—	—	R*	R*,G*
Anthurium brownii	—	—	—	—	—	—	—	R*,G*
Ardisia bartletti**	—	—	—	—	—	—	—	—
Capparis frondosa	—	—	—	—	—	—	—	—
Carludovica palmata	—	—	—	—	—	—	—	G*
Casearia sylvestris	—	—	—	—	—	—	—	—
Cassipourea elliptica	—	—	—	—	—	—	—	—
Coccoloba acuminata**	G*	—	—	—	G#	—	—	—
Coccoloba manzanillensis**	—	—	—	—	—	—	R#,G#	R*,G*
Cupania sylvatica**	—	—	—	—	—	G#	—	—
Dendropanax arboreus	—	—	—	—	—	—	—	—
Didymopanax morototoni**	—	R*,G#	G#	R*,G#	—	—	—	—
Dolicarpus major**	—	—	—	—	—	—	—	G*
Erythroxylum panamense**	G*	—	—	—	—	—	—	—
Faramea occidentale	—	—	—	—	—	—	—	—
Ficus sp.	—	—	—	—	—	—	—	—
Guatteria amplifolia**	R*,G*	—	—	R*	—	—	—	—
Hasseltia floribunda	—	—	—	—	—	—	R*,G#	R*,G#
Heisteria longipes**	—	—	—	—	—	R#	—	—
Heliconia latispatha	—	—	—	—	—	—	—	G*
Heliconia marie	—	—	—	—	—	—	—	—
Heliconia vaginalis**	—	—	—	—	—	—	—	—
Hieronima laxiflora	—	—	—	—	—	—	—	—
Lacistema aggregatum**	—	—	—	—	—	G#	R#	—
Lindackeria laurina**	G#	R#	—	—	—	—	—	—
Miconia argentea**	—	—	—	R*,G#	R#,G#	—	—	—
Ossaea quinquenervia	—	—	—	—	—	—	—	—
Ouratea lucens**	—	—	—	—	—	R#,G#	—	—
Palicourea elliptica**	—	—	—	—	—	—	—	—
Passiflora sp.	—	—	—	—	—	—	—	—
Paullinia sp.	—	—	—	—	—	—	—	—
Protium panamense	—	—	—	—	—	—	—	G*
Psychotria deflexa**	—	—	—	—	—	—	—	—
Psychotria horizontalis**	—	—	—	—	—	—	—	—
Psychotria marginata**	G#	—	—	—	R*	—	R#	R#*,G#
Psychotria racemosa	—	—	—	—	—	—	—	—
Quassia amara**	—	R#	—	—	—	—	—	—
Renealmia cernua	—	—	—	—	—	—	—	—
Sorocea affinis	—	—	—	—	—	—	—	—
Tetracera volubilis**	—	—	G#	—	—	—	—	—
Trichilia cipo	—	—	—	—	—	—	—	—
Unknown spp. (4)	G*	—	—	—	—	—	—	G*
Insects	—	—	—	—	—	—	R*	R#,G*

Direct observations of feeding (#) or collection of seeds in feces (*) of red-capped manakins (R) and golden-collared manakins (G) during the period August 1978 to December 1979. Far right columns give, for each plant species, in the total number of feeding observations by R and G on Orchid and Barro Colorado islands. ** indicates plant species for which fruit production was monitored; a = George Angehr, personal communication.

WORTHINGTON

Aug.	Sept.	Oct.	Nov.	Total R	G
—	—	—	G#	—	1
—	—	—	—	1	—
R*,G*	—	—	—	22	20
—	—	—	—	1	4
—	R#,G#	—	—	1	3
R*	—	—	—	1	—
—	—	—	—	—	6
G#	—	—	—	—	1
—	R#	—	—	2	—
—	—	—	G#	—	3
—	—	—	—	2	4
—	—	—	—	—	1
—	G*	—	—	—	1
—	—	—	—	4	3
—	R#,G#*	R#*,G#	—	7	10
—	—	—	R*	1	1
—	—	R*	R*	4	—
G*	—	—	R*	2	1
—	—	—	G#	3	3
—	—	—	—	2	3
—	—	R#	—	2	—
—	—	—	—	—	2
G#	—	—	G#	—	2
—	—	—	G#	—	2
—	G*	—	—	—	1
—	—	—	—	1	3
—	—	—	—	1	3
—	—	—	—	4	10
—	—	—	G#	—	1
—	—	—	—	1	1
—	R*,G*	R#*,G#	R*	5	4
—	—	G*	—	—	1
—	G#	—	R*	2	1
R*	—	—	—	2	1
—	—	R*,G*	R#*	6	1
—	—	R*	—	3	—
R*,G*	R#*,G*	R*	R*	16	26
—	—	—	R#*	2	—
—	—	—	—	a	—
—	—	G#	—	—	1
—	—	R*	—	3	—
—	—	—	—	—	4
R*,G*	—	—	—	4	1
G*	—	—	—	—	5
R*,G#	—	R*,G*	R*	15	12

time of ripening of *Didymopanax morototoni*, causing the tremendous rise in kilocalories of fruit in December and January on Orchid Island, shows little year-to-year variation (Hladik, 1970). Therefore, the onset of breeding of these two species of manakin should be predictable whether initiated by predictable abundance of insects or fruit. However, the termination of manakin breeding is less predictable, as it is subject to variations in the phenology and fruit-crop size of a diversity of plants. The timing and duration of the first significant soil-soaking rains play a large role in determining size and rate of ripening of fruit crops produced in the early rainy season and in determining pollination success and thus fruit-crop size of plants fruiting in the late rainy season (Augspurger, 1978; Foster, this volume). The disruption of synchrony of the early rainy-season fruits or the increase in fruit-crop size in the late rainy season could lengthen the breeding season of the manakins and enhance survival of manakins during the late rainy-season fruit shortage.

ACKNOWLEDGMENTS

This work was supported by a National Science Foundation predoctoral dissertation improvement grant (DEB 77 28129). I wish to thank the following people for fruitful discussions and constructive criticism of earlier drafts: Phyllis Coley, David Janos, Egbert Leigh, Robert Olberg, and Francis Putz. Also, I wish to thank Joe Wright for introducing me to Orchid Island. I am grateful for the use of the excellent facilities of the Smithsonian Tropical Research Institute.

LITERATURE CITED

Augspurger, C. K.
1978.   Reproductive Consequences of Flowering Synchrony in *Hybanthus prunifolius* and Other Shrub Species in Panama. Ph.D. thesis, University of Michigan, Ann Arbor, Michigan.

Chapman, F. M.
1935.   The Courtship of Gould's Manakin (*Manacus vitellinus vitellinus*) on Barro Colorado Island. *Bulletin of the American Museum of Natural History*, 68: 471–525.

Croat, T. B.
1969.   Seasonal Flowering Behavior in Central Panama. *Annals of the Missouri Botanical Garden*, 56: 295–307.
1978.   *Flora of Barro Colorado Island, Panama*. Stanford, California: Stanford University Press.

Davis, T. A. W.
1953.   An Outline of the Ecology and Breeding Seasons of Birds of the Lowland Forest Region of British Guiana. *Ibis*, 95: 450–467.

Fogden, M. P. L.
1972. The Seasonality and Population Dynamics of Equatorial Forest Birds in Sarawak. *Ibis*, 114: 307–343.

Foster, M. S.
1974. A Model to Explain Multi-breeding Overlap and Clutch Size in Some Tropical Birds. *Evolution*, 28: 182–190.
1977. Ecological and Nutritional Effects of Food Scarcity on a Tropical Frugivorous Bird and Its Food Source. *Ecology*, 58: 43–85.

Foster, R. B.
1973. Seasonality of Fruit Production and Seedfall in a Tropical Forest Ecosystem in Panama. Ph.D. thesis, Duke University, Durham, North Carolina.
1982. The Seasonal Rhythms in Fruitfall on Barro Colorado Island. Pages 151–172 in *The Ecology of a Tropical Forest*, edited by Egbert G. Leigh, Jr., et al. Washington, D.C.: Smithsonian Institution Press.

Hladik, A.
1970. Contribution a l'etude biologique d'une Araliaceae d'Amerique tropicale: *Didymopanax morototoni*. *Adansonia Ser. 2*, 10(3): 383–407.

Jones, P. J., and P. Ward
1976. The Level of Reserve Protein as the Proximate Factor Controlling the Timing of Breeding and Clutch Size in the Red-billed Quelea (*Quelea quelea*). *Ibis*, 118: 547–574.

Karr, J. R.
1971. Structure of Avian Communities in Selected Panama and Illinois Habitats. *Ecological Monographs*, 41: 207–233.

Kendeigh, C.
1970. Energy Requirements for Existence in Relation to Size of Birds. *Condor*, 72:60–65.

King, J. R.
1975. Seasonal Allocation of Time and Energy Resources in Birds. Pages 4–70 in *Avian Energetics*, edited by R. A. Paynter. Cambridge, Mass.: Nuttal Ornithological Club.

Kontogiannis, J. E.
1968. Effect of Temperature on Energy Intake and Body Weight of the White-throated Sparrow (*Zonotrichia albicollis*). *Physiological Zoology*, 41: 54–64.

Leck, C. F.
1972. Seasonal Changes in Feeding Pressures of Fruit- and Nectar-eating Birds in Panama. *Condor*, 74: 54–60.

Leigh, E. G., and N. Smythe
1978. Leaf Production, Leaf Consumption, and the Regulation of Folivory on Barro Colorado Island. Pages 35–50 in *The Ecology of Arboreal Folivores*, edited by G. Gene Montgomery. Washington, D.C.: Smithsonian Institution Press.

Lill, A.
1974a. Sexual Behavior in the Lek-forming White-bearded Manakin (*M. trinitatis* Hartert). *Z. Tierpsychol.*, 36: 1–36.
1974b. Social Organization and Space Utilization in the Lek-forming White-bearded Manakin, *M. manacus trinitatis* Hartert. *Z. Tierpsychol.*, 36:513–530.

Marchant, S.
1959. The Breeding Season in S.W. Ecuador. *Ibis*, 101: 137–152.

Martin, E. W.
1968. The Effects of Dietary Protein on the Energy and Nitrogen Balance of the Tree Sparrow (*Spizella arborea arborea*). *Physiol. Zoo.*, 41: 313–331.

McDiarmid, R. W., R. E. Ricklefs, and M. S. Foster
1977. Dispersal of *Stemmadenia donell-smithii* (Apocynaceae) by birds. *Biotropica*, 9: 9–25.

Miller, A. H.
1959. Reproductive Cycles in an Equatorial Sparrow. *Proceedings of the National Academy of Science*, 45: 1095–1100.
1963. Seasonal Activity and Ecology of Avifauna of an American Equatorial Cloud Forest. *University of California Publications Zoology*, 66: 1–78.

Moreau, R. E.
1936. Breeding Seasons of Birds in East African Evergreen Forest. *Proc. Zool. Soc. London*, 1936: 631–651.
1950. The Breeding Seasons of African Birds. I. Land Birds. *Ibis*, 92: 223–269.

Morton, E. S.
1973. On the Evolutionary Advantages and Disadvantages of Fruit Eating in Tropical Birds. *American Naturalist*, 107: 8–22.

Moss, R.
1973. Digestibility and Intake of Winter Foods by Wild Ptarmigan in Alaska, *Condor*, 75: 293–300.

Pullianinen, E. L., E. L. Paloheimo, and L. Syrjala
1968. Digestibility of Blueberry Stems (*Vaccinium myrtillos*) and Cowberries (*Vaccinium vitis-idaea*) in the Willow Grouse (*Lagopus lagopus*). *Ann. Acad. Sci.*, Fennicae AIV 126:1–15.

Ridgely, R.
1976. *Birds of Panama*. Princeton, New Jersey: Princeton University Press. 394 p.

Siebert, H. C.
1949. Differences Between Migrant and Non-migrant Birds in Food and Water Intake at Various Temperatures and Photoperiods. *Auk*, 66: 128–153.

Skutch, A. F.
1949. The Life History of the Yellow-thighed Manakin. *Auk*, 66: 1–24.
1950. The Nesting Season of Central American Birds in Relation to Climate and Food Supply. *Ibis*, 92: 185–222.

Smythe, N.
1970. Relationships Between Fruiting Season and Seed-Dispersal Methods in a Neotropical Forest. *American Naturalist*, 104: 25–35.
1982. The Seasonal Abundance of Night-flying Insects in a Neotropical Forest. Pages 309–318 in *The Ecology of a Tropical Forest*, edited by Egbert G. Leigh, Jr., et al. Washington, D.C.: Smithsonian Institution Press.

Snow, D. W.
1962a. A Field Study of the Black-and-White Manakin, *Manacus manacus*, in Trinidad, West Indies. *Zoologica*, 47: 65–104.

1962b.   A Field Study of the Golden-headed Manakin, *Pipra erythrocephala,* in Trinidad, West Indies. *Zoologica,* 47: 183–198.

Snow, D. W., and B. K. Snow
1964.   Breeding Seasons and Annual Cycles of Trinidad Land-birds. *Zoologica,* 49: 1–39.

Walsberg, G. E.
1975.   Digestive Adaptation of *Phainopepla nitens* Associated with the Eating of Mistletoe Berries. *Condor* 77: 169–174.

Ward, P.
1969.   The Annual Cycle of the Yellow-headed Bulbul, *Pychonotus goiavier,* in an Humid Equatorial Environment. *Journal of Zoology, London,* 157: 25–45.
1969.   Seasonal and Diurnal Changes in Fat Content of an Equatorial Bird. *Physiol. Zoöl.,* 42: 85–95.

Wetmore, A.
1972.   The Birds of the Republic of Panama. Part 3. *Smithsonian Miscellaneous Collections,* vol. 150, 1–3: 309–356.

White, S. C.
1974.   *Ecological Aspects of Growth and in Tropical Fruit-eating Birds.* Ph.D. thesis, University of Pennsylvania, Philadelphia, Pennsylvania.

Wiegert. R. G.
1970.   Energetics of the Nest-building Termite *Nasutitermes costalis* (Holmgren) in a Puerto Rican Forest. Pages 1–57 in *A Tropical Rain Forest,* edited by H. T. Odum and R. Pigeon. Springfield, Virginia: National Technical Information Service.

Willis, E. O.
1967.   The Behavior of Bicolored Antbirds. *University of California Publications in Zoology,* 79: 1–132.
1972.   The Behavior of Spotted Antbirds. *A.O.U. Monographs,* 10: 162 p.
1973.   The Behavior of Ocellated Antbirds. *Smithsonian Contributions to Zoology,* 144: 1–57.
1980.   Ecological Roles of Migratory and Resident Birds on Barro Colorado Island, Panama. Pages 205–25 in *Migrant Birds in the Neotropics,* edited by A. Keast and E. S. Morton. Washington, D.C.: Smithsonian Institution Press.

Willis, E. O., and E. Eisenmann.
1979.   A Revised List of Birds of Barro Colorado Island, Panama. *Smithsonian Contributions to Zoology,* 291: 1–31.

Zaret, T. M., and S. A. Rand.
1971.   Competition in Tropical Stream Fishes: Support for the Competitive Exclusion Principle. *Ecology* 52: 336–342.

Population Regulation in Some Terrestrial Frugivores

NICHOLAS SMYTHE   Smithsonian Tropical Research Institute, Balboa, Republic of Panama

WILLIAM E. GLANZ   Department of Zoology, University of Maine, Orono, Maine 04469

EGBERT G. LEIGH, JR.   Smithsonian Tropical Research Institute, Balboa, Republic of Panama

ABSTRACT

Two large, territorial caviomorph rodents, the diurnal agouti, with adults averaging 3 kg in weight, and the nocturnal paca, with adults averaging 9 kg, live on the forest floor of Barro Colorado Island. Both live primarily on fallen fruit, although pacas also browse leaves.

In Lutz catchment, and in other areas surrounding the laboratory clearing, there is one pair of adult territorial agoutis per 2 ha., and one pair of adult pacas per 3 ha. Late in the rainy season, there are slightly over half as many juveniles as adults. Half the newborn animals survive to trappable age, and the survival rate of trappable, nonterritorial juveniles is a third lower than that of adults.

Between November and March, the total weight per unit area of fruit dropping to the forest floor falls to a monthly low of 20 or 30 kg/ha., too little to support these animals even if they could eat it all, which they cannot. During this seasonal fruit shortage, agoutis live off seeds which they have buried over their territory during the season of plenty, while pacas browse more leaves and fall back on reserves of stored fat. The season of fruit shortage is nevertheless a time of stress: agoutis and pacas forage longer, range farther for food, are hungrier, judging by the greater ease with which one can attract them to baited traps, and cease caring for young sooner, during the shortage. If they are not actually losing weight, young animals gain weight far more slowly during the season of shortage than do animals of comparable size during the season of plenty, or captive animals of comparable size fed ad libitum. Young born during or just before the season of shortage are far more likely to die than those reared during the season of plenty.

In sum, the populations of agoutis and pacas appear limited by seasonal shortage of food. The proximate cause of death is often a predator, but the predator gets his chance because his prey is in worse condition or because hunger drives it to take greater risks finding food.

Figure 1. The agouti *Dasyprocta punctata*.

INTRODUCTION

Two large caviomorph rodents, the agouti (*Dasyprocta punctata*) (Figure 1), with adults of average weight about 3 kg, and the paca (*Cuniculus paca*), with adults averaging 9 kg, live on the forest floor of Barro Colorado Island. (For pacas, we use the generic name *Cuniculus*, even though technically *Agouti* may be more correct, to avoid confusion.) These two genera coexist in other forests from northern Argentina to Chiapas in southern Mexico. Their appearance and habits are very like those of the mouse deer (Medway, 1969) and chevrotain (Dubost, 1968), the small duikers, and the royal antelope (Dorst and Dandelot, 1969) of the Old World tropics. Like these and many other small ungulates (Eisenberg and McKay, 1974), agoutis and pacas are solitary or move in small family groups, a male and female or a mother with young, and they eat fallen fruit when it is available. Indeed, pacas appear to occupy the niche of duikers and mouse deer, for these all browse seedlings and other vegetation as well as eating fruit, while agoutis, which eat hard seeds in addition to softer fruits, are more like squirrels in their diet. Both agoutis and pacas, however, depend primarily on fallen fruit for food, perhaps more than their counterparts elsewhere.

To what extent are agouti and paca populations regulated by seasonal shortage of food? How do they coexist with other frugivores? What role might these animals play in seed dispersal? We know something of the behavior of these animals, in addition to the information available on their diet, their demography, and the seasonal changes in their food supply, so we can inquire more precisely than usual how they are affected by seasonal changes in food supply, how much they overlap competitors, and how effectively they disperse seeds.

METHODS

In the course of a study on squirrels, Glanz accumulated 326 separate feeding records for agoutis and 15 for pacas between January 1977 and June 1978. These data are biased somewhat toward areas and trees where squirrels are present and toward the larger, more easily identified fruits, but they appear representative. Concurrently, the Smithsonian Environmental Monitoring Program monitored fruit production by selected individuals of most of the species of plants from which agoutis and pacas were observed to feed, so we may compare diet with the selection of food available.

To monitor seasonal changes in the availability of fruit, Smythe (1970a, b) suspended 75 squares (152 × 152 cm) of polyethylene sheeting 6.1 m apart along 457 m of transect on the opposite side of the laboratory clearing from the Lutz catchment. He collected and weighed the fruit falling therein at least once a week. To estimate the population densities of frugivorous mammals, Smythe initiated and later supervised a trap-mark-release program operated by the Smithsonian Environmental Monitoring Program in the Lutz catchment. In October 1971, 51 live traps (23 × 23 × 81 cm) were set out around the weir trail, and, late in 1973, 49 more were set out around the perimeter of the catchment (Smythe, 1978). At intervals of 1 week to 1 month, the traps were prebaited for a few days, usually with dried corn, then baited and set (for details, see Smythe, 1978). Trappers recorded the species, sex, weight, and, if previously marked, the "tag number" of captured animals. There was a striking tendency to classify young agoutis and pacas as males: some of these revealed themselves female when fully grown. Despite this inaccuracy, the trapping records permit us to judge the population density of agoutis and pacas (from which we can infer their aggregate demand for food), and to compare mortality in young animals with that in adult territory-holders. If we assume greater hunger makes an animal more trappable, we may also assess seasonal changes in hunger stress. This assumption seemed correct for agoutis and pacas until 1977 and 1978, when peccaries acquired the habit of shaking the bait out of the traps, as they had occasionally done earlier during harsh shortages.

Smythe (1970a, 1978) has also studied the behavior of agoutis and pacas, observing interactions between animals and between marked animals attracted to baiting areas in the wild, and photographing animals with automatic recording cameras. His studies yield information on diet, territorial behavior, breeding rhythms, competitive relationships, and predator avoidance.

Table 1. Number of feeding sessions by agoutis on different species of fruit observed in successive months, January 1977–June 1978

| | 1977 | | | | | | | | | | | | 1978 | | | | |
	Jan.	Feb.	Mar.	Apr.	May	June	July	Aug.	Sept.	Oct.	Nov.	Dec.	Jan.	Mar.	Apr.	May	June
Dipteryx panamensis	16	3	0	0	0	0	0	0	0	0	2	31	29	3	1	0	0
Astrocaryum standleyanum	0	1	7	6	13	12	4	1	0	0	0	0	0	0	12	14	4
Apeiba membranacea	0	2	1	0	0	0	0	0	0	0	0	0	0	1	0	0	0
Ficus spp.	0	0	1	0	0	0	1	0	0	0	0	3	0	0	1	2	0
Scheelea zonensis	0	0	1*	0	4	4	2	9	4	0	3*	4*	2*	0	0	0	3
Tetragastris panamensis	0	0	1	0	0	0	0	0	0	0	0	0	0	0	8	3	0
Gustavia superba	0	0	1	0	2	5	0	0	0	0	0	0	0	0	2	8	0
Lacmellea panamensis	0	0	0	1	0	0	0	0	0	0	1	0	1	0	0	0	0
Cordia spp.	0	0	0	0	2	0	0	0	0	0	0	0	0	0	0	1	0
Anacardium excelsum	0	0	0	0	1	0	0	0	0	0	0	0	0	0	0	6	0
Maripa panamensis	0	0	0	0	0	1	0	0	0	0	0	0	0	0	0	0	0
Eugenia nesiotica	0	0	0	0	0	0	1	0	0	0	0	0	0	0	0	10	0
Oenocarpus panamanus	0	0	0	0	0	0	1	0	0	0	0	0	0	0	0	0	0
Spondias mombin	0	0	0	0	0	0	1	1	3	1	0	0	0	0	0	0	0
Virola surinamensis	0	0	0	0	0	0	0	1	0	0	0	0	0	0	0	0	0
Quararibea asterolepis	0	0	0	0	0	0	0	0	4	1	0	0	0	0	0	0	0
Protium spp.	0	0	0	0	0	0	0	0	4	0	0	0	0	0	0	0	0
Trichilia cipo	0	0	0	0	0	0	0	0	6	5	0	0	0	0	0	0	0
Socratea durissima	0	0	0	0	0	0	0	0	0	1	0	0	0	0	0	0	0
Spondias radlkoferi	0	0	0	0	0	0	0	0	0	2	0	0	0	0	0	0	0
Eugenia coloradensis	0	0	0	0	0	0	0	0	0	3	0	0	0	0	0	0	0
Cupania sp.	0	0	0	0	0	0	0	0	0	1	0	0	0	0	0	1	0
Calophyllum longifolium	0	0	0	0	0	0	0	0	0	0	0	2	0	0	0	0	0
Faramea occidentale	0	0	0	0	0	0	0	0	0	0	0	1	0	0	0	0	0
Ceiba pentandra	0	0	0	0	0	0	0	0	0	0	0	1	0	0	0	0	0
Sterculia apetala	0	0	0	0	0	0	0	0	0	0	0	1	1	0	0	0	0
Swartzia simplex	0	0	0	0	0	0	0	0	0	0	0	0	1	0	0	0	0
Zuelania guidonia	0	0	0	0	0	0	0	0	0	0	0	0	0	0	1	0	0
Guarea sp.	0	0	0	0	0	0	0	0	0	0	0	0	0	0	4	0	0
Inga spp.	0	0	0	0	0	0	0	0	0	0	0	0	0	0	1	1	0
Connarus sp.	0	0	0	0	0	0	0	0	0	0	0	0	0	0	0	1	0
Cecropia sp.	0	0	0	0	0	0	0	0	0	0	0	0	0	0	0	1	0
Beilschmiedia pendula	0	0	0	0	0	0	0	0	0	0	0	0	0	0	0	1	0
Rheedia madruno	0	0	0	0	0	0	0	0	0	0	0	0	0	0	0	1	0

* Old fruits

One feeding session is one instance of an individual agouti eating one species of fruit.

RESULTS

Diet

Glanz recorded agoutis eating 36 species of wild fruit (Table 1), but in over half the instances he recorded, they were eating the fruits or hard nuts of *Dipteryx panamensis, Astrocaryum standleyanum*, or, more rarely, *Scheelea zonensis*. Unlike squirrels, which relish the oily pulp surrounding *Scheelea* fruits, agoutis appear to prefer the sweeter pulp of *Astrocaryum*. Agoutis also find *Scheelea* nuts difficult to penetrate, and prefer those whose hulls have been partly chewed through by squirrels. Agoutis eat fruit at the times censused

Table 2. Number of censused trees of different species full of ripe fruit/number with a few ripe fruit, in successive months, January 1977–June 1978

	1977												1978				
	Jan.	Feb.	Mar.	Apr.	May	June	July	Aug.	Sept.	Oct.	Nov.	Dec.	Jan.	Mar.	Apr.	May	June
Dipteryx panamensis (8)	1/5	0/3	0/0	0/0	0/0	0/0	0/0	0/0	0/0	0/0	0/0	4/3	2/4	2/1	0/0	0/0	0/0
Astrocaryum standleyanum (10)	0/1	0/1	1/1	6/1	2/2	1/5	1/0	1/0	0/0	0/0	0/0	0/0	0/1	0/1	2/3	5/3	3/5
Apeiba membranacea (4)	0/0	3/0	1/2	0/0	0/0	0/0	0/0	0/0	0/0	0/0	0/0	0/0	0/0	2/1	0/0	0/0	0/0
Scheelea zonensis (6)	0/0	0/0	0/0	0/0	0/0	0/1	0/1	0/0	0/0	0/0	0/0	0/0	0/0	0/0	0/0	0/0	1/2
Tetragastris panamensis (6)	0/0	0/1	0/1	0/1	0/1	0/0	0/0	2/0	0/0	0/0	0/0	0/0	0/0	1/0	2/1	1/1	1/1
Gustavia superba (6)	0/0	0/0	0/0	0/0	0/0	0/1	0/0	0/1	0/0	0/0	0/0	0/0	0/0	0/0	0/0	0/3	2/3
Leamellea panamensis (4)	0/0	1/1	0/2	0/1	0/2	0/1	0/0	0/0	0/0	0/0	0/0	1/1	1/0	1/3	0/2	1/1	1/0
Cordia lasiocalyx (1)	0/0	0/0	0/0	1/0	0/0	0/0	0/0	0/0	0/0	0/0	0/0	0/0	0/0	0/0	1/0	0/1	0/0
Anacardium excelsum (6)	0/0	0/0	0/0	0/0	0/0	0/1	0/0	0/0	0/0	0/0	0/0	0/0	0/0	1/0	1/4	1/5	0/0
Eugenia nesiotica (1)	0/0	0/0	0/0	0/0	0/0	1/0	1/0	0/0	0/0	0/0	0/0	0/0	0/0	0/0	0/0	1/0	0/0
Oenocarpus panamanus (2)	0/0	0/0	0/0	0/0	0/0	0/0	0/0	0/1	0/0	0/0	0/0	0/1	0/1	0/1	0/0	0/0	2/0
Spondias mombin (4)	0/0	0/0	0/0	0/0	0/0	0/0	0/0	3/0	3/1	0/1	0/0	0/0	0/0	0/0	0/0	0/0	0/0
Virola surinamensis (3)	0/0	0/0	0/0	0/0	0/0	0/0	1/0	0/1	0/0	0/0	0/0	0/0	0/0	0/0	0/0	0/0	0/0
Quararibea asterolepis (5)	0/0	0/0	0/0	0/0	0/0	0/0	0/0	0/0	3/0	3/0	0/1	0/0	0/0	0/0	0/0	0/0	0/0
Protium panamensis (1)	0/0	0/0	1/0	0/1	0/0	0/1	0/0	0/0	0/0	0/0	0/0	0/0	0/0	0/0	0/0	0/0	0/0
Trichilia cipo (3)	0/0	0/0	0/0	0/0	0/0	0/0	0/0	0/0	1/0	1/0	0/1	0/0	0/0	0/0	0/0	0/0	0/0
Socratea durissima (3)	0/1	0/0	2/0	0/1	0/1	0/0	0/0	0/0	0/0	0/0	0/0	1/0	1/0	0/0	1/0	2/0	0/0
Spondias radlkoferi (6)	0/0	0/0	0/0	0/0	0/0	0/0	0/0	0/0	0/0	0/2	0/1	0/1	0/0	0/0	0/0	0/0	0/0
Calophyllum longifolium (4)	0/2	0/0	0/0	0/0	0/0	0/0	0/0	0/0	0/0	0/0	0/0	1/0	0/1	1/1	1/1	0/2	1/1
Faramea occidentale (4)	0/2	0/0	0/0	0/0	0/0	0/0	0/0	0/0	0/0	0/0	0/0	3/1	0/4	0/0	0/0	0/0	0/0
Ceiba pentandra (7)	0/0	0/0	0/0	0/0	0/0	0/0	0/0	0/0	0/0	0/0	0/0	0/0	1/1	0/2	0/0	0/0	0/0
Sterculia apetala (5)	0/0	0/0	0/0	0/0	0/0	0/0	0/0	0/0	0/0	0/0	0/1	1/1	0/2	0/0	0/0	0/0	0/0
Swartzia simplex (3)	0/0	0/0	0/0	0/0	0/0	0/0	0/0	0/0	0/1	0/1	0/1	0/1	0/1	0/2	0/0	0/0	0/0
Zuelania guidonia (4)	0/0	0/0	2/1	1/2	0/0	0/0	0/0	0/0	0/0	0/0	0/0	0/0	0/0	1/1	3/0	0/3	0/0
Guarea glabra (1)	0/0	0/0	0/0	0/0	0/0	0/0	0/0	0/0	0/0	0/0	0/0	0/0	0/0	0/0	0/0	0/0	0/0
Connarus panamensis (1)	0/0	0/0	0/0	0/0	0/0	0/0	0/0	0/0	0/0	0/0	0/0	0/0	0/0	0/0	0/0	0/0	0/0
Beilschmiedia pendula (3)	0/0	0/0	0/0	0/0	0/0	0/0	0/0	0/0	0/0	0/0	0/0	0/0	0/0	0/0	0/1	2/0	0/1
Rheedia madruno (2)	0/0	0/0	0/0	0/0	0/0	0/0	0/0	0/0	0/0	0/0	0/0	0/0	0/0	0/0	0/0	0/0	0/0

A tree is counted full of ripe fruit if it was full of ripe fruit any week that month. Total number of censused individuals appears in parentheses after the name of the species.

trees drop it (Table 2). The feeding records reflect seasonal differences in fruiting schedules, and perhaps also the differences in amount of fruit produced from year to year. For example, 1978 was a "bumper year" for the fruit of *Tetragastris panamensis*, and agoutis were more often seen eating *Tetragastris* that year. November 1977 appeared to be a hard month for the agoutis, a time when they often resorted to digging up old *Scheelea* nuts, and sought out early (either scarce or unripe) *Dipteryx* fruit. Hard times appeared to persist into the dry season.

Although the diets of pacas and agoutis overlap to a very great extent, it appears that pacas prefer the soft fruits bats do (Table 3): these are less available in the late rainy season and early dry season. Is there other evidence these animals suffer from seasonal shortage of food?

Food Availability

The fresh weight of fruit and seed falling into Smythe's traps per month varied from 2 g/sq. m, or 20 kg/ha., in December 1966 to 58 g/sq. m, or 580 kg/ha. in June 1967. A total of 2000 kg/ha. fell in the year starting in September 1966, 40% of which was dry matter. There was a late rainy season low once again in December 1967, when 30 kg of fruit and seed fell per ha. (Table 4).

A larger number of fruits were falling in May, June, and July than at other times; the fruits falling in this

SMYTHE ET AL.

Table 3. Feeding records for pacas on Barro Colorado Island, January 1977–January 1980

Species eaten	Date
*Dipteryx panamensis**	6 January 1977
*Dipteryx panamensis**	15 January 1977
*Astrocaryum standleyanum**	6 April 1977
Ficus yoponensis	6 April 1977
Ficus insipida	21 April 1977
Ficus insipida	15 May 1977
Ficus yoponensis	11 July 1977
Ficus insipida	22 July 1977
Spondias mombin	22 September 1977
Spondias radlkoferi	27 October 1977
Quararibea asterolepis	27 October 1977
Eugenia coloradensis	30 October 1977
Pseudobombax septenatum (flowers)	2 January 1980
*Dipteryx panamensis**	5 January 1980

* Record not certain: the animal was observed feeding under a tree with ripe fruit.

Table 4. Total weight of fruit and seed falling in successive months into Allee Ravine and surrounding areas, in kg dry weight per ha., as judged from the fall into 75 traps with an aggregate area of 170 sq. m

Date	Weight	Date	Weight
1966		1967	
Sept.	40	June	230
Oct.	50	July	125
Nov.	25	Aug.	80
Dec.	10	Sept.	50
		Oct.	40
1967		Nov.	20
Jan.	20	Dec.	15
Feb.	90		
Mar.	20	1968	
Apr.	40	Jan.	20
May	135		

peak season were bigger and had larger seeds, and more species of trees were dropping fruit at this time (Smythe, 1970a, b). Notice that the low in the number of species dropping fruit late in the rainy season is much less marked than the low in the amount of fruit falling.

Population Density and Energy Requirements

The number of trappable adult female agoutis known to be alive (excluding transients trapped only once, such as female #40) averaged six for the first 2 years, and nine for the 3 following years, when there was another trapline on the perimeter of the 10-ha. catchment (Table 5). Agouti territories are generally centered along streams, so the additional agoutis caught by the second trapline are presumably from neighboring catchments. These data accordingly support Smythe's (1970a) estimate, based on his work on the other side of the laboratory clearing, that a pair of adult agoutis holds a territory of about 2 ha. The number of trappable adult female pacas known to be alive averaged four in the first 2 years and six thereafter, suggesting that a pair of pacas holds a territory half again as large as a pair of agoutis (Table 6). Adult male agoutis and pacas seldom enter traps but, since agoutis are monogamous (Smythe, 1978), and probably pacas as well, we assume that there are as many adult males as adult females in the catchment. Late in the rainy season there are rather more resident juveniles than adult females (Tables 5 and 6).

To calculate how much the agoutis and pacas eat, we assume that, as is roughly true for mammals in general, their basal metabolic rate is 70 $W^{3/4}$ Kcal/day, where W is the animal's weight in kg (Eisenberg and Thorington, 1973), and that total energy expenditure is twice the basal metabolic rate (cf. Nagy and Milton, 1979). Taking 1 g dry weight of fruit and seed to represent 5 Kcal (Odum, 1970), and assuming that agoutis and pacas cannot metabolize more than half the dry matter in *edible* fallen fruit (some parts of edible fruits are not edible, and the edible portion is not completely assimilated), we find that a 3-kg agouti eats 128 g dry weight of food per day, or 4 kg per month, while a 9-kg paca eats 290 g dry weight of food per day, or 9 kg per month. A population of the one adult agouti and 0.7 adult pacas per hectare thus requires 10 kg dry weight, or 25 fresh weight, of food per hectare per month. Assuming that in the late rainy season there are half as many juveniles as adults, and that a juvenile weighs half as much as an adult, the agoutis and pacas of Lutz catchment require 32 kg fresh weight of food per hectare per month.

If the fall of fruit into Lutz catchment is similar to

Table 5. Tag numbers of agoutis trapped or known to be alive in successive half-years

	Oct. 71–Mar. 72	Apr.–Sept. 72	Oct. 72–Mar. 73	Apr.–Sept. 73	Oct. 73–Mar. 74	Apr.–Sept. 74	Oct. 74–Mar. 75	Apr.–Sept. 75	Oct. 75–Mar. 76
No. of trapping sessions	19	25	21	19	14	11	10	9	9
Adult females	1(5)	1(0)	1(0)	1(0)	1(1)	1(1)	1(1)	1(1)d	8(1)
	8(5)	7(1)	7(6)d	8(1)	8(4)	8(2)	8(2)	8(0)	24(1)
	10(7)	8(0)	8(0)	9(0)	9(1)d	10(0)	10(0)	10(1)d	28(2)
	13(7)	9(0)	9(1)	10(0)	10(0)	24(1)	24(2)	24(1)	30(1)
	21(1)d	10(0)	10(0)	11(0)	11(1)d	27(5)	27(1)	28(1)	36(0)
		13(0)	11(0)	13(0)	13(1)d	28(2)	28(0)	30(0)	60(2)
			13(0)	N27(1)	24(4)	30(1)d	31(1)d	36(2)	76(1)
			N40(1)d	N30(1)	27(5)	36(1)	36(2)	52(1)d	
					30(5)	46(1)d	52(0)		
					N47(3)D	N31(1)	76(1)		
					N54(2)D	N76(1)	N77(1)d		
					N56(1)d				
Adult males	3(2)	3(0)	3(0)	3(0)	3(6)d	17(0)	17(0)	17(1)	17(2)
	4(2)	4(0)	4(0)	4(2)d	17(4)	N65(1)d	N78(1)d	55(2)d	74(1)
	N15(1)d	17(0)	5(1)d	17(2)	24(1)d			82(0)	82(0)
	N16(1)d	19(0)D	17(0)	N25(1)	25(1)d			83(1)d	
	17(9)				N53(1)d				
	N20(1)d				N57(1)d				
Young females	7(8)x	11(0)x		N24(3)	28(9)x	52(0)x	60(2)x	N84(1)d	N91(3)
	9(9)x			N28(1)	36(7)x	N60(4)	69(2)d	N85(1)d	N97(1)
	11(10)			N36(2)	N37(5)d	N69(3)	N79(3)d	N86(2)d	N98(1)
	14(4)d				N38(2)d				
	18(6)d				N43(3)d				
					N45(3)d				
					N46(4)x				
					N48(2)d				
					N51(1)D				
					N52(3)				
					N58(1)d				
Young males	2(7)	5(0)	23(5)D	24(0)	26(2)	26(0)	26(1)	66(1)	66(2)
	5(15)	N23(1)	24(15)	N26(1)	30(1)d	55(3)	55(2)x	68(0)	68(1)
	6(7)	N24(2)	N30(2)	30(0)	N41(4)d	N66(3)	66(4)	70(1)d	84(2)
	12(5)d		N34(1)d		N42(5)d	N67(1)	67(3)d	80A(2)d	87(2)
	19(1)d				N44(3)d	N68(1)	68(1)	81(2)d	88(1)
	22(1)d				N49(2)d	N70(2)	70(0)	N84(1)	89(3)
					N50(1)d	N71(1)d	74(1)	N87(1)	90(2)
					N53(1)d	N74(1)	75(3)d	N88(1)	N92(3)
					N55(4)	N75(1)	N80A(13)	N89(2)	N93(2)
					N59(1)d		N80B(3)d	N90(1)	N95(1)
							N81(2)		
							N82(1)x		

Conventions are as in Table 6.

Table 6. Tag numbers of pacas trapped or known to be alive in successive half-years

	Oct. 71–Mar. 72	Apr.–Sept. 72	Oct. 72–Mar.73	Apr.–Sept. 73	Oct. 73–Mar. 74	Apr.–Sept. 74	Oct. 74–Mar. 75	Apr.–Sept. 75	Oct. 75–Mar. 76
No. of trapping sessions	19	25	21	19	14	11	10	9	9
Adult females	3(1)	2(2)	2(2)	2(0)	2(5)	2(2)	2(4)	2(2)	2(1)
	4(4)	3(0)	3(0)	3(0)	3(3)	3(1)	3(3)	3(0)	3(1)
	8(1)	4(1)	4(0)	4(0)	4(2)	4(1)	4(2)	4(0)	4(1)
		8(0)	8(1)d	11(0)	11(1)	11(0)	11(0)	11(0)	11(1)d
				14(1)	13(1)d	14(0)	14(1)d		31(2)
					14(2)	22(2)	22(3)d		35(3)
					N30(1)	30(0)	30(1)d		
Adult males	9(1)d	10(0)	10(0)	10(0)	10(1)d	25(0)	25(2)	25(0)	25(2)d
	10(1)	N12(1)d	N16(1)	15(0)	15(1)d	26(3)	26(3)	28(0)	28(2)d
				16(0)	16(2)d	28(0)	28(1)		34(1)d
				N18(1)	18(1)d				
				20(2)	20(2)d				
					N25(2)				
					N29(2)d				
Young females	2(10)x	N11(2)	11(10)x	13(0)x	N22(12)x	N31(3)	31(5)	31(1)x	37(2)
	7(10)D		N13(4)				N35(3)	35(0)x	38(0)x
			N14(1)x					N37(1)	47(8)
								N38(1)	
								N47(4)	
Young males	1(15)	1(2)d	N15(3)x	N17(6)	17(2)d	N32(3)	32(8)	N36(2)	46(5)d
	5(3)d		N20(7)x		N19(6)d	N33(1)d		N46(1)	N40(3)d
	6(10)D				N21(1)d			N48(1)	N48A(1)d
					N23(3)d				36(0)
					N24(4)d				
					N26(6)x				
					N28(1)x				

Number of times trapped that half-year in parentheses. Pacas trapped for the first time are prefixed by N, animals never seen again are suffixed by d, animals known to die in a given season are suffixed by D, young animals presumed to become adult in the next half-year are suffixed by x.

the fall of fruit into Smythe's traps, as we may well expect, since the character of the vegetation and the density of agoutis appear similar on the two sides of the laboratory clearing, too little fruit falls late in the rainy season to meet the needs of the agoutis and pacas. The discrepancy is greater than the numbers suggest, since some of the falling fruit will be inedible or too scattered to eat, and other animals are competing for the remainder.

Effects of Fruit Shortage

In the season of fruit shortage, pacas browse seedlings and leaves. Agoutis live primarily on seeds that they have buried over their territories in times of plenty. When fruit is abundant, agoutis often peel the sweet pulp from seeds such as *Astrocaryum*, discard it, and bury the seed. Pacas are larger than agoutis, have more extensive large intestines, and unlike agoutis, eat some of their own feces, all features that befit their more herbivorous habit. Moreover, pacas are also less active. Unlike agoutis, pacas are nocturnal, and escape their predators primarily by jumping away in a single bound, then freezing: agoutis, on the other hand, run away (Smythe, in press). Like howler monkeys and some other herbivores, pacas have specialized struc-

Table 7. Seasonal rhythms in the number of agoutis and pacas trapped in successive sessions, 1971–78

Month	1971			1972			1973			1974			1975			1976			1977			1978		
	D	A	P	D	A	P	D	A	P	D	A	P	D	A	P	D	A	P	D	A	P	D	A	P
January				7	7	4	5	3	2	4	17	4	3	10	5									
				14	8	3	12	2	2							9	8	7				13	6	3
				21	9	3	19	4	3	18	17	8							—	8	2			
				28	3	3	26	3	3				24	7	5	23	2	6						
February				4	4	4	2	1	3	1	11	10												
				11	5	3	9	3	1				7	7	7	6	3	7						
				18	1	2	16	1	2	15	6	6							—	5	3	—	2	2
				25	2	1	23	3	1				28	2	1	27	1	2						
March				3	1	1	2	3	0	1	2	2												
				10	1	2	9	2	0													10	0	1
				17	0	0	16	1	2	15	4	3	14	2	1				—	2	1			
				24	0	1	23	1	0															
										29	2	2										31	1	2
April							6	0	0				4	5	2									
				14	0	2	13	0	0							9	2	3				14	0	2
				21	0	1				19	2	3	18	3	1				—	3	2			
				28	0	0	27	0	0							23	4	4				28	0	3
May				5	0	0	4	1	0	3	1	0	2	1	0									
				12	0	0	11	0	0													12	0	1
				19	0	0	18	0	0	17	2	1	16	2	1				—	2	2			
				26	0	0	25	0	0	31	1	0												
June				2	0	0																2	0	0
				9	0	0	8	1	1				6	0	0									
				16	0	0	15	0	0	14	1	0				—	2	1	—	4	2			
				23	0	0																		
				30	0	0				28	1	0												

There are three columns for each year. Column D gives the date of the trapping session, columns A and P, the numbers of agoutis and pacas caught on that date.

tures permitting them to make a terrifyingly loud noise (Hershkovitz, 1955). Being comparatively sedate, pacas can afford to store energy as fat (Smythe, 1970a).

Since agoutis must live on buried seeds at some times of year, they must rely to some extent on seeds hard enough not to rot under these circumstances, and they have accordingly evolved the ability to hold seeds in their forepaws so as to chew them more effectively and consistently. Glanz, who has occasionally tossed *Dipteryx* fruit into a cage containing both an agouti and a paca, noticed that the paca only ate the surrounding pulp, while the agouti sometimes gnawed

through the nut to the seed.

Despite these alternate sources of food, pacas and agoutis are clearly more trappable in the season of fruit shortage (Table 7). Young agoutis and pacas gain weight more slowly, if at all, during this season (Smythe, 1975). At the ends of some years, such as 1971 and 1972, most juvenile agoutis did gain weight, although far more slowly than comparable captive animals (Smythe, 1978). The fruit crop of September 1972 was unusually low, with *Trichilia cipo* and other species failing to fruit at all (Foster, this volume): this may be reflected in the abnormally low number of juvenile

SMYTHE ET AL.

Table 7. (continued)

Month	1971			1972			1973			1974			1975			1976			1977			1978		
	D	A	P	D	A	P	D	A	P	D	A	P	D	A	P	D	A	P	D	A	P	D	A	P
July				7	0	0																		
				14	0	0	13	3	1															
				21	0	0	20	5	2							—	1	1	—	3	4			
				28	0	0	27	0	1	26	4	0												
August				4	0	0	3	1	1				1	3	5									
				11	0	0	10	0	0	9	5	1										11	5	5
				18	0	0	17	2	1				15	4	1	—	3	2	—	5	2			
				25	0	0	24	0	0	23	8	4												
							31	0	0															
September				1	0	0																1	3	2
				8	1	0	7	0	0	6	10	3	5	5	5									
				15	2	1	14	0	0							—	0	1				15	0	2
				22	0	1				20	5	4	19	4	6									
				29	1	3																29	7	3
October							5	1	2	4	7	2	3	6	5									
				13	0	1	12	0	2													13	3	2
				20	1	1	19	2	4	18	0	2				—	6	2						
	29	14	4	27	0	0	26	1	4				24	7	7							27	4	4
November										1	5	3												
	12	12	4	10	0	1	9	11	4				7	2	4				—	3	6			
	19	10	3	17	1	2	16	21	7	15	3	8	21	2	2							17	3	0
December	3	11	3	1	2	3							5	5	1							1	1	2
	10	9	5	15	1	1	14	17	4	13	7	7				—	3	3	—	5	2	15	3	3
	17	9	3	22	1	0																		
	30	8	7																					

agoutis caught in late 1972 (Table 5). A great dearth occurred in late 1973, possibly brought on by unusually dense populations of agoutis and pacas: most juveniles lost weight, and a few agoutis, juvenile and adult, were found starved to death.

Seasons of shortage are also reflected in behavior. Adult, reproductive agoutis (Smythe, 1978), and almost certainly pacas as well, have home ranges with many of the characteristics of territories. That is to say, they live on clearly defined areas from which they seldom move and from which they attempt to exclude conspecifics. The rigor with which they defend these areas varies with the abundance of falling fruit, being greatest when food is scarcest. When fruit is abundant, adult agoutis range less, foraging near the center of their territories, and they spend more time resting, while when food is short they spend more time, and go farther, looking for it (Smythe, 1970a). Although one can see young agoutis at any time of year, Smythe (1970a) noticed a sharp peak of mating activity in February and March, which would lead to a birth peak in May and June, and more agoutis were born between March and July than at other times of year. Finally, the bond between a mother agouti and its young apparently lasts longer in the season of plenty. Young agoutis normally live in burrows for their first 8 or 9 weeks. During the season of plenty, they are allowed to accompany their mother on foraging trips, and to nurse occasionally, for another 2 months; whereas, if fruit is short when they emerge, they are forced out on their own quite quickly, and almost certain death awaits them, either from predators or from starvation.

In sum, the late rainy-season food shortage exerts a major impact on the behavior of agoutis. As we shall see, it also affects their survival and may well be the agency by which agouti populations are regulated. Pacas seem less affected by vagaries in the fruit crop; a normal number of juvenile pacas was trapped after the fruit failure of September 1972. However, pacas are also stressed in the season of fruit shortage. Their populations are probably also regulated, in the ultimate sense, by the supply of suitable food, but they seem less dependent on fruit than agoutis.

Demography

Agoutis have between two and three litters a year; perhaps two-thirds of the litters consist of a single young, and the remainder, twins (Smythe, 1970a). An adult female thus bears three young a year. Counting those animals caught more than once, Table 5 shows that 55/39 or roughly 1.4 times as many young were trapped during the study as adult females, suggesting that a newborn has a chance slightly less than 50% of surviving to trappable age. The young that do so tend to be those trapped between March and July (Smythe, 1970a, 1978).

The six female agoutis caught in late 1971 which grew to adulthood survived as adults for an average of 2.5 years apiece, while adult male agoutis seem rather shorter-lived. As there were 1.4 juveniles per adult pair, on the average, trappable juveniles survived less than two-thirds as well as adults. Despite the high mortality of very young animals, the proximate mechanism by which the population is probably regulated is mortality among trappable young which fail to establish territories.

Counting all pacas caught more than once, we caught slightly less than one (26/28) trappable juvenile per adult female paca. The seven female pacas caught in the first 18 months of trapping which grew to adulthood survived as adults for an average of 3.5 years apiece. Two of these animals (#3 and #5) survived over 7 years. Male pacas appear shorter-lived, but trappable young pacas, like trappable young agoutis, survive only two-thirds as well as adults, as if the supply of suitable territories is the proximate factor that also regulates the paca population.

Relations with Competitors

Bats, monkeys, squirrels, kinkajous, guans, toucans, and the like eat a great deal of fruit before it ever has a chance to fall to the ground. However, arboreal frugivores also knock fruit to the ground, sometimes long before it would otherwise fall, thus lengthening the season when fruit is available to terrestrial frugivores. Both agoutis and pacas are attracted to the sound of falling fruit, and one often sees agoutis and other terrestrial frugivores foraging under trees where monkeys are eating (Smythe, 1970a).

In times of plenty, a great many terrestrial mammals eat fruit, including diurnal animals such as peccaries (*Tayassu tajacu*) and coatis (*Nasua narica*), and nocturnal ones such as spiny rats (*Proechimys semispinosus*) and common opossums (*Didelphis marsupialis*), as well as agoutis and pacas. These animals differ in their dependence on fruit. Coatis only eat fruit in quantity late in the dry season, when fruit is common and litter arthropods, their normal staple, are scarce (Russell, this volume). Peccaries are opportunistic, browsing regularly and occasionally killing and eating small animals such as *Proechimys* as well as eating fruit when available. Coatis and opossums, moreover, only eat the softer fruits or the softer parts of hard-seeded fruits. All these animals, however, suffer if a fruit crop fails. In 1970, when most of the plants that should have fruited in August, September, and October failed to do so, coatis, agoutis, peccaries, and common opossums died in unusual numbers. Oddly enough, pacas were less seriously affected (Foster, this volume).

In the season of fruit shortage, all these animals are hungrier. Coatis and peccaries, like agoutis, forage longer and farther (Smythe, 1970a). Peccaries will consume small piles of dried corn, which no animal would touch during the season of plenty, and root 30 cm into the ground searching for more. As in the fish population of the local rivers (Zaret and Rand, 1971), niche differentiation among these animals becomes more obvious in the season of shortage. Adult male coatis become more predatory, while females, and juvenile and subadult males, concentrate on litter arthropods (Smythe, 1970c). Peccaries root and browse more, but if they find a local abundance of fruit they will "camp out" on it, denying access to smaller animals. Spiny rats, which can eat grass, might well eat more vegetative matter. They may also depend to some extent on food stored in their burrows, which are situated under large roots or in other places where it would be difficult for a peccary or coati to dig out the occupant or its larder (Smythe, 1970a). Agoutis depend on hoarded seeds, which must be sufficiently scattered that peccaries do not find it worth their while to seek them.

The intensity of competition, however, can be judged by comparing the density of spiny rats on Orchid Island, an 18-ha. satellite of Barro Colorado (cf. Worthington, this volume), which in 1979 had monkeys and agoutis but only one peccary and perhaps no more than one coati (Worthington, personal communication), with that in Lutz catchment. Gliwicz (1973) found about eight spiny rats per hectare on Orchid Island. Judging from paired records of agoutis and spiny rats caught in a similar number of times in Lutz catchment, the home range of a spiny rat extends three-fifths as far along the inner trapline as the home range of an adult agouti. If the spiny rats are spaced along the stream bottom, there are slightly less than twice as many spiny rats as there are agoutis in Lutz catchment, or about three spiny rats per hectare. This is a little more than a third as many as there are on Orchid Island.

Seed Dispersal

Since agoutis bury seeds which they scatter over their territory, they may be effective dispersers. In time of food scarcity, agoutis rely on buried seeds as their primary source of food. Since they must find these seeds months after they have buried them, it is improbable that an animal will find every seed it has buried. We may accordingly assume that each animal buries more than it will need. Young agoutis begin burying seeds as soon as they begin foraging and many of them will not survive to exploit the seeds they have buried. Accordingly, agoutis are important dispersers of some types of seeds. They are much more effective than are pacas, which usually take fruits from the place where they have fallen to specific feeding spots where they eat the soft parts and generally leave the hard seeds.

Virola surinamensis (Howe, this volume) and *Casearia corymbosa* (Howe and Vande Kerckhove, 1979), whose fruits are adapted for dispersal by birds, secure dispersal for a far higher proportion of their seeds (60% to 90%) than seems possible for trees such as *Astrocaryum*, which rely largely on agoutis for dispersal. Most birds disperse *Virola* and *Casearia* seeds without harming them, while agoutis eat some seeds and disperse others only because they intend to eat them later. However, even inefficient dispersers can be vital. Elephants, the primary dispersers of many West African fruits (Alexandre, 1978), defecate many seeds into a single fecal clump, of which only one can grow (cf. Howe, 1982), yet in forests where these elephants have been hunted out, some of these trees are failing to replace themselves (Alexandre, 1978).

ACKNOWLEDGMENTS

Miguel Estribí, Gerald Chen, Gary Stump, and Bonifacio de León trapped and marked the animals for us and maintained the traps. Some of the animals they handled were rather formidable; we are grateful for the help. The trapping program was supported by the Environmental Sciences Program of the Smithsonian Institution.

LITERATURE CITED

Alexandre, D. Y.
1978. Le role disseminateur des éléphants en forêt de Tai, Côte-d'Ivoire. *La Terre et la Vie*, 32: 47–72.

Dorst, J., and P. Dandelot
1970. *A Field Guide to the Larger Mammals of Africa*. Boston: Houghton Mifflin Co.

Dubost, G.
1968. Les niches écologiques des forêts tropicales sud-americaines et africaines, sources de convergences remarquables entre rongeurs et artiodactyles. *La Terre et la Vie*, 22: 3–28.

Eisenberg, J. F., and G. M. McKay
1974. Comparison of Ungulate Adaptations in the New World and Old World Tropical Forests with Special Reference to Ceylon and the Rain forests of Central America. In *The Behavior of Ungulates and Its Relation to Management*, edited by V. Geist and F. Walther. *International Union for Conservation of Nature and Natural Resources Annual Report*, new series, 24: 585–602.

Eisenberg, J. F., and R. W. Thorington, Jr.
1973. A Preliminary Analysis of a Neotropical Mammal Fauna. *Biotropica*, 5: 150–161.

Foster, R. B.
1982. Famine on Barro Colorado Island. Pages 201–212 in *The Ecology of a Tropical Forest*, edited by Egbert G. Leigh, Jr., et al. Washington, D.C.: Smithsonian Institution Press.

Gliwicz, J.
1973. A Short Characteristics of a Population of *Proechimys semispinosus* (Tomes, 1860): A Rodent Species of the Tropical Rain Forest. *Bulletin de l'Academie Polonaise des Sciences, Serie des sciences biologiques*, Cl. II, 21: 413–418.

Hershkovitz, P.
1955. On the Cheek Pouches of the Tropical American Paca, *Agouti paca. Saugetierk. Mitteil.*, 3: 66–70.

Howe, H. F.
1980. Monkey Dispersal and Waste of a Neotropical Fruit. *Ecology*, 61:944–959.
1982. Fruit Production and Animal Activity in Two Tropical Trees. Pages 189–199 in *The Ecology of a Tropical Forest*, edited by Egbert G. Leigh, Jr., et al. Washington, D.C.: Smithsonian Institution Press.

Howe, H. F., and G. A. Vande Kerckhove
1979. Fecundity and Seed Dispersal of a Tropical Tree. *Ecology*, 60: 180–189.

Medway, Lord
1969. *The Wild Mammals of Malaya.* Kuala Lumpur: Oxford University Press.

Nagy, K. A., and K. Milton
1979. Energy Metabolism and Food Comsumption by Wild Howler Monkeys (*Alouatta palliatta*). *Ecology,* 60: 475–480.

Odum, H. T.
1970. Summary: an Emerging View of the Ecological System at El Verde. Pages I–191–289 in *A Tropical Rain Forest,* edited by H. T. Odum and R. Pigeon. Springfield, Va: U.S. Atomic Energy Commission.

Russell, J. K.
1982. Timing of Reproduction in Coatis (*Nasua narica*) in Relation to Fluctuations in Food Resources. Pages 413–431 in *The Ecology of a Tropical Forest,* edited by Egbert G. Leigh, Jr., et al. Washington, D.C.: Smithsonian Institution Press.

Smythe, N.
1970a. Ecology and Behavior of the Agouti (*Dasyprocta punctata*) and Related Species on Barro Colorado Island, Panama. Ph. D. thesis, University of Maryland, College Park, Maryland.
1970b. Relationships between Fruiting Seasons and Dispersal Methods in a Neotropical Forest. *American Naturalist,* 104: 25–35.
1970c. The Adaptive Value of the Social Organization of the Coati (*Nasua narica*). *Journal of Mammalogy,* 51:818–820.
1975. Mammal Trapping. In *1974 Environmental Monitoring and Baseline Data, Tropical Studies,* edited by D. Windsor. Unpublished report, Smithsonian Institution, Washington, D.C.
1978. The Natural History of the Central American Agouti (*Dasyprocta punctata*). *Smithsonian Contributions to Zoology,* 157: 1–52.
In press. Agoutis and Pacas. In *Primer of Terrestrial Ecology,* edited by D. Janzen.

Worthington, A.
1982. Effects of Seasonal Changes in Food Supply on the Breeding Rhythms of Two Frugivorous Birds. Pages 213–225 in *The Ecology of a Tropical Forest,* edited by Egbert G. Leigh, Jr., et al. Washington, D.C.: Smithsonian Institution Press.

Zaret, T. M., and A. S. Rand
1971. Competition in Tropical Stream Fishes: Support for the Competitive Exclusion Principle. *Ecology,* 52: 336–342.

Seasonal Food Use and Demographic Trends in *Sciurus granatensis*

WILLIAM E. GLANZ, Department of Zoology, University of Maine, Orono, Maine 04469

RICHARD W. THORINGTON, JR. Division of Mammals, National Museum of Natural History, Smithsonian Institution, Washington, D.C. 20560

JACALYN GIACALONE-MADDEN Department of Biology, Upsala College, East Orange, New Jersey 07019

LAWRENCE R. HEANEY Museum of Zoology, University of Michigan, Ann Arbor, Michigan 48109

ABSTRACT

Although red-tailed squirrels on Barro Colorado Island have been observed to eat from 58 species of plants, they feed primarily on the heavily armored nutlike fruits of the palms *Scheelea zonensis* and *Astrocaryum standleyanum,* and the legume *Dipteryx panamensis,* and pulp from the large fruits of *Gustavia superba.* Although many kinds of animals feed on the pulp surrounding the seeds of *Scheelea, Astrocaryum,* and *Dipteryx,* squirrels are among the few vertebrates that eat the seeds themselves. On Barro Colorado Island, at least one of the four fruits favored by these squirrels is available between December and July or August. Squirrels begin mating in December, when *Dipteryx* fruit ripens, and they cease mating in July and August, when the supply of *Scheelea* fruit is nearly exhausted. In drier areas, where among the four favored species of food tree only *Scheelea* is common, red-tailed squirrels breed only when *Scheelea* fruit is available. On Barro Colorado, red-tailed squirrels eat many more kinds of fruit between September and November, yet, judging by the relative ease with which they can be trapped, they are hungrier then; their growth rates are lower, and mortality, particularly of young, is higher.

Adult female squirrels bear an average of two litters a year, with a mean of nearly two young per litter. Young born in the first litter survive better than those born in the second; juvenile survival appears to reflect the availability of fruit between September and November. Survival rate of adult squirrels is about 60% per year. The demography of red-tailed squirrels on Barro Colorado is comparable to that of tree squirrels in the north temperate zone.

In 1978 there were roughly 2.5 squirrels per hectare near the laboratory clearing on Barro Colorado; the squirrel population increased roughly tenfold between 1965 and 1971 and has changed little since.

INTRODUCTION

During early studies of the mammal fauna of Barro Colorado Island, Enders (1930, 1935) found two squirrel species, the pygmy squirrel *Microsciurus alfari* and the red-tailed squirrel *Sciurus granatensis*. Since that time, the pygmy squirrel has evidently become extinct on the island, while the red-tailed squirrel has fluctuated greatly in abundance and is, at present, one of the commonest mammal species on the island (Eisenberg, 1980). The diurnal census data of Eisenberg and Thorington (1973) document the dramatic increase in *S. granatensis* abundance during the past 20 years. This squirrel species was sighted very infrequently in 1964 and 1965, but by 1971 it was the mammal species most frequently encountered on the census routes. Similar census data by Glanz (this study and unpubl.) in 1977–78 and Thorington (this study) in 1979 reveal that *S. granatensis* has persisted at high densities on Barro Colorado.

The squirrel species of Central and South America have not been studied as extensively as their north temperate counterparts, and few data are available on their life histories, population dynamics, and community interactions. Of these neotropical species, *S. granatensis* is comparatively well known. It ranges from Costa Rica to Venezuela and Ecuador (Hall and Kelson, 1958; Cabrera, 1960), and is common in many habitats in Panama. Numerous observations of its ecology and behavior in the Panama Canal region have been published (Chapman, 1938; Enders, 1930, 1935; Fleming, 1970; Smith, 1975), but none of these studies has included intensive observation and systematic sampling throughout the year.

To obtain more information on the *S. granatensis* population on Barro Colorado Island, Heaney and Thorington (1978) conducted the first intensive study of this species in 1976 and 1977. Glanz, Giacalone-Madden, and Thorington have continued these studies on Barro Colorado through 1979, emphasizing population dynamics, feeding ecology, and social behavior. In this paper we will summarize the demographic and dietary patterns of this species during the seasonal cycle on Barro Colorado. Our data are entirely from the relatively high-density population levels of recent years. Lacking comparable data at low densities, we cannot definitively explain the recent increase of this species. We can, however, identify the principal food resources of this squirrel population and can show that annual changes in these resources are correlated with distinct demographic trends. With this information we can postulate mechanisms that might produce drastic population fluctuations.

Our data permit a detailed analysis of the seasonal responses of *S. granatensis* to the phenological changes in the Barro Colorado ecosystem. The forests of central Panama have been studied extensively, and strong seasonal rhythms are evident in rainfall, flowering, and fruit production (Croat, 1975; Fleming, 1971a; Foster, 1973, this volume; Rand and Rand, this volume; Smythe, 1970). Kaufmann (1962) and Russell (this volume) working on coatis and Fleming (1971b) and Bonaccorso (1979) working on bats have shown close coordination between reproduction and fruit availability in these animals. Fleming (1973) categorized the reproductive cycles of most central Panamanian mammals and found seasonal patterns in a majority of species, with peak activity during the most favorable fruiting season. Mortality patterns have also been related to seasonality. Both Fleming (1971a) and Smythe (1978) found higher mortality rates in different terrestrial rodents during the season of fruit scarcity. We have intensively investigated the food habits of *S. granatensis*, and we can examine the influence of fruit availability on mortality and reproductive rate with some precision.

METHODS

Intensive studies of Barro Colorado squirrels were conducted in a 10-ha. study area established by Heaney and Thorington (1978). The area is mostly young forest, 50 to 70 years old, and includes Snyder-Molino ridge and western portions of the Lutz Creek catchment. Studies by Heaney and Thorington extended from May to August 1976 and from December 1976 to January 1977. Glanz continued trapping and observations in the study area from January 1977 to January 1978 and from March to June 1978. Giacalone-Madden studied squirrel ranging patterns in this area in December 1977 and January 1978 and again in December 1978 and January 1979, while Thorington recensused the area in July 1979.

On the intensive study area, squirrels were livetrapped and individually marked to facilitate identification in the field. Forty-five squirrels were marked with numbered metal ear tags, and with colored plastic beads on a ball-chain collar (see Heaney and Thorington, 1978, for details). After release, squirrels were identified and observed with binoculars when encountered during repeated trips to the study area. Many individuals became relatively tame during the study and could usually be approached closely enough for positive identification.

Between January 1977 and June 1978, Glanz censused squirrels at monthly intervals along additional trails on Barro Colorado Island. Most of these census routes radiated out from the intensive study area, permitting occasional observations of marked squirrels from that area. Feeding patterns and mating behavior were also studied along these census routes.

Feeding observations reported here were collected between May 1976 and June 1978. Data are compiled as feeding sessions (Heaney and Thorington, 1978); a feeding session is defined as one squirrel feeding on one food species until it either left the observer's viewing range or switched to a second food species, or until the observer left the area. Most feeding sessions were recorded on transects through the study area or along the census routes. Under these circumstances, squirrels were rarely observed for more than several minutes, and the feeding session records represent foods eaten when first encountered.

Reproductive data were obtained from observations of mating bouts, weights, and reproductive condition of live-trapped squirrels, and sightings of females with accompanying young animals. Survivorship estimates were determined from the number of resident marked squirrels known to be alive in 15-day sampling intervals. Animals were termed "residents" if they were recorded in the intensive study area at least twice after being marked. They were assumed to have disappeared from the study area in the sample period after they were last seen. The disappearance rate provides a measure of mortality that includes both deaths and emigration from the study area. To assess the importance of emigration, Glanz examined all squirrels encountered along the census routes away from the intensive area and recorded all observations of marked animals.

Beginning in January 1977, population density estimates were calculated using a modified Lincoln Index based on sightings of marked animals. The density estimate used was the number of marked individuals known to be alive during the sampling interval divided by the proportion of marked animals among all squirrel sightings in the study area during that interval.

Seasonal Food Use

During approximately 19 months of field work on Barro Colorado, we recorded 1917 feeding sessions (including the 261 recorded from the intensive study area by Heaney and Thorington, 1978). Food types eaten are categorized in Table 1. Fifty-eight species of trees, shrubs, and lianas were identified as food sources; at least 47 of these were eaten on the intensive study area. The number of species eaten is considerably higher than those recorded from comparable studies of temperate squirrels (Smith, 1968; Nixon et al., 1968), but is not surprising considering the diversity of plants in the Barro Colorado forest where over 1400 species have been recorded (Croat, 1978).

Fungi and animal material were relatively minor food sources, constituting only 1.2% and 0.4% respectively of all feeding sessions. These food types, however, were eaten primarily by juveniles and reproductive females and may have important sources of protein or other nutrients.

In spite of this variety of foods taken, just four food species made up the vast majority (73%) of the feeding sessions observed. The three fruits most frequently eaten are among the most heavily armored nutlike fruits in the forest: the palms *Scheelea zonensis* and *Astrocaryum standleyanum*, and the legume *Dipteryx panamensis*. Each of these has a large seed enclosed in a very hard, woody endocarp. These structures are surrounded by a pulpy mesocarp which many mammals eat, few of which can damage the seed. The red-tailed squirrel is the principal arboreal seed predator of these species on Barro Colorado (Bonaccorso et al., 1980; Bradford and Smith, 1975; Heaney and Thorington, 1978), while another rodent, the agouti *Dasyprocta punctata*, is their principal terrestrial seed predator (Smythe, 1978). The fourth primary food species is *Gustavia superba* (Lecythidaceae) which has a large (10–20 cm diam.), firm, oily fruit. Squirrels eat the pulpy mesocarp of this fruit and frequently damage the seed, but eat the seed very infrequently. *Gustavia* is also eaten by the white-faced monkey *Cebus capucinus* (Oppenheimer and Lang, 1969), and by the agouti (Smythe, 1978), but by few other vertebrates. Thus, *S. granatensis* shows a high degree of dietary specialization on food sources used by few other vertebrates, including three of the hardest, best-protected seeds available in the forest, and a fourth hard, but massive, fruit.

Dietary specialization is even more evident if one examines seasonal patterns of food use. Figure 1 plots the seasonal importance of each of the four primary foods over 15-day sample periods during the studies by Glanz. In the early dry season from December to February (in 1977) or March (in 1978), *Dipteryx panamensis* accounts for 50% to 80% of the feeding sessions observed. The two palm species reach similar levels of importance later in the year, *A. standleyanum* from March to May (late dry and early wet seasons) and *S. zonensis* from May to August (mid wet season). The fruiting season of *Gustavia superba* overlaps those of the two palms, but it is generally less important in the squirrel's diet, constituting from 5% to 35% of all feeding sessions from March to August.

During this seasonal cycle, however, there is a period in the late wet season, from September to November, when these primary food trees are not in fruit. This period includes the months of heaviest rainfall on Barro Colorado (October and November) and of lowest fruit availability (Smythe, 1970; Foster,

Table 1. Species eaten by *Sciurus granatensis* on Barro Colorado Island between May 1976 and June 1978

Species	Number of feeding sessions	% of total sessions	Highest % diet	Dates of observations
Acanthaceae				
Mendoncia retusa	1	0.05	*	Jan. 1977
Anacardiaceae				
Anacardium excelsum	3	0.16	*	May 1977, Apr. 1978
Astronium graveolens	1	0.05	*	July 1977
Mangifera indica	4	0.21	*	July–Aug. 1977
Spondias mombin	20	1.04	18	Aug. 1976; Aug.—Oct. 1977
Spondias radlkoferi	35	1.83	19	Sept.–Dec. 1977
Annonaceae				
Annona spraguei	2	0.10	*	Oct. 1977
Desmopsis panamensis	1	0.05	*	Nov. 1977
Bignoniaceae				
Jacaranda copaia	1	0.05	*	June 1976
Tabebuia rosea	1	0.05	*	July 1976
Bombacaceae				
Quararibea asterolepis	43	2.24	49	Sept.–Nov. 1977
Boraginaceae				
Cordia bicolor	23	1.20	11	Apr.–June 1977; May 1978
Cordia lasiocalyx	2	0.10	*	Apr. 1978
Burseraceae				
Protium tenuifolium	20	1.04	19	Aug.–Sept. 1977
Protium panamense	2	0.10	*	Aug. 1977
Tetragastris panamensis	13	0.68	10	Jan.–Feb. 1977; Apr.–May 1978
Chrysobalanaceae				
Hirtella triandra	7	0.37	*	June 1976; Mar., May–June 1977; May 1978
Hirtella americana	1	0.05	*	June 1977
Connaraceae				
Connarus spp.	2	0.10	*	Jan. 1977; Dec. 1977
Convolvulaceae				
Maripa panamensis	19	1.00	9	June–July 1976; May 1977; May–June 1978
Dilleniaceae				
Doliocarpus spp. (incl. *olivaceus* and *major*)	3	0.16	*	July, Sept. 1977
Euphorbiaceae				
Croton billbergianus	1	0.05	*	Oct. 1977

* = never more than 5% of all feeding sessions in one 15-day sample period; ** = includes 43 observations of chewing and feeding on the bark of unidentified trees and vines.

Table 1. (continued)

Species	Number of feeding sessions	% of total sessions	Highest % diet	Dates of observations
Guttiferae				
Rheedia madruno	11	0.57	19	June 1976; May 1978
Lauraceae				
Beilschmiedia pendula	3	0.16	*	Apr.–May 1978
Lecythidaceae				
Gustavia superba	185	9.65	33	May–July 1976; Feb.–Aug. 1977; Mar.–June 1978
Leguminosae				
Clitoria arborescens	6	0.31	*	Jan. 1977; Dec. 1977–Jan. 1978
Dipteryx panamensis	339	17.68	78	Dec. 1976–Feb. 1977; Nov. 1977–Apr. 1978
Inga spp. (incl. *fagifolia, pezizifera,* and other spp.)	17	0.89	6	May–July 1976; Oct.–Dec. 1977; April–May 1978
Platypodium elegans	1	0.05	*	May 1977
Pterocarpus spp.	1	0.05	*	Sept. 1977
Melastomataceae				
Miconia argentea	3	0.16	*	Apr.–May 1977; Apr. 1978
Meliaceae				
Guarea glabra	8	0.42	6	Apr.–May 1978
Trichilia cipo	2	0.10	*	Sept.–Oct. 1977
Moraceae				
Ficus yoponensis	6	0.31	*	Dec. 1976; Nov.–Dec. 1977
Olmedia aspera	5	0.26	5	Aug.–Sept. 1977
Sorocea affinis	1	0.05	*	Nov. 1977
Myristicaceae				
Virola sebifera	1	0.05	*	Sept. 1977
Myrtaceae				
Eugenia coloradensis	10	0.52	10	Oct.–Nov. 1977
Eugenia nesiotica	10	0.52	7	June–July 1977; May 1978
Myrcia fosteri	2	0.10	*	Oct. 1977
Palmae				
Astrocaryum standleyanum	401	20.92	81	May–June 1976; Dec. 1976–June1978
Bactris barronis	1	0.05	8	Sept. 1977
Bactris major	1	0.05	*	Dec. 1977
Oenocarpus panamanus	13	0.68	6	June, Aug. 1976; June–Aug. 1977; Apr. 1978
Scheelea zonensis	472	24.62	86	May–Aug. 1976; Dec. 1976–Jan. 1977; Mar. 1977–Jan. 1978; Apr.–June 1978
Socratea durissima	1	0.05	*	Apr. 1978
Polygonaceae				
Coccoloba parimensis	18	0.94	11	Sept.–Dec. 1977
Coccoloba manzanillensis	1	0.05	*	Aug. 1977

Table 1. (continued)

Species	Number of feeding sessions	% of total sessions	Highest % diet	Dates of observations
Rubiaceae				
Alseis blackiana	1	0.05	*	Dec. 1976
Faramea occidentale	57	2.97	16	Dec. 1976–Jan. 1977; Sept. 1977–Jan. 1978
Coussarea impetiolaris	1	0.05	*	Dec. 1977
Guettarda foliacea	8	0.42	9	Oct.–Nov. 1977
Randia armata	1	0.05	*	Sept. 1977
Sapindaceae				
Cupania latifolia	1	0.05	*	Sept. 1977
Talisia nervosa	2	0.10	*	Sept. 1977
Sapotaceae				
Chrysophyllum panamense	1	0.05	*	Apr. 1978
Sterculiaceae				
Sterculia apetala	2	0.10	*	Jan. 1978
Tiliaceae				
Apeiba membranacea	8	0.42	18	Feb. 1977; Mar.–Apr. 1978
Fungi:				
Tricholomataceae	16	0.83	6	Aug., Dec. 1976; Jan., Oct., Dec. 1977; Apr.–June 1978
Other fungi	7	0.37	*	July–Oct., Dec. 1977
Animal material:				
Insects	7	0.37	*	May, July 1977; Apr.–May 1978
Frog (*Eleutherodactylus*) eggs	1	0.05	*	May 1977
Unidentified plant material**	80	4.18	11	
Total	1917	—	—	

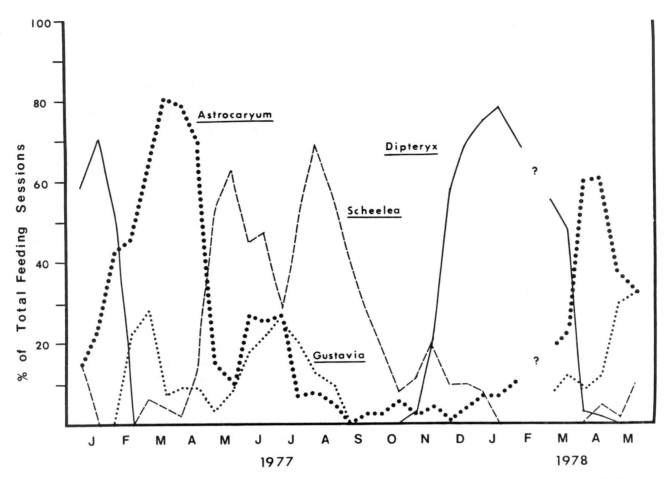

Figure 1. Seasonal trends in the utilization by *S. granatensis* of its four preferred food species: *Dipteryx panamensis* (Leguminosae), *Gustavia superba* (Lecythidaceae), *Astrocaryum standleyanum* (Palmae), and *Scheelea zonensis* (Palmae). See methods for definition of feeding sessions.

1973). At this season the squirrels alter their feeding habits in two major ways. First, they eat more stored palm nuts, particularly those of *Scheelea zonensis*. *Sciurus granatensis* begins scatterhoarding these nuts as early as April, and these activities continue as long as palm fruits are available. When squirrels later eat the buried nuts, they are easily distinguished in the field from fresh nuts by the adhering soil and the lack of a fleshy mesocarp. They are relatively unimportant in the diet while fresh fruits are available, constituting only 3% of all feeding sessions in July. These stored nuts, however, become increasingly important later in the season, making up 20% of the total feeding observations in late November. Table 2 compares the proportion of stored foods in the diet in these 3 months with comparable 3-month periods at other times in the study. The use of stored foods is considerably higher in the late wet season months.

The second way in which the squirrels deal with this shortage of primary foods is to eat a greater variety of the softer, smaller-seeded fruits that are usually taken by other mammal and bird species. In Tables 2 and 3, food species are categorized as "primary" if they constitute over 25% of all feeding sessions in at least one 15-day sample period, and as "secondary" if they make up 10% to 25% of such feeding sessions. During the 3 months from September to November 1977, squirrels used more secondary food species than in all other study periods combined (Table 3) and included one additional primary food, *Quararibea asterolepis*, in their diet. The total of primary and secondary foods in these 3 months (nine species) and the mean number of identified species taken per 15 days both exceed the comparable values for all other 3-month periods (Table 2). This greater dietary diversity then appears to be a response to low availability

Table 2. Summary of feeding patterns

Time period	Mean % stored foods in diet	Number of primary and secondary foods eaten in 3 months[1]	Mean number of species[2] eaten/2 weeks
May to Aug. 1976	5	4	5.0
Dec. 1976 to Feb. 1977	5	5	5.0
Mar. to May 1977	2	4	6.5
June to Aug. 1977	4	3	8.5
Sept. to Nov. 1977	14	9	13.2
Dec. 1977 to Feb. 1978[3]	9	3	7.3
Mar. to May 1978	1	6	10.2

[1] See text for definitions.
[2] Identified plant species only.
[3] No quantification of feeding Feb. 1978.

Table 3. Primary and secondary food species

Primary foods	Secondary foods
Dec. to Aug.:	
Dipteryx panamensis	*Apeiba membranacea* (1977 and 1978)
Gustavia superba	*Cordia bicolor* (1977 only)
Astrocaryum standleyanum	*Tetragastris panamensis* (1978 only)
Scheelea zonensis	*Faramea occidentale* (1977–78 only)
Sept. to Nov.:	
Quararibea asterolepis	*Spondias mombin*
Scheelea zonensis	*Spondias radlkoferi*
	Protium tenuifolium
	Dipteryx panamensis
	Eugenia coloradensis
	Coccoloba parinensis
	Faramea occidentale

of the harder primary foods.

We have feeding data from various times in 3 years, and it is interesting that the primary foods show comparable degrees of use from year to year, but most secondary foods in the December to August period are not used with equal intensity in different years (Table 3). *Cordia bicolor* and *Tetragastris panamensis* are disparennial species, alternating small fruit crops in some years with very large crops in others. Each was used extensively by squirrels only when abundant. *Rheedia madruno* fruited in 1976 and 1978, but not at all in 1977. It was an important squirrel food in early June 1976 (19% of diet), but constituted only 5% of the May 1978 diet. *Faramea occidentale* is a common understory tree, which fruited abundantly in both 1976–77 and 1977–78. It never constituted more than 5% of the feeding sessions in the former season, but reached 16% in November 1977, and exceeded 10% in December 1977 and January 1978. All of the above species produce fleshy fruits used by a number of other vertebrates. *Apeiba membranacea* produces a dry, spiny fruit eaten by parrots but few other vertebrate species. It was a locally important squirrel food between the *Dipteryx* and *Astrocaryum* fruiting seasons in both years. Unfortunately, we have feeding data between September and November in only one year (1977). Several of the late wet-season secondary foods, however, are known to be disparennial species (*Spondias mombin*, *Protium tenuifolium*).

All of the fruit species listed in Table 3 for the late wet season are also taken by primates, coatis, and other arboreal frugivores. The pulpy mesocarp of *Scheelea* is a preferred food of coatis and *Cebus* monkeys, which, however, usually do not damage the seed. *Quararibea asterolepis* has an acorn-shaped fruit, with a tough exocarp surrounding considerable pulp and a large seed. *Protium tenuifolium* has an arillate fruit with a dehiscent capsule, while all of the other late wet-season fruits listed are drupes. Squirrels were observed to eat both fruit pulp and seeds of all of these species. Since other vertebrate frugivores eat the fruit pulp of these species and frequently ingest the seeds of all but *Scheelea*, their impact on squirrel food resources during these months is potentially greater than at other times.

Several kinds of evidence indicate that these late wet-season fruits are not preferred by the squirrels and that this period may be a season of dietary stress for these animals. First, the caching of palm nuts and their higher rate of use from September to November (Table 2) suggest that these stored foods are relatively more valuable at this season than at other times. Second, some *Scheelea* individuals produce fruit late into September, and these trees apparently attract the largest feeding aggregations of squirrels in this season. Up to seven squirrels were seen feeding at such trees, while other species of tree never had more than three animals feeding at one tree during this period.

From March 1977 to June 1978, live-traps were baited with *Astrocaryum* and *Scheelea* nuts, and the trapping success rate (number of squirrels captured per trap per day, with four trap-checks per day) can be taken as a crude measure of the value of this bait to the squirrels. From June to early August 1977, trap success ranged from 0.08 to 0.11 squirrels per trap-day. Fresh *Scheelea* were exhausted in the intensive study area by 25 August, and immediately trap success rose to 0.22 squirrels per trap-day. This measure declined to 0.13 and 0.14 later in September and October, as certain individuals became very adept at stealing bait from the traps, but remained above previous rates. Trap success was significantly greater ($p < 0.05$ for all comparisons, U-test) when no fresh palm nuts or *Dipteryx* fruits were available locally (25 August to 15 November, three trapping sessions), than in any other 3-month period (Table 4).

The attractiveness of palm nuts is supported by observations of food choice by trapped squirrels. *Gustavia superba*, *Protium tenuifolium*, *Spondias radlkoferi*, *Faramea occidentale*, and feed corn were offered as supplementary bait with *Scheelea* nuts during the late wet season. Temporarily caged individuals always ate the *Scheelea* nuts first.

Growth rate data from a limited number of young squirrels also suggest that the late wet season is a less favorable period for the squirrels. Between May and August 1977, seven subadult squirrels gained an average of 40 g in body weight; between August and November, the mean weight gain for six comparable individuals was only 16 g ($p < .05$, U-test). Other population characteristics of red-tailed squirrels on Barro Colorado also indicate unfavorable conditions during this season, and these are discussed in the next section.

Reproduction, Mortality, and Density Trends

The mating behavior of *Sciurus granatensis*, like that of most other tree squirrels (Bakken, 1959; Farentinos, 1972; Smith, 1968; Thompson, 1977), is easily detected in the field and general seasonal patterns are readily quantified. An estrous female is receptive to males for only a portion of 1 day per reproductive cycle. Numerous males congregate around her, follow her through her home range, and vie for access to her. Such mating bouts are very obvious, as the males frequently call, threaten, and chase each other in their attempts to approach the female.

The number of mating bouts observed between De-

Table 4. Seasonal population parameters

Time period	Mean trap[1] success	Mating bouts observed	Number of disappearances[1]
May to Aug. 1976	n.c.	2	n.c.
Dec. 1976 to Feb. 1977	n.c.	8	0
Mar. to May 1977	0.05	6	0
June to Aug. 1977	0.09	5	2
Sept. to Nov. 1977	0.16[2]	0	5
Dec. 1977 to Feb. 1978	0.12	10	2
Mar. to May 1978	0.05	8	2

n.c. = Not calculated.

[1] Definitions in text.

[2] Includes 29 August to 1 September trapping period (see text).

cember 1976 and June 1978 is given in Table 4 and arranged by 3-month periods. Mating bouts were observed in all months from December 1976 to August 1977, but they ceased abruptly after 8 August, and were not observed again until December. Thus, no mating activity occurs within the season of low availability of preferred foods.

Within this breeding season, a *Sciurus granatensis* female can potentially produce three litters per year (Heaney and Thorington, 1978). Gestation and lactation together occupy 15 to 16 weeks, which is a time span comparable to the 7-week gestation period and 8- to 9-week weaning period found in temperate *Sciurus*. Recently, however, Emmons (1979) has found longer gestation periods and precocial young in African tropical squirrels. We do not have precise measurements of gestation length in *S. granatensis*, and we cannot exclude the possibility of prolonged pregnancies in this species. Nevertheless, our observations of the duration from mating to weaning indicate that three litters per year are possible within a reproductive season of normal length. While some females may have bred three times during 1976 (Heaney and Thorington, 1978, p. 849), no female on the intensive study area produced more than two litters in 1977.

The onset of reproductive activity and conception of the first litter was relatively synchronous in each year. First mating bouts of the season were recorded on 24 December 1976, 31 December 1977, and 26 December 1978, and most parous females in the study area had mated within 1 month of these dates. During the 1976–77 season most females produced a second litter, but mating activity was less synchronized than the first litter, extending from late April to July. Of

Table 5. Long-term survivorship

1. Of 10 marked animals alive in July 1976,
   6 survived to Jan. 1977   (40% mortality)

2. Of 6 marked animals alive in Jan. 1977,
   5 survived to July 1977   (17% mortality)

3. Of 24 animals alive in July 1977,
   17 survived to Jan. 1978   (29% mortality)

4. Of 22 marked animals alive in Jan. 1978,
   20 survived to June 1978   (10% mortality)

5. Of 22 marked animals alive in June 1978,
   15 survived to Jan. 1979   (32% mortality)

6. Of 17 marked animals alive in Jan. 1979,
   14 survived to July 1979   (18% mortality)

the three females in the area that mated after 15 July, all were young and two evidently had not bred before. These latest litters (conceived in July or early August) would be suckling well into October and the young would emerge from the nest at a presumably unfavorable time of year. Young females, then, are more likely to show delayed reproductive activity, and this could result from asynchronous maturation of these individuals, or from nutritional or social factors. In contrast, all mature females had produced their second litter by the end of the palm fruiting season in 1977. In the previous year at least one mature female bred after 15 July (Heaney and Thorington, 1978), but the size distribution of young animals in December indicated that few or no young were weaned in the late wet season.

Litters from the first mating period (December to February) in 1976–77 were apparently more productive than later litters. Eight juveniles from seven early litters on the intensive study area survived to trappable size, while only three juveniles from eight litters conceived between April and August were eventually trapped. Most litters seen in the field consisted of two young (mean = 1.9, N = 12), but many disappeared before litter size was accurately determined.

The above data, then, show seasonal trends in the timing and success of reproduction that can be related to seasonal patterns of food availability and rainfall. The onset of mating activity coincides with the availability of Dipteryx panamensis, the earliest of the preferred nuts, and reproductive processes cease in the late wet season when nuts are scarce and rainfall is

heaviest. Young from earlier litters have a greater chance of survival than later offspring, and this may also result from the same seasonal factors.

Survivorship data from the marked population also show seasonal variation. The data available permit two levels of analysis, the monthly disappearance rate of marked animals during 1977–78, and a semiannual assessment of mortality between 1976 and 1979. Only 11 animals disappeared from the marked population between January 1977 and June 1978, but 5 of these disappeared in the late wet-season months (September through November). Other 3-month periods showed no more than two disappearances (Table 4).

Survivorship estimates from longer, 6-month intervals indicate a similar pattern (Table 5). Although sample sizes of marked animals are very low for certain periods, the data show a consistent pattern of higher survivorships between January and June (mean = 85% per 6 months) than from July through December (mean = 66%). This analysis, then, also suggest that mortality is greater in the 6 months that include the late wet season.

There are substantial differences in survivorship between years (50% to 64% on an annual basis), and these appear directly related to juvenile mortality. Of the 11 juveniles trapped from 1977 litters, 6 (55%) were present in June 1978. In contrast, of the small samples of juveniles marked in 1976 and 1978 (N = 3 in both years), none survived more than 6 months on the study area. These figures may overestimate juvenile mortality in 1976, as five unmarked subadults (6 to 12 months old) were captured in early 1977, and three of these remained in the area for at least 1 year. Juvenile survivorship in 1978–79 was apparently low, as field observations in December 1978 and July 1979 revealed few young animals.

In contrast to these patterns in juvenile survivorship, adult Sciurus granatensis, particularly mature females, often show excellent survivorship. Of ten mature females and eight mature males on the study area in December 1977, six females and three males survived to at least July 1979.

Most disappearances from the intensive study area were evidently due to mortality rather than dispersal, as virtually none of the missing squirrels reappeared on the census routes away from the study area. Heaney and Thorington (1978) report a move of at least 800 m by an immature female, and in 1977 a young marked female relocated her home range 300 m from the study area. Mature males, however, frequently moved similar distances to enter mating bouts and yet returned to their original home ranges shortly thereafter.

Estimates of population density in the intensive study

area generally confirm these seasonal trends in reproduction and mortality, but also suggest long-term changes. Heaney and Thorington (1978) estimated a density of 2.5 squirrels per hectare in the study area during 1976, basing this calculation on home range size and overlap. Subsequent density estimates by Glanz (1977–78) and Thorington (1979) were determined from resightings of marked animals (see Methods). Study area densities rose from 2.1/ha. in January and February 1977 to 3.0/ha. in May and 3.2/ha. in July, reflecting the recruitment of juveniles into the population. The population then declined during the late wet season to 2.3/ha. in November. A slight rise to 2.5/ha. in December 1977 was apparently related to the large number of adult males attracted to fruiting *Dipteryx* trees and mating bouts in the area at this time. During the next 6 months the population showed very little change in density (2.5/ha. in May and June 1978), with reproduction barely compensating for losses through mortality and the emigration of unmarked males from the area. By July 1979 the population had declined to about 1.9/ha. with a low proportion of young animals. Thus, density estimates generally show an increase during the reproductive season and a decline late in the rainy season, but these seasonal variations are superimposed on a pattern of longer-term population changes.

DISCUSSION AND CONCLUSIONS

These studies demonstrate that the diet of *Sciurus granatensis* on Barro Colorado is remarkably specialized, considering the variety of foods available in this tropical rain forest. Just four food species constitute most (73%) of the annual diet of this squirrel, and these include three of the most heavily armored nuts in this forest. The shells of both *Dipteryx* and *Scheelea* nuts are usually 4 to 5 mm thick and extremely hard; virtually no north temperate nuts have shells as hard or thick. We know of no unique morphological adaptations of *S. granatensis* for such foods.

The relative unimportance of insects and fungi in the diet of this squirrel is also unusual. Insects are an important food source for many tropical squirrels in Africa and Asia (Emmons, 1975; Medway, 1969). Both fungi and insects are also seasonally important for many north temperate species (Nixon, et al., 1968; Smith, 1968).

Our data show clear evidence of seasonality in the population processes of *S. granatensis,* and the periods of reproductive activity and low mortality coincide almost precisely with the availability of primary foods. Reproduction begins in the *Dipteryx* season, continues through the *Astrocaryum* fruiting period, and ends as *Scheelea* fruits are declining in abundance. Mortality apparently increases in the late wet season when preferred foods are scarce and reproductive activity has ceased. This seasonal cycle corresponds closely to that found for general fruit production by Smythe (1970) and Foster (1973). The favorable season for squirrels, however, begins earlier than the first peaks shown by these workers, probably because *S. granatensis* can utilize *Dipteryx* fruits before they ripen (up to 1 month before primates and coatis begin to use them: Glanz, unpubl.). The favorable season for squirrels also ends before the final fruiting peaks of Smythe (1970) and Foster (1973), undoubtedly because the fruits ripening at this time are not among the hard-shelled nuts preferred by this animal.

The squirrel annual cycle also corresponds to the normal patterns of seasonal reproduction in many Panamanian mammals noted by Fleming (1973) and of mortality demonstrated in agoutis by Smythe (1978) and in *Proechimys* by Fleming (1971a). Most of these other animals, however, utilize additional fruit species and are probably more generalized than *Sciurus granatensis* in their food habits. Their seasonal patterns may be tied more closely to the general patterns of fruitfall (Smythe, 1970), rather than the specific food requirements seen in the squirrel.

Most of these studies show clear reductions in both fruit availability and reproductive success in the late wet season (October and November), and the squirrel data definitely agree with these trends. This period is the time of greatest rainfall in central Panama, and the mammals could conceivably be responding directly to climatic factors. While rainfall may be a proximal cue for reproduction in many of these mammals, it seems unlikely that rainfall alone would be an ultimate cause of population timing in these rain forest animals. *Sciurus granatensis* evidently does not breed in the dry season in an area near Paraiso (30 km SE of Barro Colorado), where *Dipteryx* is not present and *Astrocaryum* is uncommon (Glanz, unpubl.). This population appears to produce only one litter per year closely timed with *Scheelea* fruit production. Fleming (1973) categorized *S. granatensis* as seasonally monestrous, with breeding restricted to the early wet season. His classification may be based on populations like that at Paraiso, which are primarily dependent on *Scheelea,* but his own published observations (Fleming 1970, p. 475) certainly indicate mating activity during other times of the year, as we have found on Barro Colorado.

Extensive demographic data are available from temperate North American *Sciurus* populations, and it is interesting that they greatly resemble those observed in *S. granatensis* on Barro Colorado. Nixon and

McClain (1975) report two distinct breeding periods in *S. carolinensis* in Ohio. The first litter is conceived in December or January, and the second in May or June. The pattern in Barro Colorado *S. granatensis* is very similar, but with less synchrony in the second litter. Mature *S. carolinensis* females produce an average of 3.7 young per year (68% breed in the first period, producing a mean of 2.7 young/litter; 53% breed in the second, producing 3.5/litter). Almost all *S. granatensis* females breed twice per year (mean litter size is 1.9), producing an average of 3.8 young per year. Other North American *Sciurus* produce very similar numbers of young per year (Heaney, unpubl.).

Annual survival rates in *Sciurus granatensis* also appear very similar to those in more northern species. Barkalow et al. (1970) calculated a mean annual survival rate of 0.52 (range 0.33–0.68 for 7 years) for adult (1 year old or more) *S. carolinensis* in an unhunted North Carolina population. Our mean annual survival rate of marked animals is 0.57 (range 0.50 to 0.64 for 3 years; see Table 5), but was calculated in a somewhat different manner. Younger animals were included, but their effect was minimized by the shorter time interval (6 months instead of 1 year) and by the exclusion of vagrant animals. Other estimates confirm this survivorship calculation. The proportion of juveniles and subadults in the population from 1976 to early 1977 averaged 42% (Heaney and Thorington, 1978). Assuming a roughly stable population (as density estimates indicate at this time), the overall survival rate is 58% (100–42), also very close to the North Carolina figure.

Annual juvenile survival is also highly variable in *Sciurus carolinensis*, ranging from 0.2 to 0.68 (mean = 0.25, Barkalow et al., 1970, p. 497, as compared with *S. granatensis* values of 0 to 0.55 (mean = 0.18). The principal times of juvenile mortality, however, may be different in the two species. More than half of the *S. granatensis* litters disappeared before leaving the nest (Glanz, unpubl.), while survival of *S. carolinensis* nestlings appears to be greater, and mortality is heavier after the period of parental care. Emmons (1979) has discussed the evolution of small litter sizes in tropical squirrels and has indicated that a high predation rate on juveniles in the nest may be an important selective factor in this process.

The year-to-year fluctuations of juvenile mortality in *Sciurus carolinensis* are apparently related to annual variations in the supply of food from disparennially fruiting species and result in corresponding fluctuations in squirrel densities (Barkalow et al., 1970). The similar fluctuations in *S. granatensis* density and juvenile mortality are not as easily related to the food supply. Most *Astrocaryum* and *Gustavia* individuals fruit every year, and although many *Scheelea* and *Dipteryx*

individuals do not fruit in consecutive years, the population is not synchronous and some fruits are available each year (Bonaccorso et al., 1980; Glanz, unpubl.). These four primary foods are much more predictable from year to year than many disparennially fruiting species on Barro Colorado. Should any of them fail completely in a certain year, squirrel reproduction could be curtailed and mortality might increase greatly if no other appropriate foods are available. Foster (1973) reported climatic events that severely disrupted the fruiting seasons of many Barro Colorado plants with serious effects on vertebrate populations. Several disparennial species, such as *Spondias mombin*, are important foods in the nonreproductive season. Failure of suitable foods at this time may also substantially increase squirrel mortality. Thus, variations in fruit supplies are potential causes of population fluctuations in *S. granatensis*, but we have few data to support this hypothesis. The population decline since 1977 may be related in part to poor *Dipteryx* fruit production in the 1978–79 season (Giacalone-Madden, unpubl.), but the population levels are still much higher than the densities observed between 1964 and 1970 (Eisenberg and Thorington, 1973; Smythe, 1978, p. 46). Certainly, long-term studies of *S. granatensis* on Barro Colorado would be helpful in understanding population regulation patterns in this species.

The broad geographic range of *Sciurus granatensis* in Central and South America may permit further assessments of the role of food in its population dynamics. This species lives in a wide variety of habitats in Panama, Colombia, and Venezuela (Handley, 1966, 1976; Hershkovitz, 1947) with different climatic patterns and available food species. Comparative studies of dietary specialization and demographic patterns in this squirrel species could contribute greatly to our understanding of the seasonal constraints on tropical mammals.

ACKNOWLEDGMENTS

Our research on Barro Colorado Island has been supported by a Smithsonian Postdoctoral Fellowship to Glanz, grants from the Smithsonian Environmental Sciences Program to Thorington and Heaney, and a Sigma Xi grant to Giacalone-Madden from Upsala College.

LITERATURE CITED

Bakken, A.
1959.   Behavior of Gray Squirrels. *Proceedings of Southeastern Association of Game and Fish Commissioners*, 13:393–406.

Barkalow, F. J., Jr., R. B. Hamilton, and R. F. Soots, Jr.
1970. The Vital Statistics of an Unexploited Gray Squirrel Population. *Journal of Wildlife Management*, 34: 489–500.

Bonaccorso, F. J.
1979. Foraging and Reproductive Ecology in a Panamanian Bat Community. *Bulletin of the Florida State Museum, Biological Sciences*, 24:359–408.

Bonaccorso, F. J., W. Glanz, and C. Sandford
1980. Feeding Assemblages of Mammals at Fruiting *Dipteryx panamensis* Trees: Seed Predation, Dispersal and Parasitism. *Revista de Biología Tropical*, 28:61–72.

Bradford, D. F., and C. C. Smith
1977. Seed Predation and Seed Number in *Scheelea* Palm Fruits. *Ecology*, 58: 667–673.

Cabrera, A.
1961. Catálogo de los mamíferos de America del Sur. *Revista del Museo Argentino de Ciencias Naturales "Bernardino Rivadavia,"* 4:309–732.

Chapman, F. M.
1938. *Life in an Air Castle.* New York: Appleton-Century.

Croat, T. B.
1975. Phenological Behavior of Habit and Habitat Classes on Barro Colorado Island (Panama Canal Zone). *Biotropica*, 7:270–277.
1978. *Flora of Barro Colorado Island.* Stanford, California: Stanford University Press.

Eisenberg, J. F.
1980. The Density and Biomass of Tropical Mammals. Pages 35–55 in *Conservation Biology: An Evolutionary-Ecological Perspective*, edited by M. Soulé and B. Wilcox. Sunderland, Mass.: Sinauer Associates.

Eisenberg, J. F., and R. W. Thorington, Jr.
1973. A Preliminary Analysis of a Neotropical Mammal Fauna. *Biotropica*, 5: 150–161.

Emmons, L. H.
1975. Ecology and Behavior of African Rainforest Squirrels. Ph. D. thesis, Cornell University, Ithaca, N.Y.
1979. Observations on Litter Size and Development of Some African Rainforest Squirrels. *Biotropica*, 11:207–213.

Enders, R. K.
1930. Notes on Some Mammals from Barro Colorado Island, Canal Zone. *Journal of Mammalogy*, 11:280–292.
1935. Mammalian Life Histories from Barro Colorado Island, Panama. *Bulletin of the Museum of Comparative Zoology*, 78:383–502.

Farentinos, R. C.
1972. Social Dominance and Mating Activity in the Tassel-eared Squirrel (*Sciurus aberti ferreus*). *Animal Behavior*, 20:316–326.

Fleming, T. H.
1970. Notes on the Rodent Faunas of Two Panamanian Forests. *Journal of Mammalogy*, 51: 473–490.
1971a. Population Ecology of Three Species of Neotropical Rodents. *Miscellaneous Publications of the Museum of Zoology, University of Michigan*, 143:1–77.
1971b. *Artibeus jamaicensis:* Delayed Embryonic Development in a Neotropical Bat. *Science*, 171:402–404.
1973. The Reproductive Cycles of Three Species of Opossums and Other Mammals in the Panama Canal Zone. *Journal of Mammalogy*, 54:439–455.

Foster, R. B.
1973. Seasonality of Fruit Production and Seed Fall in a Tropical Forest Ecosystem in Panama. Ph.D. thesis, Duke University, Durham, North Carolina.
1982. The Seasonal Rhythm in Fruitfall on Barro Colorado Island. Pages 151-172 in *The Ecology of a Tropical Forest*, edited by Egbert G. Leigh, Jr., et al. Washington, D.C.: Smithsonian Institution Press.

Hall, E. R., and K. R. Kelson
1958. *The Mammals of North America.* New York: Ronald Press.

Handley, C. O., Jr.
1966. Checklist of the Mammals of Panama. Pages 753–795 in *Ectoparasites of Panama*, edited by R. L. Wenzel and U. J. Tipton. Chicago: Field Museum of Natural History.
1976. Mammals of the Smithsonian Venezuelan Project. *Brigham Young University Science Bulletin, Biological Series*, 20:1–91.

Heaney, L. R., and R. W. Thorington, Jr.
1978. Ecology of Neotropical Red-tailed Squirrels, *Sciurus granatensis*, in the Panama Canal Zone. *Journal of Mammalogy*, 59:846–851.

Hershkovitz, P. H.
1947. Mammals of Northern Colombia. Preliminary Report No. 1: Squirrels. *Proceedings of the United States National Museum*, 97:1–40.

Kaufmann, J. H.
1962. Ecology and behavior of the coati, *Nasua narica* on Barro Colorado Island, Panama. *University of California Publications in Zoology*, 60:95–222.

Medway, Lord
1969. *The Wild Mammals of Malaysia and Offshore Islands, Including Singapore.* London: Oxford University Press.

Nixon, C. M., and M. W. McClain
1975. Breeding Seasons and Fecundity of Female Gray Squirrels in Ohio. *Journal of Wildlife Management*, 39:426–438.

Nixon, C. W., D. M. Worley, and M. W. McClain
1968. Food Habits of Squirrels in Southeast Ohio. *Journal of Wildlife Management*, 32:294–305.

Oppenheimer, J. R., and G. E. Lang
1969. *Cebus* monkeys: Effects on Branching of *Gustavia* trees. *Science*, 165:187–188.

Rand, A. S., and W. M. Rand
1982. Variation in Rainfall on Barro Colorado Island. Pages 47–59 in *The Ecology of a Tropical Forest*, edited by Egbert G. Leigh, Jr., et al. Washington, D.C.: Smithsonian Institution Press.

Russell, J. K.
1982. Timing of Reproduction by Coatis (*Nasua narica*) in Relation to Fluctuations in Food Resources. Pages 413-431 in *The Ecology of a Tropical Forest*, edited by Egbert G. Leigh, Jr., et al. Washington, D.C.: Smithsonian Institution Press.

Smith, C. C.
1968. The Adaptive Nature of Social Organization in the Genus of Tree Squirrels *Tamiasciurus*. *Ecological Monographs*, 38:31–63.
1975. The Coevolution of Plants and Seed Predators. Pages 53–77 in *Coevolution of Animals and Plants*, edited by L. E. Gilbert and P. H. Raven. Austin: University of Texas Press.

Smythe, N.

1970.   Relationships between Fruiting Seasons and Seed Dispersal Methods in a Neotropical Forest. *American Naturalist,* 104:25–35.

1978.   The Natural History of the Central American Agouti, *Dasyprocta punctata. Smithsonian Contributions to Zoology,* 257:1–52.

Thompson, D.C.

1977.   Reproductive Behavior of the Grey Squirrel. *Canadian Journal of Zoology,* 55:1176–1184.

Cebus capucinus: Home Range, Population Dynamics, and Interspecific Relationships

JOHN R. OPPENHEIMER The College of Staten Island, The City University of New York, Staten Island, New York 10301

ABSTRACT

Capuchins on Barro Colorado Island have a highly diverse diet consisting primarily of fruit and insects. The availability of these prey items varies seasonally and from year to year. Births occur throughout the year, but certain types of activities, like play and time spent on the ground, are strongly seasonal. Food availability in a poor year is suggested to be the factor that determines the size of the core area and home range. Although the subpopulation studied in greatest detail had an annual growth rate of 0.20 between 1966 and 1969, it may be that this was a local phenomenon as there was no adult mortality up through 1973 and no emigration. It is suggested that the island capuchin population has been in a phase of dynamic stability that is at least in part controlled by competition from other mammalian frugivores. Relationships with other vertebrates range from competitive to predatory and commensal.

INTRODUCTION

This paper is concerned with the population dynamics of *Cebus capucinus imitator* on Barro Colorado Island and its relationships with prey and nonprey species. It will also consider how these factors may in turn dictate the size and location of areas occupied by capuchin troops.

Moynihan (1976) and Oppenheimer (1977a) have recently reviewed the ecology and behavior of New World primates in general, and Freese and Oppenheimer (1981) and Oppenheimer (1973, in press) have treated capuchins in particular. Various workers have reported on aspects of capuchin ecology and behavior, and these papers can be found cited in the above reviews.

Reports specifically relating to capuchins on Barro Colorado have already appeared (Hladik and Hladik, 1969; Hladik et al., 1971; Oppenheimer, 1967a,b, 1968, 1969a,b, 1974, in press a; Watts, 1977). Capuchins are important active and passive dispersers of seeds, and ingestion of some species of seeds results in earlier or increased rates of germination (Hladik and Hladik, 1969). Capuchins prune certain species of trees and thereby increase the number of branches and possibly the number of sites for later production of fruit (Oppenheimer and Lang, 1969). Similar behavior has also been reported for baboons in Africa (Lock, 1972). Capuchins play a major role in the biological control of insect populations and in the dispersal of seeds. It may be because of seed dispersal that tree species included in the capuchin diet are more abundant in the Barro Colorado Island forest than species not eaten by these monkeys. At least one plant species, *Apeiba membranacea*, may be dependent upon beetle grubs that infest its fruit and, in turn, attract capuchins who disperse the seeds (Oppenheimer, 1977b).

METHODS

The data were collected on Barro Colorado Island during the following periods: March 1966 to August 1967, July to November 1968, January to May 1969, March to April 1970, February 1973, and June to July 1979. Information was recorded by hand, with tape recorder, and with still and movie cameras. Observation time varied from day to day and month to month and was concentrated on three troops, though other troops were observed. Data were gathered as opportunity allowed and consequently a standard time base was lacking. Quantification, as presented here, was achieved by dividing field notes into 15-minute periods according to quarter clock hours. A behavior that was performed once by one individual during a 15-minute period was treated as equal to a behavior

that was performed throughout the 15-minute period by several individuals. The distortion caused by this is partially compensated for by the fact that a behavior performed by several individuals throughout a 15-minute period would usually continue on into the next quarter-hour period. A total of 609 contact hours was obtained with troop A–A_1 between 1966 and 1973.

OBSERVATIONS

Home Range and Population Dynamics

In 1966 troop A had a home range of approximately 164 ha., though most of its movements were confined to an area of 87.8 ha., the core area. Troops B and D had similar sized core areas, which abutted directly onto troop A's core area (Figure 1). Consequently, home ranges overlapped but intrusions into another troop's core area were infrequent. When the intruding troop was discovered, the adult males (Figure 2) would interact, while the remainder of the intruding troop would move back toward its core area.

By the end of 1966 troop A was in the process of fission. The two oldest females of the troop along with a juvenile and an infant started to concentrate their movements in the eastern third of troop A's core area. By May 1967 a number of individuals previously unknown to me, including a fully adult male, had joined the females and young. These individuals were designated troop A_2, whereas the remaining individuals of troop A were designated as troop A_1. Up through 1970 troop A_2 moved away whenever troop A_1 came near and consequently troop A_1 continued to use most of the original core area. When the balsa (*Ochroma pyramidale*) flowered, A_2's adult male came to the clearing to obtain the nectar, and in 1973 A_2 was found on the west side of troop A's original core area. Because of this, it is simplest to consider troops A_1 and A_2 as a single subpopulation occupying 87.8 ha.

Between 1966 and 1970 this subpopulation grew from 15 individuals to a minimum of 33 (Table 1). This includes, in addition to 18 births, the immigration of 3 adult males, 1 adult female, and 1 juvenile. One infant died, but this death is considered to be human-induced. (The mother was captured pregnant, and by the time she was released almost a year later the infant's locomotory abilities were poorly developed because of the confines of the cage.) Of three young females whose ages were generally known, one had her first infant during her fourth year and the other two had theirs in their fifth year. Most mature females had one infant every other year, though one female had four infants in four consecutive years. Between 1966 and 1969 six mature females had on the average 0.67 infants per year each. Between 1965

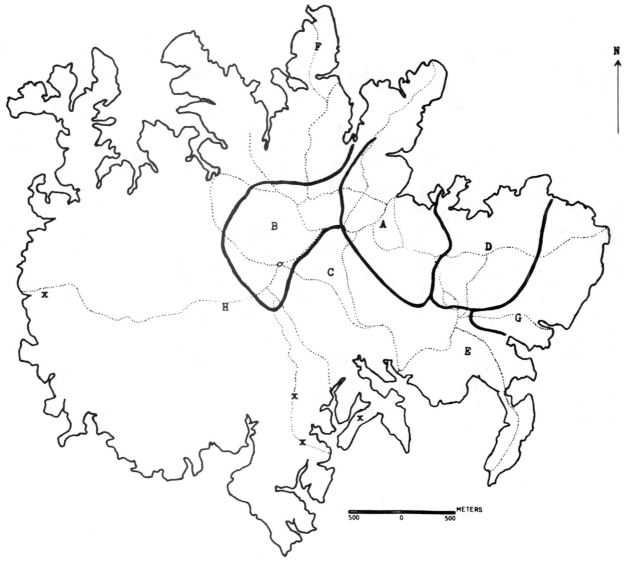

Figure 1.   Core areas and locations of eight capuchin troops in 1966. Heavy lines enclose core areas, and dotted lines show major trails.

and 1969 five of these females had on the average 0.56 infants per individual per year. If we assume that the five juveniles present in 1966 were offspring of the five adult females then present in the troop, the average number of infants per female per year between 1964 and 1969 was 0.60. Assuming that the average female continues to be reproductive to age 20, she would produce 9–10 offspring in a lifetime. The annual growth rate of this subpopulation was 0.20 between 1966 and 1969, based on births and ignoring the single infant death.

In 1966, if we assume an average core area per troop of 88 ha., there would have been at maximum

18 troops on the island. With a mean troop size of 15, the total population for the island would have been 270 individuals. Since we do not know the rate at which troops fission, we can estimate the size of the island population on the basis of the average number of hectares available per individual for the troop A subpopulation. By 1970 the population would have increased to 513 (Table 2). This, however, is probably an overestimate for the population, because some areas on the island appeared to be rarely or intermittently used. For instance, troop C, was apparently absent from the area immediately south of troop A's core area (Figure 1) between June 1966 and February 1967,

Figure 2. Chapman, the adult male of troop G on 10 August 1966. Note the square face, white flame on forehead, and muscular build.

possibly because it had moved south of Balboa trail toward American Museum of Natural History (AMNH) trail. In July and August 1979, 4 weeks were spent searching troop A's original home range; no troops were found to be resident there, even though troop A_1 and A_2 had been in residence there from 1966 to 1973.

During the first month of life infants have gray, rather than white, hair on the face and they ride across their mother's shoulders. Seventeen such infants were observed between 1966 and 1979 in five or more troops. The births of these infants occurred in all months, except for September, November, and December. These latter months were ones with fairly lush vegetation, consequently lower visibility, and less than the average monthly observation time.

Behavior

Only a portion of the behavioral data have been analyzed for seasonality so far, but some comments can be made. Allogrooming occurred throughout the year; however, grooming of adult females greatly increased when they gave birth and remained high for about 1 month thereafter. Social play was strongly seasonal; it was most frequently observed in the hot dry and early wet months of March to June (0.82 bouts/hr.), and least frequently observed in the remaining months of the year (0.18 bouts/hr.) ($p < 0.001$).

Capuchins used the ground for a number of activities: movement from one site to another (53%), playing (19%), obtaining food on or near the ground (17%), and while engaged in other activities (11%). A conservative estimate of the average number of individuals on the ground per observation hour was 1.6; however, this varied during the year from 3.5 between April and June to 1.3 between July and November and 0.7 between December and March ($\chi^2 = 462$, $p < 0.001$). There were no significant seasonal trends in types of use of the ground, although feeding was highest from April to June and lowest from December to March.

Interaction with Prey Species

Of 1291 15-minute periods during which feeding was observed between March 1966 and February 1973, capuchins ate plant matter during 83% and animal matter during 22%; however, this varied during the year (Figure 3).

Capuchins ate plant matter in 83 to 97% of the feeding periods per month during 9 months of the year, and during less than 75% of the periods during the remaining 3 months: February, March, and December (Figure 3).

The monkeys were observed feeding from a total of 110 species of plants (Table 3), with as many as 11 species being eaten on any given day. Most of the species eaten contributed fruit to the diet, though the percentage of species that did this varied during the year (Figure 4). Between February and September 80% or more of the species contributed fruit, with the maximum proportion of species contributing fruit in May and least in December.

Capuchins ate animal matter (mostly insects) throughout the year, but this varied from less than 10% of the feeding periods in June and July to over 40% in March and December (Figure 3). Harvesting of insect larvae and nymphs was most important during the dry season and accounted for 48% of the periods during which animals were eaten. The insects harvested occurred in abundance in a few selected species of trees. The bruchid beetle, *Amblycerus cen-*

Table 1. Changes in population size and structure, and area available per individual for troop A (A₁/A₂) between 1966 and 1970

Age-sex category	1966	1967	1968	1969	1970[1]
Adult male (9 years +)	1	2[2]/1[2]	2/2[2]	2/2	2/2
Subadult male (4–8 years)	0	0/0	2/0	2/0	3/1
Adult female (4 years +)	5	3/3[2]	5/3	6/4	7/5
Juveniles (1–3 years)	5	7/3[2]	5/4	6/6	7/4
Infants (0–1 year)	4	2/1	3[3]/3	3/0	1⁺/1⁺
Subtotal	15	14/8	17/12	19/12	20⁺/13⁺
Total	15	22	29	31	33⁺
Core area per individual (ha.)	5.9	4.0	3.0	2.8	2.7⁻

Core area = 87.8 ha.

[1] Observations only made in Mar. and Apr.
[2] Immigration of one individual.
[3] One infant died (see text).

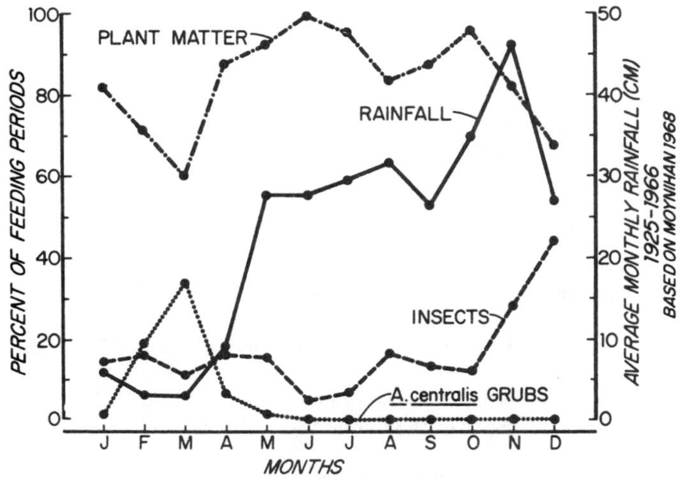

Figure 3. Changes in dietary composition and monthly rainfall during year (based on means for 1966–70).

Table 2. Estimated maximum population sizes for island between 1966 and 1969

	1966	1967	1968	1969	1970
Area per individual[1]	5.9	4.9	3.7	3.3	3.0
Total population	266	319	425	478	513

Based on data for troop A and total area for island of 1555 ha.

[1] Basing population increase on births only, since there would be no gain or loss to island because of migration.

Table 3. A partial list of angiosperm plants eaten or interacted with by *Cebus* on Barro Colorado Island

	1	2	3	4	5
MONOCOTYLEDONS					
Palmae					
1. *Astrocaryum standleyanum* Bailey	T	F	P	—	6
2. *Bactris* spp.	GP	NG	VT	—	21
3. *Desmoncus isthmius* Bailey	V	NG	VT	—	3
		F	P	—	1
4. *Oenocarpus panamanus* Bailey	T	F	P	N	6
5. *Scheelea zonensis* Bailey	T	F	P	C	109
6. *Socratea durissima* (Oerst.) Wendl.	T	F	P	—	2
Araceae					
7. *Dieffenbachia oerstedii* Schott	GP	L	(a)	—	0
8. *Monstera dubia* (H.B.K.) Engler & Krause	E	F	P, S	—	7
9. *Philodendron* sp.	E	F	P, S	—	3
Bromeliaceae					
10. *Aechmea setigera* Mart.	E	Fl	?	—	1?
11. *Tillandsia* sp.	E	Fl	?	—	1?
Musaceae					
12. *Musa sapientum* L.	GP	F	P	—	+
Zingiberaceae					
13. *Costus laevis* Ruiz and Pavon	GP	Fl	S	S	1
14. *Costus pulverulentis* Presl.	GP	Fl	S	—	4
15. *Renealmia cernua* (Swartz) Macbride	GP	Fl	S	—	7
Marantaceae					
16. *Ischnosiphon pruinosus* (Regel) Petersen	GP	B	B	—	2
DICOTYLEDONS					
Lacistemaceae					
17. *Lacistema aggregatum* (Berg) Rusby	ST	B	?	—	+
		F	P	A	11

Taxonomy follows Croat, 1978.

Columns and Symbols:

1. Plant type: T = medium to large tree, ST = small tree, GP = ground plant, V = vine or liana, E = epiphyte, H = herb, S = shrub, Sl = seedling.

2. Object of attention: F = fruit, R = receptacle, Fl = flower, L = leaf, B = flower bud, NG = new growth of branch or shoot, St = stem or trunk, Rt = root.

3. Part swallowed: P = pulp, aril, seed cover, mesocarp; VT = vascular tissue; S = seed; L = nectar or juice from pulp or seed; F = small berry; B = flower bud; Sta = stamen; I = insect pupae; (a) = rubbed on fur; (b) = open fruit during play and release air-borne seeds. When symbol is underlined, it pertains to information in column 4.

4. Taste of part swallowed (When more than one part mentioned in column 3, pertains to part underlined.): S = sweet, O = sour, B = bitter, U = turpentine, P = stewed prunes, N = crisp unsalted nut, C = soft cheese, A = astringent, T = pepper (makes tongue tingle), D = dry or powdery, L = tasteless.

5. Number of 15 minute periods in whch species was observed eaten by one or more individuals. Since observation time varied across months, data for species eaten at different times of year are not directly comparable. Symbol "+" indicates species eaten at least once by one individual.

Table 3. (continued)

	1	2	3	4	5
Moraceae					
18. *Brosimum alicastrum* Sw.	T	F	S	—	2
19. *Cecropia* spp.: a. *C. longipes* Pittier	T	F1	?	—	+
		F	P, S	—	23
20. *Ficus* spp. a. *F. citrifolia* P. Mill.	T	R, F	L	—	
b. *F. colubrinae* Standl.	E	R, F	L	—	111
c. *F. insipida* Willd.	T	R, F	L	—	
21. *Maquira costaricana* (Standl.) Berg	T	F	P	—	4
22. *Olmedia aspera* Ruiz & Pavon	S	B&F	B&F	—	14
23. *Poulsenia armata* (Miq.) Standl.	T	F	S	S	3
Polygonaceae					
24. *Coccoloba parimensis* Benth.	V	F	F	A, O	2
		St	VT	—	
Nyctaginaceae					
25. *Neea amplifolia* Donn. Smith	T	F	P	B, S	4
Annonaceae					
26. *Annona hayesii* Safford	ST	F	(a)	—	0
27. *Annona spraguei* Safford	T	F	P	—	3
28. *Desmopsis panamensis* (Rob.) Safford	ST	F	P	—	7
29. unidentified	?	F1	Sta	—	1
Myristicaceae					
30. *Virola surinamensis* (Rol.) Warb.	T	F	P, S	—	19
Monimiaceae					
31. *Siparuna pauciflora* (Beurl.) A. DC	S	F	P	—	1
Lauraceae					
32. *Nectandra purpurascens* (R. & P.) Mez	T	F	F?	—	1
33. *Ocotea cernua* (Nees) Mez	ST	F	P	—	2
Ocotea skutchii C.K. Allen	ST	F	P	—	1
Capparidaceae					
34. *Capparis frondosa* Jacq.	ST	F	P, S	S	3
Rosaceae					
35. *Hirtella triandra* Swartz.	ST	F	L	L	6
Connaraceae					
36. *Connarus turczinanowii* Triana & Planch	V	F	P, S	—	1
Leguminosae					
Mimoseae					
37. *Entada monostachya* DC	V	F	P?	—	1
38. *Inga* spp.: a. *I. fagifolia* (L.) Willd.	T	F	P	S	
b. *I. goldmanii* Pittier	T	F	P	S	
c. *I. minutula* (Schery) Elias	T	F	P	S	68
d. *I. pezizifera* Benth.	T	F	P	S	
e. *I. sapindoides* Willd.	T	F	P	S	
Caesalpinieae					
39. *Prioria copaifera* Griseb., (Hladik & Hladik, 1969)	T	F	?	—	—
Papilionatae					
40. *Clitoria javitensis* H.B.K.	V	F1	L	S	10

Table 3. (continued)

	1	2	3	4	5
41. *Dipteryx panamensis* (Pittier) Rec. & Mell	T	F	P	S	47
	—	NG	VT	—	1
42. *Erythrina costaricensis* Micheli var. *panamensis*	S1	St	VT	—	1
Rutaceae					
43. *Zanthoxylum* spp.: a. *Z. setulosum* P. Wilson	T	F	F	O, T	6
b. unidentified	T	F	F	—	1
Simaroubaceae					
44. *Quassia amara* L.	ST	R, F	P	—	4
Burseraceae					
45. *Protium panamense* (Rose) I. M. Johnson	T	F	P̲, S	S	5
46. *P. tenuifolium* Engler subsp. (Hladik & Hladik, 1969)	T	L?	?	—	—
47. *Tetragastris panamensis* (Engl.) Kuntze	T	F	P̲, S	S	62
Meliaceae					
48. *Trichilia cipo* (Adr. Juss.) DC. (Hladik & Hladik, 1969)	T	F	P	—	—
Euphorbiaceae					
49. *Croton* sp.	S	B	B	—	1
50. *Hura crepitans* L.	T	F	L̲, S	S	3
51. *Hyeronima laxiflora* (Tul.) Muell.-Arg.	T	F	F	S	13
52. *Mabea occidentalis* Benth.	ST	F	S	N	29
53. *Sapium caudatum* Pittier	T	F	P	—	13
Anacardiaceae					
54. *Anacardium excelsum* (Bert. & Balb.) Skeels.	T	R	VT	S	28
55. *Mangifera indica* L.	T	F	P	U, S	5
56. *Spondias mombin* L.	T	F	P	U, S	10
57. *Spondias radlkoferi* J. Donn. Sm.	T	F	P	U	1
Sapindaceae					
58. *Allophylus psilospermus* Radlk.	ST	F	P	S, D	6
59. *Cupania rufescens* Triana & Planch.	ST	F	P	—	1
60. *Cupania sylvatica* Seem.	T	F	P	O	23
61. *Paullinia turbacensis* HBK.	V	F	P, S	—	2
62. *Talisia nervosa* Radlk.	ST	F	P, S	—	2
Elaeocarpaceae					
63. *Sloanea terniflora* Standl.	T	F	P, S	—	1
Tiliaceae					
64. *Apeiba membranacea* Spruce ex Benth.	T	F	I, S	—	115
65. *Apeiba tibourbou* Aubl.	T	F?	I, S?	—	1
		F1	F1?	—	1
Bombacaceae					
66. *Bombacopsis* sp.?	T?	F1?	L?	—	7
67. *Ochroma pyramidale* (Cav. ex Lam.) Urban	T	F1	L	—	32
	—	F	(b)	—	1
68. *Quararibea asterolepis* Pittier	T	F	P	—	8
Sterculiaceae					
69. *Sterculia apetala* (Jacq.) Karst.	T	F	P	D	14

Table 3. (continued)

	1	2	3	4	5
Dilleniaceae					
70. *Doliocarpus dentatus* (Aubl.) Standl.	T	F	P, S	L, T	2
71. *Doliocarpus major* Gmel.	T	F	P, S	S, T	40
Guttiferae					
72. *Calophyllum longifolium* Willd.	T	F	P	—	2
73. *Rheedia edulis* (Seem.) Triana & Planch.	T	F	P, S	S, O	17
74. *Rheedia acuminata* (R. & P.) Planch. & Tr.	T	F	P, S	S, O	6
75. *Symphonia globulifera* L.f.	T	F	—	—	+
76. *Tovomita stylosa* Hemsl.	ST	F	S	—	1
Violaceae					
77. *Hybanthus prunifolius* (Schult.) Schulze	S	F	L, S	S	4
78. *Rinorea squamata* Blake	S1	Rt	VT	—	2
Flacourtiaceae					
79. *Casearia guianensis* (Aubl.) Urban	ST	F	P	—	2
80. *Hasseltia floribunda* HBK	T	F	F	—	12
81. *Laetia thamnia* L.	ST	F	P, S	—	2
82. *Lindackeria laurina* Presl.	T	F	P	—	4
83. *Zuelania guidonia* (Swartz) Britt. & Millsp.	ST	F	P	—	14
Passifloraceae					
84. *Passiflora ambigua* Hemsl.	V	F	L	—	3
Cactaceae					
85. *Epiphyllum* sp.	E	F	P?	S	1
Lecythidaceae					
86. *Gustavia superba* (H.B.K.) Berg	T	NG	VT	—	61
		F	P	—	71
Myrtaceae					
87. *Eugenia chepensis* Standley	T	F	F	O	1
88. *Eugenia nesiotica* Standley	T	F	P	—	4
89. *Psidium guajava* L.	ST	F	P	—	32
Melastomaceae					
90. *Miconia argentea* (Swartz) DC	T	F	F	S	84
91. *Mouriria myrtilloides* (SW.) Poir.	ST	F	S	S	6
Araliaceae					
92. *Dendropanax arboreus* (L.) Dec. & Planch., (Hladik & Hladik, 1969)	T	F	?	—	—
Sapotaceae					
93. *Chrysophyllum cainito* L.	T	F	L, S	—	6
94. *Chrysophyllum panamense* Pittier	T	F	L, S	—	6
Apocynaceae					
95. *Tabernaemontana arborea* Rose	T	F	P	—	1
96. *Thevetia ahouai* (L.) A. DC.	S	F	P	T	3
Convolvulaceae					
97. *Maripa panamensis* Hemsl.	V	F	P	P	13

Table 3. (continued)

	1	2	3	4	5
Boraginaceae					
98. *Cordia bicolor* A. DC	T	F	<u>P</u>, S	S, A	36
99. *Cordia lasiocalyx* P.H.	T	F	<u>P</u>, S	S, A	21
Bignoniaceae					
100. *Tabebuia guayacan* (Seem.) Hemsl.	T	F	P	—	—
Acanthaceae					
101. *Mendoncia* sp., (T. Struhsaker, pers. comm.)	V	F	P	—	1
Rubiaceae					
102. *Alibertia edulis* (L. Rich.) A. Rich., (Hladik & Hladik, 1969)	S	F	P?	—	—
103. *Coussarea curvigemmia* Dwyer	ST	F	P, S	—	2
104. *Faramea occidentale* (L.) Rich.	S	F	F	T	24
105. *Guettarda foliacea* Standl.	S	F	P	T, B	1
106. *Pentagonia macrophylla* Benth.	S	Fl	S	—	2
107. *Randia armata* (Swartz) DC	S	F	P, S	—	17
108. *Tocoyena pittieri* Standl.	T	F	<u>P</u>, S	P	2
Cucurbitaceae					
109. *Gurania megistantha* Donn. Sm.	V	F	F?	—	1?
Compositae					
110. *Mikania tonduzii* Robinson	V	Fl	Fl?	—	1?

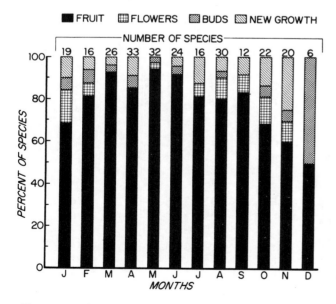

Figure 4. Changes in composition of plant diet during year (based on means for 1966–70).

tralis, accounted for 79% of the harvesting; its larvae were obtained from the fruit of *Apeiba membranacea* each year for 8 to 12 weeks between February and April. Froghopper nymphs (spittlebugs) were obtained from infested trees each year for 8 to 10 days in May. Two infestations of microlepidopteran caterpillars were harvested over periods of 5 to 7 days: *Atteva punctella* (Yponomentidae) in February 1969 and *Eulepitotis mabis* (Noctuidae) in March 1970. In both cases the caterpillars were eating leaves in the crowns of a few, widely dispersed, large canopy trees. The entire crown of the tree and some of the lower branches were entwined in silk. Though a tremendous number of larvae were eaten, others were able to escape by dropping to lower branches or the ground on silk threads.

The remaining 52% of the animal feeding periods involved foraging for individual arthropods, for nests of wasps and ants, and for small vertebrates, and occurred primarily at the end of the rainy season (Figure 3). The arthropods eaten included orthopterans (Tettigonidae); cockroaches; phasmids; termites; homopterans; coleoptera; lepidoptera (caterpillars); six or more species of ants; seven or more species of wasps, ticks, and spiders; and possibly flies. A lizard, *Anolis frenatus*, and several nestling squirrels, *Sciurus granatensis*, were observed being caught and eaten. On one occasion, a capuchin was observed with what appeared to be a nestling bird in each hand, but no body parts or feathers were obtained and thus the species was unidentified.

Large insects (orthopterans and phasmids) and small vertebrates were searched for and captured similarly, and then specific body parts were eaten in a methodical manner. However, eating of nestling squirrels drew the attention of other, usually younger, troop members (Figure 5). This may have been brought about by the initial vocalizations of the nestlings, odor, and/ or because the process of nibbling off the skin (the only part eaten) took so long, up to 20 minutes per nestling. Although the nestlings may be touched and sniffed at by others, the bodies were usually not released until most or all of the skin had been removed. Other capuchins then picked up the bodies and investigated them, and sometimes found some skin to eat.

Availability of food items in this study, as presented in Table 4, is based on observations of when a species or item was eaten by the monkeys, rather than on the amount of time present in the environment. There are advantages, as well as disadvantages, in this procedure. The advantage is that an item is scored as present only when it is partially or completely edible (fruit usually when ripe, but for some seeds when fruit is unripe). The disadvantage is that the observer should be present from dawn to dusk every day, and this was not done here. To compensate for the low level of field time in any one year, the data for all years can be combined (Table 4), and the longest period that a species was eaten in any one year can be assumed to be its period of availability (with reservations to be cited below). If the maximum periods of availability are used for all species, one ends up with what I will call the "ideal year." In such an ideal year the average species would provide food for 7 weeks, although over 36% of the species would do so for 2 weeks or less during the year. Species would provide flowers for about 6 weeks, fruit for 7, and new growth or shoots for 13 weeks. Ideal years do not exist, however, because conditions that might be optimum for one species would not be optimum for others. Thus the amount of time that any species provides food in any one year would be less than that given above.

The period during which a species provides food for the capuchins depends on how long an individual food item is available on individual trees and on whether the individuals (assuming more than one) of a species within a home range provide that food item synchronously or asynchronously. Good examples of asynchronous fruiting were *Desmopsis*, *Faramea*, and *Scheelea* (nos. 28, 104, and 5 in Table 4). In 1967 the two *Sterculia apetala* (no. 69) trees known to be in troop A's core area bore fruit in January, and at least one individual of this species in troop B's core area bore fruit at the end of March and beginning of April.

Although some species provided fruit every year, such as *Spondias mombin* (no. 56), *Apeiba* (no. 64), *Gustavia* (no. 86), and *Maripa* (no. 97), other species were less dependable or predictable. *Tetragastris* (no. 47) was a major food species for the capuchins (Table 3), and five individuals were known to be located in troop A's core area. This species fruited in 1966, 1969, 1970, and 1973, but it did not fruit in 1967 (Table 4). Similar irregularities in fruit production occurred in at least ten other species.

Interactions with Nonprey Species

Two plant species were rubbed into the fur by capuchins: the leaves of *Dieffenbachia* and the fruit of *Annona hayesii* (nos. 7 and 26, Table 3). Both plants gave off strong odors, at least immediately after being broken open, and may have been mildly irritating to the skin.

Large reptiles were only encountered twice while I was with the capuchins. A single alarm call was given when an adult iguana was seen on the ground, and a large boa resting on the ground was mobbed (without contact) by several troop members.

Except for large birds that swooped over the canopy (potential predators), adult birds were usually ignored (Table 5). A domesticated macaw sitting on a branch was lunged at by a juvenile female, possibly in play, but the bird got airborne immediately. A white hawk, which flew in and landed near a capuchin, elicited a single alarm call, but on five other occasions, when stationary or flying overhead, it was ignored. The double-toothed kite frequently accompanied capuchin troops, but was rarely recorded in the notes. During a total of 52 15-minute periods recorded with four troops, a double-toothed kite elicited an alarm call once when it flew near a surprised capuchin. On other occasions, kites were within 1 m of adult male capuchins and were ignored. On rare occasions kites were observed to capture prey while following capuchin troops: once an insect and once a good-sized lizard.

Adult red squirrels were often seen in the forest, but only once was one seen near capuchins, in this instance troop A$_2$. An adult female gave an alarm call

Figure 5.   Adult female capuchin, Ocean, eating nestling squirrel in left hand and holding second live nestling in right hand, while being watched by juvenile.

and then shook a branch at the squirrel, which immediately went down the tree and ran off on the ground.

In March 1970 a juvenile capuchin encountered a spiny rat on a branch (Table 5). As the rat ran away the capuchin grabbed its tail three times, but when the rat finally turned to face the juvenile, the juvenile retreated and the rat ran off.

Agoutis and collared peccaries are attracted by the sounds of capuchins feeding, because they eat the fruit dropped by capuchins (Table 5). Both species were usually ignored, but on two occasions an agouti alarm call (possibly stimulated by the presence of the observer) caused a capuchin near the ground to dash up a tree. Once a capuchin gave alarm calls oriented toward the ground where a couple of agoutis were located, though something else may have been the stimulus. Capuchins and agoutis can be on the ground close to one another without interacting, even when they are interested in the same food item. On one occasion, a juvenile *Cebus* chatter-screamed when it saw a peccary below it (Table 5), but again both species can be on the ground together.

Coatis also eat fruit dropped by the monkeys, but are equally adept in obtaining food in the trees. As a consequence, some agonistic interactions occur involving threats and retreats on both sides, and some chases of coatis by capuchin adults (Table 5).

Sloths and anteaters may have been encountered more often than indicated because they were usually ignored by the monkeys, and their slow movements would have been less likely to draw my attention. Once a juvenile capuchin came up to a sloth hanging below a branch. The sloth drew back an arm as if to strike, and the capuchin jumped away.

I rarely saw marmosets between 1966 and 1970, and then primarily in the old forest southwest of the tower, but in 1979 at least two different troops were commonly encountered: one in the old core area of troop A_1 and one to the northeast of the tower clearing. The only time I saw capuchins come in sight of marmosets was on 25 March 1970. Four capuchins (the active adult male, the two subadult males, and a juvenile) were play-chasing and grappling on the

OPPENHEIMER

ground to the west of Fairchild 2 from 12:38 P.M. through 12:48 P.M. At 12:55 P.M., marmoset screams were heard and immediately the adult capuchins moved in that direction. From then until 1:07 P.M. the two subadult male capuchins chased two marmosets back and forth, cornering first one and then the other marmoset when they hid in the leaf litter. By 1:08 P.M. the four capuchin males were back to chasing and grappling among themselves, and only marmoset contact calls were being made. These capuchins continued to play until 2:02 P.M.

Except for a lone capuchin male on Orchid Island, who in 1970 was living with a troop of howler monkeys, capuchin troops had only brief encounters with howlers. Most involved moving through a tree already occupied by howlers at the same level as or lower than the howlers. Less often, both species ate fruit in the same tree. In 88% of the encounters the two species ignored each other. Once a juvenile capuchin tried to play with a howler infant, but the infant retreated until it finally was able to escape. In 11% of the encounters, adults of the two species traded threats and usually the howler retreated (Table 5).

Troop A–A₁ was unusual in comparison to other capuchin troops on the island. Its core area included the laboratory clearing where a group of captive red spider monkeys was formed and released during the early 1960s. As a consequence, the adult spider male spent many of his diurnal hours moving with the capuchin troop, and at certain times all members of the two troops were together and functioned as a single unit (Table 5). They traveled, ate, rested, and played together. Adult female spider monkeys solicited grooming (5%) and sex (1%) from capuchin males. There were also displacements (4%) and agonistic interactions (10%). Most of the agonistic interactions were mild and involved repulsions of the solicitations of the female spider monkeys. However, in June 1966 the adult male spider monkey severely gashed a captive capuchin and in January 1967 he grabbed and tried to maul a juvenile capuchin from troop A₁. (Luckily, by then the male spider had lost three of his canine teeth, and the juvenile escaped without visible injury.) By late 1968, most agonistic interactions involved screams and threats from capuchins on the approach of spider monkeys, though capuchins continued to groom adult spiders. The two troops continued to associate through April 1970, including some play. During the 28-plus hours I spent with troop A₁ in 1973, the two species were together only twice, both times on 13 February. At 10:28 A.M., near Wheeler trail 1, some adult spiders appeared and went into a "rage," emitting intense raucous vocalizations; the capuchins moved quickly away making chatter-screams indicating fear. By 10:44 A.M. the capuchins had moved

sufficiently away to settle down to feeding and foraging on the ground and in the trees. At 11:31 A.M. the capuchins broke out with chatter-screams and alarm calls (grrahs), and three adult spiders, including the old adult male, appeared on the ground. They immediately chased the capuchins northward out of the area. I lost contact at 11:33 A.M. but continued to hear the raucous spider calls up to 11:49 A.M.

In 1979, the spider monkeys were seen repeatedly throughout the entire original core area of troop A, and no capuchins were present to associate with. There were capuchin troops along the eastern and southern borders of the area, however. Both species were found at different times at the intersections of T. Barbour and J. Van Tyne trails, and of F. Miller and Lake trails.

DISCUSSION

The diet of capuchins on Barro Colorado Island changes constantly during the year. This reflects the seasonal change in availability of food items. Matured fruit, as collected in traps, was most abundant during the months of March to June and September to October, and was much less abundant from November to February than in July and August (Foster, 1973; Smythe, 1970). The months of lowest fruit availability are the months when the capuchins eat more apical meristems and succulent bases of new shoots. Insects are generally less abundant in February and March (Smythe, this volume) though this varies depending on the species and weather conditions (Wolda, 1978). Insects attracted to light-traps were most abundant during May, June, and July, and least abundant during September to November (Smythe, 1974). Thus the major peak in insects (numbers and biomass) coincides with the maximum availability of fruit. It is the smaller postmonsoon peak in insects during December and January (Smythe, 1974) that is important for the capuchins. It should be pointed out that capuchins seek certain species of fruit and insects and certain stages of development, which either are masked by other species occurring in traps or which would not occur in traps. An example of the latter is the grubs of *Amblycerus centralis*, which would be represented in traps only by adults at a later time of the year if adults were attracted to lights. It is also important to remember that what appears in litter traps and insect traps has already been filtered by frugivores and insectivores.

Chapman (1938, p. 170) had suggested that capuchins on Barro Colorado Island might give birth seasonally. The data reported here indicate that births occur throughout the year, though it is possible that a larger sample would show seasonal concentration.

Table 4. Seasonal and annual changes in the plant diet based on species observed eaten or defecated five or more times between 1966 and 1973 with each month divided into two halves, before and after the 15th day (A = 1966, B = 1967, C = 1968, D = 1969, E = 1970, F = 1973)

	Part[1]	Jan. I	Jan. II	Feb. I	Feb. II	Mar. I	Mar. II	Apr. I	Apr. II	May I	May II
Years present		BD	BD	BDF	BDF	ABD	ABE	ABE	BDE	ABD	AB
No. of data days		10	15	15	19	10	20	18	14	10	10
No. and species[2]											
91. *M. myrtilloides*	F	B	B	D	?	?	B	—	—	—	—
41. *D. panamensis*	F	B	B	BF	BDF	B	AB	A	—	—	—
52. *M. occidentalis*	F	B	?	?	F	B	BE	B	B	—	—
20. *Ficus* spp.	F, R	B	?	D	BD	D	ABE	AB	BD	AB	AB
64. *A. membranacea*	F	—	D	BDF	BDF	ABD	ABE	ABE	BE	?	A
38. *Inga* spp.	F	—	B	?	D	?	E	AB	B	AB	AB
93–4. *Chrysophyllum* spp.	F	—	—	B	BF	—	AE	A	—	—	—
47. *T. panamensis*	F	—	—	F	F	—	AE	AE	DE	A	A
5. *S. zonensis*	F	—	—	F	F	D	E	B	BD	ABD	AB
1. *A. standleyanum*	F	—	—	—	D	B	?	?	D	—	—
90. *M. argentea*	F	—	—	—	F	D	ABE	BE	BD	ABD	B
60. *C. sylvatica*	F	—	—	—	—	D	?	?	D	—	AB
45. *P. panamense*	F	—	—	—	—	B	—	—	—	—	—
19. *Cecropia* spp.	F	—	—	—	—	B	B	ABE	BD	ABD	?
54. *A. excelsum*	R	—	—	—	—	—	AB	BE	?	ABD	B
86. *G. superba*	F	—	—	—	—	—	B	B	BD	BD	AB
83. *Z. guidonia*	F	—	—	—	—	—	—	B	BE	—	—
99. *C. lasiocalyx*	F	—	—	—	—	—	—	B	BE	B	—
17. *L. aggregatum*	B, F	—	—	—	—	—	—	B	?	?	B
4. *O. panamanus*	F	—	—	—	—	—	—	A	B	?	?
74. *R. acuminata*	F	—	—	—	—	—	—	—	B	?	B
51. *H. laxiflora*	F	—	—	—	—	—	—	—	E	D	AB
98. *C. bicolor*	F	—	—	—	—	—	—	—	E	A	AB
2. *Bactris* spp.	NG	B	B	—	F	—	—	—	B	?	?
15. *R. cernua*	F	—	—	—	—	—	—	—	—	B	—
73. *R. edulis*	F	—	—	—	—	—	—	—	—	—	B
97. *M. panamensis*	F	—	—	—	—	—	—	—	—	—	B
8. *M. dubia*	F	—	—	—	—	—	—	—	—	—	B
30. *V. surinamensis*	F	—	—	—	—	—	—	—	—	—	A
80. *H. floribunda*	F	—	—	—	—	—	—	—	—	—	—
35. *H. triandra*	F	—	—	—	—	—	—	—	—	—	—
58. *A. psilospermus*	F	—	—	—	—	—	—	—	—	—	—
53. *S. caudatum*	F	—	—	—	—	—	—	—	—	—	—
107. *R. armata*	F	—	—	—	—	—	—	—	—	—	—

Roman numerals indicate first and second half of each month.

[1] Part of plant which attracts attention or is handled: B = bud, F = fruit, Fl = flower, NG = new growth, R = receptacle.

[2] Use number to find complete name and classification of species in Table 3.

? Species may have been available, but was not observed being eaten.

* Flowers were inspected.

	June		July		Aug.		Sept.		Oct.		Nov.		Dec.	
	I	*II*	*I*	*II*	*I*	*II*	*I*	*II*	*I*	*II*	*I*	*II*	*I*	*II*
	AB	AB	AB	ABC	ABC	AC	AC	A	AC	AC	AC	AC	A	A
	5	11	6	9	17	9	3	2	5	13	14	6	1	5
	—	—	—	—	—	—	—	—	—	—	—	—	—	—
	—	—	—	—	—	—	—	—	—	—	—	—	—	—
	A	B	A	?	A	—	C	—	—	AC	A	C	—	—
	—	—	—	—	—	—	—	—	—	—	—	—	—	—
	A	AB	A	?	AC	A	—	—	—	AC	—	—	A	—
	—	—	—	—	—	—	—	—	—	—	—	—	—	—
	—	—	—	—	—	—	—	—	—	—	—	—	—	—
	AB	AB	AB	C	AC	A	A	?	A	—	—	—	—	—
	—	—	—	—	—	—	—	—	—	—	—	—	—	—
	B	B	—	—	—	—	—	—	—	—	—	—	—	—
	—	A	?	?	A	C	—	—	—	—	—	—	—	—
	?	?	?	AC	C	A	—	—	—	—	—	—	—	—
	—	—	—	—	—	—	—	—	—	—	—	—	—	—
	A	AB	AB	?	BC	—	—	—	—	—	—	—	—	—
	—	—	—	—	—	—	—	—	—	—	—	—	—	—
	—	—	—	—	—	—	—	—	—	—	—	—	—	—
	B	B	—	—	—	—	—	—	—	—	—	—	—	—
	?	AB	?	C	—	—	—	—	—	—	—	—	—	—
	?	AB	—	—	—	—	—	—	—	—	—	—	—	—
	AB	B	—	—	—	—	—	—	—	—	—	—	—	—
	A	A	—	—	—	—	—	—	—	—	—	—	—	—
	?	B	—	C	?	C	C	?	?	C	?	C	—	—
	—	—	—	—	—	A	?	?	A	A	A	—	—	—
	B	AB	—	—	—	—	—	—	—	—	—	—	—	—
	A	B	A	C	AC	—	—	—	—	—	—	—	—	—
	—	—	—	—	C	C	?	?	?	C	—	—	—	—
	A	AB	AB	C	A	?	?	?	?	A	—	—	—	—
	—	AB	—	—	—	—	—	—	—	—	—	—	—	—
	—	B	B	—	—	—	—	—	—	—	—	—	—	—
	—	—	A	—	—	—	—	—	—	—	—	—	—	—
	—	—	—	C	C	A	A	?	?	?	A	—	—	—
	—	—	—	C	C	AC	A	?	AC	C	A	—	—	—

Cebus capucinus

Table 4.   (continued)

	Part[1]	Jan.		Feb.		Mar.		Apr.		May	
		I	II	I	II	I	II	I	II	I	II
Years present		BD	BD	BDF	BDF	ABD	ABE	ABE	BDE	ABD	AB
No. of data days		10	15	15	19	10	20	18	14	10	10
No. and species[2]											
86. G. superba	NG	B	B	D	D	D	BE	B	BE	B	—
56. S. mombin	F	—	—	—	—	—	—	—	—	—	—
43. Zanthoxylum spp.	F	—	—	—	—	—	—	—	—	—	—
68. Q. asterolepis	F	—	—	—	—	—	—	—	—	—	—
71. D. major	F	—	—	—	—	—	—	—	—	—	—
89. P. guajava	F	?	D	D	—	—	—	—	—	—	—
104. F. occidentale	F	B	B	—	—	—	E	—	—	—	—
28. D. panamensis	F	B	?	?	?	?	?	B	?	B	—
40. C. javitensis	Fl	B	B	—	—	—	—	—	—	—	—
69. S. apetala	F	B	B	?	?	?	B	B	—	—	—
22. O. aspera	B, F	B	?	D	?	B	?	B	B	—	—
66. Bombacopsis sp.?	Fl	B	—	—	—	—	—	—	—	—	—
67. O. pyramidale	Fl	B	BD	BD	B	?	B*	—	—	—	—

Cebus apella females studied in central Brazil were found to menstruate continuously at 18-day intervals, though examination of reproductive tracts indicated a greater frequency of potential births in May-June and October-November (Hamlett, 1939).

The core area was defined as the area within which a troop confined most of its movements and which it defended against other troops. After fission, however, troop A_2's activities were primarily within the core area of troop A_1, though A_2 was unable to defend its area from intrusion by A_1. This suggests that there is a minimal core area size, which is unrelated to the number of individuals in a troop. Further, it appears that fissioning of a troop is related to social relationships rather than to troop size; that is, fission occurs in a small troop with old females, but not in a larger troop with young females.

The factors responsible for determining core area size may be related to food availability; that is, the core area should have enough species of food plants and individuals per species to provide a continuous supply of food throughout the year. The strategy would be to have several species of plants supplying food at any one time of the year in a good year, so that at least one of them might provide food in a bad year; that is, the supply of food should be sufficient to allow survival of the reproductive nucleus of the troop in the periodic poor year. Such a poor year occurred in 1970 when the September–October peak in fruiting failed, and at least one capuchin died (Foster, 1973). There is a buffer in the amount of insect prey, but this may also be smaller in a year or portion of the year with poor weather as herbivorous insects are dependent upon the vegetation. It might be possible with the current botanical knowledge of species composition and density of the forest on Barro Colorado Island and information about the seasonality and duration of food availability (particularly fruit) to predict the minimum-sized feeding area that could support a capuchin troop over the long term. One further input into such a model would be the nutritional requirements of capuchins. Presumably the large variety of fruit species eaten per day in part relates to obtaining an appropriate mix of amino acids and trace elements and avoiding a metabolic overload of secondary compounds that might be present. The dietary requirements for capuchins are already well established (Mann, 1970; Oppenheimer, in press; Samonds and Hegsted, 1973).

On Barro Colorado, animals are responsible for dispersing seeds of 72% of the plant species, including 76% of the canopy trees and 89% of the understory trees (Foster, 1973). Capuchins may be able to increase the frequency of trees that serve as their major sources of fruit by increasing dispersal of seeds and increasing the rate of successful seed germination

	June		July		Aug.		Sept.		Oct.		Nov.		Dec.	
	I	II	I	II	I	II	I	II	I	II	I	II	I	II
	AB	AB	AB	ABC	ABC	AC	AC	A	AC	AC	AC	AC	A	A
	5	11	6	9	17	9	3	2	5	13	14	6	1	5
	—	—	—	C	AC	AC	?	?	AC	AC	AC	?	?	?
	—	—	—	—	ABC	AC	C	?	A	—	—	—	—	—
	—	—	—	—	—	A	?	A	—	—	—	—	—	—
	—	—	—	—	—	A	?	A	—	—	—	—	—	—
	—	—	—	—	—	C	A	?	AC	AC	—	—	—	—
	—	—	—	—	—	C	?	?	C	C	C	?	?	?
	—	—	—	—	—	A	?	A	?	A	A	A	?	?
	—	—	—	—	—	—	—	—	—	C	A	C	—	—
	—	—	—	—	—	—	—	—	—	—	—	C	—	—
	—	—	—	—	—	—	—	—	—	—	—	C	—	—
	—	—	—	—	AC	—	—	—	—	—	—	—	A	?
	—	—	—	—	—	—	—	—	—	—	—	—	—	A
	—	—	—	C*	C*	—	—	—	—	—	—	—	—	A

(Oppenheimer, 1977b). If true, this would allow core area or home range size to be reduced. The effects of seed predators on seed survival, however, would act as a counterpressure (Janzen, 1969), and consequently would keep core areas fairly large.

The data for troops A_1 and A_2 show that the population was increasing in size between 1966 and 1970. If projected backward the data would indicate a population low in 1960–62 and, if projected forward, a population that would continue to grow up through the early 1980s. In the summer of 1976 one troop south of the tower consisted of only 16 members (Watts, 1977), and in the summer of 1979 troops appeared to be in the 15–25 range, although accurate counts were not made. However, as pointed out earlier, troop size is more likely controlled by age structure than by density relationships. The crucial data about population size would be the amount of home range and core area overlap between troops, and this information does not currently exist. An assumption here is that core area defense breaks down to allow overlap, and in turn this might lead to lower fertility.

It is possible that growth in one subpopulation might be balanced by a decrease in another subpopulation on the island. The increase of subpopulation A_1–A_2 was in part due to births and in part to an influx of adults from neighboring areas. That such migration might be due to high density in other parts of the island is suggested by the lack of emigration from the troop A subpopulation. By 1973, troop A_1 had four fully adult males and at least one subadult male, which suggests that age alone among males is insufficient to cause migration.

Why then the high rate of growth in the A subpopulation? Presumably the growth rate is genetically determined and would have allowed for survival in the face of predator pressure—eagles, cats, and boa constrictors. Eagles and cats (large species) are no longer present on the island.

A differential in growth rates in different portions of the island might be brought about by an uneven distribution of other fruit-eating (competing) species, and possibly by loss of major fruit trees because of treefalls. At the least, major treefalls might cause a change in the location of the home range. Interference competition from spider monkeys may have changed the population growth rate by excluding troop A's subpopulation from its core area of 1966 to 1973. Certainly information about current interactions between spider monkeys and surrounding capuchin troops would be helpful in testing this hypothesis. Further pressure from competitors could come from the howler monkeys. Fruit makes up 42% of the howler diet, and figs are a major component of this (Milton, 1977); even fruit-eating bats might play a role here (Morrison, 1975). The howler population has

Table 5. Types of interactions that occurred between troop A-A₁ and nonprey animal species during 501 15-minute periods

Nonprey animal species	Type of interaction				Total no.	% of grand total
	Neutral	Friendly	Play	Agonistic		
Reptilia						
Iguana iguana (iguana)	—	—	—	1	1	0.2
Constrictor constrictor (boa)	—	—	—	2	2	0.4
Aves						
Ara sp. (macaw)	—	—	—	1	1	0.2
Ramphastos sulfuratus (toucan)	2	—	—	—	2	0.4
Coragyps atratus (vulture)	3	—	—	—	3	0.6
Leucopternis albicollis (white hawk)	3	—	—	1	4	0.8
Harpagus bidentatus (double-toothed kite)	24	—	—	—	24	4.8
Mammalia						
Sciurus granatensis (red squirrel)	—	—	—	—	0	0.0
Proechimys semispinosus (spiny rat)	—	—	1	—	1	0.2
Dasyprocta punctata (agouti)	15	2	—	1?	18	3.6
Tamandua tetradactyla (anteater)	1	—	—	—	1	0.2
Bradypus infuscatus (3-toed sloth)	—	—	—	—	0	0.0
Choloepus hoffmani (2-toed sloth)	2	—	—	1	3	0.6
Tayassu tajacu (collared peccary)	30	—	—	1	31	6.2
Nasua narica (coati mundi)	33	—	—	13	46	9.2
Saguinus geoffroyi (marmoset)	—	—	2	—	2	0.4
Alouatta palliata (howler monkey)	50	—	1	6	57	11.4
Ateles geoffroyi (spider monkey)	230	22	8	45	305	60.9
Total number of 15-minute periods	393	24	12	72	501	—
Percentage of total	78.4	4.8	2.4	14.4	—	100.0

Based on 2323 periods between 1966 and 1970.

fluctuated over the years and was estimated to be at a peak from 1967 (Chivers, 1969) to 1970 (Mitter-meier, 1973).

It may be that the growth rate calculated earlier is a local short-term phenomenon. This is suggested by the lack of any natural deaths between 1966 and 1973. If one assumes that capuchins have a life span of 20 years in the forest, then some of the adults may have died after 1974. Two natural deaths have been recorded among capuchins on Barro Colorado, an individual of unknown age in 1970 (Foster, 1973) and an infant (possibly newborn) in 1976 (Watts, 1977).

The shifting of home ranges of capuchins may affect many other species. In the absence of capuchins, the efficiency of seed dispersal may decrease (though other frugivores, such as spider monkeys, may serve as adequate replacement), and the damage to vege-tation by insect herbivores may increase. With release from predation on nestlings, the red squirrel population should increase. Ground mammals, such as agoutis and peccaries, that are somewhat dependent on capuchins for their supply of fruit may spend more time in other areas where capuchins are present, and consequently the effects of their activities will decrease. Spider monkeys may be able to provide this fruit where and when they are present, but they may also direct some of their aggression toward terrestrial frugivores. The apparent resurgence of marmosets in the old core area of troop A also raises questions as to whether the capuchins' intentions are always playful toward this species. In raising the above points, I wish to indicate the complexity of capuchin interactions within the forest ecosystem of Barro Colorado Island and the dynamics of these relationships.

OPPENHEIMER

ACKNOWLEDGMENTS

A list of the individuals who have aided in one way or another with this study might be longer than the paper. The STRI staff, particularly M. H. Moynihan, A. S. Rand, B. and M. H. Robinson, N. G. Smith, and N. Smythe, has helped in many ways, as has the multitude of visitors to Barro Colorado Island during my various stays. I especially thank E. M. Banks, J. F. Eisenberg, and C. H. Southwick for their moral and other types of support over the years. Many experts on plant and animal taxonomy have also lent their knowledge: C. J. Bottimer, T. B. Croat, D. Duckworth, J. A. Duke, R. B. Foster, C. O. Handley, Jr., A. and M. Hladik, P. B. Kannowski, W. H. Lewis, M. Naumann, and O. Sexton. I also wish to thank E. C. Oppenheimer for her help some years ago in reading all the field notes and putting the various types of data into almost endless lists. Without her help, much of this present paper could not have been written at this time.

This reseach was supported from 1966 to 1967 by a Smithsonian Institution Predoctoral Internship and from 1968 to 1970 by U.S. Public Health Service Postdoctoral Training Grant 5 TO1 MH 11110–01 to the Johns Hopkins University under C. H. Southwick.

LITERATURE CITED

Chapman, F. M.
1938.   *Life in an Air Castle.* New York: D. Appleton-Century Co.

Chivers, D. J.
1969.   On the Daily Behavior and Spacing of Howling Monkey Groups. *Folia primat.,* 10:48–102.

Foster, R. B.
1973.   Seasonality of Fruit Production and Seed Fall in a Tropical Forest Ecosystem in Panama. Ph.D. Thesis. Duke University, Durham.

Freese, C. H., and J. R. Oppenheimer
1981.   The Capuchin Monkey, Genus *Cebus.* Pages 331–390 in *Ecology and Behavior of Neotropical Primates,* vol. 1, edited by A. F. Coimbra-Filho and R. A. Mittermeier. Rio de Janeiro: Brazilian Academy of Sciences.

Hamlett, G. W. D.
1939.   Reproduction in American Monkeys. I. Estrous Cycle, Ovulation and Mestruation in *Cebus. Anat. Rec.,* 73:171–187.

Hladik, A., and C. M. Hladik
1969.   Rapports trophiques entre végétation et primates dans la forêt de Barro Colorado (Panama), *La Terre et la Vie,* 23:25–117.

Hladik, C. M., A. Hladik, J. Bousset, P. Valdebouze, G. Viroben, and J. Delort-Laval
1971.   Le regime alimentaire des Primates de l'ile de Barro Colorado (Panama): Resultats des analyses quantitatives. *Folia primat.,* 16: 85–122.

Janzen, D. H.
1969.   Seed-eaters Versus Seed Size, Number, Toxicity and Dispersal. *Evolution,* 23:1–27.

Lock, J. M.
1972.   Baboons Feeding on *Euphorbia candelabrum. E. Afr. Wildl. J.,* 10: 73–76.

Mann, G. V.
1970.   Nutritional Requirements of *Cebus* Monkeys. Pages 143–157 in *Feeding and Nutrition of Nonhuman Primates,* edited by R. S. Harris. New York: Academic Press.

Milton, K.
1977.   The Foraging Strategy of the Howler Monkey in the Tropical Forest of Barro Colorado Island, Panama. Ph.D. thesis, New York University, New York.

Mittermeier, R. A.
1973.   Group Activity and Population Dynamics of the Howler Monkey on Barro Colorado Island. *Primates,* 14: 1–19.

Morrison, D. W.
1975.   The Foraging Behavior and Feeding Ecology of a Neotropical fruit bat, *Artibeus jamaicensis.* Ph. D. thesis, Cornell University, Ithaca, N.Y.

Moynihan, M. H.
1968.   Smithsonian Tropical Research Institute: 1967 Annual Report. Pages 171–182 in *Smithsonian Year 1967.* Washington, D.C.: Smithsonian Institution Press.
1976.   *The New World Primates.* Princeton, N.J.: Princeton University Press, 262 p.

Oppenheimer, J. R.
1967a.   The Diet of *Cebus capucinus* and the Effect of *Cebus* on the Vegetation. *Bull. Ecol. Soc. Amer.,* 48: 138 (Abstr.).
1967b.   Vocal Communication in the White-faced Monkey *Cebus capucinus. Bull. Ecol. Soc. Amer.,* 48: 149 (Abstr.)
1968.   Behavior and Ecology of the White-faced Monkey, *Cebus capucinus,* on Barro Colorado Island, C.Z. Ph.D. thesis, University of Illinois, Urbana (University Microfilms, Ann Arbor, Michigan 69–10, 811).
1969a.   *Cebus capucinus:* Play and Allogrooming in a Monkey Group. *Amer. Zool.,* 9: 1070 (Abstr.).
1969b.   Changes in Group Composition and Forehead Patterns of the White-faced monkey, *Cebus capucinus.* Pages 36–42 in *Proceedings of the Second International Congress of Primatology, Atlanta 1968, Vol. 1, Behavior,* edited by C. R. Carpenter. Basel: S. Karger.
1973.   Social and Communicatory Behavior in the *Cebus* Monkey. Pages 251–257 in *Behavioral Regulators of Behavior in Primates,* edited by C.R. Carpenter. Lewisburg, Pa.: Bucknell University Press.
1974.   Cebus Monkeys of Barro Colorado Island: Behavior and Ecology, Film PCR 2258 K, Pennsylvania State University, University Park.
1977a.   Communication in New World Monkeys. Pages 851–889 in *How Animals Communicate,* edited by T. A. Sebeok. Bloomington: Indiana University Press.
1977b.   Forest Structure and Its Relation to Activity of the Capuchin Monkey (*Cebus*). Pages 74–84 in *Use of Nonhuman Primates in Biomedical Research,* edited by M. R. N. Prasad and T. C. A. Kumar. New Delhi: Indian National Science Academy.
1979.   Social Behavior and Structure in a Forest Dwelling Troop of White-faced Monkeys (*Cebus capucinus*). Presented at the Seventh Congress of the International Primatological Society, Bangalore, India.

In press. Diets (Natural and Synthetic) for Capuchin Monkeys (Cebidae: *Cebus*). In *Handbook Series in Nutrition and Food*, edited by M. Rechcigl, Jr. West Palm, Fla.: CRC Press.

Oppenheimer, J. R., and G. E. Lang
1969.   *Cebus* monkeys: Effect on Branching of *Gustavia* trees, *Science*, 165: 187–188.

Samonds, K. W., and D. M. Hegsted
1973.   Protein Requirements of Young Cebus Monkeys (*Cebus albifrons* and *apella*). *Am. J. Clin. Nutr.*, 26: 30–40.

Smythe, N.
1970.   Relationships Between Fruiting Seasons and Seed Dispersal Methods in a Neotropical Forest. *American Naturalist*, 104:25–35.
1974.   Terrestrial Studies—Barro Colorado Island. Pages 1–127 in *Smithsonian Institution Environmental Sciences Program 1973: Environmental Monitoring and Baseline Data*, edited by R. W. Rubinoff. Unpublished Report. Washington, D.C.: Smithsonian Institution.
1982.   The Seasonal Abundance of Night-flying Insects in a Neotropical Forest. Pages 309–318 in *The Ecology of a Tropical Forest*, edited by Egbert G. Leigh, Jr., et al. Washington, D.C.: Smithsonian Institution Press.

Watts, D. P.
1977.   Activity Patterns and Resource Use of White-Faced *Cebus* Monkeys (*Cebus capucinus*) on Barro Colorado Island, Panama Canal Zone. M.A. thesis, University of Chicago, Chicago.

Wolda, H.
1978.   Seasonal Fluctuations in Rainfall, Food and Abundance of Tropical Insects. *Journal of Animal Ecology*, 47:369–381.

Dietary Quality and Demographic Regulation in a Howler Monkey Population

KATHARINE MILTON   Department of Anthropology, University of California, Berkeley, California 94720

ABSTRACT

Factors influencing the size of the howler monkey population (*Alouatta palliata*) on Barro Colorado Island, Republic of Panama, were investigated by analyzing annual changes in troop size and composition and comparing these with temporal patterns of their principal dietary resources, the young leaves and fruits of canopy tree species. Data indicate that this essentially closed population is not increasing in size. Although population numbers are stable through time, there is considerable turnover of individuals because of high mortality among members of particular age classes. The higher quality dietary items preferred by howlers are subject to seasonal and multi-annual fluctuations in relative abundance. Consequent resource shortages may be a principal factor limiting population size. Although births add new members to the population, data suggest that most new individuals do not survive to reproduce. The inability to predict many periods of resource shortage may have resulted in the observed pattern of continuous and aseasonal births.

INTRODUCTION

There is little direct evidence of density-regulating mechanisms in natural populations. Indeed, some schools would question that regulation occurs at all. It seems clear, however, that many natural populations manage to maintain their numbers within relatively narrow limits for long periods of time. Various hypotheses have been put forth to explain such regulation, with discussion centering on the relative importance of density-independent versus density-dependent factors, including extrinsic factors such as predators, food shortage, or disease and intrinsic factors such as social behavior and genetic polymorphism. Recent population studies, such as those of Sinclair (1974; 1977), make it clear that a combination of factors interact in different intensities at different times to regulate many natural populations. The problem thus becomes one of identifying the regulation mechanisms at work in any particular population and demonstrating how these in fact function to set limits to population size.

In 1974, when I began my examination of the ecology of free-ranging howler monkeys (*Alouatta palliata*) on Barro Colorado Island in central Panama, it was popularly believed that this population was regulated primarily by an extrinsic factor—periodic outbreaks of sylvan yellow fever. Yet yellow fever had not been reported on Barro Colorado since at least the mid-1940s. Further, the disease is not endemic to the neotropics but rather was introduced to it from Africa some 500 years ago. Many howler populations live at elevations where yellow fever does not occur. For these reasons, it seemed likely that if this primate population was being regulated, some factor(s) other than yellow fever must be involved.

Prior to my work, various studies had been carried out on different aspects of howler behavior on Barro Colorado. However, data on population parameters were sketchy at best; no life table data had been compiled; the current size of the population was unknown; and estimates differed by more than 100%. Thus my initial investigation was directed toward answering several basic questions, namely: (1) what is the size of the current population, (2) is there evidence that the population is being regulated; and (3) if so, what possible factors might be involved in such regulation?

Below I present data collected with respect to these questions during 1977, 1978, and 1979, supplemented by data from 1974–75. Annual changes in population size are discussed both in terms of my own work and that of earlier researchers. Results indicate that this primate population is not increasing in size to any detectable degree and that mortality rather

than curtailment of reproduction is the principal factor limiting further growth. It is suggested that such mortality is due, at least in part, to periodic but often unpredictable scarcity of higher quality dietary items. The lack of these items, singly and in combination with other factors such as parasitism, produces mortality in all age classes but particularly among immature individuals. As yet, it is not known whether such mortality comes about primarily as a result of intraspecific competition for limited high-quality dietary items or whether available food is abundant but simply too inferior in quality to support certain members of the population.

BACKGROUND

The howler population on Barro Colorado consists of a number of discrete troops, each of which occupies a clearly defined home range (Smith, 1977; Milton, 1977). Home ranges of neighboring troops typically overlap. There is a strong and persistent tendency for troops to average around 19 individuals and to consist of 3 to 4 adult males, 7 to 10 adult females, and 6 to 10 immature animals (Carpenter, 1934, 1962; Milton 1975, 1977). Each troop is an essentially closed social unit. However, some individuals, particularly subadult and adult males, do transfer from one troop to another.

Of more interest, in terms of population size, is the possible movement of howler monkeys to and from Barro Colorado and the surrounding islands and mainland. Interviews with people working on Barro Colorado and/or living in the Lake Gatun area for the past two decades resulted in only three reports of howler monkeys seen swimming in the lake. Thus movement of animals to and from the island appears rare and should exert little influence over the size of the resident population, which thus can be regarded as essentially closed. From this it follows that changes in the size of this population come about through only two factors, births and deaths.

To appreciate the current status of the population it is useful to know something of its origin. Howlers living on the island today are the descendants of animals occurring naturally in the area prior to its transformation from mainland to island during the construction of the Panama Canal. In 1923, Barro Colorado Island was declared a nature preserve, and since that time there has been little human interference in its ecology. Howlers and other animals are not hunted, and there is no evidence that howlers are poached.

Various sections of the forest are known to have been cleared in the past. In the early 1930s, there were sections of older forest as well as very young growth uninhabited by howler monkey troops (Carpenter, 1934). Today virtually the entire island is densely forested (an estimated 1475 ha.; E. Willis, pers. comm.); some areas are estimated to be in primary condition while other sections are composed of old second growth (Knight, 1975; Foster and Brokaw, this volume).

CENSUSES

Estimates of Population Size, 1932–70

The Barro Colorado howler monkey population was first censused by C. R. Carpenter in 1932. This census was repeated in 1933 and in 1959. A partial census was carried out in 1935. Results of these and all other censuses are presented in Table 1. The population was small in the 1930s, consisting of some 400 to 500 monkeys distributed in 23 to 28 troops. At that time the population was estimated to be increasing at a rate of 15% per annum (Carpenter, 1934).

The next island-wide census took place 18 years later in 1951 (Collias and Southwick, 1952). The population had decreased rather than increased in size and appeared to consist of only some 240 animals. It is hypothesized that an outbreak of yellow fever, known to have passed through central Panama in the mid 1940s, may have reduced the howler population to a very low level from which it was only beginning to recover in 1951 (Collias and Southwick, 1952; P. Galindo, pers. comm.; C. Handley, pers. comm.).

Between 1951 and 1958, the population increased by more than 200% to a size of 814 animals distributed in 44 troops (Carpenter, 1959). Over the next decade, however, growth amounted to only some 23%. Various estimates made between 1967 and 1970 placed the population at around 1000 animals (Chivers, 1967; Mittermeier, 1973; Eisenberg and Thorington, 1973; Smith, 1977). It was suggested that the island might well be approaching a saturation point with respect to the number of howlers that could viably be supported (Smith 1977, work carried out in 1967–68). In the 1930s, however, Carpenter (1934) had speculated that the island might be able to support as many as 2000 howlers; Chivers (1967) estimated that a population of 3860 monkeys might be possible; Hladik and Hladik (1969) suggested that there appeared to be sufficient dietary resources on Barro Colorado to support a population of some 3000 monkeys.

Estimates of Population Size, 1974–80

In 1974, I censused my first howler troops on Barro Colorado. A count of all members in each of six troops living in the northwestern sector of the island gave a mean troop size of 18.2 ± 2.8 (standard deviation). These data were combined with a 1974 island-wide troop count by R. Mittermeier (see Mittermeier, 1973, for discussion of censusing technique) to give an estimated population size of 1211 monkeys.

In March 1977, I organized an island-wide troop count with the help of 25 participants. Each participant was assigned a particular "station" in the forest, selected so as to give coverage of all parts of the island. For two consecutive mornings, between 5:40 A.M. and 6:20 A.M., participants listened for the traditional dawn choruses of the various howler troops in their area (see Chivers, 1969, for a discussion of the howler dawn chorus) and recorded the time of each chorus, the approximate distance of the chorusing troop from the participant and its compass direction. These data were later used to triangulate troop locations on a map for each of the two mornings of the census. Counting all overlapping points placed on the map gave an estimate of the total number of troops on the island (see Figure 1).

To determine population size, I then counted all individuals in each of 13 troops living in different areas of the island. Mean troop size and composition were calculated from these data and multiplied by the total number of troops to give an estimate of total population size. This same process was repeated again in late February-March-April 1979. The 1977 census gave a total of 65 troops with an estimated total population of 1331 monkeys, while the 1979 census showed 60 troops and a population size of 1212.

These estimates were further verified by work carried out by W. Glanz, who censused various species of nocturnal and diurnal mammals from January 1977 through April 1978 on Barro Colorado. His estimates for total number of troops and total population size fall well within the range of mine (see Glanz, this volume).

ANALYSIS OF RECENT CENSUS DATA

Data from the various censuses taken during the 1970s indicate that the howler population on Barro Colorado Island is not increasing in size to any detectable degree. It appears to fluctuate between some 1250 to 1350 monkeys distributed in some 60 to 70 troops. Since the population is not increasing in size, some factor or factors must therefore be functioning to limit its growth.

Troop Distribution

Figure 1 shows the locations of the 65 howler troops counted on day 2 of the March 1977 island-wide census. A similar spacing pattern was found on other

Table 1. Mean troop size for howler monkeys on Barro Colorado, 1932–80

Observer	Date	Number of troops counted to estimate troop size	Average troop size ($\overline{X} \pm SD$)	Range	Estimated no. of troops, island-wide	Estimated total population
Carpenter	Apr. 1932	23	17.3 ± 7.1	4–35	23	398
Carpenter	Apr. 1933	28	17.4 ± 6.8	4–29	28	490
Carpenter	Jan. 1935	15	18.2 ± 7.1	6–34	n.a.	n.a.
Collias & Southwick	Mar.–Apr. 1951	30	8.0 ± 3.6	2–17	30	240
Carpenter	June–Aug. 1959	44	18.5 ± 9.4	3–45	44	814
Chivers	June–Aug. 1967	12	14.8 ± 2.4	11–18	63	926*
Smith	Sept.–Nov. 1967	27	13.8 ± 6.5	6–31	n.a.	n.a.
Mittermeier	Sept.–Oct. 1970	6	16.2 ± 4.3	13–23	57	923
Milton & Mittermeier	Apr. 1974	6	18.2 ± 2.8	n.a.	66	1201
Milton	Mar.–Apr. 1977	13	20.8 ± 6.5	9–32	65	1352
Milton	July–Aug. 1977	13	23.0 ± 5.5	17–35	n.a.	n.a.
Milton	Nov.–Dec. 1977	13	21.4 ± 7.2	16–35	n.a.	n.a.
Milton	Mar.–Apr. 1978	13	20.2 ± 5.6	9–32	60	1212
Milton	July–Aug. 1978	13	18.9 ± 4.9	10–29	n.a.	n.a.
Milton	Nov.–Dec. 1978	13	18.7 ± 5.9	8–28	n.a.	n.a.
Milton	Mar.–Apr. 1979	13	20.4 ± 6.8	12–35	n.a.	n.a.
Milton	July–Aug. 1979	13	18.9 ± 5.5	11–30	n.a.	n.a.
Milton	Jan. 1980	13	21.3 ± 4.5	16–28	n.a.	n.a.

n.a. = data not available for this calculation

* See Chivers (1969) for other estimates as well.

Table 2. Troop composition for howler monkeys on Barro Colorado, 1932–80 ($\overline{X} \pm SD$)

Observer	Date	Adult males	Adult females	Juveniles	Infants
Carpenter	Apr. 1932	2.7 ± 1.3	7.4 ± 3.0	4.0 ± 2.6	3.1 ± 1.5
Carpenter	Apr. 1933	2.7 ± 1.3	7.4 ± 2.8	4.2 ± 2.2	3.5 ± 2.1
Carpenter	Jan. 1935	3.3 ± 1.7	7.0 ± 2.9	5.4 ± 2.5	2.5 ± 1.2
Collias & Southwick	Mar.–Apr. 1951	1.2 ± 0.4	4.5 ± 2.1	1.0 ± 1.0	1.1 ± 1.1
Carpenter	June–Aug. 1959	3.3 ± 1.7	9.1 ± 4.8	3.1 ± 2.5	3.0 ± 2.1
Chivers	June–Aug. 1967	3.4 ± 1.1	6.1 ± 0.9	2.8 ± 1.1	2.6 ± 1.0
Smith	Sept.–Nov. 1967	2.9 ± 1.4	7.0 ± 3.5	1.8 ± 1.2	2.1 ± 1.7
Mittermeier	Sept.–Oct. 1970	3.2 ± 1.0	5.8 ± 1.7	4.3 ± 1.2	2.8 ± 1.2
Milton & Mittermeier*	Apr. 1974	3.8 ± 0.8	7.7 ± 1.5	2.0 ± 1.4	4.0 ± 1.4
Milton	Mar.–Apr. 1977	3.5 ± 1.4	9.2 ± 2.4	2.6 ± 1.6	5.5 ± 2.6
Milton	July–Aug. 1977	3.8 ± 1.1	8.9 ± 2.3	3.1 ± 1.6	7.2 ± 2.3
Milton	Nov.–Dec. 1977	3.9 ± 1.7	8.5 ± 3.0	3.1 ± 2.3	6.0 ± 2.9
Milton	Mar.–Apr. 1978	3.1 ± 0.8	7.9 ± 3.0	2.3 ± 1.0	6.9 ± 2.3
Milton	July–Aug. 1978	3.3 ± 1.3	7.4 ± 2.4	2.7 ± 1.5	5.4 ± 2.2
Milton	Nov.–Dec. 1978	3.0 ± 1.0	7.5 ± 2.9	2.3 ± 1.1	5.9 ± 2.0
Milton	Mar.–Apr. 1979	3.7 ± 1.9	8.5 ± 3.2	2.7 ± 1.9	5.3 ± 2.1
Milton	July–Aug. 1979	3.1 ± 1.3	7.9 ± 2.5	2.4 ± 1.1	5.4 ± 1.9
Milton	Jan. 1980	3.9 ± 1.1	8.4 ± 2.7	2.6 ± 1.3	7.0 ± 1.3

* Six troops counted to get means for adult males and females; two troops counted to get means for juveniles and infants.

Table 3. Mean number of juveniles per class per troop per census ($\overline{X} \pm SD$)

Researcher	Date	Juvenile class		
		I	II	III
Carpenter	Apr. 1932	1.3± 1.1	1.8± 1.4	0.9± 1.1
Carpenter	Apr. 1933	1.3± 0.9	1.8± 1.1	1.0± 1.1
Carpenter	Jan. 1935	0.9± 1.0	1.4± 1.2	3.1± 1.5
Collias & Southwick	Mar.–Apr. 1951	0.2± 0.4	0.2± 1.2	0.6± 0.7
Carpenter	June–Aug. 1959	1.0± 1.2	1.0± 1.2	1.1± 1.1
Chivers	June–Aug. 1967	n.a.	n.a.	n.a.
Smith	Sept.–Nov. 1967	0.5± 0.7	0.8± 0.8	0.5± 0.5
Mittermeier	Sept.–Oct. 1970	n.a.	n.a.	n.a.
Milton & Mittermeier	Apr. 1974	n.a.	n.a.	n.a.
Milton	Mar.–Apr. 1977	1.1± 0.9	0.4± 0.7	0.9± 1.2
Milton	July–Aug. 1977	1.8± 2.9	1.1± 1.2	1.0± 0.9
Milton	Nov.–Dec. 1977	1.4± 1.6	0.9± 1.0	0.7± 1.0
Milton	Mar.–Apr. 1978	0.5± 0.5	1.3± 1.1	0.4± 0.7
Milton	July–Aug. 1978	1.5± 1.2	1.2± 1.0	0.3± 0.6
Milton	Nov.–Dec. 1978	1.4± 1.1	0.6± 0.8	0.3± 0.6
Milton	Mar.–Apr. 1979	1.7± 1.0	1.0± 1.2	0.2± 0.4
Milton	July–Aug. 1979	1.5± 0.9	0.8± 0.7	0.2± 0.4
Milton	Jan. 1980	1.5± 0.8	0.5± 0.6	0.7± 0.5

Estimates are based on the appearance of the animals, as in Carpenter (1934). My chronological estimates of these classes do not necessarily conform to Carpenter's (1934) and cannot be used in comparison with Glander's (1980) chronological data. I estimate that the total juvenile stage probably lasts some 2½–3 years. Juvenile-I is from around 14 to 20 months; J-II, 20 to 28 months; J-III, 28 months through subadulthood and sexual maturity. A marked cohort is needed to obtain accurate data on these time intervals.

n.a. = data not available for this calculation.

Table 4. Mean number of infants per class per troop per census ($\overline{X} \pm SD$)

Observer	Date	Infant class[1]		
		I	II	III
Carpenter	Apr. 1932	0.7± 0.7	1.1± 0.9	1.3± 1.4
Carpenter	Apr. 1933	0.8± 0.7	1.6± 1.8	1.2± 1.4
Carpenter	Jan. 1935	0.8± 0.8	1.6± 0.7	0.1± 0.4
Collias & Southwick	Apr. 1951	0.4± 0.8	0.4± 0.6	0.4± 0.6
Carpenter	June–Aug. 1959	1.0± 1.2	1.5± 1.5	0.5± 0.8
Chivers	June–Aug. 1967	n.a.	n.a.	n.a.
Smith	Sept.–Nov. 1967	0.4± 0.8	1.1± 1.1	0.6± 0.6
Mittermeier	Sept.–Oct. 1970	n.a.	n.a.	n.a.
Milton & Mittermeier	Apr. 1974	n.a.	n.a.	n.a.
Milton	Mar.–Apr. 1977	1.5± 1.4	2.4± 1.6	1.6± 1.0
Milton	July–Aug. 1977	2.0± 1.4	2.9± 1.6	2.2± 1.2
Milton	Nov.–Dec. 1977	0.9± 0.9	2.6± 1.4	2.5± 1.7
Milton	Mar.–Apr. 1978	1.0± 0.6	2.8± 1.3	3.2± 1.7
Milton	July–Aug. 1978	0.9± 0.7	2.7± 0.9	1.8± 1.4
Milton	Nov.–Dec. 1978	0.5± 0.8	3.3± 1.7	2.1± 1.3
Milton	Mar.–Apr. 1979	0.6± 1.1	2.3± 1.4	2.3± 0.9
Milton	July–Aug. 1979	1.3± 1.3	2.5± 1.7	1.5± 1.1
Milton	Jan. 1980	1.7± 1.0	2.7± 1.0	2.0± 1.4

[1] Estimates are based on the appearance of the animals, as in Carpenter (1934). My chronological estimates of these classes do not necessarily conform to Carpenter's (1934) and cannot be used in comparison with Glander's (1980) chronological data. I estimate that the infant stage lasts approximately 14 months. Infant-I is from birth to around 2 months of age; Infant-II, from 2 to around 8 months; Infant-III, from 8 to around 14 months.

n.a. = data not available for this calculation.

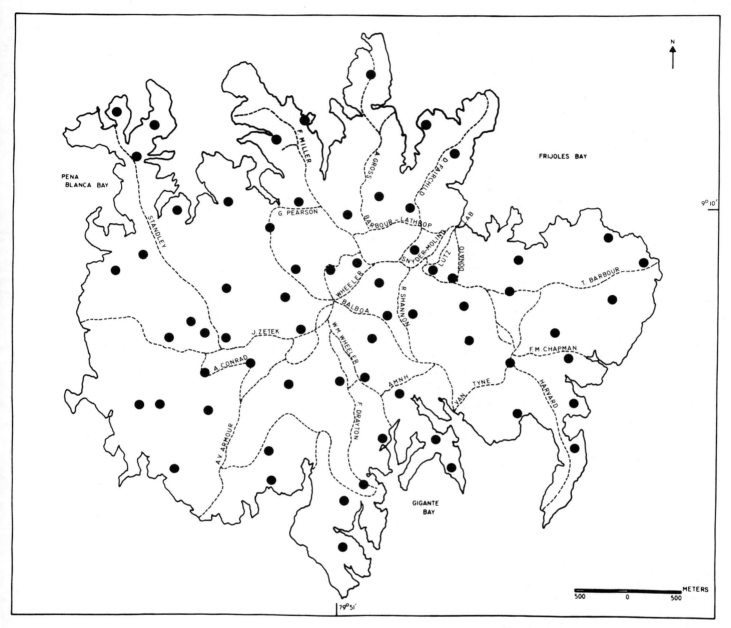

Figure 1. Map of Barro Colorado Island showing approximate locations of the 65 howler monkey troops counted on day 2 of the March 1977 island-wide troop count. See text for details of censusing technique.

census days. As can be seen in the figure, virtually the entire island is well saturated with howler troops. Furthermore, troops do not appear to be distributed in a random or aggregated pattern (allowing for certain temporary clumping effects presumably induced by clumping of some particular seasonal food source), but rather tend toward a relatively even distribution. A uniform distribution pattern of this nature between conspecific units indicates that the prior establishment of a unit in one area has a negative effect on the establishment of another unit in this same area (Bernstein, 1974). Such a distribution pattern implies intense competition for some limiting resource, generally food (Brian, 1965; Bernstein, 1974).

Troop Size

Different estimates for mean troop size, 1932–80, are presented in Table 1. Estimates should be compared with reference to time of year since these data indicate that troop size becomes smaller in the mid to late rainy season. My estimates (March–April 1977 and July–August 1979) were obtained by counting all individuals in each of 13 troops three times per year. Two known troops were always counted and the other 11 were randomly selected.

A comparison of Carpenter's April 1932 data with my March–April 1977 data show no significant difference in mean troop size between these two years 45 years apart ($t = 1.455$, $p \leq 0.05$). A further test comparing Carpenter's January 1935 data with my January 1980 data gave the same result. Though troop size fluctuates, there appears to be a strong central tendency for it to stabilize again around 19 individuals per troop (Carpenter, 1959; Southwick, 1963). The persistence through time of this mean troop size suggests that this is the optimal size for most troops on Barro Colorado, that conditions selecting for this size were the same in the 1930s that they are now and that there is strong selective pressure to maintain troop size around this mean.

Troop Composition

Different estimates for mean troop composition from 1932 to 1980 are presented in Table 2. As with troop size, data should be compared with reference to time of year at which the estimate was made. A comparison of Carpenter's April 1932 data with my March–April 1977 data showed a significant difference in troop composition between these two years ($\chi^2 = 14.66$, d.f. = 3, $p \leq .05$). Observed and expected values for adult males and adult females in both years were similar, but there were more juveniles than expected in 1932

and fewer in 1977. The opposite trend was shown for the infant class with underrepresentation of infants in 1932 and overrepresentation in 1977.

The ratio of adult males to adult females in the population was approximately the same in the 1930s as in the 1970s as was the ratio of adult animals to immatures. However, the relative proportion that infants and juveniles contribute to the immature class has shifted in favor of infants (see also Tables 3 and 4).

Births

As noted, the only input into this population can come about through births. Howlers do not have a discrete birth season on Barro Colorado and births can occur in any month of the year. As shown in Table 3, however, the input of new infants into the population varies between years. Furthermore, in some years births appear more clustered (December–June) than in others. Finally, it appears that, in general, fewer infants are born during the late rainy season than during other censusing periods. All of these observations relate to the differential survivorship of the previous generation of infants (see Altmann et al., 1977). If many females in the population wean or lose their infants at approximately the same time in one year, most will probably produce new young again at approximately the same time. Conversely, if young are weaned or lost at different times during the year, the following year's birth pattern will reflect this. In effect, the pattern of natality in any given year reflects the pattern of mortality the previous year. In addition, different troops show notably different compositions at the same time with respect to the number and ages of infants they contain. These different patterns suggest that infant survivorship varies between troops.

The gestation period for *Alouatta palliata* in Guanacaste Province, Costa Rica, averages 186 days (Glander, 1980). Receptive females cycle every month and from 1 to 4 months are generally required for impregnation. If a female loses a young infant, she generally begins cycling within 3 weeks and gives birth again within 10 months (Glander, 1980). The interbirth interval for howlers in Costa Rica is reported to be 22.5 months. The patterns reported for howlers in Costa Rica are similar in many respects to those I have observed for *A. palliata* in Panama. Data on marked adult females indicate that they are generally either nursing or expecting an infant. I estimate, judging from a small sample of three marked females monitored over a 4-year period, that the interbirth interval for howlers on Barro Colorado may average only around 17 months, but more data on marked indi-

Table 5. Howler monkey mortality by month

Year	Jan.	Feb.	Mar.	Apr.	May	June	July	Aug.	Sept.	Oct.	Nov.	Dec.	Total
1977	—	no data collected			—	J M	—	A F I F	I F	J ?	—	A F A ? *	7
1978	A M A F	SA F	—	J F A M	—	—	A M **	A F SA M J ? 2 ? ***	A F SA ? J ? 2I ?	A F 2SA F J F J ? A ?	—	—	22
1979	—	—	—	—	—	J F	—	2A M SA F J M I ?	A ?	—	A M	—	8
1980	A M	End of sample period											1

Based on cadavers found in forest. F = female; M = male; A = adult animal, all permanent teeth erupted and worn; SA = subadult, 3rd molars erupting or recently erupted, unworn; J = juvenile; I = infant; ? = dead howler, data on age and sex not obtained.
*Adult female seen badly wounded, with small infant; presumably both died. Also wounded young adult male seen, presumably died.
**Adult female seen ill, presumably died; Adult, sex unknown, seen crippled, presumably died.
***Infant seen crippled, presumably died.

viduals over a longer period of time are needed to confirm this.

As shown in Table 2, the relative proportion of adult females in the population is approximately the same now as it was in the early 1930s, but the relative proportion of infants has increased. Thus the birth rate now is higher, which in turn suggests that the interbirth interval is shorter. This shorter interbirth interval suggests that infant mortality may be higher now than it was in the 1930s.

Mortality

The ratio of adult females to infants, the large number of infants, and the small number of juveniles suggested that the death rate among immature animals might be high. To test this assumption, I totaled the number of newborn monkeys per troop for all six censuses in 1977 and 1978 (assuming that a newborn counted in one census would have ceased to be classified as a newborn by the next, but that no newborn would escape census) and divided by two to estimate the mean number of births per troop per year. I also calculated the mean number of adult females per troop observed during these six censuses. Dividing the mean number of newborns per troop (3.4) by the mean number of adult females per troop (8.23), I estimate that 0.41 monkeys were born per adult female per year. Assuming that monkeys are sexually immature for around 4 years and that the birth rate and total population size of these monkeys had not changed

over the past 4 years, the average number of immature animals per troop should be 0.41 × 8.23 × 4, or 13.5, if none die. During these six censuses, I only observed an average of 8.23 immature monkeys per troop, so that 39% of the expected number of juvenile and infant monkeys were missing from the population. It should be stressed that this is a minimum estimate of mortality since the actual birth rate is probably higher than those used in these calculations. Thus censusing data support the view that a considerable number of newborn individuals do not survive to adulthood.

There are no data to suggest that howlers do not have an equal sex ratio at birth and some that suggest they do (Glander, 1980). Yet censusing data (1932–80) consistently show that the adult sex ratio is skewed in favor of females (Table 2). There are no all male howler bands on Barro Colorado nor are lone males encountered with sufficient frequency to correct for this unequal sex ratio. Because of their white scrotum, adult male howlers are unmistakable as a class. The probability that immature males may be counted as females cannot be ruled out. In my two study troops, however, where many individuals are known, there are more adult females than adult males. This imbalance is not due to immature males' being mistaken for females. These data suggest that a female infant born into this population has a higher probability of attaining adulthood than a male infant.

To quantify patterns of howler mortality, records were kept of all dead howlers found in the forest between June 1977 and January 1980 (see Table 5). Most cadavers were found either by me or by long-term residents carrying out monthly sampling activities in the forest who reported any dead animals to me. During the total sampling period, 38 dead howlers were found. Thirty-six of the cadavers were identified as to age, sex, or both; 56% were full adults, and 44% were subadults, juveniles, or infants.

Twenty-seven of the 38 deaths occurred in the mid to late rainy season between the months of August and October. The significantly higher ($\chi^2 = 10.77$; d.f. = 1; $p < 0.01$) number of howler monkey deaths at this time of year indicates that this is the peak in overall howler mortality. Data collected by Chivers (July–August 1967) and Smith (September–November 1967) show that mean troop size decreased during 1967 (Table 1). In addition, in the two troops that I observed intensively between 1974 and 1975, mean troop size declined from 17 animals in July to 13 animals by the end of November, with most animals disappearing between September and November.

Cause of death in most cases could not be determined. Of six adult males, four appear to have died primarily of old age (teeth were very heavily worn), and one young male appeared to have died from a fall. Old age was implicated in the deaths of two adult females. Falls were implicated in two other adult deaths. A total of four subadult females were found, but cause of death could not be determined. One juvenile and two infants appear to have died from massive screwworm infestations of former botfly cavities (N. Gale, pers. comm.). One infant female apparently suffered a physiological malfunction. It is not surprising that few infants and juveniles were found, in spite of census evidence indicating a high mortality of immatures. The smaller size and softer skeletal materials of younger animals would be harder to find and more completely destroyed in the forest than the harder and more obvious skeletal materials of older animals.

Predation

The role of predation in the regulation of this population is not known. I have never seen a howler on Barro Colorado attacked by a predator, though Carpenter (1934) reported one ocelot attack on a juvenile. Eagles, big cats, and other large potential predators on howler monkeys are no longer seen on Barro Colorado. A certain percentage of immature animals may be lost to predation each year, perhaps by ocelots, tayras, or large snakes. Mammalian and avian predation on howlers on Barro Colorado, however, does not appear to be intense and probably has a negligible effect on overall population size.

Disease

The effects of disease on the howler population are not known. As discussed above, occasional attacks of yellow fever can decimate howler populations, but such events occur infrequently. Howlers on Barro Colorado may suffer from any number of as yet undetected diseases, and such diseases may well show seasonal patterns. Personal observation confirms that howlers on Barro Colorado have endoparasites in both the stomach and hindgut. The parasite loads borne by individual animals must affect their general health, but I have no means of assessing such effects on howler mortality. The possible role played by ectoparasites in regulating this population is discussed in detail below.

In summary, the data presented above indicate that the Barro Colorado howler population is not increasing in size and that mortality rather than curtailment of reproduction is the principal factor limiting growth. Mortality affects all age classes but seems particularly heavy among younger individuals. Senescence, falls, parasitism, physiological malfunctions, and predation have been implicated as possible causes of death. The high percentage of deaths during the mid to late rainy season, the scarcity of births at this time, and the relative paucity of juvenile animals in the population at all times suggest that there may be another factor involved in howler mortality: namely, the profound effect that poor diet can have on the survivorship of particular individuals in the population depending on age, general health, and other factors.

DIETARY QUALITY

Dietary quality is being increasingly implicated as a density regulating mechanism in studies of herbivore populations (see Westoby, 1974; Parra, 1978; Grant, 1978; Milton, 1979, for a discussion of the importance of dietary quality to herbivores). The supposed superabundance of food at this trophic level has been shown to be largely a myth, since most vegetation is not of suitable quality to support life. Primary consumers as disparate as pond snails (Eisenberg, 1970), desert ants (Bernstein, 1974), Canadian voles (Grant, 1978), and African buffalo (Sinclair, 1974) have been shown to be regulated, at least in part, by the relative availability of suitable food items.

The types and amounts of particular plant foods in the diet in any one day, and even the time scale on which such foods are eaten and combined in the gut, serve to define dietary quality for that particular day. Plant parts vary considerably in nutritional quality. Some items such as young leaves contain considerable protein of high biological value; other items such as fruits are rich in ready energy components. Nonetheless, many plant parts are deficient in one or more of the essential nutrients, are high in indigestible cell wall materials and contain secondary compounds that can interfere with the digestion of essential nutrients or be toxic to the feeder. Primary consumers, particularly relatively large arboreal animals such as howler monkeys, must generally mix and match foods of different categories and species together each day to obtain the proper complementary amounts of the various essential nutrients. If the animal eats poor quality food, it obtains inadequate nutrition. Moreover, it makes a temporal commitment based on its passage rate of ingesta (Milton, 1981), that is, it cannot eat another meal until a certain amount of time has elapsed. The body size of the feeder and its metabolic and other requirements thus define the range of potential dietary items (Parra, 1978; Bauchop, 1978; Van Soest, 1981). For example, few small mammal species can rely on diets high in bulky, low energy foods while many larger mammals can do quite well on such diets.

If dietary quality persistently falls below the required level, starvation is the inevitable result. If energy intake is insufficient to meet daily requirements, stored body fat as well as amino acids in foods will be catabolized for energy. Thus particular amino acids needed for protein synthesis in the body will become less available. When amino acid intake is insufficient there is a rapid decrease of liver protein and a lowering of resistance to toxic injury (Albanese and Orto, 1968, citing work by Gyorgy and Goldblatt, 1949). The liver is believed to be a major detoxication site for plant secondary compounds (Scheline, 1968; Williams, 1969). High foliage diets, being low in ready energy and containing toxic materials, may thus cause difficulty to any herbivore that cannot satisfy its energetic needs. Additionally, studies show that diets insufficient in protein reduce overall food intake which in turn simply intensifies the original energy deficit (Roe, 1968).

Physiological data on the energy and protein requirements of howler monkeys confirm that they require plant foods of a relatively high nutritional quality to remain in energy and nitrogen balance each day (Nagy and Milton, 1979a, b; Milton et al., 1979; Milton, 1979; Milton et al., 1980). An estimated 25 to 36% of their required daily energy (estimated at 355.8 kJ/kg/day for an adult animal) can apparently be provided by end products of fermentation, but data suggest that the majority must come from their foods (Nagy and Milton, 1979a; Milton et al., 1980; Milton and McBee, 1982). The estimated protein threshold for an adult howler is 10 to 14% protein per unit dry weight and howlers generally have to take in some 24

g of protein each day to remain in positive nitrogen balance (Milton et al., 1980). Transit time of food averages 20 hours for time of first appearance and an estimated 30+ hours to clear the tract (Milton et al., 1980). Thus data show that howler monkeys, which are entirely primary consumers, are best nourished when they have a variety of high quality dietary items available, particularly young leaves with a high protein-to-cell-wall ratio and fruits with considerable ready energy. If the relative abundance of foods from either of these two categories drops below certain acceptable levels, the howler diet may well become imbalanced.

PEAKS, VALLEYS, AND GAPS IN PRIMARY PRODUCTIVITY

The forest on Barro Colorado is characterized by high species diversity with low densities of particular species (Knight, 1975; Milton, 1977, 1980). Nonetheless, many species show a significant tendency toward a clumped spatial distribution of individuals (Milton, 1977, 1980; Thorington et al., this volume). Phenological data collected over a 5-year period (Leigh and Windsor, this volume) show that there are pronounced island-wide peaks and valleys in the production of new leaves, fruits, and flowers by canopy tree species in this forest, both overall and by category. In particular, during the mid to late rainy season (August–November) and the transition to dry season (December–January), production of seasonal foods from one or all of these categories may be depressed.

Data show that the percentage of feeding time a howler monkey spends per month on a given food category is influenced by the relative availability of food from that category in the forest (Milton, 1977). On a monthly basis, there was a significant positive correlation between the time howlers spent eating fruit and the number of tree species bearing fruit ($r_s = 0.93$, $p < 0.01$, $n = 7$); there was a significant negative correlation between the time spent eating new leaves and the number of tree species bearing new leaves ($r_s = -0.89$, $p = 0.01$, $n = 7$), but there was a stronger negative correlation between time spent eating leaves and the number of tree species bearing fruit ($r_s = -1.00$, $p < 0.002$, $n = 7$). Thus it would appear that howlers eat more leaves when there is less fruit available. Data show that at certain times of year when fruit is in short supply howlers may spend more than 80% of monthly feeding time eating only leaves. Since leaves are a very poor source of ready energy (averaging only around 3 to 4% nonstructural carbohydrates per unit dry weight), and howlers apparently can derive only some one-fourth to one-third of daily energetic requirements from fermentation end products, at such times they may be particularly taxed with respect to remaining in positive energy balance. If the available leaves are low in protein as well, howlers may also have problems remaining in positive nitrogen balance. Younger individuals require nutrients not only for maintenance but also for growth and have a proportionately higher demand for energy per unit body weight than adults. Thus, they might have considerably more difficulty than larger animals in meeting their nutritional demands at such times.

Phenological data show that these lows in overall food production are persistent annual patterns. However, the peaks and valleys vary in their intensity from year to year. For example, the mid to late rainy season of 1974 seemed relatively severe in terms of food limitations. The laboratory clearing was often full of smaller (and larger) mammals looking for supplementary food and I noted a marked drop in troop size in my two study troops. Conversely, the mid to late rainy season of 1977 seemed particularly benign with little food stress noted. Certain years are unusually severe. Kaufmann (1962), in his work with coatis on Barro Colorado Island, noted extremely high mortality during the late rainy season and remarked on the apparent food shortage. Both Foster (1973; this volume, 1982b) and Mittermeier (1973) worked on Barro Colorado during the late rainy season of 1970 and noted very high mortality with unusual numbers of dead animals both seen and detected by odor. The 1970 food shortage seemed due to an unusually rainy dry season that year. The rain interfered with pollination and fruit set by many tree species with the result that fruit crops never materialized or were too poor to provide much food (Foster, 1973; this volume, 1982b).

Times other than the mid to late rainy season also show evidence of producing food stress. In January 1975, for example, when little fruit or new leaves appeared to be available, howler troops were noted in competitive encounters over leaf sources in two different areas of the island.

A finer level of analysis of fruit production by particular tree species shows that food availability, both island-wide and in particular areas, can be markedly affected if a particular tree species does not produce an anticipated fruit crop. For example, in 1977 *Trichilia cipo* (mean nonstructural carbohydrates = 16% per unit dry weight of aril, mean crude fat = 38% per unit dry weight of aril) produced a massive fruit crop during September–October and was heavily fed on by howlers. Considerable *Trichilia cipo* fruit was also available during my study in 1974 (September–October) and during a study carried out by M. and D. Leighton in 1976 (pers. comm.). In 1978, however, no fruit of this species was available on the island (pers. obser.). Animals accustomed to using the en-ergy-rich arils of this fruit during September–October had to find supplementary energy sources.

This example can be amplified by many others. *Coccoloba parimensis* (no data on nutritional content) provided a food buffer for many mammals during the late rainy season of 1977 by producing a massive fruit crop from October into December. In 1978, however, I noted no fruit of this species; nor was any noted during my work in 1974. *Brosimum alicastrum*, a rich ready-energy source (per unit dry weight of fruit pulp, mean nonstructural carbohydrate content = 21%), produced a massive island-wide fruit crop in June–July 1974, and was a food highly preferred by howlers. No data on ripe fruit production by this species are available for 1975 or 1976. In 1977 and 1978, however, this species did not appear to produce ripe fruit anywhere on the island. A moderate crop was produced in 1979 but was quickly exhausted, in contrast to the long duration of the 1974 crop (pers. obser.).

Not only species but also individal trees of particular species or clumps of such trees may skip years in fruit production. *Spondias mombin*, for example (mean nonstructural carbohydrate content = 40% per unit dry weight of fruit pulp), has fruited island-wide for at least the past 6 years. However, I have noted that particular individuals or clumps of individuals of this species have skipped years in fruit production. Nonvolant mammals, loyal to particular home range areas and dependent on crops of *Spondias* fruit during August–September, may thus be faced with little or no fruit of this species in their supplying area.

Data on similar fluctuations in production of new leaves (or flowers) are not available, but these dietary categories may well show similar variability under closer examination. The fruiting patterns discussed above imply that howler monkeys and other animals which preferentially exploit soft-pulped sugary fruits are often on uncertain ground with respect to year-to-year availability of such resources. These animals presumably have mechanisms that help them cope with such shortages. In the case of howler monkeys, their generally sedentary mode of life and digestive physiology (see Nagy and Milton, 1979a; Milton, 1980; and Milton and McBee, 1982) allow them to supplement their diet to a certain extent with leaves when fruit is scarce.

All howlers may feel dietary stress during the mid to late rainy season for this is the most prolonged single low point in the overall production of higher quality seasonal food. Certain sex and age classes, however, may be stressed far more severely than others. Younger animals, because of elevated metabolic and other nutritional demands, require high quality foods and further can be displaced from limited rich food sources by larger animals. In addition, old animals

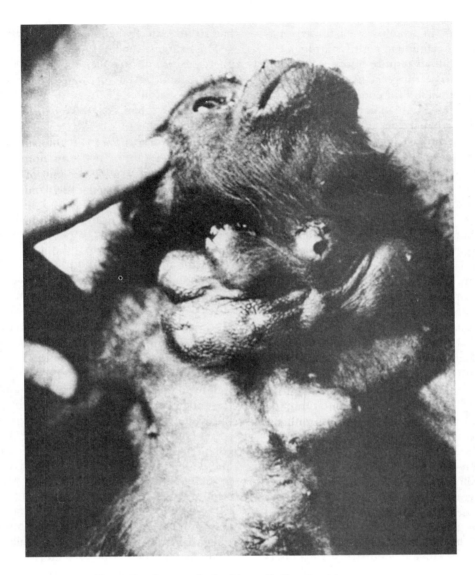

Figure 2. An anesthetized juvenile female with numerous botfly infestations in late instar stages. Scars of former botfly infestations can also be seen. The animal survived this botfly attack but disappeared at a later date.

whose teeth are worn might have problems reducing tough leaf tissues to fine enough particles for maximal fermentation activities; pregnant or lactating females might likewise suffer hardship. If, however, howler mortality on Barro Colorado is due primarily to the effects of lowered dietary quality, one cannot help but wonder why no more obvious evidence of nutrient deprivation is noted in the population. This suggests that the effects of stress may be subtle and that more than one factor, acting in combination with nutrient stress, may contribute to howler mortality. The most

likely factor would appear to be parasites, either primary infestations of botfly larvae or secondary infestations of screwworm larvae in abandoned botfly cavities.

PARASITES

Howler monkeys on Barro Colorado are persistently infested with larvae of the botfly *Dermatobia hominis* (Figure 2). In his 1967–68 work, Smith (1977) noted that botfly infestations differed in intensity, depend-

MILTON

ing on the time of the year monkeys were examined. Parasitism was higher from May through July than from October through April. In the May–July period, juvenile animals and females without infants had more botflies than other sex-age classes. It was suggested that a causal relationship might exist between botfly infestations and poor health in howlers and that botflies might limit howler population density through adult mortality and reduced reproductive success.

My data on botfly infestations, collected between 1977 and 1980, confirm that these larvae are far more evident at certain times of the year than at others. Botflies were especially prevalent during January, June, September, and October—but there was considerable variability between years, between troops, and between individuals in the degree of infestation. Based on counts of active larvae on howlers anesthetized for marking, juveniles and old adult males had more botflies per individual than other age classes. At times an individual animal carried as many as eight or ten of the parasites in late instar stages.

There is no doubt that botflies contribute to overall howler mortality but, unlike Smith (1977), I do not regard them as the principal density-regulating mechanism in this population. My reasons for thinking this are based on several factors, one of which is the actual life history of the parasite. Botfly eggs are not laid directly on howlers or other potential hosts but rather deposited by gravid females on the abdomen of mosquitos and other blood-sucking insects (Markell and Voge, 1971). These insects seek a blood meal and deposit botfly eggs on the hair or skin of their host. The body heat of the animal activates the larvae, which hatch and burrow into the skin. Howlers are typically infested in the neck and adjacent regions where hair is relatively sparse. As the larvae grow, lesions develop. After the completion of the fourth instar, the larvae drop from the body of the host to the ground to pupate. Thus in order to get to howlers, botfly eggs have to pass through an intermediary, and in effect the success of the intermediary in finding a blood meal determines the eventual success of the larvae. However, botfly larvae generally do not appear to kill their hosts. I have marked adults that have been repeatedly infested with massive crops of botfly larvae over a 7-year period, and these animals are still alive. Animals captured for marking show healed scars of former botfly larvae. How then can botfly larvae be said to contribute to howler mortality? As noted, Smith (1977) suggested that poor health and an increased botfly load might somehow be correlated and singled out juveniles and infantless adult females as the most infested classes. This raises the question of why these classes might be in generally poorer health than other sex-age classes. If these two classes of individuals are receiving a diet that is below the standard of the diet of other individuals in the population, one would expect them to be in poorer health. The reasons why juvenile animals as a class might feel special nutrient stress have already been discussed. Infantless females—which may be either younger individuals or very old animals past their reproductive prime—might also be displaced from better food sources by more reproductively active females, particularly primiparous females (Jones, 1978) or adult males. Thus it is not improbable that these two classes of individuals might well be in poorer health than other individuals in the population if dietary resources of higher quality were limited.

Though many animals survive botfly attacks each year, certainly some do not. Botfly larvae are eating the muscle tissue of howlers and animals with heavy infestations must take in sufficient food to replace these losses. Inadequate nutrition would put an even greater stress on heavily infested individuals and repeated infestations several times per year could ultimately result in debilitation and death. Of more concern in an immediate sense, however, is death due to infestations of screwworm larvae, for once these larvae enter old botfly-wound cavities, death quickly results. I have no data on the species of screwworm flies on Barro Colorado. My data suggest that June and September are peak times for fly activity. The flies apparently lay eggs in lesions left by the pupating botfly larvae, and the hatching screwworm larvae gradually eat into the spinal area, head, or brain of their host, killing it. Thus botflies could contribute to howler mortality in two ways: first, by creating or exaggerating a condition of ill health that would be further intensified by nutrient stress and, second, by providing screwworm flies with access areas for egg-laying on howlers or entry points for other secondary infections. In the mid to late rainy season, the combination of rainy weather, lowered availability of fruit and new leaves, and a high incidence of botflies and screwworm flies in the population could act in concert to produce the higher mortality rates observed.

SOCIAL FACTORS

Social factors may also contribute secondarily to howler mortality. Jones (1978; 1980) has suggested that intense competition for troop membership takes place in mantled howler monkeys living in riparian and deciduous forest in Guanacaste, Costa Rica. Young animals enter the existing dominance hierarchy with low status, whether they are natal members or immigrants, and, as stressed, "status is not conferred on young animals without effort" (Jones, 1980:395). Jones suggests that young adults not achieving positions at the top of the dominance hierarchy fail to succeed within the group as a whole. These animals, both male and female, may then emigrate and try to secure a dominant position in another troop. Emigration and immigration of juvenile animals during the dry season have also been noted (Jones, 1980). I would predict that low-ranking individuals of all ages, particularly those unable to secure a position in a troop, would suffer greater mortality than higher-ranking individuals.

The study sites in Guanacaste are more seasonal and less floristically diverse than my sites on Barro Colorado (Glander, 1975; Milton, 1980). This suggests that higher-quality dietary resources are more patchily distributed in Guanacaste and, therefore, that competition for these limited resources may be more intense. Jones suggests that the dominance system she has observed may represent a response to intense competition for a limited supply of palatable leaves. My data suggest that the same type of competition for troop membership may be occurring on Barro Colorado. Lone males are encountered in the forest, and on three occasions the same subgroup, consisting of an adult male and two juveniles, was observed. Both immigration and emigration of adult male animals have been observed in two troops where adult male members are known (pers. obs.). Movement of juvenile and adult female animals between troops may also occur. Such exchanges may take place when two troops are in proximity and thus be difficult to detect without marked animals. The underrepresentation of juveniles in this population, as well as the number of subadult female animals found dead, could have resulted, at least in part, from the presumed low status of these animals and the subsequent effects of low rank, particularly with respect to adequate access to limited higher quality dietary items. It is therefore suggested that competition for troop membership occurs on Barro Colorado and may contribute to greater mortality of lower-ranking individuals.

POPULATION STUDIES OF HOWLERS IN OTHER AREAS

A recent study by Rudran (1979) examined demography and social mobility in a population of red howlers (*Alouatta seniculus*) living in the llanos of Venezuela. Within this population, in contrast to Barro Colorado, immature individuals slightly outnumbered adults. The sex ratio favored females in the adult age class and males in the intermediate age class which may parallel the situation on Barro Col-

orado. Births and immigration were slightly greater than deaths plus emigration and the population was increasing at a rate of 1.5% per year. In this population the most frequent cause of mortality was infanticide. All male howler bands invaded established troops, drove off the resident males, and killed infants. Limited food resources were singled out as the ultimate factor promoting infanticide, viewed by Rudran as the elimination of food competitors which do not benefit the infanticidal individual or his offspring.

There are no all male howler bands on Barro Colorado, and in all the published material on this population there is only one record of a male behaving aggressively toward an infant. Collias and Southwick (1952) reported seeing an adult male attack an infant and bite off part of its tail. Their work, however, took place during a period of troop adjustment when social stress may have been more evident in the population. Given the large number of observer hours spent examining howler behavior on Barro Colorado and the lack of any reported infanticide, such deaths, if they occur, must be rare.

Food resources and dietary quality also appear to play an important role in regulating the size of the howler monkey population in Guanacaste, Costa Rica (Glander, 1975). Here data suggest that the population may currently be in a state of expansion, but the sample size is too small for any conclusive statement. As noted, Guanacaste is a more seasonal habitat than Barro Colorado and at times howlers there eat high percentages of leaves from only one or two tree species for long periods of time. During Glander's initial study, six animals died in a single 2-week period from what appeared to be massive toxemia, and an additional animal was severely convulsed. Three of these dead animals were pregnant females, and one was a juvenile female (three were unidentified). The convulsing animal was also a juvenile female. During January, when these deaths occurred, there was heavy leaf eating and little if any fruit eating. The ingestion of quantities of low-energy food over a period of days and the physiological cycle between inadequate energy, dietary protein and impaired liver function could ultimately have resulted in toxemia and death. No such dramatic incidents have been noted on Barro Colorado where the forest is less seasonal and more diverse. Howlers generally do not have to eat large quantities of leaves from one or two tree species for weeks at a time as they do in Guanacaste. Thus, on Barro Colorado, the effects of a low-energy diet are probably more subtle although ultimately, if similar dietary conditions persisted, the same results presumably would be observed.

It therefore appears that dietary quality may be the ultimate factor regulating all three of these howler

Table 6. Body weights and density estimates of howler monkeys from three different study sites

Site	Average body weight, adult male ($\overline{X} \pm SD$) (kg)	Average body weight, adult female ($\overline{X} \pm SD$) (kg)	Number of monkeys per hectare	Estimated howler biomass per hectare[1] (kg)
Guarico State, Venezuela (154.8 ha. for 176.7 monkeys: Rudran, 1979)	6.7 ± 0.33	4.5 ± 0.17	1.14	6.4
Guanacaste, Costa Rica (9.9 ha. for 11 monkeys: Glander, 1975)	6.5 ± 0.49	5.0 ± 0.22	1.11	6.4
Barro Colorado, Panama (1475 ha. for 1300 monkeys: Milton, this text)	7.9 ± 0.86	6.3 ± 0.50	0.88	6.3

[1] For this calculation, average weights of adult males and females from each site were averaged and multiplied times the number of monkeys per hectare to get a crude estimate of howler biomass per hectare.

monkey populations (Venezuela, Costa Rica, and Panama), although the proximate mechanisms appear to differ between sites. Both the Venezuelan and Costa Rican sites are vegetationally less diverse than Barro Colorado. They are also more seasonal habitats. This suggests that, per unit area, dietary quality may be lower and that seasonal fluctuations in food availability may be more severe. The impression is strengthened by the fact that adult males and adult females from both areas weigh less than adult howlers from Barro Colorado (see Table 6). In all three sites, however, the estimated howler biomass per hectare of study area appears approximately the same.

OVERVIEW OF THE BARRO COLORADO ISLAND HOWLER MONKEY POPULATION

The demographic data presented above cover a period of less than 3 years. Life table data are still scant though they are slowly being compiled. It is clear that considerably more information is required before any definitive statements can be made concerning the particular mechanisms involved in regulating the Barro Colorado howler monkey population. Material presented above, however, suggest the following overview.

The generally high species diversity characterizing the Barro Colorado forest as a whole and the persistent tendency for howler troops to stabilize at around 19 individuals suggest that higher-quality dietary resources on Barro Colorado are more or less homogeneously distributed over the entire island. Troop size and composition and the pattern of troop distribution appear to reflect adaptations to the distribution patterns of these foods and suggest that such resources are best exploited by individual howlers when they are organized in this manner. The lack of any notable growth in this population over at least the past 6 years suggests that the island is saturated with howlers. It also suggests that population size is limited in some manner. It has been demonstrated that howlers require dietary items of relatively high nutritional quality and that such items are at times in short supply in the forest. It is suggested that limitations to the amount of high-quality foods available to howlers, particularly during periods of scarcity and abnormal years, may in turn set a limit to the number of animals that can be supported on the island. The relative proportion of juvenile animals to infants suggests that natality is high but that few newborns survive to reproductive maturity. The lack of any single clearly defined birth peak for the population and the birth of at least some infants throughout the year appear to reflect a reproductive strategy oriented toward overcoming problems associated with a diet based on items that are variable in quality, patchily distributed in space, and often unpredictable or unavailable in time. Given the fact that howlers apparently cannot forecast the timing of many of these dietary shortages, the best reproductive strategy for each female would appear to be to produce a new infant as often as possible (consistent with her health, the lactation requirements of each infant, and the like), rather than wait and give birth at only one time of the year. In this manner, at least some offspring should overcome the various dietary and other problems affecting survivorship and reach adulthood. Data indicate that, on reaching adulthood, such individuals may then live an additional 10 to 15 years as reproductively active members of the population.

ACKNOWLEDGMENTS

This paper is dedicated to C. R. Carpenter in appreciation for the pioneering role he played in primate field studies and the high standards set by his meticulous observations of wild primates. Appreciation also goes to C. H. Southwick who in 1963 stressed the value of the Barro Colorado howler population with respect to the examination of many interesting demographic questions.

I thank all of the people who graciously got up at 4:00 A.M. two mornings in a row, first in 1977 and then in 1979, to help me census howler troops. For the 1977 census, Bill and Dan Glanz and Stan Rand provided special help while Mark Davis and the Dartmouth Field Class aided with the 1979 census. I thank all those who gave me data on the dead, particularly Nick Brokaw, Judy Gradwohl, Deedra McClearn, and Bonifacio de León, who really have an eye for such events. Bill Glanz, Tom Milton, Virginia Hayssen, Jeff Stelzner, and Andrew Cockburn made valuable comments on the manuscript. In particular, I thank Glenn Hausfater for his suggestions and help with data analysis. This research was supported by a postdoctoral fellowship from the Smithsonian Institution, with Egbert Leigh serving as my advisor.

LITERATURE CITED

Altmann, J., S. A. Altmann, G. Hausfater, and S. A. McCuskey
1977.   Life History of Yellow Baboons: Physical Development, Reproductive Parameters and Infant Mortality. *Primates*, 18: 315–330.

Albanese, A. A., and L. A. Orto
1968.   The Proteins and Amino Acids. Pages 95–155 in *Modern Nutrition in Health and Disease*, edited by M. G. Wohl and R. S. Goodhart. Philadelphia: Lea & Febiger.

Bauchop, T.
1978.   Digestion of Leaves in Vertebrate Arboreal Folivores. Pages 193–204 in *The Ecology of Arboreal Folivores*, edited by G. Gene Montgomery. Washington, D.C.: Smithsonian Institution Press.

Bernstein, R. A.
1974.   Seasonal Food Abundance and Foraging Activity in Some Desert Ants. *American Naturalist*, 108: 490–499.

Brian, M. V.
1965.   *Social Insect Populations*. New York: Academic Press.

Carpenter, C. R.
1934.   A Field Study of the Behavior and Social Relations of Howling Monkeys. *Comp. Psychol. Monog.*, 10:1–168.
1962.   Field Studies of a Primate Population. Pages 286–94 in *Roots of Behavior*, edited by E. L. Bliss. New York: Harper and Row.

Chivers, D.
1969.   On the Daily Behavior and Spacing of Howler Monkey Groups. *Folia Primatol.*, 10:48–102.

Collias, D. E., and C. H. Southwick
1952.   A Field Study of the Population Density and Social Organization in Howler Monkeys. *Proc. Amer. Phil. Soc.*, 96:144–156.

Eisenberg, J. F., and R. W. Thorington
1973.   A Preliminary Analysis of a Neotropical Mammal Fauna. *Biotropica*, 5:150–161.

Eisenberg, R. M.
1970.   The Role of Food in the Regulation of the Pond Snail, *Lymnaea elodes*. *Ecology*, 51:680–684.

Foster, R. B.
1973.   Seasonality of Fruit Production and Seed Fall in a Tropical Forest Ecosystem in Panama. Ph.D. thesis, Duke University.
1982a.   The Seasonal Rhythm of Fruitfall on Barro Colorado Island. Pages 151–172 in *The Ecology of a Tropical Forest*, edited by Egbert G. Leigh, Jr., et al. Washington, D.C.: Smithsonian Institution Press.
1982b.   Famine on Barro Colorado Island. Pages 201–212 in *The Ecology of a Tropical Forest*, edited by Egbert G. Leigh, Jr., et al. Washington, D.C.: Smithsonian Institution Press.

Foster, R. B., and N. V. Brokaw
1982.   Structure and History of the Vegetation of Barro Colorado Island. Pages 67–81 in *The Ecology of a Tropical Forest*, edited by Egbert G. Leigh, Jr., et al. Washington, D.C.: Smithsonian Institution Press.

Glander, K. E.
1975.   Habitat and Resource Utilization: An Ecological View of Social Organization in Mantled Howler Monkeys. Ph. D. thesis, University of Chicago.
1980.   Reproduction and Population Growth in Free-ranging Mantled Howler Monkeys. *Amer. J. Phys. Anthrop.*, 53: 25–36.

Glanz, W. E.
1982.   The Terrestrial Mammal Fauna of Barro Colorado Island: Censuses and Long-term Changes. Pages 455–468 in *The Ecology of a Tropical Forest*, edited by Egbert G. Leigh, Jr., et al. Washington, D.C.: Smithsonian Institution Press.

Grant, P. R.
1978.   Dispersal in Relation to Carrying Capacity. *Proceedings of the National Academy of Sciences, USA,* 75:2854–2858.

Hladik, A., and C. M. Hladik
1969.   Rapports trophiques entre végétation et primates dan la forêt de Barro Colorado (Panama). *Terre et Vie,* 23:25–117.

Jones, C. B.
1978.   Aspects of Reproductive Behavior in the Mantled Howler Monkey, *Alouatta palliata* Gray. Ph.D. dissertation, Cornell University.
1980.   The Function of Status in the Mantled Howler Monkey, *Alouatta palliata* Gray: Intraspecific Competition for Group Membership in a Folivorous Neotropical Primate. *Primates,* 21:389–405.

Kaufmann, J. H.
1962.   Ecology and Social Behavior of the Coati, *Nasua narica,* on Barro Colorado Island, Panama. *University of California Pub. in Zool.,* 60(3): 95–222.

Knight, D. H.
1975.   A Phytosociological Analysis of a Species-rich Tropical Forest on Barro Colorado Island, Panama. *Ecological Monographs,* 45: 259–284.

Leigh, E. G., Jr., and D. M. Windsor
1982.   Forest Production and Regulation of Primary Consumers on Barro Colorado Island. Pages 111–122 in *The Ecology of a Tropical Forest,* edited by Egbert G. Leigh, Jr., et al. Washington, D.C.: Smithsonian Institution Press.

Markell, E. K., and M. Voge
1971.   *Medical Parasitology.* Philadelphia: W. G. Saunders Company.

Mittermeier, R. A.
1973.   Group Activity and Population Dynamics of the Howler Monkey on Barro Colorado Island. *Primates,* 14:1–19.

Milton, K.
1975.   Urine-rubbing Behavior in the Mantled Howler Monkey. *Folia primatol.,* 23:105–112.
1977.   The Foraging Strategy of the Howler Monkey (*Alouatta palliata*) in the Tropical Forest of Barro Colorado Island, Panama. Ph.D. thesis, New York University.
1979.   Factors Influencing Leaf Choice by Howler Monkeys: A Test of Some Hypotheses of Food Selection by Generalist Herbivores. *American Naturalist,* 114:362–378.
1980.   *The Foraging Strategy of Howler Monkeys: A Study in Primate Economics.* New York: Columbia University Press.
1981.   Food Choice and Digestive Strategies of Two Sympatric Primate Species. *American Naturalist,* 117:496–505.

Milton, K., T. M. Casey, and K. K. Casey
1979.   The Basal Metabolism of Mantled Howler Monkeys. *Journal of Mammalogy,* 60:373–376.

Milton, K., P. J. Van Soest, and J. Robertson
1980.   Digestive Efficiencies of Wild Howler Monkeys. *Physiological Ecology,* 53:402–409.

Milton, K., and Richard H. McBee
1982.   Fermentative Digestion in the Hindgut of *Alouatta palliata. Comparative Biochemistry and Physiology* (in press).

Nagy, K., and K. Milton
1979a.   Energy Metabolism and Food Consumption by Wild Howler Monkeys. *Ecology,* 60:475–480.
1979b.   Aspects of Dietary Quality, Nutrient Assimilation and Water Balance in Wild Howler Monkeys. *Oecologia,* 39:249–258.

Parra, R.
1978.   Comparison of Foregut and Hindgut Fermentation in Herbivores. Pages 205–230 in *The Ecology of Arboreal Folivores,* edited by G. Gene Montgomery. Washington, D.C.: Smithsonian Institution Press.

Rowe, D. A.
1968.   Dietary Interrelationships. Pages 436–449 in *Modern Nutrition in Health and Disease,* edited by M. G. Wohl and R. S. Goodhart. Philadelphia: Lea & Febiger.

Rudran, R.
1979.   The Demography and Social Mobility of a Red Howler (*Alouatta seniculus*) Population in Venezuela. Pages 107–26 in *Vertebrate Ecology in the Northern Neotropics,* edited by J. F. Eisenberg. Washington, D.C.: Smithsonian Institution Press.

Scheline, H. J.
1968.   Drug Metabolism by Intestinal Microorganisms. *Journal of Pharmaceutical Sciences,* 57:2021–2037.

Sinclair, A. R. E.
1974.   The Natural Regulation of Buffalo Populations in East Africa. *East African Wildlife Journal,* 12:291–311.
1977.   *The African Buffalo.* Chicago: University of Chicago Press.

Smith, C. C.
1977.   Feeding Behavior and Social Organization in Howling Monkeys. Pages 97–126 in *Primate Ecology,* edited by T. H. Clutton-Brock. London: Academic Press.

Southwick, C. H.
1963.   Challenging aspects of the behavioral ecology of howling monkeys. Pages 185–91 in *Primate Social Behavior,* edited by C. H. Southwick. Princeton, N.J.: Van Nostrand.

Thorington, R. W., Jr., B. Tannenbaum, A. Tarak, and R. Rudran
1982.   Distribution of Trees on Barro Colorado Island. Pages 83–94 in *The Ecology of a Tropical Forest,* edited by Egbert G. Leigh, Jr., et al. Washington, D.C.: Smithsonian Institution Press.

Van Soest, P. J.
1981.   *Nutritional Ecology of the Ruminant.* Corvallis, Ore.: Washington and Oregon Press.

Westoby, M.
1974.   An Analysis of Diet Selection by Large Generalist Herbivores. *American Naturalist,* 108:290–304.

Williams, R. T.
1969.   *Detoxication Mechanisms.* New York: John Wiley & Sons.

The Genetic Structure and Socioecology of Howler Monkeys (*Alouatta palliata*) on Barro Colorado Island

JEFFERY W. FROEHLICH   Department of Anthropology, University of New Mexico, Albuquerque, New Mexico 87131

RICHARD W. THORINGTON, JR.   Division of Mammals, National Museum of Natural History, Smithsonian Institution, Washington, D.C. 20560

ABSTRACT

The howler monkeys of Barro Colorado Island exhibit very little genetic polymorphism in their serum proteins. An examination of approximately 25 loci in 80 individual animals demonstrated that there are approximately 1.5% heterozygous loci per individual. However, quantitative variation, which may be related to the detoxification of plant compounds, occurs in the serum esterases and in haptoglobin.

Variable fingerprint traits were used to examine genetic similarities and differences between *Alouatta* troops. Close genetic similarity implies common origin of troops. The pattern of differences between troops in the northeast corner of Barro Colorado suggests that two different troops of monkeys colonized one of the peninsulas. In another area, the genetic and historical data suggest that neighboring troops of presumed common origin differentiated as a result of socially mediated differences in rates of outbreeding.

Morphometric characters differ between troops in a manner which is only partly explained by the genetic relatedness of the troops. The pattern of differences is better explained as an effect of variable vegetational diversity on the growth and adult size of the animals. On Barro Colorado, howler monkeys grow biggest where they have access to the most diverse, mature forest.

Dental characteristics are linked both with fingerprint and tree diversity. They reflect both the genetic history of the troops and the vegetational differences between their home ranges, but not the same types of vegetational differences as are linked to body size.

Relationships between social and demographic factors suggested some unexpected relationships. Population density and biomass were closely linked, but troop size and home range were not allied with these. Instead, the latter two seem to be related to nonecological social factors of which adult sex ratio is one measure. Nonetheless, the proportion of subadults was closely linked to vegetational diversity and morphological traits, suggesting a moderate and variable degree of food limitation on population growth rates.

INTRODUCTION

When Barro Colorado Island was formed by the rising water of the Chagres River from 1907 to 1914, an unknown but probably small number of howler monkeys (*Alouatta palliata*) were trapped on the island and isolated from neighboring mainland populations. Half the island was covered by mature forest at that time, and the rest by various stages of second growth. During the ensuing years there was little farming, the forest regenerated, and an increasing percentage of the area of the island became habitable for howlers (Kenoyer, 1929; Bennett, 1963; Knight, 1975; Foster and Brokaw, this volume). In 1949, yellow fever swept across Barro Colorado Island. Between three-fourths and nine-tenths of the howler monkeys on the island were killed by the epidemic. The population rapidly increased again, so that now there is a dense population of howler monkeys on almost all parts of the island.

In reviewing this history, we perceived a number of questions concerning the genetic structure of this population and how it developed. First, are there distinguishable genetic differences between troops? If so, does the pattern of genetic differences and similarities merely reflect geographic proximity, due both to the common origin of neighbors and subsequent genetic exchange? If not, does the pattern also reflect the history of howler dispersion from the more central parts of the island, which were habitable when the island was formed (Chapman, 1929; Carpenter, 1934), into the peripheral peninsulas which have become habitable for *Alouatta* only more recently? Furthermore, are there other factors, such as social interactions between troops, which affect the patterns of genetic relatedness?

Finally, might environmental factors, such as nutrition, lead to phenotypic differences between howler monkeys in different areas? It seemed unlikely from the history noted above that all parts of the island would be equally suitable for howler monkeys.

In this paper we describe and analyze our data on the animals (serological polymorphisms, fingerprint variations, and morphological measurements), data on their social structure (including troop size and sex ratios) and on their local environments (such as diversity of tree species and relative isolation by water). The analyses tell us how these variables are associated one with another and suggest how they affect the biology of howler monkeys on Barro Colorado Island.

METHODS

Data Collection

This study was conducted from 1972 to 1979 on the northeast corner of Barro Colorado Island, Republic of Panama. The study area comprises approximately 165 ha., or one-tenth of the island, and includes the Lutz and Allee ravines which border the laboratory clearing, the Fairchild and Gross peninsulas, and small Orchid Island, which lies off the Gross Peninsula (Figure 1). As shown, the study area borders on the more maturely forested central plateau. It includes diverse topography and forest types.

We captured 125 animals, mostly from eight contiguous troops. The animals were captured with a CO_2 dart gun, using techniques that have been described by Scott et al. (1976) and Thorington et al. (1979). The animals were studied, marked, and released again in the vicinity of their troops. The mortality rate resulting directly from capturing, handling, and releasing the animals was 4%. Other mortality resulted from an unsuccessful attempt to use radiocollars.

While the animals were in hand, we drew blood samples, using techniques described by Froehlich et al. (1977). Red cells were separated, washed, and stored in a common freezer before shipment. These have been analyzed electrophoretically for variations in 22 red cell and serum proteins. We took weight and 11 linear measurements of each animal, using techniques described by Schultz (1929). With conventional orthodontic techniques, we prepared dental casts of most animals. Thirty-five measurements were later taken from these casts as previously used for studies of human populations (Bailit et al., 1968; Lombardi et al., 1972). We prepared impressions of the dermal ridges of the left hands and feet, using a silicone molding compound (Froehlich et al., 1976). Forty ordinal traits were scored from these fingerprints. (See Figure 2 for an illustration of these variables.) Finally, we marked the animals with unique freeze-brands and collars, so that they could be identified individually at a distance. We also marked them so that each could be identified when recaptured by tattoos, ear notches, and ear tags (Scott et al., 1976; Thorington et al., 1979).

After release, we made repeated intermittent observations of most animals in their troops for up to 5 years. We plotted the movements of the specific troops, which were identified by the marked animals they contained. Our observations of troops mingling and displacing other troops and of individuals changing troops are based on these observations of marked individuals. Our estimates of the population density and troop size are based on repeated counts of the troops, with comparisons between the numbers of animals known to be marked and the proportion of marked animals in the troops at each census, using Lincoln Index techniques (Seber, 1973).

An exploratory effort to measure floral diversity was based on transects taken through the home ranges

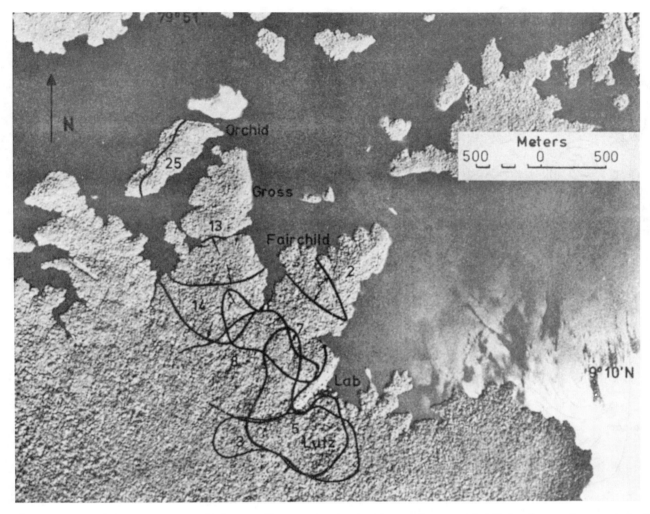

Figure 1.   Orchid and northeast Barro Colorado islands, showing locations and ranges of eight howler monkey troops and principal landmarks within the 165-ha. study area.

of the howler troops. Our transects were 10 m wide and were described at approximate right angles to the topography. On the peninsulas and Orchid Island, the transects ran from shore to shore over the central ridge. In the Lutz catchment they ran from ridge to ridge, across the ravine. We measured, identified and tagged all trees with a circumference greater than 59 cm. Our transects totaled 4600 m, and included 1000 identified trees belonging to 83 taxa.

Analyses of Data

For purposes of systematic interpretation, we simplified our data sets using standard multivariate techniques. The morphometric data for adult males and females were pooled by using scores standardized on the means for the two sexes. We then used a stepwise discriminant analysis to select eight measurements that best discriminated between the eight troops. These measurements, in ranked order of explanatory importance, were knee height, weight, jaw breadth, tail length, trunk length, cranial length, thigh length, and facial height.

The dental metric data comprised lengths and breadths of individual teeth, and measures of arcade shape and occlusal relationships. The discriminant analysis allowed us to reduce this complex data matrix to a subset of 19 important variables. Similarly, the continuous and ordinal traits derived from the fingerprint molds were reduced to 21 variables. (For a discussion of the use of discriminant analysis on nonmetric data, see Froehlich and Giles, 1981.)

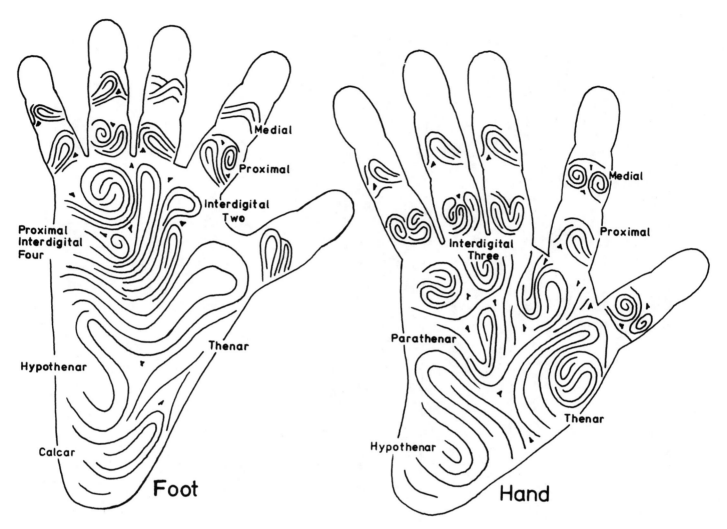

Figure 2. Schematic diagram of principal howler monkey dermatoglyphic pattern areas, emphasizing those traits that varied systematically and significantly between Barro Colorado Island populations. (Not to scale.)

The blood data were analyzed in two ways. A bivariate plot of trait frequency was sufficient to display the limited genetic variation. We then analyzed the more abundant nongenetic, quantitative variation by a statistical technique analogous to factor analysis (Harpending and Jenkins, 1973), which provided a single measure of multivariate differences between troops.

In our analysis of the tree transects we sought to reduce the effect of clumping, which could bias our samples, by counting two adjacent trees of the same species as a single individual. Since large trees have greater productivity, we counted a tree with circumference greater than 120 cm as two individuals. Transects included within the home range of each troop were pooled, the frequency of occurrence of each species was computed for each home range sample and

these frequencies were rank-ordered. Spearman rank correlations were calculated and the matrix of these correlations was factor analyzed to give a graph of floral differences between the home ranges of the eight troops.

We also calculated an index of foraging flexibility for each troop. For this index, the number of tree species per 100 m of transect was divided by the fraction of the troop's range that was bordered by water. This index gives us a combined estimate of the diversity of trees within the home range for each troop and the potential for the troop to move out of its home range if environmental conditions should require it.

From the multivariate analysis of each of the five data sets—the morphometric, and dental metric, the fingerprints, the floral transects, and the nongenetic blood variation—we calculated 2- and 3-dimensional

FROEHLICH AND THORINGTON

Euclidean distances between each pair of troops, and then rank-ordered these pairwise distances. Between-troop differences were also calculated and ranked for the social and demographic variables: home range, troop size, sex ratio, ratio of subadults to adults, density, biomass, and the proportion of the home range that was bordered by water. Geographic distances between the centers of the home ranges of the troops were also measured and ranked. The correlation coefficients between all the variables in terms of these rank orderings were computed, using Kendall's Tau. The resulting correlation matrix was factor-analyzed to describe the interrelationships between the different sets of variables and to generate hypotheses about howler monkey socioecology.

All the "factor analyses" cited above were "principal component solutions," based on the rank-order correlation matrices, with one's in the diagonal. We used quartimax rotations, maintaining orthogonality and independence between factors.

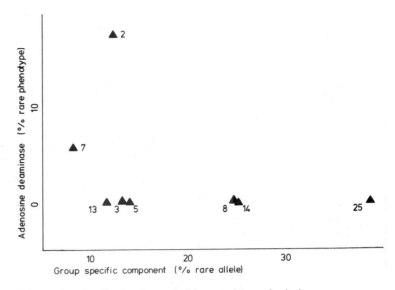

Figure 3. Qualitative (presumably genetic) serological variation between eight Barro Colorado Island howler monkey troops.

RESULTS AND DISCUSSION

Serology

In total, 22 proteins representing at least 25 loci were examined in the serum and red cell hemolysates of 80 individuals. Only three systems (group-specific component, serum esterase, and adenosine deaminase) exhibited genetic polymorphism, which is between one-half and one-third that expected for mammalian populations. Moreover, the proportion of heterozygous loci per individual was approximately 1.5%, which is dramatically less than the range, 5–15%, cited as normal (Selander et al., 1970). It is possible that these low levels of heterozygosity result from this being an island population, from the small size of the founding population, from the effects of yellow fever epidemics such as that in 1949, or from some peculiar aspects of the biology of howler monkeys. There is a similar degree of monomorphism in a sample of *Alouatta* from Guanacaste Province, Costa Rica, (Froehlich et al., 1976); thus it is possible that the last three factors are more important than the first.

In contrast to the paucity of genetic blood variation, the electrophoretic analyses showed a surprising degree of quantitative variation in all of the serum esterases and in haptoglobin. Despite similarities in genetic patterns, there were dark bands and faint bands in different individuals, most typically in Orchid Island animals. For esterase, this suggests variability in the available quantity of these digestive enzymes. For haptoglobin, *in vivo* hemolysis can lead to a depletion

of this hemoglobin-binding protein (C. Jolly, personal communication). These variations appear to have ecological interpretations with regard to plastic (i.e., homeostatic) responses to different diets and plant secondary compounds, particularly on Orchid Island.

Curiously, these monkeys from Orchid Island were remarkably resistant to the anesthetic phencyclidine HCl. We are reminded of the well-documented sensitivity of some people with low serum cholinoesterase to the anesthetic, succinyl dicholine (Harris, 1970). Is this resistance to phenocyclidine due to some detoxification mechanism connected with these esterases? Such a relationship would be quite specific, since their response to another, closely related anesthetic, ketamine HCl, showed no variability.

There is little serological genetic variation between troops. Only two serological variables were sufficiently sampled for this purpose, as shown in Figure 3. One of these, the red cell enzyme adenosine deaminase, is variable in only three animals; and, since the variant phenotype only lacks a cathodal band, it is conceivable that even this polymorphism is nongenetic. The variation of the group-specific component on Orchid Island, however, suggests genetic isolation and inbreeding.

Fingerprint Genetic Structure

In contrast with blood, there was considerable variability in dermal patterns, with significant differences between troops. These dermal systems of howlers are

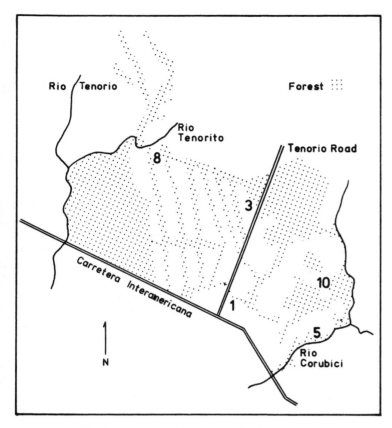

Figure 4. Costa Rican (Guanacaste) study site, showing five howler troop locations.

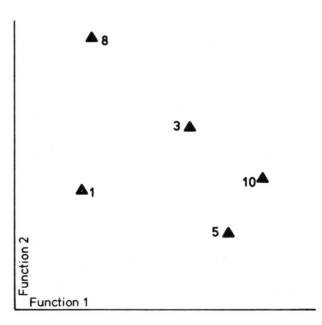

Figure 5. Discriminant analysis of Costa Rican howler fingerprints with 21 variables and five groups. The analysis was based on 57% of the between-group variance. Significance was demonstrated by a classification accuracy of 51% and a Wilk's Lambda probability below 0.0001.

probably highly heritable as they are in man (Froehlich, 1976). Close similarities in the dermatoglyphics of two troops are likely to be due to the common origin of the troops and to subsequent gene flow between them. Because of the complex, polygenic nature of fingerprints, it is improbable that gene flow between distantly related troops would lead to close dermatoglyphic resemblances between them (Froehlich and Giles, 1981).

In order to support this contention and our use of dermal patterns for studying genetic structure in the Barro Colorado Island howlers, we present an analysis conducted on 53 monkeys from five troops in Guanacaste Province, Costa Rica. These troops occurred on Finca La Pacifica, as shown in Figure 4. Their habitat consists largely of riparian strips and forested windbreaks between fields, which restrict and determine most contacts between troops (Scott et al., 1978; Froehlich et al., in prep.). Figure 5 shows the genetic relatedness of the five troops as determined from a discriminant reduction of the fingerprint data. The pattern of genetic relatedness and the geographic dis-

tribution of the five troops are very similar (compare Figures 4 and 5), especially considering the most likely migration routes of the troops. This congruence suggests that fingerprints are dependable population markers for howler monkeys and supports our contention that they can be used to study the historical and social relationships between troops. This is one case in which genetic patterns can be explained almost entirely by geographic proximity.

The dermatoglyphic data from Barro Colorado Island were analyzed in the same way as the Costa Rica data, to produce a "map" of genetic similarities between troops. There is considerable congruence between this map (Figure 6) and the geographic map of troop distribution (Figure 1), as is expected if the pattern of genetic similarities and differences are mediated primarily by the common origin of neighboring troops and gene flow between them. The geographically most isolated troops (2 and 25) occupy opposite poles in the genetic map, as they did in the genetic plot of the two blood polymorphisms (Figure 2). Also, the genetic similarities between troops 7 and 8 at the

FROEHLICH AND THORINGTON

base of Fairchild Peninsula and troops 13 and 14 of Gross Peninsula are best explained as resulting from common origin and gene flow. This hypothesis is supported by our observations of their geographic proximity, the social tolerance between these troops, and the migration of individuals between troops.

Oddly, there is more genetic similarity (as measured by dermatoglyphics) between troop 25 of Orchid Island and troop 7 of Fairchild Peninsula, than between troop 25 and its neighboring troops on Gross Peninsula. However, troop 7 is a composite of two or three semiautonomous subtroops which periodically fuse and exchange members. This unstable situation has persisted for more than a decade. It was noted by Chivers (1969) in 1967, by Mittermeier (1972) in 1970, and by us since 1972. We have observed the movement of marked individuals from troop 7 to troop 14, and even from troop 7 to Orchid Island. This social instability probably explains why troop 7 occupies a central position in our genetic map. We suggest that it has contributed more immigrants to the Orchid Island troop in the last decade than have troops that are geographically closer to Orchid Island, and that this partially explains the dermatoglyphic similarities.

Other discordances exist between the genetic map and the geographic map. Troop 3, one of the "laboratory troops" of Lutz Ravine is more similar to troop 2 at the tip of Fairchild Point than it is to troop 8, its nearest neighbor to the north. There is some evidence that the troops that presently occur between 2 and 3 have intruded between them from the west. Chapman (1938) indicates that the Fairchild Peninsula was initially colonized in 1937 by a portion of Carpenter's (1934) laboratory clan. Periodic howler censuses through the 1950s (Collias and Southwick, 1952; Altmann, 1959; Carpenter, 1965) document the existence of a troop at the base of Fairchild Peninsula, but none at the tip where troop 2 now lives. In 1959, Carpenter (1965) noted that the laboratory troop and the troop at the base of Fairchild were mutually tolerant of one another. Eight years later in 1967, Chivers (1969) found that the laboratory troop and the troop at the base of Fairchild were totally intolerant of one another and exchanged more morning calls than any other pair of troops. For the first time Chivers also noted that there was a second troop, farther out Fairchild Peninsula. It is as if a strange troop had intruded between the two related and tolerant troops. The success and subsequent fissioning of the intruding troop would explain why a troop isolated on Fairchild Point is more closely related to troops in Lutz Ravine than it is to its neighboring troops. The suggestion that this intruding troop came from the west is consistent with our data showing that these troops

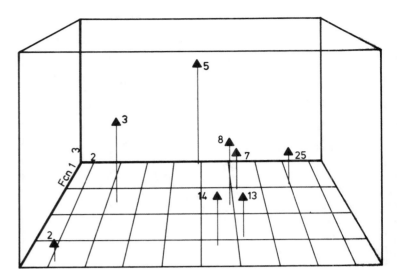

Figure 6. Fingerprint discriminant analysis with 21 variables and eight howler groups from Barro Colorado Island. Function 3 was significant at 0.003 and classification accuracy was 57%. The proportion of explained between-group variance was 70%. Troops 2 and 3 are separated by a high degree of palmar parathenar patterning, with low pattern complexity on the foot digits, particularly 4 and 5, and moderate plantar surface complexity. In axis 3, troops 3 and 5, are distinguished by low overall palmar surface complexity with very high patterning in specific interdigital areas. They also have medial digital segment simplicity and proximal complexity on the index finger. Finally, their plantar patterns show overall simplicity in combination with high patterning in specific regions, such as the second interdigital and the calcar eminence. (See Figure 2 for definitions.)

7 and 8 are closely related to and somewhat tolerant of troops 13 and 14 of Gross Peninsula. The intolerance noted by Chivers (1969) between the laboratory troop and troop 7 at the base of Fairchild Peninsula has lasted for 12 years.

The marked difference in dermatoglyphics between troops 3 and 5, which coexist in Lutz catchment and presumably derive from the former laboratory troop, is another discordance between the genetic and geographic maps. The most likely explanation is the well-documented difference in the social stability of the two troops. We know of no data to support any hypothesis suggesting that the difference is due to a recent migration of one of the troops into this area.

In 1972 the two troops were mutually tolerant and occasionally merged, leading us to believe they were sister troops. This tolerance broke down when strange males entered troop 3 in subsequent years. Instead, troop 5 would very aggressively supplant troop 3 from favored fruit trees and troop 3 would scatter, to reas-

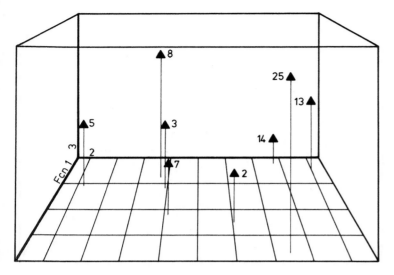

Figure 7. Morphometric discriminant analysis with eight measurements and eight howler groups from Barro Colorado Island. Function 3 is significant at 0.03 and classification accuracy was 44%. Here 84% of between-groups variance is explained. With reference to Table 1, troops 2 and 25 are allied on Function 1 by lighter body weight, relatively longer knee height, and relatively narrow jaws. Along axis 2, troop 5 is distinguished by heavier weights and absolutely longer legs. Finally, troops 8 and 25 have high loadings on Function 3 because of their lighter bodies, long knee height relative to tail length, and absolutely broader jaws.

Table 1. Standard discriminant function coefficients for an eight-variable, eight-group analysis of morphometric population patterning

Trait	Discriminant functions		
	I	II	III
Head length	0.51	−0.38	0.31
Face height	−0.03	0.33	−0.12
Jaw breadth	−0.57	−0.33	0.80
Weight	−0.70	0.59	−0.66
Tail length	−0.22	−0.06	−0.61
Trunk length	0.10	−0.54	0.04
Thigh length	−0.45	−0.17	−0.34
Knee height	0.59	1.00	0.97

See Figure 6 legend for a discussion of specific trait differences as they determine population distances.

semble later. There was evidence of internal turmoil within troop 3, in that eight marked females disappeared from the troop, two of them by documented migrations to other troops. The strange males disappeared, too, and in 1978 the relationship between the two troops had returned to the condition in 1972. Troop 5 was very stable during this period, with no strange males immigrating. Moreover, three of the four adult males and two of the three adult females we marked in 1973 were still in the troop in 1978. One of these males, which has a distinctively scarred lip, was first seen by Chivers in 1967 (Mittermeier, 1972). Thus there seems to have been a marked difference between troops 3 and 5 in rates of immigration and emigration, during the period that we have observed them. We suggest that the observed dermatoglyphic differences between these two troops result from both the socially mediated genetic isolation of troop 5 and the high rate of migration between troop 3 and other neighboring troops. In sum, social fluidity and historical population movements both seem to interact with geographical proximity in the derivation of present genetic relationships among howler troops on Barro Colorado Island.

Morphometry and Tree Transects

The analysis of the morphometric data are shown and described in Figure 7 and Table 1. The discriminant functions are standardized so distances on axes 2 and 3 are exaggerated. There are similarities between neighboring troops, such as troops 13 and 14, and troops 3, 7, and 8. However, on the graph, the nearest neighbor of troop 2 is troop 7. We have just concluded on the basis of dermatoglyphics that these adjoining troops are not genetically close. Also troop 25 has troop 2 as its nearest neighbor on the graph. This similarity seems anomalous on the basis of either geography or relatedness. Metric proportions undoubtedly have a genetic component, but in these cases it seems as if other factors are important as well.

We had a subjective impression that the morphological similarities were matched by similarities between the forest on Orchid Island, where troop 25 lives, and the forest on Fairchild Point, occupied by troop 2. These vegetational similarities probably exist because the areas have had similar histories of deforestation and reforestation, and because they have similar northern exposures to wind. Therefore we tried to quantify habitat differences by means of the vegetational transects.

The results of the analyses of the tree transects are presented in Figure 8. We consider that the vegetational patterns shown reflect relative differences in the food available to the different howler troops. The

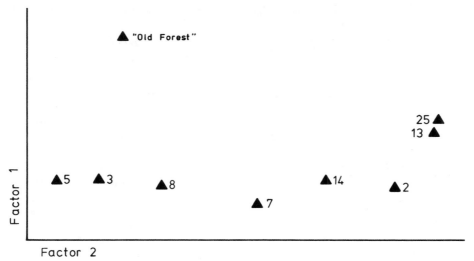

Figure 8. Factor analysis of tree transect data (with 83 taxa) from the home ranges of eight howler troops on Barro Colorado Island, with an old forest sample included for a perspective of floral maturity.

second axis provides a linear separation of the habitats of the eight troops, showing which of our transects were most similar to which others. The correspondence between this measure of vegetational similarity in Figure 8 and the pattern of morphometric differences between the troops, as seen in Figure 7, suggests that there is a correlation between the two, presumably mediated through the food available to the monkeys.

We pursued this hypothesis further, by forming an index of foraging flexibility, previously described, and comparing it with the body weights of the adult monkeys in the different troops. In Table 2 we show that there is a clear association between body weight and this index (which combines tree diversity with insularity). The Spearman correlation coefficients of 0.94 for females and 0.80 for males are both large and highly significant. Therefore, we conclude that tree diversity influences the morphometric differences that we have found between troops of howler monkeys on Barro Colorado Island. We hypothesize that animals with access to a greater diversity of trees are more buffered from food shortages and grow larger. Because all adult animals are not similar in size, we suggest that some troops are less subject to such shortages. The implication is that these troops are not as close to the carrying capacity of the habitat, if the food supply is ultimately the factor limiting population density.

Relationships between Socioecological and Genetic Variables

Table 3 is a matrix of Spearman rank-order correlations between eight variables which were measured for the eight troops. The matrix has been subdivided to show that there are two sets of positively correlated variables. The first set is troop size, sex ratio, and home range. The second set is density, biomass, female weight, foraging flexibility, and percentage of troop members that are infants. Density is a member of the second set only through its high correlation with biomass. The members of each set have predominantly nonsignificant negative correlations with the members of the other set.

In Table 4 we present a larger matrix of rank-order correlations (Kendall's Tau). For each of the 13 variables, the ranking was based on the between-group difference or distance, involving the 28 pairs of the eight troops. This has an advantage over the analysis presented in Table 3, in that we need not compress our multivariate data into a single value for each variable for each group with resulting distortion. Instead of using average female weight, we have used our multivariate analysis of morphology. Instead of using an index of foraging flexibility, we have used a multivariate analysis of floral diversity. It also enables us to compare different types of variables, for each is reduced to a ranking of the similarities between pairs

Table 2. Relationship between the average adult howler body weights in seven geographical areas and a large tree diversity/social insularity index (foraging flexibility), based on floral transects from each area

Sample area	Foraging flexibility	Rank	Body weights (kg)			
			Female	Rank	Male	Rank
Orchid Island	0.105	1	5.5	1.0	6.6	1.0
Gross Pt. Out	0.233	2	6.1	3.5	8.0	4.5
Fairchild Pt. In	0.255	3	5.6	2.0	7.9	2.5
Fairchild Pt. Out	0.351	4	6.1	3.5	7.9	2.5
Gross Pt. In	0.475	5	6.2	5.0	8.0	4.5
Lutz Ravine	1.53	6	6.3	6.0	8.8	7.0
Old forest	2.24	7	6.6	7.0	8.3	6.0
Rank-order correlation between tree index and body weight (Spearman)			.94		.80	
Significance (probability less than)			0.01		0.04	

Tree diversity was determined by the number of taxa per 100 m of 10-m wide transects. This in turn was divided by the percentage of troop home range bounded by water.

Table 3. Spearman correlations between demographic and ecological variables in eight contiguous howler troops on Barro Colorado Island

	Sex ratio	Home range	Density	Biomass	Female weight	Foraging flexibility	Infants (%)
Troop size	0.82*	0.55	−0.38	−0.70*	−0.58	−0.58	−0.53
Sex ratio		0.77*	−0.58	−0.55	−0.18	−0.16	−0.11
Home range			−0.18	−0.25	0.10	0.05	0.21
Density				0.81*	0.17	0.14	0.19
Biomass					0.64*	0.67*	0.65*
Female weight						0.92**	0.88**
Foraging flexibility							0.80*

Note that the troops compared here and the geographical areas compared in Table 2 are slightly different, thus explaining the small difference in the two correlations between female weight and foraging flexibility. Sex ratio is the number of females per adult male.

* $p<.05$; ** $p<.01$.

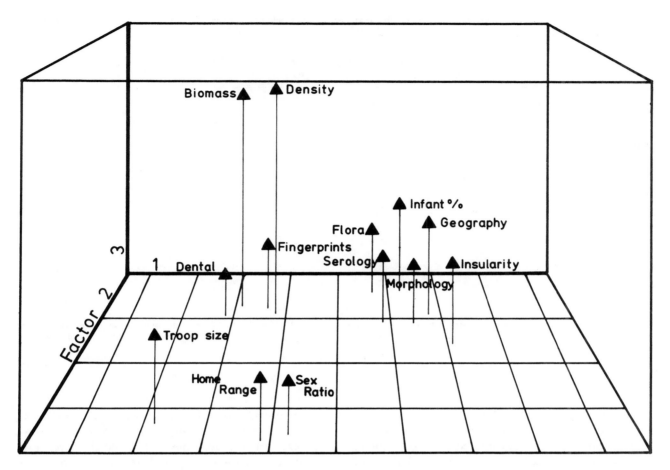

Figure 9.   Factor analysis of howler monkey population structure, using biological distances and socioecological differences among eight contiguous troops, and showing the functional relationships among variables.

of troops. The disadvantage with the matrix of Table 4 is our uncertainty about the number of degrees of freedom that are represented when 28 nonindependent paired combinations of troops are used. The overall significance of the matrix is confirmed by a sign test ($p < 0.0005$), but the bivariate significance levels, which are starred, are based on 27 degrees of freedom and therefore may be slightly inflated. A comparison of Tables 3 and 4 suggests that the estimates of the correlations between variables are decreased by the pair-wise analysis, but the estimates of their significance are slightly increased, as anticipated. The patterns of correlations seen in Table 3 are not changed in Table 4, with the exception that biomass shows a significant correlation only with density in Table 4, whereas it had significant negative correlation with troop size and positive correlations with the other variables of the second set in Table 3.

The patterns of relationshps between variables are shown in Figure 9, based on a principal component analysis of the matrix in Table 4 using a quartimax rotation. These patterns are presented and discussed here as hypotheses. Because they are generated by our data, they cannot be tested by our data. They must be tested subsequently in other howler populations.

It is evident that there are four clusters of variables in Figure 9. The first of these is biomass and density, which are clearly separated from other variables on the third axis. The close relationship between these variables, with a Kendall Tau of 0.67, was obviously predictable. But their complete lack of association with other social and ecological variables was not anticipated from the data presented in Table 3. As reported elsewhere (Froehlich and Thorington, 1982), it appears that one population (Orchid Island) is at car-

Table 4. Rank-order correlations (Kendall's Tau) between social, demographic, and biological variables in eight contiguous howler troops on Barro Colorado Island

	Insularity	Floral data	Morphology	Dental size	Fingerprints	Serology	Density
Geography	0.57***	0.33**	0.44***	0.02	0.31*	0.38**	0.28*
Insularity	—	0.42**	0.40**	0.05	0.11	0.38**	0.15
Floral data	—	—	0.27*	0.32*	0.07	0.00	0.04
Morphology	—	—	—	−0.12	0.10	0.28*	0.11
Dental size	—	—	—	—	0.16	−0.28*	−0.15
Fingerprints	—	—	—	—	—	0.06	0.08
Serology	—	—	—	—	—	—	0.04
Density	—	—	—	—	—	—	—
Biomass	—	—	—	—	—	—	—
Home range	—	—	—	—	—	—	—
Troop size	—	—	—	—	—	—	—
Sex ratio	—	—	—	—	—	—	—

The variables were measured as differences between pairs of troops and thus a sample size of 28 such combinations is reflected in the correlations. The asterisks provide a provisional measure of significance at 0.05*, 0.01**, and 0.001*** levels. See text for a discussion of significance levels.

rying capacity, while the others are still growing at a moderate rate. This binary demographic difference may account for the lack of expected associations among density, body size, infant proportion, and floral diversity. On the other hand, it is easy to conceive of conditions that would cause biomass and density to vary completely independently of the other variables, so these results will probably not be unique to our data.

A second variable cluster, well separated on the second axis, comprises troop size, home range, and sex ratio. This grouping was predictable on the basis of our familiarity with the dynamics of howler social structure, and it was evident in the correlation matrix of Table 3. To the previously hypothesized relationship between sex ratio and troop size (Scott, Malmgren, and Glander, 1976), we add the variable of home range size. Large troops inhabit large home ranges and have a relatively larger number of females for each adult male. We deduce that there is an upper limit to the number of mutually tolerant males, partially independent of troop and home range size.

The third cluster is complex and includes the most variables. The six variables are: (1) the morphometric data, (2) the tree transect data, (3) the degree of insularity in the home ranges of each troop, (4) the geographic distances between troops, (5) the quantitative serological differences, and (6) the proportion of infants and juveniles. Three of these were also seen

to be interrelated variables in the matrix of Figure 3. We consider this to be our constellation of environmental variables, together with those that are most influenced by the ecological differences between the home ranges of the different troops. The relationships between morphology, tree diversity, and troop insularity are as previously discussed. Geographic distance is included here as a peculiarity of the topography of Barro Colorado, because forests on the partially isolated northern parts of the study area are youngest and least diverse. Quantitative serological variation probably reflects enzymatic plasticity to plant secondary compounds, as discussed before. The ecological factor consequently reflects both costs and benefits of howler foraging in different areas. Finally, the proportion of young animals in this variable cluster suggests that the more food-stressed populations have lower reproductive rates. This hypothesis agrees with our conclusion that in 1976 Orchid Island animals were the most food limited and had the lowest frequency of infants and juveniles (Froehlich and Thorington, 1982).

The last cluster in Figure 9 groups fingerprints and dental metrics, which seem to be the genetic characters least influenced by environmental and social factors. A more penetrating analysis of this cluster is provided by the rotation of the five significant factors (Table 5). After quartimax rotation, the first three are similar to those of Figure 9, but the fourth factor now

FROEHLICH AND THORINGTON

Biomass	Home range	Troop size	Sex ratio	Infants (%)
0.14	0.20	−0.17	0.13	0.49***
0.06	0.22	0.00	0.31*	0.52***
0.15	−0.08	0.01	−0.03	0.22
0.00	0.10	−0.06	0.14	0.41**
0.03	−0.03	0.00	−0.07	0.10
0.07	0.09	−0.24	−0.08	0.35**
−0.19	0.14	−0.17	0.26	0.28
0.67***	−0.01	−0.10	−0.02	0.14
—	−0.16	0.05	−0.14	0.04
—	—	0.34**	0.58***	0.32*
—	—	—	0.32*	−0.14
—	—	—	—	0.21

allies dental metric traits with the data from tree transects. The latter probably reflects specific nutritional variables, and the size of teeth is likely to be influenced by these, so the association seems logical. The fourth factor also shows an inverse relationship between dental traits and the quantitative serological variation, which is probably associated with plant toxins and tannins, as previously discussed. This "dental factor" is of course orthogonal to the "morphological factor," which has a positive association with serology. The apparent contrasting effects of plant secondary compounds on these two factors suggest that different sets of nutrients are involved in the two anatomical variables. Smith (1977) provides a rationale for this hypothesis. He suggested that howlers obtain calcium primarily from old *Cecropia* leaves and figs, plant parts that may be less protected by secondary compounds than other howler foods. These problems of secondary compounds and dietary choice in howlers are complex and only partially understood (Glander, 1978, 1981; Milton, 1979), but it is evident that there is a dietary component as well as a large genetic component to tooth morphology.

The fifth principal component in Table 5 sets off dermatoglyphics from all other sets of variables. We believe that this results from the lack of influence of ecological and social structural variables on the fingerprints, corroborating our earlier conclusion that these genetic traits vary between troops in accordance with the complexities of the social and migrational histories of howler monkeys on Barro Colorado Island.

CONCLUSIONS

There is a very low level of polymorphism in the blood proteins of howler monkeys on Barro Colorado Island. The reason for this is not clear, because we lack good comparative data from populations of howler monkeys under other conditions.

The dermatoglyphics exhibit a great deal of genetically based variation. The pattern of variation in fingerprints on Barro Colorado shows that some adjacent troops are closely related to one another and are probably sister troops. In other cases, adjacent troops have quite different dermatoglyphics and appear to be more distantly related. In one such case we believe that the present geographic pattern results from the intrusion of more distantly related troops between two sister troops. In another case, we suspect that the differences have resulted from a great deal of outbreeding in one of two sister troops and greatly restricted outbreeding in the other.

A number of morphometric features, associated with adult size, vary between monkey troops on Barro Colorado. This pattern of variation is correlated with the diversity of tree species in the home ranges of the animals, such that howler monkeys seem to grow big-

Table 5. Quartimax rotated factor loadings of population structure, based on Kendall rank-order correlations for biological distances and socioecological differences between eight contiguous howler troops

Variable	Factor					Communality
	I	II	III	IV	V	
Geography	0.77	—	—	—	—	0.68
Insularity	0.81	—	—	—	—	0.71
Density	—	—	0.88	—	—	0.85
Biomass	—	—	0.91	—	—	0.86
Home range	—	0.84	—	—	—	0.79
Flora	0.55	—	—	0.63	—	0.79
Morphometrics	0.70	—	—	—	—	0.49
Dental metrics	—	—	—	0.82	—	0.74
Fingerprints	—	—	—	—	0.84	0.77
Troop size	—	0.68	—	—	—	0.72
Infant ratio	0.64	—	—	—	—	0.66
Sex ratio	—	0.78	—	—	—	0.70
Quantitative serology	0.58	—	—	−0.54	—	0.67
Sum of squares	2.98	1.87	1.73	1.53	1.32	9.43
Percent trace	22.9	14.4	13.3	11.8	10.1	72.5

For clarity, only loadings above 0.5 are shown. The factor loading for a given variable is the correlation coefficient of that variable with the factor concerned. The communality of a given variable is the proportion of its variance explained by all five factors.

gest on Barro Colorado where they have access to the greatest diversity of tree species. Another variable associated with morphometry and tree diversity is quantitative serological variation. This probably reflects an enzymatic adjustment of the monkeys to toxins and other secondary compounds in the plants they eat. It suggests that the howlers can be more selective in the more diverse forests and thus avoid toxins, but they must respond differently to secondary compounds in less diverse forests by producing more enzymes. Finally, the percentage frequency of infants and juveniles also differs between troops in a manner similar to the other five variables. This may reflect an effect of nutrition on the rates of birth or infant survival.

ACKNOWLEDGMENTS

These studies were supported by the Smithsonian's Environmental Science Program and by a grant from the secretary of the Smithsonian Institution. We are grateful to the Smithsonian Tropical Research Institute for the assistance provided by the staff, to our many colleagues who have assisted us, especially to Norman Scott and Jeff Otis, and to Katharine Milton and Arturo Tarak for allowing us to use data they collected on tree distributions in the "old forest" of Barro Colorado Island. Finally, we gratefully acknowledge the electrophoretic analyses of Clifford Jolly and his students, especially Richard Macris.

LITERATURE CITED

Altmann, S. A.
1959.   Field Observations of a Howling Monkey Society. *Journal of Mammalogy*, 40: 317–330.

Bailit, H. L., S. J. DeWitt, and R. A. Leigh
1968.   The Size and Morphology of the Nasioi Dentition. *American Journal Physical Anthropology*, 28: 271–288.

Bennett, C. F., Jr.
1963.   A Phytophysionomic Reconnaissance of Barro Colorado Island, Canal Zone. *Smithsonian Miscellaneous Collections*, 145(7): 1–8.

Carpenter, C. R.
1934.   A Field Study of the Behavior and Social Relations of Howling Monkeys. *Comp. Psychol. Monograph*, 10(2): 1–168.
1965.   The Howlers of Barro Colorado Island. Pages 250–291 in *Primate Behavior*, edited by I. DeVore. New York: Holt, Rinehart, and Winston.

Chapman, F. M.
1929.   *My Tropical Air Castle*. New York: Appleton.
1938.   *Life in an Air Castle*. New York: Appleton.

Chivers, D. J.
1969.   On the Daily Behavior and Spacing of Howling Monkey Groups. *Folia Primat.*, 10: 48–102.

Collias, N., and C. Southwick
1952.   A Field Study of Population Density and Social Organization in Howling Monkeys. *Proceedings of the American Phil. Society*, 96(2): 143–156.

Foster, R. B., and N. V. L. Brokaw
1982.   Structure and History of the Vegetation of Barro Colorado Island. Pages 67–81 in *The Ecology of a Tropical Forest*, edited by Egbert G. Leigh, Jr., et al. Washington, D.C.: Smithsonian Institution Press.

Froehlich, J. W.
1976.   The Quantitative Genetics of Fingerprints. Pages 260–320 in *The Measures of Man*, edited by E. Giles and J. Friedlaender. Cambridge, Mass.: Peabody Museum Press.

Froehlich, J. W., P. H. Froehlich, L. A. Malmgren, and N. J. Scott
1976.   Dermatoglyphic Variation in Central American Howler Monkeys (*Alouatta palliata*). *American Journal of Physical Anthropology*, 44: 179.

Froehlich, J. W., P. H. Froehlich, N. J. Scott, and R. W. Thorington
In prep.   Fingerprint Variation Within and Between Two Breeding Populations of Central American Howler Monkeys.

Froehlich, J. W., and E. Giles
1981.   A Multivariate Approach to Fingerprint Variation in Papua New Guinea. II. Perspectives on the Evolutionary Stability of Dermatoglyphic Markers. *American Journal of Physical Anthropology*, 54: 93–106.

Froehlich, J. W., W. W. Socha, A. S. Wiener, J. Moor-Janowski, and R. W. Thorington
1977.   Blood Groups of the Mantled Howler Monkey (*Alouatta palliata*). *Journal of Medical Primatology*, 6: 219–231.

Froehlich, J. W., and R. W. Thorington, Jr.
1982.   Food Limitation on a Small Island and the Regulation of Population Size in Mantled Howler Monkeys (*Alouatta palliata*). *American Journal of Physical Anthropology*, 57: 190.

Glander, K. E.
1978.   Howling Monkey Feeding Behavior and Plant Secondary Compounds: A Study of Strategies. Pages 561–574 in *The Ecology of Arboreal Folivores*, edited by G. G. Montgomery. Washington, D.C.: Smithsonian Institution Press.
1981.   Feeding Patterns in Mantled Howling Monkeys. Pages 231–257 in *Foraging Behavior*, edited by A. Kamil. New York: Garland Press.

Harpending, H., and T. Jenkins
1973.   Genetic Distance Among Southern African Populations. Pages 177–199 in *Methods and Theories of Anthropolgical Genetics*, edited by M. A. Crawford and P. L. Workman. Albuquerque: University of New Mexico Press.

Harris, H.
1970.   *The Principles of Human Biochemical Genetics.* New York: American Elsevier.

Kenoyer, L. A.
1929.   General and Successional Ecology of the Lower Tropical Rain Forest at Barro Colorado Island, Panama. *Ecology*, 10: 201–222.

Knight, D. H.
1975.   A Phytosociological Analysis of Species-rich Tropical Forest on Barro Colorado Island, Panama. *Ecological Monographs*, 45:259–284.

Lombardi, A. V., and H. L. Bailit
1972.   Malocclusion in the Kwaio, a Melanesian Group on Malaita, Solomon Islands. *American Journal of Physical Anthropology*, 36: 283–293.

Milton, K.
1979.   Factors Influencing Leaf Choice by Howler Monkeys: A Test of Some Hypotheses of Food Selection by Generalist Herbivores. *American Naturalist*, 114: 362–378.

Mittermeier, R. A.
1972.   Group Activity and Population Dynamics of the Howler Monkey on Barro Colorado Island. *Primates*, 14: 1–19.

Schultz, A.
1929.   The Technique of Measuring the Outer Body of Human Fetuses and of Primates in General. *Contributions to Embryology*, 20: 213–257.

Scott, N. J., Jr., L. A. Malmgren, and K. E. Glander
1976.   A Model for Grouping Behavior of Mantled Howler Monkeys (*Alouatta palliata*). Unpublished manuscript.
1978.   Grouping behaviour and sex ratio in mantled howling monkeys. Pages 183–185 in *Proceedings of the Sixth International Congress of the International Primatological Society*, edited by D. J. Chivers and W. Lane-Petter. New York: Academic Press.

Scott, N. J., Jr., A. F. Scott, and L. A. Malmgren
1976.   Capturing and Marking Howler Monkeys for Field Behavioral Studies. *Primates*, 17: 527–533.

Seber, G. A. F.
1973.   The Estimation of Animal Abundance. London: Charles Griffin and Co. Ltd. 506 pp.

Selander, R. K., S. Y. Yang, R. C. Lewontin, and W. E. Johnson
1970.   Genetic Variation in the Horseshoe Crab (*Limulus polyphemus*), A Phylogenetic 'Relic.' *Evolution*, 24: 402–414.

Smith, C. C.
1977.   Feeding behavior and social organization in howling monkeys. Pages 97–126 in *Primate Ecology*, edited by T. M. Clutton-Brock. New York: Academic Press.

Thorington, R. W., Jr., R. Rudran, and D. Mack
1979.   Sexual Dimorphism of *Alouatta seniculus* and Observations on Capture Techniques. Pages 97–106 in *Vertebrate Ecology in the Northern Neotropics*, edited by J. F. Eisenberg. Washington, D.C.: Smithsonian Institution Press.

INSECTS OF TREE CROWNS AND THEIR PREDATORS

The Seasonal Abundance of Night-flying Insects in a Neotropical Forest

NICHOLAS SMYTHE Smithsonian Tropical Research Institute, Balboa, Republic of Panama

ABSTRACT

From 1971 through 1973, the total weight of insects caught in light-traps near the weir in Lutz catchment peaked sharply early in the rainy season. The number of insects less than 5 mm long caught in these traps varied least from season to season, although numbers were lowest from September through November. The seasonal rhythm in numbers caught was far more marked for insects between 5 mm and 15 mm long, showing a peak early in the rainy season, and a similar, but less marked, rhythm occurred for insects over 15 mm long.

Different groups of insects have different rhythms. Flying termites emerge in huge numbers following the first few rains of each wet season, satiating their predators. Adult mayflies peak between July or August and December or January; very few are caught in May. The number of Homoptera caught tends to parallel the availability of new leaves. The catch of beetles less than 5 mm long varies greatly, but with little seasonal trend; the catch of larger beetles shows a clear seasonal peak early in the rainy season.

INTRODUCTION

Seasonal variations in food abundance are important to many aspects of the adaptation of an organism to its environment. Other factors remaining equal, a predictable season of even slightly increased food abundance would result in an adaptive advantage for those species that synchronized their breeding season to take advantage of it, and seasons of deprivation result in the favoring of those species that most satisfactorily accommodate to them. Patterns of migration, of food storage, and of the deposition of fat are affected by seasonal changes in food abundance, and they in turn may affect other behavioral and ecological aspects of the biology of a species.

There are three principal classes of food upon which the vertebrates of a tropical forest are ultimately dependent: leaves, fruits, and arthropods. There is a complex web of interdependence between and within these classes but, from the point of view of a vertebrate consumer, they may be considered as distinct. It should be possible to measure the way in which the availability of each class of food varies with time, and such measurements would aid in the understanding of the effects of seasonal abundance of food upon the evolution of various adaptations of the consumers to their environment.

I reported earlier (Smythe, 1970) on the seasonal availability of falling fruit in the moist forest of Barro Colorado Island, and commented on some of its effects upon the ecology of the terrestrial frugivorous mammals. I then became interested in attempting to measure the seasonal availability of other types of food that are important to vertebrates in the same environment and, in this paper, I describe temporal fluctuations in the numbers of certain insects over nearly 3 years.

The data are from light-traps. There is no doubt that light-traps have many shortcomings, some of which are more serious than others. They obviously sample only those insects that are attracted to the particular light source being used. The sample is practically entirely of flying insects and omits nonvolant immatures, thus neglecting an important food source for insectivores. The almost total absence of orthopterans from my data is probably due to sampling methods. This order constitutes an important food source for many animals, and its absence is lamentable.

Light-traps do not measure the total number of insects present in the sampling area, but they should show how the numbers of those species that are attracted vary with time and, if enough different species are trapped, if and when there is a season of general abundance or scarcity of food for insectivores. The relatively high annual predictability of the peaks and lows in the data presented here indicates that flying, phototropic insects do undergo seasonal changes in abundance. The timing of the breeding seasons of some insectivorous bats (Wilson, 1971) and birds (Morton, 1973; Karr, 1971) in the same general area where these data were gathered indicates (presuming that these animals find it advantageous to feed young at the times of maximum food abundance) that the seasonal variations shown by my data closely approximate the real situation.

In spite of the shortcomings inherent in light-trap data, I believe that the results presented in this paper, especially when considered in conjunction with sweep-sampling data (Janzen, 1973) or with the results of direct observational sampling (Robinson and Robinson, 1970; Elton, 1975; Windsor, 1978), are of some value as indicators of variation in abundance of an important foodstuff in the lowland forests of Central America and Panama.

METHODS

I constructed three traps (Figure 1) after the pattern of the "Pennsylvania" trap described by Southwood (1966) but with the following modifications. Four sheets of 6 mm acrylic sheet (Plexiglas) were placed around a vertical F15T8-BL fluorescent tube so that they formed walls with the tube at the center of a cross. Insects flying or circling close to the tube were thus likely to bump into the transparent walls and fall into the collecting funnel below. An additional advantage of this design was that a single light source was visible from any angle around the trap. Around the aluminum roof, which extended 30 cm beyond the outside of the acrylic center and around the top of the collecting cone, there were 10 cm walls of 1.6 mm acrylic sheet. The wide roof and the walls around its eave and around the top of the collecting cone were found to be necessary in order to prevent the entrance of spray during heavy rains. The transparency of the walls allowed the light to be seen through them and probably did not detract from the efficiency of the trap. The lid of a wide-mouthed, square, 3.8 l glass jar was fastened to the bottom of the collecting cone (with "pop-rivets") so that the jar itself could be screwed onto the cone. A 200 ml glass bottle, filled with carbon tetrachloride, was placed inside the larger jar. It had a small hole drilled in its top, through which projected the wick of an alcohol lamp. The carbon tetrachloride was thus evaporated slowly into the collecting jar. A bag, made of unbleached muslin, fit tightly in the mouth of the jar and hung inside it. The insects that fell down the collecting cone fell into the bag, which was immersed in the fumes of the evaporating poison, where they were quickly killed.

Figure 1. The three traps hanging in place.

Subjective observations, and the fact that some insectivores habitually forage at a particular height above the ground, indicate that there is considerable difference between the abundance of insects at different levels in the forest. I therefore decided to sample at three different levels: level I is about 2 m above the forest floor, II at about 20 m (in the thickest part of the canopy) and III is above most of the canopy at about 26 m. The traps were raised into position on a 12 mm nylon rope that passed over a pulley that was fastened high on a branch of a canopy-emergent *Pseudobombax* tree. The electrical cord that supplies current to the traps was led up the same rope.

Preliminary trapping indicated that a trap that remained lit during an entire night caught so many insects that (1) analysis of the sample with the available time and personnel was impossible and (2) the collecting sack became so full that the poison ceased to work efficiently, leaving some of the larger insects alive. A single large beetle thrashing about among thousands of smaller insects can render many of them unidentifiable. Because of these factors I decided to switch the traps on for 1 hour about half an hour after sunset and for another hour at midnight, for 4 out of the 7 days in each week. The traps were connected to a timeswitch and hoisted into position each Friday afternoon; each Tuesday morning they were lowered and the catch was removed for analysis.

The insects were dried to a constant weight at about 60°C. They were then separated into taxonomic orders, and each order was divided into three size classes. The choice of the limits for each size class was somewhat arbitrary but was influenced by the following rationale (bearing in mind that my primary interest was in the insects as food items for vertebrates): on the average, the capture of a very small insect probably requires the same expenditure of energy as does the capture of a somewhat larger one. The return from the energy expended thus increases with the size of the insect captured, but only up to a certain point. As they exceed a certain size, insects seem to have a disproportionate increase in their ability to defend themselves. Thus, while marmosets (*Saguinus geoffroyi*) or common opossums (*Didelphis marsupialis*) would probably totally ignore a small dipteran as a food item, each would eat a medium-sized cricket, but both are unable to deal with very large beetles. Small insectivorous bats, lizards, and frogs eat many of the smallest insects, but they get more value for their energy expenditure from those prey items near the upper end of their prey size range; and they are unable to deal with the larger insects. The question is where to place the limits in the light of these very broad generalizations? Whether the generalizations are valid or not, I found it convenient and, as it turned out, inform-

ative, to divide the trapped insects into three size classes: those of less than 5 mm, those of 5–15 mm, and those of greater than 15 mm total length. The measurements were taken from the front of the head to the tip of the gaster or to the tip of the closed wings, whichever was longer.

RESULTS AND DISCUSSION

To reduce confusion, the figures that follow were derived from the data by (1) dividing the total catch of the appropriate category by the number of times the traps were emptied that month, (2) adding five to the resulting quotient, and (3) taking the logarithm. Adding five to the quotients smooths the lower ends of the curves.

Figure 2 (part a) illustrates the monthly average of the grand total number of all insects collected. No clearly defined, predictable, seasonal peak appears, although numbers are lower during the late wet season months of September, October, and November (Figure 3). By comparison, there is a pronounced, predictable seasonal peak in the total biomass of insects collected (Figure 2, part b). Reference to Figure 4 shows the reason for this apparent paradox: the two larger classes, which contribute most of the weight of the sample, show the most pronounced and predictable seasonality. Although the smallest insects also show some seasonality, they are often most abundant at times when the largest ones are scarcest. The peak in total biomass occurs in the early wet season and corresponds with the season of greatest fruit abundance (Smythe, 1970). The magnitude of the peak is variable, but it is at least six to eight times that for the period of October through March.

Figure 4 represents the number of insects of each size class at each level in the forest. In general there are more insects and their numbers are more variable at the higher levels. Abundance appears to be inversely proportional to size. There are about 50 times as many insects in the smallest size class as there are in the largest. All sizes show some evidence of seasonal fluctuations, but these are most pronounced in the 5–15 mm class (Figure 4, part b). This is significant because the insects within this size range are probably the most important food for vertebrates. A very strong, predictable increase in numbers occurs in May and June. As I mentioned earlier, this is also the time that falling fruit is at its greatest abundance, and it is interesting to note that it is also the time of greatest abundance of new, green leaves (Leigh and Smythe, 1978).

Figure 4 also shows a much smaller, but still predictable, peak of abundance in December and January. This second peak is less pronounced in the larger

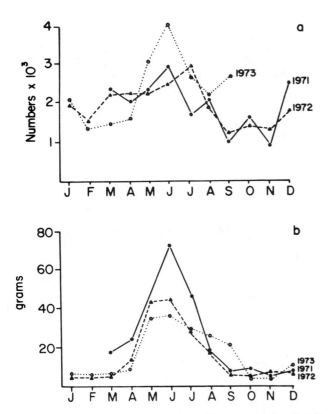

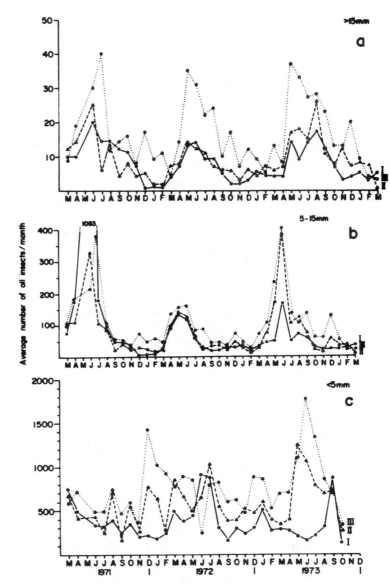

Figure 2. Part A: Total number of insects caught. Part B: Weight of insects caught.

Figure 4. Total numbers of insects caught.

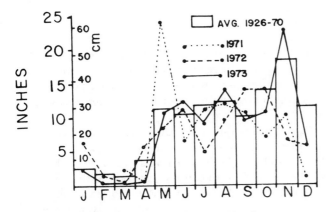

Figure 3. Rainfall on Barro Colorado Island.

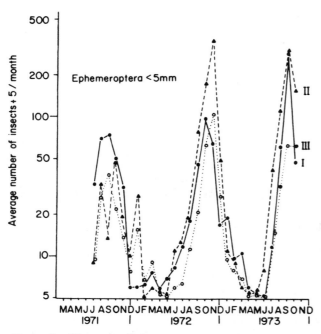

Figure 5. The order Ephemeroptera.

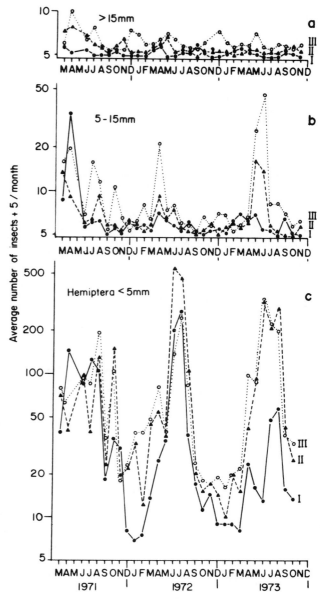

Figure 6. The order Hemiptera.

size classes, and also at level I, closest to the ground.

Figures 5 through 11 illustrate some of the more abundant orders of insects that were trapped. The Isoptera are conspicuously absent from these graphs, and termites are probably the most seasonal of all the insects in this habitat. There is a seasonal peak in abundance of flying termites: there are generally huge emergences of these insects following the first few showers of each wet season. (The abnormally high peak in numbers during May 1971 that appears in Figure 4, part b, was due to a flight of termites.) This mass emergence is undoubtedly effective as a predator saturation mechanism. For 3 successive years, near a small lake in Las Cumbres, about 35 km from the insect sampling site, I observed mass termite emergences following evening showers in the early wet season. On each occasion a flock of approximately 150 martins (*Progne chalybea*) began feeding on the termites as soon as they emerged. Each year the birds gorged themselves to the point that, after 30 to 45 minutes of feeding, every bird was perched on an overhead wire, and none was foraging, while the apparently undiminished clouds of termites continued flying. At other times, when there were no termite emergences, the flock of martins would continue foraging an hour or more longer, until it became almost completely dark.

The order Ephemeroptera (Figure 5), practically all of which were less than 5 mm long, shows very

distinct seasonal peaks during the mid wet- and early dry-season and practically no flying adults from February through May (which constitutes most of the dry season). There is little difference between forest levels.

Figure 6 illustrates the order of Hemiptera. Greater numbers, with more pronounced seasonal variation, were caught at the higher levels than at level I. The smallest size class, in contradistinction to that class in general, shows the most pronounced seasonality. In the 5–15 mm size class, by far the largest number of

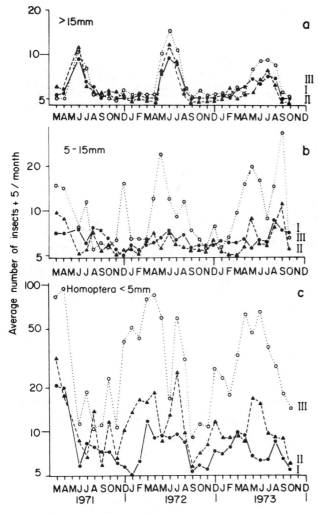

Figure 7.   The order Homoptera.

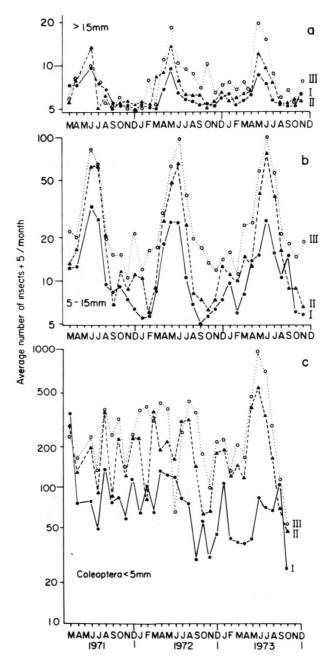

Figure 8.   The order Coleoptera.

insects were found at the higher levels. Their peaks in abundance occur during the same season, but not necessarily during the same month, of each year. The numbers are low, however, which could cause a considerable sampling error. Figure 6, part a, illustrates the Hemiptera of greater than 15 mm in length. The numbers are too low to be meaningful but, recalling that all data points on the graph are +5, the figure shows that practically all of the larger Hemiptera occur in levels II and III.

Figure 7 illustrates the Homoptera, all of which are plant feeders. In Figure 7, part c, it is evident that the numbers of homopterans less than 5 mm in length are much larger at the highest level of the forest; the same is true of the 5–15 mm class, but is less true of the over 15 mm class. Once again, the numbers are so low for the largest class that this may be a sampling

error. Most of the large Homoptera caught were *Fidicina mannifera*, a cicada that tends to occur only in the lower level of the forest (H. Wolda, pers. comm.). Cicadas emerge from fossorial nymphs, usually at night, fairly low on forest vegetation. The newly emerged adults may fly straight to the lower level traps). There is a strong seasonal pattern in all size classes, but this is distinguished more by sharp troughs than by peaks.

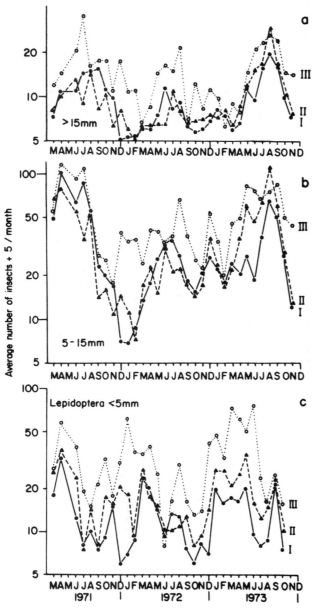

Figure 9.　The order Lepidoptera.

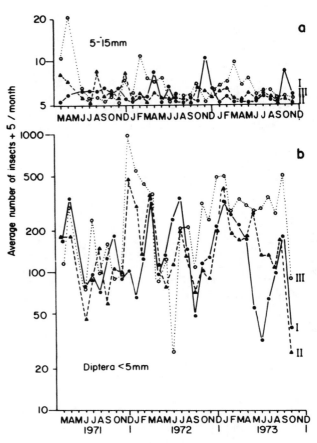

Figure 10.　The order Diptera.

The seasons of greatest abundance are coincident with the periods of greatest plant activity, as would be expected.

Since this work was done, Wolda (1977, 1978a, b, this volume) has worked extensively on seasonal abundance in homopterans. Reference should be made to the works cited for more detail.

The beetles, order Coleoptera, are illustrated in Figure 8. These are probably the most reliable data of this project, since beetles are the insects most easily caught in the type of traps that I used. Their hard

exoskeletons and the habit of many of them of closing their wings when they hit an object while in flight probably results in a greater proportion of beetles that approach the traps being caught than is true for other orders. The general conclusion that numbers are greater, but also more seasonally variable at the higher levels, holds true for all size classes of beetles. The 5 mm class shows no distinct seasonal variation, but the 5–15 mm class shows two distinct, predictable, seasonal peaks each year. An early wet season peak is followed by a late wet season low, and then a small early dry season peak. The peak in the early wet season can probably be ascribed to the general abundance of all types of food at that time, but the early dry season peak is more difficult to understand. Without a breakdown into finer taxonomic categories it is difficult to generalize, but it is interesting to note that in the late wet season there are often local storms of high intensity that blow down many trees. It is also common to find mammals that have died, apparently of starvation or related causes, at that time of the year. Both the broken trees and the dead animals would

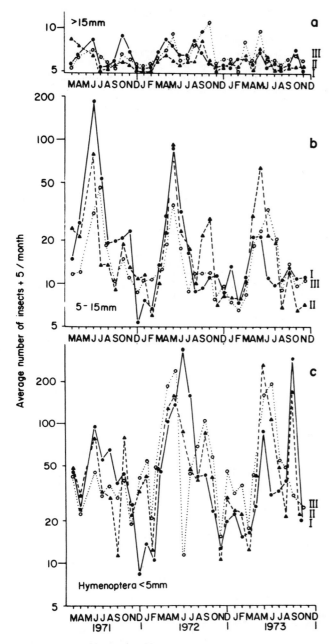

Figure 11. The order Hymenoptera.

in general. The abundance of lepidopterans is clearly highest at level III, but there is little difference between the two lower levels. There is a general increase in numbers during the early wet season, but at level III numbers remain high during much of the dry season. This is also the time when conspicuous flowers are most abundant and, since the adults of this order are principally nectar feeders, there is probably a correlation between the two phenomena. There was a sharp drop in the number of lepidopterans during the dry season of 1971–72, and it is interesting to note that in March 1971, a time when many trees were flowering, there was a brief period of exceptionally heavy rain (on 4 successive days there was more than 100 mm). It is possible that these rains washed pollen and nectar out of many of the flowers at that time and that the resulting shortage of food for adult lepidopterans lowered their reproductive ability, which resulted in a drop of numbers during the following season.

The Diptera are illustrated in Figure 10. Very few larger than 15 mm were trapped, so only the two smaller classes are illustrated. The stratification in abundance is much less pronounced in the Diptera than it is in most of the other orders, as is the consistency of fluctuation from one level to another. In general, the numbers show a small peak during the dry season (December through March). This may be because it is advantageous for nectar-feeding flying adults to be present at the time of maximum flower abundance. Or it may be that small bodies of water, less likely to harbor predators, are more abundant during dryer weather, and it is advantageous for some flies with aquatic larvae to breed at that time. Figure 10, part a, illustrates the very low numbers of larger Diptera. When they are present at all they are at the higher levels (a situation that is apparently reversed during daylight, when many large tabanid flies may be active near the forest floor).

The Hymenoptera (Figure 11) are characterized by a bimodal peak similar to that of the Coleoptera. There is little stratification in abundance, but the lower levels appear to show a slightly greater number than the upper. The periods of greatest abundance coincide with the times when food is generally abundant, but is slightly earlier than with most other insects, perhaps because of the large numbers of flowers that are usually present during the dry season.

As a general conclusion then, these data show that there is a predictable peak in seasonal abundance of some kinds of night-flying, phototropic insects. This peak is most pronounced among those insects of between 5 and 15 mm body length, which is probably the most important size of prey for the general insectivorous vertebrate.

constitute a source of food for beetle larvae. It may be that the peak in the early dry season is due to the increased food supply that was available during the previous October and November. The largest size class of beetles follows a pattern similar to that of the 5–15 mm class, except that the early dry season peak was absent in 1971–72.

The Lepidoptera (Figure 9) show rather less seasonal abundance variations than do the other orders

ACKNOWLEDGMENTS

This work was supported by the Environmental Sciences Program of the Smithsonian Institution. Gerald Chen assisted with collecting the data.

LITERATURE CITED

Elton, C. S.
1975.   Conservation and the low population density of invertebrates inside Neotropical rainforest. *Biological Conservation*, 7: 3–15.

Janzen, D. H.
1973.   Sweep samples of tropical foliage insects: effects of season, vegetation types, elevation, time of day and insularity. *Ecology*, 54: 687–708.

Karr, J. R.
1971.   Structure of avian communities in selected Panama and Illinois habitats. *Ecological Monographs*, 41: 207–233.

Leigh, E. G., and N. Smythe
1978.   Leaf production; leaf consumption, and the regulation of folivory on Barro Colorado Island. Pages 33–50 in *The Ecology of Arboreal Folivores*, edited by G. G. Montgomery. Washington, D.C.: Smithsonian Institution Press.

Morton, E. S.
1973.   On the evolutionary advantages and disadvantages of fruit-eating in tropical birds. *American Naturalist*, 107: 8–22.

Robinson, M. H., and B. Robinson
1970.   Prey caught by a sample population of the spider *Argiope argentata* (Araneae: Araneidae) in Panama—a year's census data. *Zool. J. Linn. Soc.*, 49: 345–358.

Smythe, N.
1970.   Relationships between fruiting seasons and seed dispersal methods in a neotropical forest. *American Naturalist*, 104: 25–35.

Southwood, T. R. E.
1966.   *Ecological Methods, with Special Reference to Insect Populations*. London: Methuen. 391 pp.

Wilson, D. E.
1971.   Food habits of *Micronycteris hirsuta* (Chiroptera: Phyllostomidae). *Mammalia*, 35: 107–110.

Windsor, D. M.
1978.   The feeding activities of tropical insect herbivores on some deciduous forest legumes. Pages 101–113 in *The Ecology of Arboreal Folivores*, edited by G. G. Montgomery. Washington, D.C.: Smithsonian Institution Press.

Wolda, H.
1977.   Fluctuations in abundance of some Homoptera in a neotropical forest. *Geo-Eco-Trop.*, 3: 229–257.
1978a.   Fluctuations in abundance of tropical insects. *American Naturalist*, 112: 1017–1045.
1978b.   Seasonal fluctuations in rainfall, food and abundance of tropical insects. *Journal of Animal Ecology*, 47: 369–381.
1982.   Seasonality of Homoptera on Barro Colorado Island. Pages 319–330 in *The Ecology of a Tropical Forest*, edited by Egbert G. Leigh, Jr., et al. Washington, D.C.: Smithsonian Institution Press.

Seasonality of Homoptera on Barro Colorado Island

HENK WOLDA   Smithsonian Tropical Research Institute, Balboa, Republic of Panama

ABSTRACT

The Homoptera on Barro Colorado Island were studied with the aid of light-traps. The 87,547 individuals caught include at least 717 species. Almost one-quarter of these species are represented by only a single individual, showing that many more species are probably present. The species, on average, have longer seasons and less well-defined seasonal peaks than leaf-hoppers from temperate or subarctic areas, but some species have seasons as short, and seasonal peaks as sharp, as species from northern Finland. Species with shorter seasons, with more defined seasonal peaks, tend to change more in abundance from year to year than species that demonstrate less seasonal variation in abundance. The distribution of the seasonal peaks over the year suggests that the species tend to reduce the presence of other species to a minimum because of a strong interaction between the species.

INTRODUCTION

Pronounced seasonal fluctuations have been shown to exist in many kinds of tropical insects (for references, see Wolda, 1978a). Until recently, however, no efforts have been made to describe these fluctuations in such a way that quantitative comparisons between different data sets, such as between different geographic areas, can profitably be made. I select two parameters, the seasonal range (*SR*) and the seasonal maximum (*SM*), which indicate the length of the season a given species is present in a given year, in weeks, and the sharpness of the seasonal peak, respectively, taking the effect of sample size into account, albeit in a somewhat crude manner. Applying these to light-trap data from Las Cumbres, Panama, an area strongly affected by man, 35 km east of Barro Colorado Island in Gatun Lake, Panama, I showed that Homoptera (leafhoppers) tend to have longer seasons and less sharp seasonal peaks than leafhoppers from Kansas, U.S.A., from England, or from Finland (Wolda, 1980a). This result is hardly surprising. In fact, about one-third of the species in Las Cumbres occur year round. Some species, however, in Las Cumbres have seasons as short as those found in northern Finland. There are a few species that do not seem to have any seasonal fluctuations at all, but such species are rare. These species show distributions in abundance that are similar to those of *Charaxes* butterflies in Sierra Leone (Owen and Chanter, 1972) or that of *Heliconia ethilla* in Trinidad (Ehrlich and Gilbert, 1973). The vast majority of leafhopper species, however, even of those that are found throughout the year, have well-defined fluctuations in abundance that are clearly related to the alternation of wet and dry seasons. Relatively small changes in rainfall pattern can appreciably change the seasonal distribution of many species (Wolda, 1978a).

It is conceivable that leafhoppers from a residential area like Las Cumbres are not representative of tropical leafhoppers in general. After all, the natural habitat in which these species evolved, at least in Panama, is the tropical forest, and it seems possible that the insects there behave in quite a different manner. This idea will be tested in the present paper, using light-trap data collected since 1973 in the forest on Barro Colorado Island. It will be shown that, although there are major differences in the species composition of the samples taken in both places, only 35 km apart, the general picture of the seasonal distribution of these species is very similar in two localities.

It was suggested that there might be an inverse correlation between the length of the season of a given species and the amount of change in abundance that occurs between successive years. A preliminary analysis of available data supported that hypothesis (Wolda, 1978b). A detailed analysis of the data from Las Cumbres also supported that hypothesis (Wolda, 1980a), and the same analysis will be shown here for the Barro Colorado leafhoppers. They again lend support to the hypothesis.

METHODS

The present study is being carried out on Barro Colorado Island in Gatun Lake, Panama, at 9°9′19″N; 79°45′19″W, on a ridge in the forest that is 121 m above sea level and 96 m above the level of the lake. The site is surrounded by tropical forest.

In a large tree (*Tachigalia versicolor* Standl. and Wms.; Leguminosae-Caesalpinoideae), a set of two light-traps was installed in June 1973, one at about 3 m above ground level and the other in the canopy at some 27 m above the forest floor, overlooking a large area of the Lutz catchment and of the Fairchild Peninsula. In November 1978 the traps were moved some 30 m. This small move is not expected to affect the results in any significant way. The light-traps used are of the Pennsylvania type, modified for the tropics by my colleague Nicholas Smythe. The insects are attracted by a Sylvania F15T8 BL fluorescent tube, fall through a funnel and, until early March 1977, fell into a cloth bag where they were killed by carbon tetrachloride. The trap was modified in March 1977 in that the insects now fall directly into preservative fluid; a mixture of alcohol, formaldehyde, and acetic acid (Kahle's solution; Borror et al., 1971). The insects that were collected dry were stored in a freezer for later sorting, those collected in liquid were stored in that liquid until sorting.

The traps operate all night every night, and the insects are collected every morning by Bonifacio de León, who sends them to my office where Saturnino Martínez takes care of the first sorting. Here the insects are sorted to groups; in some cases orders, in others families. Most of these groups have been or are being analyzed to species by specialists, while some groups are being analyzed to the species level in my office by Miguel Estribí and myself. The present paper deals only with Homoptera, for the analysis of which Miguel Estribí deserves most of the credit. The data on other groups will be dealt with elsewhere.

The average rainfall for Barro Colorado over the last 50 years is roughly 250 cm per year, some 91.5% of which falls in the 8 months of the rainy season, which is May through December (Windsor, 1977). The actual distribution of the rain over the year in the last 5 years is shown in Figure 1, where the rain per week is plotted against time. The time scale used merits some explanation. Because most insects have an annual low in their abundance in March, the insects' year

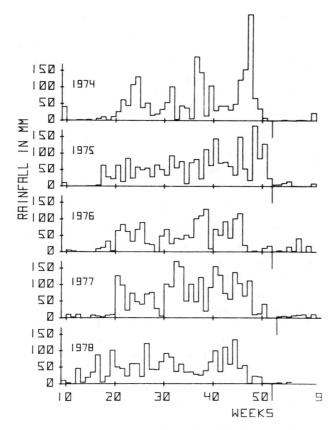

Figure 1. Seasonal distribution of rainfall, in mm per week, on Barro Colorado Island, Panama.

was taken to begin with the tenth Wednesday in the calendar year. Because of this convention, a year which usually has 52 weeks sometimes, as in 1977, has 53 weeks.

Temperature probably is not an important factor causing seasonality in insect populations, although it cannot definitely be discarded. Mean minimum temperature does not vary seasonally and remains at 22°C near the forest floor and some 0.5°C higher above the canopy. The mean maximum temperature near the forest floor is 27.5°C during most of the year, but may reach 30°C in April–May (Windsor, 1977). In the open, the mean maximum temperature is some 2°C higher, but has the same seasonal pattern. Relative humidity is high, especially near the forest floor, but it does have a seasonal rhythm in that it is lower in the dry season, with an annual minimum in April (Windsor, 1977).

Wind speed, which may affect the flight activity of insects, is, on the average, much higher in the dry season (January through April) than in the wet season, but this effect seems to be stronger during the day than during the night, when the light-traps are op-

erating (Windsor, 1977).

The relative abundance of species in light-trap samples may differ from the real relative abundance in the forest. Some species that are often seen in the forest rarely, if ever, are found in the trap (Wolda, 1979b). In species richness, the light-trap samples give an underestimate, and in relative abundance of the species the samples are probably biased. As long as there are no better data available, however, these samples will do to give an impression of what the fauna looks like. Comparisons are made with similar light-trap samples from Las Cumbres (Wolda, 1980a), and, as those are probably biased in the same direction, the comparison might be valid. For the study of annual and seasonal variations in abundance at the level of individual species, light-trap data are probably good for the vast majority of species, although some problems may sometimes arise (Wolda, 1978b).

Variation in abundance from year to year is measured using the annual variability (AV) parameter described in Wolda (1978b). It is the variance of the distribution of $\log R_i$, where $R_i = N_i(t + 1)/N_i(t)$ and $N_i(t)$ is the number of individuals caught of species i in year t.

For comparing faunal composition of different samples, two parameters are used: the coefficient of community (CC) and the percentage similarity (PS). The first is an indication of similarity in the kind of species present in the samples irrespective of their abundance (Pielou, 1975). $CC = 200C/(A + B)$ where A and B are the number of species present in the two samples to be compared, and C is the number of species both samples have in common. CC is very sensitive to presence or absence of some rare species. On the other hand, PS is mostly influenced by the more abundant species (Whittaker, 1952; Whittaker and Fairbanks, 1958).

$$PS = 100 \left(1 - 0.5 \sum_i |P_{ix} - P_{iy}|\right)$$
$$= 100 \sum_i \min (P_{ix}, P_{iy})$$

where P_{ix} and P_{iy} are the number of individuals of species i as a proportion of the total number of individuals in samples x and y.

The seasonal distribution is also measured by two parameters. SR and SM. The length, in weeks, of the period of a year when the species is present or, rather, 52 minus the longest stretch of weeks in which the species was not observed, is called the season length (SL). Season length depends on sample size, which can, to some extent, be taken into account using the relation between SL and sample size as found in seasonally normal distributions with known seasonal standard deviations (SSD), through computer simulations. Seasonal range (SR) is the corrected season length, the length of the period in which 99% of the individuals of the species are expected to occur; $SR = 5.1 \times SSD$. For further details, see Wolda (1979a, 1980a).

The seasonal maximum (SM) is the number of individuals found in the peak 4 consecutive weeks of a year divided by the average number per 4 weeks for that year. SM varies between 13, when all individuals are found within one 4-week period, to a minimum of unity when the same number of individuals is caught each week of the year. Because of stochastic variation, both in the natural populations and in the sampling, the actual minimum will never reach unity even in species that are completely nonseasonal. SM is also affected by sample size, and this is taken into account by using, in a plot of SM on N, lines indicating the relationship SM versus sample size as given by simulated seasonally normal distributions with different SSD (Wolda, 1979a; 1980a).

For deciding when an annual peak in the distribution occurs, a number of conventions have been adopted. Basically, it is the week with the most individuals within the 4-week period that constitutes the maximum of the season. In smaller samples this does not always work, and then the midpoint of the season was chosen. In some cases there was clearly more than one peak, and in such cases the peaks were all included in the plot. The decision on whether there is "clearly" more than one peak is necessarily subjective.

RESULTS

In 1974–77, a total of 87,547 individual leafhoppers were obtained, belonging to at least 717 species. In the vast majority of the cases there is little question of the integrity of the species recognized; but, in some cases, there are doubts, e.g., two taxa on the subfamily Typhlocybinae, including the green *Empoasca*, each probably represents a number of species. Anyway, the distribution of these individuals and species over the various (sub)families of the Homoptera involved is given in Table 1. The Cicadellidae are listed per subfamily (Cicadellinae–Coelidiinae in the table), while the various families within the Fulgoroidea (Achilidae–Issidae in Table 1) are left intact, as is customary and convenient, considering the number of individuals involved. For about the same number of individuals, the Barro Colorado samples have some 33% more species than the samples from Las Cumbres. The subfamilies of the Cicadellidae in Las Cumbres tend to have many more individuals than they have on Barro Colorado, while most other groups are better represented on Barro Colorado. In terms of numbers of species, the same difference exists, but to a lesser extent. On Barro Colorado, only 8.5% of the species are common enough in the trap so that after 4 years

more than 100 individuals were obtained as compared with 20.4% in Las Cumbres (Wolda, 1980a). On the other hand, the number of species in which only a single individual was caught in 4 years is 168, which is 23.4% of all the species, as compared with 19.8% in Las Cumbres (Wolda, 1980a). The fact that almost a quarter of the species are represented by only one individual shows that many more species can be expected to appear in the traps in the future. The number of 717 for the species present on Barro Colorado Island is a gross underestimate (cf. Wolda, 1979b).

A comparison between the faunas of Barro Colorado and Las Cumbres is also made in Table 2. The CC, indicating the overlap in species, is 56.6, while the PS is only 25.4, showing that, of the species that are found in both places, many tend to be common in one place and rare in the other. As a basis for comparison, Table 2 also lists the values of CC and PS for consecutive years on Barro Colorado Island. The values for the comparison 1976–77, especially for PS, are lower than for the other years. It is premature to decide about the causes for these lower values, i.e., the larger changes that occurred between 1976 and 1977. It could have to do with the unusually long dry season at the beginning of 1977, but it could also be explained by the change in collecting technique, i.e., the change from carbon tetrachloride to Kahle's solution.

Annual Variability

The change in abundance of the individual species as summarized by AV is given in Table 3. The values for AV for the statistically more reliable data, i.e., when NS is at least equal to 5, for 1974–75 and for 1975–76 are slightly smaller than the corresponding data from Las Cumbres (Wolda, 1980a), but not significantly so. A smaller value for AV means a greater numerical stability of the species involved, but such a greater stability in the forest on Barro Colorado as compared with an open area much affected by human activities is at this moment only a suggestion, not supported by the statistical analysis of the available data. From 1976 to 1977 the changes in abundance were larger, resulting in a significantly larger AV ($p < 0.01$). This, again, is probably due to the unusually long dry season at the beginning of 1977, but an effect of the change in collecting technique at the beginning of 1977 cannot be ruled out at this stage.

As I have discussed before (Wolda, 1978b), one might expect species with a sharp seasonal peak to be more variable in abundance from year to year, to give larger values for AV, than species that do not have well-defined seasonal fluctuations in abundance. The data from Las Cumbres supported this hypothesis (Wolda,

Table 1. Homoptera collected during 4 years on Barro Colorado Island, Panama, as compared with similar samples from Las Cumbres, Panama

	Individuals			Species			BCI species	
	Number BCI	% BCI	% LC	Number BCI	% BCI	% LC	N>100	N=1
Cicadidae	3163	3.6	2.1	14	2.0	1.8	2	2
Membracidae	1936	2.2	0.3	66	9.2	5.5	1	15
Cercopidae	3021	3.4	0.1	17	2.4	2.0	2	6
Psyllidae	2254	2.6	0.1	36	5.0	2.8	2	13
Cicadellinae	6482	7.4	22.2	40	5.6	6.5	4	14
Agalliinae	52	0.06	7.1	8	1.1	1.8	—	3
Xestocephalinae	3347	3.8	11.2	11	1.5	2.0	2	1
Hecalinae	—	—	0.001	—	—	0.2	—	—
Nirvaniinae	55	0.06	0.005	2	0.3	0.4	—	—
Ledrinae	—	—	0.002	—	—	0.2	—	—
Deltocephalinae	3826	4.4	10.3	52	7.2	13.0	3	13
Typhlocybinae	11023	12.6	15.5	81	11.3	16.5	4	15
Idiocerinae	534	0.6	1.4	14	1.9	2.4	1	2
Gyponinae	804	0.9	5.7	56	7.8	6.1	—	16
Neocoelidiinae	118	0.1	0.08	9	1.3	0.9	—	2
Coelidiinae	37	0.04	0.01	3	0.4	0.7	—	1
Achilidae	13845	15.8	5.3	38	5.3	3.9	7	4
Cixiidae	9756	11.1	2.6	40	5.6	5.9	6	9
Acanaloniidae	53	0.06	0.02	2	0.3	0.4	—	—
Achilixiidae	19	0.02	0.1	1	0.1	0.2	—	—
Fulgoridae	941	1.1	0.07	19	2.6	0.4	1	5
Flatidae	6445	7.3	3.8	38	5.3	4.2	8	8
Nogodinidae	4	0.005	0.02	2	0.3	0.2	—	1
Kinnaridae	92	0.1	0.02	3	0.4	0.5	—	—
Derbidae	3709	4.2	3.9	87	12.1	10.4	3	22
Tropiduchidae	240	0.3	0.007	3	0.4	0.4	—	—
Delphacidae	14239	16.2	7.7	59	8.2	8.7	13	10
Dictyopharidae	1546	1.8	0.4	12	1.7	1.8	2	4
Issidae	6	0.07	—	4	0.6	—	—	2
Total	87547		86039	717		540	61	168

BCI denotes Barro Colorado Island; LC denotes Las Cumbres.

Table 2. Similarity between samples of Homoptera in successive years on Barro Colorado Island, Panama, and between the total collected on Barro Colorado Island and Las Cumbres, Panama

	Community coefficient (CC)	Percentage similarity (PS)
BCI 1974 vs. 1975	75.5	76.4
BCI 1975 vs. 1976	75.5	76.6
BCI 1976 vs. 1977	74.2	61.3
BCI vs. LC	56.6	25.4

BCI denotes Barro Colorado Island; LC denotes Las Cumbres.

Table 3. Change in abundance from year to year in Homoptera from Barro Colorado Island, Panama, as measured by the annual variability index

	1974/75	1975/76	1976/77
$NS \geq 5$			
N	186	206	205
Mean $\log R_i$	0.146	−0.022	0.127
Var. $\log R_i = AV$	0.084	0.092	0.150
All NS			
N	392	412	446
Mean $\log R_i$	0.181	0.016	0.137
Var. $\log R_i$	0.249	0.273	0.396

The annual variability index (AV) is the variance of the distribution of $\log R_i$, where R_i is $N_i(t + 1)/N_i(t)$ for the ith species. The mean of the distribution of $\log R_i$ is also given. The statistically more reliable data are those where the smallest of the two N values (NS) is at least equal to 5.

1980a). This hypothesis is now tested with the present data. For those species that, in 2 successive years, have a not-well-defined seasonal peak, i.e., have values for SM smaller than 4, AV was calculated and compared with the species that have, in 2 successive years, values for SM of at least 6.5. Values of $SM = 6.5$ are only accepted if the number of individuals in that year was at least 10. In all other cases, N was at least equal to 6, the minimum value accepted to calculate SM. For the data with the sharp seasonal peaks ($SM \geq 6.5$), AV is 0.208, which is significantly higher than for the

data with $SM \leq 4$, where $AV = 0.082$ ($p < 0.01$). The present data thus again support the hypothesis. Species that do not show pronounced seasonal variation in abundance tend to vary little in abundance from year to year as compared with species that have well-defined seasonal fluctuations.

Seasonal Distribution

The number of individuals per week in two major groups of Homoptera, the Cicadellidae and the Fulgoroidea, is plotted in Figures 2 and 3. The Delphacidae are not included because of the often erratic seasonal distribution (Wolda, 1977, 1978a, 1980a). As explained above, the time scale is such that each year begins with week 10 of the calender year.

There is a pronounced cycle in abundance, especially in the Fulgoroidea, with a period of about 4 weeks. This is an artifact produced by the cycle of the moon and has nothing to do with real variations in abundance in the populations (Wolda, 1977). As can be seen in Figure 1, the dry season 1976–77 was extremely long. It started at a record early date, 21 November 1976, according to the Meteorological Branch of the Panama Canal Commission (formerly Panama Canal Company), and lasted until the middle of May 1977. The first major peak in abundance of Homoptera did not occur until week 21, which is from 18–24 May, about 1 week after the rains started. In 1978, on the other hand, the rains started unusually early, in the first few days of April, and so did the leafhoppers. The year 1976 is somewhat intermediate. The occurrences in 1974 and 1975 have been discussed before (Wolda, 1978a). In that paper it was shown that rain strongly affects the seasonal pattern of the production of new leaves in the forest, the major source of food for many leafhoppers and, thus, indirectly affects the seasonal distribution of those leafhoppers. This effect can again be shown with the present data. In Figure 4, the production of new leaves in 1976, 1977, and 1978 is given. A large number of trees are examined every week by Bonifacio de León, including many species, and for each tree he determines whether the tree has new leaves on some branches (partial flush), leaves all over (full flush), or no new leaves to speak of. The percentage of all the trees examined with full flush of new leaves is plotted as a histogram in Figure 4 and the partial flush by a continuous undulating line. The relationship between the time of the rains at the beginning of the wet season and the timing of the first major peak in leaf production is striking. Again the causal sequence (rain–leaf production–insect abundance) suggests itself rather strongly.

Table 4. Distribution of the seasonal maximum (*SM*) of Homoptera taken with light-traps on Barro Colorado Island, Panama, in 1974–77

SM classes	Seasonal standard deviation							N
	<1	1–2	2–4	4–7	7–11	11–20	>20	
1974	1.6	7.3	15.0	32.6	29.0	10.9	3.6	193
1975	0.9	6.1	20.4	35.2	20.9	10.4	6.1	230
1976	0.4	7.4	16.9	38.1	25.1	7.4	4.8	231
1977	1.2	12.4	18.5	26.3	23.6	11.6	6.6	259
Cicadidae	—	20.7	41.4	37.9	—	—	—	29
Membracidae	—	—	13.2	47.2	26.4	11.3	1.9	53
Cercopidae	—	—	33.3	53.3	13.3	—	—	15
Psyllidae	3.1	34.4	28.1	21.9	6.3	3.1	3.1	32
Cicadellidae	2.0	10.5	18.4	34.0	21.8	8.2	5.1	294
Fulgoroidea–Delph.	0.3	2.8	11.6	30.4	32.2	14.9	7.8	395
Delphacidae	1.1	18.9	31.6	30.5	14.7	2.1	1.1	95
All Barro Colorado Island	1.0	8.4	17.9	32.9	24.4	10.1	5.4	913
All Las Cumbres	0.5	4.1	14.7	39.1	27.0	11.3	3.3	637

For comparison the distribution of *SM* for Homoptera taken by a similar light-trap during 3½ years at Las Cumbres, Panama, is also given. The data are presented as percentages.

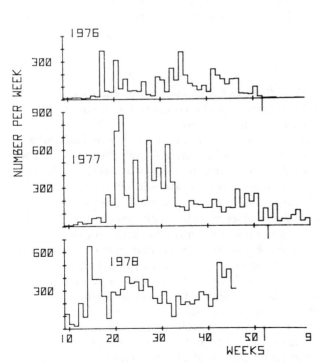

Figure 2. Seasonal distribution of Cicadellidae (Homoptera) in number of individuals per week in the light-traps on Barro Colorado Island, Panama.

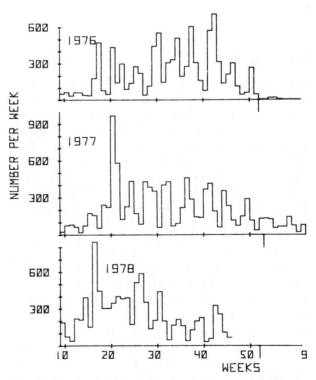

Figure 3. Seasonal distribution of Fulgoroidea (less the Delphacidae) (Homoptera) in individuals per week in the light-traps on Barro Colorado Island, Panama.

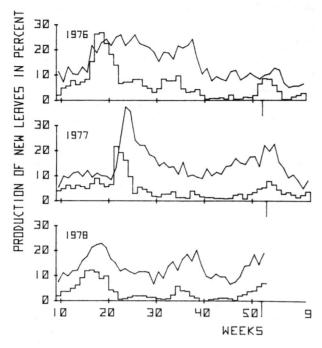

Figure 4. Seasonal distribution of the production of new leaves in the forest on Barro Colorado Island, Panama. Given are the percentages of the total number of trees in the census that are fully producing new leaves (histogram) or that are only producing new leaves on some branches (continuous line).

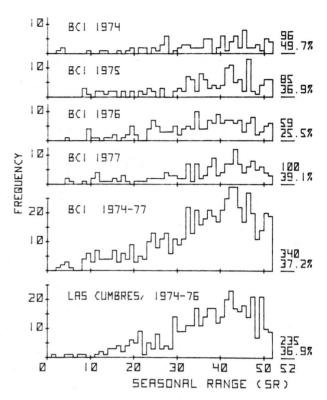

Figure 5. The length of the active season of the adults of the Homoptera on Barro Colorado Island, Panama, as measured by the seasonal range. The data are given per year and for the 4 years combined. Data from Las Cumbres are included for comparison. The week numbers refer to the calendar year.

Seasonal Range

For each species that in a given year had at least six individuals in the trap, the SR was determined, which is equivalent to the time span in weeks in which 99% of the individuals are expected to be found. The effect of sample size is taken into account (Wolda, 1979a, 1980a). The results for the leafhoppers from Barro Colorado Island are plotted, per year, in Figure 5. Differences between years are tested by lumping the weeks 0–10, 10–20, . . .40–51.9, keeping the species with an SR of 52 separate, and then different years, or different groups, are compared, using chi-square. The 4 years are significantly different ($p < 0.001$), which is almost entirely because 1976 had shorter seasons, i.e., having more species with SR values between 20 and 40. The year 1976 was relatively dry with a wet season that ended on 21 November, a record early date for the beginning of a dry season. It is, therefore, not surprising that 1976 should have relatively more species with short seasons, with low values of SR. Unfortunately, the data for 1978 are not available yet, but, considering the early start of the wet season, one might predict that there will be relatively many large values for SR.

The SR values for all 4 years combined are also plotted in Figure 5, to be compared with the SR values from Las Cumbres, covering 3 years. The data show that Barro Colorado Island has relatively more SR values between 0 and 30 and relatively fewer between 30 and 53, as compared with Las Cumbres, but the difference is not significant statistically ($p = 0.28$).

The SR values per (super)family are plotted in Figure 6, and differences between families are tested using chi-square. The only nonsignificant differences are those between Membracidae and Cercopidae ($p = 0.13$), between Membracidae and Fulgoroidea ($p = 0.20$), and between Cercopidae and Delphacidae ($p = 0.24$). All other differences are significant, most of them highly significant ($p < 0.01$). Cicadas have rather short seasons while membracids and fulgoroids have, on the average, very long seasons. The other groups are intermediate. Compared with Las Cumbres (Wolda, 1980a), the values for the cicadas are about the same. The SR values for the Cicadellidae are, on the average, smaller than in Las Cumbres, while for

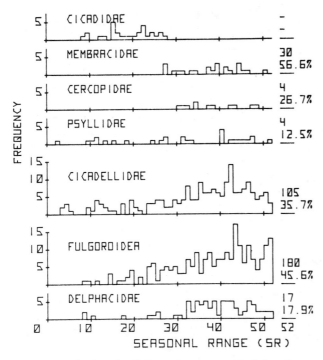

Figure 6. The length of the active season of adults of various groups within the Homoptera as measured by the seasonal range, on Barro Colorado Island, Panama.

Membracidae, Fulgoroidae, and Delphacidae they tend to be larger. The data for Psyllidae and Cercopidae in Las Cumbres are insufficient to allow a comparison.

Seasonal Maximum

The seasonal maximum (SM), an indication of the sharpness of the seasonal peak, is plotted against sample size in Figure 7. Simulation experiments with seasonally normal distributions with various seasonal standard deviations (SSD) were carried out in order to determine the relationship between SM and sample size at a number of SSD values. The lines in Figure 7 illustrate this relationship. For further details see Wolda (1980a). The number of data points between each two lines was determined and given, in percentages, in Table 4. The column headings refer to the SSD values belonging to each line. There are no significant differences in SM values between the years ($p = 0.14$).

The difference between Barro Colorado Island and Las Cumbres is significant ($p = 0.003$), which means that, on the average, Homoptera on Barro Colorado tend to have sharper seasonal peaks (have higher values for SM, which means tend to occur in the left-hand columns of Table 4) than those from Las

Cumbres. Many of the differences between families are significant. Cicadas, psyllids, and delphacids tend to have relatively sharp seasonal maxima, while fulgoroids and membracids tend to have peaks that are less well defined. Cicadellids and cercopids occupy intermediate positions.

Comparing again Las Cumbres with Barro Colorado, one can say that the SM values for cicadas tend to be the same in both places, that membracids, cicadellids, and delphacids tend to have sharper seasonal peaks on Barro Colorado, while the fulgoroids tend to have, on the average, slightly sharper peaks in Las Cumbres (Wolda, 1980a).

Timing of the Peaks

For each species in each year it was decided in what week the populations reached a peak, or, if there were more than one peak, in what weeks they occurred (see above). The results for all species combined are plotted, per year and the years combined, in Figure 8. Some peaks occur in the dry season, but those are rare; most peaks are found in the rainy season. Because of the seasonal pattern in the production of new leaves (Figure 4) with its peak during the early part of the rainy season, one might expect that most Homoptera species, at least those who depend on those new leaves for food, would also have their annual peaks during those months. In fact, the peaks are rather evenly distributed over the rainy season, which suggests that there is an interaction between the species, which causes them to be spread out over the wet season rather than to be concentrated in the most favorable months. Some species have their seasonal peak right at the beginning of the rainy season and, as one might expect, the date of these first peaks varies between years (Figure 8) because of the variation in starting date of the wet season (Figure 1). The data for 1978, with its early start of the rainy season, are not yet available.

The data for all 4 years combined are also given in Figure 8, together with similar data from Las Cumbres, covering 3 years (Wolda, 1980a). There is one major difference: in Las Cumbres there are many species that reach their peak of abundance in the trap in the early dry season. These are species that have an increased activity during that period as their habitat deteriorates. This phenomenon does not occur on Barro Colorado, but otherwise the data from the two localities are rather similar.

DISCUSSION

As one might expect, the fauna of leafhoppers in a relatively undisturbed forest on Barro Colorado is

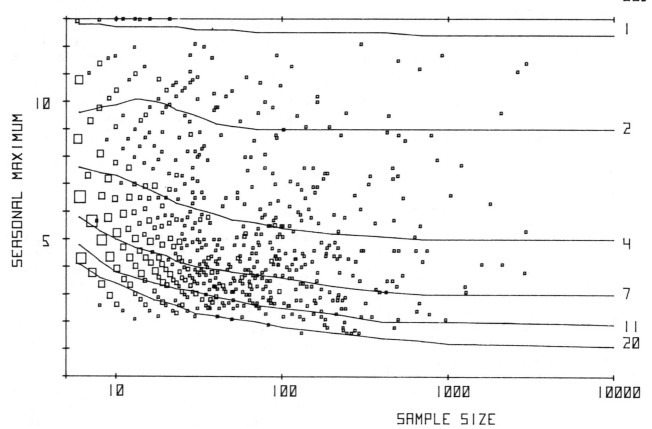

Figure 7.   A plot of the values for the seasonal maximum, a measure of the sharpness of the seasonal peak, against sample size. The size of each point is proportional to the number of data points it represents. The lines give the theoretical relation between *SM* and *N* for simulated seasonally normal distributions with seasonal standard deviations (*SSD*) as indicated.

richer in species than that in Las Cumbres, in an environment strongly affected by man. The difference is not impressive, however, especially if one takes into account that both collections are far from complete (as evidenced by the high percentage of species represented by a single individual only) and that on Barro Colorado insects are trapped with two traps, as opposed to only one in Las Cumbres, and represent one more year of collecting. Nevertheless, the difference between Barro Colorado and Las Cumbres in species richness is undoubtedly real. The relatively high number of individuals caught in Las Cumbres is partly to be attributed to many Cicadellidae, and some other species, having a major flight at the beginning of the dry season when the lawns where they live dry out.

The difference in species composition between Barro Colorado Island and Las Cumbres (Table 2), however, is only partly because Las Cumbres is impoverished as a result of the cutting of the forest. The distance between the two sites, as the crow flies, is only 35 km, but Las Cumbres is just on the Pacific slope of the isthmus of Panama while Barro Colorado is on the Atlantic side, and, in many aspects, the fauna and flora of one side are different from those on the other (Standley, 1928; Ridgely, 1976, among others). The leafhoppers are no exception. Many species known from Las Cumbres and not from Barro Colorado, classified initially as "open country species," are really "Pacific species" as they are also found in good forest on Majé Island in the Bayano area (unpublished data), some 100 km east from Las Cumbres.

The fluctuations in abundance from year to year on Barro Colorado Island are similar to those in the more disturbed area of Las Cumbres. On Barro Colorado Island, as found before in Las Cumbres, the changes in abundance from year to year are correlated with the seasonal fluctuations in that shorter seasons with sharper seasonal peaks tend to have larger

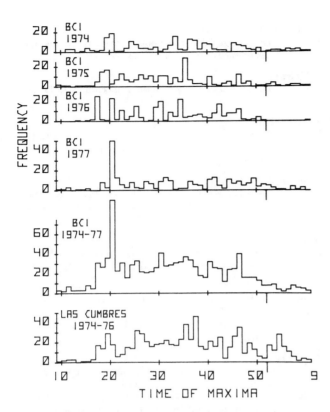

Figure 8. The timing of the seasonal peaks given as the week in which the peak occurs for the Homoptera on Barro Colorado Island, Panama. Data are given per year and for 4 years combined. Data on Homoptera from Las Cumbres (Panama) are included for comparison.

fluctuations in abundance from year to year. Extrapolating from this finding to insects in temperate areas, where all species have well-defined seasonal peaks and have relatively short season, is not justified. Such extrapolation would predict that the changes in abundance in temperate areas are much greater from one year to another than in the tropics, and this is not true (Wolda, 1978b).

A strong correlation was found (Wolda, 1978a) between the occurrence of rain in the dry seson, the production of new leaves, and the seasonal distribution of Homoptera in the forest on Barro Colorado. Now an additional 2 years of data are available and these 2 years happen to be very different in the time of the first rains of the wet season. As predicted, this had a large infuence on the seasonal pattern of both leaf production and, indirectly, Homoptera abundance.

The seasonal distribution of the species of leafhop-

pers on Barro Colorado is very similar to that found in Las Cumbres (Wolda, 1980a). On the average, the length of the seasons, as measured by the SR, is slightly, but not significantly, shorter than in Las Cumbres ($p = 0.28$), and the sharpness of the seasonal peaks, as measured by the SM, is slightly more pronounced on Barro Colorado Island ($p = 0.003$). This difference stands even if one analyses only the data on those 129 species that are sufficiently abundant in the samples from both localities to give values for SR and SM. In 55.0% of these species the season in Las Cumbres was longer than on Barro Colorado (larger SR in Las Cumbres), which is not significantly different from 50–50. On the other hand, 66.7% of the species had sharper seasonal peaks (higher SM values) on Barro Colorado Island, which is significant ($p < 0.01$). If one takes only those species where the difference between the two sites is relatively large, i.e., smallest SR at most 75% of largest and difference between SM values more than 2, 74.2% of the species have shorter seasons on Barro Colorado and 72% have sharper peaks, which is significant in both cases ($p < 0.01$). The difference is especially clear in the Cicadellidae, but almost nonexistent in the Fulgoroidea, with the possible exception of the Delphacidae. Much of the difference may have to do with the extra activity peak of Homoptera, especially some Cicadellidae, at the beginning of the dry season in Las Cumbres, a peak which is not found on Barro Colorado Island. In spite of these differences, the general conclusion is that, in terms of SR and SM, the Homoptera in Las Cumbres and Barro Colorado are very similar.

On a larger geographic scale, large differences are found (Wolda, 1980a) with shorter seasons and sharper seasonal peaks as one goes farther north.

Ricklefs (1966) has shown that the nesting season of birds is not staggered as one would expect if the bird species were to avoid or reduce interspecific interactions. A preliminary analysis of my data on leafhopper abundance (Wolda, 1977) leads to a similar conclusion in that I found no tendency to reduce interspecific interactions by occurring at different times of the year. The longer series of data and the more detailed analysis of these data now lead to the opposite conclusion. Both on Barro Colorado Island and in Las Cumbres the seasonal peaks seem to be more evenly distributed over the entire rainy season than one might expect, which suggests a maximum of interspecific avoidance (Figure 8). Biological interactions between leafhopper species are evidently strong enough to force the seasonal peaks to be spread all over the wet season. There are new leaves being produced the year round, but there are well-defined seasonal maxima and minima (Figure 4). It could thus be that some species are forced to occur at times when the production of their food is not at a maximum, but whether this is true cannot be decided as long as life history data on these species are lacking. It seems highly likely that many of the Homoptera species are specific to one or a few species of food plants, but data for the species under consideration here are almost completely lacking (Fennah, 1953; Claridge and Reynolds, 1972; Claridge and Wilson, 1976, 1978).

ACKNOWLEDGMENTS

I am deeply grateful to the help received in sorting and identifying the insects from Mr. Miguel Estribí and Mr. Saturnino Martínez. I also gratefully acknowledge the work of Bonifacio de León who took care of the daily operation of the light-traps and who collected the data on leaf phenology. The work is partially supported by the Environmental Sciences Program of the Smithsonian Intitution.

LITERATURE CITED

Borror, D. J., D. M. DeLong, and C. A. Triplehorn
1971.   *An Introduction to the Study of Insects.* 3rd ed. New York: Holt, Rinehart and Winston. 812 pp.

Claridge, M. F., and W. J. Reynolds
1972.   Host Plant Specificity, Oviposition Behaviour and Egg Parasitism in Some Woodland Leafhoppers of the Genus *Oncopsis* (Hemiptera Homoptera:Cicadellidae). *Transactions of the Royal Entomological Society of London,* 124: 149–166.

Claridge, M. F., and M. R. Wilson
1976.   Diversity and Distribution Patterns of Some Mesophyl-feeding Leafhoppers of Temperate Woodland Canopy. *Ecological Entomology,* 1: 231–250.
1978.   Seasonal Changes and Alternation of Food Plant Preference in Some Mesophyl-feeding Leafhoppers. *Oecologia,* 37: 247–255.

Ehrlich, P. R., and L. E. Gilbert
1973.   Population Structure and Dynamics of the Tropical Butterfly *Heliconius ethilla. Biotropica,* 5: 69–82.

Fennah, R. G.
1953.   Some Aspects of the Food Problem of Homoptera in the Humid Areas of the Neotropical Region. *Transactions of the Ninth International Congress of Entomology,* 2: 260–265.

Levins, R.
1968.   *Evolution in Changing Environments.* Princeton, N.J.: Princeton University Press.

Owen, D. F., and D. O. Chanter
1972.   Species Diversity and Seasonal Abundance in *Charaxes* butterflies (Nymphalidae). *Journal of Entomology (A),* 46: 135–143.

Pielou, E. C.
1975.   *Ecological Diversity.* New York: John Wiley and Sons. 165 pp.

Ricklefs, R. E.
1966.   The Temporal Component of Diversity Among Species of Birds. *Evolution,* 20: 235–242.

Ridgely, R. S.
1976.   *A Guide to the Birds of Panama.* Princeton, N.J.: Princeton University Press. 394 pp.

Standley, P. C.
1928.   *Flora of the Panama Canal Zone.* Contribution to the U.S. National Herbarium, No. 27. New York: J. Cramer. 410 pp.

Windsor, D. M. (ed.)
1977.   *Environmental Monitoring and Baseline Data from the Isthmus of Panama, 1976.* Vol. 4. Washington, D.C.: Smithsonian Institution. 267 pp.

Whittaker, R. H.
1952.   A Study of the Summer Foliage Insect Communities in the Great Smoky Mountains. *Ecological Monographs,* 22: 1–44.

Whittaker, R. H., and C. W. Fairbanks
1958.   A Study of Plankton Copepod Communities in the Columbia Basin, Southeastern Wisconsin. *Ecology,* 39: 46–65.

Wolda, H.
1977.   Fluctuations in Abundance of Some Homoptera in a Neotropical Forest. *Geo-Eco-Trop,* 3: 229–257.
1978a.   Seasonal Fluctuations in Rainfall, Food and Abundance of Tropical Insects. *Journal of Animal Ecology,* 47: 369–381.
1978b.   Fluctuations in Abundance of Tropical Insects. *The American Naturalist,* 112: 1017–1045.
1979a.   Seasonality Parameters for Insect Populations. *Researches on Population Ecology,* 20: 247–256.
1979b.   Abundance and Diversity of Homoptera in the Canopy of a Tropical Forest. *Ecological Entomology,* 4: 181–190.
1980a.   Seasonality of Tropical Insects. I. Leafhoppers (Homoptera) in Las Cumbres, Panama. *Journal of Animal Ecology,* 49: 277–290.

Population Irruptions and Periodic Migrations in the Day-flying Moth *Urania fulgens*

NEAL G. SMITH Smithsonian Tropical Research Institute, Balboa, Republic of Panama

ABSTRACT

In Central America and throughout lowland tropical South America, day-flying moths of the genus *Urania* undertake unidirectional flights every year, usually between early August and late November. The movement may be synchronous over 34° of transequatorial latitude. In some years the numbers involved in this movement are many times greater than in others. The periodicity may be 8 years between very large flights and 4 years between lesser ones. The reasons for this are not understood. Their reproductive success in dry-season refugia may be the determinant of the number of individuals that will be involved in the rainy-season movement. Not all individuals in any area leave, thus several migratory generations may originate from one locality.

The adults require nectar to live and to reproduce. If there are no suitable flowers available when the adults emerge, they leave (migrate?). As larvae, they eat only *Omphalea* spp. (Euphorbiaceae), that are lianas and trees. These moths are the only insects that regularly eat the leaves of *Omphalea* spp. Observational and experimental data suggest that repeated grazing by three or more generations of *Urania* larvae on an individual *Omphalea* vine results in a response, presumably chemical, which greatly lowers the chances of survival and prolongs the development time of *Urania* that attempt to eat it. There is nothing known about the cost of this response to an individual *Omphalea* vine. It is suggested that flights by *Urania* are an adaptive response to locate *Omphalea* vines, outside their dry-season refugia, which have either low toxicity and/or higher nutritional value and are thus more suitable for *Urania* reproduction.

INTRODUCTION

Urania fulgens is a handsome butterfly-like moth which displays periodic, and often spectacular, population outbursts and movements. The unidirectional flights of this insect are a more or less annual event throughout Central and South America, but the numbers involved vary enormously, from a few in some years to hundreds of millions in others (Smith, 1972). In some years, such as 1969, these population outbursts have occurred within the same week over 34° of latitude, from Mexico to Bolivia. In those years of major population movement, the diurnal flight of millions of these conspicuous insects constitutes a spectacle that is perhaps without equal, at least in the neotropics. Why do these animals migrate?

This moth provides an unusually spectacular instance of population outbreak in tropical leaf-eating insects. Wolda and Foster (1978) discussed the outbreaks of another migratory moth, *Zunacetha annulata*, on Barro Colorado Island. This moth's caterpillars can defoliate shrubs of the common understory species *Hybanthus prunifolius* four times in a year. Wolda and Foster (1978) and Oppenheimer (this volume) mention other such outbreaks. *Urania*, however extreme, is by no means unique.

I will focus on aspects of the life history of this moth that may affect its migratory behavior and discuss the relationship of this moth to its larval food plant and the plants providing nectar to adults. Next I will summarize population fluctuations of *Urania* since my last compilation (Smith, 1972), which covered the period from 1850 to 1971. Finally, I present the results of a series of rearing experiments designed to elicit the factors in the larval environment that might affect an individual's behavior when it becomes adult.

DESCRIPTION, CLASSIFICATION, AND RANGE

Urania fulgens is a diurnal moth (Lepidoptera, Uraniidae) which as an adult resembles a swallow-tailed butterfly. It is black with iridescent green bars across each wing and white "tails" on the hind wings. Sexes may be distinguished in the field, for the females are larger (gravid females weigh 0.9–1.3 g; males weigh 0.2–0.3 g) and thus are more ponderous flyers, have bright green wing bars rather than the bronzy-green bars of the males, and have broader hind wings than the rather "kite-like" males.

Urania is restricted to the neotropics, but its subfamily occurs in East Africa, Madagascar (*Chrysiridia madagascariensis* is perhaps the most handsome moth in the world), the southern Philippines, Papua New Guinea, and northern Australia. This peculiar distribution reflects that of the larval food plant: species of the genus *Omphalea* (Euphorbiaceae) which are mainly lianas, but occasionally trees.

Some classifications considered that there are as many as eight species of *Urania* (Westwood, 1879). Seitz and Gaede (1930) treated *Urania* as being divided into four allopatric species, namely: *U. fulgens* (Veracruz, Mexico, throughout lowland Central America to northern Ecuador west of the Andes), *U. boisduvalii* (Cuba), the rare *U. sloanus* (Jamaica), and finally *U. leilus* (South America east of the Andes). The morphological differences are slight, and they might be best treated as races of one biological species; if so, *U. leilus* (L.) would be the name. The distribution of *Urania* precisely matches that of *Omphalea* in the lowland neotropics.

Larval Food Plant

Several species of *Omphalea* are reported from the neotropics, but the only one in Panama is the widespread *O. diandra*, which also occurs in Cuba, Jamaica, Central America, and throughout the lowlands of South America to Bolivia and Brazil. *Omphalea diandra* is an often huge, canopy liana of wet and swamp forest, often occurring in coastal areas behind the White Mangrove zone (*Laguncularia* sp.). I have also found it on 150 m high granite massifs in Surinam, and it occurs in various localities on Barro Colorado Island. It is difficult to recognize in heavy forest, and most individuals that I have studied were at forest edges. Its huge, tendril-like climbing organs often stick up above the canopy and provide the best field mark for recognizing the vine.

No botanical report, that I know of, lists it as a dominant species anywhere (e.g., Standley, 1928; Kenoyer, 1928; Holdridge and Budowski, 1956; Duke and Porter, 1970), and most fail to list it at all. Only Johnston (1949), writing about San Jose Island in the Bay of Panama, addresses himself to the biology of *Omphalea;* its hard, black seeds, still viable, were relatively common on the beach there. Johnston (1949), and Guppy (1917), writing about Trinidad, suggest that its seeds are dispersed by ocean-currents. While I think that this is partly true, I suspect that mammals are the chief dispersers, but I have no direct evidence. The fruits are the size of grapefruits and remain on the vine for many months before turning light orange and falling. I have never seen a vine, however large, with more than three fruits. In various areas of Central and South America, the seeds are roasted and eaten by man. *Omphalea oleifera*, a tree, is cultivated for its seeds in El Salvador (Calderon and Standley, 1941) and *O. triandra*, also a tree, has been introduced into Haiti for this purpose as well (Adams, 1972).

I have seen *O. diandra* occurring in "pockets" of from 1 huge vine almost 90 m long to groups of 20 vines contained in an area of about 1.5 sq. km of forest. I suspect that such pockets may be separated from other such areas by many kilometers.

While man, and perhaps other mammals, may eat the seeds, in 10 years of observing individual plants in the wild in Panama, Surinam, Venezuela, and Costa Rica, and, in my garden in Panama City, I have seen no lepidopteran larvae eating the leaves of *Omphalea diandra* save those of *Urania fulgens*. Several hemipterans suck on the stems and occasionally small beetles (Chrysomelidae) were found to nip pieces of the youngest emerging leaves. Except for leaf-cutting ants (*Atta* sp.), no insect other than *Urania* larvae regularly attack the leaves of *O. diandra*, yet *Urania* larvae apparently eat nothing else. I have tried raising *Urania* larvae from eggs that I placed on the fresh leaves of 11 other species of Euphorbiaceae from Panama, and they refused to feed. This, and the complete coincidence of the distribution of *Urania* with that of *Omphalea* spp., suggests that, as was first supposed by MacLeay (1834) and later by Guppy (1907), *Urania* is completely dependent on *Omphalea* spp. *Urania* larvae also display choice between species of *Omphalea*. Second and later instars (five in total) of *U. fulgens* from Panama refused to eat the leaves of *O. triandra* from Jamaica. Newly hatched first instars did eat it, but grew more slowly than first-instar siblings fed *O. diandra*.

As many as three species of *Omphalea* may occur together (e.g., Cuba), but I do not know if the *Urania* adults there display any preference. This point is almost a moot one, for I will later present data suggesting that individuals of *U. fulgens* may show very fine oviposition discrimination within a single population of *O. diandra*.

Adult Food Plant

What is the relevance of the kinds of flowers upon which the adults feed to the questions of population fluctuation and migration? The answer is simply that if adults do not have a nectar meal within 4 days of emergence, they die. Water alone is apparently insufficient. This conclusion is based on observations of individuals that I have reared, and I assume that it is true for *Urania* in the wild. Females do not accept males until the females are around 9 days of age.

Hence, if the females do not feed, they do not breed.

Urania are attracted to white "fluffy" flowers like those of the mimosoid legumes, such as *Inga* spp., *Leucaena* spp., and the composite *Eupatorium*. I have never seen them feeding on other types of flowers. I do not understand why they are so specific. The proboscis of a *Urania* is about 15–17 mm long, which may restrict their exploitation of flowers with longer corollas. There are many species of *Inga* in the wet Atlantic lowlands of Panama where *Urania* breeds. Individuals of some species flower several times a year during the rainy season and may represent a relatively secure food source. Repeated censuses of areas with both *Omphalea* and *Inga* spp. have shown that, if the *Inga* spp. are in flower, the *Urania* will be there. If they are not in flower, no *Urania* will be found. They have gone. Any consideration of the reason for their migratory behavior must take this into consideration.

Urania Movements, 1900–1979

Background I have directly observed *Urania* movements in Panama and elsewhere in Central and South America since 1964. For information on previous flights, I surveyed a wide range of scientific and popular literature. Very large flights were, and are still, almost always mentioned in newspapers. I therefore searched through all the July, August, and September copies of two local newspapers from 1915 onward. Documentation of these flights up to 1971 is presented in Smith (1972), and Table 1 here documents *Urania* movements from 1972 to 1979.

Rainy-season Movement The following generalizations may be given for the autumnal or rainy-season migration. *Urania* moths begin to migrate in late July and may continue in this phase until late October. The movement is usually to the east, southeast, or northeast depending on the location in Central America. *Urania* move down through Central America and then southward, west of the Andes to northern Ecuador. To the east of the Andes, the *U. leilus* population also usually fly eastward, and often in complete synchrony with the Central American and Cuban populations. In Cuba, they move southward. I know nothing about the movements of *U. sloanus* on Jamaica. In Trinidad, the moths cross the Gulf of Paria from Venezuela, west to east. Individuals have been recovered after storms in Florida (Emmel, 1974), Barbados, and Dominica (Williams, 1958).

Urania fly only during the day, but are occasionally attracted to lights at night. They are powerful fliers and can exceed 40 km/hr., but I estimate that 20 km/hr. for a 12-hr. day is the average speed while on

Table 1. Summary of the migration and population fluctuations of the day-flying moths *Urania fulgens* and *U. leilus* in Central America and northern South America from 1972 to 1979

Year and place	Dates and direction of flight	Comments
1972		
Panama	6–13 May, flying to both the east and west 2 Aug., residents present on Atlantic side	A standard migratory flight, not a big year. Probably only two generations involved.
Panama City	9–18 Aug., migrants flying eastward	
Panama, Cocle del Norte	19–20 Aug., flying east in A.M. and west in P.M.	
Panama, Pacora	21–24 Sept., large flight, to NNE; none after 25 Sept.	
1973		
Surinam	27 Jan.–20 Feb., eastward	Not a big flight
Panama/Costa Rica	30–31 Mar., flying from NW Panama to SW Costa Rica (Osa Peninsula)	About 50 per minute for 3 hr. near San Vito, Costa Rica (N.G. Smith and N. Smythe)
Guatemala, Flores, Petin	7 June, flying eastward from Mexico into Guatemala and Honduras	Flight reached Honduras but no reports from Nicaragua (H. Loftin)
Panama, Mexico, Veracruz	21 July–21 Oct., eastward	Scattered individuals moving in late July, 10–28 Aug. enormous numbers with dropoff until 16 Sept. when large numbers again move until 30 Sept. (second generation); fewer after that
Surinam	20–31 Aug., late Sept. to 25 Oct., all moving eastward	A very large movement, probably two generations (F. Feekes, pers. comm.)
1974		
Panama	18–25 June, eastward; 7 Sept.–26 Oct., eastward	Larvae on *Omphalea* in late May, but no adults present. Adults present mid June on Atlantic side and on Barro Colorado Island. 4–6 Oct. was a heavy flight. The migration was not large.
1975		
Panama, San Blas	18–29 June, mostly eastward, but some flew to west	Odd eastward flight on Atlantic side (R. Robertson)
Panama	19 Aug.–8 Nov., eastward	A relatively large movement involving two generations (H. Wolda)
1976		
Panama, Coiba Is.	9–14 April	*Urania* abundant and not migrating (R. Ridgely). No migration noted in 1976

Table 1. (continued)

Year and place	Dates and direction of flight	Comments
1977		
Panama	Jan.	A few individuals present on Atlantic side, residents
	Feb.–Mar.	Scattered individuals noted, perhaps migrants
	18 June	Several individuals flying NE near Cerro Campana (H. Wolda)
	1–20 Aug.	Very large movement with a dropoff of numbers by the end of Aug.
Costa Rica, La Selva	13–18 Aug., eastward	A large movement (A.S. Rand)
Panama	8–25 Sept., eastward	A very large movement. All known *Omphalea* vines on side heavily eaten. Eggs laid on vines in garden in Panama City, 10–12 Sept.
Panama, Gamboa	20 Oct., a few flying eastward	The migration in 1977 was the largest of the 1970s, but did not exceed the flight of 1969
1978		
Panama	Apr., eastward	A few flying eastward in Panama City. Adults present on Barro Colorado Island
Costa Rica	17 Aug., eastward	Large numbers moving in onto the Osa Peninsula over water from west to east (A.S. Rand)
Panama, Veraguas	18–19 Aug., eastward	*Urania* swarming in the hundreds on *Inga* flowers near Santa Fe
Panama	22 Aug.–7 Sept., eastward none until 30 Sept., Continued until 15 Oct.	Large movement through Panama City and in the Pearl Islands. *Omphalea* on Atlantic side untouched; hence adults not locally derived. Eggs laid on 30 Aug.
Panama, Almirante	13–17 Nov., westward	Scattered individuals which appeared to be flying westward (H. Wolda)
1979		
Panama, Atlantic side	10 Jan.	*Omphalea* vines untouched, no adults or larvae present
Panama, Pearl Is.	14–16 Mar., NW to W	Small numbers moving westward on the mainland as well
Panama, Chiriquí	15 Aug., NE	Scattered individuals flying northeastward (H. Wolda)
Panama	27 Aug., westward	Thousands of adults flying westward over Gatun Lake
Panama	3 Sept.–10 Oct., both to east and to the west	Peculiar westward flight on Pacific side and over Gatun Lake but eastward in San Blas
Panama, Atlantic side	21 Oct.	Most *Omphalea* not touched. Several third instar larvae and no adults

migration. They are little influenced by the variable winds of the rainy season and can fly distances of at least 240 km over open water. That they emerge with large amounts of fat and feed during migration suggests that they can and do fly enormous distances. But we still do not know how far an individual actually migrates.

Perhaps the most important aspect of this rainy season movement is that the individuals are in reproductive condition. Females are laden with well-developed eggs, and much courtship activity is observed (Smith, 1972). When I caught migrating females and put them in a screened cage (1 cu. m) with a fresh branch of *Omphalea*, they almost always laid about half their eggs that night on the screen and seldom on the plant. Dissection showed that they were inseminated. *Urania* spermatophores are large, and I have dissected females with as many as five spermatophores, but the average is two ($n = 120$). Migrating and hand-reared virgin females usually do not lay their eggs in this fashion and, if kept isolated, either begin to lay sterile eggs after about 14 days or die without laying. Dissection of three such females, which died at ages 39, 50, and 53 days, indicated that they had not resorbed their eggs.

In 1977, I randomly selected 30 wild-caught, inseminated females and 30 wild-caught, virgin females and counted the number of recognizable eggs in their ovarioles. The mean number of eggs in the virgins was 198.6 ($SD = 77.02$, range 65–315), while for the inseminated females the mean was 85.33 ($SD = 66.27$, range 0–230). The difference is significant ($t = 6.14$, $p < 0.0005$). If *Urania* do not resorb eggs, then this implies that some female *Urania* oviposit in more than one locality.

Dry-season Movement There are return movements, but these contain the grandchildren of individuals in the last (October) movement to the east. I do not know how long individuals may live in the wild, but two caged females lived 61 days. Central American *Urania* apparently survive the dry season (January–April) in areas that are relatively aseasonal, such as certain areas on the Atlantic side of Central America. These are areas that have tall mountains to the south which catch the moisture in the strong dry-season trade winds. In some years they appear to go into reproductive diapause, while in others they breed during this period and produce a generation, some of which move out, usually westward, in March. I have never observed courtship during this movement, and the females do not have well-developed eggs. The next generation appears in early June.

In those years when *Urania* found conditions suitable to reproduce in the dry season and were thus successful in producing a flight to the west, e.g., 1964, 1969, and 1977 (Smith, 1972 and Table 1), a large eastward migration almost always occurred in the following rainy season. It is the third or the fourth generation of the year that commences the eastward flight. In big flights, two or even three generations are produced in the migratory phase and are easily detected by lulls in the migration and the appearance of recently emerged individuals. The normal generation time for *Urania* in the wild is 42 days from egg to adult. The *Urania* populations throughout Central America are sufficiently out of phase that the lulls are usually less than 51 days for an observer anywhere in the migration path.

Within a particular year the numbers of individuals produced in these migratory generations usually do not differ significantly. Thus the important point to stress here is that the big migrations of *Urania* are apparently determined by their success in the dry season and not by variations in conditions when reproducing during migration.

Directionality That *Urania* fly eastward in the rainy season and westward in the dry season has perhaps been overstressed. They do, at times, fly the "wrong" way (e.g., Table 1, 1979). What I think is significant is that they all fly in the same direction. It seems clear why *Urania* in southern Veracruz, Mexico, should have been subject to selection for flying eastward (Williams, 1958). This area represents the northern edge of the range of *Omphalea*. Individuals flying in any other direction, except to the east or southeast, would simply not reproduce. But it is less clear why *Urania* originating near, say Manaus, in the middle of Brazil, should fly basically eastward (Williams, 1958). Keith Brown (pers. comm., 1980) informs me that he is not sure that this is true. In northern South America, Guiana, Surinam, French Guiana, and Brazil to Belem, the migration path appears to be as in Central America. But reports from the vast central area are too few and, in some cases, too anecdotal to serve as evidence for pronounced directionality in that huge area. The uraniid of Madagascar, *Chrysiridia madagascariensis*, also undergoes population fluctuations and also migrates west to east (Griveaud, 1959).

Another point may possibly be drawn from consideration of Table 1 and from below. The occurrence of several migrating generations *throughout* its entire range in Central America from southern Mexico to Panama (e.g., 1973) may suggest that not all individuals in a population emigrate upon emergence. They may lay some of their eggs locally (on the *Omphalea* that they themselves ate?) and then begin their migration. Alternatively, some may never migrate and may lay all their eggs locally. In 1977, I collected 40 fifth instar larvae from several *Omphalea* vines near Achiote, Panama, on the wet, Atlantic coast of the former Canal Zone. These were placed in four cages and left to pupate in the forest. Upon emergence, they were marked with bright green spray paint on their right forewings and allowed to escape. There were 28 females and 9 males. Three did not emerge. Censuses taken 2, 7, and 14 days later showed that at least some marked individuals remained. Five were seen 2 days later, 7 at day 7, and 5 on day 14. During this period, thousands of migratory individuals were pouring through the area without any apparent pause.

One of the problems in determining whether some individuals in a population migrate while others do not, is deciding what constitutes a biologically meaningful population in *Urania*. In the later portion of this paper I will offer data that suggest that such a population may be the individuals that ate the leaves of but a single *Omphalea* vine.

The Question of Periodicity Figure 1 indicates the years in which major flights of *Urania* occurred, principally in Central America and northern South America. Before 1954, the commonest interval is 8 years (mean is 7.57). If one examines the intervals after the early 1950s, the commonest interval is 4 years (mean is 3.83).

It is difficult to get a real idea of just how large *Urania* flights were from the literature. Several authors indicated that 1924 was the largest flight of the 1920s and that of 1932 was even larger; 1954 was said to have been the largest since the end of World War II, but 1955 was said to have been even larger (Smith, 1972). Thus, only once in the record have major flights occurred in successive years. Bear in mind that there is always some migration *every* year. My own observations indicate that 1969 was the year of the largest flight of the 1960s and the 1970s as well. It was followed in magnitude by 1977 and, to a lesser extent, by 1964 and 1973 respectively.

I am not sure what all of this tells us, or even if it has any biological sense at all. Are we seeing really big flights every 8 years, and lesser flights every 4? What does even a 4-year interval mean when discussing an animal that lives 6 weeks as an immature, 2–3 months as an adult, and which produces perhaps five to seven generations per year? If there is a correlation with some climatic phenomenon, I have not yet attempted to seek it out. But, if I found such a correlation, I am unsure how I might interpret it in terms of the biology of *Urania fulgens*.

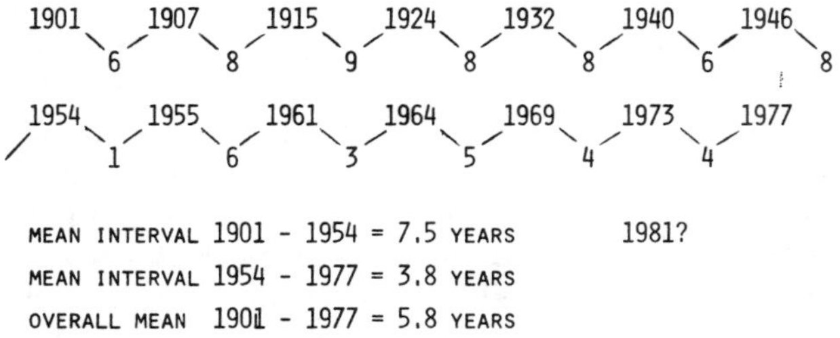

MEAN INTERVAL 1901 - 1954 = 7.5 YEARS   1981?
MEAN INTERVAL 1954 - 1977 = 3.8 YEARS
OVERALL MEAN 1901 - 1977 = 5.8 YEARS

Figure 1. Intervals between major flights of the day-flying moth *Urania* in Central and South America.

REARING EXPERIMENTS

Assumptions

When I began to raise *Urania* in captivity, I made a number of assumptions which have proven to be either too simplistic, partly false, or completely erroneous.

Chief among these assumptions were:

1. There is a migratory type and a sedentary type.
2. These types could be discriminated by some series of morphological characters such as eggs-to-fat ratio, wing size, etc.
3. Caged individuals of the migratory type would display a directional flying activity whose orientation would match that of the free-living migrating individuals while the sedentary type would not.
4. Finally, conditions during the larval stage were the chief factor in determining whether the adult migrated or not.

Initial Experiments

By August 1973, I had clones from a single *Omphalea* vine from the Atlantic side of Panama growing in pots outside my office in a screened-in hallway, and eight large (3 m high) individuals of one clone growing in my garden in Panama City. I decided to test the idea that the amount of *Omphalea* that the larvae experience determines whether they as adults would migrate or not.

I caught migrating females which laid in my cages as previously described. I placed 200 first instar larvae from those eggs on vines in my garden, and another 200 were divided and placed into two 1-cu. m screen cages in the same area as the potted *Omphalea* (hereafter "lab"). Finally I monitored at 3-day intervals the larvae that had hatched on a low *Omphalea* near Achiote, Panama. When the "garden" and "wild" larvae reached fifth instar, and thus stopped eating, I collected as many as possible and brought them to the lab area to pupate and emerge. All adults at that time were kept in separate, covered, cardboard cups and were tested for the presence or absence of migratory behavior when they were between 2 and 4 days of age. The testing cages were completely exposed to the sky and single individuals were placed in them for 5 minute periods between 0730–0939 hr. and between 1500–1700 hr. A positive migratory behavior was scored when an individual behaved as did migrating individuals when placed in the same cages—constant fluttering on the east side of the cage in both the morning and the afternoon. A negative score resulted if an individual showed any deviation from the behavior, e.g., sitting on the shaded side in the morning or on the sunlit side in the afternoon. The procedure was crude, but subsequent experience has suggested that it is reliable.

The lab population was given fresh *Omphalea* leaves *ad lib.;* they never lacked for food. The wild population had to deal with an already damaged vine. The plants in my garden were untouched. The lab population was protected against ants and wasps, which are major predators on eggs and early instars of *Urania*. *Omphalea diandra*, like all *Omphalea* spp., has extrafloral nectaries at the base of each leaf which attract ants to patrol the vine. At the approach of an ant, the larvae jump off into the air and hang by silklike threads (Figure 2). They return to the leaf by crawling back up this thread, which they eat. The important point is that larvae exposed to ants cannot eat at nearly the same rate as those not exposed. This may, partially, explain the differences in the development times shown in Table 2.

My prediction was that the laboratory-reared *Urania* would: (1) have more eggs and less fat than those produced in the other groups, and (2) that they would not display migratory behavior. I predicted (1) that the garden and wild adults would have fewer eggs and more fat than the lab group, and (2) that they would display migratory behavior.

The average fed *ad lib.* completed development between 30–34 days, significantly faster than the rates of either garden or wild larvae (Table 2). There was no significant difference among the groups in the dry weights of the adults, but the lab females had significantly more eggs ($t = 8.59$, $p < 0.0005$) than did the females of either of the other groups. These data were in accord with the predictions. But when tested for flight behavior, all individuals showed a very strong migratory behavior.

I was puzzled by these results and put aside this line of questioning in order to get more data on growth rate. Again I secured larvae (60) as before and raised each in its own cup, using *Omphalea* from my garden. The 38 females that emerged were much like the previous lab generation in weight (mean = 0.272) but

had slightly fewer eggs (mean = 254). As almost an afterthought, I decided to test these individuals for migratory behavior. Wild *Urania* were still migrating at that time. None of the 57 adults so raised showed any migratory activity. I immediately concluded that larval density was, at least, one important factor determining migratory behavior.

I therefore repeated this experiment, using cups of 1 pint, 1 quart, and 1 gallon capacity, respectively. I placed single first instar larvae in 80 pint-size cups, 5 in 16 quart-size cups, and 20 in each of 4 gallon-size cartons. The amount of *Omphalea* on hand was too little to feed this many larvae and I therefore mixed this supply with freshly cut *Omphalea* from the Atlantic side. This, I believe, was an unfortunate decision. I did not make detailed records of their growth rates. But it was clear that singletons grew more quickly than those in groups of 5, which in turn grew more quickly than those in groups of 20. *Urania* larvae were given a leaf per day up to late second instar and then two leaves per day for the later instars. The groups of five were given six leaves per day throughout, and those in the gallon containers got all the *Omphalea* that I could stuff in. None exhausted their food in 24 hours.

Mortality was higher than in any other group of *Urania* that I had ever raised: 51 out of 80 (64%) of the singletons, 69 of 80 (86%) of the fives, and 43 (54%) of the larvae in the gallon containers failed to attain adulthood. I attributed this to the onset of the dry season (possibly because of low humidity), disease of some sort, or perhaps to an inbreeding effect of some kind. While some of these factors may have contributed to the high mortality, I now believe that this was the wrong interpretation for reasons that I will present later.

I predicted that the singletons would not show migratory behavior, while those in the other groups would be migratory. Singletons emerged first and were tested first, followed by the adults from the other two treatments. There were 29 adults from the single cups, 11 from the groups of 5, and 37 from the groups of 20. All exhibited migratory behavior. This anomalous result suggested that there was at least some other variable that I was not considering.

Nonmigratory Populations

In June 1974, J. Waage and I began to examine a resident population of *Urania* in a swamp forest near Achiote, on the Atlantic coast of the former Canal Zone. Waage also studied the behavior of larvae at Barro Colorado Island. At both Achiote and Barro Colorado, adult *Urania* flew about, often ignoring large *Omphalea* vines. Few larvae were evident and I suspected that many of the adults were in reproductive

Figure 2.   First instar larvae of *Urania fulgens*, which have just jumped off an *Omphalea* vine on silklike threads in response to a patroling ant. Note the characteristic strip-mine damage produced by these 4-mm long larvae.

Table 2. Development times and subsequent flight behavior of *Urania* raised under different conditions

	Laboratory	Garden	Wild
Egg to hatching	3–4 days	3–4 days	3–4 days
Larval stage	$N = 184$	$N = 109$	$N = 133$
	mean = 15	mean = 22	mean = 27
	$R = 14$–17	$R = 20$–25	$R = 25$–31
Pupal stage	13 days	14 days	13 days
Total	30–34 days	37–43 days	41–48 days
Adult female dry weight (g)	$N = 89$	$N = 47$	$N = 42$
	mean = 0.26	mean = 0.22	mean = 0.23
	$R = 0.23$–0.29	$R = 0.22$–0.23	$R = 0.21$–0.26
Adult male, dry weight (g)	$N = 75$	$N = 24$	$N = 48$
	mean = 0.11	mean = 0.10	mean = 0.13
	$R = 0.10$–0.12	$R = 0.10$–0.11	$R = 0.10$–0.15
Number of eggs per individual	mean = 263	mean = 181	mean = 188
	$R = 191$–393	$R = 110$–284	$R = 94$–290
Behavior	Migratory	Migratory	Migratory

diapause. We brought back to the lab some larvae and adults in an attempt to initiate another breeding program. The larvae (mostly second instars) were fed *Omphalea* from my garden and, after 2 weeks, the adult females began to lay. We quickly realized that the supply of *Omphalea* on hand would not be sufficient. I returned to Achiote to collect *Omphalea,* which was flushing new leaves at that time. These plants had been heavily damaged by the *Urania* generations of the previous migration. I chose a vine that covered a *Ficus* sp. tree on the west side of Achiote road, 2.5 km from the point where the Achiote road breaks off from the Gatun-Escobal road, a plant that I had used to make my clones 4 years before. I knew that first instar larvae did not like mature leaves and so I was careful to select branches with the light green, soft new leaves. I also collected branches with more mature leaves for the older larvae. First instar larvae essentially "strip mine" a leaf, and it is not until late second or early third instar that they are capable of actually biting through at the edge of a leaf.

The new *Omphalea* leaves were distributed to each of the 53 wild-caught larvae, mainly second and third instars that had been eating what was genetically the same *Omphalea.* After 3 days, I noticed that they were eating very little of the new leaves and appeared to be rather sluggish. On day 4, 17 were dead in their cups, which contained untouched leaves. In the following 12 days, 13 more larvae died. The last of the living larvae pupated 33 days later. Of these 23 pupae, only 7 produced adults.

My initial reaction to this unprecedented mortality and greatly attenuated growth rates was to assume that there had been aerial spraying of insecticides in the Achiote area. But the pertinent agencies indicated to me that the area had not been sprayed in recent years. Disease seemed the next possible choice. Y. Marciacq, a parasitologist at the Gorgas Memorial Laboratory, examined the dead larvae and pupae. She found no evidence of viral, bacterial, or fungal infection. She did find that they were all infected with a sporozoan, *Gregarina* sp. Most gregarine parasites are thought to be relatively benign, but some species apparently cause damage to the epithelial cells of their hosts and have adverse effects on development when their hosts are reared on a suboptimal diet (Brooks, 1974).

The coincidence of the nadir in reproduction in the wild with this low success in the laboratory suggested that these parasites might be one of the factors causing *Urania* populations to fluctuate. But subsequent examinations of preserved larvae and pupae from previous generations also revealed gregarine infections. These had been healthy. In addition, when the eggs of the wild-caught females hatched, I put some larvae on the *Omphalea* from my garden. These grew normally and, when examined, also proved to be positive for gregarines. I concluded that it was something about the plant, and not these parasites, that caused this mortality and drawn-out development times.

Omphalea Manipulation Experiment

I was not able to continue work with *Urania* until 1977. By that time I had become aware of the rapidly developing field of research on plant defensive mechanisms (e.g., Feeney, 1976). This research approach completely reversed my ideas about *Urania* and *Omphalea*. I know nothing about the chemical compounds in *Omphalea*. The vine has a reddish purple sap that causes black stains to appear on my hands in about 10 minutes. If it is allowed to remain on cotton trousers, the stains become more or less permanent until the material breaks down, leaving a hole, in about 30 days. That essentially nothing eats its leaves except *Urania* argues that *Omphalea* must be full of toxins. With the earlier results in mind, I now asked the question, Was *Omphalea* displaying some sort of "wound response" (Green and Ryan, 1972; Ryan and Green, 1974) to repeated attacks by raising its level of toxicity to a point where *Urania* were unable to deal with it?

By early 1977, the 13 *Omphalea* vines in my garden—genetically identical and the same individual as the apparently supertoxic (and/or deficient in some critical substance for *Urania* growth) vine of Achiote in 1974—were in good condition and had not been touched since 1974. I decided to simulate several generations of *Urania* attack on some vines, and to test the new leaves that resulted on *Urania* larvae. I proceeded in a manner to mimic as closely as possible the way *Urania* larvae attack the plant—strip mining and eventually consuming the youngest leaves, and strip mining and partly eating the older leaves. Except for the young leaves, the petioles are seldom consumed. Thus I did not simply pluck leaves from the vine. I used razor blades to scrape, and a hand-held paper punch to cut. Each vine was photographed to obtain a before-treatment estimate of leaf development. Each vine was attacked over a 20-day period and then allowed to recover until the amount of new leaves matched the previous amount. I deviated from this procedure by putting a limit on the number of days to recover. Plants were always attacked by day 65. Leaf production on other growing leads did not stop during attack, but I always waited a "*Urania*" generation before attacking these. Since I began in the early dry season, I watered the plants daily.

Urania began migrating through Panama City in early August and I immediately decided to see whether females would oviposit differently on the vines in my garden. Would they show a preference for untouched vines and discriminate against, as oviposition sites, the vines that had been attacked? By that time, three vines had been attacked three times, four had been attacked twice, three once, and the remaining six had been left untouched.

Scanning-electron-microscope pictures had revealed that adult *Urania* have well-developed "gustatory pores" on the tips of their legs. In the wild, gravid females fly about, often flitting down to touch the vegetation. When they touch an *Omphalea* leaf, they go into flight gyrations and then touch down again in another spot. The gyrations are apparently triggered only when they land on *Omphalea*. This may go on for several days before the first eggs are laid. The explanation of this behavior remains unclear. The eggs are deposited on the underside of the leaves, apparently at night. I have found single eggs and clutches of up to 80. I do not know what determines whether they lay few or many eggs on an individual leaf.

By 4 September, *Urania* had found my vines and as many as six at one time could be seen gyrating around the vines. I found the first eggs on September 7 and the last on September 20. I thought a pattern was emerging when only one of the three thrice-treated vines received any eggs. But I then discovered that ants were eating the eggs at night and, short of spraying the vines to kill the ants, the problem was unsolvable at the time. No interpretation of those oviposition data is possible. These efforts will be repeated again with vines suitably protected against ants.

To investigate the effects of these various treatments on the larvae, I divided 120 first instar larvae into four groups: those to be fed leaves from untouched vines and those to be fed leaves from vines that I attacked once, twice, and three times. Each larva was placed in its own 1-pint container and was fed *ad lib*. Table 3 records the mortality which occurred at various stages in their development. The highest mortality occurred in the group fed the leaves of the vine that had been attacked three times. The seven larvae that died between hatching and second instar (Table 3) never ate any of the leaves offered. Mortality in the pupal stage was also high in this group. Table 3 also records the development rates among the four groups. Again, the fourth group grew significantly more slowly than did those exposed to the other treatments. There were no significant differences among the first three groups in either growth or mortality rate.

I conclude that changes took place in the vine attacked three times which caused this slowing down of development and high mortality. I further suggest

Table 3. Mortality and growth rates of *Urania* larvae fed leaves from *Omphalea* vines that received different growing treatments

Larval stage	Untouched vines	Number of attacks on vines		
		One	Two	Three
Mortality:				
Instar 2	30	30	30	23
Instar 3	29	30	30	20
Instar 4	29	30	29	20
Instar 5	29	30	28	20
Pupating	29	29	28	20
Emerging	29	29	28	13*
Percentage surviving	97	97	94	43
Growth rate:				
Larvae	29	30	28	20
Mean larval period (days)	16.2	15.7	16.9	27.6
Range	14–19	14–18	14–18	22–33

*Chi square = 40.73 with 3 d.f.; $p < 0.005$

that this is exactly what happens in the wild. The details of these changes, presumably chemical, are still unknown and will be investigated. The effects of repeated, but small, amounts of grazing on really large *Omphalea* vines are also unknown. This response by heavily grazed *Omphalea* vines may explain why *Urania* emigrates. I suggest that as a vine becomes more and more unsuitable for *Urania* development, more and more emigrants will be produced. The *Urania* may be seeking less toxic vines and/or vines *not* lacking critical nutrients for larval development. I do not yet know that adults can make this discrimination.

SUMMARY AND CONCLUSIONS

Diurnal moths of the genus *Urania* undergo annual, often massive, unidirectional flights in Central and South America. In Central America, the major movement occurs during the rainy season usually sometime between late July and November, and is basically from north to south. But the curvature of this land mass is such that, as in Panama, much of the flight is from west to east, that is, toward South America. In South America it is much the same, with a strong east to southeast component except for the populations west of the Andes, which fly southward. The moths involved in this flight are in reproductive condition and

the females apparently lay their eggs in clutches throughout the flight. It is not known how far an individual moth flies. The moths often attain speeds exceeding 50 km/hr., but it was concluded that the average daily speed was 18 km/hr. for a 12-hr. day. Adults in captivity lived as long as 74 days.

The numbers of individuals involved in such flights varied enormously between years. Between 1900 and the 1950s, large flights occurred roughly every 8 years and after that around every 4 years. The reasons for this apparent periodicity are not understood. During really large flights extending over several months, as many as four generations may be produced throughout the range before the flight stops. Flights in the opposite direction occur in the dry season (usually in March) but usually relatively few individuals are involved and they normally are not in reproductive condition. Exceptions occurred and in Panama, when the westward movement was large and had reproductive individuals, a very large eastward movement usually followed several months later in the rainy season. Flights in the opposite direction to that of the rainy season flight were rare following the periodic, really massive, eastward flights. This and the seeming nonreplacement of the northern populations by return flights argues that not all of the individuals that emerge at one locality participate in the emigration flight.

Adult *Urania* feed on white "fluffy" flowers of mimosoid legumes, particularly *Inga* spp., *Leucaena* sp., and on the composite *Eupatorium* sp. The reason for this apparent specificity for white flowers is not known. In captivity they will not live longer than 4 days if fed only water. In cages, females do not copulate until they are at least 9 days from eclosion. Hence, if they are not provided with a nectarlike food (I used a boiled mixture of water, sugar, honey, and bouillon cubes), they do not breed. I assume that this is true of the free-living individuals. Thus one possible reason for emigration from the area of eclosion might be the lack of a suitable adult food source. Yet I doubt that this could explain mass flights over long distances.

The sole larval food plant of *Urania* is *Omphalea* (Euphorbiaceae), species of which are mainly woody lianas, but also some trees. The occurrence of *Omphalea* spp. and *Urania* coincides almost exactly in the lowland neotropics. *Urania* apparently are the only insects that regularly graze the leaves of *Omphalea* spp. *Omphalea diandra* was the only species that I studied and, with the exception of the clones growing in my garden, were huge lianas which often climbed 20–30 m up into the forest canopy. In some cases, the biomass of *Omphalea* leaves seemed to be a sizable fraction of the total canopy vegetation, especially in forest-edge situations. Yet even during the massive population explosions of 1969 and 1973, none of these vines were completely defoliated. Thus I feel that depletion of the larval food plants in an area is probably not a major factor in producing mass flights.

I assumed that the dichotomy in adults of mass unidirectional emigration versus nondirectional and presumed more or less sedentary behavior reflected some difference in the conditions during larval development. I further assumed that this dichotomy could be produced and detected under lab conditions. I also envisioned that there would be some sort of morphological as well as behavioral difference in the adults. For example, the so-called sedentary type might have put more energy into egg production and less into fat. Two series of experiments were devised, in which the first (Table 2) varied the amount of *Omphalea* that the larvae had at their disposal, and the second in which larval density was varied but all groups were fed *ad lib*. Larvae grew faster and eclosed as adults faster when raised at either low densities or when provided with large amounts of *Omphalea*. Adult females from such groups also had significantly more eggs than did females raised under higher density or less abundant food regimes. There were no significant differences among adults from any treatment in body weight. These results taken alone might have suggested that good conditions during larval development produced adults in which most of the *Omphalea* intake had been converted into eggs rather than into fat. But no correlation was obtained between the conditions during larval development and the behavior of the adults when tested in flight cages. In the first series (Table 2), all individuals showed migratory behavior while in the second, none did. During both these experiments the wild populations continued their massive flight eastward through Panama.

Between 1969 and 1973, I took cuttings from 19 *Omphalea* vines from the Atlantic side of Panama and transferred these clones into my garden in Panama City. In 1977 I discovered that *Urania* larvae would not eat the fresh leaves taken from the mother plant in the wild but would eat the leaves of the clones made from the plant in my garden. The only difference between these genetically identical plants, aside from the size, was that the wild vine had been heavily grazed while the vine in my garden had not.

I simulated *Urania* grazing on several clones of the same *Omphalea* individual. These were subjected to simulated grazing by one, two, or three generations of *Urania* larvae. The new leaves that emerged from each clone were given to larvae. Growth and mortality rates were measured. Larvae grew well on leaves from control clones (not grazed) and also grew well on leaves from clones grazed once or twice (Table 3). But those that were given leaves from clones grazed three times showed significantly slower growth rates and higher

mortality as compared with the other groups. I concluded that *Omphalea* clones that had been subjected to three *Urania* "generations" either increased their toxicity to a level that made larval growth difficult or that repeated grazing resulted in the production of leaves that lacked certain nutrients critical for normal larval growth. The chemistry of *Omphalea diandra* remains to be studied.

Experiments designed to detect whether *Urania* females could discriminate among *Omphalea* clones that received different grazing treatments were inconclusive. I speculate that females may be able to do this, and that flights by *Urania* represent an adaptive response to locate *Omphalea* vines of low toxicity or higher nutrient value than the vines which gave rise to those adults. Indeed, the apparent periodicity of massive *Urania* flights may be a reflection of the timing of biochemical changes in *Omphalea* vines.

LITERATURE CITED

Adams, C. D.
1972. *Flowering Plants of Jamaica*. Mona, Jamaica: University of the West Indies.

Brooks, W. M.
1974. Protozoan Infections. Pages 237–295 in *Insect Diseases*, edited by G. E. Cantwell. New York: Marcel Dekker, Inc.

Calderon, S., and P. C. Standley
1941. *Lista Preliminar de Plantas de El Salvador*. San Salvador: Imprenta Nacional. 450 p.

Duke, J. A., and D. M. Porter
1970. *Darien Phytosociological Dictionary*. Columbus, Ohio: Battelle Memorial Institute. 70 p.

Emmel, T.
1974. *Urania fulgens* (Uraniidae) Captured in Florida. *Journal of the Lepidopterists' Society*, 28(3): 292.

Feeny, P.
1976. Plant Apparency and Chemical Defense. Pages 1–40 in *Biochemical Interaction Between Plants and Insects. Recent Advances in Phytochemistry*, vol. 10, edited by J. W. Wallace and R. L. Mansell. New York: Plenum Press.

Green, T. R., and C. A. Ryan.
1972. Wound-induced Proteinase Inhibitor in Plant Leaves: A Possible Defense Mechanism Against Insects. *Science*, 175: 776–777.

Griveaud, P.
1959. Sur les deplacements de *Chrysiridia madagascariensis* (Lepidoptera: Uraniidae). *Le Naturaliste Malgache*, 11(1–2): 107–109.

Guppy, H. B.
1907. Life history of *Cydimon (Urania) leilus*. L. Trans. Royal Ent. Soc., 1907: 405–410.
1917. *Plants, Seeds and Currents in the West Indies and Azores*. London: Williams and Norgate. 531 p.

Holdridge, L. R., and G. Budowski
1956.   Report of An Ecological Survey of the Republic of Panama. *Caribbean Forestry*, 17: 92–110.

Johnston, I. M.
1949.   The Botany of San Jose Island (Gulf of Panama). *Sargentia*, 8: 1–306.

Kenoyer, L. A.
1928.   General and Successional Ecology of the Lower Tropical Rain Forest at Barro Colorado Island, Panama. *Ecology*, 10: 201–222.

MacLeay, W. S.
1834.   A Few Remarks Tending to Illustrate the Natural History of Two Annulose Genera, *viz. Urania* of Fabricus, and *Mygale* of Walckenaer. *Trans. Zool. Soc.*, 1: 179–195.

Oppenheimer, J. R.
1982.   *Cebus capucinus*: Home Range, Population Dynamics, and Interspecific Relationships. Pages 253–271 in *The Ecology of a Tropical Forest*, edited by Egbert G. Leigh, Jr., et al. Washington, D.C.: Smithsonian Institution Press.

Ryan, C. A., and T. R. Green
1974.   Proteinase Inhibitors in Natural Plant Protection. Pages 123–140 in *Metabolism and Regulation of Secondary Plant Products. Recent Advances in Phytochemistry*, vol. 8, edited by V. C. Runecklees and E. E. Conm. New York: Academic Press.

Seitz, A., and M. Gaede
1930.   Uraniidae; *Urania*. Pages 829–831 in *The Macrolepidoptera of the World*, II division: *The Macrolepidoptera of the American Region*, vol. 6: *The American Bombyces and Sphinges*, edited by A. Seitz. Stuttgart: Alfred Kernan Verlag.

Smith, N. G.
1972.   Migrations of the Day-flying Moth *Urania* in Central and South America. *Carib. J. Sci.*, 12(1–2): 45–58.

Standley, P. C.
1928.   Flora of the Panama Canal Zone. *Contributions of the United States National Herbarium*, 27: 1–416.

Westwood, J. D.
1879.   Observations on the Uraniidae, a family of Lepidopterous insects, with a synopsis of the family and a monograph of *Coronidia*, one of the genera of which it is composed. *Trans. Zoological Society of London* 12: 507–545.

Williams, C. B.
1958.   *Insect Migration*. London: Collins. 235 pp.

Wolda, H., and R. B. Foster
1978.   *Zunacetha annulata* (Lepidoptera, Dioptidae), an outbreak insect in a neotropical forest. *Geo-Eco-Trop.*, 2: 443–456.

The Breeding Season of Antwrens on Barro Colorado Island

JUDY GRADWOHL   Museum of Vertebrate Zoology and Department of Zoology, University of California, Berkeley, California 94720

RUSSELL GREENBERG   Museum of Vertebrate Zoology and Department of Zoology, University of California, Berkeley, California 94720

ABSTRACT

We censused antwren groups monthly from November 1978 to August 1979 to determine the timing of breeding activity and juvenile production of the three species of antwrens on Barro Colorado Island. While nest building and courtship feeding continued from March at least through September, most new young appeared in late July and early August, suggesting that most successful nests were initiated in mid to late June. The rainy season and associated increase in arthropod prey abundance started in April. Why was there a 2-month delay in successful breeding?

Samples of arthropod abundance showed high numbers throughout the rainy season. The amount and composition of food brought to dot-winged antwren nestlings varied little between nests or from month to month during the rainy season, so delayed buildup in nesting prey abundance is not the answer. We suggest that high activity by snakes early in the rainy season, eating eggs and nestlings, accounts for the delay in successful nesting. This would explain why antwrens with very different diets produced successful nests at the same time.

INTRODUCTION

The nesting activity of insectivorous birds on Barro Colorado Island peaks near the beginning of the rainy season (Eisenmann, 1952). This is the season when insects are most abundant (Wolda, this volume; Smythe, this volume). Such a pattern is found in many tropical forests: in Trinidad (Snow and Snow, 1964), Costa Rica (Skutch, 1950), and Malaya (Fogden, 1972), nesting activity was found to be greatest at the onset of a rainy season, when new leaves are common and insects plentiful. Food supply, however, may not be the only factor influencing the timing of the successful production of young: competition and predation may also be involved. Miller (1963) suggested that competition from winter residents from North America affected the breeding cycles of songbirds in an equatorial cloud forest. Morton (1971) hypothesized that clay-colored robins (*Turdus grayi*) nested in the dry season, before insect abundance peaked, to avoid the higher nest predation in the early wet season.

During the period of November 1978 to September 1979, we monitored the breeding activities of three species of antwrens (family Formicariidae) on Barro Colorado Island: white-flanked antwren (*Myrmotherula axillaris*), checker-throated antwren (*Myrmotherula fulviventris*), and dot-winged antwren (*Microrhopias quixensis*). We also gathered extensive data on the diets of dot-winged antwren nestlings, and on the foraging habits of the adults of all three species, and related these to seasonal changes in food abundance.

The Antwren Species

The three species of antwrens on Barro Colorado Island form the nucleus of mixed species flocks in the understory and middle levels of the forest. All three species are wholly insectivorous; the smaller (8 g) dot-winged and white-flanked antwrens glean insects from live leaves, while checker-throated antwrens probe into dead leaves hanging in understory foliage.

Pairs or families of checker-throated and dot-winged antwrens ("antwren groups") travel together and jointly defend 1.5-ha. territories (Gradwohl and Greenberg, 1980). Both species display simultaneously at the territorial border. These displays usually occur several times daily. The territories appear to be centered on the presence of dense vine tangles. White-flanked antwrens spend more time in the open understory and maintain territories of 3 to 5 ha.

While these antwrens all build nests woven of dead leaves and rootlets, each species differs in nest shape and placement. Dot-winged antwrens build deep cup nests which hang tenuously from a thin vine, over or inside a vine tangle. Heights of dot-winged antwren nests ($n = 19$) ranged from 3.5 to 10 m and averaged 5.2 m. Checker-throated antwrens build pendant-shaped nests which hang from branches in vine tangles or understory shrubs. Heights of nests ranged from 0.5 to 8 m ($n = 25$). We were able to locate only three white-flanked antwren nests. These were each deep cups placed in understory shrubs 1 m from the ground.

Most studies of breeding seasonality have concentrated on active nests (Snow and Snow, 1964; Willis and Eisenmann, 1979), but this does not provide an accurate picture of successful breeding in antwrens. Antwrens build multiple nests and active nests are difficult to find. Most nests are empty, either not yet used or already abandoned. Moreover, as we will discuss below, the season of nesting activity is far longer than the season when young are successfully fledged. To learn when antwrens were nesting and producing young, we censused 13–65 groups of each antwren species each month. This census took 400+ field hours. Since antwren pairs forage with their young, this census allowed us to determine when young fledged. We were also able to estimate the age of young by comparing morphology and behavior with individuals of known ages.

We walked 15–25 km of trail each month to locate different antwren groups. Antwrens defend small territories (Gradwohl and Greenberg, 1980), so we avoided recounting the same group within a month by visiting new areas. Each antwren group was followed for 10–30 minutes to determine with certainty if any juveniles were present. Young juveniles of all three species had a species-specific begging note, so we could usually determine rapidly if a young bird (less than 8–10 weeks old) was present. We kept notes on any nesting activities of adults, including courtship feeding, nest building, copulation, or feeding of young in nests. Several of these activities were commonly seen in dot-winged antwrens, which showed little shyness near the nest; checker-throated antwrens were observed building nests and courtship feeding, but breeding activity was rarely observed in white-flanked antwrens.

Nestling diet was determined for dot-winged antwrens during 120 hr. of observation at nine different nests (of eight pairs). Dot-winged antwrens habituated rapidly to our presence so we could watch nests within 2–3 m without a blind. Prey were carried singly, crosswise in the tip of the bill, and were generally larger than 4 mm (total body length excluding wings). We identified 539 prey of the 679 we saw taken to order (to family or subfamily for orthopterans) and estimated the sizes of 592 prey using the length of the bird's bill for comparison. Nests were watched at all stages of development, but generally including the last 2–3 days of the 8–10-day nestling period. Checker-

Table 1. Seasonality of courtship activity and production of juveniles in three species of antwrens

	Nov.	Dec.	Jan.	Feb.	Mar.	Apr.	May	June	July	Aug./Sept.
Dot-winged antwren										
Total groups	32	33	33	25	30	47	40	46	65	54
Total groups with juveniles	2	1	4	0	1	1	3	2	12	8
Total groups in courtship activity[1]	1	0	0	1	1	6	10	13	7	7
Checker-throated antwrens										
Total groups	26	28	40	27	29	24	39	36	51	56
Total groups with juveniles	1	0	0	0	0	0	0	0	12	13
Total groups in courtship activity	0	0	0	1	1	6	8	2	5	6
White-flanked antwren										
Total groups	19	13	17	15	29	21	27	28	35	40
Total groups with juveniles	0	0	0	0	0	1	0	1	12	20

[1] Courtship activity = courtship feeding, nest building, and copulation.

throated antwrens foraged characteristically (98%, n = 600) by probing their bills into dead, curled leaves hanging in foliage and vine tangles (this study; Wiley 1971). We observed them eating and feeding mates (courtship feeding) mainly orthopterans and spiders and assume that they also feed nestlings prey taken from dead curled leaves.

Data on light-trap insects was provided by the Smithsonian Environmental Sciences Program (ESP). The biomass of insects in dead leaves was determined from five samples of 100 leaves (approximately 60 g dry weight) in November 1978, January, March, July, and August 1979. Further details on the census technique will be published in a later paper.

RESULTS

Breeding Seasonality

Dot-winged antwrens produced juveniles through the wet season (see Table 1 for seasonality of juvenile production). Two juveniles observed in January were probably 2 months old and fledged in November or early December 1978. Of the 39 total dot-winged antwren juveniles, 66% were first observed in July or August, resulting from nests in June or July. This mid

wet-season peak in the production of young is more pronounced in the two species of *Myrmotherula*. Ninety-four percent ($n = 35$) of new juvenile white-flanked antwrens and 100% of juvenile checker-throated antwrens ($n = 25$) were found in late July and early August. During 9–24 July, 13 of 24 white-flanked antwren groups observed (54%) had young juveniles. Before 9 July, only two groups were seen with new juveniles. This requires approximately half of all white-flanked antwren pairs to start successful nests between 14 and 28 June.

Dot-winged antwrens were observed courtship feeding from April to August, and checker-throated antwrens courtship fed from February to August. Courtship feeding was rarely observed in white-flanked antwrens. Nest building was most commonly observed in June for dot-winged and checker-throated antwrens, and, for three pairs of dot-winged antwrens which were marked or recognizable, we observed successive nest building with no indication that the nests were used (up to six nests for one checker-throated antwren pair). Because we checked nests for eggs or incubating birds every 1–2 days, we assume that the nests were never used, or that the clutches were lost quickly. In checker-throated antwrens our handling of the few low nests may have disturbed the adults and caused them to build new nests, but all of the dot-winged antwren nests and most of the checker-throated antwren nests were inaccessible to us and were examined through binoculars, causing little or no disturbance.

Nestling Food

The proportions of various types and size classes of prey items brought to dot-winged antwren nests remained fairly constant over the 4-month observation period. Dot-winged antwrens fed their young relatively large prey items (mean = 10.1 mm, range = 2–40 mm, Table 2). This facilitates a low number of trips to the nest, which may render the nest less conspicuous to predators. Most arthropod prey visible through binoculars were cryptically colored, green or brown (47%). We identified prey of nine different arthropod orders (plus one *Anolis* lizard). Most of the prey items were orthopterans (total = 57% of the

identified arthropods), with 16% spiders and 9% Lepidoptera larvae.

Seasonality of Nestling Food

We examined light-trap data from the ESP project as an indicator of the seasonality of occurrence of the major orthopteran groups which make up a majority of prey items brought to dot-winged antwren nests. Roaches (Blattidae) showed a strong early wet-season pulse and decreased into the mid wet season. Katydids were generally common through the wet season, declining gradually. Table 3 presents seasonal patterns of orthopterans in each group for 3 or 4 years (1976–79; these data were not collected for the crickets during the year of our study) for 10-week periods from February to November. All groups increased in the wet season; in roaches, early wet-season figures exceeded mid wet season in all 3 years. In katydids, early

Table 2. Size and type of prey fed to young at dot-winged antwren nests

Prey items identified to order	Nest 1 No.	Nest 1 %	Nest 2 No.	Nest 2 %	Nest 3 No.	Nest 3 %	Nest 4 No.	Nest 4 %	Nest 5 No.	Nest 5 %
Arachnida	10	17	9	17	4	5	5	15	10	10
Unidentified	12	20	7	13	13	17	5	15	27	27
Orthoptera	26	43	25	47	44	58	14	42	46	46
Tettigoniidae	1	2	5	9	8	10	2	5	12	12
Gryllidae	13	21	7	14	14	19	4	12	18	18
Mantidae	0	—	1	2	2	2	4	12	0	—
Phasmatidae	0	—	0	—	1	1	1	2	0	—
Blattidae	13	21	12	22	20	26	4	12	16	16
Isoptera	1	1	0	—	0	—	0	—	1	1
Homoptera	0	—	1	2	1	1	0	—	4	4
Neuroptera	0	—	0	—	0	—	0	—	1	1
Coleoptera	4	7	7	12	3	4	5	15	5	5
Lepidoptera larvae	1	1	4	8	8	10	3	8	4	4
Lepidoptera adult	7	11	1	2	4	5	2	5	3	3
Malacostraca (isopod)	0	—	0	—	0	—	0	—	0	—
Vertebrate *Anolis limifrons* lizard	0	—	0	—	0	—	0	—	0	—
Sample size (number of prey items)	61	—	54	—	76	—	33	—	101	—
Mean prey size (mm)	10.8	—	11.1	—	11.9	—	8.9	—	9.5	—
Standard deviation of prey size	4.9	—	3.8	—	5.8	—	4.5	—	4.4	—

wet-season figures exceeded mid wet-season figures in 3 out of 4 years. In crickets, mid wet-season figures exceeded early wet-season figures in 1977, and the two seasons were equivalent in 1978. Generally, orthopterans declined through the wet season.

The total weight of arthropods found in our samples of dead leaves increased greatly from March to May. Total biomass of arthropods remained high (2.8–1.1 g dry weight arthropods/500 leaves) through the end of August (Table 4).

DISCUSSION

The data on seasons of antwren breeding pose several paradoxes: (1) Why is successful production of young restricted to nests started in late June or early July when abundances of Orthoptera at light-traps and of arthropods in dead leaves peak early in the rainy sea-

Table 3. Numbers of orthopterans captured in ESP light-traps in 10-week periods

	1976	1977	1978	1979
Roaches				
6 Feb.–8 Apr.	?	182	690	392
9 Apr.–28 June	?	654	1795	1763
29 June–6 Sept.	?	371	512	461
7 Sept.–15 Nov.	?	159	185	?
Katydids				
6 Feb.–8 Apr.	118	98	513	186
9 Apr.–28 June	429	341	759	326
29 June–6 Sept.	235	468	468	244
7 Sept.–15 Nov.	99	285	291	?
Crickets				
6 Feb.–8 Apr.	?	?	814	?
9 Apr.–28 June	?	1204	3075	?
29 June–6 Sept.	?	1535	3076	?
7 Sept.–15 Nov.	?	1966	1434	?

Nest 6		Nest 7		Nest 8		Nest 9	
No.	%	No.	%	No.	%	No.	%
11	16	6	12	21	21	8	17
9	13	6	12	13	13	8	17
41	58	23	48	41	41	22	44
9	13	7	16	6	6	3	6
10	14	5	10	15	15	8	17
0	—	0	—	0	—	0	—
0	—	1	2	1	1	0	—
22	31	9	20	19	19	10	21
0	—	0	—	1	1	0	—
1	1	1	2	2	2	2	4
0	—	0	—	0	—	0	—
5	7	1	2	6	6	1	2
3	4	6	12	10	10	7	14
1	2	4	8	4	4	0	—
0	—	0	—	2	2	1	2
0	—	1	2	0	—	0	—
71	—	47	—	100	—	49	—
9.1	—	10.9	—	7.9	—	10.5	—
3.6	—	6.7	—	3.8	—	4.9	—

Table 4. Seasonality of biomass of spiders and orthopterans in aerial leaf litter (dry weight in grams per 500 leaf sample)

	Jan.	Mar.	May	July	Aug.
Spiders	0.18	0.32	0.77	0.94	1.42
Roaches, katydids, and crickets	0.39	0.29	1.45	2.01	1.70
Total	0.57	0.61	2.22	2.95	3.12

son? (2) Why is the season of nest building and courtship feeding so much longer than the season when young are successfully fledged? (3) Why do birds with very different feeding habits produce young at nearly the same time of year?

Food supply may limit the breeding season, otherwise we would expect to see more antwrens breeding during the dry season when arthropod prey is less common. However, breeding does not occur over the entire period when food supply is abundant, so we must look for other factors that could affect breeding seasonality. We have shown that prey items for young birds, mainly large orthopterans, occur seasonally and were present in large numbers through August. Because arthropod abundance is generally elevated in the wet season (Leigh and Smythe, 1978), ample food is probably available for self-maintenance as well. Sinclair (1978) found a similar delay in birds' breeding on the African savanna and attributed the delay to the need for adult birds to build body condition in preparation for breeding. This explanation may hold for antwrens on Barro Colorado Island, but, if this was the sole cause of delay, we might not expect to see such a sharp peak of successful breeding across the entire population and in different species. There should be enough individual variation in body condition within a species, because of the differing quality of territories, that such precise timing would be unexpected. Moreover, checker-throated antwrens, foraging in dead leaves, and white-flanked antwrens, foraging on live foliage, and presumably relying on an entirely different food supply, exhibited almost the exact same peak of successful breeding. This would be less likely than synchronized breeding within a species if food supply alone determined breeding seasonality.

If food was present in appropriate amounts and the adult birds did not need 2 to 3 months to build body condition, then adverse weather conditions could cause a delay in successful breeding. Heavy rains could affect all species by leaving adults less time for foraging (Foster, 1974) and causing thermoregulatory problems for young birds. It rained 290 mm in the last half of April, and 295 mm in May; these figures are not excessive for wet season months.

Miller (1963) suggested that wintering migrants from the northern temperate zone reduce food availability for residents and stimulate breeding by their departure in the spring. This is probably not applicable to the pattern we observed. The last migrants left in late April to early May, which does not correspond with the initiation of successful breeding. While chestnut-sided warblers show high foraging-site overlap with dot-winged antwrens, we observed chestnut-sided warblers handling Orthoptera only rarely in three winters of close observation, and Morton (1980) found none in stomach contents. White-flanked antwrens, and particularly checker-throated antwrens, showed little or no foraging overlap with any migrants. Finally, some dot-winged antwrens bred in the early fall after the migrants arrived.

We suggest that few antwren nests were successful before mid-June because a pulse of high nest predation occurred in the early wet season. Such a pulse would explain why the period of successful nesting is more restricted than the season of available food. It would also provide a reasonable explanation for the reproductive synchrony of checker-throated and white-flanked antwrens. While the foraging microhabitats of these species are quite distinct, their nests are quite similar in placement.

What might be responsible for such a pulse of predation? Morton (1972) proposed in a similar model for clay-colored robins that in the early wet season omnivores were switching to high-protein food resources and robbing more nests in preparation for their own breeding. The main omnivores on Barro Colorado Island are mammals (e.g., coatis, tayras, *Cebus* monkeys) and possibly birds (toucans), but the placement and construction of antwren nests makes predation by large-bodied animals very difficult. The bold behavior of dot-winged antwrens around nests may indicate that they are fairly safe from mammalian and avian predators.

Snakes have been reported to be major nest predators for many species of tropical birds (Willis, 1967, 1972; Oniki, 1975; Snow, 1962). Snow found that early nests of black and white manakins (*Manacus manacus*) on Trinidad were considerably less successful than late nests and attributed the failure to snake predation. Much of the evidence of snake predation is based on observations that eggs or young disappeared without a trace and without visible signs of disturbance to nests. This type of predation is also consistent with our observations; none of the nests that failed looked disturbed. Since it was not possible to tell if a nest was active without looking inside, some of the multiple nests built by dot-winged and checker-throated antwrens may have been used and subjected to predation during the early egg stage.

If snakes were causing the pulse of predation seen in the early wet season, why was the predation so concentrated in time? There is evidence that the incidence of snakes may be seasonal in tropical forests (Henderson et al., 1978). In Iquitos, a forest with a seasonal rainfall regime, many snakes were seen more commonly when the rains started at the end of the dry season. We observed snakes more commonly during a period in the early wet season on Barro Colorado Island. Although this phenomenon has not been studied on Barro Colorado, other observers have noted it (A. Jaslow, pers. comm.), and this may be a viable explanation for the pulse of nest predation at the beginning of the wet season.

It appears that while seasonality in food supply determines the period in which breeding is attempted, predation may further limit the period of successful breeding. We propose this hypothesis because it best explains the pattern of juvenile production in antwrens. The hypothesis that predation is heaviest at the onset of rain can probably be tested through field experiments with artificial clutches.

ACKNOWLEDGMENTS

The order of authorship was determined by the toss of a coin. We thank Egbert Leigh for his continued support of our research. Henk Wolda and the Environmental Sciences Program provided data on insect abundance at light-traps. Financial support was provided by a National Science Foundation dissertation improvement grant, and fellowships from the Smithsonian Tropical Research Institute and the John Tinker Foundation through the Center for Latin American Studies, University of California, Berkeley.

LITERATURE CITED

Eisenmann, E.
1952.   Annotated List of Birds of Barro Colorado Island, Panama Canal Zone. *Smithsonian Misc. Coll.*, 117: 1–62.

Fogden, M. P. L.
1972.   The Seasonality and Population Dynamics of Equatorial Forest Birds in Sarawak. *Ibis*, 114: 307–343.

Foster, M.
1974.   Rain, Feeding Behavior and Clutch Size in Tropical Birds. *Auk*, 91: 722–726.

Gradwohl, J., and R. Greenberg
1980.   The Formation of Antwren Flocks on Barro Colorado Island, Panama. *Auk*, 97: 385–395.

Henderson, R. W., J. R. Dixon, and P. Soini
1978.   On the Seasonal Incidence of Tropical Snakes. *Milwaukee Public Museum Contributions in Biology and Geology*, 17: 1–15.

Leigh, E. G., and N. Smythe
1978.   Leaf Production, Leaf Consumption, and the Regulation of Folivory on Barro Colorado Island. Pages 33–49 in *The Ecology of Arboreal Folivores*, edited by G. Montgomery. Washington, D.C.: Smithsonian Institution Press.

Miller, A. H.
1963.   Seasonal Activity and Ecology of the Avifauna of an American Equatorial Cloud Forest. *University of California Publ. Zool.*, 66: 1–78.

Morton, E. S.
1971.   Nest Predation Affecting the Breeding Season of the Clay-colored Robin. *Science*, 181: 920–921.
1980.   Adaptations to Seasonal Changes in Migrant Land Birds in the Panama Canal Zone. Pages 437–457 in *Migrant Birds in the Neotropics: Ecology, Behavior, Distribution and Conservation*, edited by A. Keast and E. Morton. Washington, D.C.: Smithsonian Institution Press.

Oniki, Y.
1975.   The Behavior and Ecology of Slaty Antshrikes (*Thamnophilus punctatus*) on Barro Colorado Island, Panama Canal Zone. *An. Acad. brasil. Cienc.*, 47: 477–515.

Sinclair, A. R. E.
1978.   Factors Affecting the Food Supply and Breeding Season of Resident Birds and Movements of Palearctic Migrants in a Tropical African Savannah. *Ibis*, 120: 480–498.

Skutch, A.
1950.   The Nesting Period of Central American Birds in Relation to Climate and Food Supply. *Ibis*, 92: 185–222.

Smythe, N.
1982.   The Seasonal Abundance of Night-flying Insects in a Neotropical Forest. Pages 309–318 in *The Ecology of A Tropical Forest*, edited by Egbert G. Leigh, Jr., et al. Washington, D.C.: Smithsonian Institution Press.

Snow, D. W.
1962.   A Field Study of the Black and White Manakin, *Manacus manacus*, in Trinidad. *Zoologica*, 47: 65–107.

Snow, D. W., and B. K. Snow
1964.   Breeding Season and Annual Cycles of Trinidad Land Birds. *Zoologica*, 49: 1–39.

Wiley, R. H.
1971.   Cooperative Roles in Antwren Flocks on Barro Colorado Island, Panama Canal Zone. *Auk*, 88: 881–892.

Willis, E. O.
1967.   The Behavior of Bicolored Antbirds. *University of California Publ. Zool.*, 79: 1–132.
1972.   *The Behavior of Spotted Antbirds*. A.O.U. Ornithological Monog. 10. Lawrence, Kans.: American Ornithologists Union.

Willis, E. O., and E. S. Eisenmann
1979.   A Revised List of Birds of Barro Colorado Island, Panama. *Smithsonian Contributions to Zoology*, 291: 1–31.

Wolda, H.
1982.   Seasonality of Homoptera on Barro Colorado Island. Pages 319–330 in *The Ecology of a Tropical Forest*, edited by Egbert G. Leigh, Jr., et al. Washington, D.C.: Smithsonian Institution Press.

LITTER ARTHROPODS
AND THEIR PREDATORS

Seasonal and Annual Variation in Litter Arthropod Populations

SALLY C. LEVINGS   Museum of Comparative Zoology, Harvard University, Cambridge, Massachusetts 02138

DONALD M. WINDSOR   Smithsonian Tropical Research Institute, Balboa, Republic of Panama

ABSTRACT

Results from 30 months of weekly Berlese samplings of litter are reported for major arthropod groups. Seasonal and annual variation in populations was found to be considerable and to vary in extent between groups. It is hypothesized that the length of the wet season and the distribution of dry-season rains have critical effects on litter arthropods. The extent of seasonal and annual population fluctuations is comparable with that reported from other tropical and temperate studies.

INTRODUCTION

Prior studies on Barro Colorado Island and elsewhere in the tropics have shown that litter arthropod populations vary seasonally and between locations (Willis, 1976; Macfadyen, 1969; Bullock, 1967). Most litter falls during the dry season, but litter decomposition appears to begin only when the rains do (Smythe, 1970). At the same time, litter arthropod populations increase, perhaps fed by the release of nutrients from decomposing litter (Madge, 1965; Willis, 1976). The timing and extent of seasonal population fluctuations and their relationship to physical factors has not yet been adequately studied.

Our study was designed to (1) determine the extent and nature of seasonal population change in major groups of litter arthropods, (2) examine the relationships between various biotic and abiotic factors that influence litter arthropods, and (3) evaluate the magnitude of population variation between years. Using Lutz catchment on Barro Colorado Island, we sampled macroarthropod groups to answer these questions.

METHODS

In order to sample a range of macrohabitats within the Lutz catchment, samples were taken in a transect line starting at the stream bottom and moving up the slope. The watershed was divided into four 100-m sections by drawing lines perpendicular to the stream and then dividing each 100-m section into 10 transect lines at 10-m intervals. Each week a transect was sampled in consecutive order: 10, 110, 210, 310, 20, 120, etc. The side of the slope sampled was chosen by tossing a coin. We thereby sampled from the entire catchment without resampling any given site less than 40 weeks apart. Samples were taken in pairs, the first pair next to the stream, succeeding pairs at 10-m intervals up the slope. Members of a pair were 3 m apart. Each sample was taken by placing a frame 50 cm on a side upon the ground and collecting all leaves and leaf fragments that were more than half under the frame, discarding twigs and wood. This procedure somewhat overestimates the amount of leaf litter, and the number of litter arthropods, per unit area. Litter was collected, bagged, returned to the laboratory, and weighed wet. It was then placed in Berlese funnels and processed under lights for 24 hours. Arthropods fell into alcohol, which was then extracted with kerosene to remove debris and dirt (Southwood, 1966). Arthropods with nonwettable exoskeletons were removed from the debris by hand. Samples were stored in 70% alcohol until they could be sorted. After removal of the arthropod samples, litter was allowed to dry (at 35°–45° C) in the funnels for the rest of the week and then weighed dry.

When litter samples were collected from the catchment, a sample of the top 3 cm of soil was taken with a corer to determine its moisture content. Percentages of soil and litter moisture were calculated using the equation:

$$\frac{\text{Wet weight} - \text{dry weight}}{\text{Wet weight}}$$

Extracting litter in kerosene after Berlese processing provided a check on the efficiency of our Berlese funnels. Efficiency varied greatly from group to group (Table 1). Large mobile arthropods were sampled relatively efficiently while most small groups, such as enchytraeids and nematodes, were killed by heat in the funnels before they could move out. Mites and Collembola were so poorly sampled that they are not included in sample counts. The extent of sampling bias for major arthropod groups sampled cannot be ascertained, and counts are presented without alteration. Sampling efficiency in soil and litter arthropod populations is a continuing problem because no one method is suitable for all groups (Southwood, 1966; Macfadyen, 1962, 1963, 1971; Edwards and Fletcher, 1971; Healey, 1971; Strickland, 1944; Phillipson, 1971). By restricting our attention to larger mobile arthropod taxa, we lessen the dependence of our counts on efficient extraction of relatively delicate groups, but do not sample small, common, and important decomposer groups, especially mites and Collembola. More detailed treatment of sampling problems for individual groups will be discussed when results for these groups are presented.

The exact methods of litter collection and processing differed somewhat with time. Errors were minimized in several ways. The same person, Bonifacio de León, collected the litter samples for the entire period of study, and we are exceedingly grateful to him. His methods were checked occasionally and were never found to depart significantly from his instructions. From time to time funnels were plugged or samples were contaminated by insects attracted to the lights, perhaps causing some part of the weekly variation in counts. The few samples where plugged funnels were discovered were discarded. Unfortunately we were unable to place the funnels indoors; they were housed in a screen building. They were also covered in fine-mesh netting and sealed as well as possible, but some light-attracted Diptera and Coleoptera were found from time to time. Obviously contaminated samples—such as those where the cover was found off the jar—were discarded. Delays in counting samples led to some

Table 1. Classification of major groups extracted from litter and an estimate of relative sampling efficiency

Group	Sampling efficiency
Annelida	
Lumbricidae[1]	+
Mollusca	
Pulmonata[1]	+
Arthropoda	
Onychophora[1]	+ + ?
Crustacea	
Isopoda[2]	+ + +
Amphipoda[2]	+ + +
Myriapoda	
Chilopoda[2]	+ + +
Diplopoda[2]	+ + +
Apterygota	
Thysanura[1]	+
Diplura[1]	+
Collembola	+
Insecta	
Coleoptera *[2]	+ + +
Hymenoptera	
Formicidae ***[2]	+ + +
Others *[1]	+ +
Orthoptera	
Blattaria **[2]	+ + +
Gryllidae **[2]	+ + +
Diptera *[1]	+ ?
Isoptera **[1]	+ +
Lepidoptera *[1]	+ ?
Hemiptera **[2]	+ + +
Homoptera **[2]	+ + +
Thysanoptera **[2]	+ +
Psocoptera **[2]	+ +
Neuroptera[1]	+ + +
Dermaptera **[1]	+ + +
Embioptera **[1]	+ + ?
Holometabolous larvae[2]	+ +
Arachnida	
Scorpionida[1]	+ + +
Araneae and Opiliones[2]	+ + +
Pseudoscorpionida[2]	+ + +
Acari	+

+   Less than 50% sampling efficiency.
+ +   50% to 75% sampling efficiency.
+ + + Greater than 75% sampling efficiency.

*   Adults only.
**   Adults and nymphs.
*** Adults and larvae included.

[1] These and other obscure groups and pupae (excluding pupae of ants) are combined and graphed in Figure 6d as "Others." Our sampling methods are inappropriate for these groups. Data on these groups are available from the authors upon request.

[2] Groups that are discussed separately.

loss from decomposition. Sample loss from all these sources meant that fewer than 10 samples per week were available for some parts of the study.

Some dirt contamination and slight overcollection of litter is inherent in the method of litter collection. Rapid tropical decay rates do not produce a distinct litter horizon like those found in the temperate zone (Madge, 1965). There is very little ambiguity in separating the litter layer from the underlying soil. In the rainy season, some mud and mud splash is incorporated when the samples are collected; more is picked up in periods of heavy rain after the ground has saturated and the litter has decayed into relatively small pieces. A dry-weight error estimate of 10% in the dry season and 15–20% in the wet season is reasonable after examination of samples. Soil insects added to the collections appear to be few; no effort has been made to remove them.

Arthropods were sorted into size classes and broad taxonomic categories. Most adults were sorted to order. All holometabolous larvae were lumped into a single class. Hemimetabolous nymphs were placed with adults of the same order until December 1976. After December 1976, nymphs and adults were scored separately for those groups. Spiders and phalangids, pseudoscorpions, scorpions, centipedes, and millipedes were sorted to class. All arthropods were grouped into size classes: (1) 0.5–1.49 mm, (2) 1.5–2.49 mm, (3) 2.5–3.49 mm, (4) 3.5–5.49 mm, (5) 5.5–7.49 mm, (6) 7.5–11.49 mm, (7) 11.5–17.49 mm, (8) 17.5–23.49 mm, (9) 23.5–31.49 mm, and (10) over 31.5 mm.

Estimated dry weight for major groups was calculated from length-weight regressions. Regressions were based on arthropods that were collected on Barro Colorado Island, measured, dried, and weighed. Values for size classes greater than 1 mm in width were calculated from the midpoint of the class range (C.A. Toft, unpublished data). Dry-weight estimates are therefore only approximate.

Table 2 lists sample dates and number of samples collected. The samples have been grouped by month and season. A total of 1153 samples have been grouped into 30 months. One month (no. 22) contains 5 weeks in order to avoid a gap in our sampling which occurred immediately before the start of the rainy season in 1977. Monthly grouping of samples includes results from all sections of the watershed and will be used for the most part in the analysis.

Seasonal Divisions

Seasons were defined by convention, since no exact cutoff point is obvious. The dry season was defined

Table 2. Month of study, date of collection, and number of litter arthropod samples collected

Mo. no.	Yr.	Mo.	Day	No. of samples		Mo. no.	Yr.	Mo.	Day	No. of samples
1	1975	Aug.	10	10		11	1976	May	30	8
		Aug.	17	10				June	7	10
		Aug.	24	10				June	13	10
		Aug.	31	10				June	20	10
2	1975	Sept.	7	10		12	1976	June	27	10
		Sept.	13	10				July	4	7
		Sept.	21	10				July	11	10
		Sept.	28	9				July	18	10
3	1975	Oct.	5	10		13	1976	July	25	10
		Oct.	12	10				Aug.	1	10
		Oct.	19	10				Aug.	8	10
		Nov.	2	4				Aug.	15	10
4	1975	Nov.	9	9		14	1976	Aug.	24	9
		Nov.	18	5				Aug.	29	8
		Nov.	23	10				Sept.	5	9
		Nov.	27	6				Sept.	12	9
5	1975	Dec.	7	10		15	1976	Sept.	19	10
		Dec.	14	10				Sept.	26	10
		Dec.	21	10				Oct.	3	10
		Dec.	25	10				Oct.	12	10
6	1976	Jan.	4	10		16	1976	Oct.	17	10
		Jan.	11	10				Oct.	24	10
		Jan.	18	10				Oct.	31	10
		Jan.	25	10				Nov.	7	10
7	1976	Jan.	31	10		17	1976	Nov.	15	10
		Feb.	7	9				Nov.	23	10
		Feb.	17	8				Nov.	28	10
		Feb.	22	10				Dec.	5	10
8	1976	Feb.	29	9		18	1976	Dec.	12	10
		Mar.	7	10				Dec.	24	8
		Mar.	21	10			1977	Jan.	4	10
		Mar.	28	10				Jan.	9	10
9	1976	Apr.	10	10		19	1977	Jan.	18	9
		Apr.	11	9				Jan.	23	10
		Apr.	21	10				Jan.	30	9
		Apr.	25	9				Feb.	6	8
10	1976	May	2	10		20	1977	Feb.	13	9
		May	9	10				Feb.	21	10
		May	16	10				Feb.	28	10
		May	23	8				Mar.	6	8

Table 2. (continued)

Mo. no.	Yr.	Mo.	Day	No. of samples
21	1977	Mar.	14	10
		Mar.	19	9
		Mar.	28	8
		Apr.	3	10
22	1977	Apr.	12	9
		Apr.	17	10
		Apr.	24	10
		May	1	9
		May	7	10
23	1977	June	1	10
		June	4	10
		June	12	10
		June	18	7
24	1977	June	27	10
		July	2	10
		July	9	10
		July	18	10
25	1977	July	25	10
		July	30	10
		Aug.	7	7
		Aug.	14	9
26	1977	Aug.	20	10
		Aug.	28	10
		Sept.	3	10
		Sept.	12	10
27	1977	Sept.	18	10
		Sept.	25	10
		Oct.	1	10
		Oct.	8	10
28	1977	Oct.	15	10
		Oct.	24	10
		Oct.	30	10
		Nov.	7	10
29	1977	Nov.	14	10
		Nov.	23	10
		Nov.	28	10
		Dec.	4	10
30	1977	Dec.	10	10
		Dec.	19	10
		Dec.	27	10
		Dec.	31	9

to begin on the first of 4 consecutive weeks when average litter moisture fell below 45%. Similarly, the wet season was defined to begin on the first of 4 consecutive weeks when litter moisture rose above 45%. By convention, the first and last 12 sample weeks of the wet season were designated the early and late wet season, respectively. Dates for seasons as defined above are found in Table 3. Although any seasonal definition is arbitrary, the examination of the percentages of litter moisture and the extent of rainfall shows there is little ambiguity in assigning any particular period to the appropriate season. The dry season is delineated to the nearest month (Table 3) in order to include samples from all areas of the watershed. In 1976, 1 week (4 January) which would otherwise be included in the late wet season falls in the dry season; the weeks of 15 and 23 November 1976 are included with the dry season of 1977. Inclusion of these weeks does not alter the seasonal pattern significantly and corresponds more accurately to the end of the rains. There is no change in the timing of the end of the dry season.

Statistics

The frequency distributions of numbers collected per sample was examined for all arthropods and for major arthropod groups. The distribution of all groups differed significantly from normal, using chi-square statistics. In addition, major taxa were examined for fit to the Poisson distribution, and all groups were significantly more aggregated than predicted using chi-square tests. In the light of this finding, the distribution of numbers over time has been examined, using nonparametric tests, following a suggestion made by Bullock (1967). More detailed information on statistical methods and the occasional use of parametric statistics will be included where it is applicable. Most accumulations and comparisons will be made using monthly data from all areas of the watershed (see Methods for details). Months and a detailed sample listing are found in Table 2. All density data is reported for areas of 0.25 sq. m.

RESULTS

Physical Factors

Rainfall and Soil and Litter Moisture Timing and amount of rainfall varied strongly between years during the period of sampling. Total rainfall was 2514 mm in 1975, 1762 mm in 1976, and 2575 mm in 1977 (ESP rain gauge, Figure 1, part d). Distribution of rainfall within years also varied. In particular, the tim-

Table 3. Seasonal definition: August 1975 through December 1977

Season	Dates	Months of study
Wet 1975*	10 Aug. 1975 – 4 Jan. 1976	1–5
Late wet 1975	12 Oct. 1975 – 4 Jan. 1976	3–5
Dry 1976	11 Jan. 1976 – 25 Apr. 1976	6–9
Wet 1976	2 May 1976 – 21 Nov. 1976	10–16
Early wet 1976	2 May 1976 – 18 July 1976	10–12
Late wet 1976	5 Sept. 1976 – 21 Nov. 1976	14–16
Dry 1977	28 Nov. 1976 – 7 May 1977	17–22
Wet 1977	1 June 1977 – 4 Dec. 1977	23–29
Early wet 1977	1 June 1977 – 14 Aug. 1977	23–25
Late wet 1977	18 Sept. 1977 – 4 Dec. 1977	27–29
Dry 1978	10 Dec. 1977 –	30

* Sampling initiated 10 July 1975.

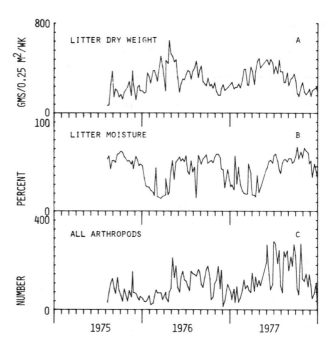

Figure 2. Part A: litter dry weight (gm/sq. m, average of 10 samples/week), Part B: percent litter moisture (average of 10 samples/week), Part C: total number of arthropods (average of 10 samples/week).

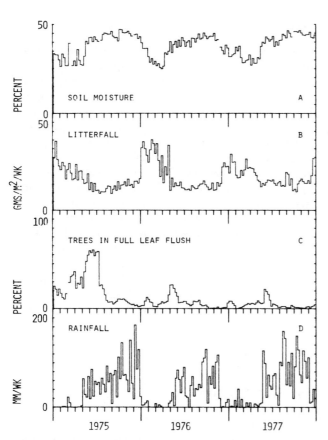

Figure 1. Part A: soil moisture (average of 10 samples/week), Part B: litterfall (gm/sq. m/week), Part C: percent full flush (% of all censused trees in full flush/week), and Part D: rainfall (mm/week) (data from the STRI-ESP study, used with permission).

ing and duration of dry-season rains was substantially different. Although the dry season of 1976 was about average in length (4 months, based on Panama Canal Company—now Panama Canal Commission—averages), there were only two heavy rains (one in February and one in April), and average litter moisture remained quite low (Figure 2, part b). In 1977, the dry season was 5.5 months long but was punctuated with rainfall at more or less regular intervals. Dry-season rains both moisten the litter temporarily and increase the underlying heterogeneity in litter moisture. Litter moisture is more variable in the dry season than in the wet season (one factor analysis of variance, performed on the variances of weekly litter moisture percentages for all weeks in the nine or more sample values, $n = 103$ weeks, $p = 0.05$). Wet-season litter moisture varied from around 45% to 60%, but did not change between years. During the dry periods in the wet season, litter moisture occasionally dropped to around 40%. During periods in the dry season without rain, average litter moisture was between 15% and 25%. Rain in the dry season immediately increased litter moisture to wet-season levels, but unless followed by other showers, it quickly dropped to previous lows. Litter moisture was significantly higher in the dry season of 1977 than in 1976 (mean = 26.7%,

1976; mean = 32.1%, 1977; *t*-test, $p < 0.001$).

The seasonal pattern of soil moisture parallels that of rainfall. Within a week or so after the end of the rains, soil moisture begins to drop. Moisture content remains low through most of the dry season and begins to rise when the rains begin again. Dry-season soil moisture averages between 20% and 30%; in the wet season it ranges between 35% and 45%.

Litterfall and Litter Accumulation

Litterfall and litter accumulation are highly seasonal and correlated with rainfall (Dietrich et al., this volume; Leigh and Smythe, 1978; Foster, 1973; Haines and Foster, 1977). The end of the rains in November or December and the consequent fall in soil moisture content initiates heavy dry-season litterfall. Forty percent of total litter falls between January and March (Dietrich et al., this volume). Litter accumulates through the dry season; average litter dry weight increases by a factor of two to three from November to May (Figures 1, part b, and 2, part a; Table 4). Litter accumulation is highest at the start of the rainy season and lowest in the last month of the rainy season (Table 4). Decomposition appears to stop during the period when litter is dry.

Litterfall is correlated with the amount of leaf flush in the preceding year (Wolda, 1978). The pattern of litter accumulation is similarly correlated with the amount of litterfall and leaf flush (Figures 1, parts b and c, and 2, part a). Litterfall and litter accumulation followed the same pattern: both were highest in 1975, lower in 1976, and lowest in 1977. Maximum and minimum litter accumulations, figured as the average of the 4 weeks of samples immediately preceding and following the dry season, are presented in Table 4. Minimum accumulation decreases each year, but only the difference between 1975 and 1977 is significant (*t*-test, $p = 0.01$). Litter accumulations at the start of the rainy season in 1976 are higher than in 1977, but the difference is not significant.

Seasonal Patterns in Individual Taxa

There are several inherent difficulties in the interpretation of general arthropod sampling data. Some of these difficulties are multiplied in our case because so little is known about litter arthropods in the tropics. For some levels of classification, trophic and ecological information may safely be inferred (all spiders, for example, are predaceous). In other cases, the level of classification that was possible provides little or no information about the ecology of the group (almost anything found on Barro Colorado Island, for ex-

Table 4. Maximum and minimum litter accumulation, 1975–77

Sample weeks	Grams per 0.25 sq. m	95% CI	Number of samples
Maximum:			
2–9–16–23 May 1976	493.2	45.5	38
1–4–12–18 June 1977	464.9	32.4	37
Minimum:			
14–21–25 Dec. 1975;			
4 Jan. 1976	218.8	23.5	40
31 Oct.; 7–15–23 Nov.			
1976	198.0	20.1	39
14–23–28 Nov.; 4 Dec.			
1977	182.8	15.3	40

Average dry weight of litter in the first 4 weeks and the last 4 weeks of the wet season in 1975, 1976, and 1977.

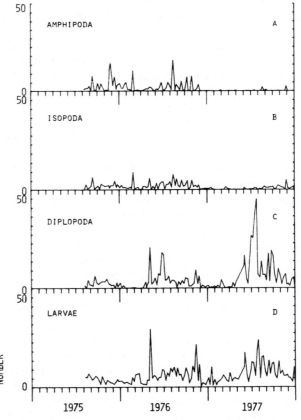

Figure 3. Part A: Amphipoda, Part B: Isopoda, Part C: Diplopoda, Part D: holometabolous larvae (average 10 samples/week, all figures).

Table 5. Seasonal comparisons of density of Amphipoda and Isopoda

Season	N	Amphipoda		Isopoda		Probability
		Number of samples without group	Median of samples with group	Number of samples without group	Median of samples with group	
Late wet 1975	104	33	3	29	2	0.09
Dry 1976	154	89	2	75	2	0.21
Early wet 1976	113	62	2	47	3	* 0.02
Late wet 1976	115	68	2	41	3	* 0.01
Dry 1977	236	210	1	177	2	* 0.003
Early wet 1977	113	105	1	92	2	*<0.001
Late wet 1977	120	108	1.5	60	2	*<0.001

* More isopods than amphipods in these comparisons.

All tests were made using the Mann–Whitney U test, using the correction for ties (Siegel, 1956).

ample, is food for some beetle, and most beetles hide in the litter from time to time). Group patterns and relevant ecological characteristics will be discussed as possible, but many cases await further, detailed study.

Crustacea: Isopoda and Amphipoda Isopods and amphipods are potentially significant detritivores on Barro Colorado Island (Healey, cited in Willis, 1976). Even at low average densities, they may constitute an important fraction of arthropod biomass (Figure 3, parts a,b). Both groups feed mainly on decaying leaf litter or other decomposing substances such as wood or occasionally carrion. Isopods are widely reported to have developed effective behavioral mechanisms for avoiding dessication, allowing them to move into relatively arid habitats (Paris, 1963; Wallwork, 1970). Terrestrial amphipods are more generally confined to littoral, freshwater, or extremely moist habitats (Birch and Clark, 1954). In Australia, amphipods may be responsible for most litter decomposition in some forests (Birch and Clark, 1954). Some authors feel that isopods and amphipods in general are an important part of the decomposition process in tropical forests (Lawrence, 1953; Birch and Clark, 1954).

Although numbers in both groups changed substantially over time, average weekly density remained highly correlated (Spearman rank correlation coefficient = 0.589, $p < 0.001$, $n = 121$ weeks). Seasonal density varied but, until 1977, the minimum combined density per sample was two to three animals (Figure 3, parts a,b). At the start of the 1977 dry season, isopods and amphipods essentially vanished and remained rare until the end of the rainy season

when isopod density rose to a median of 0.5 per sample. Populations differed in some seasons despite the close correspondence between groups (Table 5). Isopods are significantly more common than amphipods in all seasons after the 1976 early wet season. Densities do not differ significantly in either the 1975 late wet or 1976 dry seasons. Amphipods have been generally reported to be more affected by desiccation than isopods (Hurley, 1959) and have been reported to disappear during dry years in some Australian forests (Birch and Clark, 1954). It is possible that the low average rainfall in 1976 and the long dry season in 1977 affected amphipods more than isopods, although both populations declined.

The pattern of population change differed between groups (Table 6). Amphipod populations decreased at the start of the dry season in both 1976 and 1977, but did not change significantly from the dry-season level through the following wet season. Amphipod populations showed a general decrease between years in seasonal comparisons. Isopod populations also decreased at the beginning of the dry season, but in 1976 they increased at the start of the wet season. During the 1976 wet season, populations remained at the same level. In 1977, density dropped during the dry season and remained the same when the rains began. Only at the end of the rainy season did density finally begin to increase. The general pattern of population decrease between years is similar to that of amphipods.

Judging by the presence of some individuals 3 mm or smaller, recruitment occurred during most of the wet-season months for both isopods and amphipods. In the 1975 and 1976 wet seasons, 20% or more of the

LEVINGS AND WINDSOR

collected amphipods were small in 8 of 12 months. Small amphipods constituted 40% and 45%, respectively, of all amphipods collected in the last 2 months of the 1976 wet season. Numbers collected dropped to fewer than 10 per month from month 17 to month 29. During month 29, 29 amphipods were collected, 13 of which were 3 mm long or smaller. During the 1976 dry season, the proportion of small individuals collected ranged from 0% to 11% of the total number of amphipods sampled.

Isopods showed a slightly different pattern of recruitment. Individuals 3 mm long or smaller composed 20% or more of the isopods sampled during the 1975 late wet season in only 1 month (no. 3). During the 1976 dry season, 9 of 30 isopods collected in month 7 and 66 of 107 caught in month 8 were small, but in months 6 and 9 they form 7/63 and 8/51 of the individuals collected. During the 1976 wet season, populations were relatively high, and the smallest three size classes constituted 18–44% of the collections. After the population drop in 1977, small individuals formed 20–50% of the isopods caught as numbers increased slowly through the wet season.

Chilopoda Centipedes are almost entirely predacious forms, many of which are restricted to cryptic habitats such as logs or soil crevices (Lawrence, 1953; Kuhnelt, 1961). Most species are reported to be intolerant of desiccation; some temperate species migrate up and down in soil and litter in response to environmental conditions (Lloyd, 1963).

The seasonal distribution of centipedes is marked (Figure 4, part b; Table 6). Individuals are rare in the dry season, increasing in density somewhat at the beginning of the rains. There is a strong recruitment of small individuals in the first or second month of the rainy season. Median size then increases throughout the rainy season, although a few small individuals may be collected later in the season. There appears to be one cohort of young produced each year which grows through the wet season and then either lays eggs which remain dormant over the dry season or which move down in the dry season and reproduce when the rains return. In 1977, a few small individuals were collected in the last month of the dry season, and the large cohort of young were produced earlier in the wet season than in 1976.

The pattern of recruitment varies between years. In 1976, populations increased significantly after the rains began and continued to increase through the rainy season (Table 6). In 1977, populations increased quickly and showed no further average increase during the wet season.

Between years, the distribution of centipede numbers differed. There were higher populations in the 1977 dry and early wet seasons, but 1976 late wet-season centipede density was higher than 1977 late wet-season density.

Diplopoda Millipedes feed predominantly on dead plant material. Different kinds and ages of litter are taken selectively; leaves with high calcium or low secondary compound content or which have been exposed to leaching for some period appear to be preferred (Lyford, 1943; Birch and Clark, 1954). Although they prefer aged litter, millipedes may reject litter if it has decomposed for too long a period (Neuhauser and Hartenstein, 1978). Most species are unable to tolerate dry conditions (Barnes, 1968), but at least some tropical species have developed limited physiological mechanisms for coping with desiccation (Sundara-Rajulu and Krishnan, 1968).

Millipede density shows a strong seasonal pattern (Figure 3, part c). During the dry season, millipedes are very rare. A large recruitment of individuals 2 mm long or smaller takes place in the second or third month of the wet season; some recruitment of small individuals may continue throughout the rainy season. Density drops as the wet season continues; most millipedes abruptly disappear when the rains cease.

Changes in density between all seasons are statistically significant (Table 6). The major period for recruitment occurs early in the wet season, but some small millipedes continue to be collected throughout the wet season. During the 1976 dry season, a few large individuals were collected in the first 3 months (median size 4.5 mm, 64 individuals, 109 samples). After a 10-mm rain on 10 April 1976, 45 individuals, with a median size of 3 mm, were collected in 38 samples. In the 1977 dry season, catches varied from month to month, but some individuals less than 3 mm long were collected each month. The changes in size patterns between years suggest that small individuals are more active or more viable during wetter dry seasons.

Araneae and Opiliones Spiders are common predators, employing a wide variety of prey capture and handling techniques (Robinson, Lubin, and Robinson, 1974; Lubin, 1978). Seasonal behavior patterns for some web-spinning spiders has been studied on Barro Colorado Island (Lubin, 1978; Robinson and Robinson, 1970); species-level separation is currently in progress for our collections (Opell, in prep.). A wide variety of prey are taken by spiders. Most litter arthropods are probably spider prey at some time, and spider predation has potentially important community effects (Robinson and Robinson, 1970, 1974).

Spider populations are lower in the dry season and

Table 6. Comparisons of litter arthropod densities between consecutive seasons (a) and between years (b)

Season	Year	No. of samples without group	Median no. of specimens per sample	Range, minimum and maximum no. of specimens per sample	Total no. of samples	Season	Year	No. of samples without group	Median no. of specimens per sample
Amphipoda[1]									
a.									
LW	1975	33	3	0–52	104	D	1976	89	2
D	1976	89	2	0–23	154	EW	1976	62	2
EW	1976	62	2	0–19	113	LW	1976	68	2
LW	1976	68	2	0–66	115	D	1977	210	1
D	1977	210	1	0–21	236	EW	1977	105	1
EW	1977	105	1	0–5	113	LW	1977	108	2
b.									
D	1976	89	2	0–23	154	D	1977	210	1
EW	1976	62	2	0–19	113	EW	1977	105	1
LW	1976	68	2	0–66	115	LW	1977	108	2
Isopoda[1]									
a.									
LW	1975	29	2	0–22	104	D	1976	75	2
D	1976	75	2	0–19	154	EW	1976	47	3
EW	1976	47	3	0–24	113	LW	1976	41	3
LW	1976	41	3	0–15	115	D	1977	177	2
D	1977	177	2	0–8	236	EW	1977	92	2
EW	1977	92	2	0–8	113	LW	1977	60	2.5
b.									
D	1976	75	2	0–19	154	D	1977	177	2
EW	1976	47	3	0–24	113	EW	1977	92	2
LW	1976	41	3	0–15	115	LW	1977	60	2.5
Chilopoda[1]									
a.									
LW	1975	69	1	0–4	104	D	1976	138	1
D	1976	138	1	0–3	154	EW	1976	74	1
EW	1976	74	1	0–10	113	LW	1976	44	3
LW	1976	44	3	0–20	115	D	1977	167	1
D	1977	167	1	0–11	236	EW	1977	55	2
EW	1977	55	2	0–30	113	LW	1977	58	2
b.									
D	1976	138	1	0–3	154	D	1977	167	1
EW	1976	74	1	0–10	113	EW	1977	55	2
LW	1976	44	3	0–20	115	LW	1977	58	2
Diplopoda[2]									
a.									
LW	1975	—	2	0–17	104	D	1976	—	0
D	1976	—	0	0–21	154	EW	1976	—	4
EW	1976	—	4	0–79	113	LW	1976	—	1
LW	1976	—	1	0–29	115	D	1977	—	0
D	1977	—	0	0–35	236	EW	1977	—	7
EW	1977	—	7	0–157	113	LW	1977	—	3

D = dry season, EW = early wet season, LW = late wet season. Each comparison occupies one row of the table. The Mann-Whitney U test was applied in each comparison. Population increase, decrease, and no change are indicated by +, –, and ns.

[1] Number of samples with zero animals is given; median is the value for samples with at least one animal.

[2] Median reported is for all samples.

Range, minimum and maximum no. of specimens per sample	Total no. of samples	Level of significance determined by Mann-Whitney U test	Direction of change
0–23	154	<0.001	−
0–19	113	0.410	ns
0–66	115	0.350	ns
0–21	236	<0.001	−
0–5	113	0.120	ns
0–9	120	0.190	ns
0–21	236	<0.001	−
0–5	113	<0.001	−
0–9	120	<0.001	−
0–19	154	<0.001	−
0–24	113	0.037	+
0–15	115	0.079	ns
0–8	236	<0.001	−
0–8	113	0.104	ns
0–12	120	<0.001	+
0–8	236	<0.001	−
0–8	113	<0.001	−
0–12	120	<0.001	−
0–3	154	<0.001	−
0–10	113	<0.001	+
0–20	115	<0.001	+
0–11	236	<0.010	−
0–30	113	<0.001	+
0–11	120	0.090	ns
0–11	236	<0.001	+
0–30	113	0.001	+
0–11	120	0.020	−
0–21	154	<0.001	−
0–79	113	<0.001	+
0–29	115	<0.001	−
0–35	236	0.001	−
0–157	113	<0.001	+
0–61	120	<0.001	−

Table 6. (continued)

Season	Year	No. of samples without group	Median no. of specimens per sample	Range, minimum and maximum no. of specimens per sample	Total no. of samples	Season	Year	No. of samples without group	Median no. of specimens per sample
b.									
D	1976	—	0	0–21	154	D	1977	—	0
EW	1976	—	4	0–79	113	EW	1977	—	7
LW	1976	—	1	0–29	115	LW	1977	—	3
Araneae and Opiliones[2]									
a.									
LW	1975	—	2	0–11	104	D	1976	—	2
D	1976	—	2	0–24	154	EW	1976	—	4
EW	1976	—	4	0–42	113	LW	1976	—	4
LW	1976	—	4	0–52	115	D	1977	—	2
D	1977	—	2	0–101	236	EW	1977	—	6
EW	1977	—	6	0–53	113	LW	1977	—	4
b.									
D	1976	—	2	0–24	154	D	1977	—	2
EW	1976	—	4	0–42	113	EW	1977	—	6
LW	1976	—	4	0–52	115	LW	1977	—	4
Pseudoscorpionida[2]									
a.									
LW	1975	—	1	0–34	104	D	1976	—	1
D	1976	—	1	0–20	154	EW	1976	—	4
EW	1976	—	4	0–86	113	LW	1976	—	4
LW	1976	—	4	0–54	115	D	1977	—	3
D	1977	—	3	0–68	236	EW	1977	—	5
EW	1977	—	5	0–120	113	LW	1977	—	4
b.									
D	1976	—	1	0–20	154	D	1977	—	3
EW	1976	—	4	0–86	113	EW	1977	—	5
LW	1976	—	4	0–54	115	LW	1977	—	4
Psocoptera[1]									
D	1976	83	2	0–28	154	D	1977	110	4
EW	1976	68	2	0–64	113	EW	1977	46	2
LW	1976	89	1	0–12	115	LW	1977	73	1
Thysanoptera[1]									
D	1976	72	3	0–107	154	D	1977	69	7
EW	1976	62	2	0–10	113	EW	1977	44	4
LW	1976	79	2	0–39	115	LW	1977	81	1
Coleoptera[2]									
a.									
LW	1975	—	3	0–25	104	D	1976	—	2
D	1976	—	2	0–27	154	EW	1976	—	4
EW	1976	—	4	0–44	113	LW	1976	—	6
LW	1976	—	6	0–51	115	D	1977	—	3
D	1977	—	3	0–35	236	EW	1977	—	8
EW	1977	—	8	0–146	113	LW	1977	—	9

Range, minimum and maximum no. of specimens per sample	Total no. of samples	Level of significance determined by Mann-Whitney U test	Direction of change
0–35	236	<0.001	+
0–157	113	<0.001	+
0–61	120	<0.001	+
0–24	154	0.140	ns
0–42	113	<0.001	+
0–52	115	0.220	ns
0–101	236	<0.010	−
0–53	113	<0.001	+
0–33	120	0.150	ns
0–101	236	0.180	ns
0–53	113	0.140	ns
0–33	120	0.290	ns
0–20	154	0.424	ns
0–86	113	<0.001	+
0–54	115	0.380	ns
0–68	236	0.038	−
0–120	113	<0.001	+
0–87	120	0.028	−
0–68	236	<0.001	+
0–120	113	<0.001	+
0–87	120	0.433	ns
0–150	236	<0.001	+
0–65	113	<0.001	+
0–11	120	<0.010	+
0–111	236	<0.001	+
0–38	113	<0.001	+
0–11	120	0.480	ns
0–27	154	0.176	ns
0–44	113	<0.001	+
0–51	115	<0.010	+
0–35	236	<0.001	−
0–146	113	<0.001	+
0–85	120	0.090	ns

Table 6. (continued)

Season	Year	No. of samples without group	Median no. of specimens per sample	Range, minimum and maximum no. of specimens per sample	Total no. of samples	Season	Year	No. of samples without group	Median no. of specimens per sample
b.									
D	1976	—	2	0–27	154	D	1977	—	3
EW	1976	—	4	0–44	113	EW	1977	—	8
LW	1976	—	6	0–51	115	LW	1977	—	9

Holometabolous larvae[2]
a.

LW	1975	—	2	0–25	104	D	1976	—	2
D	1976	—	2	0–27	154	EW	1976	—	5
EW	1976	—	5	0–113	113	LW	1976	—	4
LW	1976	—	4	0–36	115	D	1977	—	3
D	1977	—	3	0–47	236	EW	1977	—	8
EW	1977	—	8	0–124	113	LW	1977	—	6

b.

D	1976	—	2	0–25	154	D	1977	—	3
EW	1976	—	5	0–27	113	EW	1977	—	8
LW	1976	—	4	0–113	115	LW	1977	—	6

Formicidae[2]
a.

LW	1975	—	25	1–305	104	D	1976	—	9
D	1976	—	9	0–218	154	EW	1976	—	60
EW	1976	—	60	0–454	113	LW	1976	—	50
LW	1976	—	50	0–351	115	D	1977	—	26
D	1977	—	26	0–501	236	EW	1977	—	68
EW	1977	—	68	0–527	113	LW	1977	—	56.5

b.

D	1976	—	9	0–218	154	D	1977	—	26
EW	1976	—	60	0–454	113	EW	1977	—	68
LW	1976	—	50	0–351	115	LW	1977	—	56.5

Blattaria: adults and nymphs[1]
a.

LW	1975	80	1	0–5	104	D	1976	103	1
D	1976	103	1	0–4	154	EW	1976	78	1
EW	1976	78	1	0–6	113	LW	1976	80	2
LW	1976	80	2	0–5	115	D	1977	192	1
D	1977	192	1	0–6	236	EW	1977	94	1
EW	1977	94	1	0–3	113	LW	1977	100	1

b.

D	1976	103	1	0–4	154	D	1977	192	1
EW	1976	78	1	0–6	113	EW	1977	94	1
LW	1976	80	2	0–5	115	LW	1977	100	1

Gryllidae: adults and nymphs[1]
a.

LW	1975	73	1	0–6	104	D	1976	87	1
D	1976	87	1	0–6	154	EW	1976	61	2
EW	1976	61	2	0–8	113	LW	1976	67	2
LW	1976	67	2	0–16	115	D	1977	142	2
D	1977	142	2	0–8	236	EW	1977	42	3
EW	1977	42	3	0–16	113	LW	1977	52	2

b.

D	1976	87	1	0–6	154	D	1977	142	2

Range, minimum and maximum no. of specimens per sample	Total no. of samples	Level of significance determined by Mann-Whitney U test	Direction of change
0–35	236	<0.010	+
0–146	113	<0.001	+
0–85	120	<0.001	+
0–27	154	0.280	ns
0–113	113	<0.001	+
0–36	115	0.310	ns
0–47	236	<0.010	−
0–124	113	<0.001	+
0–53	120	0.230	ns
0–47	236	0.095	ns
0–124	113	<0.001	+
0–53	120	0.010	+
0–218	154	<0.001	−
0–454	113	<0.001	+
0–351	115	0.280	ns
0–501	236	<0.001	−
0–527	113	<0.001	+
1–529	120	0.310	ns
0–501	236	<0.001	+
0–527	113	0.075	ns
1–529	120	0.054	ns
0–4	154	0.015	+
0–6	113	0.413	ns
0–5	115	0.337	ns
0–6	236	0.001	−
0–3	113	0.341	ns
0–4	120	0.464	ns
0–6	236	<0.001	−
0–3	113	0.006	−
0–4	120	0.001	−
0–6	154	0.007	+
0–8	113	0.192	ns
0–16	115	0.233	ns
0–8	236	0.390	ns
0–16	113	<0.001	+
0–11	120	0.100	ns
0–8	236	0.413	ns

Table 6. (continued)

Season	Year	No. of samples without group	Median no. of specimens per sample	Range, minimum and maximum no. of specimens per sample	Total no. of samples	Season	Year	No. samples without group	Median no. of specimens per sample
EW	1976	61	2	0–8	113	EW	1977	42	3
LW	1976	67	2	0–16	115	LW	1977	52	2

Homoptera: adults and nymphs[1]

a.

Season	Year	No. of samples without group	Median no. of specimens per sample	Range, minimum and maximum no. of specimens per sample	Total no. of samples	Season	Year	No. samples without group	Median no. of specimens per sample
LW	1975	68	1	0–8	104	D	1976	100	1
D	1976	100	1	0–6	154	EW	1976	75	1
EW	1976	75	1	0–7	113	LW	1976	75	1
LW	1976	75	1	0–8	115	D	1977	164	1
D	1977	164	1	0–6	236	EW	1977	51	2
EW	1977	51	2	0–8	113	LW	1977	70	1

b.

Season	Year	No. of samples without group	Median no. of specimens per sample	Range, minimum and maximum no. of specimens per sample	Total no. of samples	Season	Year	No. samples without group	Median no. of specimens per sample
D	1976	100	1	0–6	154	D	1977	164	1
EW	1976	75	1	0–7	113	EW	1977	51	2
LW	1976	75	1	0–8	115	LW	1977	70	1

Hemiptera: adults and nymphs[1]

a.

Season	Year	No. of samples without group	Median no. of specimens per sample	Range, minimum and maximum no. of specimens per sample	Total no. of samples	Season	Year	No. samples without group	Median no. of specimens per sample
LW	1975	69	1	0–4	104	D	1976	101	1
D	1976	101	1	0–16	154	EW	1976	46	2
EW	1976	46	2	0–19	113	LW	1976	45	2.5
LW	1976	45	2.5	0–11	115	D	1977	108	2
D	1977	108	2	0–39	236	EW	1977	24	5
EW	1977	24	5	0–40	113	LW	1977	53	2

b.

Season	Year	No. of samples without group	Median no. of specimens per sample	Range, minimum and maximum no. of specimens per sample	Total no. of samples	Season	Year	No. samples without group	Median no. of specimens per sample
D	1976	101	1	0–16	154	D	1977	108	2
EW	1976	46	2	0–19	113	EW	1977	24	5
LW	1976	45	2.5	0–11	115	LW	1977	53	2

All arthropods[2]

a.

Season	Year	No. of samples without group	Median no. of specimens per sample	Range, minimum and maximum no. of specimens per sample	Total no. of samples	Season	Year	No. samples without group	Median no. of specimens per sample
LW	1975	—	53.5	1–359	104	D	1976	—	35
D	1976	—	35	2–308	154	EW	1976	—	108
EW	1976	—	108	6–509	113	LW	1976	—	88
LW	1976	—	88	1–663	115	D	1977	—	69.5
D	1977	—	69.5	1–615	236	EW	1977	—	123
EW	1977	—	123	3–789	113	LW	1977	—	121

b.

Season	Year	No. of samples without group	Median no. of specimens per sample	Range, minimum and maximum no. of specimens per sample	Total no. of samples	Season	Year	No. samples without group	Median no. of specimens per sample
D	1976	—	35	2–308	154	D	1977	—	69.5
EW	1976	—	108	6–509	113	EW	1977	—	123
LW	1976	—	88	1–663	115	LW	1977	—	121

Nonformicid arthropods[2]

a.

Season	Year	No. of samples without group	Median no. of specimens per sample	Range, minimum and maximum no. of specimens per sample	Total no. of samples	Season	Year	No. samples without group	Median no. of specimens per sample
LW	1975	—	26	2–179	104	D	1976	—	26
D	1976	—	26	1–278	154	EW	1976	—	38
EW	1976	—	38	4–347	113	LW	1976	—	33
LW	1976	—	33	1–408	115	D	1977	—	31
D	1977	—	31	0–318	236	EW	1977	—	70
EW	1977	—	70	2–547	113	LW	1977	—	43.5

b.

Season	Year	No. of samples without group	Median no. of specimens per sample	Range, minimum and maximum no. of specimens per sample	Total no. of samples	Season	Year	No. samples without group	Median no. of specimens per sample
D	1976	—	26	1–278	154	D	1977	—	31
EW	1976	—	38	4–347	113	EW	1977	—	70
LW	1976	—	33	1–408	115	LW	1977	—	43.5

Range, minimum and maximum no. of specimens per sample	Total no. of samples	Level of significance determined by Mann-Whitney U test	Direction of change
0–16	113	0.002	+
0–11	120	<0.001	+
0–6	154	0.400	ns
0–7	113	0.421	ns
0–8	115	0.437	ns
0–6	236	0.292	ns
0–8	113	<0.001	+
0–5	120	<0.001	−
0–6	236	0.230	ns
0–8	113	0.001	+
0–5	120	0.166	ns
0–16	154	0.448	ns
0–19	113	<0.001	+
0–11	115	0.334	ns
0–39	236	0.029	−
0–40	113	<0.001	+
0–17	120	<0.001	−
0–39	236	<0.001	+
0–40	113	<0.001	+
0–17	120	0.058	ns
2–308	154	0.050	−
6–509	113	<0.001	+
1–663	115	0.290	ns
1–615	236	0.001	−
3–789	113	<0.001	+
8–758	120	0.090	ns
1–615	236	<0.001	+
3–789	113	0.008	+
8–758	120	0.030	+
1–278	154	0.295	ns
4–347	113	<0.001	+
1–408	115	0.239	ns
0–318	236	0.082	ns
2–547	113	<0.001	+
3–498	120	0.016	−
0–318	236	0.028	+
2–547	113	<0.001	+
3–498	120	0.006	+

increase in the wet season (Figure 4, part d). Dry season populations in 1976 and 1977 were similar and did not differ significantly from the 1975 late wet season (Table 6). Density increased at the beginning of both wet seasons sampled, but did not differ over the course of the wet season. Of all possible wet-season comparisons within and between years, none are significant (Table 6). Spider populations in the years studied appear to be very similar in the extent of seasonal fluctuations.

Although the average numbers of spiders do not change appreciably through the wet season, estimated dry weight increases as the wet season progresses. A peak is reached in both years in the fourth wet season month at 4–5 mg/sample. Dry- and late wet-season values vary between 2 and 3 mg/sample. Average size remains 1–2 mm, showing no seasonal trend during the period of the collections. There is a general increase in number in all size classes in the middle of the rainy season.

Pseudoscorpionida Pseudoscorpions are small predators (rarely longer than 4 mm), usually found in crevices in litter, bark, or soil. They prefer situations of high humidity, are not tolerant of desiccation, and are rarely active in the open (Weygoldt, 1969). Temperate species construct silken hibernation chambers which they are unwilling to leave, even under the heat stress of Berlese funnels (Gabbutt, 1967). Some species are gregarious and, for most temperate forms, nymphs overwinter and emerge in favorable spring conditions (Gabbutt and Vanchon, 1963). Prey items include collembolans, small dipterans, psocopterans, larvae, beetles, ants, mites, and occasionally small earthworms (Weygoldt, 1969).

Pseudoscorpion numbers varied strongly between seasons and years (Figure 4, part c). Maximum populations were collected at the beginning of the rainy season. Numbers declined slowly during the wet season; lowest population density was found in the dry season. In 1976, the early and late wet seasons do not

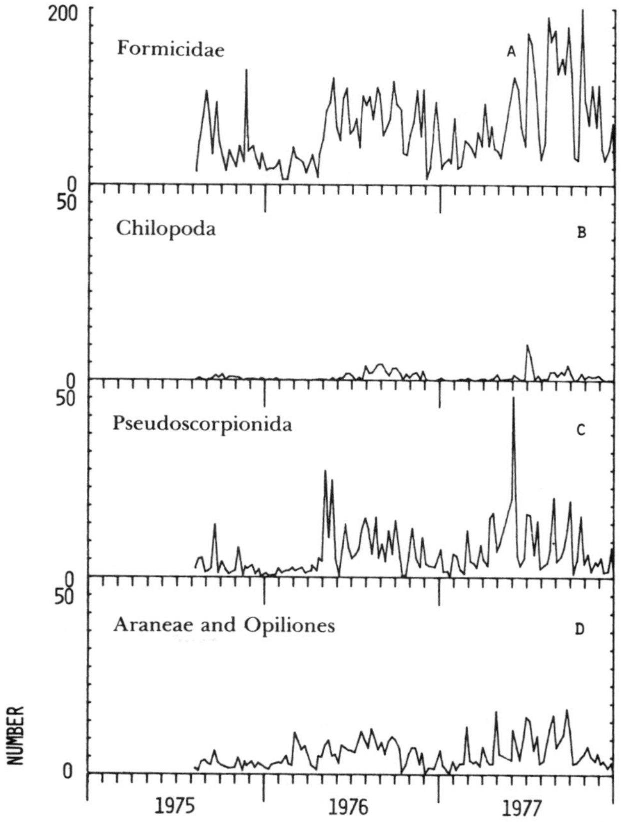

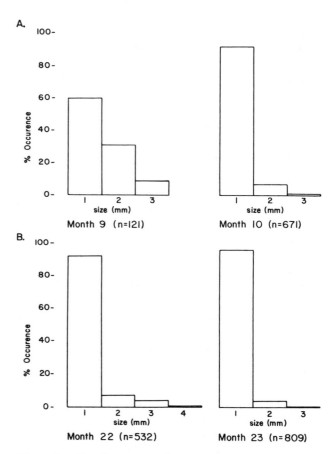

Figure 4. Part A: Formicidae, Part B: Chilopoda, Part C: Pseudoscorpionida, Part D: Araneae and Opiliones (average 10 samples/week, all figures).

Figure 5. Size frequency of Pseudoscorpionida collected the last month of the dry season and the first month of the wet season: chi-square test for heterogeneity; Part A: 1976, Part B: 1977.

differ significantly in density (Table 6). However, in 1977, significantly more pseudoscorpions were collected in the early wet season. Decreases in populations between the late wet and dry seasons were significant in 1976–77, but not in 1975–76. The 1975 late wet and 1976 dry seasons have the lowest overall population density (Table 6).

In general, population size was greater in 1977 than in 1976 (Table 6). Pairwise comparisons between seasons in 1976 and 1977 showed significant increases between seasons in the dry and early wet season, but the late wet seasons do not differ significantly (Table 6). Late wet season 1975 has significantly fewer individuals collected than either 1976 or 1977.

Population increase at the start of the rainy season is extremely rapid, and there is a significant shift in size toward the 1-mm size class (Figure 5). The rapidity of the shift indicates that emergence from dry-season hibernation by small individuals is probably responsible. The shift is more pronounced in 1976

than in 1977, suggesting that more small individuals remain active during a wetter dry season. It appears that tropical pseudoscorpions may aestivate during the dry season and emerge at the beginning of the favorable season as their northern brethren do.

Psocoptera Psocids are small (less than 4 mm long) insects which feed mostly on organic matter such as fungal spores or algal cells (Kevan, 1962; Kuhnelt, 1961). Some gregarious species spin webs on the underside of litter or wood and live in groups. Egg masses may be wrapped in silk, and hatching nymphs remain together until reaching adulthood (Borror and DeLong, 1971).

Psocid populations are low in the wet season, increasing only under dry-season conditions (Figure 6, part b). Late wet-season density is consistently low, fewer than one individual per sample, but between years density distributions differ significantly, with 1977 exceeding 1976 and 1975 (Table 6). Maximum density between dry seasons differed significantly (Table 6). The length of the dry season appears to be critical in determining maximum population density. Month-by-month comparison of psocid density in 1976 and 1977 shows that populations differ significantly for only one of four comparisons when dry-season months are considered in order (Table 7). In that case, populations were higher in 1976 than in 1977. In 1976, density remained high through the first month of the rainy season (month 10); it did not differ significantly from the fifth month of the 1977 dry season. However, months 21 and 22 in 1977 show a continued population increase, reaching a higher density than at any time in 1976. When early wet-season months are compared in order (Table 7), 1977 density was significantly higher than 1976 for two of three comparisons. Populations dropped in both years, but the decline was slower in 1977. Between years, populations built up at about the same rate, but in 1977, since the dry season was longer, higher population levels were produced.

The effect of dry-season rains on psocid populations is unknown, but they may be important in increasing psocid survivorship or available food resources. It is also possible that the increase in populations between years is related to increased psocid populations at the start of the dry season. This appears to be unlikely because 1977 psocid populations do not appear to differ significantly from those in 1976 until late in the dry season (Table 7). Any effect appears to be either delayed or too small to be detectable by our sampling methods.

Thysanoptera Thysanoptera are small (usually less

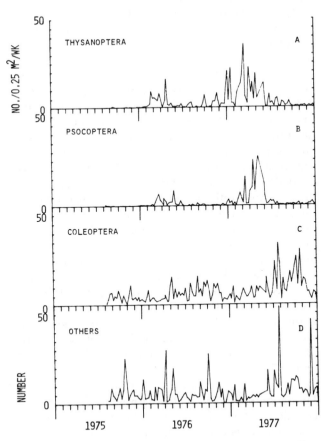

Figure 6. Part A: Thysanoptera, Part B: Psocoptera, Part C: Coleoptera, Part D: Others (average 10 samples/week, all figures).

than 3 mm long) foliage, flower, and bark feeders. Flower-feeding groups are very common and may be serious pests in the temperate zone (Strickland, 1944; Borror and DeLong, 1971). There are a few litter thrips which prey on mites, and others feed on various algae and fungi (Kuhnelt, 1961). Immature thrips tend to live in groups and to move and feed together (Borror and DeLong, 1971).

Thysanoptera on Barro Colorado Island are mainly associated with dry conditions, which corresponds to the period when most trees flower (Figure 6, part a; Windsor, 1977; Foster, 1973; Croat, 1978). However, the length of time that flowers are collected in litterfall differs between years (Windsor, 1977). The major period of flowerfall in 1976 was January to April, but in 1977 flowers fell from December 1976 to August 1977 (Windsor, 1977; unpublished ESP litterfall data). Densities of thrips are correlated with the period of flowering (Spearman rank correlation coefficient = 0.544, $0.001 < p < 0.01$, using average monthly flowerfall versus median monthly thrip density, $n = 30$ months), but are uncorrelated with litter moisture. Some thrips were collected throughout the period of flowerfall in 1977 (Figure 6, part a), but maximum densities were found during the dry season.

Thysanoptera were more common in 1977 than in 1976. Month-by-month comparison of the dry and early wet seasons (Table 7) shows that density of thrips was generally higher in 1977 than in 1976 (seven of nine comparisons significantly different). Total populations in the dry and early wet seasons were significantly higher in 1977 than 1976 (Table 6). However, the late wet seasons of 1976 and 1977 do not differ significantly in density, although populations are significantly higher than those found in 1975. The importance of non-flower-feeding groups cannot be evaluated until a more detailed examination of samples is possible; their contribution to seasonal population fluctuations is unknown. In addition, some groups may migrate up in the foliage when the rains begin after sheltering in litter or soil during the dry season (Kevan, 1962).

Coleoptera The category Coleoptera contains all species of beetles collected. The enormous diversity of species, families, and life styles makes any ecological generalization about the group impossible. Two families, Curculionidae and Carabidae, are being separated to species and the results will be reported separately (Erwin and Stockwell, in prep.).

Coleoptera form an average of 10% of all individuals collected throughout the year. The average number collected weekly is highly correlated with the number of other arthropods collected (Spearman rank correlation coefficient = 0.683, $p < 0.001$, $n = 121$ weeks). The seasonal distribution of Coleoptera therefore closely parallels that of the general litter fauna (Figure 6, part c).

Coleoptera density drops in the dry season and increases in the wet season. However, instead of reaching peak abundance in the early wet season as combined arthropods do (see All Arthropods), density increases through the wet season and is highest at the end of the wet season (Table 6). In 1976, the increase between the early and late wet seasons is highly significant; in 1977, median density increases from eight to nine individuals per sample, but the increase is not statistically significant (Table 6).

In general, Coleoptera density was greater in 1977 than in 1976 (Table 6). The late wet season 1975 had significantly lower density than either 1976 or 1977.

Holometabolous Larvae Larvae for all holometabolous groups except ants are lumped into a single category because of the extreme difficulty of lower level identification. Larvae form an average of 6% of all arthropods collected, and average larval density is highly correlated with the average density of other arthropods (Spearman rank correlation coefficient = 0.749, $p < 0.001$, $n = 121$ weeks). Some larvae are present in the litter all year round; seasonally, larval abundance parallels that of all arthropods (Figure 3, part d).

The number of larvae drops in the dry season and increases in the early wet season (Figure 3, part d, Table 6). Median density more than doubles in the first 2 months of the rainy season and then declines slowly through the wet season and into the dry season. However, the wet season decline is small and is not statistically significant in either 1976 or 1977 (Table 6). In 1975, late wet- and dry-season densities do not differ significantly, although the drop at the beginning of the dry season is significant in 1976. There is no seasonal trend in median size for the 30 months of collections. Median size was 2–3 mm for 26 months and was 4 mm for 4 months. Size was not correlated with seasonal changes, and some small larvae were collected every month. Between years, larval density increased in the late 1977 wet season, but remained at the same level for the two dry-season periods sampled. There were fewer larvae in the late wet season of 1975 than in the corresponding periods of 1976 and 1977 (Table 6).

Hymenoptera: Formicidae Ants are an extremely common and important part of the litter fauna. Nearly any type of food has an ant that will eat it (Wilson, 1971). Many common litter groups are generalists, taking sugar, scavenged material, and prey. Some species are extreme specialists and eat only a few re-

Table 7. Comparisons of litter arthropod densities by month for wet (a) and dry seasons (b) using the Mann–Whitney U test

Month, 1976	No. samples with 0 animals	Median of samples with 1 or more animals	Number of samples	Month, 1977	Number of samples with 0 animals	Median of samples with 1 or more animals	Number of samples	Probability	Direction of change
Psocoptera									
a.									
6	28	1.0	40	17	32	1.0	40	0.138	ns
7	24	1.0	37	18	21	3.0	37	0.074	ns
8	13	2.0	39	19	24	2.0	36	<0.001	−
9	18	2.0	38	20	14	3.0	37	0.138	ns
10	15	2.0	38	21	12	4.0	37	0.090	ns
11	22	1.0	38	22	7	8.0	48	<0.001	+
b.									
10	15	2.0	38	23	12	5.5	37	0.067	ns
11	22	1.0	38	24	14	2.0	40	<0.001	+
12	31	1.0	37	25	20	1.0	37	<0.001	+
Thysanoptera									
a.									
6	33	2.0	40	17	24	3.5	40	0.018	+
7	14	2.0	37	18	17	8.0	37	0.164	ns
8	7	4.5	39	19	11	4.0	36	0.068	ns
9	18	3.0	38	20	6	6.0	37	<0.001	+
10	16	2.0	38	21	3	9.0	37	<0.001	+
11	21	1.0	38	22	8	5.5	48	<0.001	+
b.									
10	16	2.0	38	23	11	8.0	37	<0.010	+
11	21	1.0	38	24	16	3.0	40	<0.050	+
12	25	2.0	37	25	17	3.0	37	<0.050	+

Population increase, decrease, and no change are indicated by +, −, and ns.

stricted prey types. Several genera collected in litter samples culture fungus for food on a variety of substrates. In general, most ants collected are at least partially predaceous and most types of litter arthropods are probably eaten by one species or another (Levings, unpublished data). Ants as social insects present special sampling problems (Brian, 1978). Colonies persist for far longer than 1 year; many live 10 or more years (Wilson, 1971). Ant workers found in samples are probably mostly foragers, although females, males, and brood (indicating the presence of nests) are also frequently collected. Species-level identification and seasonal patterns will be considered in detail elsewhere (Levings, in prep.).

On the average, ants compose about half the number of arthropods caught (Figure 4, part a). Ant density is correlated with density of other arthropods (Spearman rank correlations coefficient = 0.635, $p < 0.001$, $n = 121$ weeks). Although ant numbers show a strong negative response to dry conditions, ant density does not change over the wet season in either 1976 or 1977 (Table 6). Between years, numbers are significantly greater in the dry season in 1977 than at the same period in 1976. Both early and late wet-season density is similar between years; but, in 1977, density is marginally larger in the late wet season ($p = 0.054$, Mann-Whitney U test) and just misses significance in the early wet season ($p = 0.075$, Mann-Whitney U test).

Short-term seasonal conditions appear to affect ants

Table 8. Occurrence of ants as a function of litter moisture

	Number of weeks with litter moisture ≥45%	Number of weeks with litter moisture <45%	Total
Number of weeks with <50% ants	19 (1)	23 (21)	42 (22)
Number of weeks with ≥50% ants	66 (9)	13 (10)	79 (19)
Total	85 (10)	36 (31)	121 (41)

Data in parentheses are dry-season weeks.
$\chi^2 = 19.25$, 1 d.f., $p < 0.001$
($\chi^2 = 10.14$, 1 d.f., $0.01 > p > 0.001$)

proportionately more than most other groups. The relative percentage of ants per sample week drops substantially in the dry season. During the wet season, ants average about 60–70% of the samples by number; in almost all weeks, they constitute more than 50% of the samples. In the dry season, the proportional abundance of ants drops to 20–40% of the samples.

Ant abundance is strongly correlated with litter moisture (Spearman rank correlations coefficient = 0.428, $p < 0.001$, $n = 121$ weeks), but is only weakly correlated with litter dry weight (Spearman rank correlation coefficient = 0.213, $p < 0.05$, $n = 121$ weeks). Ant response to moist conditions is very rapid. Table 8 shows the number of weeks in which litter moisture was above or below 45% compared with the number of weeks in which ants were 50% or less of the total sample counts. There is a significant association between litter moisture and the proportional occurrence of ants, for both the entire sample period and the dry seasons alone (Table 8). Dry-season rains immediately increase the proportion of ants in samples. This short-term, facultative response on the part of the long-lived colonial species is not surprising. Ant colonies do not have inactive stages in which they can escape poor conditions, such as a diapause or prolonged pupation. Colonies may use brood as a stored food resource and maintain low-level activity even under very dry conditions (Levings, unpublished data). Many ants forage whenever conditions are acceptable, and shifts in activity periods have been shown for many species (Hunt, 1974; Levings, unpublished).

Orthoptera Orthoptera have been separated into two main groups: roaches, and crickets and grasshoppers.

Phasmids, mantids and other groups are rare and are not included in the counts. After December 1976, counts are reported separately for nymphs and adults. Both roaches and crickets feed on plant material. Roaches are potentially important detritivores and/or omnivores, crickets eat both living and dead plant material, and grasshoppers feed predominantly on living plants (Borror and DeLong, 1971). Grasshoppers were rarely collected and almost all the individuals in the cricket and grasshopper category were crickets.

Roaches were always uncommon and density remained lower than one per sample during the period of our sampling. Few adults were collected. There was almost no trend in roach abundance (Figure 7, parts c, d; Table 6) although fewer roaches were collected in 1977. Populations increased at the start of the 1976 dry season, remained the same through the start of the following dry season and then decreased. There

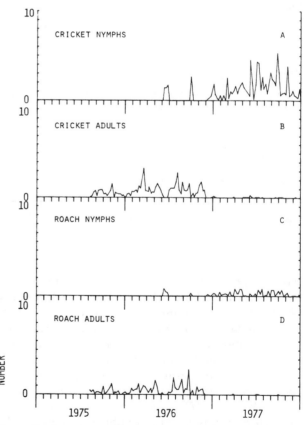

Figure 7. Part A: Gryllidae nymphs, not separated before December 1976; Part B: Gryllidae, all prior to December 1976; after December 1976, adults only; Part C: Blattaria nymphs, not separated before December 1976; Part D: Blattaria adults, all prior to December 1976, after December 1976, adults only (average 10 samples/week, all figures).

were no further changes in density during the 1977 sampling. Some individuals 3 mm long or less were collected each month, but there was no peak period of recruitment. The ratio of small to large individuals collected did not vary between seasons in a consistent way. During the wet-season periods sampled, small individuals formed 35–45% of the total collected. In the 1976 dry season they formed only 28% of the total; in the 1977 dry season, they constituted 63% of the total. Catches were always low, so that any conclusions about population fluctuations are risky.

Although the distributions of crickets showed some distinct seasonal trends, like the roaches, relatively few adults were collected once the samples were separated into adult and nymphal categories. The data were thus combined for treatment (Table 6; Figure 7, parts a, b). Cricket density increased between the 1975 late wet season and the 1976 dry season, but then remained the same until the start of the 1977 wet season.

At that time, it increased and stayed at the same level through 1977. Thus, although populations changed somewhat between seasons, there was no regular seasonal pattern of population fluctuation. Populations on the whole were larger in the 1977 wet season than in 1976 (Table 6). Recruitment was similarly irregular. The proportion of individuals 2 mm or less varied, but some were collected each month. During the 1975 late wet season and the 1976 dry season, small individuals formed 46% of the 50 collected and 38% of 130 collected, respectively. During all other seasons, the proportion ranged from 55% to 69%. Recruitment was high in the 1977 dry season (68% of those collected) and remained high in the 1977 early wet season (69% of those collected). The proportion was somewhat lower in other periods. Thus, although density did not differ between dry-season periods sampled, more small individuals were collected in 1977, indicating higher recruitment.

Homoptera and Hemiptera Various groups of Hemiptera and Homoptera were regularly collected, but were never very common. Most Homoptera collected appear to be temporary inhabitants of the litter, perhaps seeking shelter. Some of the Hemiptera collected eat seeds as adults (see below) and feed as nymphs in the litter during the dry season. Very little can be said about their position in the litter ecosystem; most are probably transients (Kuhnelt, 1961).

Homoptera populations did not change significantly from the 1975 late wet season until the 1977 early wet season (Figure 8, parts a, b; Table 6). In 1977 they increased in the early wet season, but decreased significantly by the late wet season. In collections separated into nymphal and adult categories, the overwhelming majority of individuals proved, in all seasons, to be nymphs. Density of adults did not change significantly from the 1977 dry season to the end of the sampling reported here (Mann-Whitney U test, $p > 0.1$ for all comparisons), while numbers of nymphs changed significantly and caused the changes recorded in total Homoptera (Table 6). Between years, only the early wet seasons differ significantly; more Homoptera were collected in 1977 than 1976 (Table 6).

Hemiptera numbers changed significantly between most seasons (Table 6). There was a general decrease during the dry season, increase during the wet season, and slow decrease to the next dry season. In collections separated into adult and nymphal categories, we find a large recruitment of nymphal Hemiptera during the late dry season and early wet season. More are collected in the early wet season than in the dry season (Mann-Whitney U test, $p < 0.01$). Numbers of adults

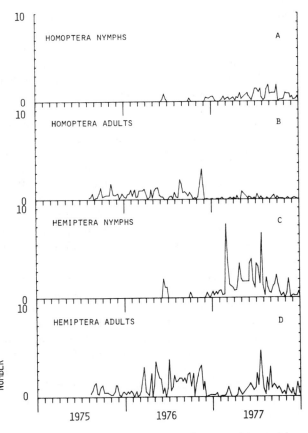

Figure 8. Part A: Homoptera nymphs, not separated before December 1976; Part B: Homoptera adults, all prior to December 1976, after December 1976, adults only; Part C: Hemiptera nymphs, not separated before December 1976; Part D: Hemiptera adults, all prior to December 1976, after December 1976, adults only (average 10 samples/week, all figures).

Table 9. Taxa collected per week, by season

Wet 1975

Wet 1976 > Dry 1976

Wet 1977   Dry 1977   Wet 1975 < Wet 1976 < Wet 1977

    $p < 0.001$ $p = 0.045$ $p = 0.038$

    (Taxa collected per week

    in any wet season   Dry 1976 = Dry 1977

    exceeds those collected in $p = 0.444$

    any dry season.)

All comparisons were made using Mann–Whitney U tests on the distributions of the number of taxa collected per week.

increase during the early wet season, but reach a peak later than numbers of nymphs (Figure 8, parts c, d). Both nymphs and adult numbers then decline for the rest of the year. More nymphs than adults are collected in both the dry and early wet seasons (Mann-Whitney U test, $p < 0.01$, both tests), but numbers do not differ in the late wet season (Mann-Whitney U test, $p > 0.10$). Some nymphs are collected all year; there is no period without recruitment. It appears from the population changes that dry- and early wet-season nymphs turn into early and late wet-season adults, which may or may not reproduce immediately. At least some of the dry-season nymphs appear to represent species related to *Dysdercus,* which feed on various seeds produced during the dry season.

All Arthropods The distribution of the number of arthropods collected per sample shows a strong seasonal pattern (Figure 2, part c). There is a significant decrease in total arthropod abundance during the dry season, followed by a strong and immediate increase in total number when the rains begin (Table 6). Although there is a downward trend in numbers during the wet season, overall density does not differ between the early and late wet seasons in either 1976 or 1977. Numbers collected in 1977 were higher for all three seasonal comparisons, showing a general increase in arthropod activity in 1977.

Total Number of Taxa The total number of taxa collected per week varied seasonally, in partial correlation with the total number of arthropods. The median number of taxa collected in both dry seasons was 19 (range 1976, 17–21, 16 weeks; range 1977, 14–23, 25 weeks). In the three wet seasons sampled, the median number of taxa collected was 20, 20, and 23, respectively (range 1975, 14–25, 20 weeks; range

1976, 14–26, 28 weeks; range 1977, 16–25, 33 weeks). The number of taxa collected differed significantly between wet and dry seasons (Table 9), but the ranges overlap broadly. In general, the largest number of taxa per week were collected in the 1977 wet season. Differences between years in the number of taxa collected are significant between the 1977 wet season and both other wet seasons. The two dry seasons sampled are statistically indistinguishable (Table 9).

Nonformicid Arthropods When nonformicid arthropods are considered separately, a slightly different seasonal pattern emerges (Table 6). There is no significant decrease in arthropod density at the start of the dry season in either 1975–76 or 1976–77. Density increases significantly at the start of the rainy season and remains at a high level throughout the rainy season in 1976. Arthropod density drops gradually from the early wet season 1976 to the 1977 dry season. Although comparisons of the early wet season with the late wet season of 1976 and the late wet season of 1976 with the dry season of 1977 are not significant, the comparison between the early wet season of 1976 and the dry season of 1977 is highly significant ($p < 0.01$, Mann-Whitney U test). In 1977 the decline from early to late wet season is significant. Between-year comparisons show that populations in 1977 were, on the whole, greater than those in 1976 (Table 6), although the dry-season comparison is only weakly significant.

Summary Trends Table 10 summarizes the direction of population changes in major arthropod taxa over the period of study. The general increase in arthropod abundance between years is composed of increases in most groups sampled, not the overwhelming effect of a few. Only roaches, isopods, and amphipods, which declined, and homopterans, ants, and spiders, which remained about the same, did not show increases in average population size over two or more seasons (Table 10). Changes in abundance reflect an increase in the average number of samples in which a taxon is collected as well as an increase in the number collected per sample.

Correlation between Physical Factors and Arthropod Abundance

Table 11 lists the Spearman rank correlations between litter dry weight, litter moisture, and major arthropod taxa. Most groups are significantly associated with both factors. Total arthropod abundance is highly seasonal, which is reflected in a positive association with both factors. When nonformicid arthropods are considered separately, the correlation between the percentage of litter moisture and the abundance of such arthropods disappears, and the strength of the correlation between litter dry weight and nonformicid arthropod abundance increases. Ant abundance, however, is only weakly correlated with litter dry weight, but is strongly correlated with litter moisture.

Groups that are present mainly in the wet season show strong correlations with litter moisture. In general, the correlation between litter dry weight and number is weaker than the correlation between litter moisture and number. This is because litter dry weight is high during the dry season and at the start of the rainy season, periods when many litter arthropod groups are changing rapidly in abundance. The spiders and the pseudoscorpions are an exception to this generalization. Neither is correlated with litter moisture, but both are correlated with litter dry weight. This is related to the relatively large number of spiders collected in the late dry season and to the extremely rapid increase in pseudoscorpion numbers when the rains begin and litter dry weight is high (Figure 4, parts c, d; see Araneae and Opiliones, and Pseudoscorpionida).

In general, the pattern of correlation tracks seasonal changes summarized in Table 10, but the correlation is far from exact and does not provide a good predictor of litter arthropod populations.

Trophic Structure

Although many litter groups are difficult or impossible to classify ecologically at our level of analysis, a rough breakdown into predaceous and nonpredaceous groups can be made. Ants are the overwhelming numerical dominants throughout the year, constituting roughly half the total number collected; most of these are predaceous. Consequently, total predators are 60–70% of the arthropods collected in the wet season and 40–60% of the total number collected in the dry season. Nonformicid predators average 10–15% of the samples; occasionally in the dry season they make up 20% of the samples. After ants, pseudoscorpions are the most common predator, followed by spiders and centipedes. The proportion of rare predators (Onychophora, Embioptera, Scorpionida, Neuroptera, and nonformicid Hymenoptera) is seldom even 1% of the total sample. Coleoptera, larvae, and Hemiptera are excluded from consideration since the ecology of these groups is mixed and predator abundance cannot be separated from other feeding types by our level of analysis.

Ant number does not change during the wet season (see Hymenoptera: Formicidae), but other predator groups peak during different periods of the year. Pseudoscorpions peak early in the wet season, spiders during the middle, and centipedes during the last months of the rainy season (see Chilopoda, Araneae and Opiliones, and Pseudoscorpionida).

Major decomposer groups sampled are amphipods, isopods, millipedes, and some portion of the larvae collected. Larvae are excluded from consideration because some do not consume litter. The exact definition of a decomposer is very loose in this system and encompasses those groups that consume litter and those that consume fungi and microbes that are growing on the litter (see Discussion section). Other potential detritivores that are not considered here are Orthoptera, Psocoptera, and Thysanoptera.

There were large and possible compensatory changes in density between the major decomposer groups we sampled. In 1975–76, isopods and amphipods formed a significant fraction of the total arthropods collected (see Crustacea). At the start of the dry season in 1977, both groups essentially disappeared until the end of the following rainy season. Diplopoda were relatively common in 1975–76, but density increased dramatically at the start of the 1977 wet season, and late wet-season density was triple that of the 1976 late wet season (see Diplopoda). One possible interpretation of these changes is that the decline in isopod and amphipod populations was responsible for the increase in millipede density. Such an explanation would require that isopods and amphipods were competing with each other and with millipedes for some resource or were otherwise interfering with millipede populations (by eating millipede eggs, for instance). It is also possible that increased millipede populations in 1977 were unrelated to crustacean population fluctuations or that both were responding to another controlling influence. We unfortunately have no direct

Table 10. Summary of trends in arthropod abundance, 1975–77

Between seasons	All arthropods	Ants	Non ants	Isp.	Amp.	Cen.	Mil.	Col.
Late wet 1975–Dry 1976	−	−	ns	−	−	−	−	ns
Dry 1976–Early wet 1976	+	+	+	+	ns	+	+	+
Early wet 1976–Late wet 1976	ns	ns	ns	ns	ns	+	−	+
Late wet 1976–Dry 1977	−	−	ns	−	−	−	−	−
Dry 1977–Early wet 1977	+	+	+	−	ns	+	+	+
Early wet 1977–Late wet 1977	ns	ns	−	+	ns	ns	−	ns
Between years								
Dry 1976–77	+	+	+	−	−	+	+	+
Early wet 1976–77	+	ns	+	−	−	+	+	+
Late wet 1976–77	+	ns/+	+	−	−	−	+	+

+ = increase, − = decrease, ns = no significant change.

Isp. = Isopoda, Amp. = Amphipoda, Cen. = Chilopoda, Mil. = Diplopoda, Col. = Coleoptera, Pso. = Psocoptera, Thr. = Thysanoptera, Lar. = holometabolous larvae, Spi. = Araneae and Opiliones, Psc. = Pseudoscorpionida, Bla. = Blattaria, Gry. = Gryllidae, Hem. = Hemiptera, Hom. = Homoptera.

evidence on this point, and experimental data would be very difficult to gather.

Seasonal Distribution of Arthropod Size

Median size of the collections does not change significantly during the period of study. As pointed out by Williams (1941), small individuals predominate throughout the year. Median size is 1 mm in 25 of 30 months; in 5 scattered months it is 2 mm. Inclusion of mites and Collembola would have lowered median size to 1 mm in all months.

The proportion of individuals 11.5 mm and longer (size classes 7–10) was always low; the grand mean for the period of study was 0.0082%. The proportion of large arthropods did change seasonally over the period of study (one factor analysis of variance performed on the arcsin transformed percentage occurrence of arthropods in size classes 7–10, $n = 7$ seasons, 101 weeks, d.f. = 6, 96, $F = 6.61$, $p < 0.001$). Aposteriori comparison of seasonal subsamples, using the Student-Newman-Keuls test, shows that only one subsample differs from the rest. A significantly lower proportion of large individuals was collected during the 1977 dry season than at any other time ($p < 0.01$, 0.0044% vs. 0.006 to 0.0154%).

The distributions of the number of large arthropods per sample shows a similar pattern. The distribution of numbers of large individuals differs between all wet and dry periods, although there is less heterogeneity within either wet or dry seasons. The two dry-season periods do not differ significantly from each other (median = 0, Mann-Whitney U test, $p > 0.10$), but the number of arthropods collected is lower than during any wet-season period (Mann-Whitney U tests, $p < 0.01$ or smaller, all comparisons). Between wet-season periods there is some heterogeneity. The 1976 late wet-season sample had more large arthropods than the 1975 late wet-season sample (Mann-Whitney U test, $p = 0.0091$), but there are no other significant differences in pairwise comparisons. Median number of large arthropods per sample is one, in all wet season periods.

The pattern of insect size was thus relatively constant between years although the numbers of arthropods were changing significantly (Table 10).

DISCUSSION

There is an obvious seasonal cycle in litter arthropod populations. Numbers of most groups decrease at the beginning of the dry season, increase when the rains begin, and then decrease, more or less slowly during the wet season. There is no detailed correspondence between litter arthropod populations and changes in physical factors (see Correlation between Physical Factors and Arthropod Abundance). The beginning of the rainy season initiates most decomposition, and the

Pso.	Thr.	Lar.	Spi.	Psc.	Bla.	Gry.	Hem.	Hom.	Total		
									+	ns	−
+	+	ns	ns	ns	+	+	ns	ns	4	7	6
−	−	+	+	+	ns	ns	+	ns	11	4	2
−*	−	ns	ns	ns	ns	ns	ns	ns	2	12	3
+	+	−	−	−	−	ns	−	ns	2	3	12
−	−	+	+	+	ns	+	+	+	12	2	3
−	−	ns	ns	−	ns	ns	−	−	1	9	7
+	+	ns	ns	+	−	ns	+	ns	10	4	3
+	+	+	ns	+	−	+	+	+	12	2	3
+	ns	+	ns	ns	−	+	ns/−	ns	7	6	4

subsequent flush of food fuels, directly or indirectly, the subsequent increase in arthropod populations.

Fluctuations in litter arthropod populations must be examined in relation to seasonal and annual changes in physical factors, especially rainfall and litter dry weight. Rainfall and litter accumulations are connected through the process of decomposition. The importance of litter moisture in determining the rate of decay has been shown in a wide variety of tropical and temperate habitats (Hopkins, 1966; Gupta and Singh, 1977; Klinge, 1977; Ewel, 1976; Neilsen, 1959; Madge, 1965, 1969, and included references). In addition to moisture content, a wide variety of other factors influence decomposition rates. The amount of fragmentation, concentration of secondary compounds, leaf toughness, and position on the forest floor may all have important effects (Edwards and Heath, 1974; Heath and Arnold, 1966; King and Heath, 1967). Decomposition rates vary between species and between locations within species (Heath et al., 1965; Madge, 1969; Ewel, 1976). Our sampling is not detailed enough to examine these factors, but it is clear that decomposition is largely restricted to the wet season and that, on the whole, litter arthropod activity is higher during the periods when litter is moist.

Although the amount of litter present on the forest floor must ultimately control the food supply of litter arthropods (McBrayer et al., 1977), the small decrease in litterfall and accumulation between years did not seem to affect litter arthropod populations strongly. Both litterfall and litter accumulations fell over the period of study, but litter arthropod populations increased (Tables 4 and 10). However, the observed differences are small, and maximum litter accumulation did not differ significantly between years (see Litterfall and Litter Accumulation). Although the total amount of litter did not change greatly between years, its suitability as a food source may have changed, thus affecting the populations of both predators and decomposers. This possibility cannot be excluded with the information at hand.

The timing and amount of rainfall affects litter arthropods both directly and indirectly. Directly, it changes the amount of moisture available to litter organisms. Indirectly, it affects the timing, duration and (possibly) amount of litterfall (Dietrich, et al., this volume). Leaching by rainfall also affects the suitability of litter as food. We are unable to evaluate the effects of rainfall on the amount or chemical composition of litter. However, the timing and amount of dry-season rains had a significant effect on litter moisture (see Rainfall, Soil, and Litter Moisture). In turn, we hypothesize that this difference had important effects on litter arthropod populations.

There are several mechanisms through which dry-season litter moisture content may affect litter arthropod populations. Survivorship may be reduced by desiccation, either of the animals themselves or their prey. The susceptibility of litter arthropods to

Table 11. Spearman rank correlations between litter dry weight, litter moisture, and major arthropod groups

	Arthropods	Non-ant arthropods	Ants	Col.	Lar.	Psc.
Litter dry weight	0.327	0.400	0.213	0.156	0.201	0.432
Probability	<0.01	<0.001	<0.05	ns	<0.05	<0.001
Litter moisture (percent)	0.308	0.117	0.428	0.337	0.281	0.117
Probability	<0.01	ns	<0.001	<0.001	<0.01	ns

$N = 121$ weeks, mean number collected weekly versus weekly average dry weight or moisture content. Abbreviations follow Table 10.

desiccation has been shown for a wide variety of tropical and temperate groups (Kuhnelt, 1961; Wallwork, 1970; Birch and Clark, 1954). Small reductions in average relative humidity may be fatal for many litter species. Behavioral responses to desiccation may also have important effects on arthropod distributions. Some groups have been shown to move up and down in soil and litter in response to changes in moisture content (Usher, 1975; Strickland, 1947), and some groups may remain active longer in moister sections of the forest (Macfadyen, 1969). Ants, at least, respond immediately to wet conditions (see Hymenoptera: Formicidae). The effect of migration to favorable patches of litter has not been studied but is a possible consideration (Lloyd, 1963). Moist patches of litter may attract mobile invertebrates in the dry season or be the site of enhanced survivorship or activity when conditions in the litter are generally poor. The variance in average litter moisture is higher in the dry season than in the wet season (see Rainfall, Soil, and Litter Moisture). In addition, wetter areas of litter occur during the dry season and may persist for considerable periods of time (Levings, pers. observation). An increase in survivorship or in the length of the potential breeding season may have important effects in determining population levels during the next period of population increase.

The timing and severity of dry periods may vary in effect, depending upon whether microhumidity drops rapidly or slowly. During a slow change in litter moisture, litter invertebrates are able to seek shelter or aestivate. In addition, the length of dry periods that different groups of arthropods can survive differs—some cannot survive extended dry conditions. The relative severity of the dry season will thus vary with both the length of the dry season and with the distribution of showers within the dry season. Regular showers maintain litter moisture content at a higher level than heavy, infrequent storms. In 1977 the long dry season was punctuated with frequent showers. In 1976 there was almost no rain during the dry season. Litter moisture content was an average of 6% higher in 1977 than in 1976 during the dry season, but wet-season litter moisture did not differ significantly (see Rainfall, Soil, and Litter Moisture).

Litter arthropod populations were extremely low during the severe dry season of 1976. The longer, wetter 1977 dry season had generally higher arthropod populations (Table 10). However, more groups decreased in abundance at the start of the dry season in 1976–77 than in 1975–76 (6 versus 12, Table 10), because arthropod populations were lower in the 1975 late wet season and 1976 dry season than at any other time. One possible cause is the longer 1975 wet season. In 1976 and 1977, the wet season was only 6 months long, but in 1975 it was 8 months long. The end of the rainy season is usually characterized by extremely heavy rainfall (Rand and Rand, this volume), which may adversely affect many relatively delicate litter arthropods.

Because the start of the dry season is unpredictable (Rand and Rand, this volume), many groups may have life histories with dispersal, aestivation, or pupation before the start of the dry season. They will thus tend to disappear before the dry season begins.

In fact, some groups do decline over the wet season (Table 10). Unfortunately, we did not sample during the early parts of the wet season in 1975. However, when the first 2 months of sampling, which immediately precede the 1975 late wet season, are compared with the 1975 late wet season, six groups declined in abundance, nine stayed the same, and only two increased (Table 12). In 1976 and 1977, most groups stayed the same, but a few decreased signifi-

	Spi.	Mil.	Pso.	Gen.
	0.471	0.187	0.497	0.149
	<0.001	<0.05	<0.001	ns
	0.100	0.428	−0.403	0.329
	ns	<0.001	<0.001	<0.001

cantly. Some that did not decrease significantly showed a decreasing trend. Thus, although the data do not allow us to accept this hypothesis, they generally support it. The length of the wet season and/or heavy late wet-season rains may have important effects on litter arthropod populations.

If the preceding analysis is correct, litter arthropod populations are strongly influenced by rainfall patterns, in particular the length of the rainy season and the distribution of rainy periods in the dry season. Sexton has argued that *Anolis* population fluctuations are related to the severity of the preceding dry season (Sexton, 1967). Wolda (1977, 1978a) has suggested that dry-season rains may have either positive or negative effects on homopteran catches in light-traps, depending upon the life history of the species involved. He has also pointed out that many species begin to disperse or disappear before the rains actually stop in the late wet season, presumably to seek refuge. Some litter arthropods appear to do the same thing (Macfadyen, 1969; Strickland, 1947).

Direct comparisons with other tropical studies are difficult because differences in sampling techniques have important effects on estimates of density (see Methods). In addition, most published studies have concentrated on the microarthropod fauna; few have dealt convincingly with the macrofauna. In spite of these limitations, litter arthropod populations appear to change in approximately the same ways in different tropical habitats. Dry conditions have always been found to reduce arthropod activity. Where both wet- and dry-season periods have been sampled, more arthropods were collected in wet periods. Unfortunately, there are no studies that cover as long a period as this one, and we are unable to examine the magnitude of changes between years. On Barro Colorado Island, populations may vary two- to threefold between years.

If species identifications were possible, estimates of the amount of fluctuation could be larger (Wolda, 1978b).

There are several published studies of the litter fauna on Barro Colorado Island. Williams (1941) sampled litter from the forest floor in the early wet season and examined species distributions using differently sized quadrats. He noted that some groups were more likely to be found in large than small quadrats and interpreted this as evidence for the nonrandom spatial separation of some species. Macfadyen (1969) sampled soil and litter at wetter and dryer sites during the dry season. He showed that some species were found closer to the surface in wetter areas and interpreted this as evidence that some groups moved up and down in the soil in response to moisture levels. Willis (1976) sampled for 12 months at several sites. He found strong seasonal patterns of growth and recruitment in major arthropod groups with a peak in the total number of arthropods at the start of the rainy season.

Scattered reports from other tropical areas confirm that marked seasonal variation in arthropod number and biomass is common in litter groups and that dry conditions severely reduce arthropod activity (Dammerman, 1925, 1937; Salt, 1952, 1955; Van Der Drift, 1963; Singh and Singh, 1975; Hazra, 1978; Plowman, 1979; Madge, 1965; Bullock, 1967 and included references). Strickland and Bullock documented the downward migrations of some animals from the surface layers into the soil as the dry season began (Bullock, 1962; Strickland, 1945, 1947). Madge (1965) reported an increase in microarthropod number in Nigeria as the wet season began. The overall density of individuals collected in tropical areas is similar to

Table 12. Comparison of months 1 and 2 with months 3–5 (1975 late wet season), using Mann–Whitney U tests, with correction for ties (Siegel, 1956)

Groups that decreased in abundance	Groups that remained the same	Groups that increased in abundance
Psocoptera	Araneae and Opiliones	Isopoda
Holometabolous larvae	Thysanoptera	Amphipoda
All arthropods	Coleoptera	
Ants (±)	Chilopoda	
Pseudoscorpionida (±)	Diplopoda	
Hemiptera	Non-ant arthropods	
	Homoptera	
	Orthoptera:	
	Blattaria	
	Gryllidae	

that reported from the temperate zone (Greenslade and Greenslade, 1968), but, as with many other groups, there is some evidence that tropical faunas are more diverse (Stanton, 1979).

Recent temperate litter arthropod work has been summarized in a series of reviews (Anderson and Macfadyen, 1976; Edwards et al., 1970; Kuhnelt, 1961, 1963; Wallwork, 1970; Graff and Satchell, 1967; Kevan, 1962; Burges and Raw, 1967; Dickinson and Pugh, 1974; Doeskin and Van Der Drift, 1963). In general, temperate litter arthropods are active through all moist periods of the year. In areas with heavy frost, winter ice may depress arthropod activity, and populations peak in the spring and the fall. In areas without severe frost, arthropod populations remain high and in many cases actually peak during winter months. In most areas, the heat and relative dryness of summer conditions lower arthropod numbers.

Superficially, at least, litter arthropods in tropical and temperate areas change seasonally in similar ways. Moisture availability is more important than temperature in influencing population levels. Beck (1971), working in Amazonia, has pointed out that there are major differences in the function and number of various litter groups between the two regions. In the temperate zone, there are many groups of primary decomposers, which ingest, fragment, and partially digest litter. These groups differ between temperate forest types (Kuhnelt, 1961), but the basic pattern of decomposition is similar. Their feces and undigested leaf fragments form the start of a complex food web, with secondary, tertiary, and even higher levels of decomposer activity not uncommon (Wallwork, 1970). However, Beck (1970, 1971) found that most or all of the function of temperate primary decomposer groups had been taken over by fungi. He hypothesized that because fungi could compete favorably with most primary decomposers under tropical conditions, the primary decomposers began to feed on fungi. In turn, secondary decomposers lacked sufficient pretreated litter to feed upon and shifted to fungi as a food source. In particular, Beck discussed diplopods, which he found to be exclusively fungivorous in Amazonia. In the temperate zone, diplopods are important primary decomposers (Wallwork, 1970; Kevan, 1962). Madge (1965), working in Nigeria, found that decomposition was retarded in mesh bags that did not admit microarthropods. Although the bags may create anomalous situations by altering physical conditions within them, it appears that some microarthropod activity is necessary to maintain high rates of decomposition. The effect of microarthropods could be direct, through cropping of fungi, or indirect, through fragmentation of leaf material which would create more surface area for fungal activity. Other authors have suggested similar hypotheses (Eidmann, 1942, 1943; Maldague, 1958) or have discussed the incidence of fungivorous tropical arthropods (Strickland, 1945; Meyer and Maldague, 1957).

Other tropical–temperate differences in the roles of decomposers involve earthworms. In temperate areas, burial and fragmentation of fallen leaves by earthworms is critical in the production of mull humus (Wallwork, 1970; Kuhnelt, 1961). Two studies have shown that some groups of large tropical earthworms do not participate in leaf burial or feed on organic detritus, although they may cast large amounts of soil on the surface (Madge, 1965; Beck, 1971).

Any critical discussion of the functions of decomposers in tropical–temperate comparisons is risky. The data base is small, but reports from widely separated areas are fairly consistent. The combination of high temperatures and heavy rainfall are close to optimal for fungal growth. This in turn appears to have set up a situation in which many groups of litter arthropods have had to shift their preferred food type to fungi. The rapidity of litter decomposition in the tropics lends some indirect support to this hypothesis (Madge, 1965; Ewel, 1976). The generality of these results needs to be tested in other tropical areas.

The results of this study further reinforce the conclusion that tropical and temperate insect populations fluctuate at similar levels (Wolda, 1978a,b). Although exact comparisons are not possible since we were unable to separate litter groups to species, the extent of fluctuations between years is as large as that reported for many groups, including data from many kinds of sampling. In addition, the pattern of fluctuations with respect to rainfall reinforces Wolda's (1977, 1978a) conclusion that water availability at critical points in the life cycle of various groups can have major consequences on population levels.

ACKNOWLEDGMENTS

The successful completion of the sampling program would not have been possible without the careful assistance of Bonifacio de León, to whom we are exceedingly grateful. Technical assistance was provided by Juan Barria Cruz, Carlos Ramos, Julio Jaen, L. S. Kimsey, R. Kimsey, and D. Kourany. C. A. Toft was instrumental in starting and continuing the project. Stan Rand, Stephen Garrity, and Henk Wolda helped throughout the project. Stan Rand and Henk Wolda have generously provided unpublished data for citation. E. G. Leigh, B. L. Thorne, and S. D. Garrity read and helpfully commented upon various versions of the manuscript. Funding was provided by the Smithsonian Environmental Sciences Project, the Hines Fund of the University of Chicago, the Anderson Fund of Harvard University, a National Science Foundation predoctoral fellowship, and the Exxon and Noble Foundation funds of the Smithsonian Tropical Research Institute. Finally we would like to thank the staff of the Smithsonial Tropical Research Institute, especially Thomas Borges and Ricardo Cortez, who provided electricity when it was needed most.

LITERATURE CITED

Anderson, J.M., and A. Macfadyen (eds.)
1976. *The role of terrestrial and aquatic organisms in decomposition processes.* Oxford, England: Blackwell Scientific Publications. 474 pp.

Barnes, R.D.
1968. *Invertebrate Zoology.* 2nd ed. Philadelphia: Saunders. 743 pp.

Beck, L.
1970. *Zur Ökologie der Bodenarthropoden in Regenwaldgebiet des Amazonasbeckens.* Habilitationsschrift. Ruhr-Universität Bochum.
1971. Boden zoologische glaedirung und characterisierung des amazonischen Negenwaldes. *Amazonia,* 3:69–132.

Birch, L.C., and D.P. Clark
1954. Forest soil as an ecological community with special reference to the fauna. *Quart. Rev. Biol.* 1:13–36.

Borror, D.J., and D.M. DeLong.
1971. *An introduction to the study of insects.* 3rd ed. New York: Rhinehart and Winston. 812 pp.

Brian, M.V. (ed.)
1978. *Production Ecology of Ants and Termites.* Cambridge, England: Cambridge University Press. 409 pp.

Bullock, J.A.
1962. *Nematocerus* sp.—a Pest of Cereals in Kenya. IV. The Estimation of Larval Populations and the Distribution of Larvae on a Farm. *E. Afr. Agric. For. J.,* 28:29–34.
1967. The Arthropoda of Tropical Soils and Leaf Litter. *Trop. Ecol.,* 8:74–87.

Burges, A., and F. Raw (eds.)
1967. *Soil Biology.* London: Academic Press.

Croat, T.B.
1978. *Flora of Barro Colorado Island.* Stanford, Calif: Stanford University Press. 943 pp.

Dammerman, K.W.
1925. First Contribution to the Study of the Tropical Soil and Surface Fauna. *Treubia,* 6:107–139.
1937. A Second Contribution to a Study of the Tropical Soil and Surface Fauna. *Treubia,* 16:121–147.

Dickinson, C.H., and G.J.H. Pugh (eds.)
1974. *Biology of plant litter decomposition.* vol. 2. London: Academic Press. 175 pp.

Dietrich, W., D.W. Windsor, and T. Dunne
1982. Geology, Climate, and Hydrology of Barro Colorado Island. Pages 21–46 in *The Ecology of a Tropical Forest,* edited by Egbert G. Leigh, Jr., et al. Washington, D.C.: Smithsonian Institution Press.

Doeskin, J., and J. Van Der Drift (eds.)
1963. *Soil Organisms.* Amsterdam: North Holland Publishing Co.

Edwards, C.A., and K.E. Fletcher
1971. A Comparison of Extraction Methods for Terrestrial Arthropoda. Pages 150–186 in *Methods of Study in Quantitative Soil Ecology,* IBP Handbook No. 18, edited by J. Phillipson. Oxford: Blackwell Scientific Publications. 297 pp.

Edwards, C.A., and G.W. Heath
1974. Studies in Leaf Litter Breakdown. III. The Influence of Leaf Age. *Pedobiol.,* 15:348–354.

Edwards, C.A., D.E. Reichle, and D.A. Crossley, Jr.
1970. The Role of Soil Invertebrates in the Turnover of Organic Matter and Nutrients. Pages 147–172 in *Analysis of Temperate Forest Ecosystems,* edited by D.E. Reichle. New York: Springer Verlag.

Eidman, H.
1942. Der tropische Regenwald als Lebensraum. *Kolonialforstl. Mitt.,* 5:91–147.
1943. Zur Ökologie der Tierwelt. *Beitr. Kolonialf.,* 2:25–45.

Ewel, J.J.
1976. Litterfall and Leaf Decomposition in a Tropical Forest Succession in Eastern Guatemala. *J. Ecol.,* 64:293–307.

Fittkau, E.J., and H. Klinge.
1973. On Biomass and Trophic Structure of the Central Amazonian Rain Forest Ecosystem. *Biotropica,* 5:2–14.

Foster, R.B.
1973. Seasonality of Fruit Production and Seed Fall in a Tropical Forest Ecosystem in Panama. Ph.D. dissertation, Duke University, Durham, North Carolina.

Gabbutt, P.D.
1967. Quantitative Samplings of the Pseudoscorpion *Chthonius ischnocheles* from beech litter. *J. Zool. Lond.,* 151:465–478.

Gabbutt, P.D., and M. Vanchon
1963. The External Morphology and Life History of the Pseudoscorpion *Chthonius ischnocheles* (Herman). *Proc. Zool. Soc. London,* 140:75–98.

Graff, O., and J.E. Satchell (eds.)
1967. *Progress in Soil Biology.* Amsterdam: Braunschweig.

Greenslade, P.J.M., and P. Greenslade
1968. Soil and Litter Fauna Densities in the Solomon Islands. *Pedobiol.,* 7:362–370.

Gupta, S.R., and J.S. Singh
1977. Decomposition of Litter in a Tropical Grassland. *Pedobiol.,* 17:330–333.

Haines, B., and R. B. Foster
1977. Energy Flow Through Litter in a Panamanian Forest. *J. Ecol.,* 65:147–155.

Hazra, A.K.
1978. Ecology of Collembola in a Deciduous Forest Floor of Birbhum District, West Bengal, in Relation to Soil Moisture. *Oriental Insects,* 12:265–274.

Healey, I.
1971.   Apterygotes, pauropods and symphylans. Pages 209–233 in *Methods of Study in Quantitative Soil Ecology*, IBP Handbook No. 18, edited by J. Phillipson. Oxford: Blackwell Scientific Publications. 297 pp.

Heath, G.W., and M.K. Arnold.
1966.   Studies in Leaf Litter Breakdown. II. Breakdown Rate of Sun and Shade Leaves. *Pedobiol.*, 6:238–243.

Heath, G.W., M.K. Arnold, and C.A. Edwards.
1965.   Studies in Leaf Litter Breakdown. I. Breakdown Rates of Different Species. *Pedobiol.*, 6:1–12.

Hopkins, B.
1966.   Vegetation of the Olokemeji Forest Reserve, Nigeria. IV. The Litter and Soil with Special Reference to Their Seasonal Changes. *J. Ecol.*, 54:687–702.

Hunt, J.H.
1974.   Temporal activity patterns in two competing ant species. *Psyche*, 81:237–242.

Hurley, P.E.
1959.   Notes on the Environmental Adaptations of Terrestrial Amphipoda. *Pacific Science*, 13:107–129.

Kevan, D.K.
1962.   *Soil Animals*. London: Witherby Ltd. 244 pp.

King, H.G.C., and G.W. Heath.
1967.   The Chemical Analysis of Small Samples of Leaf Material and the Relationship Between the Disappearance and Incorporation of Leaves. *Pedobiol.*, 7:192–197.

Klinge, H.
1977.   Preliminary Data on Nutrient Release from Decomposing Leaf Litter in a Neotropical Rain Forest. *Amazonia*, 6:193–202.

Kuhnelt, W.
1961.   *Soil Biology*. London: Faber. 397 pp.
1963.   Soil Inhabiting Arthropoda. *Ann. Rev. Entomol.*, 8:115–136.

Lawrence, R.F.
1953.   *The Biology of the Cryptic Fauna of Forests with Special Reference to the Indigenous Forests of South Africa*. Cape Town. 408 pp.

Leigh, E.G., Jr., and N. Smythe
1978.   Leaf Production, Leaf Consumption and the Regulation of Folivory on Barro Colorado Island. Pages 33–50 in *The Ecology of Arboreal Folivores*, edited by G.G. Montgomery. Washington, D.C.: Smithsonian Institution Press.

Lloyd, M.
1963.   Numerical Observations on the Movements of Animals Between Beech Litter and Fallen Branches. *J. Anim. Ecol.*, 32:157–163.

Lubin, Y.D.
1978.   Seasonal Abundance and Diversity of Web-building Spiders in Relation to Habitat Structure on Barro Colorado Island, Panama. *J. Arachnol.*, 6:31–51.

Lyford, W.H.
1943.   The Palatability of Freshly Fallen Forest Tree Leaves to Millipedes. *Ecology*, 24:252–261.

Macfadyen, A.
1962.   Soil Arthropod Sampling. *Adv. Ecol. Res.*, 1:1–34.
1963.   *Animal Ecology*. London: Pitman. 344 pp.
1969.   The Systematic Study of Soil Ecosystems. Pages 191–199 in *The Soil Ecosystem*, edited by J.G. Sheals. London: Systematics Association. 247 pp.
1971.   The Soil and Its Total Metabolism. Pages 1–14 in *Methods of Study in Quantitative Soil Ecology*, IBP Handbook No. 18, edited by J. Phillipson. Oxford: Blackwell Scientific Publications. 297 pp.

Madge, D.S.
1965.   Leaf Fall and Litter Disappearance in a Tropical Forest. *Pedobiol.*, 5:273–288.
1969.   Litter Disappearance in Forest and Savanna. *Pedobiol.*, 9:288–299.

Maldague, M.
1958.   Relations entre microfaune et microflore du sol dans la région de Yangambi (Congo-Belge). *Agricultura*, 2:340–351.

McBrayer, J.F., et al.
1977.   Decomposer Invertebrate Populations in U.S. Forest Biomes. *Pedobiol.*, 17:89–96.

Meyer, J., and M. Maldague
1957.   Observations simultanées sur la microflore et microfaune de certains sols du Congo Belge. *Pédologie*, 7:110–117.

Neilson, C.O.
1959.   Soil Fauna and the Moisture Regime of Its Environment. *Proc. 15th Int. Congress Zoology*. 394 pp.

Neuhauser, E.F., and R. Hartenstein
1978.   Phenolic Content and Palatability of Leaves and Wood to Soil Isopods and Diplopods. *Pedobiol.*, 18:99–109.

Paris, O.
1963.   Ecology of *Armadillidium vulgare* in a California Grassland. *Ecol. Monogr.*, 33:1–22.

Phillipson, J.
1971.   Other Arthropods. Pages 262–288 in *Methods of Study in Quantitative Soil Ecology*, IBP Handbook No. 18, edited by J. Phillipson. Oxford: Blackwell Scientific Publications. 297 pp.

Plowman, K.P.
1979.   Litter and Soil Fauna of Two Australian Subtropical Forests. *Aust. J. Ecol.*, 4:87–104.

Rand, A. S., and W. M. Rand
1982.   Variation in Rainfall over Barro Colorado Island. Pages 47–59 in *The Ecology of a Tropical Forest*, edited by Egbert G. Leigh, Jr., et al. Washington, D.C.: Smithsonian Institution Press.

Robinson, M., Y.D. Lubin, and B. Robinson
1974.   Phenology, Natural History, and Species Diversity of Web-building Spiders on Three Transects at Wau, New Guinea. *Pacific Insects*, 16:117–163.

Robinson, M., and B. Robinson
1970.   Prey Caught in a Sample Population of the Spider *Argiope argentata* (Araneae: Araneiidae) in Panama: A Year's Census Data. *Zool. J. Linn. Soc.*, 49:345–358.
1974.   A Census of Web-building Spiders in a Coffee Plantation at Wau, New Guinea and an Assessment of Their Insecticidal Effect. *Tropical Ecology*, 15(1&2):95–107.

Salt, G.
1952. The Arthropod Population of the Soil in Some East African Pastures. *Bull. Ent. Res.*, 43:203–220.
1955. The Arthropod Population of the Soil Under Elephant Grass in Uganda. *Bull. Ent. Res.*, 46:539–545.

Sexton, O.J.
1967. Population Changes in a Tropical Lizard *Anolis limifrons* on Barro Colorado Island, Panama Canal Zone. *Copeia*, 1967, 1:219–222.

Siegel, S.
1956. *Non-parametric Statistics.* New York: McGraw-Hill Book Co. 312 pp.

Singh, J., and U.R. Singh
1975. An Ecological Study of Soil Microarthropods from Soil and Litter of the Tropical Deciduous Forest of Varanasi. *Tropical Ecology*, 16:81–85.

Smythe, N.
1970. Relationships Between Fruiting Seasons and Seed Dispersal Methods in a Neotropical Forest. *Amer. Nat.*, 104:25–35.

Southwood, T.R.E.
1966. *Ecological Methods.* London: Chapman and Hall. 391 pp.

Stanton, N.
1979. Patterns of Species Diversity in Temperate and Tropical Litter Mites. *Ecology*, 60:295–304.

Strickland, A.H.
1944. The Arthropod Fauna of Some Tropical Soils. *Tropical Agric.*, 21:107–114.
1945. A Survey of the Arthropod Soil and Litter Fauna of Some Forest Reserves and Cacao Estates in Trinidad, British West Indies. *J. Anim. Ecol.*, 14:1–11.
1947. The Soil Fauna of Two Contrasted Plots of Land in Trinidad, British West Indies. *J. Anim. Ecol.*, 16:1–10.

Sundara-Rajulu, A., and D. Krishnan
1968. The Epicuticule of Millipedes Belonging to the Genera *Cingabolus* and *Alvacobolus* with Special Reference to Seasonal Variations. *Z. Naturforsch.*, 23B:845–851.

Usher, M.B.
1975. Seasonal and Vertical Distribution of a Population of Soil Arthropods: Cryptostigmata. *Pedobiol.*, 15:364–374.

Van Der Drift, J.
1963. A Comparative Study of the Soil Fauna in Forests and Cultivated Land on Sandy Soils in Suriname. Studies on the Fauna of Suriname and the Other Guyanas. vol. 6. *Uitg. Naturw. Studkring Suriname*, 32:1–42.

Wallwork, J.A.
1970. *Ecology of Soil Animals.* London: McGraw-Hill Co. 293 pp.

Weygoldt, P.
1969. *The Biology of Pseudoscorpions.* Cambridge, Mass.: Belknap Press. 145 pp.

Williams, E.C.
1941. An Ecological Study of the Floor Fauna of the Panamanian Rain Forest. *Bull. Chicago Acad. Sci.*, 6:63–124.

Willis, E.O.
1976. Seasonal Changes in the Invertebrate Litter Fauna on Barro Colorado Island, Panama. *Rev. Brasil Biol.*, 36:643–657.

Wilson, E.O.
1971. *The Insect Societies.* Cambridge, Mass.: Belknap Press. 548 pp.

Windsor, D.M.
1976. *1976 Environmental Monitoring and Baseline Data from the Isthmus of Panama.* vol. 4. Washington, D.C.: Smithsonian Institution Press.

Wolda, H.
1977. Fluctuations in Abundance of Some Homoptera in a Neotropical Forest. *Geo-Eco-Trop.*, 3:229–257.
1978a. Seasonal Fluctuations in Rainfall, Food and Abundance of Tropical Insects. *J. Anim. Ecol.*, 47:369–381.
1978b. Fluctuations in abundance of tropical insects. *Amer. Nat.*, 112:1017–1045.

Ecology and Population Regulation in the Army Ant
Eciton burchelli

NIGEL FRANKS   Department of Pure and Applied Zoology, University of Leeds, Leeds LS29JT, England

ABSTRACT

Barro Colorado Island has had about 50 colonies of the army ant *Eciton burchelli* for the last few decades. Each colony includes a single queen and about 400,000 soldiers and workers. Each colony lives to a rhythm of roughly 35 days, spending 21 days raiding out from a central bivouac, and the other 14 moving to a new site. On the average, 55,000 workers hatch per 35 days, but larger colonies produce fewer new workers per colony member.

An army ant colony eats roughly 40 g dry weight of animal matter per day, of which half are prey ants and their brood. An ant raid reduces the abundance of crickets and roaches in the leaf litter by a half, but immigrants replace these animals within a week. The army ants also greatly reduce the abundance of their principal ant prey, making space for new prey colonies; it takes the prey ants 100 days to recover to half their original abundance.

The raiding pattern of an army ant colony is designed to prevent the same area from being swept twice within a week and to ensure that the raids from one central bivouac do not impinge on areas swept from the previous month's central bivouac.

Although army ant populations seem to be strongly self-regulated, and army ants exert a major impact on the abundance of their principal and favored prey, they appear to exert less effect on the litter fauna as a whole than the antbirds that follow them, the lizards of the forest floor, or coatis.

INTRODUCTION

Several species of doryline ant on Barro Colorado Island raid in swarms or columns, thus earning the name of army ant. Of these, by far the most conspicuous is *Eciton burchelli*, where a raid can consist of up to 200,000 ants moving along a front 15 m wide (Willis, 1967), flushing arthropods out from the leaf litter. They flush out so many insects and other animals that there is a special guild of birds whose members glean the insects trying to escape from the army ants. These ants are interesting for three reasons. First, their feeding rate and foraging behavior, and the effects of their foraging on prey populations, can be described rather precisely, so that one can discuss the relation between these army ants and their food supply with something approaching rigor. Second, the seasonal rhythms of these army ants may tell us something of the underlying rhythms of the litter fauna on which they feed. Finally, the population of *Eciton burchelli* is one of the most stable on Barro Colorado Island: there have been about 50 colonies of *Eciton burchelli* on that island for the last 20 years or more (Willis, 1967; personal observations).

I have accordingly been studying the ecology of *Eciton burchelli* on Barro Colorado for the last 2 years. This chapter is a preliminary summary of my results: more authoritative reports will appear later, as I analyze my data more completely.

NATURAL HISTORY

Eciton burchelli live in colonies of about 400,000, including a single queen and 400,000 soldiers and workers ranging in dry weight from 1 to 10 mg apiece, averaging 2.7 mg; one can count them by filming them as they move from one nest site or "bivouac" to another. Each colony lives to a 35-day rhythm, documented in detail by Willis (1967, pers. comm.). For an average of 21 days (ranging from 17 to 25 days in 48 observations) they live in a "statary bivouac," staging an average of 13 diurnal raids during the 21 days. During the 10 middle days of their stay, they raid on only 5, and the raid distance averages 57 m ($SD = 18$, $N = 9$). During the statary period as a whole, the raid distance averages 89 m ($SD = 41$, $N = 25$). For 14 days (ranging from 10 to 18 in a sample of 38) they live in "nomadic phase," raiding an average distance of 116 m ($SD = 48$, $N = 38$) during the day and, usually, shifting the entire colony—workers, brood, and all—to a new bivouac during the night. The new bivouac is distant an average of 81 m ($SD = 43$, $N = 395$) along the line of the previous day's raid from the old. The rhythm is correlated with worker production: the queen lays eggs in the middle of sta-

tary phase, and the larvae hatch at the end of that phase. The larvae pupate at the beginning of the next statary phase, and the workers hatch, ready to march, at its end. An average of 55,000 workers hatch per 35 days, as one can judge by counting the empty pupal cases at the site of a newly abandoned statary bivouac.

DIET AND FEEDING RATE

In the nomadic phase, the average army ant raid lasts 10 hours and extends 116 m. When not interrupted by rain or other adversity, the swarm front moves forward at an average rate of 14.8 m/hr. (Willis, 1967). The raiding swarm contains about 100,000 ants, on the average, with a dry weight of 2.7 mg apiece, and these raiders must feed 300,000 adults and 55,000 larvae at the bivouac. In the statary phase, a raid extends 89 m, on the average, and raids occur on only 13 of the 21 days, so, remembering that the swarm front averages 6 m wide, over the whole cycle the ants raid for an average of nearly 7 hours a day, sweeping out 475 sq. m in the 7 hours. As there are 300,000 sq. m of forest per colony, assuming random search, *Eciton burchelli* will return to a newly swept area after 630 days, on the average. Thus there is a 31% chance that a newly swept area will escape the attention of army ants for 2 years, and a 10% chance that it will escape for 4.

During raids, army ants are perpetually returning to the bivouac with food items, bringing back an average of 10 food items per 12.4 seconds ($SD = 5.4$, $N = 100$). The majority of these items are ants and ant brood, as Rettenmeyer (1963) first pointed out. Ant and wasp brood form a larger proportion of the diet of army ants in the rainy season than in the dry, while the reverse is true for crickets and roaches (Table 1).

The average food item carried back by *Eciton burchelli* contains 2.14 mg of dry matter; social Hymenoptera adults and fragments thereof average 2.8 mg dry matter apiece ($N = 35$), brood items average 1.0 mg dry matter apiece ($N = 44$), and items of other arthropods average 2.9 mg dry matter apiece ($N = 310$). Except for ant larvae, army ants rarely carry back items weighing much less than themselves. Extrapolating, one finds that the average day's nomadic raid brings 29,000 items, with a total dry weight of 62 g, back to the bivouac. The food brought back is proportional to the area raided, so that a statary bivouac receives about half as much food per day as a nomadic one: the average feeding rate of an *Eciton burchelli* bivouac is 42 g dry weight of animal matter per day. Taking feeding rate as 3.6 times basal metabolic rate, and assuming that the basal metabolic rate of an animal weighing W kg is $70W^{0.75}$ kcal per day, and that 1 g dry weight of insects represents 6.5 kcal (Eisenberg and Thorington, 1973; Wiegert, 1970), a 3 kg coati eats roughly 100 g dry weight of food per day, over twice as much as an army ant colony weighing the same amount.

There are several other ways to estimate the feeding rate of an army ant colony. First, one can calculate the average energy expenditure for animals of this type and size. Nielsen (1972) found that workers of the temperate-zone ant *Lasius alienus* consumed $0.27008(1.0493)^T$ microliters of oxygen per mg live weight per hour when at temperature T. Applying this relation to army ants at 28°C, and assuming that a thousand microliters of O_2 consumed represents 4.825 calories spent (Wiegert, 1970), a colony of *Eciton burchelli* spends 360 kcal, or the energy content of 55 g dry weight of insects, per day. This seems typical of other temperate zone ants at tropical temperature (Peakin and Josens, 1978). Bartholomew and Casey (1977) report that in the tropics a beetle weighing x grams consumes $230x^{0.86}$ microliters of oxygen per hour when resting, and $3760x^{1.17}$ when walking. Applying this relation to an army ant weighing 7 mg when live, this ant spends 0.373 calories per day when at rest, and 1.31 calories per day when constantly walking. On the average, one-fourth of the colony raids each day, for two-sevenths of the day, so the colony expends 176 kcal, or 27 g dry weight worth of insect food per day. The observed feeding rate falls well within the limits of error of such calculations. Another check is provided by the refuse deposited at a bivouac: like spiders (Robinson and Robinson, 1973), army ants discard the exoskeletons of their prey at the bivouac. These data are only now being analyzed.

In theory, one could also check these figures by comparing them with the abundance of prey just before and just after army ants have raided. Berlese samples from 60 plots of 0.25 sq. m suggest that where army ants have not raided recently, there are 15 ± 4.3 mg dry weight (mean ± s.e.m.) of roaches and crickets per square meter, and that immediately after a raid there is only half that much (see Levings and Windsor, this volume, for an explanation of Berlese sampling). Since an ant colony raids 500 sq. m in an average day, one would conclude that they, and the antbirds that followed them, ate somewhat less than 4 g dry weight of crickets and roaches in a day. Judging from items carried back to the bivouac, the army ants themselves eat nearly 20 g of these animals: the discrepancy may reflect the fact that army ants sometimes climb stems, perhaps reaching wads of dead leaves caught in the understory shrubbery, which are unusually rich in crickets and roaches (J. Gradwohl, pers. comm.), and that they sometimes enter other rich areas which my Berlese funnels did not sample.

Table 1. Proportion of *Eciton burchelli* food items, by category

	Social Hymenoptera		Crickets and roaches	Other arthropods
	Adults	Brood		
Rainy season (N = 522)	0.10	0.44	0.34	0.12
Dry season (N = 520)	0.21	0.34	0.30	0.15

IMPACT UPON FOOD SUPPLY

A colony of *Eciton burchelli* apparently eats less than 50 g dry weight of insects per day. A raid, however, attracts several kinds of antbirds, wood-creepers, and the like which eat insects flushed from the litter by the ants. Barro Colorado has 1 army ant colony per 30 ha., or 3.3 colonies per square kilometer. Willis (1974, 1971) has calculated the number of individuals per square kilometer of the different species of ant-following birds on Barro Colorado Island and has discussed their diets. From these data we may calculate the number of birds of each species per ant swarm. Lasiewski and Dawson (1967) find that the standard metabolic rate M of a bird weighing W kg is roughly $129W^{0.724}$ kcal per day. Assume, with Holmes and Sturges (1975), that a bird's total feeding rate is $2.5M/0.7$ kcal per day, or $2.5M/4.6$ g dry weight of insect matter per day. In 1961, six species of birds secured over half their food by following ant swarms (Table 2). Assuming that all of these species derived all their food from swarms of *Eciton burchelli*, except for spotted antbirds, which derive only a little over half their food from ant swarms, and only about one-fifth of their food from *Eciton burchelli*, then these birds eat roughly 50 g dry weight of insects, including many crickets and roaches, per ant swarm per day. As these birds eat only arthropods other than ants, they exert a far greater effect on these other arthropods than do the army ants themselves.

A colony of *Eciton burchelli* and its attendants eats nearly 100 g dry weight of insects per day; as there is one swarm per 30 ha., they eat 3 g dry weight of insects per hectare per day. Litterfall amounts to a little under 20,000 g dry weight of leaves and 10,000 g of other matter per hectare per day. One might conclude either that army ants matter very little or that, small as they are, they live very high up in the decomposer food chain. How does the impact of *Eciton burchelli* and their birds compare with that of other

Table 2. Numbers and feeding rates of ant-following birds, and the proportions of their diet flushed by army ants

	Weight (g)	Number of birds per 30 ha.		Proportion of diet flushed by ants	Dry weight of food per bird per day (g)
		1961	1971		
Barred woodcreeper	65	0.1	0.0	70	10.6
Ocellated antbird	50	1.0	0.0	100	8.8
Plain-brown woodcreeper	40	2.0	2.0	80	7.5
Bicolored antbird	32	2.0	1.0	80	6.4
Grey-headed tanager	30	0.7	0.7	80	6.1
Spotted antbird	18	12.0	12.0	60	4.2

forest floor insectivores? How lasting is the impact of the army ants?

Aside from *Eciton burchelli* and its attendant antbirds, the best known insectivores of the forest floor are the lizard *Anolis limifrons* and the coati *Nasua narica*. *Anolis limifrons* eats arthropods 3 to 10 mm long (Sexton et al., 1972). This lizard's diet includes far fewer ants and ant brood, is otherwise far more varied, and changes far more from season to season than that of *Eciton burchelli*. An adult *Anolis limifrons* eats roughly 20 mg dry weight of insects per day, of which over a quarter is crickets and roaches, and another quarter small caterpillars (Andrews, pers. comm.). The number of these lizards varies from 170 to 1100 per hectare (Andrews and Rand, this volume), so their aggregate feeding rate varies from 2 to 15 g dry weight of insects per hectare per day.

A coati *Nasua narica* eats roughly 100 g dry weight of food per day. Most of this food is invertebrates it finds in the leaf litter, or digs from the ground or from rotten sticks and logs: principally beetles and beetle larvae, but also ant brood and a variety of other animals (Russell, this volume). Coatis eat far larger items, of course, than do army ants. There are 600 coatis on Barro Colorado (Eisenberg and Thornton, 1973), or two-fifths of a coati per hectare, so these animals eat over 30 g dry weight of litter animals per hectare per day. *Eciton burchelli* seems to eat far less than its principal competitors.

Eciton burchelli lowers the abundance of crickets, roaches, etc., by 50% when it sweeps through, but the levels of these animals recover in a week. The abundance of one of the more common and conspicuous ant prey, however, takes 100 days to recover to half of its original level. Assuming random search, the average time between *Eciton burchelli* raids over a given point is 630 days; hence, populations of this ant prey over a quarter of the area of Barro Colorado are re-

covering from raids of these army ants. Moreover, if one puts out pieces of bamboo as potential nest sites, these sites are more likely to be colonized by founding queens of ants eaten by *Eciton burchelli* if these army ants have recently raided. This suggests that these army ants have lowered competition among their prey. Army ants do make a difference, however little they seem to eat.

FORAGING BEHAVIOR

The impact of army ants upon their food supply shows up in their foraging behavior. During the 21 days of statary phase, an army ant colony stages about 13 raids, averaging 89 m long. Each swarm-raid tends to be in a straight line: its successive changes of direction tend to compensate each other to keep to that line. If one maps these 13 raids, the last raid of the preceding nomadic phase, and the first raid of the following nomadic phase, one has 15 lines radiating out from the statary bivouac, their directions seemingly distributed at random. The direction of a statary raid is shifted an average of 123° (SD about 40°) from the previous one, thereby avoiding raids over habitat raided during the previous week or so: presumably, the army ants can remember the direction of the previous few raids as they lay down a trail substance that lasts at least 4 days.

During the 14 days of nomadic phase, the bivouac is moved an average of 81 m a day. Seemingly to avoid crossing the previous day's path and to ensure that the area raided from one statary bivouac does not overlap the area raided from the one previous, a nomadic raid is in much the same direction as that of the day before, the mean root square change in direction being 60° (N = 65). The mean distance between successive statary bivouacs is 529 ± 267 m, which is significantly farther than the ants would have achieved if they had simply engaged in a 14-step random walk, with each step being 81 m long. In such a random walk, the average distance between statary bivouacs would be $14^{1/2} \times 80$, or about 300 m, and the danger of overlap would be much greater.

The more food the army ants need, the farther they raid. Daily raid distance z increases with t, the number of days after the beginning of nomadic phase, because the larvae are growing: $z = 65.2 \exp (0.027t)$ ($r = 0.75$). Raid distance z also increases with x, the number of ants in the bivouac: $z = 23 + 0.0003x$ ($r = 0.57$).

Each army ant colony avoids crossing its own path and avoids reworking areas it has recently worked, and army ant colonies of different species raid independently of each other. If two such raiding colonies intersect, one crosses over the other along a suitable root or vine. Each colony thus moves over the entire island: it does not have a specific home range. The simplicity of their foraging patterns greatly eases the analysis of how their populations are regulated.

REPRODUCTIVE CYCLE

In the dry season, about 15 of the 50 colonies of *Eciton burchelli*, usually the largest, split (Schneirla and Brown, 1950, 1952). It does not pay an army ant colony to increase indefinitely, even though many ants are better than one at flushing and overrunning prey. The death rate of workers (due primarily to encounters with prey and accidents along the trail) is presumably unaffected by colony size as long as the size of the raiding party is proportional to the size of the colony as a whole. On the other hand, when a statary bivouac with x ants terminates, $31,754 + 0.0743x$ ($r = 0.92$) pupal cases are left behind. Thus a bivouac of 200,000 produces 0.23 new workers per capita per 35 day cycle, while a bivouac of 400,000 produces 0.15. Thus some intermediate colony size, neither too small to catch prey nor too large to replace its workers, is best. As in intertidal sea anemones of the Pacific Northwest, which split at the beginning of winter, the season of food shortage (Sebens, 1977), one may expect a smaller colony size to be more suitable when food is in shorter supply. Indeed, litter arthropods are less abundant in dry season (Levings and Windsor, this volume). The origin of the dry season seems to be the cue for laying eggs that will grow into males, while the colonies actually split in late February. In some of the splitting colonies, the old queen dies, while in the others, she joins one of the daughter colonies.

STABILITY OF POPULATION

For the past 20 years or more, Barro Colorado Island has had about 50 colonies of *Eciton burchelli*. Willis (1967) found 12 statary bivouacs in 11 months of intensive search over a 40-ha. plot in 1961, representing 3.2 colonies per square kilometer; he believes colonies were rather more numerous in succeeding years. I counted colonies by assuming that at any moment raiding columns are distributed at random over Barro Colorado Island, and inferring the total length R of the raiding columns from N, the number of columns I crossed walking a known length H of trail, and the total area A of the island, using the formula $R = \pi NA/2H$ (Newman, 1966). Plugging in the appropriate length of column per army ant colony, I, too, found there were about 50 colonies on this island. Why is the population so stable?

Army ant populations do not seem to be affected much by competition for cockroaches, crickets, foraging ants, etc. These insects form part of a common pool which lizards, frogs, toads, etc., also exploit. The numbers of some of these competitors fluctuate greatly, partly, at least, because they are more sensitive to physical factors (Andrews and Rand, this volume; Toft et al., this volume). These fluctuations seem to have had little effect on *Eciton burchelli*, which suggests that the army ants are not stabilized by their relationship with arthropods other than ants.

Eciton burchelli obviously affect the ants they prey upon. These populations recover far more slowly from army ant raids, yet these raids do facilitate the founding of new colonies of prey ants. On Orchid Island, a 19 ha. satellite of Barro Colorado, where I introduced *Eciton burchelli* in July 1978, colonies of suitable prey ants were closely packed in a hexagonal arrangement, the result of perfect, undiluted competition. Moreover, the effect of a raid on prey ant populations clearly matters to the army ants, which go to obvious lengths to avoid overlap in areas raided from successive statary bivouacs. *Eciton burchelli* populations may well be stabilized by their relation with prey ant populations, which have such a strong self-regulatory mechanism yet are so responsive to openings.

The stability of army ant populations is extraordinary in view of the marginal nature of their economy. When I introduced a colony of *Eciton burchelli* to the previously virgin Orchid Island, the proportion of ant brood among the items in their diet was twice as high as on Barro Colorado, while they ate only a third as many nonsocial arthropods. Despite the apparent richness of the area, the Orchid Island colony failed to grow, for the singular reason that the prey colonies they encountered were mature and well defended. The proportion of injured among the workers returning to bivouac was twice as high as on Barro Colorado Island; worker mortality was unusually high; and worker production was unusually low. Since a normal colony of 400,000 produces only 55,000 new workers per 35 days, the average worker must live 250 days if the colony is to break even. This is a long time: workers of the wasp *Mischocyttarus* (West Eberhard, 1978) and of the bees *Apis* and *Melipona* (Roubik, pers. comm.) live about 30 days. That so seemingly marginal a predator can exert such an influence on its prey seems very odd indeed, yet the strength of its influence on prey ant populations is largely responsible for the stability of *Eciton burchelli*.

ACKNOWLEDGMENTS

I am greatly indebted to Edward Broadhead for bringing the existence of Barro Colorado Island to my attention and for his guidance of my research. Carl Rettenmeyer and Edwin Willis have welcomed me to their field with enormous generosity. They have opened wide their storehouses of knowledge and intuition. Moreover, Dr. Willis has allowed me to analyze further the data he summarized in his work on bicolored antbirds (Willis, 1967). Egbert Leigh helped me to shape this paper and drew attention to the fact that the impact of these ants includes that of their attendant birds. For 2 years he has asked embarrassing questions about the ecology of *Eciton burchelli*, for which, in retrospect, I will remain most grateful.

This work was supported by the Natural Environment Research Council, U.K.

LITERATURE CITED

Andrews, R.M., and A.S. Rand
1982.   Seasonal breeding and long-term population fluctuations in the lizard *Anolis limifrons*. Pages 405-412 in *The Ecology of a Tropical Forest*, edited by Egbert G. Leigh, Jr., et al. Washington, D.C.: Smithsonian Institution Press.

Bartholomew, G. A., and T. M. Casey
1977.   Body temperature and oxygen consumption during rest and activity in relation to body size in some tropical beetles. *Journal of Thermal Biology*, 2:173–175.

Eisenberg, J. F., and R. W. Thorington, Jr.
1973.   A preliminary analysis of a neotropical mammal fauna. *Biotropica*, 5: 150–161.

Holmes, R. T., and F. W. Sturges
1975.   Bird community dynamics and energetics in a northern hardwoods ecosystem. *Journal of Animal Ecology*, 44: 175–200.

Lasiewski, R. C., and W. R. Dawson
1967.   A re-examination of the relation between standard metabolic rate and body weight in birds. *Condor*, 69: 13–23.

Levings, S., and D. M. Windsor
1982.   Seasonal and annual variation in litter arthropod populations. Pages 355-387 in *The Ecology of a Tropical Forest*, edited by Egbert G. Leigh, Jr., et al. Washington, D.C.: Smithsonian Institution Press.

Newman, E. I.
1966.   A method of estimating the total length of root in a sample. *Journal of Applied Ecology*, 3: 139–145.

Nielsen, M. G.
1972.   An attempt to estimate energy flow through a population of workers of *Lasius alienus* (Forst.), (Hymenoptera, Formicidae). *Natura Jutlandica*, 16: 97–107.

Peakin, G. J., and G. Josens
1978.   Respiration and energy flow. Pages 111–163 in *Production Ecology of Ants and Termites*, edited by M. V. Brian. Cambridge: Cambridge University Press.

Rettenmeyer, C. W.
1963.   Behavioral studies of army ants. *Kansas University Science Bulletin*, 44: 281–465.

Robinson, M. H., and B. Robinson
1973.   Ecology and behavior of the giant wood spider *Nephila maculata* (Fabricius) in New Guinea. *Smithsonian Contributions to Zoology*, 149: 1–76.

Russell, J. K.
1982.   Timing of reproduction by coatis (*Nasua narica*) in relation to fluctuations in food resources. Pages 413-431 in *The Ecology of a Tropical Forest*, edited by Egbert G. Leigh, Jr., et al. Washington, D.C.: Smithsonian Institution Press.

Schneirla, T. C., and R. Z. Brown
1950.   Army ant life and behavior under dry season conditions. Further investigation of cyclic processes in behavioral and reproductive functions. *Bulletin of the American Museum of Natural History*, 95: 263–353.
1952.   Sexual broods and the production of young queens in two species of army ants. *Zoologica, New York*, 37: 5–32.

Sebens, K. P.
1977.   Habitat suitability, reproductive ecology, and the plasticity of body size in two sea anemone populations (*Anthopleura elegantissima* and *A. xanthogrammica*) Ph. D. dissertation, University of Washington, Seattle.

Sexton, O. J., J. Bauman, and E. Ortleb
1972.   Seasonal food habits of *Anolis limifrons*. *Ecology*, 53: 182–186.

Toft, C. A., A. S. Rand, and M. Clark
1982.   Factors affecting the time of breeding in *Bufo typhonius* and *Colostethus nubicola* (Anura). Pages 397-403 in *The Ecology of a Tropical Forest*, edited by Egbert G. Leigh, Jr., et al. Washington, D.C.: Smithsonian Institution Press.

West Eberhard, M. J.
1978.   Polygyny and the evolution of social behavior in wasps. *Journal of the Kansas Entomological Society*, 51: 832–856.

Wiegert, R. G.
1970.   Energetics of the nest-building termite, *Nasutitermes costalis* (Holmgren) in a Puerto Rican forest. Pages 1–57–64 in *A Tropical Rain Forest*, edited by H. T. Odum and R. Pigeon. Washington, D.C.: U.S. Atomic Energy Commission, Division of Technical Information.

Willis, E. O.

1967.   The behavior of bicolored antbirds. *University of California Publications in Zoology*, 79: 1–127.

1972.   *The behavior of spotted antbirds.* Ornithological Monograph no. 10, 1–127, Lawrence, Kans.: American Ornithologists Union.

1974.   Populations and local extinctions of birds on Barro Colorado Island, Panama. *Ecological Monographs*, 44: 153–169.

Population Dynamics and Seasonal Recruitment in *Bufo typhonius* and *Colostethus nubicola* (Anura)

CATHERINE A. TOFT   Department of Zoology, University of California, Davis, California 95616

A. STANLEY RAND   Smithsonian Tropical Research Institute, Balboa, Republic of Panama

MILTON CLARK   Smithsonian Tropical Research Institute, Balboa, Republic of Panama

ABSTRACT

Numbers of *Bufo typhonius* and *Colostethus nubicola* in the leaf litter on Barro Colorado Island varied throughout the year of study, with both species more abundant in the dry season than in the wet. The sudden increase in numbers at the beginning of the dry season was due to seasonal recruitment of juveniles emerging from streams. Cohorts of *Bufo typhonius* appeared to reach maturity in 8–10 months, those of *Colostethus nubicola* in 4–5 months. Causes for the timing of recruitment are not clear, but evidence presented in this study most strongly supports the hypothesis that suitable water levels for the aquatic tadpoles influence the timing and duration of recruitment in both *B. typhonius* and *C. nubicola*.

INTRODUCTION

Several common species of diurnal frogs and toads occur in the leaf litter in lowland tropical forest on Barro Colorado Island (Myers and Rand, 1969). The most conspicuous of these are *Bufo typhonius* and *Colostethus nubicola*, but this group also includes *Physalaemus pustulosus* and several species of *Eleutherodactylus*. This group of species is representative of the widespread anuran fauna in the litter of neotropical forests. As many as 20 or more species, typically representing the families Bufonidae, Dendrobatidae and Leptodactylidae, may occur at any given location in the neotropical rain forest (personal observations of the authors; Crump, 1974; Duellman, 1978; Toft, 1980a, 1980b, 1981; Toft and Duellman, 1979). The fauna of Barro Colorado Island contains only five or six species, fewer than any rain forest with which we are familiar. However, some species (for example, *Dendrobates minutus*) have become extinct since the formation of the island (Myers and Rand, 1969); and others that do not occur on Barro Colorado Island, such as *Colostethus inguinalis* occur in the nearby Pipeline Road area (Toft, personal observation) in habitats not well represented on the island.

The litter anurans are very similar to one another ecologically, and those on Barro Colorado Island share the characteristics of this assemblage in general. These species are typically diurnal. All forage in the litter for arthropods; however, species differ in the degree to which they eat ants and in the sizes of prey that they take (Toft, 1980a, 1981). Unlike many of the anurans that occur in other habitats in the rain forest, some of the litter species usually do not migrate to breeding areas distant from the habitat of the adult. Instead, they complete their life cycles within the confines of the forest floor. *Eleutherodactylus* and the dendrobatids deposit their eggs in the litter of the forest floor (personal observations; Crump, 1974). *Eleutherodactylus* then emerge directly as juveniles into the litter. The dendrobatids carry their tadpoles to water; *Colostethus nubicola* deposit their tadpoles in small pools of forest streams (Heyer, 1976) and *Dendrobates auratus* deposit their tadpoles in water in tree holes or other cavities (personal observations; C. Myers, pers. comm.). *Bufo typhonius* and *Physalaemus pustulosus* deposit their eggs directly into pools of forest streams (Heyer, 1976; Wells, 1979). Thus for all or most of the life cycle, these species are confined to the litter of the forest floor.

As one might expect in a seasonal environment, the populations of *Bufo typhonius* and *Colostethus nubicola* appear to fluctuate both seasonally and from year to year. Despite differences in their breeding biologies, both species have major recruitment into the population during the dry season. Both also show changes in distribution with season. In this paper we will document these seasonal fluctuations and discuss some of the factors that may be responsible.

METHODS

Populations of *Bufo typhonius* and *Colostethus nubicola* were monitored from November 1976 through December 1978 in the Lutz Creek watershed of Barro Colorado Island, Panama. Frogs were censused weekly by walking along a standard route. All frogs within 1 m of the center of the trail were identified and, when possible, caught and measured for snout-vent length (SVL). Size estimates were made for frogs that escaped without being measured. Casual notes were made on breeding activity in the two species.

Leaf litter and soil characteristics change with topography (Toft and Levings, 1979) so that three areas were sampled: the margins at the main stream channel, known herein as "stream bottom"; the slopes of ravines, or "slope"; and the crest of ridges and upland plateaus, or "ridge top" (Table 1).

Routes of different lengths were censused in the three areas, 20 m in the stream bottom, 700 m along the slope, and 1100 m on the ridge tops (Figure 1). In addition to these three census routes, a fourth census route was monitored from a ridge top near the laboratory clearing to the Lutz stream.

Rainfall, soil moisture, leaf litter, runoff, and abundance of arthropods were measured and supplied to us by concurrent projects in the Lutz Creek catchment (courtesy of Environmental Sciences Program, Smithsonian Institution).

RESULTS

The seasonal fluctuations in population sizes of both species in both years were primarily due to seasonal recruitment, as the changing distributions of body sizes indicate, and in both species this recruitment occurred in the dry season. Lateral movements were also significant in *C. nubicola*.

The extent of wet-season recruitment is probably underestimated in our results because individuals newly transformed during the dry season tend to stay along the stream to be counted, while in the rainy season they disperse immediately. Until further data are collected, we cannot estimate the magnitude of this bias but believe it to be small.

When *Bufo typhonius* increased greatly in numbers at the end of the wet season, there was a large proportion of juveniles, that is, individuals under 30 mm (Wells, 1979). The majority of these juveniles ap-

Table 1. Estimated mean weekly density, per 10 m of census route, of *Colostethus nubicola* and *Bufo typhonius* by month for each census route

Month	Bufo typhonius			Colostethus nubicola		
	Stream	Midslope	Ridgetop	Stream	Midslope	Ridgetop
Nov. 1976	2.50	0.22	0.01	1.00	0.01	0.01
Dec.	8.15	0.13	0.01	23.50	0.12	0
Jan. 1977	5.10	0.13	0	35.00	0.48	0
Feb.	0.75	0.08	0.003	24.50	0.07	0
Mar.	2.15	0.02	0	29.50	0.07	0
Apr.	0.75	0.02	0	18.50	0.12	0
May	1.10	0.004	0.002	27.00	0.07	0
June	0	0.02	0.01	0.75	0.01	0.002
July	0	0	0	0	0.01	0
Aug.	0	0	0	2.00	0.004	0
Sept.	0.70	0.01	0.004	0.75	0.03	0
Oct.	0	0	0	0.40	0.01	0
Nov.	0	0.01	0	0.10	0	0
Dec.	0	0	0	0.85	0.02	0
Jan. 1978	17.50	0	0	0.75	0.06	0
Feb.	8.50	0.01	0	26.00	0.07	0
Mar.	9.50	0.01	0	40.00	0.04	0
Apr.	0.60	0.01	0	9.00	0.04	0
May	0	0.01	0.003	1.50	0.02	0
June	0	0	0	1.75	0.02	0
July	0	0.01	0	1.20	0.04	0
Aug.	0	0	0	1.25	0.03	0
Sept.	0	0.01	0.002	0.90	0.03	0
Oct.	0.15	0	0	0.25	0.04	0.003
Nov.	0.35	0	0.003	0	0	0
Dec.	1.50	0.01	0.01	1.45	0.04	0

peared in a pulse in November, and juveniles continued to be present until May in both years (Figure 2). During that time, we found tadpoles to be abundant in various ponds and streams from August through December. These results are consistent with details of the breeding biology of *Bufo typhonius* on Barro Colorado Island reported by Wells (1979). Smaller peaks of recruitment occurred outside of the dry season each year; these juveniles were primarily from census route 4, indicating that they had emerged from the artificial pond, which always contained water, in the laboratory clearing at the head of that census route.

As body size increased during the dry season in both years, population size decreased, representing a combination of dispersal and mortality during the period of growth of juveniles in the cohort. Time to adulthood in *B. typhonius* is much greater than in *C. nubicola*;

B. typhonius not only transforms at a much smaller proportion of its adult size, but attains a much greater adult size (Wells, 1979). We estimate this time to be between 8 and 10 months for *B. typhonius* on Barro Colorado Island.

Juveniles (under 12 mm) of *C. nubicola* began to appear at the beginning of the dry season in December the first year, slightly later the second; sizes increased during the dry season, presumably because of growth of that cohort (Figure 2). The pulse in numbers of *C. nubicola* each year was due not only to recruitment, but also to movement of adults into the stream bottom during the dry season. Further, breeding, as evidenced by calling males and by tadpoles on the backs of males, occurs over a much longer period in *C. nubicola* than in *B. typhonius*. This agrees well with the more prolonged period of higher numbers

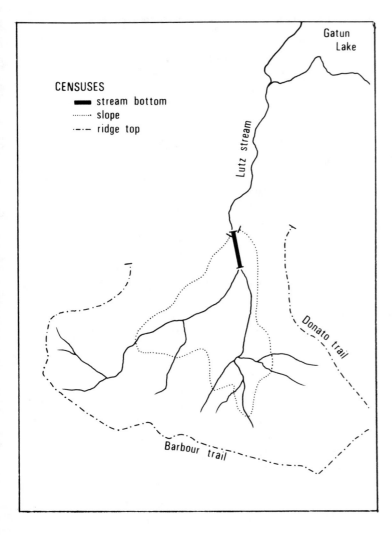

Figure 1.   Three census routes in the Lutz watershed, Barro Colorado Island.

of individuals in the censuses, as well as the presence of small-sized individuals over a longer period (Figure 2).

The sudden decrease in population size in the early rainy season was accompanied by lowered proportions of juveniles and thus was probably due to mortality and to dispersal of the new adults to midslopes and ridges. The disappearance of *C. nubicola* from the stream bottom coincides with the first rains of the wet season and suggests that they move back up the slopes as soon as the litter is wet, though they are very seldom seen during the ridge-top census even during the wet season. These horizontal movements are also suggested by our observations that calling males are heard throughout the forest during the wet season, but that during the dry season the only calls heard come from along the stream. That the number of juveniles seen during the rainy season is small may be due at least in part to the immediate dispersal following transformation at this season.

The census data do not show the growth of these frogs as clearly as they do for *B. typhonius*, in part because the size between transformation and adulthood is less, in part because the longer period of recruitment means that cohorts are less clearly defined. Still, Figure 2 suggests that it takes *C. nubicola* about 4–5 months to reach adulthood.

Finally, increases in numbers of frogs and, therefore, recruitment were correlated with several environmental factors—rainfall, leaffall, and food abundance (Figure 3)—which themselves covaried either directly or inversely (Table 2). Numbers of individuals of both species were inversely correlated with rainfall and arthropod numbers, and positively correlated with leaffall.

Table 2.   Covariance of selected environmental factors and numbers of *B. typhonius* and *C. nubicola* by month during the study period

Environmental factors		Covariance			
	n	*B. typhonius*	*C. nubicola*	Rain-fall	*Leaffall*
Rainfall (mm)	26	−0.48	−0.61	—	—
Leaffall (gm)	26	0.67	0.63	−0.74	—
Arthropod numbers	15	−0.58	−0.75	0.50	−0.59

A correlation of 0.39 between 24 pairs of observations is significant at $p = 0.05$, as is a correlation of 0.54 between 15 pairs of observations.

TOFT ET AL.

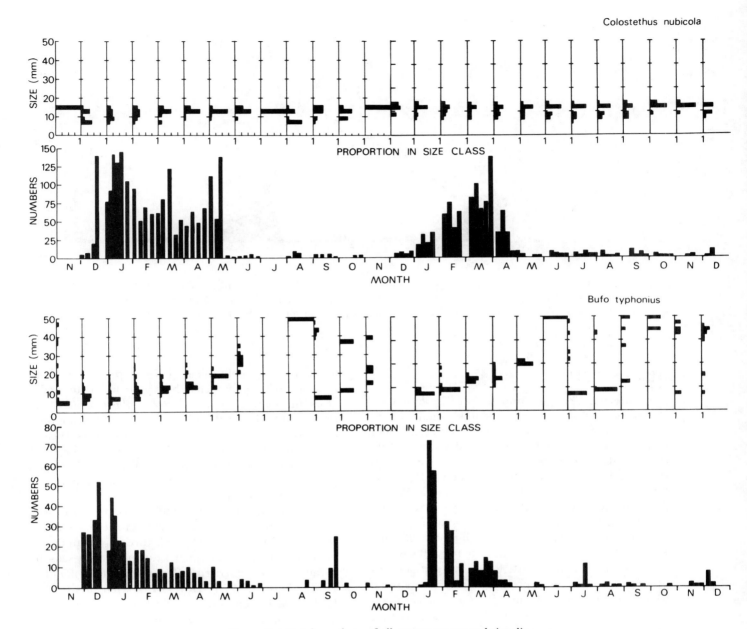

Figure 2. Total numbers of all census routes and size distribution in *Colostethus nubicola* (A) and *Bufo typhonius* (B) in the Lutz watershed by week from November 1976 through December 1978.

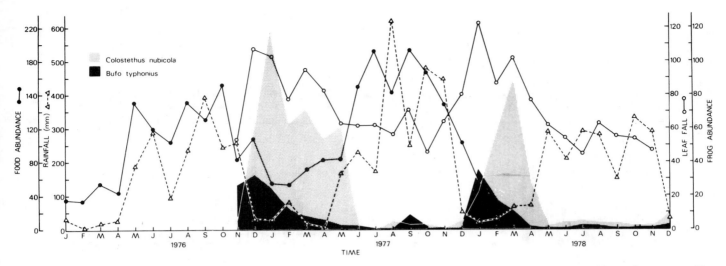

Figure 3. Total rainfall (mm) and mean weekly numbers of arthropods by month from January 1976 and mean weekly leaffall (gm) from November 1976 through December 1978. Monthly numbers of *B. typhonius* and *C. nubicola* during the study period are shaded in for reference. Data were provided by the Environmental Sciences Program, Smithsonian Institution.

DISCUSSION

The pattern of changing numbers of *B. typhonius* and *C. nubicola* on Barro Colorado Island is similar to that of litter anurans in other parts of Panama (Toft, 1980b); frogs are also more abundant in the dry season in the Pipeline Road area, which is near Barro Colorado Island and similar climatically, and the El Llano-Cartí Road area, which has much greater annual rainfall. At Barro Colorado Island and the Pipeline Road the seasonal increase in numbers is due to a pulse of recruitment in the dry season, though that on Pipeline Road is perhaps less pronounced than on Barro Colorado Island; at the "Cartí Road," recruitment appears to be much more prolonged and occurs somewhat later than at the former locations (according to Toft's personal observations). Thus, a similar pattern of increased numbers of litter anurans of a variety of species in the dry season occurs at these three sites despite differences in the timing of recruitment.

The seasonal change in numbers of litter anurans on Barro Colorado, however, is dominated by recruitment, and contrasts between the two species, *B. typhonius* and *C. nubicola*, may help to reveal causes for the timing of recruitment.

Bufo typhonius has a very short period of recruitment, compared with *C. nubicola*, reflecting the shorter breeding period in the former species (Wells, 1979); further, in *B. typhonius*, time from when the eggs are laid to the emergence of juveniles is very short, 2–3 weeks (according to Clark's personal observations), so these pulses of breeding and recruitment follow one

another very closely. Wells (1979) hypothesized that *B. typhonius* breed in such a short pulse to satiate predators, in this case larvae of *Leptodactylus pentadactylus*, though tadpoles of *B. typhonius* are probably poisonous and therefore not taken by most predators (Wells, 1979). *Bufo typhonius* is more likely to deposit eggs in larger, more permanent ponds (Wells, 1979). Such ponds may be maintained at sufficient size only when runoff is at a certain level.

The tadpoles of *C. nubicola* tend to occur in smaller pools of forest streams, especially in the dry season (Heyer, 1976), when the tadpoles are most abundant. Pools would tend to be smaller during the dry season because of decreased runoff at that time (Rubinoff, 1974; Windsor, 1976). Heyer (1976) felt that *C. nubicola* deposit their tadpoles, which are not poisonous, in ponds of this size because these ponds do not contain predators of *L. pentadactylus*, such as fish or tadpoles.

Thus the level of water in streams, which determines conditions such as the probability of predation for tadpoles, may influence the timing and duration of breeding and recruitment in both *B. typhonius* and *C. nubicola*. Several types of evidence support this possibility. First, the negative correlation between rainfall and numbers of juveniles of both species is consistent with this hypothesis because runoff is strongly correlated with rainfall (Rubinoff, 1974; Windsor, 1976; Dietrich et al., this volume); otherwise it is difficult to explain why juveniles, which are highly susceptible to desiccation because of their small size, would emerge during the driest period of the year. Second, during

402

this study, juveniles of *B. typhonius* emerged at unusual times from an artificial pond, the level of which is kept constant relative to forest ponds. Lastly, there is a suggestion, based on only 2 years of data, that the numbers of juveniles emerging in a particular dry season is inversely correlated with the amount of rainfall during the *preceding* wet season (Figure 3); data from additional years would be necessary to discover if such an inverse correlation really exists.

However, conditions for terrestrial juveniles may also be relevant to the timing and duration of recruitment. One result of the differences between *B. typhonius* and *C. nubicola* in both duration of recruitment and time spent as tadpoles and juveniles is that juveniles of both species are present in the litter at the same period of time. This fact suggests that growth to adulthood might either be favored at this time, or might have to be completed, for some reason, well before the onset of the next breeding season.

We investigated only two environmental factors that might be relevant during growth of juveniles. Leaf litter might provide some kind of protection for juveniles, and leaffall was positively correlated with numbers of juveniles; however, we do not yet feel that this relationship is directly causal.

Food abundance was negatively correlated with numbers of juveniles, but there are numerous problems with interpreting this result. First, the true availability of prey suitable for juveniles is not known since the techniques used (Levings and Windsor, this volume) do not sample very small prey accurately (Toft and Levings, 1979). Second, the numerical response in juvenile anurans is not clear; for instance, should they appear when food is measured to be most abundant, or is measured abundance of food irrelevant because it represents what is "left over" and ignores renewal rates? Lastly, there is some indication that the seasonal trends in arthropod abundance in the Lutz watershed may not be representative of what occurs in other parts of Panama (Toft, 1980b), where patterns of recruitment are similar.

Thus, the distinct seasonal pattern of recruitment in *B. typhonius* and *C. nubicola* on Barro Colorado Island perhaps represents the best compromise between conditions for tadpoles and for juveniles. The evidence presented herein supports the contention that conditions for the aquatic tadpoles influence the timing and duration of recruitment in both *B. typhonius* and *C. nubicola*.

LITERATURE CITED

Crump, M. L.
1974.   Reproductive strategies in a tropical anuran community. *Miscellaneous Publications*. Lawrence, Kans.: University of Kansas, Museum of Natural History.

Dietrich, W. E., D. M. Windsor, and T. Dunne
1982.   Geology, climate, and hydrology of Barro Colorado Island. Pages 21–46 in *The Ecology of a Tropical Forest*, edited by Egbert G. Leigh, Jr., et al. Washington, D.C.: Smithsonian Institution Press.

Duellman, W. E.
1978.   The biology of an equatorial herpetofauna in Amazonian Ecuador. *Miscellaneous Publications*. Lawrence, Kans.: University of Kansas, Museum of Natural History.

Heyer, R. W.
1976.   Studies in larval amphibian habitat partitioning. *Smithsonian Contributions to Zoology*, 242:1–27.

Levings, S., and D. W. Windsor
1982.   Seasonal and annual variation in litter arthropod populations. Pages 355–387 in *The Ecology of a Tropical Forest*, edited by Egbert G. Leigh, Jr., et al. Washington, D.C.: Smithsonian Institution Press.

Myers, C. W., and A. S. Rand
1969.   Checklist of amphibians and reptiles of Barro Colorado Island, Panama, with comments on faunal change and sampling. *Smithsonian Contributions to Zoology*, 10:1–11.

Panama Canal Company
1968.   *Climatological data. Canal Zone and Panama. Annual-1968*. vol. 60. Panama City: Engineering and Construction Bureau, Meteorological and Hydrographical Branch.

Rubinoff, R. W. (ed.)
1974.   *1973 Environmental Monitoring and Baseline Data*. Washington, D.C.: Smithsonian Institution Environmental Science Program.

Toft, C. A.
1980a.   Feeding ecology of 13 syntopic species of anurans in a seasonal tropical environment. *Oecologia*, 45:131–141.
1980b.   Seasonal variation in populations of Panamanian litter frogs and their prey: a comparison of wetter and drier sites. *Oecologia*, 47:34–38
1981.   Feeding ecology of Panamanian litter anurans: patterns in diet and foraging mode. *Journal of Herpetology*, 15:139–144.

Toft, C. A., and W. E. Duellman
1979.   Anurans of the lower Rio Llullapichis, Amazonian Peru: a preliminary analysis of community structure. *Herpetologica*, 35(1):71–77.

Toft, C. A., and S. Levings
1979.   Seasonal trends in litter arthropod populations. Pages 559–76 in *Actas del IV Symposium International de Ecología Tropical, marzo 7–11,1977*, vol. 2, edited by H. Wolda.

Windsor, D. M.
1976.   *1975 Environmental Monitoring and Baseline Data*. Washington, D.C.: Smithsonian Institution Environmental Sciences Program.

Wells, K. D.
1979.   Reproductive behavior and male mating success in a neotropical frog, *Bufo typhonius*. *Biotropica*, 11(4):301–307.

Seasonal Breeding and Long-term Population Fluctuations in the Lizard *Anolis limifrons*

ROBIN M. ANDREWS   Department of Biology, Virginia Polytechnic Institute and State University, Blacksburg, Virginia 24061

A. STANLEY RAND   Smithsonian Tropical Research Institute, Balboa, Republic of Panama

ABSTRACT

Anolis limifrons is a small lizard; adults weigh an average of 1.6 g. It feeds on arthropods in the leaf litter and the shrub layer. On a 25 × 35 m plot in Lutz catchment, the density of these lizards fluctuated from one per 58 sq. m to one per 10 sq. m over 10 years. Similar fluctuations occurred elsewhere on the island in apparent synchrony. Food is probably not limiting in the study population. The survival rate in these lizards was 74% per 28 days regardless of sex or time of year and did not vary over the 10-year period. Changes in numbers of lizards probably reflect changes in rate of recruitment. In these lizards, recruitment is concentrated at the beginning of the rainy season. Numbers of lizards are correlated ($r = 0.70$) with the length of the dry season.

INTRODUCTION

Anolis limifrons is a small arboreal lizard found in the understory of moist and wet tropical forest throughout much of Central America. On Barro Colorado Island, both males and females reach maximum snout-vent lengths of 50 mm. These lizards eat small invertebrates of all trophic levels, which they capture in the leaf litter and in shrub-level vegetation. The prey of adults averages 8–9 mm in length (Sexton et al., 1972). Adult *A. limifrons* averaging 1.6 g in weight and 46 mm in length eat an average of 94 calories or 0.016 g dry weight of food per day (Andrews, Rand, and Guerrero, 1982). Because lizard densities approach one per 9 sq. m in Lutz catchment, and one per 6 sq. m in the old forest of Barro Colorado Island (Andrews, Rand and Guerrero, 1982), they may well play an important part in the ecology of the forest floor. These lizards are eaten in turn by motmots, trogons, toucans, their larger congener *Anolis frenatus*, and snakes such as *Oxybelis* and *Dendrophidion*. Juvenile *A. limifrons* are vulnerable to spiders, mantids, predaceous tettigoniids, and other invertebrates.

Both male and female *A. limifrons* appear to be territorial, although social and aggressive behavior have been described only for males (Hover and Jenssen, 1976). Residents exhibit strong site tenacity; adult females and adult males captured four or more times had median distances of 4 m and 8 m, respectively, between successive captures (Andrews and Rand, in preparation).

These lizards appear very sensitive to seasonal changes in the weather. Populations of *A. limifrons* contain a far smaller proportion of young in the dry season than they do during the wet season (Sexton et al., 1963). Seasonal changes in population composition result from a concentration of reproductive activities early in the wet season (Sexton et al., 1971). The average female lays an egg every 8–9 days early in the wet season and every 19 days in the dry season (Andrews and Rand, 1974; Andrews, 1979). The reason lizards concentrate reproduction early in the wet season is not known. Dry-season conditions may lower egg survival through desiccation (Sexton et al., 1979). Lizards may lay fewer eggs later in the rainy season and in the dry season because of seasonal food shortage. Litter arthropods are largest and most abundant early in the wet season (Willis, 1976; Toft and Levings, 1979; Levings and Windsor, this volume) and herbivorous insects (Wolda, 1978a) and other arthropods (Wilson, 1970; Robinson and Robinson, 1970; Smythe, this volume) also peak at this time.

The numbers of *A. limifrons* fluctuate greatly from one year to the next (Sexton, 1967). As individuals rarely live longer than 1 year, annual changes in population size are presumably related to variation in reproductive success. Moreover, the sensitivity of lizard reproduction to dry-season conditions suggests that variation in the length and intensity of the dry season might be related to the fluctuations in their numbers. And indeed, Sexton (1967) found one lizard per 8 sq. m in April 1963, after a 2-month dry season, and one lizard per 26 sq. m in April 1965, after a 5-month dry season. In this paper we report fluctuations in the number of *A. limifrons* on a 25 × 35 m (875 sq. m) plot at Barro Colorado Island over 10 years and relate these fluctuations to the length and intensity of the dry season.

METHODS

Study Area and Census Methods

The study area was located in the N–O, W–1 quadrat of Lutz catchment (Thorington et al., this volume; Rubinoff, 1974). Lutz Stream forms the lower boundary of the site and the inner loop trail of Lutz catchment the upper boundary. Although in most places the understory was sparse enough to walk through easily, the site included several clumps of dense and tangled vegetation. Marked trees were used as reference points for capture data.

We censused *Anolis* in this plot between November 1971 and January 1981, as shown in Figure 1 and Table 1. The site was consistently censused between November and January of each year. Intensive monthly to bimonthly censusing was conducted from May 1976 to July 1977. Most censuses included two collecting periods separated by 4–6 days to allow use of the Lincoln Index to estimate population size.

During censuses, anoles were captured by hand, individually placed in plastic bags, and transported to a laboratory building where an individual identification number was recorded, snout-vent length (SVL) measured to the nearest millimeter, and weight determined to the nearest one-hundredth of a gram. Individuals were identified by clipping the terminal phalange of toes in unique combinations that required only one toe per foot. On the day after capture lizards were released at the spot where they were caught.

The lizards were divided into classes based on age, size, and reproductive attributes. Individuals with SVL of 40 mm or more were considered adult because most are sexually mature at these sizes (Sexton et al., 1971). The juvenile I class consisted of individuals with SVL of 29 mm or less (0–50 days old) and the juvenile II class consisted of individuals with SVL of 30–39 mm (ca. 50–110 days old).

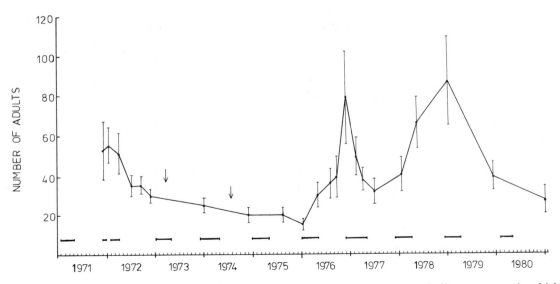

Figure 1. Population size of *Anolis limifrons* on the Lutz study area, 1971–81. Arrows indicate censuses in which too few individuals could be collected for reliable estimation of population size. Vertical lines through each estimate indicate plus and minus one standard deviation. The filled squares on the horizontal axis indicate the months with less than 100 mm of rainfall.

Population Estimates

The number of adult *A. limifrons* on the Lutz site was estimated for each census that included two collecting periods using Bailey's modification of the Lincoln Index (Poole, 1974). The number of juveniles was not estimated. Too few juveniles were present in most censuses for reliable use of the Lincoln Index. Moreover, the survivorship of the juvenile I class was very low (Andrews, Rand, and Guerrero, 1982). This inflated the estimate of juvenile numbers in censuses where this class was well represented.

Survivorship

Survivorship on the plot was determined as

$$S = 1 - (\ln N_o - \ln N_t)/t$$

where S is the daily survivorship, N_o is the number of individuals present or known to be alive in one census period, N_t is the number of individuals included in the first census period present or known to be alive in a successive census period, and t is the interval between censuses in days. This formula assumes that the probability of death or disappearance is equal in each time interval. Survivorship was determined separately for adult females, adult males, and juveniles.

Seasonality and Population Size

Seasonal designations were based on rainfall. Dry-sea-

son months were those with less than 100 mm of rain (Janzen, 1967). Although the average dry season at Barro Colorado Island extends from January through April, its length varies considerably from year to year. During our study the dry season ranged from 3 to 5 months beginning as early as December and ending as late as mid-May. We used regression techniques to determine the relationship between rainfall and population size of *A. limifrons*. Population size in late wet-season censuses was used as the dependent variable and monthly rainfall records (Rand and Rand, this volume) for the months of December through May prior to each census were used as the independent variables. Population size used was the estimated adult numbers plus the number of juveniles in class II.

RESULTS

Population density of *A. limifrons* fluctuated greatly during the 10 years of census (Figure 1, Table 1). Estimates of adult density on the study area ranged from 15 in January 1976 to 86 in January 1978 (171 and 983 adults/ha., respectively). Total population size during each census interval can be estimated by adding the total number of juveniles captured to the Lincoln Index for adults. This conservative estimate indicated that the population density of *A. limifrons* on the study site reached maximum values of about 100 individuals (1143/ha.) in the late wet seasons of 1971, 1976, and 1978.

Changes in the age and composition of the popu-

Table 1. Numbers of *Anolis limifrons* of different ages captured in successive censuses, November 1971– January 1981, and Lincoln Index estimates of numbers of adults

Census interval	Juveniles		Adults		Total captured	Lincoln Index estimates of adults[1]
	I	II	Female	Male		
30 Nov. 1971–26 Jan. 1972	15	27	16	39	97	53, 56[2]
7 Apr. 1972–28 Apr. 1972	0	4	18	22	44	51
6 June 1972–19 July 1972	7	3	17	12	39	35
29 Aug. 1972–21 Sept. 1972	9	19	13	16	57	36
22 Nov. 1972–13 Dec. 1972	13	7	12	15	47	29
14 Apr. 1973–18 Apr. 1973	0	2	3	10	15	—
30 Dec. 1973–9 Jan. 1974	7	5	6	16	34	25
1 Aug. 1974–12 Aug. 1974	2	3	4	5	14	—
22 Nov. 1974–4 Dec. 1974	8	6	5	8	27	20
9 Aug. 1975–27 Aug. 1975	1	5	7	6	19	20
12 Jan. 1976–25 Jan. 1976	7	1	7	6	21	15
6 May 1976–14 May 1976	1	3	8	17	29	30
28 July 1976–6 Aug. 1976	22	7	12	15	56	36
13 Oct. 1976–21 Oct. 1976	9	12	10	18	49	39
19 Nov. 1976	3	4	5	4	16	—
1 Dec. 1976–9 Dec. 1976	5	12	14	23	54	79
12 Jan. 1977–13 Jan. 1977	3	9	12	12	36	—
9 Feb. 1977–17 Feb. 1977	4	9	12	25	50	49
16 Mar. 1977	1	6	3	4	14	—
20 Apr. 1977–28 Apr. 1977	2	8	17	18	45	38
25 May 1977–26 May 1977	2	4	12	8	26	—
29 June 1977–7 July 1977	5	1	11	14	31	32
18 Jan. 1978–26 Jan. 1978	15	6	9	21	51	40
17 May 1978–25 May 1978	3	5	25	21	54	66
17 Jan. 1979–25 Jan. 1979	14	12	23	31	80	86
13 Dec. 1979–21 Dec. 1979	8	11	13	17	49	38
23 Jan. 1981–30 Jan. 1981	2	11	8	10	31	26

[1] Adults ≥ 40 mm SVL.

[2] Separate estimates were made for the first and second half of the 30 Nov. 1971–26 Jan. 1972 interval.

lation during the period of intensive study indicated that breeding was concentrated at the beginning of the wet season (Table 2). The juvenile I class was most abundant in July and August; judging by the growth rates of juveniles in field studies (Andrews, 1976), these juveniles hatched in early July, and the eggs from which they hatched were laid 44 days earlier (Andrews and Sexton, 1981), in late May, soon after the rains began. These lizards would have attained adult size in early November. The small proportion of juveniles late in the rainy season suggests that the rate of egg laying had decreased considerably by late July or that the survival of eggs fell off drastically as the wet season progressed.

The survival rate of *A. limifrons* individuals averaged 74% per 28 days (Table 3), and was independent of sex, age, season, year, or rate of population growth. Mann-Whitney U tests revealed no significant differences in survivorship between adults and juveniles ($p > 0.05$), between dry-season and wet-season intervals ($p > 0.05$), or between intervals of population increase and those of decrease ($p > 0.05$). Population fluctuations in these lizards must therefore be ascribed primarily to fluctuations in the rate at which young lizards hatch into the population.

Because *A. limifrons* reproduces more slowly in the dry season (Sexton et al., 1971), we assumed that either the quantity of rainfall during the dry season, the length of the dry season, or some combination of these variables would be related to population size.

Preliminary analyses indicated that neither the total rainfall from January through April, months that are usually "dry," nor the length of the dry season, judged by the number of months with less than 100 mm of rainfall, were correlated with population size ($r = 0.17$ and -0.27, respectively, d.f. $= 8$, $p > 0.05$). In contrast, total rainfall from December, a month that is usually "wet," through April resulted in a significant correlation between rainfall and population size ($r = 0.65$, $p < 0.05$). This relationship was improved somewhat ($r = 0.70$) when the sum of December and April rainfall alone was used in the analysis. The relationship between population size at the end of the wet season (N) and rainfall during the preceeding December and April (R) is

$$N = 16.1 + 0.143\,R$$

DISCUSSION

Until recently, ecologists thought that tropical rain forest environments were more stable than those of the temperate zone, and that species diversity bred community stability; they concluded accordingly that populations of the tropical forest were stable (MacArthur, 1955; Hutchinson, 1959; Elton, 1958). However, there is no necessary relation between species diversity and community stability (May, 1973; Goodman, 1975; Connell, 1978) or between climatic stability and the degree of population fluctuation (Leigh, 1975a). The timing of reproduction and leaf flush in tropical plants, and its consequent effects on the timing of mortality and reproduction in animal populations, is largely controlled by the seasonal distribution of rainfall (Frankie et al., 1974; Fogden, 1972; Leigh, 1975b; Wolda, 1978a). Moreover, the distribution of rainfall changes sufficiently from one year to the next to generate population fluctuations in tropical animals every bit as striking as those in the temperate zone (Wolda, 1978b).

Anolis limifrons fits this pattern. The almost sixfold fluctuation in population density we observed is considerably greater than has been observed for lizards of temperate regions. *Uta stansburiana* in Texas, which like *A. limifrons* exhibits almost complete population turnover each year, showed a less than twofold fluctuation in population density over 4 years of study (Tinkle, 1967). A population in Nevada, where annual adult survivorship is higher, about 20%, showed less than fourfold fluctuation in population density over 8 years of study (Turner, 1977). Other, longer-lived lizards of the temperate zone censused for 3 or more years mostly exhibited maximum population fluctua-

Table 2. Proportional representation of *Anolis limifrons* classes during the intensive census period, 1976–77

Census	Juvenile I	Juvenile II	Adult female	Adult male
May 1976	0.034	0.103	0.276	0.586
July–Aug. 1976	0.393	0.125	0.214	0.268
Oct. 1976	0.184	0.245	0.204	0.367
Dec. 1976	0.093	0.222	0.259	0.426
Jan. 1977	0.083	0.250	0.333	0.333
Feb. 1977	0.080	0.180	0.240	0.500
Apr. 1977	0.044	0.178	0.378	0.400
May 1977	0.077	0.154	0.462	0.308
June–July 1977	0.161	0.032	0.355	0.452

Total numbers are given in Table 1.

Table 3. Survivorship of *Anolis limifrons* adults and juveniles

Census interval	Survivorship (N)			
	Adults		Juveniles	
Dec. 1971–Apr. 1972	0.762	(55)	0.809	(42)
Apr. 1972–June 1972	0.752	(44)	—	(4)
June 1972–Aug. 1972	0.855	(32)	0.736	(10)
Aug. 1972–Nov. 1972	0.750	(31)	0.592	(29)
Nov. 1972–Apr. 1973	0.598	(27)	0.688	(20)
Apr. 1973–Dec. 1973	0.817	(13)	—	(2)
Dec. 1973–Aug. 1974	0.665	(22)	0.834	(12)
Aug. 1974–Nov. 1974	—	(9)	—	(5)
Nov. 1974–Aug. 1975	0.866	(15)	0.846	(14)
Aug. 1975–Jan. 1976	0.760	(14)	—	(6)
Jan. 1976–May 1976	0.871	(14)	—	(8)
May 1976–July 1976	0.798	(27)	—	(4)
July 1976–Oct. 1976	0.761	(29)	0.670	(29)
Oct. 1976–Dec. 1976	0.658	(31)	0.671	(24)
Dec. 1976–Feb. 1977	0.743	(44)	0.786	(20)
Feb. 1977–Apr. 1977	0.736	(42)	0.766	(14)
Apr. 1977–June 1977	0.613	(37)	—	(11)
June 1977–Jan. 1978	0.745	(25)	—	(6)
Jan. 1978–May 1978	0.752	(30)	0.630	(21)
May 1978–Jan. 1979	0.829	(46)	—	(8)

Adults are those with snout-vent length ≥ 40 mm; juveniles are those with snout-vent length < 40 mm. Daily survivorship has been converted to survivorship over a 28-day period ($= S^{28}$). The total number of individuals included in the initial census follows survivorship in parentheses.

tions of twofold or less (Blair, 1960; Fitch, 1954; Tinkle, 1972; 1973; Tinkle and Ballinger, 1972; Vinegar, 1975; Whitford and Creusere, 1977; Turner, 1977, and included references).

Annual recruitment into the *A. limifrons* population appeared to depend on the amount of rainfall in December and April. Rainfall in January, February, and March was not related to the number of lizards present at the end of the following rainy season. This indicated that success in recruitment was related to both the length of the dry season and to its severity.

However, the precise mechanism by which the length of the dry season affects lizard recruitment is not known. The length of the dry season may determine population size through its influence on the timing of reproduction. Because the end of the dry season determines when most eggs are laid, variability in the time of this event will affect recruitment in two ways. First, female survivorship is about 75% each month (Table 3), thus, the longer the dry season, the fewer the number of females that will be alive to produce eggs when the rains begin. For example, at the end of a 3-month dry season, 42%, or $(0.75)^3$, of the initial number would be alive and at the end of a 5-month dry season, only 25%, or $(0.75)^5$, would be alive. Second, the interval between oviposition and the attainment of adult size (40 mm SVL) is about 5.5 months. Therefore, only eggs laid by 15 July would produce adults by 1 January. Thus, if the oviposition rate is constant during the reproductive period prior to 15 July, more eggs would be produced in years when the dry season ended early than when it ended late. For example, if the dry season ended on 15 March, eggs laid during 4 months would contribute to the adult population in a late wet-season census. On the other hand, if the dry season ended on 15 May, eggs laid during only 2 months would contribute to the adult population in the late wet-season census.

On the other hand, the length of the dry season may determine population size through an effect on food chains which include *A. limifrons* as an intermediate link. Perhaps the decomposition of the litter accumulated during a longer dry season allows higher populations of the invertebrates that eat eggs of *A. limifrons*. Conversely, reduced arthropod abundance following a long dry season might reduce the availability of food for females. At the moment we cannot dismiss any of these ideas.

Climate, a density-independent factor, clearly has an important influence on population dynamics of *A. limifrons*. The large changes in population density we observed can be attributed to density-independent factors that determine when eggs are laid, their number, and their survival. This conclusion does not exclude effects of density-dependent factors. However,

the strong relationship between rainfall and recruitment probably indicates that density-dependent factors can be detected only when a population density is either very low or very high. Although we have no evidence that food limited the number of *Anolis limifrons* in Lutz catchment during any part of our study, lower food intake and slower growth suggests that a denser population in mature forest on the other side of the island at least occasionally suffered food shortage (Andrews, Rand, and Guerrero, 1982).

ACKNOWLEDGMENTS

This study was funded by NSF grants B019801X and GB37731X to E. E. Williams and NSF grant 76–05758 to A. S. Rand and S. Ayala. We would like to thank N. Fetcher and E. G. Leigh for their comments on the manuscript, and S. Guerrero for assistance with censusing from 1976 through 1979.

LITERATURE CITED

Andrews, R. M.
1976.   Growth rate in island and mainland anoline lizards. *Copeia*, 1976:477–482.
1979.   Reproductive effort of female *Anolis limifrons* (Sauria: Iguanidae). *Copeia*, 1979:620–626.

Andrews, R. M., and A. S. Rand
1974.   Reproductive effort in anoline lizards. *Ecology*, 55:1317–1327.

Andrews, R. M., A. S. Rand, and S. Guerrero
1982.   Seasonal and spatial variation in the annual cycle of a tropical lizard. In a festschrift for Ernest E. Williams, edited by A. G. J. Rhodin and K. Miyata. Cambridge, Mass.: Museum of Comparative Zoology (in press).

Andrews, R. M. and O. J. Sexton
1981.   Water relations of the eggs of *Anolis auratus* and *Anolis limifrons*. *Ecology*, 62:556–562.

Blair, W. F.
1960.   *The rusty lizard: A population study.* Austin: University of Texas Press.

Connell, J. H.
1978.   Diversity in tropical rain forests and coral reefs. *Science*, 199:1302–1310.

Elton, C. S.
1958.   *The ecology of invasions by animals and plants.* New York: John Wiley. 181 p.

Fitch, H. S.
1954.   Life history and ecology of the five-lined skink, *Eumeces fasciatus*. *University of Kansas, Museum of Natural History Publications*, 8:1–156.

Fogden, M. P. L.
1972.   The seasonality and population dynamics of equatorial forest birds in Sarawak. *Ibis*, 114:307–343.

Frankie, G. W., H. G. Baker, and P. A. Opler
1974.   Comparative phenological studies of trees in tropical wet and dry forests in the lowlands of Costa Rica. *Journal of Ecology*, 62:881–919.

Goodman, D.
1975.   The theory of diversity-stability relationships in ecology. *Quarterly Review of Biology*, 50:237–266.

Hover, E. L., and T. A. Jenssen
1976.   Descriptive analysis and social correlates of agonistic displays of *Anolis limifrons* (Sauria, Iguanidae). *Behaviour*, 58:173–191.

Hutchinson, G. E.
1959.   Homage to Santa Rosalia or why are there so many kinds of animals? *American Naturalist*, 93:145–159.

Janzen, D. H.
1967.   Synchronization of sexual reproduction of trees with the dry season in Central America. *Evolution*, 21:620–637.

Leigh, E. G., Jr.
1975a.   Population fluctuations, community stability, and environmental variability. Pages 51–73 in *Ecology and Evolution of Communities*, edited by M. L. Cody and J. M. Diamond. Cambridge, Mass.: Belknap Press of Harvard University Press.
1975b.   Structure and climate in tropical rain forest. *Ann. Rev. Ecol. Syst.*, 6:67–86.

Levings, S., and D. M. Windsor
1982.   Seasonal and Annual Variation in Litter Arthropod Populations. Pages 355–387 in *The Ecology of a Tropical Forest*, edited by Egbert G. Leigh, Jr., et al. Washington, D.C.: Smithsonian Institution Press.

MacArthur, R. H.
1955.   Fluctuations of animal populations, and a measure of community stability. *Ecology*, 36:533–536.

May, R. M.
1973.   *Stability and Complexity in Model Ecosystems*. Princeton, N. J.: Princeton University Press.

Poole, R. W.
1974.   *An introduction to quantitative ecology*. New York: McGraw-Hill.

Rand, A. S., and W. M. Rand
1982.   Variation in Rainfall over Barro Colorado Island. Pages 47–59 in *The Ecology of a Tropical Forest*, edited by Egbert G. Leigh, Jr., et al. Washington, D.C.: Smithsonian Institution Press.

Robinson, M. H., and B. Robinson
1970.   Prey caught by a sample population of the spider *Argiope argentata* (Araneae: Araneidae) in Panama: a year's census data. *Zool. Journal of the Linnean Society*, 49:345–357.

Rubinoff, R. W.
1974.   *Environmental monitoring and baseline data (1973)*. Washington, D.C.: Smithsonian Institution Environmental Sciences Program, Tropical Studies.

Sexton, O. J.
1967.   Population changes in a tropical lizard *Anolis limifrons* on Barro Colorado Island, Panama Canal Zone. *Copeia*, 1967:219–222.

Sexton, O. J., J. Bauman, and E. Ortleb
1972.   Seasonal food habits of *Anolis limifrons*. *Ecology*, 53:182–186.

Sexton, O. J., J. Heatwole, and E. Meseth
1963.   Seasonal population changes in the lizard, *Anolis limifrons*, in Panama. *American Midland Naturalist*, 69:482–491.

Sexton, O. J., E. P. Ortleb, L. M. Hathaway, R. E. Ballinger, and P. Licht
1971.   Reproductive cycles of three species of anoline lizards from the Isthmus of Panama. *Ecology*, 52:201–215.

Sexton, O. J., G. M. Veith, and D. M. Phillips
1979.   Ultrastructure of the eggshell of two species of anoline lizards *Journal of Experimental Zoology*, 207:207–236.

Smythe, N.
1982.   The Seasonal Abundance of Night-flying Insects in a Neotropical Forest. Pages 309–318 in *The Ecology of a Tropical Forest*, edited by Egbert G. Leigh, Jr., et al. Washington, D.C.: Smithsonian Institution Press.

Thorington, R. W., Jr., B. Tannenbaum, A. Tarak, and R. Rudran
1982.   Distribution of trees on Barro Colorado Island: a five-hectare sample. Pages 83–94 in *The Ecology of a Tropical Forest*, edited by Egbert G. Leigh, Jr., et al. Washington, D.C.: Smithsonian Institution Press.

Tinkle, D. W.
1967.   The life and demography of the side-blotched lizard, *Uta stansburiana*. *Miscellaneous Publications of the Museum of Zoology, University of Michigan*, 132:1–182.
1972.   The dynamics of a Utah population of *Sceloporus undulatus*. *Herpetologica*, 28:351–359.
1973.   A population analysis of the sagebrush lizard, *Sceloporus graciosus*, in southern Utah. *Copeia*, 1973:284–295.

Tinkle, D. W., and R. E. Ballinger
1972.   *Sceloporus undulatus*: A study of the intraspecific comparative demography of a lizard. *Ecology*, 53:570–584.

Toft, C., and S. C. Levings
1979.   Seasonal trends in leaf litter arthropod populations. Pages 559–576 in *Actas del IV Simposium International de Ecologia Tropical, Panama*, edited by H. Wolda. Panama City: La Nación, INAC.

Turner, F. B.
1977.   The dynamics of populations of squamates, crocodilians, and rhynchocephalians. Pages 157–264 in *Biology of the Reptilia, Vol. 7: Ecology and Behaviour A*, edited by C. Gans and D. W. Tinkle. New York: Academic Press.

Vinegar, M. B.
1975.   Demography of the striped plateau lizard, *Sceloporus virgatus*. *Ecology*, 56:172–182.

Whitford, W. G., and F. M. Creusere
1977.   Seasonal and yearly fluctuations in Chihuahuan desert lizard communities. *Herpetologica*, 33:54–65.

Willis, E. O.
1976.   Seasonal changes in the invertebrate fauna on Barro Colorado Island, Panama. *Rev. Brasil. Biol.*, 36:643–657.

Wilson, D. E.

1970.   The food habits of *Micronycteris hersuta* (Mammalia: Chiroptera). *Mammalia*, 35:307.

Wolda, H.

1978a.   Seasonal fluctuations in rainfall, food, and abundance of tropical insects. *Journal of Animal Ecology*, 47:369–381.

1978b.   Fluctuations in abundance of tropical insects. *American Naturalist*, 112:1017–1045.

Timing of Reproduction by Coatis (*Nasua narica*) in Relation to Fluctuations in Food Resources

JAMES K. RUSSELL   Department of Zoology, University of North Carolina, Chapel Hill, North Carolina 27514

ABSTRACT

Coatis (*Nasua narica*) on Barro Colorado Island breed synchronously once a year. The proportion of adult females that attempt reproduction varies markedly from year to year. Seasonal variations in food availability understandably play a role in the timing of reproductive events within years. The precision of the response to seasonality in coatis is due to the complexity and fluidity of their social system. Year-to-year differences in food availability have a strong influence on the age at first reproduction in coatis and thereby affect population size, age structure, and potential growth.

INTRODUCTION

Coatis (*Nasua narica*) on Barro Colorado are seasonally monoestrous. Although seasonal breeding is common among Panamanian mammals (Fleming, 1973), coatis are distinguished by their high degree of synchrony in breeding within and among social groups (Chapman, 1938; Kaufmann, 1962; Russell, 1979). Judged by the synchrony with which adult females bring juveniles down from their nests in May, it appears that all mating in the population occurs within a 1-week to 2-week period within any year, although this period may shift slightly from year to year. Given this constraint, an adult female coati's control over the timing of her reproductive effort is limited to whether she reproduces in a particular year. The proportion of adult females that reproduces varies dramatically in different years.

A comprehensive understanding of the timing of reproductive attempts by coatis thus requires explanation of the advantages of breeding seasonally, of the importance of synchrony in breeding within and among social groups, and of the factors governing the choice of whether to reproduce in a given year or to defer reproduction until the next year. An explanation of seasonal breeding will require information about seasonal changes in the distribution and abundance of food and about the growth and development of juveniles. Selection for synchronous breeding can be understood in relation to the social organization. Understanding the choice of whether to undertake or defer reproduction requires information about the dependence of the costs and benefits of reproduction on age and variations among years in food availability.

METHODS

The Study Animal

Coatis are the only gregarious species of the carnivore family Procyonidae. With the exception of the nesting season (April–May), adult females and their offspring up to 2 years of age are found in small bands with stable membership. Adult males are solitary, except during the mating season in mid-February, when some of them temporarily succeed in joining bands. During the rest of the year adult males, which occasionally prey on juveniles, are aggressively chased away from bands by the adult females (Figure 1).

Gregariousness in coatis has apparently evolved as a response to predation on juveniles (Russell, 1979). Coatis do not cooperate in foraging, other than in mutual protection and shared vigilance.

While foraging, bands typically assume an elliptical

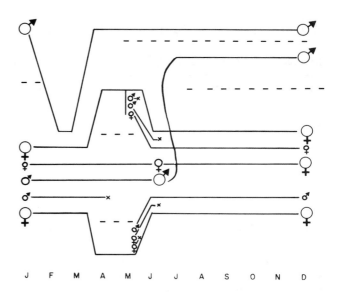

Figure 1. The yearly cycle of social events in a coati band. The smallest circles represent juveniles, next largest are subadults, and largest are adults. Dashed lines represent separation between social units. Xs represent mortality.

outline, with subadults and adults forming the periphery and juveniles aggregated in the center. Individuals forage about five body lengths from their nearest neighbors, somewhat more than twice the distance at which they regularly detect food items. In addition to interposing themselves physically between juveniles and potential predators, animals on the peripheries of bands, especially adults, protect juveniles through specialized vigilance behavior, by cooperative attack on potential predators, and by assuming protective positions during flight from alarming stimuli (for details, see Russell, 1979).

Because breeding is strictly seasonal on Barro Colorado, females have their first opportunity to breed at 22 months of age. In their first breeding season, at 10 months of age, females weigh only 1.3 kg (*n* = 4), much less than the 3.7 kg average for fully adult females (*n* = 29). Depending on ecological conditions, all 2-year-old females may breed, or as little as 20% may breed. Females that fail to breed at 22 months have their next opportunity at 34 months. A few females do not reproduce before they are 46 months old. Males have their first reproductive opportunity at 34 months of age. At 22 months they are still members of their natal band and weigh only about 3.5 kg (interpolated), substantially less than the average 4.75 kg weight of fully mature adult males (*n* = 18). Because of the polygynous mating system and concommitant high level of competition among males for mates, most males probably do not breed until their fourth or fifth year, and many males may never breed.

In captivity, litter size is from four to six (Kaufmann, 1962; McToldrige, 1969; Smith, 1977). However, on Barro Colorado females bring an average of only 3.5 juveniles down from the nest. This difference may be due to lower litter size in nature, mortality in the nest, or a combination of these factors.

Foods

I recorded the identity of animal food items and collected scats only when it was possible to do so without disturbing the animals. Scats were washed with sodium hydroxide, and the animal fragments found in them were identified to order. Samples of fruits that I observed coatis eating were identified through the kindness of several botanists that resided on Barro Colorado during various portions of my stay there.

I estimated the density of fruiting *Scheelea* trees by a census of all individuals within 100 m of the trails in the main study area. Estimates of the densities of fruiting individuals of other tree species, which were much rarer, are from records of the locations of individual trees either visited by coatis while I accompanied them or located by me during extensive searches for favorable trapping sites. These estimates are not intended to measure the entire population of these species, but rather refer to that portion of the population which affects coati foraging behavior: the fruit-bearing individuals.

Behavior

Observations of coati foraging behavior were collected in August and September 1975, from June 1976 to October 1977, and from January to July 1978. I thoroughly habituated two bands of coatis so that I could follow and observe them without disturbing their behavior. Rates of behaviors are from 10-min. focal animal samples (J. Altmann, 1974). Spatial organization was recorded during periodic scans of the group. The number of individuals per band in the several age classes are derived from records of the membership of the two fully habituated bands, supplemented whenever possible by complete counts of three neighboring bands which were partially habituated. Calculations referring to the wet season include data collected from June through November. Those referring to the dry season include data collected from January to April. Data from December and May, which are transitional months, are excluded from these calculations. For details of habituation procedure and observation technique, see Russell (1979).

At 1-hr. intervals I recorded the location of the band I was observing on a grid with 20 × 20 m units superimposed on a topographical map of the study area. These locations have been lumped into 1-ha. units. I estimated the number of hectares a band visited in each 2-mo. period by fitting the frequency distribution of hectare usage to a truncated log-normal distribution (Cohen, 1961; Bliss, 1965; Robinson, 1979). This procedure provides a correction for the number of hectares that are "missed" during sampling because they are used infrequently. I have multiplied the estimated number of hectares in the 0–1 usage class by the midpoint of that interval (0.5), and added this product to the total number of hectares in which a band was observed in any 2-mo. period. The truncated log-normal distribution provided a good fit to the observed frequency distribution. The average χ^2 value for goodness-of-fit tests was 4.09, (range 0.0 − 10.9, d.f. = 9), with an associated probability of 0.94 (range 33.8–100; $p < 0.05$ would indicate an unacceptable fit; Hays, 1973).

Age and Reproductive Condition

Recruitment into the juvenile, subadult, and adult age-classes occurs in late May when bands reaggregate after the nesting season. From the time of birth until they begin foraging with bands, young coatis are considered infants. At band reaggregation, they become juveniles. Juveniles surviving from the previous year achieve subadult status at reaggregation and, similarly, surviving subadults become adults. These nomenclatural conventions reflect social position rather than physiological maturation. Although subadult females may become sexually mature before they are defined as adults, they do not assume a fully adult role in cooperative vigilance and in the settlement of intraband disputes until their third year. Adult males do not have an opportunity to breed until many months after reaggregation, but they become solitary at the time their band reaggregates in their third year.

Because coatis breed only once a year on Barro Colorado, it was relatively easy to separate adults into 2-year-olds, 3-year-olds, and animals 4 or more years old on the basis of tooth wear. Tooth wear was recorded by assigning points for wear of each of the cusps and ridges on the third and fourth premolars and the first and second molars of the upper tooth row. Each cusp or ridge was assigned one point if dentine was exposed and two points if the pulp cavity was exposed. Tooth-wear scores were calibrated with records of animals of known age, which were either juveniles or subadults when I first identified them. Juveniles and subadults were easy to distinguish from each other and from adults on the basis of size.

I judged whether a female had ever bred by evidence of lactation. Females that have never bred can

Table 1. Foraging activities of coatis

	Wet season	Dry season
% of daytime spent foraging[1]	91	89
% of foraging time spent on ground[1]	99	91
% of terrestrial foraging spent under fruiting trees	12	45
Estimated % of foraging time spent searching for animals	89	54
Rate of intake of animals while foraging away from fruiting trees (items/ 10 min.)	2.4	1.6
Rate of intake of animals while foraging under fruiting trees (items/ 10 min.)	1.2	0.8
Rate of intake of fruits while foraging under fruiting trees (items/10 min.)	6.4	7.6

[1] from Kaufmann (1962: Figure 5).

be separated from parous females by this criterion, but since evidence of lactation may persist for more than 1 year it is not possible to be sure by this criterion alone whether a parous female, a female that has bred at least once in its life, has given birth in the year it is captured. Of the females for which I have records extending over several years, all continued to reproduce in each year once they had started.

RESULTS

The Coati Diet

Throughout the year coatis spend about 90% of their daytime hours foraging (Kaufmann, 1962). The remainder is spent in rest periods. They sleep at night. At least 90% of this foraging time is spent on the ground; the remainder is spent foraging for fruit in trees. In the wet season almost 90% of the time spent foraging on the ground is devoted to searching for animal foods. In the dry season only slightly more than half of terrestrial foraging is spent searching for animal foods; the remainder is spent under fruiting trees. There, almost all food items taken are fallen fruits, although the coatis continue to take animal foods

at a low rate. As a result, nearly 90% of foraging time is spent collecting animal foods in the wet season, and slightly more than half of foraging time is spent on animal foods in the dry season (Table 1).

Coatis discover most animal food items in the forest litter by scent and quickly excavate and eat them. They capture a few animals from foliage within a meter of the ground. An observer can identify only a few of these animals before they are eaten: one must judge the animal part of the coati diet largely from scats. However, some animals are more likely than others to leave identifiable traces in scats, and some animals important to coatis, such as beetle larvae, leave no trace at all.

Most coati scats consisted primarily of beetle fragments. Parts of spiders and millipedes occurred in smaller amounts, in half of the scats. Fragments of ants (apparently lapped up with brood), land crabs, and bits of snail shell occurred in about a quarter of the scats. No other type of animal fragment occurred in more than 1 of the 16 scats I examined. I often saw coatis eating soft-bodied animals excavated from rotting wood. These were probably beetle larvae. I also regularly saw coatis eating caterpillars, orthopterans, snails, and ant brood. I rarely saw them eat vertebrates, such as caecilians, frogs, lizards, and small rodents. It may be safely assumed that vertebrates contribute only a small amount to the diet.

Coatis eat a wide variety of fruits (Table 2). Five species (*Scheelea zonensis*, *Dipteryx panamensis*, *Spondias mombin*, *Tetragastris panamensis*, and *Ficus insipida*) were relatively common in my study area and produced fruits that were highly palatable to coatis. The pattern of availability of fruits of these species is described below. *Astrocaryum standleyanum* was both common and palatable, but most of its fruits were inaccessible to coatis because they could not climb its densely spined trunk. The few fruits usually present on the ground under an *Astrocaryum* tree were not attractive enough to divert an entire band's attention from foraging for arthropods, although solitary males foraged under *Astrocaryum* trees fairly regularly, and bands would stop to feed under them when foraging *Cebus* monkeys knocked down larger numbers of fruits. *Cecropia*, *Brosimum*, and *Guapira* fruits were attractive to coatis, but fruit-bearing individuals of these species were uncommon in my study area. Kaufmann's (1962) coatis ate much more *Cecropia* than mine, probably because there were more mature *Cecropia* trees in his study area, which was mostly in the "young forest," than in mine, which contained more "old forest" (Foster, 1973). The other species in Table 2 produced small crops of fruit (*Coccoloba*, *Faramea*, *Randia*, *Maguira*), or produced fruits that were unattractive to coatis (*Quararibea*), or were rare in the study area (the remainder):

Faramea produced a large crop of fruit in November and December 1977, while I was away from Barro Colorado, and coatis were frequently observed eating it then (Wm. Glanz, pers. comm.).

Periodicity in the Availability of Food Resources

Animals The animal portion of the coati diet consitutes a broad cross section of the arthropod litter fauna. The abundance of the litter fauna undergoes an annual cycle associated with the abundance and suitability of the litter layer on the forest floor (Willis, 1976; Levings and Windsor, this volume). Litter accumulates during the dry season, since the dry weather increases leaffall and slows decomposition, and peaks at the beginning of the wet season. Increased rainfall then moistens the litter and decomposer organisms proliferate. The litter layer is effectively saturated with moisture, and local differences in litter fauna are minimized as well. Leaffall decreases sharply with the beginning of the wet season and the litter layer gradually thins. The abundance of litter fauna decreases gradually with the thinning of the litter layer and then falls off sharply at the onset of the dry season because of desiccation. The litter fauna also becomes less evenly distributed during the dry season as local differences in moisture, due to differences in drainage and exposure, become more pronounced.

The magnitude of the cycle of abundance of litter fauna varies markedly from year to year, depending on variations in the pattern of rainfall (Levings and Windsor, this volume). Densities of arthropods in the litter were substantially lower in the late wet season in 1975 and in the dry season in 1976 than they were in the corresponding seasons in 1976 and 1977. In terms of litter fauna availability, 1977 appeared to be an even better year than 1976, judging from the early and late wet seasons.

Fruits Five species of trees, *Scheelea zonensis*, *Dipteryx panamensis*, *Spondias mombin*, *Ficus insipida*, and *Tetragastris panamensis*, had important effects on the behavior of the coati bands I observed. These species represent two different fruiting strategies.

Scheelea is a large common palm that bears fruit over a long period, about 4 months, coinciding with the early wet season. Each tree bears relatively few fruits: approximately 200 (Wm. Glanz, pers. comm.). Eleven of 31 trees bore fruit annually; the others bore fruit less often (see also Croat, 1978). *Scheelea* occurs at a high density; there were 5.6 fruit-bearing individuals per hectare in the 5.2-ha. area I censused. The long fruiting period, low number of fruits per individual,

Table 2. Fruits eaten by coatis

Species	Dates
Scheelea zonensis	28 Aug. 1975–7 Sept. 1975; 6 June 1976–23 Sept. 1976; 5 May 1977–19 Sept. 1977; 28 Apr. 1978–11 July 1978
Astrocaryum standleyanum	17 July 1977; 19 June 1978
Dipteryx panamensis	8 Jan. 1977–17 Feb. 1977; 12 Jan. 1978–3 Mar. 1978
Spondias mombin	3 Sept. 1975–5 Sept. 1975; 31 July 1977–12 Sept. 1977
Tetragastris panamensis	3 Apr. 1978–2 June 1978
Ficus insipida	3 July 1976–5 July 1976; 29 July 1976–2 Aug. 1976; 1 Oct. 1976–4 Oct. 1976; 29 June 1977; 10 July 1977; 11 July 1977; 25 Aug. 1977
Cecropia sp.	5 Apr. 1977; 3 May 1978–8 May 1978
Brosimum sp.	2 Sept. 1976; 17 Sept. 1976
Coccoloba parimensis	30 Sept. 1976; 9 Oct. 1976; 14 July 1977–18 July 1977
Faramea sp.	30 Nov. 1976; 1 Dec. 1976; 23 Dec. 1976
Hirtella triandra	11 June 1977
Guapira standleyanum	23 May 1977–27 May 1977
Quararibea sp.	18 Aug. 1976
Maguira costaricensis	26 June 1976
Randia armata	16 June 1977; 11 July 1977
Lindackeria laurina	26 Feb. 1978
Chrysophyllum sp.	17 Mar. 1978
Anthurium clavigenum	5 July 1976

Other observers report coatis eating the following additional species of fruits in the forest on Barro Colorado: *Annona acuminata, Anacardium excelsum, Mangifera indica, Cupania fulvida, Apeiba aspera, Miconia argentea, Coussarea impetiolaris, Calocarpum mammosum*, (Kaufmann, 1962); *Ficus yoponensis, Protium tenuifolium, Cupania latifolia, Eugenia coloradensis, Calophyllum longifolium*, (Wm. Glanz, pers. comm.); *Tetrathylacium johansenii* (R. Foster, pers. comm.).

and high density of fruit-bearing individuals together mean that available fruits are relatively evenly distributed across a coati band's home range.

In the other four species, *Dipteryx*, *Spondias*, *Ficus*, and *Tetragastris*, each individual produces enormous quantities of fruits. Fruit-bearing individuals are relatively rare. Average densities in my 96-ha. study area were: *Dipteryx* (0.2/ha.), *Spondias* (0.1/ha.), *Ficus* (0.1/ha.), and *Tetragastris* (0.1/ha.). These species generally bear fruit during a relatively restricted period, usually

Table 3. Weeks of maximum fruit availability for individual trees ($\overline{X} \pm SD$)

Species	1974	1975	1976	1977	1978	Overall
Spondias	3.0 ± 3.6	1.0 ± 1.5	2.0 ± 2.4	2.8 ± 3.1	2.3 ± 2.7	2.1 ± 2.5
Dipteryx	n.a.	n.a.	1.5 ± 2.1	0.9 ± 1.3	3.6 ± 6.0	2.0 ± 3.4
Tetragastris	n.a.	0.7 ± 1.0	0	0	3.0 ± 5.0	0.9 ± 2.2

From unpublished Environmental Studies Project data, courtesy of Smithsonian Tropical Research Institute.

Table 4. Seasonal weights and numbers per band of coatis

Age-class	June–July	Aug.–Sept.	Jan.–Apr.
Juvenile			
Number ($\overline{X} \pm SD$)	5.6 ± 3.8	3.4 ± 2.7	2.3 ± 1.4
Weight (kg ± SD)	0.5[1]	1.2 ± 0.2	1.7 ± 0.4
Subadult			
Number ($\overline{X} \pm SD$)	1.8 ± 1.6	1.6 ± 1.1	1.3 ± 0.8
Weight (kg ± SD)	2.0[2]	2.5 ± 0.3	3.4[2]
Adult			
Number ($\overline{X} \pm SD$)	4.1 ± 1.0	3.8 ± 1.1	3.5 ± 1.0
Weight (kg ± SD)	3.3 ± 0.4	3.6 ± 0.4	3.6 ± 0.3
Total			
Number	11.5	8.8	7.1
Weight	19.7	21.4	20.9

[1] from Kaufman (1962)
[2] estimated by interpolation

somewhat less than 2 months for the population. Individual trees have fruit available for shorter periods (Table 3). *Ficus* is an exception because although individuals bear ripe fruit for only about a week, the population is not synchronized and *Ficus* fruits are available in most months (Foster, 1973; Morrison, 1978). In these species, fruit crops vary greatly from year to year (Croat, 1978; Foster, this volume). *Spondias* was a very important source of fruits for coatis in 1975 and again in 1977, but was not used in 1976.

Tetragastris was used heavily in 1978, but not at all in 1977. *Dipteryx* appears to be a more reliable source. It was an important source of fruit for coatis in both 1977 and 1978. Individual trees, however, were less reliable. Only 2 of 14 *Dipteryx* trees used in 1977 produced enough fruit in 1978 to attract coatis to them. The high variability in fruit production by these species is reflected in the high standard deviations in Table 3. The large number of fruits on individuals of these species, their relative rarity, the short period during which they produce fruits, and their unreliability together produce a highly clumped and unpredictable distribution of available fruits.

Seasonal Changes in Foraging Behavior and Home Range Utilization

Although the numbers of individuals in coati bands change through the year, due to recruitment and mortality, the average total biomass of bands changes little with the seasons because growth roughly compensates mortality (Table 4). Seasonal changes in foraging behavior thus reflect not gross changes in food requirements so much as changes in the abundance and distribution of food and in the foraging ability of young coatis.

Juveniles change in two important ways during the year, as far as foraging ability is concerned: they learn and they grow. As juveniles gain experience in foraging, their efficiency at finding and excavating food items increases. Throughout the year, juveniles approach adults that are excavating or eating animals more often than would be expected on the basis of the overall rate of approaches of juveniles to adults and the amount of time adults spend excavating and eating animal foods: 25% of juvenile approaches to adult females occur during these behavioral states, which constitute only 11% of an adult female's time budget ($G = 27.8$, d.f. $= 1$, $p < 0.005$).

Although adults usually threaten subadults and other adults that approach them while they are excavating or eating, they tolerate the approach of juveniles, and juveniles can often be seen sniffing the muzzles of adults that are eating. Although virtually no food sharing occurs in coati bands, this tendency to approach and smell the food items that adults capture probably enhances the rate at which juveniles learn about animal food characteristics.

Together with the accumulated benefits of trial-and-error learning, the effects of these learning opportunities can be seen by comparing the foraging performance of juveniles and adults in the wet and dry seasons (Table 5). The rate at which both age-classes attempt to excavate animal prey declines from the wet to the dry season, presumably as a result of decreased availability of suitable prey. The rate at which adults capture prey undergoes a commensurate decline indicating that the proportion of predation attempts that are successful changes little for adults over the year. On the other hand, the rate at which juveniles capture prey items remains constant indicating an increase in the proportionate success of predation

Table 5. Seasonal foraging success of adults and juveniles

Age class and season	Attempt rate (attempts/ 10 min ± SD)	Capture rate (items/ 10 min ± SD)	Success proportion
Juvenile			
Wet	7.4 ± 5.3[1]	2.1 ± 1.9[2]	0.28
Dry	2.6 ± 4.8[1]	2.1 ± 1.9[2]	0.79
Adult female			
Wet	5.7 ± 4.4[3]	2.9 ± 2.3[4]	0.51
Dry	2.2 ± 3.8[3]	1.2 ± 1.2[4]	0.55
Solitary adult female			
Dry	2.6 ± 4.4	1.7 ± 1.3	0.65

[1] $t = 3.1$, d.f. $= 58$, $p < .01$
[2] $t = 0.001$, d.f. $= 37$, n.s.
[3] $t = 4.5$, d.f. $= 108$, $p < .001$
[4] $t = 3.1$, d.f. $= 60$, $p < .01$

attempts for juveniles. Juvenile predation success in the dry season actually exceeds that for adults, probably because juveniles interrupt predation attempts for vigilance less frequently than adults (Russell, 1979). When adults become solitary, during the nesting season, their predation success rises.

From the time they begin foraging with bands to the time bands break up in the following dry season, juveniles roughly triple in size. As juveniles grow longer limbs and develop larger muscles, their mobility increases. They can both travel more rapidly and sustain longer journeys without interruption. Search area also increases with size. Juveniles forage farther from their neighbors after the first 2 months with their band (mean = 1.6 m) than during the first 2 months (mean = 1.3 m, $t = 2.05$, d.f. $= 30$, $p < 0.05$). Increased size also makes juveniles less vulnerable to predators. Juveniles become bolder, spending 34% of their time on the periphery of the group after the first 2 months, as compared with 21% during the first two months ($G = 5.34$, d.f. $= 1$, $p < 0.05$). The distances to nearest neighbor during foraging and the proportion of time spent on the peripheries of bands do not change significantly for the older age classes over the same period.

Because of the changes in juvenile foraging behavior associated with growth, the overall proportion of

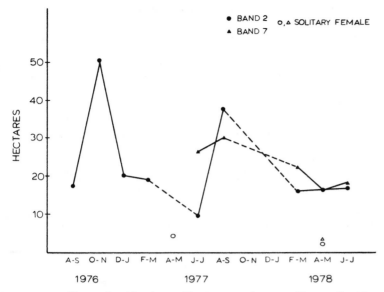

Figure 2.   Numbers of hectare quadrats used by coati bands in 2-month periods.

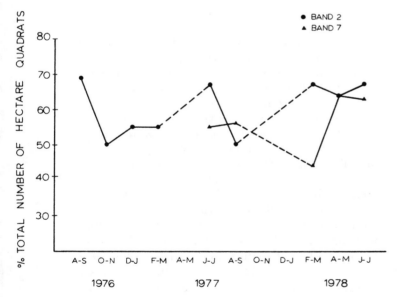

Figure 3.   Percentage of total number of hectare quadrats required to account for 75% of the activity of coati bands in 2-month intervals. High values indicate even usage of the home range, low values indicate that the utilization is clumped. In February–March, 1978, band 2 used two *Tetragastris* trees which were beyond the normal boundaries of its home range. They remained at either tree for several hours, but usually returned to their normal home range before nightfall. Sampling during movements to and from these trees has made this band's utilization of its home range appear more even than it would if the distribution of eating was plotted.

individuals on the periphery of bands and the overall average distance between foraging neighbors both increase, and thus the diameter of the entire band increases. Because of the increased spacing, the band can effectively search a larger cross-sectional area per unit of path length.

Furthermore, the increased mobility of juveniles allows bands to move more rapidly, increasing the path length searched per unit time. As a result, the swept area (diameter of cross-sectional area times path length) per unit time increases throughout the year. Over the same period, experience improves the foraging ability of juveniles, and consequently improves the average foraging ability of the band. In combination these effects mean that the overall foraging efficiency of the band increases throughout the year. If food distribution and density did not vary seasonally, we would expect the rate of food intake to increase substantially through the year.

The distribution and density of food items does not remain constant throughout the year, however. Early in the wet season the litter fauna is most abundant and most evenly distributed. Because *Scheelea* fruits are relatively evenly distributed as well, the total available food crop in the early wet season is dense and evenly distributed.

Later in the wet season, declining abundance of litter fauna and the termination of fruiting by *Scheelea* combine to produce a general decline in the density of available food. This decline is offset, in part and to varying extent, by the *Spondias* fruit crop. In years in which *Spondias* produces a substantial fruit crop, it modifies the distribution of available foods because its fruits are clumped. The distribution of animal foods remains fairly even, however, so that late wet-season foods are fairly evenly distributed, but with lower density.

With the arrival of the dry season, both the density and the distribution of food items change more remarkably. The litter fauna declines in abundance and becomes more patchily distributed. At the same time highly clumped crops of fruits become a more important part of the diet. On the whole, in the dry-season food is clumped and sparse. The degree of sparseness varies from year to year with the length of the dry season and the size of the fruit crops.

The effects of these seasonal changes in food distribution and abundance are manifest in seasonal changes in the pattern of home-range utilization. Early in the wet season the home range a band uses is relatively small (Figure 2 and Figure 4, parts f and k), and they use this range relatively evenly (Figure 3 and Figure 4, parts f and k). As the wet season progresses bands exploit larger areas, and their usage becomes less even (Figures 2, 3, and 4, parts a, g, and b). When

420

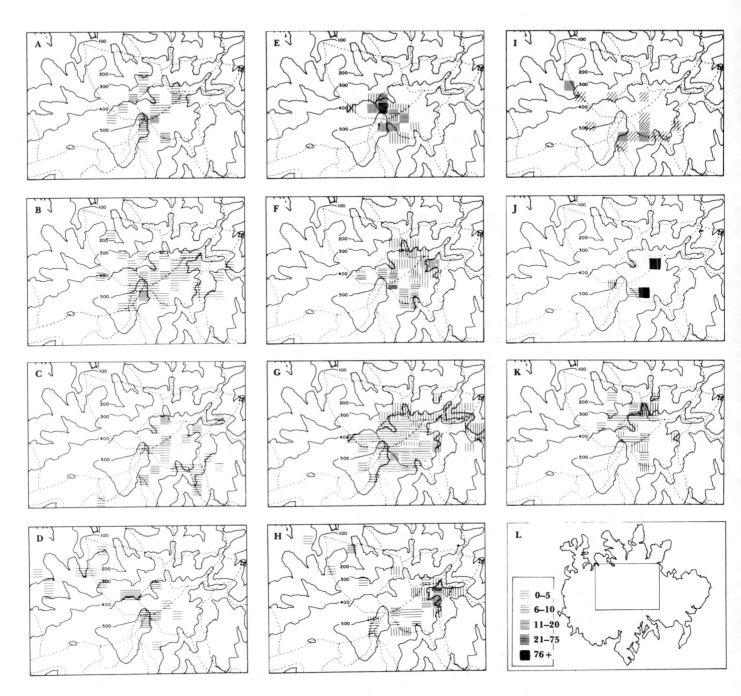

Figure 4. Home ranges of two habituated coati bands. Horizontal bars represent band 2, vertical bars band 7. Band 7 originated in May 1977 (see Figure 5). Parenthetical numbers indicate the percentage of the total number of hectares the map is estimated to represent, according to the truncated log-normal distribution (see Methods section of the text). Hectares not appearing in the maps were used infrequently. A. Aug.–Sept. 1976 (85%). B. Oct.–Nov. 1976 (56%). C. Dec. 1976–Jan. 1977 (93%). D. Feb.–Mar. 1977 (80%). E. Apr.–May 1977 (horizontal—a single nesting female in band 2, 100%; vertical—combined range of two communally nesting females in band 7, 46%). F. June–July 1977 (band 2—86%, band 7—72%). G. Aug.–Sept. 1977 (band 2—66%, band 7—82%). H. Feb.–Mar. 1978 (band 2—90%, band 7—55%). I. Apr.–May 1978 (range of combined group of immatures from bands 2 and 7—100%). J. Apr.–May 1978 (ranges of two nesting females; vertical bars and upper black square, band 7—100%; horizontal bars and lower black square, band 2—100%). K. June–July 1978 (band 2—81%, band 7—78%). L. Outline of Barro Colorado Island, with area covered by detailed maps indicated.

the dry season arrives, usage becomes even more clumped (Figure 3 and Figure 4, parts c, d, and h). The actual number of hectares used declines because more time is spent in each (Figure 2). The areas of intense usage are not contiguous with each other, however, and bands must move long distances from time to time even though the area exploited is relatively small.

During the nesting season home-range size drops to its lowest level. In this season an adult female forages alone, near the nest, for a small fraction of each day (Figure 2 and Figure 4, parts e and j). Most of each day is spent on the nest. The immature band members remain together in a group and may even unite with another group of immatures. These groups use a relatively small home range, which they exploit with an intermediate degree of evenness (Figures 2, 3, and 4, part i). My data regarding the home-range utilization of immatures during this period may be atypical, as the immature members of bands 2 and 7 merged into a single unit of seven to nine individuals during much of the nesting season in 1978. In 1977 band 2's two juveniles appeared to forage in a small area, but I do not have enough data concerning them to make any quantitative statement regarding their habits.

Patterns of Population Change within and among Years

Rates of recruitment are affected by three factors: reproduction, migration, and mortality. Variations in recruitment among years will produce changes in the size and age structure of the population.

Reproduction An individual female's schedule of reproduction has two components: seasonality in parturition and age at first breeding. Parturition is strictly seasonal on Barro Colorado, occurring in early May. Age at first breeding varies from nearly 2 to nearly 4 years. During my study, once a female began reproducing, she continued to bear young in each successive year until she died or reached postreproductive age. Two females in my study population and one in Kaufmann's (1962) appeared to be postreproductive. The postreproductive animals I observed continued to participate in their bands in an apparently normal manner. The one Kaufmann observed left its group and became dependent on food in the laboratory clearing. I have no detailed data on the behavior of postreproductive animals, as they did not belong to bands that I had habituated thoroughly. Their teeth

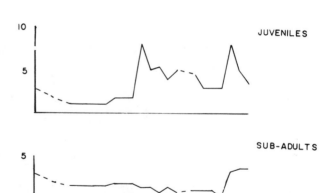

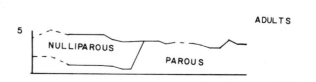

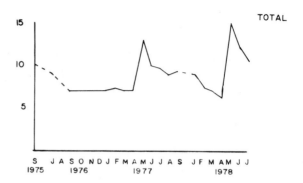

Figure 5. Variations in average size of bands and component age classes over the course of the study.

Table 6. Yearly parity in 2- and 3-year-old females

Age	Parity	1975	1976	1977	1978
2	Nulliparous	5	6	0	*
2	Parous	1[1]	2[1]	6[1]	*
3	Nulliparous	*	4	0	0
3	Parous	*	2[2]	6[2]	2[2]

[1] 1975, 1976 vs. 1977, $G = 15.0$, d.f. $= 1$, $p < .01$

[2] 1976 vs. 1977, 1978, $G = 4.9$, d.f. $= 1$, $p < 0.5$

* no individuals in this age class in this year.

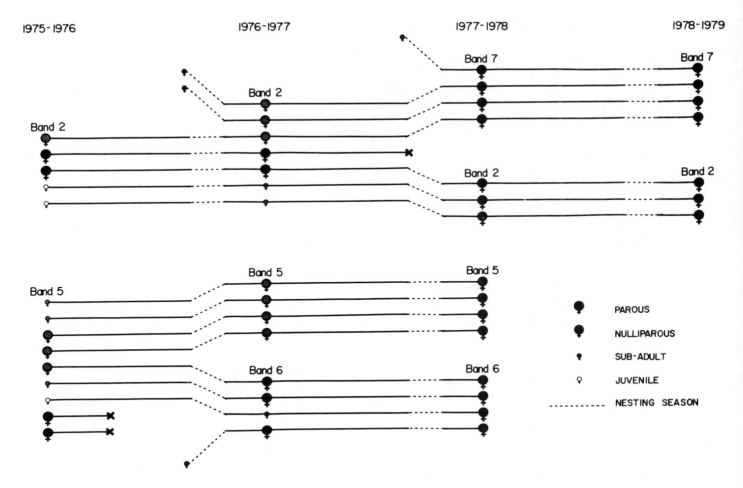

Figure 6. Histories of association among females in four habituated bands. Only females that were adult at some point during the study are shown.

were more extremely worn than others I examined. Extrapolating from rates of tooth wear in known-age individuals I would judge them to have been at the very least 7 years old. Interestingly, I never caught males with teeth this extremely worn. This may reflect a real sex difference in survival to older ages or may simply be a result of the small numbers of old individuals that I captured.

The proportion of adult females that had never bred varied dramatically from year to year (Figure 5, Table 6). In 1975 and 1976 half or more of the adult females were nulliparous (had never bred), while in 1977 and 1978 all had bred. Most nonbreeding females were 2-year-olds (11 of 15, including captures from other bands), although a few females delayed reproduction past their third year as well. The percentage of 2-year-old females that reproduced in 1975 (17%) and 1976 (25%) was significantly lower than in 1977 (100%). There were no 2-year-old females in my bands in 1978. The percentage of 3-year-olds that reproduced in 1976 (33%) was significantly lower than in 1977 and 1978. There were no 3-year-olds in my bands in 1975.

The decision to reproduce appears to depend on nutrition. Nulliparous females, which forgo the costs of producing and nursing a litter, weigh 14% more (mean = 4.16 kg ± $S\,D$. 0.24) than parous females (females which had bred at least once) (3.57 ± 0.36 kg, t = 4.30, d.f. = 21, p < 0.001). The only 3-year-old nullipara I captured weighed 4.6 kg, well over the average (4.12 ± 0.18; t = 2.87, d.f. = 6, p < 0.05) for 2-year-old nulliparae. Probably as a consequence, nulliparous females also appear to suffer a lower incidence of mortality per year (1 in 11 coati-years) than parous females (4 in 21 coati-years), although the difference is not statistically significant and other factors, such as the age distribution of nulliparous as compared with parous females, would also contribute to

Table 7. Composition of coati bands

Year/month	Band 2 J	Band 2 S	Band 2 A	Band 5 J	Band 5 S	Band 5 A	Band 6 J	Band 6 S	Band 6 A	Band 7 J	Band 7 S	Band 7 A	Band 8 J	Band 8 S	Band 8 A	Mean J	Mean S	Mean A	Total
1975																			
Sept	5	2	3	1	4	5	—	—	—	—	—	—	—	—	—	3.0	3.0	4.0	10.0
1976																			
July	2	2	5	—	—	—	—	—	—	—	—	—	—	—	—	2.0	2.0	5.0	9.0
Aug.	—	—	—	—	—	—	—	—	—	—	—	—	—	—	—	—	—	—	—
Sept.	2	2	5	0	1	4	—	—	—	—	—	—	—	—	—	1.0	1.5	4.5	7.0
Oct.	2	2	5	0	1	4	—	—	—	—	—	—	—	—	—	1.0	1.5	4.5	7.0
Nov.	2	2	5	0	1	4	—	—	—	—	—	—	—	—	—	1.0	1.5	4.5	7.0
Dec.	2	2	5	0	1	4	—	—	—	—	—	—	—	—	—	1.0	1.5	4.5	7.0
1977																			
Jan.	2	2	5	0	1	4	—	—	—	—	—	—	—	—	—	1.0	1.5	4.5	7.0
Feb.	2	2	5	0	1	4	3	2	3	—	—	—	—	—	—	1.7	1.7	4.0	7.3
Mar.	2	2	4	0	1	4	3	2	3	—	—	—	—	—	—	1.7	1.7	3.7	7.0
Apr.	2	2	4	0	1	4	3	2	3	—	—	—	—	—	—	1.7	1.7	3.7	7.0
May	5	2	3	14	0	4	3	3	4	10	0	4	—	—	—	8.0	1.3	3.8	13.0
June	5	2	3	6	0	4	3	3	4	6	0	4	—	—	—	5.0	1.3	3.8	10.0
July	4	2	3	6	0	4	—	—	—	6	0	4	—	—	—	5.3	0.7	3.8	9.7
Aug.	4	2	3	5	0	4	1	3	3	6	0	4	—	—	—	4.0	1.3	3.5	8.8
Sept.	4	2	3	5	0	4	—	—	—	6	0	4	—	—	—	5.0	0.7	3.7	9.3
1978																			
Jan.	4	2	3	—	—	—	—	—	—	5	0	4	—	—	—	4.5	1.0	3.5	9.0
Feb.	4	2	3	—	—	—	—	—	—	3	0	4	2	1	3	3.0	1.0	3.3	7.3
Mar.	4	2	3	—	—	—	—	—	—	3	0	4	2	1	2	3.0	1.0	3.0	7.0
Apr.	4	0	3	—	—	—	—	—	—	3	0	4	2	1	2	3.0	0.3	3.0	6.3
May	—	—	—	—	—	—	—	—	—	8	3	4	—	—	—	8.0	3.0	4.0	15.0
June	3	4	3	—	—	—	—	—	—	7	3	4	—	—	—	5.0	3.5	3.5	12.0
July	3	4	3	—	—	—	—	—	—	4	3	4	—	—	—	3.5	3.5	3.5	10.5

J = Juveniles.   S = Subadults.   A = Adults.

the difference.

Migration   Migration probably has little net effect on the coati population on Barro Colorado. Although it is not inconceivable that individual coatis could move to or from the island, one would expect that they would only do so rarely and under substantial stress. Migration within the Barro Colorado population does occur. Males routinely leave their natal bands at adulthood. Their movements thereafter have not been studied, although my trapping records indicate that considerable movement occurs. There may be stationary and mobile parts of the adult male population. Some females change groups during adulthood. All of the instances of adult female migration that I observed (Figure 6) involved nulliparous or newly parous females joining or separating from bands at the time of reaggregation.

The process of breakage and formation of social bonds among adult females is treated elsewhere (Russell, 1979). Females apparently adjust their social relationships in such a manner as to ensure reciprocity in aid-giving behavior and maintain band size within a narrow optimum range. The net effect of migration on population size is probably small. Figure 6 appears to emphasize migration into the study area. However, both of the original bands in the study split, resulting in a total of four bands. These four bands occupied a larger area than the original two, and my study area expanded as I moved with these familiar groups.

Mortality Most mortality in this population appears to be due to predation. I saw little evidence of starvation or disease during my study. However, the decline in food availability in the dry season may be indirectly responsible for some mortality by forcing animals to take greater risks in the search for food.

Juveniles undergo heavy mortality early in life (Figure 5, Table 7). Over 90% (20 of 22) of the disappearances of individual juveniles I recorded occurred between May and August. This figure underestimates early juvenile losses because bands are difficult to census immediately after reaggregation in May and the earliest losses are not recorded. The small numbers of juveniles in bands that were not censused until later in the year also indicate heavy early losses. Incomplete counts of unhabituated bands also evidenced large numbers of juveniles in the early wet season and small numbers later. During the early wet season, juveniles are extremely vulnerable to predation because of their small size. When juveniles first begin foraging with bands they weigh only about 500 g (Kaufmann, 1962) and have not achieved full locomotory competence (Figure 7).

During the late wet season, mortality is apparently very moderate for all age classes. I recorded no disappearances during this period, and average band-size changed little as well.

Some additional mortality occurs during the dry season. The magnitude of these losses is difficult to estimate because of the small numbers of individuals in each age class at the beginning of the dry season. Two juvenile disappearances occurred in January, two subadult disappearances occurred in March (one of these may actually have been in early April) and two adult disappearances occurred in February. The two subadult disappearances were the only losses of subadults I recorded. The two adult disappearances in February are the only adult disappearances that I am confident were losses due to mortality (the one disappearance in July may have been a late emigration).

A hypothesis of dry-season mortality finds some confirmation in the overall census records as well. Average numbers of subadults and adults were 25% and 9% lower, respectively, in April than in February, although no such difference appears in the records of numbers of juveniles (I have used February, instead of December or January, as a starting point here because of the larger numbers of records available). Dry-season mortality may reflect declining food availability, as suggested above, and, for subadults, the withdrawal of adult protection. Without the adults to surround them, bands of immatures do not forage with the elliptical formation that is typical of bands during the rest of the year. Rather, they tend to move as a rank, a spatial organization that is efficient for foraging (S. A. Altmann, 1974), but not for defense (Treisman, 1975). Attacks by adult male coatis on immatures increase markedly during this period. These attacks are probably responsible for some mortality and at the same time reflect the increased vulnerability of the immatures to predators in general. Direct observation of predation attempts is generally very difficult. I could observe predation attempts by male coatis because several in the study area were habituated. Russell (1979) describes mechanisms by which adult males avoid eating their own offspring.

Age Structure

As a result of the differences among years in reproduction by young adult females, and to a lesser extent migration and mortality, the age profile of the female component of the population changed during the study (Figure 8). In 1975 the adult females were all either 2 years old or 4 or more years old. We can infer that a general reproductive failure, similar to the one that occurred in 1976 (see below), had occurred in 1972. Although only one 2-year-old reproduced in 1975, the large number of older females provided a large number of juveniles. The intermediate size of the subadult component suggests that reproduction had been at roughly replacement level in the preceding year. In 1976 the high incidence of nulliparity in 2- and 3-year-olds, combined with some mortality of older females, resulted in a very small number of juveniles. Parity, and therefore production of juveniles, was high in the following year, 1977, but no subadult females survived from the small juvenile cohort of the preceding year. At the end of the study, in 1978, parity was again high. All age classes except 2-year-olds are well represented therefore. It is easy to see how an age distribution like that in 1978 could lead to one like that at the beginning of the study. Interestingly, the major differences in age structure among years can be attributed to changes in the age at first reproduction. In comparison, the effect of adult mortality was relatively minor.

Population Size and Density

A quantitative estimate of the density of the coati population is difficult to make, even if we restrict our attention to band members. The home ranges of bands overlap extensively (see Figure 4, parts e–k). My data concerning range overlap do not include all bands

Figure 7. A. Juvenile immediately after descent from the nest. Note its relatively large head and small body and limbs. The object it is climbing over is the base of a *Scheelea* palm leaf. B. Appearance of a juvenile in September. Note resemblance to adult features and proportions. The adult behind it is standing on a rotten *Scheelea* leaf base, for scale comparison.

RUSSELL

that frequented the study area and are probably not typical of overlap between neighboring bands because of the special relations between the bands concerned. These bands (2 and 7) were the products of a band fission (see Figure 6) and maintained an unusually amicable relationship for neighbors, frequently foraging as a mixed group in areas of range overlap.

If we consider only the numbers of adult band members in the bands under observation, we can see evidence for an increase in population size over the course of the study. In 1975–76 there were 8 adults in the two bands. By 1976–77 there were 12 adults in three bands. Most of the difference between the years was due to immigration (3 individuals). Internal recruitment (3 individuals) barely exceeded mortality (2). By 1977–78 the number of adults had increased to 15, the number of bands to four. Only one death occurred, which was outbalanced by internal recruitment (3 individuals) and one case of immigration. Although the final four bands occupied a larger area than the original two, the areal increase was probably not commensurate with the numerical increase because the relations within the two pairs of bands that were derived from the two original bands were unusually friendly and their home ranges overlapped to an unusual degree. Thus, there probably was a moderate increase in population density in the study area as well.

DISCUSSION

The degree of seasonality in tropical forest ecosystems and its effects on the organisms that live in them have been generally underestimated. Once we recognize the degree to which food resources vary during the year, it is not hard to understand why many tropical mammals breed seasonally. Monoestrous animals with high juvenile mortality must time their reproductive effort within any year so as to maximize survivorship through the first year of life. The youngest age class is generally the least buffered against environmental stress. Coatis time their reproductive effort so that juveniles begin foraging with the bands at the beginning of a long-lasting peak in availability of animal foods. This timing affords the juveniles the longest possible period in which to gain foraging experience before the marked decline in abundance of animal foods in the dry season. The experience juveniles gain during the wet season, amplified by numerous opportunities to learn the scent of appropriate foods from successful older animals, permits them to maintain a nearly constant level of intake of animal foods despite the decline in availability that comes with the

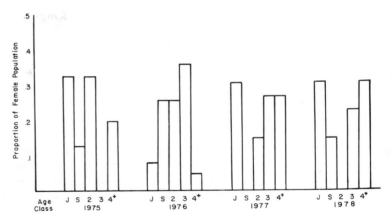

Figure 8. Variation in age composition of the female component of the coati population, 1975–78. Juveniles that died within 2 months of reaggregation have been excluded. Unsexed juveniles, which were few, were counted as half female.

dry season. The rate of intake of animal foods by adults, in contrast, declines in the dry season.

The season of high availability of animal foods coincides with an important fruit crop provided by the palm *Scheelea zonensis*. The relatively even dispersion of this fruit nicely complements the even dispersion of animal foods. During the early wet season, bands move slowly and more or less constantly throughout the day, foraging for animals in the litter layer. They interrupt litter foraging to eat *Scheelea* fruits for a half hour or so when they encounter a fruiting tree, and then return to litter foraging. In this manner, bands can find adequate food in relatively small home ranges.

As the wet season progresses, bands exploit larger and larger home ranges. This requires longer or more rapid movement and increased foraging efficiency. The growth and early foraging experience of juveniles facilitate this adaptation to declining food availability by increasing the general foraging efficiency, the rate of movement, and the foraging diameters of bands, thereby reducing intragroup competition. In some years the increase in home-range size in the wet season is moderated somewhat by the availability of crops of the fruit of *Spondias mombin* in the middle of the wet season. This is a short-lived respite, however, and the size of home ranges continues to increase through the wet season.

With the onset of the dry season the availability of animal foods declines still further. At this time coatis rely much more heavily on fruits than in the wet season. The principal fruits available during the dry season, *Dipteryx* and *Tetragastris*, are disparennially fruiting species, that is, species whose fruit crops vary greatly from year to year. Individual trees of these species produce so much fruit that a band may restrict its foraging to one or two trees for a period of several days, with occasional excursions on the ground to forage for animals. As a result, the home range a band uses declines in area, but is broken up into a number of noncontiguous areas of intense utilization. Long moves between these areas are often required.

There are several problems inherent in the exploitation of these disparennially fruiting species which are not posed by the evenly dispersed palms (*Scheelea* and *Astrocaryum*). Bands must undertake long "treks," during which all band members move constantly and do not forage for animals, much more often when they are using disparennially fruiting species than at other times. These treks would be more difficult earlier in the year when juveniles are relatively small and weak. Furthermore, such fruit crops attract large numbers of competitors, some of which, such as tayras (*Eira barbara*) and adult male coatis, occasionally prey on juveniles. A third limitation to the exploitation of disparennially fruiting species is their unreliability. Many of these species produce substantial crops only in alternate years or at even longer intervals. Food sources with this characteristic, alternating "boom" and "bust" years, would clearly be unsuitable for getting an annually reproducing consumer through a crucial stage of its life cycle each year (Janzen, 1971).

The social organization of coatis is well suited for exploitation of disparennially fruiting species. Young individuals benefit from the experience of older group members, who may have been through one or several of the boom-bust cycles, in finding fruiting trees. The occurrence of females past reproductive age in bands may reflect the value of accrued knowledge about the location of intermittently fruiting trees. Further, the communal maternal care in coati bands permits individual adults to leave the group periodically without jeopardizing the safety of their offspring. These independently moving adults must be more effective scouts of rich food sources than are entire bands or single adults accompanied by immature offspring. The long treks outside the normal home range to reach fruiting trees, also noted by Kaufmann (1962), give an observer the strong impression that at least one member of the band knows the location of a rich source of food and induces the rest of the band to move there directly. These adaptations, however, do not outweigh the disadvantages of disparennially fruiting species for timing seasonal reproduction.

The most important feature of the wet season for the timing of reproduction by coatis is the increased availability of animal foods. The coincident availability of a species of fruit with a dispersion pattern similar to that of the animals coatis eat is perhaps fortuitous. The intermittent availability of fruit during the dry season may also be fortuitous. Nonetheless, it may be advantageous to disparennially fruiting species to bear fruit when facultative frugivores are under food stress, because at these times they will be able to attract dispersal agents from greater distances, which may provide more effective dispersal of their seeds.

The coati's adaptation to seasonal fluctuations in food supply is in some ways similar to those of other tropical mammals. Rudran (1973), in a study of langur (*Presbytis senex*) reproduction in Sri Lanka, showed how one subspecies in an area with a pronounced dry season had a seasonal birth peak timed such that most juveniles began taking solid foods at the beginning of the period of greatest food availability. In contrast, a subspecies in a nonseasonal habitat had no distinct birth peak. The majority of seasonally breeding mammal species in Panama have their birth peak near the beginning of the wet season (Fleming, 1973). However, coatis are distinguished from most seasonally breeding tropical mammals by the high degree of synchrony in breeding within and among social groups. The birth peaks described by Rudran (1973) and Fleming (1973) are probabilistic and extend over several months. All coatis on Barro Colorado, in striking contrast, breed within a period of less than 1 month. Seasonality in food resources cannot explain this synchrony. Are there special features of coati social organization that might provide an explanation?

Coatis are unusual for gregarious mammals because they have a very rapid transition between a period of total dependence of juveniles on their mothers for food and the following period in which juveniles depend on their own foraging for nutrition. During the nesting period juveniles locomote only in play. Once nesting is over they are rapidly called upon to travel under their own power. Adults rarely carry juveniles after the nesting season, and then only to help them negotiate a particularly difficult arboreal pathway. Even this kind of carrying stops after the juveniles have been out of the nest for a week or so. Bands forage actively and are on the move for about 90% of the day when this transition occurs. Exceptionally young juveniles would be slower than other juveniles and would probably tend to be left behind the band, where they would be exposed to predators.

An unusual incident helps to illustrate this point. In September 1977 one of the young juveniles in band 7 suffered debilitation from a bot-fly wound. Juveniles usually recover quickly from bot-fly wounds with the aid of much grooming by all band members, but in this case the damage was too severe and the juvenile became weaker and weaker and gradually spent more time behind the band. His mother would sometimes remain with him briefly, then usually encourage him to catch up by uttering the contact vocalization and walking toward the band. She never remained with him for more than a few seconds. None of the other adults helped him and the band moved on whether or not he attempted to follow. Within a week the juvenile disappeared. Although the unusual slowness of the juvenile came about through parasitism, we can see how selection against late breeders might operate.

There is also selection against breeding too early. A mother whose offspring required solid foods before those of the other adults in her band would be hard put to defend them by herself while they foraged. Together, these two sources of selection lead to convergence in the time of breeding within bands.

Selection for synchrony among bands may derive from another distinctive feature of coati social organization. The social bonds among adult females that provide stability to coati bands can be formed and broken several times during adulthood. Individual adult females adjust their social relationships to ensure reciprocity in aiding behaviors and to maintain band sizes within rather narrow limits (Russell, 1979). Social bonds among adult females are weakened each year during the nesting season and then either reestablished or changed at the time of band reaggregation. Since females may change social groups at this time, there is an advantage to being in synchrony with neighboring groups. This synchronization among groups may be facilitated through olfactory communication. Adult females perform perineal drags, apparently a scent-marking behavior, more frequently just prior to the mating season than at any other time. Because home ranges overlap broadly at this season, neighboring groups could communicate reproductive readiness to each other as well as to adult males in this manner.

Nongregarious mammals, like most of those that Fleming (1973) studied, are obviously not constrained by the requirement of synchronizing activity in a social group. Most primates, including Rudran's langurs (1973), carry their offspring while they are very young. Because a juvenile's ability to stay with the group is not critically dependent on its own mobility, selection for synchronous reproduction does not appear to have been important for primates in general.

Because of the ecological and social constraints that bring about synchronous seasonal reproduction, a female coati's choice is reduced to whether to reproduce in any particular year. Although physically mature at 2 years, many females defer reproduction until their third or fourth year. Animals that defer reproduction are at a selective disadvantage unless they derive some benefit in later fecundity or in early survivorship (Wiley, 1974, in press). What benefits might coati females derive by delaying reproduction?

In many gregarious vertebrates, young, subordinate adults defer reproduction in response to social inhibition (Mech, 1970; Rasa, 1973; Brown, 1978; Frame et al., 1979; Wiley, in press). In these species, reproduction is the prerogative of the dominant pair. Younger adults must forgo reproduction or leave the group. In such systems, an explanation for deferred reproduction must be sought in the long-term benefits of group membership. Such dominance relationships do not occur among adult coatis, however (Kaufmann, 1962; Russell, 1979). Any number of adult females in a band may breed. In some years in some bands, none does; in other cases, all do. Clearly, social inhibition cannot explain deferment of reproduction in coati bands.

Animals that are not inhibited socially from reproduction must still weigh the advantages of present reproduction against the probability that it will impair their future reproductive success. The resources demanded by reproduction, the resources the animal has available, and the animal's age will affect this evaluation. As is true for most female mammals, the resources demanded of coati females by reproduction are great. A successful female bears a litter that weighs 20–30% of her postpartum weight. She then nurses it for 3 to 5 weeks on a nest, until its surviving members together weigh 45–60% of her weight. Throughout the nesting period her foraging time is reduced to less than 2 hours a day. During the first week of nesting she may not leave the nest at all. The cost this demand on resources imposes can be seen in weight loss through the nesting season and in a persistent difference in weight between females that have reproduced in a given year and those that have not.

The ability to meet this demand will depend on the amount of resources the animal has available. Available resources include currently available forage and stored fat. Thus, the amount of resources available for reproduction depends on the density of prey organisms at and for several months before the point at which a reproductive decision is made. For coatis on Barro Colorado, this period is the late wet season of the preceding year and the dry season of the year in which reproduction occurs.

Although data are not available for 1974, the year in which reproduction by females in 1975 was determined, the correspondence between low availability of litter fauna in late 1975 and early 1976 and high incidence of nulliparity in 1976, followed by increased availability of litter fauna in late 1976 and early 1977 and in late 1977 associated with universal parity in 1977 and 1978, is unlikely to be mere coincidence. Young adult females in 1975 and 1976 apparently found that the expected costs of reproduction outweighed the benefits of early reproduction. In 1977 and 1978, when nutrition was good, expected costs of reproduction were lower and all young adults reproduced.

In iteroparous organisms, reproductive effort generally increases with age (Gadgil and Bossert, 1970). Old adults put fewer future reproductive opportunities at risk than do young adults when they reproduce. This may explain why parity in older adults was unaffected by differences among years in food availability.

Thus, coati reproduction responds to fluctuations in food availability, not through territorial preemption of resources and social inhibition, but through facultative deferment of reproduction by young adults in years of scarcity. In 2 of the 4 years of this study most young females did not reproduce. The lack of 3-year-olds in 1975 suggests a similar restriction of reproduction in 1972. Kaufmann (1962) also found a nearly complete failure of reproduction in 1959, in contrast to much reproduction in 1960.

The high frequency with which 2- and 3-year-olds defer reproduction indicates that the cost of reproduction for these age-classes is presently nearly in balance with its benefits. It is interesting to note the effect of gregariousness on this balance. By banding together and sharing vigilance and defense responsibilites, coati females improve their offspring's chances of surviving early predation. At the same time, they reduce the cost of reproduction to themselves by shortening the period of exclusive dependence of juveniles on milk. Raccoon (*Procyon lotor*) young, which are reared by a single adult female, depend on their mothers totally for food for 7–12 weeks (Montgomery, 1969; Montgomery et al., 1970; Schneider et al., 1971), considerably longer than the 3–5 weeks of coatis (Kaufmann, 1962; Russell, 1979). Females that raise their young in bands will thus be more capable of enduring the cost of reproduction than females that raise their young alone.

The timing of reproduction by coatis, then, can be seen as the result of interactions between fluctuations in food availability and a complex, cooperative, social organization. Seasonal breeding, a common response to seasonality in food availability, is refined into highly synchronous breeding in coatis because of the dependence of adult females on one another for the protection of their offspring. The dynamic nature of social bonds among adults leads to synchrony among as well as within groups. Variation among years in food availability raises and lowers the costs of reproduction, but the costs are, in general, lowered by cooperative maternal care.

ACKNOWLEDGMENTS

The data for this paper were collected during a study of the social organization of coatis, which was undertaken as part of the requirements for the degree of Ph.D. in the Department of Zoology, University of North Carolina at Chapel Hill. I would like to thank the many people who helped me to conduct the study, especially my wife, Ann, for her help in the field and her continuing moral support; my advisor, Haven Wiley, for his encouragement and guidance; Gene Montgomery, for introducing me to radiotelemetry techniques and generously sharing his equipment and expertise; Gary Stump, for help with the logistics of catching coatis; Bob Silberglied, for patiently enhancing my rudimentary knowledge of insect morphology; Nancy Garwood and Robin Foster, for helping to identify the fruits and seeds; and Stan Rand and Bert Leigh, for encouragement and illuminating discussions. Bill Glanz and Robin Foster kindly provided their observations of coatis foraging on fruits. The interpretation of seasonal and yearly variations in coati behavior and ecology could not have been complete without the long-term ecological data collected by the Environmental Sciences Program. I thank Bert Leigh for access to the data and for his thorough and helpful criticism of the manuscript. Finally, I thank the Smithsonian Tropical Research Institute for providing a stimulating intellectual environment and, with the National Science Foundation, for providing financial support for the study.

LITERATURE CITED

Altmann, J.
1974. Observational study of behavior: Sampling methods. *Behav.*, 49:227–65.

Altmann, S. A.
1974. Baboons, space, time and energy. *Amer. Zool.*, 14:221–48.

Bliss, C. I.
1965. Analysis of some insect trap records. Pages 385–97 in *Classical and Contagious Discrete Distributions*, edited by G. P. Patil. Calcutta: Statistical Publishing Society.

Brown, J. L.
1978. Avian communal breeding systems. *Ann. Rev. Ecol. Syst.*, 9:123–55.

Chapman, F. K.
1938. *Life in an Air Castle.* New York: Appleton-Century.

Charlesworth, B.
1973. Selection in populations with overlapping generations. V. Natural selection and life histories. *Amer. Natur.*, 107:303–11.

Cohen, A. C.
1961.   Tables for maximum likelihood estimates: Singly truncated and singly censored samples. *Technometrics*, 3:535–41.

Croat, T. B.
1978.   *Flora of Barro Colorado Island*. Stanford, Calif.: Stanford University Press.

Fleming, T. H.
1973.   The reproductive cycles of three species of opossums and other mammals in the Panama Canal Zone. *Jour. Mamm.*, 54:439–55.

Foster, R. B.
1973.   Seasonality of fruit production and seed fall in a tropical forest ecosystem in Panama. Ph.D. thesis. Durham, N.C.: Duke University.

1982. Famine on Barro Colorado Island. Pages 201–212 in *The Ecology of a Tropical Forest*, edited by Egbert G. Leigh, Jr., et al. Washington, D.C.: Smithsonian Institution Press.

Frame, L. H., J. R. Malcolm, G. W. Frame, and H. van Lawick
1979.   Social Organization of African Wild Dogs (*Lycaon pictus*) on the Serengeti Plains, Tanzania 1967–1978. *Z. Tierpsychol.*, 50:225–49.

Gadgil, M., and W. H. Bossert
1970.   Life historical consequences of natural selection. *Amer. Natur.*, 104:1–24.

Hays, W. L.
1973.   *Statistics for the Social Sciences*. 2nd ed. New York: Holt, Rinehart, and Winston.

Janzen, D. H.
1971.   Seed predation by animals. *Ann. Rev. Ecol. Syst.*, 2:465–492.

Kaufmann, J. H.
1962.   Ecology and social behavior of the coati, *Nasua narica*, on Barro Colorado Island, Panama. *Univ. Calif. Publ. Zool.*, 60:95–222.

Levings, S., and D. M. Windsor
1982.   Seasonal and annual variation in litter arthropod populations. Pages 355-387 in *The Ecology of a Tropical Forest*, edited by Egbert G. Leigh, Jr., et al. Washington, D.C.: Smithsonian Institution Press.

Mech, L. D.
1970.   *The Wolf*. Garden City, N.Y.: Natural History Press.

McToldridge, E. R.
1969.   Notes on breeding ring-tailed coatis, *Nasua narica*, at Santa Barbara Zoo. *Int. Zoo Yearb.*, 9:89–90.

Montgomery, G. G.
1969.   Weaning of captive raccoons. *J. Wildl. Mgmt.*, 33:154–59.

Montgomery, G. G., J. W. Lang, and M. E. Sunquist
1970.   A raccoon moves her young. *J. Mamm.*, 51:202–203.

Morrison, D. W.
1978.   Foraging ecology and energetics of the frugivorous bat *Artibeus jamaicensis*. *Ecology*, 59:716–23.

Rasa, A.
1973.   Intra-familial sexual repression in the dwarf mongoose. *Naturwissenschaften*, 60:303–304.

Robinson, J. G.
1979.   Vocal regulation of use of space by groups of Titi monkeys *Callicebus moloch*. *Behav. Ecol. Sociobiol.*, 5:1–15.

Rudran, R.
1973.   The reproductive cycles of two subspecies of purple-faced langurs (*Presbytis senex*) with relation to environmental factors. *Folia primatol.*, 19:41–60.

Russell, J. K.
1979.   Reciprocity in the social behavior of coatis, *Nasua narica*. Ph. D. dissertation, University of North Carolina, Chapel Hill.

Schneider, D. B., L. D. Mech, and J. R. Tester
1971.   Movements of female raccoons and their young. *Anim. Behav. Monogr.*, 4:3–43.

Smith, H. J.
1977.   Social behavior of the coati (*Nasua narica*) in captivity. Ph.D. dissertation, University of Arizona, Tucson.

Treisman, M.
1975.   Predation and the evolution of gregariousness. I. Models for concealment and evasion. *Anim. Behav.*, 23:779–800.

Wiley, R. H.
1974.   Effects of delayed reproduction on survival, fecundity, and the rate of population increase. *Amer. Natur.*, 108:705–09.

Wiley, R. H.
In press. Social structure and individual ontogenies: Problems of description, mechanism, and evolution. In *Perspectives in Ethology*, vol. 4, edited by P.P.G. Bateson and P. Klopfer.

Willis, E. O.
1976.   Seasonal changes in the invertebrate litter fauna on Barro Colorado Island, Panama. *Rev. Brasil. Biol.*, 36:643–57.

LONG-TERM CHANGES

Introduction: The Significance of Population Fluctuations

EGBERT G. LEIGH, JR. Smithsonian Tropical Research Institute, Balboa, Republic of Panama

The fluctuations in numbers of individuals of different species are of topical interest to anyone concerned with reserves of finite size (Wilson and Willis, 1975). The fewer individuals there are of a given species, the more likely that species is to die out, either from environmental change or through chance variation in numbers. Thus, the smaller a reserve, the more rapidly one may expect the number of species it contains to decline, and the more isolated this reserve, the fewer species immigrate to replace those that die out. As on an island (MacArthur and Wilson, 1967), diversity expresses a balance between immigration and extinction. On Barro Colorado Island, a relatively small reserve, the diversity of birds, mammals, reptiles, and amphibians has declined noticeably since the island was isolated from the surrounding mainland (Willis, 1974; Glanz, this volume; Myers and Rand, 1969).

Time to extinction, however, is affected not only by the average size of a population, but also by the extent and rapidity of fluctuations in its size. To understand the capacity of a reserve for preserving different kinds of organisms, one must know something about the nature and causes of fluctuations in their populations.

There is another reason for studying fluctuations, however. In theory, one can learn a lot about how communities are organized by studying the mechanisms that maintain their diversity (Hutchinson, 1959, 1965; MacArthur, 1972). On a continent (as opposed to a small reserve), diversity presumably represents a balance between the tendency of its species to give rise to more specialized descendants and the more rapid extinction of small, specialized populations (Fisher, 1930; MacArthur and Wilson, 1967; Leigh, 1975). This balance may represent a true steady state (Boucot, 1978). Presumably, the stabler the environment, the more specialized a species can be and still survive, and the more species can coexist (MacArthur, 1972, p. 179).

The Smithsonian Institution's environmental monitoring program appeared to provide a very natural test of this proposition. Its participants proposed to measure the stability of various aspects of the environment, and the fluctuations of representative populations, on Barro Colorado Island and in a temperate-zone forest on the shores of Chesapeake Bay. Some hoped such data would allow one to decide whether the greater stability of tropical environments is what allows the greater diversity of tropical communities.

The proposition proved too vague to test, however. To begin with, environmental stability does not only promote greater specialization. As was noted in the introduction to the papers on the biotic setting, tropical conditions may promote tree diversity by permitting a more even supply of fruit, flowers, and leaves throughout the year, which allows a far greater diversity of pollinators and dispersers and far heavier pressure from insect pests, and thereby provides many more different ways for trees to coexist than there are in the temperate zone. The same is no doubt true for other organisms. Moreover, the notion that species are "packed" into a community until the tendency to specialize just balances the more rapid extinction of the specialized, is too abstract to mean much. To flesh out the remark, one must try to judge (a) how rapidly species originate or immigrate, (b) how species resist competitive displacement, and (c) how specialization affects a population's prospects of extinction.

SPECIATION

Consider an area so large that most new species appear by speciation within it rather than by immigration from outside it. This appears true, for example, for the insects and plants of the New World tropics as a whole. It is hard to tell for how small a subregion of the neotropics this remains true. How might speciation rate be related to preexisting diversity, and how does this affect the relation between the number of species on a continent, say, and the extinction rate per species?

In the simplest view, the more species there are, the more opportunities there are for speciation; so one might expect the rate at which new species form to be proportional to the number of species already present (Leigh, 1975). This may not always be true; after a major biotic crisis, when there is a multitude of opportunities to exploit, speciation rates appear to be much higher than usual (Boucot, 1978). If the speciation rate per preexisting species c is constant, however, we may express the rate at which the number S of species in the community changes as

$$dS/dt = cS - E(S)S$$

where t is time and $E(S)$ is extinction rate per species, which is presumably higher the higher S and the less stable the environment. If so, then $dS/dt = 0$, and the number of species is at equilibrium, when the extinction rate per species is equal to the speciation rate c. If environmental stability does not affect speciation rate, then, at equilibrium, the extinction rate per species is the same no matter how unstable the environment. In effect, the number of species S in the community is adjusted so that $E(S) = c$. Thus, in a community at equilibrium, environmental stability is reflected, not by the extinction rate per species, but by the number of species in the community. In particular, one cannot argue the instability of a community's environment from the vulnerability to extinction of its populations. Notice that this argument only applies to communities at equilibrium: the geologist is perfectly correct to infer a "biotic crisis" from a sudden sharp increase in extinction rate.

COMPETITION AND SPECIALIZATION

Much thought has been given to how species resist competitive displacement. It is not worth distinguishing competitive displacement from extinction by predators because a predator so rarely extinguishes its only prey; a prey species is likely to be eaten to extinction only when alternative food permits the predator to attain intolerable levels, a process which can be viewed as the competitive exclusion of one prey by another.

A species can attain competitive superiority by exploiting some foods, some combination of foods, or some aspect of a particular habitat better than any of its fellows. This crude idea embraces the ocellated antbird of Panama, which only knows how to eat insects flushed out from the litter of the forest floor by swarms of army ants, but is big enough so that other birds cannot chase it from ant swarms (Willis, 1973); the *Cecropia* tree, which colonizes large gaps opened in the canopy of the tropical forest by windthrows, and reproduces quickly before competitors or consumers kill it (Brokaw, this volume); the mangrove, which can grow under conditions ordinary rain forest trees cannot tolerate; and the seaweed *Lessoniopsis* of exposed rocky shores in the Pacific Northwest, which

is so shaped that, in a surge channel, waves cause it to sweep away its competition (Dayton, 1975). Notice that in all these cases, specialization is essential to the achievement of competitive superiority. Ocellated antbirds cannot feed effectively except at ant swarms, *Cecropia* can grow only where abundant light allows it to sprout and reproduce quickly, mangroves can grow only where saltwater excludes other competition, and *Lessoniopsis* can survive only where waves are strong enough to transform it into a scourge for its competitors.

SPECIALIZATION AND EXTINCTION

To see how specialization enhances the prospects of extinction, remember the saying that "the jack of all trades is master of none" (MacArthur and Connell, 1966, p. 181) and its converse, that specialization implies more limited opportunities, chancier food supplies, and smaller population sizes, rendering the specialist more sensitive to environmental change. The idea is superbly illustrated by the ocellated antbird of Barro Colorado, which has no peer at ant swarms but cannot feed elsewhere. Since Barro Colorado has become an island, the ocellated antbirds there have dwindled to the vanishing point, although they have maintained their numbers on the surrounding mainland. The more generalized, more numerous, spotted antbird, which cannot outface ocellated antbirds at ant swarms but can feed effectively elsewhere, even surviving in habitats without army ants, has kept up its numbers on the island (Willis, 1972, 1974). Theory suggests that in a constant environment, smaller populations die out more rapidly than large (MacArthur and Wilson, 1967), and we will soon inquire how sensitivity to environmental change might affect the time it takes a population to go extinct.

To know more precisely how specialization affects a population's chances of extinction, we need to know more precisely how specialization might restrict that population's numbers and affect its sensitivity to environmental change, and how, in turn, these effects alter its prospects of extinction. We hardly even know the different senses in which a population can specialize, let alone the consequences of different types of specialization; these are issues that cannot be settled in an introductory note. One can make a few remarks, however, about the relative importance of environmental change as opposed to the chance effects of finite population size in causing population fluctuations, and one can predict how sensitivity to environmental change reduces a population's prospective lifetime.

436

THE CAUSES OF POPULATION FLUCTUATIONS

To what extent do a population's fluctuations represent sheer chance? Even in a constant environment, there will be chance variation in the number of offspring per parent; as noted in the introduction to the section on the biotic setting, Hubbell (1979) believes that fluctuations in the numbers of different species of tropical tree are governed primarily by the statistical consequences of such variation.

How extensive are the fluctuations such a mechanism can account for? Some mathematical theory is needed to help answer the question. Let $N(t)$ be the number of mature individuals in the population at generation t. If the number of offspring of different parents are distributed independently about the same mean, then in a constant environment the change $N(t + 1) - N(t)$ in the number of individuals over one generation has mean 0 and variance kN (Leigh, 1975), where k lies between 1 and 2 (Crow and Kimura, 1970, p. 363). As changes in successive generations are uncorrelated, the variance in $N(t + s) - N(t)$ will be skN, and the probability that the population's numbers will change by more than $2\sqrt{skN}$ in s generations is less than 0.05. According to this criterion, most population fluctuations on Barro Colorado Island which are big enough to notice are too big to have occurred by chance; they are *caused*. For example, the number of adult squirrels on Barro Colorado changed from 120 to 1200 in 10 years (Glanz, this volume). A squirrel generation is about 1 year (Glanz et al., this volume): taking $N = 1200$, $s = 10$, $k = 2$, we find that chance cannot account for a change of more than 320 individuals during this period. The number of adult howler monkeys on Barro Colorado increased from about 175 to about 550 in 8 years, and a howler generation is 4 years or more (Milton, this volume). Taking $N = 550$, $k = 2$, $s = 2$, we find that chance cannot account for a change of more than 100 individuals during this period. And, indeed, we know the cause of this increase: the population was recovering from a disastrous epizootic of yellow fever (Glanz, this volume).

It is hardly a surprise that population fluctuations reflect environmental causes. The mortality of agoutis and pacas (Smythe et al., this volume) and the reproductive rates of coatis (Russell, this volume) and anoline lizards (Andrews and Rand, this volume) change significantly from year to year. In other words, these changes too are caused, although we do not know what caused them. Patterns in changes from year to year in the species composition of netted birds suggest that these changes are also caused (Karr et al., this volume). The populations of Barro Colorado and surrounding areas are clearly sensitive to year-to-year variation in their environment.

THE AVERAGE LIFETIMES OF POPULATIONS

How might sensitivity to environmental variation affect a population's prospective lifetime? To answer, consider a population with N individuals at time t, where time is measured in generations, and assume that if the time interval dt is so short that the population cannot change by more than one individual, then the chance it has $N + 1$ individuals at time $t + dt$ is $Nb(N)dt$ where $b(N)$ is the per capita birth rate when the population has N individuals, and the chance it has $N - 1$ individuals at time $t + dt$ is $Nd(N)dt$, where $d(N)$ is the per capita death rate. Here, $M(N)dt$, the expected change in numbers during time dt, is $Nb(N)dt - Nd(N)dt$, while $V(N)dt$, the mean square change in numbers during this interval, is $Nb(N)dt + Nd(N)dt$, which is also the probability that the population's numbers will change during this interval. We assume that $V(N)$ greatly exceeds $M(N)$, so that $V(N)$ is roughly the variance in population change over one generation.

Given these assumptions, what is the average length of time it takes a population now possessing N individuals to die out? Following MacArthur and Wilson (1967), remember that $T(N)$ is the average length of time $1/V(N)$ it takes for the population to change its numbers, plus the average time it takes to go extinct after the change has taken place, which latter is $T(N + 1)$ times the probability $Nb(N)/V(N)$ that the change is an increase, plus $T(N - 1)$ times the probability $Nd(N)/V(N)$ that the change is a decrease. Thus

$$T(N) = 1/V(N) + Nb(N)T(N + 1)/V(N) + Nd(N)T(N - 1)/V(N)$$

Multiplying by $V(N)$, and remembering that $Nb(N) + Nd(N) = V(N)$; $Nb(N) - Nd(N) = M(N)$ imply $Nb(N) = \frac{1}{2} V(N) + \frac{1}{2} M(N)$, $Nd(N) = \frac{1}{2} V(N) - \frac{1}{2} M(N)$, we obtain

$$\begin{aligned} V(N)T(N) = \ & 1 + \tfrac{1}{2} V(N)T(N + 1) \\ & + \tfrac{1}{2} M(N)T(N + 1) \\ & + \tfrac{1}{2} V(N)T(N - 1) \\ & - \tfrac{1}{2} M(N)T(N - 1) \end{aligned}$$

$$\begin{aligned} & \tfrac{1}{2} V(N)[T(N + 1) - T(N)] \\ & - \tfrac{1}{2} V(N)[T(N) - T(N - 1)] \\ & + \tfrac{1}{2} M(N)[T(N + 1) - T(N - 1)] = -1 \end{aligned}$$

Under some circumstances, this can be approximated by the differential equation

$$\tfrac{1}{2} V(N)d^2T/dN^2 + M(N)dT/dN + 1 = 0$$

(see also Kimura and Ohta, 1971, pp. 174–175). Although, strictly speaking this derivation assumed a constant environment, this differential equation also applies for variable environments when the effects of the environment on the per capita growth rate of successive generations are uncorrelated. If we assume $T(1) = 0$, $\lim(N \to \infty)\, dT/dN = 0$, then the solution to this differential equation is (Leigh, 1981)

$$T(N) = \int_1^N dL \int_L^\infty [2dx/v(x)]\exp \int_L^x 2M(y)dy/V(y)$$

To apply this equation, we must decide how the mean change $M(N)$ in population size over one generation depends on the size of the population. This requires us to decide how closely the population is regulated by its own density. This is a matter of some controversy (Lack, 1954; Ehrlich and Birch, 1967). On Barro Colorado Island, howler monkeys (Milton, this volume) and army ants (Franks, this volume) appear very closely regulated by their own numbers, while density regulation appears undetectable in many insect populations, and appears rather weak (but not insignificant) in anoline lizards (Andrews and Rand, this volume).

One extreme model is to suppose that the world consists of a very large number P of places to be divided up among its species, and to assume that the average change in numbers $N(t + 1) - N(t)$ of a given species over one generation is 0. If we assume that environmental variation dominates a population's fluctuations, then we may set $N(t + 1) - N(t) = e(t)N(t)$, where $e(t)$ is sampled anew each generation from a normal distribution with mean 0 and variance v. Here, $M(N) = 0$, $V(N) = vN^2$, and $T(N)$ is roughly $(2/v) \ln N$ generations. On the other hand, if the environment is constant and chance fluctuations dominate, then $V(N) = kN$, as discussed earlier, and the median time to extinction will be roughly as many generations N as there are individuals now in the population. Sensitivity to environmental variation greatly hastens extinction, as one might expect.

Notice that v measures the response of the population to the variation in its environment. It will be the higher, the less stable the environment. It will also be the higher, the more sensitive the population is to the variation in its environment, that is to say, the more specialized the population. Schematically, v is a function $v(S)$ of the number S of species in the community. I assume that when S is larger, the community's species will be more specialized and more sensitive to environmental variation, so $v(S)$ will be higher.

However, v also measures the relative amplitude of a population's fluctuations. If, as seems to be the case, most changes of population size that matter are caused, this theory suggests that a population's prospective lifetime is more sensitive to the relative amplitude v of its fluctuations than to its size N, which enters the formula for $T(N)$ only as a logarithm. I argued earlier that if, in a community at equilibrium, speciation is a far more important source of new species than immigration, then the extinction rate per species will be equal to the speciation rate c, regardless of the stability of the environment. This implies that the number of species S adjusts to changes in environmental stability in such a way that v assumes the value that maintains the extinction rate per species equal to c. Thus, one cannot measure the instability of an environment from the amplitude of fluctuation of its populations. Wolda (1978) compared the amplitude of fluctuation in tropical and temperate-zone insects and found that tropical insect populations fluctuate just as much as their counterparts in the temperate zone, suggesting that the amplitude of fluctuation is not correlated with environmental instability.

Conversely, instead of assuming that a population's numbers fluctuate purely at random, responding to an ever-changing environment, we may suppose that the species has an *equilibrium* population size to which it returns after disturbance. Assume, to be specific, that

$$N(t + 1) - N(t) + [r + e(t)]\mathrm{N}(t) - aN^2(t) + s(t)$$

where r is the population's per capita rate of increase when rare, which is assumed positive, a is a positive constant measuring the diminution in per capita growth rate imposed by adding a single individual to the population, $e(t)$ is a random variable representing the effects of environmental change, sampled anew each generation from a normal distribution of mean 0 and variance v, and $s(t)$ represents chance fluctuations unrelated to environmental change, and is sampled anew each generation from a normal distribution with mean 0 and variance $N(t)$ (cf., Leigh, 1975). Here, $M(N) = rN - aN^2$, and $V(N) = N + vN^2$. Here, the population has an *equilibrium* size, $K = r/a$, and if Kv far exceeds 1, $v/2r$ is a rough measure of the amplitude of a population's fluctuations relative to its equilibrium numbers. When $v = 0$, $T(K)$, the average time to extinction of a population now at its equilibrium size K, increases very rapidly with K while, if Kv is large, time to extinction increases far more slowly with K, and is more sensitive to the relative amplitude in the population's fluctuations than to its average numbers (Leigh, 1981: Table 1).

CONCLUDING REMARKS

If, as it seems, a population's fluctuations reflect its sensitivity to environmental variation, then sensitivity to such variation will largely govern vulnerability to extinction. Thus the causes, as well as the magnitudes, of population fluctuations are of great concern to the managers of reserves. To learn why a population fluctuates, one must know how its numbers are regulated. Some of the earlier chapters of this book were concerned with population regulation in animals as varied as agoutis (Smythe, Glanz and Leigh, this volume), lizards (Andrews and Rand, this volume), and army ants (Franks, this volume). These studies were based primarily on how these populations responded to the seasonal rhythm of the forest, but studies are now under way on how some populations are affected by differences between years. The two papers to follow summarize information on the magnitudes of population fluctuations in the mammals of Barro Colorado (Glanz, this volume) and in the birds of a small plot on the nearby mainland (Karr, Schemske, and Brokaw, this volume).

To what extent does the greater diversity of tropical communities reflect the greater stability of their environments? There are more spectacular instances of specialization and more complex relationships between species in the tropics than in the temperate zone (Robinson, 1978), as theory would suggest. Moreover, the relative amplitude of population fluctuation is as great in the tropics as in the temperate zone, as if species do specialize to the limits their environments permit, and environmental stability is reflected solely in the diversity of the community. Nonetheless, we know little about how, or how often, such specialization evolves or how it affects sensitivity to environmental change. At this stage, understanding the diversity of tropical communities may depend more on detailed studies of natural history from an evolutionary standpoint than on general mathematical arguments.

LITERATURE CITED

Andrews, R. M., and A. S. Rand
1982.   Seasonal Breeding and Long-term Population Fluctuations in the Lizard *Anolis limifrons*. Pages 405-412 in *The Ecology of a Tropical Forest*, edited by Egbert G. Leigh, Jr., et al. Washington, D.C.: Smithsonian Institution Press.

Brokaw, N. V. L.
1982.   Treefalls: Frequency, Timing, and Consequences. Pages 101-108 in *The Ecology of a Tropical Forest*, edited by Egbert G. Leigh, Jr., et al. Washington, D.C.: Smithsonian Institution Press.

Boucot, A. J.
1978.   Community Evolution and Rates of Cladogenesis. *Evolutionary Biology*, 11:545–654.

Crow, J. F., and M. Kimura
1970.   *An Introduction to Population Genetics Theory*. New York: Harper and Row.

Dayton, P. K.
1975.   Experimental Evaluation of Ecological Dominance in a Rocky Intertidal Community. *Ecological Monographs*, 45:137–159.

Ehrlich, P. R., and L. C. Birch
1967.   The "Balance of Nature" and "Population Control." *American Naturalist*, 101:97–107.

Fisher, R. A.
1930.   *The Genetical Theory of Natural Selection*. Oxford: Clarendon Press.

Franks, Nigel
1982.   Ecology and Population Regulation in the Army Ant *Eciton burchelli*. Pages 389-395 in *The Ecology of a Tropical Forest*, edited by Egbert G. Leigh, Jr., et al. Washington, D.C.: Smithsonian Institution Press.

Glanz, W. E.
1982.   The Terrestrial Mammal Fauna of Barro Colorado Island: Censuses and Long-term Changes. Pages 455-468 in *The Ecology of a Tropical Forest*, edited by Egbert G. Leigh, Jr., et al. Washington, D.C.: Smithsonian Institution Press.

Glanz, W. E., R. W. Thorington, Jr., Jacalyn Giacalone-Madden, L. R. Heaney
1982.   Seasonal Food Use and Demographic Trends in *Sciurus granatensis*. Pages 239-252 in *The Ecology of a Tropical Forest*, edited by Egbert G. Leigh, Jr., et al. Washington, D.C.: Smithsonian Institution Press.

Hubbell, S. P.
1979.   Tree Dispersion, Abundance and Diversity in a Tropical Dry Forest. *Science*, 203:1299–1309.

Hutchinson, G. E.
1959.   Homage to Santa Rosalia, or, Why Are There So Many Kinds of Animals? *American Naturalist*, 93:145–159.
1965.   *The Ecological Theater and the Evolutionary Play*. New Haven: Yale University Press.

Karr, J. R., D. W. Schemske, and N. V. L. Brokaw
1982.   Temporal Variation in the Understory Bird Community of a Tropical Forest. Pages 441-453 in *The Ecology of a Tropical Forest*, edited by Egbert G. Leigh, Jr., et al. Washington, D.C.: Smithsonian Institution Press.

Kimura, M., and T. Ohta
1971.   *Theoretical Aspects of Population Genetics*. Princeton, N.J.: Princeton University Press.

Lack, D.
1954.   *The Natural Regulation of Animal Numbers*. Oxford: Clarendon Press.

Leigh, E. G., Jr.
1975.   Population Fluctuations, Community Stability, and Environmental Variability. Pages 51–73, in *Ecology and Evolution of Communities*, edited by M. L. Cody and J. M. Diamond. Cambridge, Mass.: Belknap Press.
1981.   The Average Lifetime of a Population in a Varying Environment. *Journal of Theoretical Biology*, 90:213–239.

MacArthur, R. H.
1972.   *Geographical Ecology: Patterns in the Distribution of Species*. New York: Harper and Row.

MacArthur, R. H., and J. H. Connell
1966.   *The Biology of Populations.* New York: John Wiley and Sons.

MacArthur, R. H., and E. O. Wilson
1967.   *The Theory of Island Biogeography.* Princeton, N.J.: Princeton University Press.

Milton, Katharine
1982.   Dietary Quality and Demographic Regulation in a Howler Monkey Population. Pages 273-289 in *The Ecology of a Tropical Forest,* edited by Egbert G. Leigh, Jr., et al. Washington, D.C.: Smithsonian Institution Press.

Myers, C. W., and A. S. Rand
1969.   Checklist of Amphibians and Reptiles of Barro Colorado Island, Panama, with Comments on Faunal Change and Sampling. *Smithsonian Contributions to Zoology,* 10:1–11.

Robinson, M. H.
1978.   Is Tropical Biology Real? *Tropical Ecology,* 19:30–50.

Russell, J. K.
1982.   Timing of Reproduction by Coatis (*Nasua narica*) in Relation to Fluctuations in Food Resources. Pages 413-431 in *The Ecology of a Tropical Forest,* edited by Egbert G. Leigh, Jr., et al. Washington, D.C.: Smithsonian Institution Press.

Smythe, Nicholas, W. E. Glanz, and E. G. Leigh, Jr.
1982.   Population Regulation in Some Terrestrial Frugivores. Pages 227-238 in *The Ecology of a Tropical Forest,* edited by Egbert G. Leigh, Jr., et al. Washington, D.C.: Smithsonian Institution Press.

Willis, E. O.
1972.   *The Behavior of Spotted Antbirds.* Ornithological Monograph No. 10. Lawrence, Kans.: American Ornithologists' Union.
1973.   The Behavior of Ocellated Antbirds. *Smithsonian Contributions to Zoology,* 144:1–57
1974.   Populations and Local Extinctions of Birds on Barro Colorado Island, Panama. *Ecological Monographs,* 44:153–169.

Wilson, E. O., and E. O. Willis
1975.   Applied Biogeography. Pages 522–534 in *Ecology and Evolution of Communities,* edited by M. L. Cody and J. M. Diamond. Cambridge, Mass.: Belknap Press.

Wolda, H.
1978.   Fluctuations in Abundance of Tropical Insects. *American Naturalist* 112:1017–1045.

Temporal Variation in the Understory Bird Community of a Tropical Forest

JAMES R. KARR   Department of Ecology, Ethology, and Evolution, University of Illinois, Champaign, Illinois 61820

DOUGLAS W. SCHEMSKE   Department of Biology, University of Chicago, Chicago, Illinois 60637

NICHOLAS V.L. BROKAW   Department of Biology, University of Chicago, Chicago, Illinois 60637

ABSTRACT

Mist-net samples of forest understory birds in central Panama taken in 10 months between August 1968 and July 1969, and once every month from May 1977 through January 1978, yielded similar numbers of species in both years. The species composition of the two samples was very different, however, primarily because of changes in rare species. A few abundant species (about 10% of the species) changed significantly in abundance between years. In some cases, shifts seem due to habitat changes (increased area of treefall gaps) while in others, seasonal movement of temperate-tropical migrants are responsible.

The manakin *Pipra mentalis* is the most abundant species in both years (20% of each sample). However, its abundance shifts markedly from month to month within each year (from 7% to 35% of captures), peaking in the early wet season. The only major guild showing significant shifts in abundance (for the guild and for several species) was the professional ant-followers. The only abundant ant-follower not showing a significant increase in abundance was the relatively more territorial spotted antbird. Not coincidentally, this species is much less dependent on ants than are the other species.

A few species are captured at higher rates in the wet season than in the dry season. The insectivore-nectarivore guild is more common in the dry season, a period of peak flowering activity, while species that follow army ants are more common in the wet season. Samples from three dry seasons show that a number of species change in abundance from year to year with a general correlation related to the severity of the dry season. Species characteristic of dry forest increase in years with relatively drier dry seasons.

Samples taken in successive months differ significantly. These differences are particularly marked during the transition between the wet and the dry season, and during the period when migrants are arriving from North America. These and other striking changes in the structure of a forest understory avifauna, both within and between years, are clear evidence that the popular notion of population and/or community stability in tropical ecosystems should not be extrapolated to all species, guilds, and communities.

INTRODUCTION

How does the composition and abundance of a tropical-forest avifauna change over time? To answer, we will consider mist-net censuses conducted at Limbo Hunt Club, Pipeline Road, Panama, by Karr in 1968–69 (10 months, 643 captures, 65 species) and by Schemske and Brokaw in 1977–78 (9 months, 826 captures, 74 species). After demonstrating that the avifauna does vary, we will inquire into possible causes.

Study Area

The study area is a 2–3 ha. plot of lowland, moist forest adjacent to the Limbo Hunt Club about 8 km NW of Gamboa, Panama. Karr (1971a) described the area in 1968: "Many trees rise to heights of 40 m or more and the undergrowth is generally open. Canopy trees indicate the area is structurally mature. . . . Annual precipitation averages about 2600 mm. There are distinct wet and dry seasons, but the forest remains predominantly green throughout the year." Since then, the composition of the flora has changed relatively little, but a number of large trees have fallen. No precise quantitative data are available from 1968–69 on size of treefall (gap) areas. However, new treefalls indicate a three- to fourfold increase in gap area, especially as a result of a large treefall of 569 sq. m. Several other small gaps have expanded in size, apparently because of the increased susceptibility to wind of trees exposed by an earlier treefall. In general, the forest at Limbo Hunt Club is similar to the forest on Barro Colorado Island (Foster and Brokaw, this volume) in structure, species composition, and number of lianas, but with more understory palms and perhaps more epiphytes than on Barro Colorado.

METHODS

The Karr study was part of a detailed analysis of a tropical avifauna (Karr, 1971a, 1976; Karr and Roth, 1971). During that study, about a dozen mist nets (12 m, 30 and 36 mm mesh) were operated at ground level (Karr, 1979) from dawn to early afternoon for 3 to 5 days each month (Table 1). Net locations were varied from month to month within the boundaries of a 2-ha. intensive-study plot. In addition, Karr netted in the study plot during the dry seasons of 1975, 1977, and 1978 and briefly during the wet season 1977 (Table 1).

The Schemske and Brokaw study was designed to compare avifauna composition in treefall gaps with that of adjacent, intact forest. Census data are based on 16 nets (12 m, 36 mm mesh) set in the same locations each month from May 1977 to January 1978.

Nets were run from dawn to dusk the first day of each sampling period and often the second. The netting period never exceeded 2.5 days, as capture rates declined precipitously after the second day. Net locations were determined by the availability of gaps greater than or equal to 10 m in length. Of the gaps on the study area that met this criterion, two were long enough to accommodate two nets. A forest net was located at a randomly chosen compass direction (from eight possible directions) about 18 m from and parallel to each gap net. Twelve of the nets operated by Schemske and Brokaw were within the boundaries of the 2-ha. study plot netted by Karr in 1968–69. Two were associated with a gap at the boundary of the Karr study plot, and two were located about 175 m from the study plot. The species composition of captures in nets outside the Karr study plot were very similar to those inside the plot. Thus data from all Schemske and Brokaw nets (eight gap and eight forest) are included in this analysis.

We assume that capture rates from these net data can be used as estimates of local abundance. The diversity of spatial distribution patterns (Karr, 1971; Willis, 1972) and the presence of many very rare species (Karr, 1977) preclude simple, direct estimates of densities of each of the many species. Further, as we will show below, densities fluctuate considerably between seasons and among years, thereby minimizing the utility of such density estimates.

We compare samples by calculating PD_s, the percentage difference in species present, and PD_c, the percentage difference in species composition weighted by number of captures.

$$PD_s = \frac{100\,(a' + b')}{a' + b' + c'}$$

$$PD_c = \frac{100 \sum |(x_i - y_i)|}{x + y}$$

where a' and b' = number of species in samples A and B only, respectively, c' = number of species common to both samples A and B; x and y = number of individuals in samples A and B, respectively; x_i and y_i = number of individuals of species i in samples A and B, respectively.

To evaluate the significance of measured differences in community composition, we generate hypothetical communities by drawing randomly from the data sets used in each comparison. For example, in comparing our two periods of data, 30 random pairs of communities are generated of sizes equal to the number of captures in the first (643) and second (826) years of study.

RESULTS

Between Years

To compare the number of species in the Karr and the Schemske-Brokaw samples, we plotted cumulative number of species versus cumulative number of captures (not the number of different individuals captured), beginning with the first wet-season sample from each year (Figure 1). These curves are virtually identical for two samples taken nearly a decade apart, but there are striking differences in species composition between these samples. Karr caught 65 species in 643 captures, and Schemske-Brokaw caught 64 species in a seasonally equivalent 637 captures, but these 1280 captures included a total of 84 species. When all data from 1968 through 1978 are combined (Table 1), a total of 97 species (1907 captures) have been captured in mist nets (Figure 1, "combined sample").

Species composition differs least for samples taken at different seasons of the same year, more for samples taken at the same season of different years, and most for different years (Table 2). The differences for nearly all comparisons are well above those for randomly generated communities, suggesting that these differences are not just accidents of sampling a community with many rare species. Indeed, an analysis based on 100 captures per sample yields a similar scale of differences (Karr, 1980).

Table 1. Summary of mist-net data from the Limbo Hunt Club study plot, 1968–78

Month and year	Season	Number of Captures	Number of Species	Cumulative number of Captures	Cumulative number of Species
Aug. 1968	Wet*	40	13	40	13
Sept. 1968	Wet*	61	26	101	30
Oct. 1968	Wet*	119	36	220	42
Nov. 1968	Wet*	79	32	299	50
Dec. 1968	Dry*	75	26	374	52
Feb. 1969	Dry*	44	24	418	56
Mar. 1969	Dry*	67	30	485	58
Apr. 1969	Dry*	38	20	523	59
May 1969	Wet*	57	20	580	62
July 1969	Wet*	63	27	643	65
Apr. 1975	Dry*	147	45	790	71
Feb. 1977	Dry*	123	39	913	78
May 1977	Dry**	112	32	1025	83
June 1977	Wet**	106	30	1131	84
June 1977	Wet*	41	26	1172	84
July 1977	Wet**	82	21	1254	86
Aug. 1977	Wet**	80	32	1334	87
Sept. 1977	Wet**	83	30	1417	88
Oct. 1977	Wet**	96	33	1513	93
Nov. 1977	Wet**	87	32	1600	94
Dec. 1977	Dry**	103	38	1703	96
Jan. 1978	Dry**	77	33	1780	96
Mar. 1978	Dry*	127	32	1907	97

* Data collected by JRK.
** Data collected by DWS & NB.

Table 2. Percentage difference in avian community structure by species (PD_s) and species weighted by number of captures (PD_c) for mist-net data and for communities generated at random

Comparison	Number of captures	PD_s Observed	PD_s Random	PD_c Observed	PD_c Random
Between years (1968–69 vs. 1977–78)	643 vs. 826	52.9	26.0 ± 4.5	56.5	18.7 ± 1.0
Dry (1968–69) vs. Dry (1977–78)	224 vs. 542	49.4	36.0 ± 4.5	64.9	45.0 ± 1.3
Wet (1968–69) vs. Wet (1977–78)	419 vs. 575	49.4	30.6 ± 3.2	49.4	23.4 ± 1.7
Wet (1968–69) vs. Dry (1968–69)	419 vs. 224	40.0	35.9 ± 4.3	37.7	36.8 ± 1.4
Wet (1977–78) vs. Dry (1977–78)	575 vs. 542	38.6	28.8 ± 3.9	57.4	17.0 ± 1.6

Random communities were generated with replacement from a universe equivalent to the combined 1-year samples (1469 captures, 92 species). Random communities (mean ± SD, N = 30) always contained the same number of captures as the field data for each comparison.

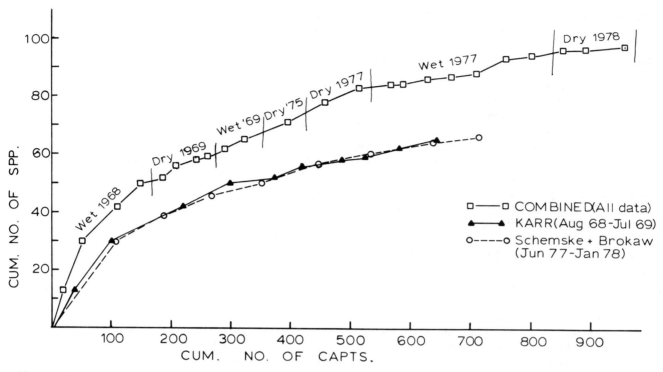

Figure 1. Species accumulation rates for 1968–69 (Karr), 1977–78 (Schemske and Brokaw), and all data (1968–78) from mist-nets in the undergrowth at Limbo Hunt Club. The cumulative number of captures for combined data is twice the abscissa value.

In both years there was a high proportion of species captured only rarely (Figure 2). Most of these species forage near the ground; therefore, rarity in our samples is indicative of their frequency in our study plot. However, others (like the cotingid *Laniocera rufescens*) appeared "rare" because they typically forage at levels above those sampled by our ground-level nets. The percentage difference in species present in the two samples is due primarily to rarely captured species. If we call rare those species constituting less than 2% of the sample (Karr and Roth, 1971), 75% and 85% of species are rare in the first and second samples, respectively. Using a 1% definition, 55% and 62% of species are rare. (A summary of the raw data by species is provided in Appendix 1.) These are very similar to results of a Brazilian study (Novaes, 1970) where 78% and 64% of the species captured in nets were less than 2% and 1% of a mist-net sample, respectively.

A few species were captured in 1977–78 as a result of differences in sampling regime—gap and forest habitats were sampled equally in 1977–78, but gaps were avoided in 1968–69. However, only one species (*Dysithamnus puncticeps*) not captured in 1968–69 is significantly associated with gaps (Schemske and Brokaw, 1981). Several species in the 1977–78 sample are represented only because they descend from their normally high foraging level in areas where treefall gaps exist. These include *Notharchus pectoralis*, *Tityra semifasciata*, *Cacicus uropygialis*, *Euphonia fulvicrissa*, *Tachyphonus luctuosus*, *Pitylus grossus*, and *Xiphorhynchus lachrymosus*. Each of these species was captured only once (*Pitylus* twice) in nets during 1977–78 but was recorded on the study plot more or less regularly from 1968 to 1978. A number of species were caught in one but not both sample years (19 in 1968–69, 13 in 1977–78); these birds showed no association with habitat. Thus, the pronounced between-year differences in mist-net samples are not primarily a function of differential sampling.

Ten species were captured more frequently ($p<0.05$) in one year than the other (Table 3). To attain the 5% level of significance, over five captures are required (binomial exact test), and 45 of the 97 species captured meet this criterion. By random processes, we would expect only 2.3 species (0.05×45) to show significant between-year differences. Our findings that 10 species vary significantly between years (Table 3) is striking evidence that differences in community composition are not statistical artifacts.

Seven of the 10 species were more abundant in the

second year, and 3 were more abundant in the first. We only caught *Dysithamnus* in 1977–78 when nets were placed in gaps. All other differences appear unrelated to how we placed our nets. Two temperate-tropical migrants were captured significantly more often in 1968–69. Schemske and Brokaw did not catch *Oporornis formosus* (Kentucky warbler), but Karr caught it every month he netted between October 1968 and April 1969, when an individual established a territory in the study plot (Karr, 1971b). The second migrant, the thrush *Catharus minimus*, was very abundant in the study plot in October 1968 (18 of 119 captures), but only 4 captures were recorded by Schemske and Brokaw in October 1977. *Catharus* seems to be a transient, recorded only in the late wet season.

Of the eight permanent residents that changed significantly in abundance, only the woodcreeper, *Glyphorynchus spirurus*, was more abundant in the first year. The species was not captured (or seen) in the 1977–78 sample of Schemske and Brokaw. However, Karr did capture at least one individual in each of his 1977 and 1978 dry-season samples. An examination of the capture locations for this species does not account for the differences between the two years, and no other woodcreeper seems to have changed in abundance. The increased abundance of *Myrmeciza* is probably due to the number of treefalls occurring on the study plot in that period (Karr, 1980). Both *Damophila* (hummingbird) and *Hylophilus* (greenlet) were not represented in the year 1 sample, but composed more than 1% of all captures in year 2. Causes for their increase are unknown.

A total of seven species of professional ant-followers have been netted in the study plot, and their abundance increased almost twofold (1968–69, 81 captures; 1977–78, 149 captures) between the two samples. Only five of the seven were caught in sufficient numbers (six captures) to allow tests of significance. These were the spotted (*Hylophylax*), bicolored (*Gymnopithys*), and ocellated (*Phaenostictus*) antbirds, the gray-headed tanager (*Eucometis*), and the plain-brown woodcreeper (*Dendrocincla fulginosa*). All but the spotted antbird and the woodcreeper increased significantly ($p < 0.05$). The number of woodcreeper captures increased by 50% (10 versus 15) between the sample periods, but the difference is not statistically significant.

Of the professional ant-followers, only the spotted antbird (*Hylophylax naevioides*) was captured commonly and at essentially the same rate in the two years. It is noteworthy that, among the ant-followers, this species is the most territorial and least dependent on ants for their foraging activities (Willis, 1972).

Although the two years differed dramatically in the capture rates of some species (Table 3), the rank (and/

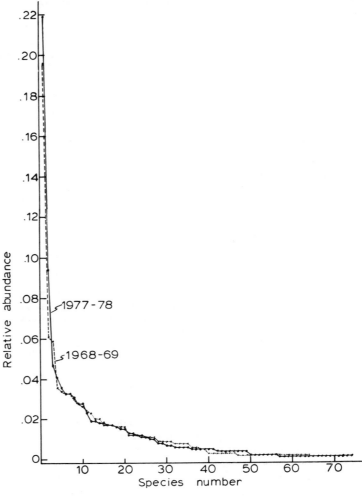

Figure 2. Proportion of captures per species from most abundant to least abundant species in two samples from Limbo Hunt Club. 1968–69: 65 species, 643 captures; 1977–78: 74 species, 826 captures.

or proportion) in abundance of the most common species was similar (Table 4). Only 4 of the 15 most common species were not represented in both samples, and the relative position of 8 species varied no more than two places (Table 4). The manakin *Pipra mentalis* and the antbird *Gymnopithys leucaspis* were, respectively, first and second in abundance in both years, despite the significantly higher capture rate of *Gymnopithys* in 1977–78 (Table 3).

Between Seasons

Rainfall is the primary physical variable that changes seasonally in central Panama. The nearest long-term records are from Barro Colorado Island, 9 km east of our forest study plot. The mean annual rainfall at

Table 3. Bird species captured at significantly different rates, 1968–69 and 1977–78

Species[1]	Number of captures	
	1968–69	*1977–78*
Damophila julie (hummingbird)	0	8
Glyphorynchus spirurus (woodcreeper)	6	0
Dysithamnus puncticeps (antvireo)	0	7
Myrmeciza exsul (antbird)	0	7
Gymnopithys leucaspis (antbird)	39	78
Phaenostictus mcleannani (antbird)	8	39
Catharus minimus (thrush)	18	4
Hylophilus ochraceiceps (greenlet)	0	9
Oporornis formosus (warbler)	10	0
Eucometis penicillata (tanager)	1	10
Total number of captures	643	826

All significant at $p < .05$ by binomial probability test (*Gymnopithys* and *Phaenostictus* by χ^2). The between-year difference in total number of captures was incorporated into the statistical calculations.
[1] With common name of group.

Table 4. Relative ranks and proportion of sample for the 15 most frequently captured species in mist-net samples from Limbo Hunt Club

Rank in 1977–78	Species (proportion)	Rank in 1968–69 (proportion)	
1.	*Pipra mentalis* (21.9)	1.	(19.6)
2.	*Gymnopithys leucaspis* (9.4)	2.	(6.1)
3.	*Phaenostictus mcleannani* (4.7)		(<2.0)
4.	*Pipromorpha oleaginea* (4.1)	4.	(5.9)
5.	*Cyphorhinus phaeocephalus* (3.6)	15.	(2.0)
6.	*Hylophylax naevioides* (3.3)	7.	(3.3)
7.	*Sclerurus guatemalensis* (3.3)	8.	(3.3)
8.	*Pipra coronata* (3.1)	3.	(5.9)
9.	*Geotrygon montana* (3.8)		(<2.0)
10.	*Phaethornis superciliosus* (2.8)	12.	(2.3)
11.	*Platyrinchus coronatus* (2.3)	9.	(3.0)
12.	*Automolus ochrolaemus* (1.9)	5.	(3.6)
13.	*Terenotriccus erthyrurus* (1.9)	13.	(2.3)
14.	*Dendrocincla fuliginosa* (1.8)		(<2.0)
15.	*Myrmotherula axillaris* (1.8)		(<2.0)
(<1.8)	*Myobius sulphureipygius*	6.	(3.4)
(<1.8)	*Catharus minimus*	10.	(2.8)
(<1.8)	*Cyanocompsa cyanoides*	11.	(2.6)
(<1.8)	*Myrmotherula fulviventris*	14.	(2.0)

Barro Colorado Island is 2727 mm, with 2253 mm falling during the wet season (May–November) and 474 mm in the dry season (December–April). Rainfall in the wet season of 1968 was about 10% below normal (2037 mm), while during the dry season of 1969 rainfall was 46% below normal (256 mm). In contrast, the 1977 sample followed an especially dry dry season (155 mm; 33% of normal) and included a somewhat wet (2410 mm; 7% above normal) wet season.

In 1968–69, two species, a migrant thrush, apparently present as a passage migrant briefly in October, and an ant-follower (*Phaenostictus*), were caught significantly more often in the rainy season (Table 5). In 1977–78, the tyrannid *Rhynchocyclus* was more frequently captured in the wet season. Pooling data from both years reveals other species whose catch rate varies with season (Table 5). The frugivorous tyrannid *Mionectes olivacea*, for example, is captured primarily in the wet season. Only 3 of 18 captures of *Mionectes* were in the dry season, and all 3 were in December (the first few weeks of the dry season).

Sample sizes for between-season comparisons are small, but species with a significant difference for combined samples displayed similar preferences in each year. Of the 95 species in the combined data set for seasonal comparisons, 48 were captured more than five times and could therefore reflect significant seasonality. Thus, 2.9 (0.06×48) would be expected to show a significant difference by chance alone, compared with the 5 species with significant differences in our sample (Table 5).

Grouping species according to foraging guilds shows that insectivore-nectarivores were caught more often in the dry season (cf. Leck, 1972) when many plants were flowering (Croat, 1978), while ant-following birds were more common in the rainy season, when litter fauna is more abundant (Willis, 1976).

Comparisons among the Three Dry Seasons

Sufficiently large samples are available from the dry seasons of 1969, 1977, and 1978 for comparisons of those years with markedly different rainfall (Table 6). The number of statistically significant changes among the species and guilds is small. However, we are convinced that the trends depicted here are real biologically, and we offer the following comments to account for them.

In the extreme dry season of 1977, when rainfall was one-third the normal, *Automolus* and *Gymnopithys*, both wet-forest species, and *Sclerurus guatemalensis*, the dominant leaf-tosser of wetter habitats, were caught least often (Table 6). Quail doves, *Geotrygon* spp., and

Table 5. Bird species captured at different rates in wet and dry seasons, 1968–69 and 1977–78

Species	Number of captures					
	1968–69		1977–78		Combined	
	Wet	Dry	Wet	Dry	Wet	Dry
Automolous ochrolaemus (ovenbird)	18	5	8	14	26	19
Gymnopithys leucaspis (antbird)	28	11	61	31	89	42
Phaenostictus mcleannani (antbird)	8	0*	31	11	39	11**
Rhynchocyclus olivaceus (flycatcher)	4	3	12	2*	16	5***
Mionectes olivaceus (flycatcher)	6	1	9	2	15	3*
Catharus ustulatus (thrush)	9	1	3	2	12	3***
C. minimus (thrush)	18	0*	4	0	22	0*
Total number of captures	419	224	575	542	994	766

Between-season differences in number of captures were incorporated into the statistical calculations.
  * Significant at $p <.05$ by binomial probability test.
  ** Significant at $p <.05$ by χ^2 test.
  *** Significant at $p <.06$ by binomial probability test.

other ground frugivores were caught five times as often in 1977 as in 1969 and 1978 (Table 6). Finally, the grassland finches, *Sporophila aurita* and *Oryzoborus funereus*, were captured only in the dry season of 1977.

Month-to-Month Variation

The relative capture rate of the most commonly captured species, the red-capped manakin *Pipra mentalis*, varies greatly from month to month (Figure 3). The striking seasonality in manakin activity may be due to the seasonal periodicity of fruits or to post-breeding-season movement of recently fledged young of the year. Peak capture rate each year occurs the first month of the rainy season (May 1969, June 1977). This follows after the April fruiting peak of understory shrubs (Croat, 1978) and corresponds with the early wet-season peak in availability of bird-dispersed fruits (Foster, 1973). In addition, peak manakin abundance broadly overlaps the main breeding period of March-May (Wetmore, 1972). An active manakin lek was located near our study area in both years and may have influenced capture rates in some nets. Regardless of the factors affecting manakin abundance, the marked variation in density may have important community effects. Seasonality in bird density as a function of habitat preference during the breeding season may

Table 6. Rainfall and number and percentages of captures for species and guilds in the dry season, 1969, 1977, and 1978

	1969	1977	1978
Dry-season rainfall (Dec.–Apr.)			
Amount (mm)	256	155	333
Percentage of normal rainfall	54	33	70
Species (number and percentage of captures)			
Phaethornis superciliosus	6(2.7)	12(5.1)	14(4.6)
Automolous ochrolaemus	5(2.2)	4(1.7)	10(3.5)
Sclerurus guatemalensis	9(4.0)*	1(0.4)*	10(3.3)
Gymnopithys leucaspis	11(4.9)	9(3.8)	22(7.2)
Geotrygon montana	3(1.3)	13(5.5)*	3(0.9)
Cyphorhinus phaeocephalus	4(1.8)	10(4.1)	12(3.9)
Guild (number and percentage of captures)			
Ground frugivores	3(1.3)*	16(6.8)*	4(1.3)
Insectivores–nectarivores	8(3.6)*	22(9.4)	25(8.1)
Total number of captures	224	235	307

Percentages of captures are in parentheses.
* Significant at $p<.05$ between adjacent years by binomial probability test.

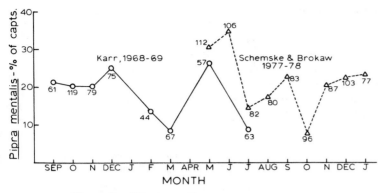

Figure 3. *Pipra mentalis* as a percentage of captures in sequential monthly mist-net samples from Limbo Hunt Club. Numbers indicate number of captures in each monthly sample.

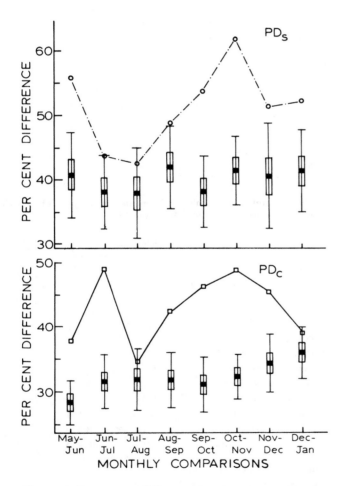

Figure 4. Percentage difference in composition of mist-net samples (Schemske and Brokaw, 1977–78) in successive months by species (PD_s) and species abundance (PD_c) for field data (open symbols) and for 30 pairs of randomly generated communities (solid symbols) with the same sample sizes. Monthly samples vary from 77 to 112 captures. Vertical bars indicate $\pm 2\ SE$; vertical lines $\pm 1\ SD$.

influence the patchiness of resources, and the distribution of other species.

One may also calculate PD_s and PD_c for samples from successive months. This is possible only for the Schemske and Brokaw data, which come from an unbroken sequence of 9 months. Comparing the observed differences for those to random samples of the same sizes (combined data for paired months), we find observed differences are always greater than random (Figure 4). Moreover, the observed differences peak during the onset of rains and during the peak influx of migrants. The low PD_c for the May–June comparison (Figure 4) is a function of the great abundance of *Pipra mentalis* during these months (Figure 3). The striking shift in the resident avifauna occurring at the dry/wet transition is additional evidence for the presence of seasonal differences in avifaunal structure.

Both PD_s and PD_c exhibit a steady increase from mid to late rainy season (Figure 4). During this interval (July–August to October–November), PD_c rose from 35% to 49% and PD_s from 43% to 62%. That two samples of birds from identical netting localities in successive months (October, 96 captures; November, 87 captures) could differ to such an extent is clear evidence that the popular notion of community stability in tropical systems must be reexamined.

DISCUSSION

Our results show striking temporal changes in the catches of both rare and common species from the undergrowth of this tropical moist forest—from month to month, season to season, and year to year, even though the number of individuals captured per species is very similar in both years (1968–69, 9.89; 1977–78, 9.95). The marked variation in the composition of species in successive months of 1977–78 shows how rapidly changes in community composition might occur (Appendix 1).

Since data used in this analysis were collected for other reasons, we cannot test a priori hypotheses. We can, however, speculate on the ecological and evolutionary causes of the patterns described above and suggest testable hypotheses for future studies.

Ecologists have recently been much concerned with the relative stability of tropical and temperate communities (cf., Wolda, 1978). The alternation of winter and summer imposes great seasonal changes in the number of insectivorous birds in temperate forest. However, the alternation of dry and rainy season has a much smaller impact on the insectivores of our plot. There were only two groups of insectivores for which catches changed greatly from 1968–69 to 1977–78: ant-followers and the species affected by treefalls and other habitat changes. Although insects shift downward toward the forest floor in dry season when many trees lose their leaves (Smythe, 1974), the birds do not, showing the precision of vertical segregation in tropical forest birds (Orians, 1969; Terborgh and Weske, 1969; Karr, 1971a). About 50% of the species known to occur on the Limbo Hunt Club study plot have been captured in nets. Data from north temperate forests (Karr, pers. observation; C. S. Robbins, pers. comm.) suggest that 80% to 90% of temperate forest species are captured in undergrowth mist-nets.

Among noninsectivorous guilds, two seem to be especially prone to changing species composition and abundance. One group, the nectarivorous hummingbirds, seems especially variable among dry seasons, a pattern observed in the clearing on Barro Colorado (Leck, 1972; G. Angehr, pers. comm.) and in other areas. Variability may be expected in this specialist guild because of their dependence on specific flowering plants. Another noninsectivorous group mentioned as temporally variable is the terrestrial frugivores (Table 6).

Other than the insectivore-nectarivore guild discussed above, all species that exhibit a seasonal trend in abundance peak in the wet season. Is there a greater bird abundance, in general, in the forest during the wet season? If so, could this be due to increased number of juveniles following the late dry/early wet season breeding season of many species? Alternatively, do many species expand foraging ranges in the wet season to include a wider array of microhabitats (ridge tops, sheltered valleys, etc.) because insects are more abundant in all these areas? A preliminary study in 1979 (Karr, unpubl.) supports the latter alternative.

Another recent ecological controversy is concerned with the time scale of changes in community structure (Diamond and May, 1977). Our measured differences in community composition between two samples are clearly greater than expected at random. However, at this point we cannot determine if they represent an accumulation of changes over 9 years, or if they are typical of year-to-year changes in the composition of the fauna. Our measures of changes over shorter time scales (month-to-month and between seasons) are nearly as great as our year-to-year variability, suggesting the latter may be closer to the truth.

Our data on the manakin *Pipra mentalis* emphasize the potential contrast in annual versus seasonal abundance patterns within a single species. *Pipra mentalis*, the most abundant species at Limbo Hunt Club in both sample years (Table 6), was strikingly consistent in the proportion of each year's sample (19.6% versus 21.9%). However, that similarity is rather deceptive, as the species experiences local changes in capture rates within each of those annual cycles (Figure 3).

Other frugivores also show considerable month-to-month variation in abundance. *Pipra coronata* varied from 0.9% to 13.6% of samples while *Pipromorpha oleaginea* varied from 1.2% to 10.4%.

Among the ant-followers, the month-to-month variation in capture rates in 1977–78 yields insight into species-specific distribution patterns. *Phaenostictus* makes up from 0 to 12.6% of the monthly samples, while *Gymnopithys* varies from 1.9% to 18.8%. The most territorial species varies only from 1.2% to 6.9% of the samples. To emphasize the short-term variation, *Phaenostictus* had the highest relative abundance in November 1977 (12.6%), when it was the second most abundant species, but was not represented at all in the next monthly sample. Thus, in addition to differences in temporal variation among guilds, temporal variation among species in the same guilds also occurs.

In some cases, seasonal fluctuations in food resources seem to correlate well with seasonal variation in bird catches (e.g., nectarivores discussed above). However, we have no data on such food resource variability from our study site to reinforce that speculation.

Species that specialize on spatially patchy resources (ant-followers, gap species) seem to be more variable in their presence and abundance than species that search more generally through a habitat. This is supported by our observations of the ant-followers discussed above.

Some final words of caution: Throughout this paper we have attempted to cite examples of temporal variation in species composition and densities of tropical forest birds at a specific study site. We do not mean to suggest that this variation is characteristic for each species throughout its range or for all species. Further, it is clear that the spatial scale of variation is likely to differ among species and guilds. More detailed information from a series of study plots is required to clarify the subtlety of these patterns.

Similarly, we do not know why capture rates change with time. The reasons are likely different among species. In some cases, regular, local migration within the isthmus of Panama seems likely, while in others, more opportunistic movements may be a reality as species exploit changing resource availability in space and time. This phenomena is well documented in grassland and savanna species (e.g., *Sporophila* spp. in Panama, *Quelea* in Africa) and may be common but difficult to document in forest birds. Further, local changes in capture rates may be a result of reproductive activities.

ACKNOWLEDGMENTS

We gratefully acknowledge financial support from the

following institutions which made this analysis possible: Smithsonian Tropical Research Institute (JRK, DWS, NB), National Geographic Society and University of Illinois Research Board (JRK), and University of Chicago, Hutchinson and Coulter Funds (NB). C. Augspurger, T. Casey, E. Eisenmann, T. Martin, N. Smith, P. Waser, and M. Willson made helpful comments on an earlier draft of the manuscript. Finally, we thank the many volunteers who aided us in the operation of mist-nets.

LITERATURE CITED

Croat, T.
1978. *Flora of Barro Colorado Island*. Stanford, California: Stanford University Press.

Diamond, J. M., and R. M. May
1977. Species turnover rates on islands: dependence on census interval. *Science*, 197:266–270.

Foster, R. B.
1973. Seasonality of fruit production and seedfall in a tropical forest ecosystem in Panama. Ph.D. dissertation, Duke University, Durham, North Carolina. 156 pp.

Foster, R. B., and N. V. L. Brokaw
1982. Structure and History of the Vegetation of Barro Colorado Island. Pages 67–81 in *The Ecology of a Tropical Forest*, edited by Egbert G. Leigh, Jr., et al. Washington, D.C.: Smithsonian Institution Press.

Karr, J. R.
1971a. Structure of avian communities in selected Panama and Illinois habitats. *Ecological Monographs*, 41:207–233.
1971b. Wintering Kentucky Warblers (*Oporornis formosus*) and a warning to banders. *Bird Banding*, 42:229.
1976. Seasonality, resource availability, and community diversity in tropical bird communities. *American Naturalist*, 110:973–994.
1977. Ecological correlates of rarity in a tropical forest bird community. *Auk*, 94:240–247.
1979. On the use of mist nets in the study of bird communities. *Inland Bird Banding*, 51:1–10.
1980. Turnover dynamics in a tropical continental avifauna. Pages 991–997 in *Proceedings of the 17th International Ornithological Congress, West Berlin*.

Karr, J. R., and R. R. Roth
1971. Vegetation structure and avian diversity in several New World areas. *American Naturalist*, 105:423–435.

Leck, C. F.
1972. Seasonal changes in feeding pressures of fruit and nectar-eating birds in Panama. *Condor*, 174:54–60.

Novaes, F. C.
1970. Distribuicao ecológica e abundanciadas aves em um trecho da mata do baixo Rio Guamá (Estado de Pará). *Boletim do Museu Paraense Emíleo Goeldi, Zoologia*, 71:1–54.

Orians, G. H.
1969. The number of birds species in some tropical forests. *Ecology*, 50:783–801.

Schemske, D. W., and N. Brokaw
1981. Treefalls and the distribution of understory birds in a tropical forest. *Ecology*, 62:938–945.

Smythe, N.
1974. Biological monitoring data—insects. Pages 70–115 in *1973 Environmental Monitoring and Baseline Date*, edited by R. W. Rubinoff. Washington, D.C.: Smithsonian Institution Environmental Sciences Program.

Terborgh, J., and J. S. Weske
1969. Colonization of secondary habitats by Peruvian birds. *Ecology*, 50:765–782.

Willis, E. O.
1972. *The Behavior of Spotted Antbirds*. Ornithological Monograph No. 10. Lawrence, Kans.: American Ornithologists' Union. 162 pp.
1976. Seasonal changes in the invertebrate litter fauna on Barro Colorado Island, Panama. *Revista Brasiliense Biologica*, 36:643–657.

Wolda, H.
1978. Fluctuations in abundance of tropical insects. *American Naturalist*, 112:1017–1045.

Appendix 1. Number of captures overall and for wet and dry seasons, 1968–69 and 1977–78 samples *(continued on next page)*

Family, genus, and species[1]	Aug. 1968 to July 1969	May 1977 to Jan. 1978[2]	Season Wet (Aug. 1968 to Mar. 1978)	Dry (Aug. 1968 to Mar. 1978)
Accipitridae				
Leucopternis semiplumbea (1)	1	1 (1)	1	1
L. plumbea (1)	2	—	2	—
Falconidae				
Micrastur mirandollei (1)	—	1	—	1
M. ruficollis (1)	—	1 (1)	1	—
Phasianidae				
Rhynchortyx cinctus (5)	1	—	1	—
Columbidae				
Leptotila cassinii (3)	—	1 (1)	—	1
Geotrygon violacea (3)	—	1	—	2
G. veraguensis (3)	—	—	—	1
G. montana (3)	7	23 (13)	21	19
Strigidae				
Glaucidium minutissimum (11)	—	1	—	1
Trochilidae				
Threnetes ruckeri (8)	5	5 (2)	7	3
Phaethornis superciliosus (8)	15	23 (18)	22	32
P. longuemareus (8)	1	—	1	2
Florisuga mellivora (8)	—	3 (3)	1	3
Chlorostilbon canivetii (8)	1	—	—	3
Thalurania colombica (8)	2	3 (3)	4	4
Damophila julie (8)	—	8 (8)	4	7
Amazilia amabilis (8)	1	1 (1)	1	1
Trogonidae				
Trogon rufus (6)	—	2 (1)	2	3
Alcedinidae				
Chloroceryle aenea (14)	1	3 (3)	4	—
C. inda (14)	—	—	—	1
Momotidae				
Baryphthengus martii (6)	1	1 (1)	1	2
Electron platyrhynchum (6)	1	—	1	—
Bucconidae				
Malacoptila panamensis (11)	11	4 (4)	11	4
Notharchus pectoralis (11)	—	1 (1)	—	1
Picidae				
Campephilus haematogaster (9)	—	2 (2)	1	1

[1] Numbers in parentheses indicate guild assignment of species as follows:
1–Raptor
3–Terrestrial frugivore
4–Undergrowth frugivore
5–Terrestrial insectivore-frugivore
6–Undergrowth insectivore-frugivore
8–Insectivore-nectarivore
9–Bark insectivore
10–Terrestrial insectivore
11–Foliage insectivore
12–Sallying insectivore
13–Ant follower
14–Miscellaneous

[2] Numbers in parentheses are for June 1977 to Jan. 1978.

Family, genus, and species[1]	Aug. 1968 to July 1969	May 1977 to Jan. 1978[2]	Season	
			Wet (Aug. 1968 to Mar. 1978)	Dry (Aug. 1968 to Mar. 1978)
Dendrocolaptidae				
Glyphorynchus spirurus (9)	6	—	4	5
Deconychura longicauda (9)	6	5 (5)	9	6
Dendrocincla fuliginosa (13)	10	15 (15)	12	16
D. homochroa (13)	1	1 (1)	1	1
Xiphorhynchus guttatus (9)	—	6 (5)	3	5
X. lachrymosus (9)	—	1 (1)	—	1
Furnariidae				
Automolus ochrolaemus (11)	23	16 (13)	26	19
Xenops minutus (9)	5	11 (10)	9	10
Sclerurus mexicanus (10)	1	2 (2)	2	1
S. guatemalensis (10)	21	27 (27)	34	20
Formicariidae				
Thamnophilus punctatus (11)	5	12 (10)	10	7
Thamnistes anabatinus (11)	2	—	1	1
Dysithamnus puncticeps (11)	—	7 (7)	4	3
Myrmotherula axillaris (11)	3	15 (12)	13	16
M. fulviventris (11)	13	10 (10)	17	13
Microrhopias quixensis (11)	2	—	2	—
Myrmeciza exsul (10)	—	7 (7)	5	6
Myrmornis torquata (10)	7	2 (2)	7	5
Gymnophithys leucaspis (13)	39	78 (73)	89	42
Hylophylax naevioides (13)	21	27 (20)	31	22
Phaenostictus mcleannani (13)	8	39 (32)	39	11
Formicarius analis (10)	11	8 (7)	14	8
Pittasoma michleri (13)	1	—	1	—
Hylopezus perspicillata (10)	3	4 (4)	5	3
Pipridae				
Pipra coronata (4)	38	26 (25)	37	41
P. mentalis (4)	126	181 (147)	202	161
Manacus vitellinus (4)	2	4 (3)	6	3
Schiffornis turdinus (11)	8	5 (3)	9	8
Sapayoa aenigma (11)	1	—	1	—
Cotingidae				
Attila spadiceus (11)	4	4 (4)	4	4
Laniocera rufescens (6)	1	—	—	2
Tityra semifasciata (6)	—	1 (1)	1	—
Tyrannidae				
Empidonax sp. (12)	—	3 (3)	2	1
E. virescens (12)	1	—	1	—
Terenotriccus erythrurus (12)	15	16 (15)	21	24
Myiobius sulphureipygius (12)	22	12 (12)	23	12
Onychorhynchus mexicanus (12)	5	—	2	8

Family, genus, and species[1]	Aug. 1968 to July 1969	May 1977 to Jan. 1978[2]	Season	
			Wet (Aug. 1968 to Mar. 1978)	Dry (Aug. 1968 to Mar. 1978)
Platyrinchus coronatus (11)	19	19 (19)	29	17
Cnipodectes subbrunneus (11)	8	6 (5)	8	8
Tolmomyias assimilis (11)	—	2 (2)	1	1
Rhynchocyclus olivaceus (11)	7	14 (13)	16	5
Oncostoma olivaceum (4)	2	3 (3)	2	3
Pipromorpha oleaginea (4)	38	34 (29)	48	50
Mionectes olivacea (4)	7	11 (11)	15	3
Troglodytidae				
Henicorhina leucosticta (11)	2	—	1	2
Cyphorhinus phaeocephalus (10)	13	30 (24)	29	26
Microcerculus marginatus (10)	6	14 (13)	14	7
Turdidae				
Hylocichla mustelina (4)	—	3 (3)	2	2
Catharus ustulatus (4)	10	3 (3)	12	1
C. minimus (4)	18	4 (4)	22	—
C. fuscescens (4)	1	—	1	—
Sylviidae				
Microbates cinereiventris (11)	11	4 (3)	10	8
Vireonidae				
Hylophilus ochraceiceps (11)	—	9 (9)	4	5
Parulidae				
Seiurus noveboracensis (10)	—	2 (2)	1	4
Oporornis formosus (10)	10	—	3	11
Wilsonia canadensis (11)	—	3 (3)	3	—
Basileuterus fulvicauda (14)	—	—	—	1
Icteridae				
Cacicus uropygialis (6)	—	1 (1)	1	—
Thraupidae				
Euphonia fulvicrissa (14)	—	1 (1)	1	—
Piranga rubra (6)	1	—	1	—
Chlorothraupis carmioli (6)	6	5 (5)	9	3
Habia fuscicauda (6)	4	—	2	2
Tachyphonus luctuosus (6)	—	1 (1)	1	—
Eucometis penicillata (13)	1	10 (8)	9	3
Fringillidae				
Pitylus grossus (6)	—	2 (1)	—	2
Cyanocompsa cyanoides (6)	17	13 (12)	15	22
Sporophila aurita (14)	—	1	—	1
Oryzoborus funereus (14)	—	1	—	1
Arremon aurantiirostris (10)	1	—	1	—

The Terrestrial Mammal Fauna of Barro Colorado Island: Censuses and Long-term Changes

WILLIAM E. GLANZ   Department of Zoology, University of Maine, Orono, Maine 04469

ABSTRACT

This paper presents estimates of the numbers of most of the nonvolant species of mammals on Barro Colorado Island. I compare these results with estimates from previous censuses, to learn how much these populations have fluctuated. Since 1930, several species of mammal have gone extinct on Barro Colorado, including pumas and white-lipped peccaries, which could not survive on so small an island after hunting pressure built up on the adjacent mainland, and pygmy squirrels, pygmy rice rats, and perhaps other rodents, which died out as areas of grassland and young second-growth grew into more mature forest.

Judging from previous censuses by Eisenberg in 1964/65 and Thorington in 1970/71, some populations have fluctuated greatly in more recent years.

During the last 15 years, populations of coatis and howler monkeys have remained stable; the numbers of tamarins, white-faced monkeys, and collared peccaries have declined; and the numbers of squirrels and agoutis have increased tenfold or more. During the year of my study, the number of four-eyed opossums declined greatly.

The normal community of Barro Colorado Island seems reasonably representative of mammal communities in other lowland neotropical forests, except for the absence of the largest cats. The mammals of this island may indeed be more abundant because jaguars and pumas are absent, but they may merely appear more abundant because they are so much less wary, as a result of protection from hunting.

INTRODUCTION

Barro Colorado Island has one of the best-studied mammal faunas in the neotropics. Many of the common diurnal species of mammals there have been studied in detail, beginning with Carpenter's (1934) early research on howler monkeys. There have also been several reviews of the mammal fauna as a whole. Enders (1930, 1935) summarized what was known of most of the mammal species of Barro Colorado, including many of the lesser-known nocturnal species. Eisenberg and Thorington (1973) have estimated population densities and weights per unit area of the different mammals of Barro Colorado, and Eisenberg (1980) has revised many of these estimates in the light of both further work on Barro Colorado and comparisons with several Venezuelan communities.

From January 1977 to June 1978 I had an opportunity to make another survey of Barro Colorado's mammal fauna, to see how much population densities had changed since Eisenberg and Thorington's time. During this period my coworkers and I were repeatedly walking transects through a variety of habitats, "strip-censusing" squirrels. As the strip-census is a quick, relatively effective way of censusing many of the mammal species on Barro Colorado, we collected appropriate census data on all species of mammals we encountered. For comparisons, we conducted a less intensive program of night censuses and observations of nocturnal animals.

In this paper I will first discuss my census methods and some potential biases and limitations associated with their use. I will then present the results of these censuses and use them to estimate the densities of certain species. Such conclusions will necessarily be preliminary, but I hope they will facilitate comparisons and stimulate further study. Finally, I will discuss fluctuations of mammal populations on Barro Colorado, drawing on qualitative information from earlier accounts and on comparisons of my results with those of Eisenberg and Thorington (1973).

METHODS

I estimated mammal populations using strip-census techniques (Robinette et al., 1974; Cant, 1977) along trails in the northeastern and central parts of the island (Figure 1), especially those trails near the squirrel intensive-study area on Snyder-Molino Ridge. The following six routes (designated by trail name and distance markers) were censused repeatedly on the diurnal surveys: (1)Snyder-Molino 0–6, Wheeler 4–12 to the tower clearing; (2) Barbour-Lathrop 0–8 to Miller to Lake; (3) tower clearing to Armour 0–9 to Zetek 3–0 and return to tower clearing; (4) Balboa 0–

7 to Shannon 5–0 to Barbour 1; (5) Lutz to Barbour 1–7 and return via Donato; (6) Fairchild 0–18. These routes usually were censused once every 2 weeks. Nocturnal surveys were conducted along four routes: the census routes (3),(4), and (5) listed above, and another route that included all of (1) above and the Lake 0–6 portion of (2). Each nocturnal census route was walked once every 4 to 6 weeks early in the study, and once every 6 to 8 weeks later.

During the diurnal censuses, we walked the trails at an average speed of 1 km/hr., stopping frequently to scan both ground and foliage levels for animals. The nocturnal censuses required a slower pace (0.8 km/hr.), headlamps, and, whenever possible, two observers for easier detection and positive identification of many mammals. Data recorded for most mammal sightings included: species, trail location, detection distance when first encountered, perpendicular distance from animal to trail, height above ground, and feeding behavior (Figure 2). Duration of census and distance walked were recorded for each transect walk. Diurnal censuses were conducted between 7:00 A.M. and 11:00 A.M., a period of peak mammal activity, while most nocturnal censuses were run between 7:00 P.M. and 11:00 P.M., the time most convenient for myself and coworkers.

For comparisons with the data of Eisenberg and Thorington (1973), we have calculated the numbers of sightings per species per hour of censusing. The population estimation techniques used in this study were two relatively simple strip-census methods recommended by Robinette et al. (1974): King's method and Kelker's method. Both techniques calculate densities based upon the number of animals encountered in a strip of land on both sides of the trail (Table 1 and Figure 2). Each assumes that animals can be censused thoroughly within this strip. In King's method, the strip width used is the mean of all sighting distances for a given species (Table 1). Kelker's method is equivalent to a bird transect method developed by Emlen (1971), based upon the perpendicular distances of animals from the trail. A frequency distribution of all perpendicular distances for a species is plotted, and a strip width is estimated in which the frequency of encounter for that species is constant, indicating that few animals were overlooked in that strip. Formulas used in each method are given in Table 1.

Social mammals, such as primates and coatis, were often encountered in groups that responded to the observer in a coordinated fashion, by scolding, mobbing, or fleeing. Under such conditions, accurate counts and distances for each animal were impossible to obtain, so I modified the techniques for social animals by recording the distance only for the first animal

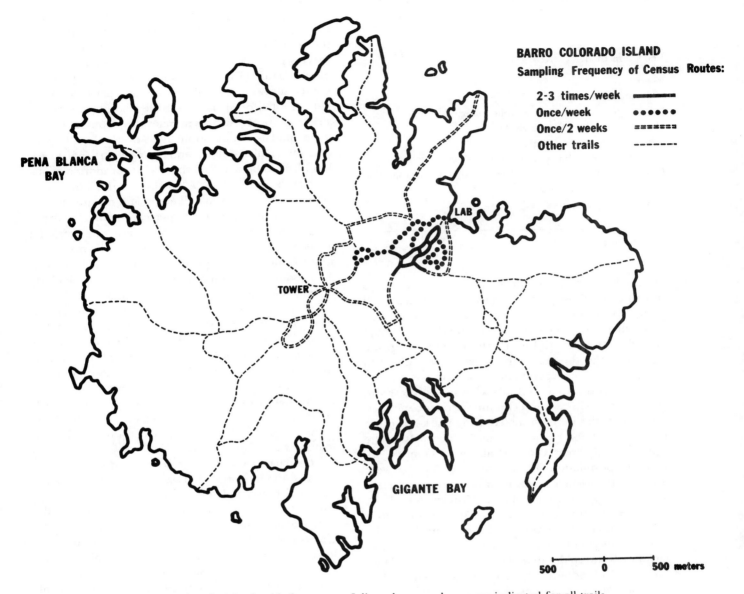

Figure 1.   Map of Barro Colorado Island, with frequency of diurnal mammal censuses indicated for all trails.

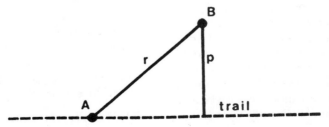

Figure 2.   Distances recorded during strip-censuses. A = observer; B = animal sighted; r = sighting distance or detection distance; p = perpendicular distance of animal from trail.

Table 1. Formulas for strip-census estimates of population size

King's method: $\qquad N = nA/2L\bar{R}$

Kelker's method: $\qquad N = n'A/2LP*$

where

A = area to be censused
L = length of census lines, in units comparable to A
N = estimate of population size
n = number of animals sighted
n' = number of animals sighted within distance $P*$
$P*$ = estimated distance beyond which a significant proportion of animals are missed
$\bar{R}$ = mean sighting distance.

From Robinette et al. (1974).

sighted in each group and by carefully observing a subsample of these groups to measure group size and group radius. In density calculations for both King's and Kelker's methods, the mean number of animals per group was multiplied by the number of group sightings, and the mean group radius was added to the sighting and perpendicular distances.

Several additional methods were used to test and verify these strip-census techniques. Rodent and marsupial densities were estimated using mark-recapture methods and observations of marked animals on the squirrel study area (Glanz et al., this volume). Estimates of population size and mean group size were available from other more intensive studies of certain species (Oppenheimer, 1982; Mittermeier, 1973; Montgomery and Sunquist, 1975; Milton, 1977; Russell, 1979), and these provided useful checks on the strip-census results. Several mammal species, particularly tapirs and spider monkeys, are rare on the island, but most individuals are recognizable; such population estimates were also used.

Several other techniques were used to monitor species that were difficult to census. Arboreal nocturnal mammals were observed from towers and platforms located 5 to 30 m above ground level. Most (87%) of these nocturnal watches were conducted from 20 to 25 m above the ground on a scaffolding tower in Lutz Ravine near the laboratory clearing. From March to May 1977, low water levels in Gatun Lake exposed extensive beaches on the perimeter of the island. Mammal tracks were monitored on beaches between Barbour Point and Fairchild Point during these months.

Before discussing the results, we should outline some biases and limitations of the methods employed, particularly the strip-census techniques. Thorington

(1972), Robinette et al. (1974), and Cant (1977) have reviewed many aspects of strip-censusing. These census methods were used primarily because they were time-efficient, they could be applied to most mammal species present, and they were appropriate for estimating squirrel densities and diets. Several factors limited the accuracy of these methods, particularly visibility in the forest. The dense vegetation severely restricts sighting distances in many directions, and even large animals can occasionally be overlooked. In general, the smaller, quieter, and more solitary species are less likely to be detected than larger or more obvious species. Because of such "missed" animals, the strip-census calculations are likely to underestimate the population levels of many species. Fortunately, trapping projects and other intensive studies in restricted areas have permitted us to calibrate our census techniques, and estimate proportions of animals missed. The rodents and some marsupials were particularly amenable to such calibration (see below).

Detection problems are particularly severe in censusing nocturnal species, since they must be located by eyeshine reflecting the observer's headlamp, or by movement. Only the largest nocturnal species (such as the brocket deer) and those that freeze under the headlamp can be reliably identified beyond 15 m. Arboreal mammals that have either poor eyeshine (such as the porcupine *Coendou*) or small body size (*Caluromys* and *Diplomys*) are almost certainly underestimated by these techniques.

The Barro Colorado forest is not homogeneous, and to estimate population sizes for the island, the animals must be sampled in habitats that are representative of the entire island. The trails sampled during the strip-censuses include most of the common forest types of Barro Colorado but are biased toward ridge tops and "young" forest (50 to 80 years old) on the northeast side of the island. Ravines and lake-edge habitats are severely underrepresented, and mammals that prefer these habitats (such as tapirs and capybaras) are surely underestimated.

Finally, the strip-census techniques presume that the animal will remain visible long enough for the observer to locate and identify it. Extremely wary species, such as the ocelot and the jaguarundi, are less likely to be detected, while unwary and noisy species are located very easily. These potential biases will be considered in evaluating the strip-census results and in deriving reasonable population estimates.

RESULTS AND DISCUSSION

Population Densities

Table 2 summarizes the strip-census estimates of population size on Barro Colorado using both King's and

Table 2. Estimates of population size of mammals on Barro Colorado Island   (*continued on next page*)

Species	Census type[1]	Number of sightings	King's estimate			Kelker's estimate			"Reasonable" estimate
			$\overline{R}$[2]	Individuals	Groups	$P*$[2]	Individuals	Groups	
Marsupialia									
Caluromys derbianus	N	3	11.7	30	—	—	—	—	300
	T	8							
Chironectes minimus	N	0	—	—	—	—	—	—	?
Didelphis marsupialis	N	41	11.0	430	—	8	432	—	700
	T	6							
Marmosa robinsoni	N	6	8.7	79	—	—	—	—	400
Metachirus nudicaudatus	T	1	—	—	—	—	—	—	?
Philander opossum	N	6	10.0	69	—	—	—	—	200
Primates									
Alouatta palliata	D	173	38.6*	1489	78	30	1227	65	1300
Aotus trivirgatus	N	4	17.5	26	10	—	—	—	40
Ateles geoffroyi	D	16	36.8*	31	—	40	23	—	14
Cebus capucinus	D	30	29.0*	172	14	25	218	17	140
Saguinus geoffroyi	D	9	20.4*	38	8	—	—	—	40
Edentata									
Bradypus infuscatus	D	18	10.1	43	—	—	—	—	8000
Choloepus hoffmanni	D	2	8.0	6	—	—	—	—	1500
	T	4							
Tamandua mexicana	D	26	15.4	40	—	10	48	—	80
	N	2	7.5	31					
Cyclopes didactylus	D	1	10.0	—	—	—	—	—	?
Dasypus novemcinctus	N	34	9.0	435	—	5	484	—	800
Cabassous centralis	N	0	—	—	—	—	—	—	?
Lagomorpha									
Sylvilagus brasiliensis	N	19	6.3	353	—	—	—	—	100
	D	1	12.0	—	—	—	—	—	—
Rodentia									
Sciurus granatensis	D	774	15.1	1220	—	15	1162	—	2700
Oryzomys spp.	N	20	4.5	512	—	5	460	—	2000
Diplomys labilis	N	2	10.0	23	—	—	—	—	?
	T	2	—	—	—	—	—	—	—
Proechimys semispinosus	N	31	5.2	687	—	5	645	—	2800
Coendou rothschildi	N	1	8.0	14	—	—	—	—	150
	T	2							
Dasyprocta punctata	D	1006	17.0	1410	—	10	1616	—	1500
	N	46	9.4	564	—	5	668	—	—
Agouti paca	N	43	16.5	300	—	10	345	—	600
Hydrochaeris hydrochaeris	D	0	—	—	—	—	—	—	?

Area of Barro Colorado Island = 1500 ha.
[1] Census types: D = diurnal; N = nocturnal; T = tower watch.
[2] Distances in Population Estimates: $\overline{R}$ = mean sighting distance; $P*$ = perpendicular strip width. Asterisk indicates group radius not included in mean sighting distance or in perpendicular strip width.

Table 2. (continued)

Species	Census type[1]	Number of sightings	King's estimate			Kelker's estimate			"Reasonable" estimate
			$\overline{R}^2$	Individuals	Groups	$P*^2$	Individuals	Groups	
Carnivora									
Nasua narica (all)	D	67	—	371	34	—	304	28	360
bands only	D	38	20.9*	323	34	20	276	28	300
singles only	D	29	14.5	48	—	15	38	—	60
Potos flavus	N	24	18.4	150	—	15	115	—	300
	T	14							
Eira barbara	D	4	17.3	6	—	—	—	—	25
Lutra annectens	N	0	—	—	—	—	—	—	?
Felis pardalis	N	0	—	—	—	—	—	—	12
Felis yagouarundi	N	0	—	—	—	—	—	—	?
Perissodactyla									
Tapirus bairdii	D	2	16.0	3	—	—	—	—	8
Artiodactyla									
Tayassu tajacu	D	28	24.0*	137	21	20	149	23	140
	N	6	19.5	163	25	—	—	—	—
Mazama americana	N	15	26.2	66	—	—	—	—	30
	D	11	20.2	13	—	—	—	—	—
Odocoileus virginianus	D	3	12.0	6	—	—	—	—	10
	N	2	15.0	15	—	—	—	—	—

Kelker's methods. Since the latter method requires a sufficiently large sample size to construct a frequency distribution of distances, it is applied to only those species with more than 20 census records. In addition, a "reasonable" estimate of numbers on the island is provided, which takes into account biases in sampling and other information on the species. Since each group presents its own problems in sampling, we will discuss these results following the phylogenetic order in Table 2.

Marsupialia All marsupials present on the island are nocturnal, give excellent eyeshine, and often freeze under the headlamp. They are therefore detectable using the night census methods employed. All are quiet, however, and most will climb into cover if disturbed; the calculations from strip-censuses, therefore, probably underestimate all to some extent. The probability of detection depends greatly on habits and body size, with the larger, more terrestrial species, such as the common opossum *Didelphis marsupialis* and the four-eyed opossum *Philander opossum*, being easily located, while smaller forms (such as the mouse opossum *Marmosa robinsoni*) and extremely arboreal forms

(the woolly opossum *Caluromys derbianus*) are much less likely to be seen. For example, during night censuses, *Caluromys* was seen approximately five times as often per hour of observation from stationary positions in the canopy as from the ground (see Tables 3 and 4). Of the species trapped on the squirrel study area, *Marmosa* was rare and restricted to vine tangles and treefalls, *Philander* decreased greatly in abundance during the study, and *Didelphis* was common at approximately 0.5/ha. These differences between species agree well with the relative abundances from strip-censuses, but calibration of censuses by using trapping results is possible only with *Didelphis*.

Primates Each of the primate species of Barro Colorado lives in social groups, ranging from the large multimale troops of the howler monkey *Alouatta palliata* to the pairs and small family groups seen in the night monkey *Aotus trivirgatus*. Only the small, nocturnal *Aotus* presents problems in detection. Nevertheless, the strip-censuses provide estimates that are remarkably close to those found by other methods.

The howler monkey is the commonest primate on the island. Recent censuses by Mittermeier (1973) and

Milton (this volume) can be used to check the strip-census results. King's method estimates 78 troops on the island, while Kelker's estimates 65 troops. Assuming a troop size of 17 animals (Milton, 1977; and this study; mean = 16.5), the Barro Colorado population would be 1326 or 1105 animals by the two methods. Milton (this volume) has more recently found a mean group size of 19 to 20 monkeys, which would produce a King's estimate of 1489 and a Kelker's estimate of 1227. These results are very close to Milton's (this volume) most recent estimate of 1300 monkeys in the population.

The other three diurnal primates are all considerably rarer than *Alouatta*. The white-faced monkey *Cebus capucinus* lives in smaller troops of approximately 8 to 15 animals, but troop members are very widely spaced as they travel through the forest, making censusing relatively difficult. The measured troop radius (21 m) is probably a conservative estimate, which would overestimate the true population density. The tamarin *Saguinus geoffroyi* presents similar problems in the measurement of both troop size and group radius. In addition, this species is wary and relatively rare.

The red spider monkeys (*Ateles geoffroyi*) on Barro Colorado are all individually identifiable, and population size (14 to 16 during this study) is easily determined by observation near the laboratory clearing, where they frequently congregate. Population estimates from strip-censusing are 1.5 to 2.0 times the actual value, undoubtedly because the census routes heavily sample areas in the northeastern portion of the island, where the monkeys concentrate their activities.

On Barro Colorado, the night monkey *Aotus* appears to be rare and unpredictable in its occurrence.

Edentata This order includes the largest proportion of mammalian biomass on the island (Eisenberg and Thorington, 1973; Montgomery and Sunquist, 1975), largely because of the great number of three-toed sloths (*Bradypus infuscatus*) and two-toed sloths (*Choloepus hoffmanni*). Walking strip-censuses are definitely inappropriate for these silent, sedentary animals (see Table 2). My personal observations of sloths in the squirrel study area lead me to believe that, while the published density estimates of Montgomery and Sunquist (1975) may be somewhat high, the recent estimates of Eisenberg (1980) are too low. My guesses at sloth population size in Table 2 are closer to those of Montgomery and Sunquist (1975).

Other Barro Colorado edentates, particularly the vested anteater *Tamandua mexicana* and the nine-banded armadillo *Dasypus novemcinctus*, are more easily detected during strip-censuses. Both are noisy and easy

to locate when moving, but can be difficult to detect when stationary. The arboreal tendencies of the anteater and the burrowing of the armadillo also limit their visibility. Strip-censusing probably underestimates both, but not to the extent seen in sloths. The data certainly reveal that *Dasypus* is common on Barro Colorado (0.2 to 0.5/ha.), with most of its activity occurring at night. *Tamandua* is less common (approximately 0.05/ha.), as one would expect from its larger size and specialized diet.

Lagomorpha In their 1973 paper, Eisenberg and Thorington noted that the tropical cottontail rabbit, *Sylvilagus brasiliensis* had not been recorded on Barro Colorado since 1964. Their obituary for this species was evidently premature, as *Sylvilagus* was sighted frequently during night censuses in 1977–78. This rabbit was particularly common near the laboratory and tower clearings. Because most census routes began or terminated at these clearings, such "edge" habitats were

Table 3. Sightings per hour on diurnal censuses, 1964–78

| Genus | Eisenberg | | Thorington | | Glanz, 1977–78 |
	1964	1965	1970	1971	
Alouatta	.455	.481	.628	.567	.561
Ateles	n.c.	n.c.	n.c.	n.c.	.052
Cebus	.473	.630	.326	.133	.097
Saguinus	.073	.185	.093	.033	.029
Tamandua	.127	.111	.023	—	.084
Cyclopes	—	—	—	—	.003
Bradypus	.018	.037	.140	.033	.058
Choleopus	—	—	—	—	.006
Dasypus	—	—	—	—	.006
Sylvilagus	—	—	—	—	.003
Sciurus	.109	.185	.186	1.100	2.509
Dasyprocta	.182	.333	.535	.967	3.261
Nasua	.145	.185	.163	.133	.223
Eira	.018	.074	—	—	.013
Tapirus	—	—	—	—	.006
Tayassu	.145	.259	.093	—	.091
Mazama	.018	—	—	—	.036
Odocoileus	—	—	—	.033	.010
Total hours	55	27	43	30	309

n.c. = not calculated.

Table 4. Sightings per hour on nocturnal censuses, 1964–78

Genus	Walking censuses from trails			Tower watches
	Eisenberg 1964–65	Thorington 1971	Glanz 1977–78	Glanz 1977–78
Caluromys	—	.109	.039	.213
Marmosa	—	—	.078	.027
Philander	.095	.055	.078	.027
Metachirus	—	—	—	.027
Didelphis	.381	.236	.532	.160
Chironectes	—	.018	—	—
Alouatta	—	—	—	.027
Ateles	—	—	.013	—
Aotus	.095	.036	.052	—
Tamandua	.048	—	.026	.027
Choloepus	.048	.036	.013	.107
Bradypus	—	—	.013	—
Dasypus	.048	.145	.442	.053
Sylvilagus	—	—	.247	—
Oryzomys	n.c.	n.c.	.260	—
Misc. small rodents	.095	.091	n.c.	—
Diplomys	—	.055	.026	.053
Proechimys	.095	—	.403	.053
Coendou	—	—	.013	.053
Agouti	.143	.127	.558	.080
Dasyprocta	—	.036	.597	.027
Potos and *Bassaricyon*	.048	.091	.312	.373
Tapirus	—	—	.013	—
Tayassu	—	—	.078	—
Mazama	—	—	.221	—
Odocoileus	—	—	.013	—
Unidentified	n.c.	n.c.	.390	.133
Total hours	21	55	77	37.5

n.c. = not calculated

overrepresented along the transects, and King's estimate of rabbit numbers on the island is undoubtedly too high.

Rodentia Several rodent species on Barro Colorado permit a direct calibration of strip-census estimates with those obtained by other techniques. During this and related studies (Glanz et al., this volume), population densities of the red-tailed squirrel, *Sciurus granatensis*, were monitored on a 10-ha. study area, using mark-recapture methods and resighting in-

dexes. Strip censuses were run through the study area frequently during this project, and these produced estimates that averaged from 40% to 60% of the mark and resighting index, depending on the season. Thus, about one squirrel was missed for every one censused, which is not surprising considering the small size and arboreal habits of this species. The strip-census estimates of 1160 and 1220 squirrels on the island, therefore, may be about half the true population size. Analysis of sightings per hour permits another calculation. About 3.1 squirrels were encountered per hour on the intensive study area, and 2.5 were sighted per hour on the census transects. Assuming that sighting rate is proportional to density and that there were an average of 2.5 squirrels/ha. on the study area, the mean density of squirrels along the census routes would be 2.0/ha., or about 3000 squirrels on the island. We have averaged these two estimates to give the "reasonable" estimate of 2700 squirrels in Table 2.

Strip-censuses probably also underestimate to a serious degree the densities of the other small rodent species on the island, the spiny rat *Proechimys semispinosus*, the arboreal spiny rat *Diplomys labilis*, and the three rice rat species *Oryzomys bicolor*, *O. capito*, and *O. concolor*, because these animals are nocturnal and are smaller and quieter than squirrels. I have assumed only one in four is seen on the strip censuses. The resultant *Proechimys* estimate of 1.8/ha. is concordant with trapping estimates from Barro Colorado, being midway between the 3.0/ha. found in good *Proechimys* habitat in Lutz Ravine (Smythe et al., this volume) and my own estimate of 1.0/ha. on Snyder-Molino ridge. The *Oryzomys* estimate is considerably greater than any obtained by trapping on the island, but the species are too small to be caught consistently by the traps used in either study cited above. *Diplomys* is arboreal and therefore more difficult to census. It is probably uncommon, as it was seen only twice during the nocturnal tower watches, twice during nocturnal censuses, and was trapped only once in squirrel traps set in trees.

Of the larger rodents, the agouti *Dasyprocta punctata* and the paca *Agouti paca* have been studied by Smythe (1978) and Smythe et al. (this volume) and numerous data are available on their numbers and habits. The agouti was the most frequently sighted mammal species on both the diurnal and nocturnal censuses in 1977–78. It is large, diurnal in habits, noisy when fleeing, and thus easily detected; there is little indication that a significant proportion of the population is missed during diurnal censusing. The nocturnal estimates are lower, presumably because most agoutis are resting in sheltered areas at that time. Smythe (1978) and Smythe et al. (this volume) estimate 1.0 to 1.5 agoutis per hectare during the annual cycle on

Barro Colorado. The strip-census estimate of about 1.0/ha., then, is very reasonable. This figure is somewhat higher than in several other neotropical areas; Eisenberg (1980) reports densities of 0.6 and 0.4/ha. at two Venezuelan localities, while Cant (1977) found less than 0.1/ha. near Tikal, Guatemala.

Pacas are nocturnal and relatively silent. They are therefore more difficult to census accurately. Smythe et al. (this volume) estimate 0.5 to 0.7/ha. Strip census calculations give 0.20 to 0.25/ha., but considering the above difficulties, 0.5/ha. is probably more reasonable.

The other large rodents of Barro Colorado are apparently much less common. The prehensile-tailed porcupine *Coendou rothschildi* is nocturnal, arboreal, and gives weak eyeshine. Eisenberg and Thorington (1973), comparing Barro Colorado with Surinam forests, suggested that *Coendou* may be very common on the island. Our very infrequent observations of this species from both canopy towers and walking surveys indicate, however, that it is rare. The capybara *Hydrochaeris hydrochaeris* is spreading throughout the Gatun Lake region (Glanz, unpubl.), and has recently (1977) reached Barro Colorado Island. The population is presently very small and is restricted to lake-edge habitat; it was not seen on any census walks.

Carnivora Coatis, *Nasua narica*, have been studied extensively on Barro Colorado (Kaufmann, 1962; Russell, 1979), and their habits are well known. Their size, boldness, and diurnal activity make them easy to detect, but their variable social structure, with group size showing marked seasonal changes, creates difficulties in censusing. In our analysis, we have separated single animals (mostly males) from group observations, and have added the two separate estimates together for total population size (see Table 2). Mean group size (9.5) is calculated from Russell (1979). This figure is greater than that obtained from groups counted on the census routes (8.4), but was determined from more precise observations of coati bands. It is interesting that the estimated number of males from strip-census calculations (38 to 48) is not much more than the number of bands calculated for the island (28 to 34). There appear to be numerous lone males, even in the mating season when males associate with the bands. The strip-censuses probably underestimate lone males, as they can be overlooked more easily than bands, particularly when in trees. The "reasonable" estimates in Table 2 are adjusted accordingly.

The kinkajou *Potos flavus* is frequently seen and heard at night on Barro Colorado, but because of its arboreal and nocturnal habits it is difficult to census. Walker and Cant (1977) censused this species in seasonal dry forest near Tikal, Guatemala, and estimated a density of 0.7/ha. Our strip-census estimate (about 0.1/ha.) is probably low, as the sighting rate from stationary positions during tower watches (0.373/hr.) was slightly greater than that from the walking censuses (0.312/hr.; see Table 4). It is unlikely that we missed more than half the kinkajous along our routes, as they are noisy and few of the unidentified animals on our nocturnal censuses were arboreal. At most, we estimate 0.2 kinkajous per hectare on Barro Colorado, considerably less than at Tikal. Barro Colorado is within the range of a similar species, the olingo *Bassaricyon gabbii*, and some "kinkajous" may have been olingos. All of those seen at close range, however, were definitely *Potos*, and if *Bassaricyon* is present on Barro Colorado, it is rare.

Other carnivores are evidently much rarer than either coatis or kinkajous. The tayra *Eira barbara* was encountered only twice during the 1977 censuses, and twice more on censuses in April and May 1978, but was seen more frequently during other observation periods. The strip-census results almost certainly underestimate this species, as other workers on the island also reported them fairly frequently. Tayras may be more common in areas away from the laboratory clearing. The ocelot *Felis pardalis* is very wary, and it was never encountered during the strip-censuses, but fresh tracks were noted on one route in late 1977. Two individuals were seen while I was on Barro Colorado, and a female with one young was reported shortly thereafter (R. Greenberg, pers. comm.). Beach transects during the 1977 dry season revealed tracks of at least three and possibly four separate individuals. These transects covered less than one-fourth of the island's perimeter, and thus a minimum population estimate of 12 is reasonable. One jaguarundi, *Felis yagouarundi*, was sighted during my stay on Barro Colorado (C. Handley, pers. comm.), and occasional otters (*Lutra annectens*) were reported in the island's estuaries.

Perissodactyla Tapirs (*Tapirus bairdii*) have been re-introduced on the island since 1950, and semi-tame individuals repeatedly visit the laboratory clearing. They were encountered only twice on the censuses, but as they prefer moist ravines and swampy habitats, they are less likely to be seen from the trails. Five individuals were distinguishable during 1977–78, and an appropriate population estimate is eight animals. Terwilliger (1978) thinks there are ten.

Artiodactyla The collared peccary *Tayassu tajacu* is common on Barro Colorado. Its large size and noisy habits make it easy to detect, but numbers per group and group radii are more difficult to measure, as the animals invariably flee from the observer. Most of our estimates of these parameters are from bands feeding under fruiting trees, and the mean group radius (8 m) may be smaller than at other times, resulting in a slight population overestimate. This source of error, however, is probably small, and a population estimate of 140 animals is reasonable.

Two species of deer, the white-tailed deer *Odocoileus virginianus* and the brocket deer *Mazama americana*, inhabit Barro Colorado. The white-tail is uncommon (6 to 15 animals estimated), while the brocket deer is more common and probably more nocturnal in its habits. The King's estimate from nocturnal censuses (66 animals) is surprisingly high and may be related to several aspects of their behavior on Barro Colorado. They were often seen on or near trails. If they concentrate their feeding or traveling activities on trails, they are more likely to be encountered. Also, they often showed little evidence of alarm when detected, and in several cases moved ahead of us or parallel to the trail, so that we might record the same individuals several times. We have attempted to eliminate such cases from the population estimate. Our "reasonable estimate" of 30 animals reflects our doubts about the strip-census results, but the true population size may be higher.

Long-term Population Changes

There is abundant anecdotal and quantitative evidence that the densities of terrestrial mammals on Barro Colorado have not been stable through time. First, several species recorded by Chapman (1929, 1938) and Enders (1930, 1935) apparently have become extinct on the island. These include the puma *Felis concolor*, the white-lipped peccary *Tayassu pecari*, and several rodents, the pygmy squirrel *Microsciurus alfari*, the pygmy rice rat *Oryzomys fulvescens*, and possibly the cotton rat *Sigmodon hispidus* (Enders, unpubl. ms.). In addition, the spider monkey was extinct before the island became a preserve and the tapir disappeared between 1935 and 1950, but both have been successfully reintroduced since 1950. The patterns of island extinction have been reviewed by Willis (1974) for Barro Colorado birds and by Wilcox (1980) and Terborgh and Winter (1980) for wildlife preserves in general, and few additional theoretical comments are necessary. Briefly, the mammalian extinctions on Barro Colorado fall into three categories: desirable and unwary game animals that may have been hunted to extinction (spider monkey and tapir), large-bodied specialists that may require home ranges greater in area than Barro Colorado (puma and white-lipped peccary), and animals of grassland and second-growth forest that have lost sufficient appropriate habitat as the forest has matured on the island (all of the rodents listed above).

In addition to these extinctions, several species have shown marked population changes. The diurnal primates have been studied repeatedly over much of the history of Barro Colorado. The tamarin *Saguinus* has declined since Ender's studies (1935), as its preferred habitat, second-growth forest, has disappeared. The howler monkey population increased greatly in the 1930s, was decimated by yellow fever in the late 1940s, and has since risen to much higher levels. Mittermeier (1973) and Heltne and Thorington (1976) have quantified these population changes, and Milton (this volume) has updated these estimates of population size very recently.

Next, we compare our results with the results of strip-censuses conducted between 1964 and 1971 by Eisenberg and Thorington (1973). Although they did not calculate density estimates directly from the census data, they reported numbers of each species seen and hours spent walking the trails. In Tables 3 and 4 we present their data in terms of sightings per hour and compare them with our 1977–78 results. Assuming that census techniques were generally similar between observers and that detectability of each species has not changed, these data roughly outline the density trends of most mammal species from 1964 to 1978.

The diurnal censuses (Table 3) probably involve the least variation between observers in methods. Among the primates, *Alouatta* population size increased until 1970 but appears to have stabilized since then, while *Cebus* and probably *Saguinus* have declined noticeably over this period. Two seed-eating rodents, *Sciurus* and *Dasyprocta*, show remarkable increases in abundance between 1964 and 1978. Heaney and Thorington (1978), Smythe (1978), and Glanz et al. (1982) have remarked on these population trends in the red-tailed squirrel, but apparently no one has previously noted the similar trend in the agouti. Smythe (1978) found agouti densities similar to those in this study (1.0 to 1.5/ha.) in 1966–68 and 1971–76 on two study areas near the laboratory clearing. Perhaps agouti densities in this area have remained high and stable over this period, while elsewhere on the island they have increased greatly. This may reflect the improving protection of the rest of the island from poachers during the past two decades (see below). In this same time span, coatis may have increased, peccaries may have decreased, while most other diurnal species are either too scarce to generalize about or show no obvious trend.

The nocturnal censuses (Table 4) are more difficult to interpret, as variations in census technique may more directly affect the number of nocturnal animals sighted and identified. No nocturnal species show a definite decline in numbers from 1964 to 1978. Armadillos, pacas, agoutis, small rodents (including *Ory-*

zomys and *Proechimys*), kinkajous, and brocket deer apparently have all increased substantially over this period, while *Didelphis* shows less of an increase, and *Philander* and *Aotus* may have decreased. The diurnal censuses certainly confirm the increase in agoutis and show indications of a similar trend in the brocket deer. *Philander* did apparently decrease during 1977–78, as none was seen or trapped after May 1977. The other density trends are less easily confirmed.

Differences in census efficiency between years may, in part, explain some of these trends. Two observers were present on about two-thirds of the nocturnal censuses in 1977–78, each scanning different heights and directions. Our census data suggest that two observers may be more likely to sight the smaller, inconspicuous species, but the encounter rate for larger species is similar with either one or two observers. Rate of travel may also influence sighting rate. Our data seem to indicate that an increased speed will decrease sightings of small species, but the encounter rate for large species may actually be increased. Table 4 illustrates another potential source of differences between observers. Comparison of nocturnal census data with nocturnal tower observations reveals that many arboreal animals are likely to have been present on the census routes, but were not seen. The woolly opossum *Caluromys* and the kinkajou *Potos* were seen at a greater rate from the towers than from the trails, even though the tower observer was stationary. Conceivably, if more attention is directed toward the canopy during night censuses, more of these animals may be seen. Observers concentrating more on arboreal habitats, then, should show a higher proportion of arboreal species in their census results.

In summary, any of the above differences in census techniques could affect the sightings per hour of many nocturnal mammal species, but if sampling methods are the only cause of the observed differences between years, biases toward certain sizes and habitat classes should be evident. Inspection of Table 4 reveals no obvious biases toward small, large, arboreal, or terrestrial species in the 1964 to 1971 data, and we must consider real population changes as an additional explanation for the trends found.

We consider it possible that the high sighting rates for many species in 1977–78 could reflect a general increase in mammal densities during a series of favorable years. Most Barro Colorado mammals use tree fruits as either a staple or a supplementary food source. Foster (this volume) observed unusual climatic events that disrupted the fruiting of many tree species on Barro Colorado in 1970, and he recorded extensive evidence for increased mortality in many mammals. The 1970–71 censuses were conducted during and after this bad year. The 1964–65 censuses suggest that

densities of some species were also relatively low. There was a severe fruit shortage in early 1959 (Kaufman, 1962), and perhaps again in early 1961 (Foster, this volume). The Barro Colorado forest, then, is not necessarily a stable environment for its mammal species, and there is evidence that many species have changed greatly in abundance.

These patterns are complicated, however, by recent changes in human poaching pressure. Prior to 1960, poaching was so widespread that tapirs introduced on the island apparently did not survive. Later, the problem was less severe and primarily restricted to the western half of the island. By 1977 evidence of poaching anywhere on the island was very infrequent. Control of poaching, therefore, may have permitted the more desirable game species to increase, but concurrent increases in nongame species are more likely due to changes in availability of fruit or other resources.

Comparisons with Other Neotropical Mammal Communities

This study provides more precise estimates of mammal population sizes and better evidence for population fluctuations than do previous surveys. Many mammal species present on the island, however, have not been adequately censused or studied, and these results must be considered preliminary. To conclude this analysis, we will consider how these results affect the generalizations of Eisenberg and Thorington (1973). In particular, we will evaluate the relative importance of different patterns of food and habitat use, and we will consider whether the Barro Colorado community can be considered representative of other neotropical mammal communities.

Eisenberg and Thorington concluded that arboreal species made up more than half the mammalian biomass of Barro Colorado, and our results are in agreement. Although we cannot provide precise estimates of tree sloth densities, they are certainly very common and contribute very heavily to the island's total biomass of mammals. In addition, our estimates of other arboreal species, particularly howler monkeys, squirrels, and kinkajous, further emphasize the importance of this habitat zone within the Barro Colorado community.

Our data also support the conclusions of Eisenberg and Thorington on the relative importance of certain trophic adaptations. The predominance of sloths and howler monkeys (folivores and frugivore/folivores, respectively) in the island's biomass indicates the importance of tree leaves as a food source. Our results indicate, however, that another potential arboreal folivore, *Coendou*, is probably unimportant, while certain terrestrial folivore/browsers, such as *Mazama* and *Syl-*

vilagus, may be more important than the previous analysis indicated. The rarest trophic categories on the island are the ant-eating species (*Tamandua* and *Cyclopes*) and carnivores (*Felis*), two groups for which Eisenberg and Thorington did not provide estimates. Eisenberg (1980) has more recently discussed these ecological groups, and his new estimates are comparable to ours for *Tamandua* but much less so for *Felis*.

Most of the remaining species present use fruit as either a primary or secondary food source, and the importance of frugivory in this community should be stressed. Of the common Barro Colorado species, howler monkeys eat fruits and leaves; agoutis and squirrels eat fruit pulp and seeds; peccaries eat fruits, seeds, and some animal material; and coatis eat fruits and animal material. Our data provide measures of the numerical importance of these species and also suggest that their abundance may be related to long-term variation in fruit availability.

One additional trophic group that has been under-represented in previous analyses is the insectivore/omnivore group, particularly the armadillos. *Dasypus* was very common on our census routes and is potentially an important factor for soil arthropod populations and nutrient cycling processes. Our revised population estimates for Barro Colorado mammals generally confirm previous hypotheses on habitat use and trophic structure in this community, but permit a more precise analysis of the importance of each group. It must be stressed, however, that more accurate and intensive studies of certain species are needed.

How representative is the Barro Colorado community of neotropical mammal assemblages in general? First, this pattern of trophic structure is probably typical only of humid forests. Eisenberg (1980) has shown that the arboreal folivore component of the mammal community becomes less important as one proceeds to ecosystems with more broken forest canopies. Other trophic and habitat-use components, however, remain comparable.

A second point to be stressed is the potential for species extinction on the island as a result of its size and isolation. As noted earlier, several species have become extinct within the past 50 years, and some of these, particularly the large carnivores, may be important functional components of other neotropical mammal communities. Considering the small numbers estimated for certain species still present—especially the ocelot, spider monkey, tapir, and white-tailed deer—further extinctions are all too likely. Nevertheless, the species list for Barro Colorado is at least as impressive as those of many other neotropical communities (see Eisenberg, 1980), and the isolation of Barro Colorado has certainly been important in the survival there of many mammal species, particularly game animals. The Pipeline Road area, a large, forested region near Barro Colorado, has been hunted so heavily that few, if any, of the large mammal species survive in significant numbers.

A final point to be discussed is whether the isolation of Barro Colorado has influenced the species proportions and densities so much that its mammal community is abnormal or unrepresentative of neotropical ecosystems. Many workers have raised this possibility. Eisenberg (1980), for instance, has suggested that the abundance of certain Barro Colorado rodents may be related to the absence of appropriate carnivores; he notes that Venezuelan communities with more carnivores have fewer rodents, but the carnivore population estimates are speculative. Terborgh and Winter (1980) have recently characterized Barro Colorado as "a veritable zoo without cages," where "large mammals are unwary and remarkably abundant." They attribute the abundance of mammals to the absence of top predators, particularly jaguars, pumas, and harpy eagles. This hypothesis implies that these predators normally regulate their prey populations at levels well below those found on Barro Colorado. While this hypothesis is plausible, it is not the only one possible. In an effort to prevent it from becoming accepted dogma without a proper test, we would like to suggest alternative explanations.

First, perhaps Barro Colorado mammals are not more abundant, but merely less wary than the mammals in comparable unhunted communities. This study has shown that tropical mammal densities, particularly for very wary species, are not easily determined. Careful census work will be required to demonstrate that mammal densities elsewhere are consistently lower than on Barro Colorado Island. The population data presented by Eisenberg (1980) for Venezuelan localities, for example, are comparable to Barro Colorado densities for many groups, differing primarily in the arboreal folivore component. Second, perhaps Barro Colorado mammals are more abundant, but such densities are determined more by resource levels than by predation. Perhaps there are more sloths and howler monkeys on Barro Colorado than at certain Venezuelan localities because the canopy is more continuous and leafy foods are more diverse in the former community (as Eisenberg, p. 49, has indicated) rather than because harpy eagles are less common there. Perhaps there is an abundance of agoutis and squirrels on Barro Colorado because appropriate foods have been abundant and dependable in the last 10 years, and because seasonally critical food sources, such as the legume *Dipteryx panamensis* are relatively common (Glanz et al., this volume; Bonaccorso et al., 1980).

Finally, perhaps the "normal" mammal communities that we observe in most of the neotropics today are heavily influenced by one predator species, *Homo sapiens*, using prey-capture techniques involving dogs, guns, and headlamps, against which most neotropical mammals species have not evolved any defenses. Smythe (1978, pp. 49–50) has discussed this hypothesis relative to the Central American agouti, but it may apply to hunted and semiprotected populations of many other neotropical mammals. Clearly, more intensive work on mammal communities on Barro Colorado and elsewhere in the neotropics will be needed to differentiate and test these explanations.

ACKNOWLEDGMENTS

I thank Dan Glanz and Jeff Brokaw for their assistance with the census work. During the course of this study I was supported by a Smithsonian Institution postdoctoral fellowship and by a short-term fellowship from the Smithsonian Tropical Research Institute. I thank Nick Smythe, Richard Thorington, Egbert Leigh, and numerous Barro Colorado residents for their advice during this study, and the Smithsonian Tropical Research Institute for logistical support.

LITERATURE CITED

Bonaccorso, F. J., W. Glanz, and C. Sanford
1980.   Feeding assemblages of mammals at fruiting *Dipteryx panamensis* trees: seed predation, dispersal, and parasitism. *Revista de Biología Tropical*, 28:61–72.

Cant, J. G. H.
1977.   A census of the agouti (*Dasyprocta punctata*) in seasonally dry forest at Tikal, Guatemala, with some comments on strip censusing. *Journal of Mammalogy*, 58:688–690.

Carpenter, C. R.
1934.   A field study of the behavior and social relations of howling monkeys. *Comparative Psychology Monographs*, 10(2):1–168.

Chapman, F. M.
1929.   *My Tropical Air Castle*. New York: Appleton-Century.
1938.   *Life in an Air Castle*. New York: Appleton-Century. 250 pp.

Eisenberg, J. F.
1980.   The density and biomass of tropical mammals. Pages 35–55 in *Conservation Biology: An Evolutionary-Ecological Perspective*, edited by M. Soulé and B. Wilcox. Sunderland, Mass.: Sinauer Associates.

Eisenberg, J. F., and R. W. Thorington, Jr.
1973.   A preliminary analysis of a neotropical mammal fauna. *Biotropica*, 5:150–161.

Emlen, J. T.
1971.   Population densities of birds, derived from transect counts. *Auk*, 88:323–342.

Enders, R. K.
1930.   Notes on some mammals from Barro Colorado Island, Canal Zone. *Journal of Mammalogy*, 11:280–292.
1935.   Mammalian life histories from Barro Colorado Island, Panama. *Bulletin of the Museum of Comparative Zoology*, 78:383–502.

Foster, R. B.
1982.   Famine on Barro Colorado Island. Pages 201–211 in *The Ecology of a Tropical Forest*, edited by Egbert G. Leigh, Jr., et al. Washington, D.C.: Smithsonian Institution Press.

Glanz, W. E., R. W. Thorington, Jr., J. Giacalone-Madden, and L. R. Heaney
1982.   Seasonal food use and demographic trends in *Sciurus granatensis*. Pages 239-252 in *The Ecology of a Tropical Forest*, edited by Egbert G. Leigh, Jr., et al. Washington, D.C.: Smithsonian Institution Press.

Heltne, P. G., and R. W. Thorington, Jr.
1976.   Problems and potentials for primate biology and conservation in the New World. Pages 110–124 in *Neotropical Primates: Field Studies and Conservation*, edited by R. W. Thorington, Jr., and P. G. Heltne. Washington, D.C.: National Academy of Sciences.

Kaufmann, J.
1962.   Ecology and behavior of the coati *Nasua narica*, on Barro Colorado Island, Panama. *University of California Publications in Zoology*, 60:95–222.

Milton, K.
1977.   The foraging strategy of the howler monkey (*Alouatta palliata*) in the tropical forest of Barro Colorado Island, Panama. Ph.D. thesis, New York University.
1982.   Dietary quality and demographic regulation in a howler monkey population. Pages 273-289 in *The Ecology of a Tropical Forest*, edited by Egbert G. Leigh, Jr., et al. Washington, D.C.: Smithsonian Institution Press.

Mittermeier, R. A.
1973.   Group activity and population dynamics of the howler monkey on Barro Colorado Island. *Primates*, 14:1–19.

Montgomery, G. G., and M. E. Sunquist
1975.   Impact of sloths on neotropial forest energy flow and nutrient cycling. Pages 69–98 in *Tropical Ecological Systems: Trends in Terrestrial and Aquatic Research*, edited by F. Golley and E. Medina. New York: Springer Verlag.
1978.   Habitat selection and use by two-toed and three-toed sloths. Pages 329–359 in *The Ecology of Arboreal Folivores*, edited by G. G. Montgomery. Washington, D.C.: Smithsonian Institution Press.

Oppenheimer, J. R.
1982.   *Cebus capucinus*: Home range, population dynamics, and interspecific relationships. Pages 253–272 in *The Ecology of a Tropical Forest*, edited by Egbert G. Leigh, Jr., et al. Washington, D.C.: Smithsonian Institution Press.

Robinette, W. L., C. M. Loveless, and D. A. Jones
1974.   Field tests of strip census methods. *Journal of Wildlife Management*, 38:81–96.

Russell, J. K.
1979.   Reciprocity in the social behavior of coatis, *Nasua narica*. Ph.D. thesis, University of North Carolina, Chapel Hill.

Smythe, N.
1970.   Ecology and behavior of the agouti (*Dasyprocta punc-tata*) and related species on Barro Colorado Island, Panama. Ph.D. thesis, University of Maryland. 201 pp.
1978.   The natural history of the Central American agouti, *Dasyprocta punctata. Smithsonian Contributions to Zoology*, 257:1–52.

Smythe, N., W. E. Glanz, and E. G. Leigh, Jr.
1982.   Population regulation in some terrestrial frugivores. Pages 227-238 in *The Ecology of a Tropical Forest*, edited by Egbert G. Leigh, Jr., et al. Washington, D.C.: Smithsonian Institution Press.

Thorington R. W., Jr.
1972.   Censusing wild populations of South American monkeys. *Pan American Health Organization, World Health Organization Scientific Publications*, 235:26–32.

Terborgh, J., and B. Winter
1980.   Some causes of extinction. Pages 119–133 in *Conservation Biology: An Evolutionary-Ecological Perspective*, edited by M. Soulé and B. Wilcox. Sunderland, Mass.: Sinauer Associates.

Terwilliger, V. J.
1978.   Natural history of Baird's tapir on Barro Colorado Island, Panama Canal Zone. *Biotropica*, 10:211–220.

Walker, P. L., and J. G. H. Cant
1977.   A population survey of kinkajous (*Potos flavus*) in a seasonally dry forest. *Journal of Mammalogy*, 58:100–102.

Wilcox, B. A.
1980.   Insular ecology and conservation. Pages 95–117 in *Conservation Biology: An Evolutionary-Ecological Perspective*, edited by M. Soulé and B. Wilcox. Sunderland, Mass.: Sinauer Associates.

Willis, E. O.
1974.   Populations and local extinctions of birds on Barro Colorado Island, Panama. *Ecological Monographs*, 44:153–169.

Epilogue: Research on Barro Colorado Island, 1980–94

EGBERT G. LEIGH, JR. Smithsonian Tropical Research Institute, Balboa, Republic of Panama

This chapter outlines some of the major directions of research at the field station of the Smithsonian Tropical Research Institute (STRI) on Barro Colorado Island after 1979, when manuscripts for the first edition of this book were submitted. Since 1979, a 50-hectare Forest Dynamics Plot has been installed on Barro Colorado, where nonliana stems ≥1 cm in diameter at breast height have been mapped, measured, and identified. New techniques have led to an explosive increase in studies on the physiology of plants, especially trees, on Barro Colorado. Finally, Allen Herre, now a member of the STRI staff, has prompted a series of studies on the ecological implications of the evolution of the mutualism between fig trees and their pollinating wasps at a variety of levels, ranging from the physiology of the fig trees and the virulence of the nematodes that parasitize their pollinating wasps to the ecology of the forest as a whole. These studies represent a precise and far-reaching analysis of the ecological consequences of natural selection on interrelationships among different populations.

The material presented in this chapter generally follows the order of the topics considered in this volume.

SOIL, GEOLOGY, AND CLIMATE

What factors govern the mode and rate at which soil forms, or the speed with which water and nutrients move from soil into plant roots and leaves? Dietrich, Windsor, and Dunne (this volume) addressed these questions in connection with the geology, soil, and climate of Barro Colorado. How do these questions stand now?

The plateau of Barro Colorado Island is capped by andesite (Johnsson and Stallard, 1989) and not by basalt, as was reported by Woodring (1958); andesite is the most abundant type of rock formed on volcanic island arcs. Yavitt and Wieder (1988) found that the total phosphorus content of the top 15 cm of soil from the Barro Colorado plateau was higher than that of the alfisols on its surrounding sedimentary slopes. They found little systematic contrast between the concentrations of "available" phosphorus and nitrogen in these two soil types, or the rate at which these soils release soluble phosphorus and nitrogen under incubation in the laboratory. They concluded that phosphorus was more readily available from the soils of Barro Colorado than from most tropical soils. And, indeed, the litter that falls on the Barro Colorado plateau is unusually rich in nitrogen, phosphorus, and calcium (Haines and Foster, quoted in Leigh and Windsor, this volume), while the vegetation of the plateau is considered representative of tropical forest on fertile soil (Foster and Brokaw, this volume).

R. F. Stallard has also initiated studies on the geology and hydrology of Barro Colorado Island. Stallard (pers. comm., 1995) finds that the mineral nutrient content of soil from the 50-hectare Forest Dynamics Plot on the Barro Colorado plateau is typical of volcaniclastics, soils weathered from volcanic island–arc debris. Eleven samples from the top 15 cm of the oxisol in this plot averaged 0.25% by weight P_2O_5 (range 0.2–0.3%), 0.14% K_2O (range 0.1–0.2%), and 0.23% CaO (range 0.1–0.4%). He finds these concentrations quite similar to those he sampled near the Bisley experimental catchments (Silver et al., 1994) in the Luquillo Mountains of Puerto Rico. Despite the remarks quoted in Leigh and Wright (1990), the soil of Barro Colorado's 50-hectare plot contains five times as much phosphorus and potassium as do soils from northern Amazonia, in Venezuela. In a summary written for Leigh and Wright (1990), Stallard contrasted the nutrient content of streams draining the well-weathered, relatively nutrient-poor oxisols on Barro Colorado's central plateau with those draining the more nutrient-rich alfisols on the sedimentary slopes surrounding this plateau. Conrad stream, which drains Barro Colorado's central plateau, is hardly richer in nitrogen and phosphorus than streams of the nutrient-poor regions of central and eastern Amazonia. Conrad stream is slightly richer in cations than streams of the relatively fertile western regions of Amazonia. Lutz stream, which drains alfisols on relatively fertile slopes near Barro Colorado's laboratory clearing, is richer in cations than the Amazon at Iquitos, which drains the rapidly eroding eastern slopes of the

Andes. The nutrient content of water from Conrad stream closely resembles that of water from Gatun Lake, but the nutrient content of water from Lutz stream is very different.

The seeming misrelation between the relative poverty in nutrients of Conrad stream and the high nutrient content of the leaf litter fall on the plateau it drains, which so puzzled Leigh and Wright (1990), is now better understood. As at La Selva, Costa Rica (Sollins et al., 1994, p. 49), and elsewhere in the tropics (Nortcliff and Thornes, 1989), soil on Barro Colorado forms aggregates separated by "macropores." Water draining into a stream flows through the macropores and has little contact with the more tightly bound, nutrient-rich water of the "micropores" within soil aggregates. Thus, the stream draining a relatively fertile soil can be quite poor in nutrients (Nortcliff and Thornes, 1989, p. 52).

The characteristics of sediments deposited in the small seasonal streams of Barro Colorado are governed more by the steepness of the slopes they drain than by the nature of the bedrock (Johnsson and Stallard, 1989). Similar bedrocks yield very different sediments depending on whether the terrain is level or steeply sloping, while different bedrocks can yield very similar sediments on similarly sloping terrain.

Similarly, the steepness of the slope is the most important influence on the richness in cations of a given soil. On Barro Colorado's slopes, erosion keeps pace with weathering, removing weathered particles rather quickly, before they have lost their cations. Soils on these slopes are only about 50 cm thick. Especially in places like Lutz catchment, where the bedrock is rich in limestone, these soils contain an abundance of cation-rich clays, such as smectites. On the relatively level plateau, however, bedrock weathers more rapidly than the resulting sediment can erode away, and the soil attains a thickness of 2 m or more. Particles remain in the soil for long periods. In these thick soils, much of the rainwater may not even reach bedrock, but may instead move laterally at the top of the groundwater table, leaching cations from the particles it washes. Thus the plateau soil is much poorer in cations than soil on the slopes. Iron and aluminum are retained in gravelly concretions called pisolites. Weathered sand grains are rich in quartz, even though the andesitic bedrock is poor in silica (Johnsson and Stallard, 1989).

Dietrich et al. (this volume, p. 44) estimated that erosion in Lutz catchment removes roughly 6 tons of sediment per hectare per year, which is equivalent to a layer of soil 0.75 mm thick, or a layer of bedrock 0.25 mm thick. On the other hand, only 0.043–0.115 mm of bedrock erodes per year from the forested Icacos basin of the Luquillo Experimental Forest,

Puerto Rico (Brown et al., 1995; calculations by R. F. Stallard from data of Clyde Asbury), and erosion rates in catchments near the El Verde field station of the Luquillo forest, drained by the Sonodora and Toronja rivers, are 0.039 and 0.029 mm/year, respectively (R. F. Stallard, pers. comm., based on data of Clyde Asbury). Why this enormous difference? R. F. Stallard (pers. comm.) believes that erosion is so much higher in Lutz catchment because there is calcium carbonate is the glue that holds the bedrock together. Percolating water dissolves calcium carbonate rather rapidly, allowing a much higher outflow of both dissolved and solid matter than from the granitic soils of the Icacos basin or the volcaniclastic soils near El Verde. The volcaniclastic soils near El Verde are similar to those of the Barro Colorado central plateau; erosion rates on this plateau are probably even lower than those near El Verde, which is frequently visited by hurricanes.

Keller et al. (1991) have also estimated the rate at which soil under different types of vegetation withdraws methane, a "greenhouse gas," from—or adds it to—the earth's atmosphere. They find that tropical forest soils slowly consume methane, while pasturelands do not.

The seasonal rhythms of rainfall on Barro Colorado have profoundly influenced the biology of that island (Rand and Rand, this volume). The rhythmic alternation between dry and rainy seasons plays an important role in timing the forest's flowering, fruiting, and production of new leaves (Foster, 1982a, this volume). Later in this chapter, we shall consider some of the mechanisms that may be involved. On a larger scale, the species composition of the forest changes quite rapidly across the isthmus of Panama from the wetter Caribbean to the drier Pacific coast, as if total annual rainfall were a decisive influence on the species composition of a forest. Therefore, Rand and Rand (this volume) considered how rainfall varied from season to season and from year to year. Windsor (1990) has analyzed this variation in more detail and discussed some of its causes.

Rainfall on Barro Colorado Island is quite seasonal. From 1925 through 1986, annual rainfall averaged about 2600 mm, while the median rainfall for the first three months of the year was 96.5 mm. The *average* rainfall for the first three months was 125 mm, suggesting that the first three months are usually quite dry, but in occasional years substantial amounts of rain can fall during this period (Table A3 in Windsor, 1990).

The seasonality of rainfall imposes a seasonal rhythm on litter decomposition and nutrient release. Many trees drop leaves during the dry season. The litter accumulates until the rains come, triggering decomposition and a sudden burst of nutrient release (Cornejo et al., 1994). The contrast between two plots of 2.25 hectares on Barro Colorado, watered through four successive dry seasons, and two nearby nonirrigated control plots has provided an opportunity to assess the effect of the alternation of rainy and dry season on various features of the soil (Yavitt, Wieder, and Wright, 1993; Kursar, Wright, and Radulovich, 1995).

Windsor, Rand, and Rand (1990) and Windsor (1990) find that rainfall also varies over longer time scales. A regression of annual rainfall against time for the period 1925–86 suggests that rainfall on Barro Colorado Island has been decreasing during this period by an average of 8 mm/year (Windsor, 1990, p. 5). Is this decline part of a cycle, in which rainfall will soon return to higher levels, or does it reflect human interference with the environment?

A few years ago, the connection between deforestation and decreasing rainfall seemed very strong. Rainfall was decreasing at inland stations near the Panama Canal, but not at coastal ones. At Barro Colorado, most rain falls in the early afternoon, as convective thundershowers, while at STRI's Caribbean marine station, rainfall is distributed more evenly through the day, as if it is primarily orographic. Converting forest to pasture or scrub increases the reflectivity of the vegetation, which should weaken convection and decrease convective rainfall, without affecting orographic rainfall. In the last few years, however, Barro Colorado's rainfall has increased again (S. Paton, pers. comm.), putting this connection in doubt.

We are also beginning to understand more how year-to-year fluctuations in rainfall reflect worldwide influences on climate. When a strong El Niño warm-water current pushes south along Peru, bringing heavy rains to that desert coast, as happened in 1982–83, the dry season in Panama is uncommonly long and/or severe (Windsor, 1990). Strong El Niños are part of an extraordinarily widespread climatic disturbance, which raises sea levels and flings storms against the west coast of North America; brings severe drought to Amazonia, Hawaii, north Australia, eastern Borneo, the Malay Peninsula, and southern Africa; lowers the level of the Nile flood in Egypt (Quinn, 1992); and weakens the summer monsoon in India (Diaz and Kiladis, 1992). In Panama, El Niño droughts are often preceded by exceptionally wet years (Windsor, 1990).

VEGETATION: THE PHYSIOLOGICAL BACKGROUND

Lowland tropical forests the world around drop roughly 6 or 7 metric tons of leaves per hectare per year (Leigh and Windsor, this volume). What controls leaf production—or, for that matter, the total production of vegetable matter—in tropical forest? To answer this question, we need to know what factors restrict the total photosynthesis of a forest plot and govern the proportion of the energy thus stored that is devoted to producing vegetable matter.

Moreover, animal populations appear to be limited by seasonal shortage of fruit and new leaves, as many papers in this book show (see also the section below on seasonal rhythms in plants). Dry-season rains can disrupt flowering and fruiting, sometimes causing mass starvation among the forest mammals (Foster, 1982b, this volume). To understand what causes seasonal shortage of food, we must know how different kinds of plants know when to flower, fruit, or produce new leaves. As flowering and leaf flush seem to be related to the onset of rainy season (Foster, 1982a, this volume), or to the timing of individual rainstorms in the dry season (Augspurger, this volume), learning what factors govern a plant's water relations may help us understand the timing of flowering and leaf flush.

Since 1979, Barro Colorado Island has witnessed an explosion of research in plant physiology, thanks largely to the efforts of the late Alan Smith. This work can help us understand what factors control forest productivity and what mechanisms allow plants to time their growth and reproduction.

Photosynthesis

All the activities of a forest community, plant and animal, are financed by the photosynthesis of its plants, particularly its canopy trees. Zotz and Winter (1993) supplied an effective tool for assessing forest photosynthesis when they discovered that in Panama the maximum photosynthetic rate of a well-lit sun leaf is a good indicator of its daily photosynthesis. Regardless of its species, a sun leaf's daily photosynthesis, A_L, in millimoles of CO_2 per square meter of leaf per day, can be estimated fairly accurately from the equation

$$A_L = 21 A_{max} - 2.1,$$

where A_{max} is the maximum photosynthetic rate, in micromoles of CO_2 per square meter of leaf per second. In other words, the daily photosynthesis of a leaf can be estimated by assuming that it photosynthesizes at its maximum rate for six hours (21,600 seconds) per day and is otherwise shut down (Zotz and Winter, 1993).

It may also be possible to predict the annual carbon gain of a leaf, in grams of carbon dioxide fixed per square meter of leaf per year, from its lifetime average nitrogen content, in milligrams of nitrogen per square meter of leaf. Based on only five plants—including one deciduous canopy tree, one evergreen hemiepiphyte, and three epiphytes (a fern, an orchid, and an incipient hemiepiphyte) in that tree's crown—Zotz and Winter (1994d) find that the annual carbon gain of a leaf can be expressed as 1.47(mean leaf N content) − 454.

The forest of Barro Colorado produces about 7 metric tons dry weight of mature leaves, 3 tons of twigs, 1 ton of fruit, 1 or 2 tons of other canopy matter (Leigh and Windsor, this volume), and about 5 tons of wood (2% of the forest's standing timber) per hectare per year. We know too little about belowground production in this, or any other, forest, but it appears that Barro Colorado produces as much weight of roots as leaves per hectare (Cavelier, 1989; Kursar, 1989). Thus, the total production of dry vegetable matter on Barro Colorado, like that of the dipterocarp forest at Pasoh, Malaya (Kira, 1978), is roughly 25 metric tons per hectare per year. Barro Colorado's 7 tons of leaves per hectare must therefore subsidize the construction of 25/7 times their own dry-matter content, while also paying for the forest's maintenance respiration.

Zotz and Winter tracked the yearly cycle of photosynthesis and water use in a variety of plants. Sun leaves of a 47-m *Ceiba pentandra* (Bombacaceae) behind the old laboratory on Barro Colorado fix 2640 g CO_2 per square meter of leaf per year. A *Ceiba* leaf fixes 13 times its own carbon content during its lifetime, 1.3 g CO_2/mg N contained in the leaf. These leaves release 409 kg water per square meter of leaf per year, 154 g water per gram of CO_2 fixed (Zotz and Winter, 1994a). Seated on the crotch of this *Ceiba* is the round crown of a hemiepiphyte *Clusia uvitana* (Guttiferae), whose roots reach the ground. Leaves on the outer edge of this *Clusia* crown fix 1780 g CO_2 per square meter of leaf per year. A *Clusia* leaf fixes six times its carbon content during its life, 1.08 g CO_2/mg N (Zotz and Winter, 1994b). A little less than one-quarter of this CO_2 is fixed by crassulacean acid metabolism (CAM), a process that saves water by opening stomates at night, when the air is more humid, to let in CO_2. These *Clusia* leaves release 75.4 kg water per square meter of leaf per year, 42 g water per gram of CO_2 fixed, hardly more than one-quarter of the water *Ceiba* leaves release to fix 1 g of CO_2.

Zotz and Winter (1994c) also followed photosynthesis and water use of three species of epiphyte in the crown of this *Ceiba*: a small, epiphytic *Clusia uvitana;* an orchid, *Catasetum viridiflavum;* and an epiphytic fern, *Polypodium crassifolium.* Despite very different leaf thickness and leaf lifetime, all these epiphytes fix roughly 1 kg CO_2 per square meter of leaf per year, about 1.1 g CO_2/mg N in leaf. Leaf pay-backs are rather different: a *Polypodium* fixes 5.3 g C/g C in leaf per leaf lifetime, while the lightweight leaves of *Catasetum* fix 16 g. The *Clusia* epiphyte, aided by CAM (from which it derives only 26% of its CO_2), releases only 37 g water per gram of CO_2 fixed, while the other two epiphytes, which lack CAM, release about 80 g water per gram of CO_2 fixed, about as much as the rooted *Clusia* mentioned above, half as much as the sun leaves of the *Ceiba* that supports them, and twice as much as the epiphytic *Clusia.*

Water Relations and Phenological Rhythms

Barro Colorado has a severe dry season (Rand and Rand, this volume). Dry-season rains appear to stimulate synchronous flowering in some plant populations (Augspurger, this volume). Many other species of plants flower after the onset of rainy season (Foster, 1982a, 1982b, this volume). Thus it became important to investigate the "water relations" of Barro Colorado's plants. This work has brought some surprises.

There seemed to be many reasons to believe that rainfall causes these plants to flower by wetting the soil. The dry season of 1970 was uncommonly wet, and the onset of the following rainy season was indistinct. That year, many of the species that flower after (in response to?) the onset of rainy season failed to flower or flowered without bearing fruit (Foster, 1982a, 1982b, this volume). Augspurger (this volume) found that watering the roots of the understory shrub *Hybanthus prunifolius* at some time in the dry season caused it to flower only if the watering was sufficiently copious *and* if a sufficiently severe dry spell preceded watering, as if the reduction in soil water tension had to exceed a certain minimum to cause flowering. Reich and Borchert (1982) successfully modeled the timing of leaf fall, flowering, and leaf flush of *Tabebuia neochrysantha* in terms of changes in water tension of these trees (as inferred from shrinkage or expansion of their trunks) in response to the onset of dry season, the leaf loss this induced, dry-season rains, and the onset of rainy season. This model seemed to explain the behavior of many other tree species in the dry forest of Costa Rica (Reich and Borchert, 1984).

To see if this were indeed true, Wright constructed a sprinkler system to provide two 2.25-hectare plots of mature forest on Barro Colorado with 6 mm of rain a day, five days a week, through five successive dry seasons. In 1986 soil water potential never fell below −0.09 MPa (megapascal; 1 MPa = 10 bars = 10.13 atmospheres of pressure) on the irrigated plots, while at the end of the 1986 dry season, soil water potential had fallen to −1.6 MPa in one of two nearby, nonirrigated control plots. Wright compared the timing of leaf fall, flowering, and leaf flush of trees on these irrigated plots with their timing among conspecifics on the nonirrigated control plots. The reader can imagine the amazement of the STRI community when, year after year, irrigation failed to affect the timing of these events in most species of canopy tree (Wright and Cornejo, 1990a, 1990b); *Tabebuia guayacan* was one of the few exceptions. We all stared astonished at this result, rather as Martin Luther imagined a cow would stare at a new barn door.

As the experiment continued, however, it became clear that irrigation was affecting the timing—but not the amount—of leaf production in understory shrubs, *Piper* spp. and *Psychotria* spp. (Wright, 1991; Tissue and Wright, 1995). As the years passed, irrigation was progressively blurring or annihilating the peaks in leaf production observed at the beginning of the rains among conspecifics in control plots. In *Psychotria furcata* leaf production, normally almost entirely restricted to the beginning of the rains, occurred progressively earlier and with progressively less synchrony on irrigated plots relative to the controls. It is as if leaf production in *Psychotria furcata* were controlled by a free-running endogenous circannual "clock," which would normally be reset by the onset of dry season. (If these *Psychotria* are indeed endowed with a circannual clock, this would be the strangest and most novel of all the phenomena plant physiologists have yet discovered on this island.)

Sternberg et al. (1989) provided a clue to the contrast between understory and canopy plants. The more CO_2 is available when photosynthesis is in progress, the more strongly the photosynthetic enzymes discriminate against C_{13} in favor of C_{12}, and the higher the ratio of C_{12} to C_{13} in the leaf's dry matter. When stomates are open, CO_2 is more abundant in the leaf, and the photosynthetic enzymes discriminate more strongly in favor of C_{12} than when stomates are closed and less CO_2 is available. Irrigation did not significantly affect the ratio of C_{12} to C_{13} in canopy leaves of the three tree species tested, but in two of these species, the ratio of C_{12} to C_{13} in leaves of 1-m saplings was significantly lower in control plots (Sternberg et al., 1989, Figure 3), as if irrigation enhanced the availability of water for small saplings, allowing them to keep their stomates open longer, but had no such effect on canopy trees.

And, indeed, even though the contrast between dry and rainy season is so sharp that the understory shrub *Psychotria marginata* makes special leaves for each (Mulkey et al., 1992), many canopy trees behave as if they always have access to adequate water. Late in the dry season, just after a new set of leaves had been flushed, measured leaves of the 47-m-tall *Ceiba pentan-*

dra behind the old laboratory building transpired up to 90 g water per second per square meter of leaf surface (Zotz and Winter, 1994a)—as high a transpiration rate as has been recorded from Barro Colorado (Machado and Tyree, 1994; Patiño, Tyree, and Herre, 1995). The transpiration rate of these *Ceiba* leaves then declines steadily throughout the rainy season, a decline that cannot reflect increasing shortage of water.

Hydraulic Architecture and Plant Phenology

Could an analysis of hydraulic architecture of the stems, branches, and petioles of tropical trees—an analysis, in effect, of the pressure differentials required to draw water through these plant parts—shed light on the contrasting effects of irrigation on canopy and understory plants? Martin Zimmermann (1983) summarized evidence for the "cohesion theory of the ascent of sap," which asserts that the evaporation of water through the stomates of leaves pulls water up from the roots through the narrow vessels of the xylem. Water in the xylem is therefore under tension. All the work on the hydraulic architecture of the plants of Barro Colorado is based on this assumption. Ulrich Zimmermann et al. (1993, 1994) devised a probe to measure water tension within xylem vessels. They found the tension much less than the cohesion theory of sap flow predicted. This discovery caused some uproar because, as we shall see, the work on the hydraulic architecture of plants inspired by Martin Zimmermann (1983) makes perfect sense. Canny (1995) suggested that compression by tissue surrounding xylem vessels reduces the tension of water in the xylem vessels. Canny summarized evidence that when transpiration exerts a stronger pull, this pull calls forth higher tissue pressures to prevent the tension in xylem vessels from being strong enough to cause "cavitation," snapping of the column of water in the xylem vessel. If Canny is correct, transpiration does pull water from the roots, but where we now speak of higher xylem tension, we should speak of higher pressure on the xylem from the surrounding tissue. Our measurements and theoretical estimates of water potential in leaves and stems would be correct, but this potential arises not from tension in xylem vessels but from the compensating pressure applied to the xylem (Canny, 1995).

Tyree et al. (1991) analyzed the hydraulic architecture of the pioneer tree *Schefflera morototoni* (Araliaceae). They found that this tree appears to have reliable access to water all year around. In full sun, 1 m² *Schefflera* leaves yields 60 mg water per second, or 216 g water per hour, to the atmosphere. What pressure differential is required to pull this water from the root collar to the leaves?

Stem conductance, k_h, may be defined as the flow of water through a stem, w, in kilograms per second, divided by the pressure differential per meter of stem, dP/dx, in megapascals per meter, required to pull it through:

$$k_h = w/(dP/dx).$$

Leaf specific conductivity, LSC, is the conductance per square meter of leaf supplied:

$$LSC = (k_h/LA) = (w/LA)/(dP/dx),$$

where LA is the area of leaves supplied by this stem. The higher the leaf specific conductivity of a tree, the lower the pressure differential required to bring water from the root collar to the leaves. Expressing w/LA as E, the rate at which a square meter of leaves yields water to the atmosphere, we find that

$$LSC = E/(dP/dx).$$

Schefflera morototoni has uncommonly high leaf specific conductivity, from two to twenty times higher than for the other species of trees and lianas recorded. The pressure gradient in the stem of the 20-m-tall *Schefflera* studied by Tyree et al. (1991) needed to supply 60 mg water per square meter of leaf per second is 12.5 kPa/m, not much above the 9.8 kPa/m required to overcome gravitational potential.

When tension in a xylem vessel exceeds a certain limit, air may be sucked into that vessel, causing a cavitation that breaks the water column and prevents the further transport of water through that vessel unless root pressure pushes water into it. In *Schefflera* the tension required to cause cavitation is remarkably low: a tension (the negative of water potential) of 1.1 MPa causes so many vessels to cavitate that stem conductance is reduced by half. During the dry season, soil moisture potential often falls below −1.5 MPa for prolonged periods (Becker, Rabenold, et al., 1988). The stem of the *Schefflera* studied by Tyree et al. (1991) contained 70 kg of extractable water, which would help tide such a tree over a few weeks of drought. Nonetheless, their deep roots must assure *Schefflera* trees a fairly reliable supply of water. Another deep-rooted pioneer tree, the balsa, *Ochroma pyramidale*, is also sensitive to water stress (a water tension of only 1 MPa reduces stem conductance by one-half) and has high leaf specific conductance, as if it, too, has reliable access to water (Machado and Tyree, 1994). The story is quite different for those understory plants whose shallow roots do not have reliable access to water. The shallow-rooted climbing bamboo *Rhipidocladum racemiflorum* is so constructed that a water tension of 4.5 MPa is required to halve its stem conduc-

tivity (Cochard et al., 1994). A water tension of 5 MPa eliminates only 30% of the stem conductivity of the understory shrub *Psychotria horizontalis*.

Studies of hydraulic architecture have presented yet another surprise. As we have seen, plants can save water by using CAM; indeed, CAM is considered a mode of photosynthesis that plants use when short of water. Yet a *Clusia uvitana* whose roots have access to lake water derives as high a proportion of its CO_2 from CAM as does the aforementioned hemiphytic *Clusia* in the *Ceiba* crown. Moreover, these two *Clusia* show the same seasonal rhythm of CAM use (Zotz and Winter, 1994b), as if CAM use is triggered by an atmospheric signal such as vapor pressure deficit. What is going on here?

To find out, Zotz, Tyree, and Cochard (1994) undertook an analysis of the hydraulic architecture of these *Clusia*. As in *Schefflera*, cavitation causes a loss of half the conductivity in *Clusia* stems when tension (the negative of water potential) is no higher than 1.3 MPa. Therefore, like *Schefflera* and the lakeside *Clusia*, the hemiepiphytic *Clusia* in the *Ceiba* crown must have reliable access to water. On the other hand, the leaf specific conductivity of *Clusia* is one-fifteenth that of *Schefflera*: 2 rather than 30 (kg/second)/[(MPa/m)m² leaf]. *Clusia* stems are nearly as conductive as *Schefflera* stems of the same diameter, but a *Clusia* stem 4.5 cm thick supports 11,000 cm² leaf per square centimeter of stem cross-section, compared to 500 for a *Schefflera* stem. In both the lakeside *Clusia* and that of the *Ceiba*, transpiration peaks at 8 A.M. and 4 P.M., as if the low leaf specific conductivity is unable to meet the demand for water imposed by the low vapor pressure deficits of midday. Is this apparent water shortage, which is caused by low leaf specific conductivity, the explanation for the lake *Clusia*'s use of CAM? If so, we have learned two lessons. First, plants with different hydraulic architecture have different responses to water stress. Indeed, adjustments of hydraulic architecture may be one way to adjust the timing of flowering, fruiting, and leaf flush, or even to choose the signals that stimulate these events. Second, CAM and the thick leaves of *Clusia*, which hold water reserves for transpiration, allow *Clusia* to economize sharply on stems, a use that was not foreseen by CAM's discoverers.

UNDERSTANDING DIVERSITY

One of the most striking mysteries of tropical forest is why it contains so many species of trees (Leigh, this volume). One hectare of old-growth forest ten miles south of Annapolis, Maryland (Burnham et al., 1992), contains 16 species among 351 trees ≥10 cm diameter at breast height (dbh). Here, Fisher's α (a measure of diversity that is relatively independent of sample size, invented by Fisher, Corbet, and Williams, 1943; see below) measures 3.5. One hectare of forest in the 50-hectare Forest Dynamics Plot contains 93 species among 417 stems ≥10 cm dbh (Foster and Hubbell, 1990; data from 1982 census), so that Fisher's α is 37. One hectare of forest in Amazonian Peru contains 283 species among 580 stems ≥10 cm dbh (Gentry, 1988); here, Fisher's α is 218.

The astonishing diversity of tropical trees raises the more general question, why are the tropics so replete with biodiversity, plant and animal? This section considers the various processes or circumstances that might allow different species to coexist and reviews evidence for each. The next section reviews evidence from the Barro Colorado Forest Dynamics Plot concerning the factors that allow so many tree species to grow there.

Tradeoffs and Diversity

On Barro Colorado Island, some trees can only colonize large clearings, while others are restricted to mature forest (Brokaw, this volume). More generally, different species can coexist because no one species can do everything perfectly: "the jack of all trades is master of none" (MacArthur, 1961), because improvement in one ability necessarily involves sacrifices in others. Identifying such tradeoffs is the basis for understanding biotic diversity (Leigh, 1990).

Clear-cut tradeoffs are rarely easy to identify. An organism faces many conflicting demands: obtaining resources, escaping consumers, reproducing (Cody, 1966). Under extreme conditions, however, a tradeoff between two factors may stand out. One such example is provided by Sevenster and van Alphen (1993a, 1993b). Among those species of *Drosophila* on Barro Colorado whose larvae live in rotting fruit, those with slower development are longer lived as adults; apparently, the adults of species with fast developing larvae cannot live long. This circumstance imposes a tradeoff: faster developing larvae have a greater chance of completing development before the fruit in which they are growing is eaten up, but especially when fruit is scarce, longer lived adult females are more likely to find a suitable patch of fallen fruit in which to lay eggs. When fruit is abundant, finding suitable sites to lay eggs is not a problem, and those *Drosophila* whose larvae develop more quickly are the better competitors; scarcity of fruit favors long-lived *Drosophila*. On Barro Colorado, fruit abundance varies in space and time, and this tradeoff allows *Drosophila* species of different longevity to coexist.

Plants face a tradeoff between the capacity to survive drought and the ability to take full advantage of continuously moist habitats. Coping with drought imposes the expense of constructing and maintaining deep roots or leaves and xylem vessels capable of withstanding severe water stress, which reduces aboveground growth rate.

The most familiar tradeoff plants face, however, is that between growing rapidly in full light or surviving under shadier conditions. This tradeoff is most obvious among pioneer trees. *Trema micrantha* can grow 14 m during its first two years of life, but only in gaps of area >376 m² did they survive eight years or more. *Cecropia insignis* can grow 10 m during its first two years of life, but can survive eight years or more only in gaps >215 m² in area. *Miconia argentea* (Melastomaceae) can grow no more than 5 m during its first two years, but can survive over eight years in gaps >102 m² in area (Brokaw, 1987).

The light–shade tradeoff seems to be imposed primarily by herbivores. Seedlings of light-demanding species grow faster than seedlings of shade-tolerant species in both sun and shade, but they are unable to survive long in the shade (Kitajima, 1994). Shade-tolerant seedlings have deeper roots and tougher stems and leaves, which slows their growth but allows them to resist herbivores and pathogens more effectively (Kitajima, 1994). Larger plants also face a tradeoff between fast growth and both the amount and type of anti-herbivore defense they employ (Coley et al., 1985). A leaf's best defense against herbivores is to be tough and poor in nitrogen. Such leaves are necessarily long-lived because photosynthesis is limited by nitrogen content; it takes a long time for leaves with low nitrogen content to pay back the costs of the cellulose and lignin that toughen their leaves (Coley, 1988). There is a clear contrast between fast growing, light-demanding plants with short-lived, rapidly eaten leaves, and slow growing, shade-tolerant plants with tough, well-defended leaves. This contrast reflects the tradeoff between "pioneers" and "persistents" (Coley, this volume, 1987, 1988). Toward the shade-tolerant end of the spectrum, this tradeoff is reflected in some physiological characteristics: although most tropical shade leaves increase photosynthesis quite rapidly when lit by a sunfleck, long-lived leaves take much longer to bring their photosynthetic rate to its maximum level (Kursar and Coley, 1993). Toward the sunlit end of the spectrum, this tradeoff is reflected in the allocation of photosynthate: the species of sapling that grow fastest in large clearings devote most of their energy to stem growth (King, 1994) and can survive only if their relatively few leaves are well enough lit to subsidize this stem growth.

Another tradeoff involves the nitrogen content of young leaves and their rate of maturation. As we have seen, herbivores prefer leaves that are tender and rich in nitrogen (protein). Because young leaves are more tender and (usually) richer in nitrogen than older ones, both insects and vertebrate herbivores prefer young leaves. Young leaves are more attractive to herbivores the richer they are in nitrogen, but the longer it takes a young leaf to mature and toughen, the longer it remains available to herbivores. Since fast leaf expansion requires high nitrogen levels, plants face a tradeoff between keeping their young leaves low in nitrogen and maturing them rapidly (Kursar and Coley, 1991). This tradeoff is illustrated by a tree, *Gustavia superba,* which expands and toughens a new leaf in less than a week—so quickly that many caterpillars of its specialist herbivore fail to grow big and strong enough to tackle mature foliage before their leaf matures (Aide and Londoño, 1989). The price for such rapid expansion is high nitrogen levels, which presumably make the young leaves attractive to a range of vertebrate leaf-eaters.

Aide (1993), however, examined 32 species of understory shrubs and saplings and found no correlation between the mean proportion of the area of a leaf a species loses to herbivores during the first month of that leaf's life and the rapidity with which that species matures its leaves. Aide's observation does not disprove the role of rapid leaf expansion as a defense against herbivores. Species that expand leaves slowly may well defend them in other ways. There are a variety of possible defenses against herbivores, and this presumably increases the number of tree species that can coexist in a herbivore-rich setting.

Specialized Pests and Plant Diversity

Leaves have two general types of chemical defense against pests. Some leaves have high contents of long-lived compounds such as cellulose or tannin, which require a large initial investment but little maintenance (Coley, 1988). As we have seen, such leaves must be long-lived to repay the investment in their construction, and plants with long-lived leaves are slow growing. Conifers with such leaves can be locally very common (Regal, 1977). When tough, tannin-rich leaves do fall, they decompose slowly and often acidify the soil, slowing or blocking the recycling of nutrients (Waring and Schlesinger, 1985; Hobbie, 1992).

Other leaves employ low concentrations of short-lived compounds with low molecular weight, such as alkaloids, monoterpenes, and cardiac glycosides, which require less initial investment but may need more rapid replacement. Such defenses are appropriate to shorter lived leaves on faster growing plants. When they fall, such leaves are much better for the soil. Unlike tannins and cellulose, these metabolically active defensive compounds can be detoxified by spe-

cialized pathogens and pests. One would expect trees of a mature forest species whose leaves are defended by short-lived compounds to be scattered, kept rare by specialist insects (or diseases).

A most controversial question is whether insect pests (at least the most damaging ones) face tradeoffs between the abilities to detoxify different compounds. This is a crucial assumption in Janzen's (1970) and Connell's (1971) explanation of why there are so many kinds of tropical trees. Janzen and Connell's argument can be summarized as follows: (1) The absence of winter in the tropics permits pest populations to exert a steadier and more intense pressure on their host plants than occurs in the temperate zone. (2) Specialist pests are most damaging where their host plants are most dense. (3) At least where a tree species is most common, specialist pests attack seeds and seedlings within a sufficiently wide radius of their parent that trees of other species grow up between a parent and its surviving young.

Basset (1992) asserted that most of the insect herbivores in the crown of a tropical tree are "generalists" that feed on many plant species. On Barro Colorado Island John Barone, of the University of Utah, is trying to assess whether or not most of the damage to the leaves of seedlings is inflicted by specialist herbivores. If it turns out that this is true in general, can we conclude that pest pressure helps species of tropical trees to coexist?

The relation between pest pressure and tree diversity has inspired much of the research on Barro Colorado. Before describing this research, we should clear away two misconceptions. First, Janzen (1970) made the ill-judged remark that pest pressure would cause trees of a given species to be "hyperdispersed" (dispersed more evenly than random). Thus, clumping among adult conspecific trees was considered evidence against Janzen's hypothesis (Hubbell, 1979). In the null case where herbivores are absent, however, adult trees of a species will be clumped, because seeds disperse only a finite, often short, distance from their parents (Howe et al., 1985). The question of how many tree species can coexist by virtue of a given pattern of bias among pests toward attacking seeds and seedlings near parent trees is one of the thorniest problems of theoretical biology.

Second, Hubbell (1980) argued that species-specific herbivores could not maintain high tree diversity. Using just three species, Hubbell constructed a hexagonal lattice of tree crowns where conspecific crowns never share a common edge (Figure 1); he concluded that species-specific herbivory sufficient to prevent conspecifics from ever being nearest neighbors would not allow many tree species to coexist. This argument convinced many researchers that "seed predation near parent trees is probably not sufficient to promote high species diversity in tropical forests" (Howe et al., 1985; see also Tilman and Pacala, 1993; Gilbert et al., 1994). Becker, Lee, et al.'s (1985) refutation of Hubbell's argument was well founded but unduly prolix. It suffices to recall that in Hubbell's three-species lattice, a dead adult can be replaced only by a conspecific: a hypothetical invader, immune to the pests of the residents, has a threefold advantage over these residents because it can replace *any* dead adult. Hubbell's lattice implies nothing about how many tree species can coexist if species-specific herbivores prevent conspecific crowns from touching.

Several case histories of pests spacing trees have been established on Barro Colorado. Augspurger (1983) showed that a fungal disease, "damping-off," inflicted heavier mortality on those shaded seedlings of the canopy tree *Platypodium elegans* that were near their parent. Moreover, shaded seedlings far from their parent were more likely to die from this fungus where they were more densely aggregated. Where the seed crop was copious, this fungus eliminated nearly all shaded seedlings within 20 m of the parent. It appeared that near parent trees the ground was more heavily stocked with spores of this fungus and that where seedlings were close together, they also infected each other (Augspurger and Kelly, 1984). On the other hand, seedling survival was much higher, and the incidence of damping-off much lower, in light gaps, even in those close to the parent. Does fungal disease limit those *Platypodium* seedlings that fall near their parents to light gaps?

Augspurger (1984) also followed the fate of seedlings in eight other species of tree with wind-dispersed seeds. For five of these species, no marked seedlings survived one year in the shade; whether their seedlings survived better in distant light gaps than in nearby ones is not known. Among the three remaining species, nearly all shaded seedlings of a *Lonchophyllus pentaphyllus* (Leguminosae) tree within 20 m of their parent died within one year, but shaded seedlings farther from their parent survived better. The canopy tree, *Aspidospermum cruentum* (Apocynaceae), dispersed its seeds so effectively that seedlings were rarer near their parent (0.2 per square meter) than 30–40 m away (30–40 per square meter). *Aspidospermum* seedlings did not suffer from damping-off, and the few seedlings near their parent survived as well as those farther away. Shaded seedlings of *Triplaris cumingiana* (Polygonaceae) were also immune to damping-off, and *Triplaris* seedlings nearer their parent did not suffer conspicuously higher mortality. Augspurger's (1984) data demonstrate a decided advantage to seed dispersal. Her data would

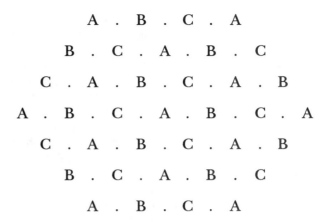

Figure 1. Hexagonal lattice of trees of three species, *A*, *B*, and *C*, where conspecific crowns never share a common edge.

support Janzen and Connell's hypothesis, however, only if seedlings of her first five species were restricted to light gaps by diseases or pests.

Seeds of the canopy tree *Virola surinamensis* (Myristicaceae) attract toucans, which carry them 30–50 m away and drop them after mouthing off the aril (Howe, this volume). *Virola* seeds placed on the ground 40–49 m from a fruiting conspecific were 3.6 times more likely to become six-week-old seedlings than were seeds placed less than 10 m away (Howe et al., 1985, Table 1). Six-week-old seedlings transplanted from a laboratory to sites 30–49 m from a fruiting tree were fifteen times more likely to survive the following twelve weeks than were seedlings planted within 10 m of a fruiting conspecific (Howe et al., 1985, Tables 3 and 4). In a different year, Forget and Milleron (1991) found no established *Virola surinamensis* seedlings that had germinated from unburied seeds; unburied *Virola* seeds were invariably attacked by weevils or rot. Even so, it is clear that *Virola* seeds near their parents and those in dense aggregations, even far from their parents, have vanishingly poor prospects (Howe, 1989, 1990), in full accord with the predictions of Janzen (1970) and Connell (1971). As one might expect from the quality of the reward *Virola* offers its seed dispersers and the effectiveness of the principal dispersers of their seeds (Howe, this volume), *Virola* seeds benefit overwhelmingly from being dispersed far from their parents and the pests they attract.

Howe (1990) found that three-month-old seedlings of the canopy tree *Tetragastris panamensis* (Burseraceae) less than 20 m from their parent tree have a 44% chance of surviving their next year, compared to 3% for *Virola surinamensis* seeds of comparable age and situation. *Tetragastris* seeds survived as well near their parent as farther away. An isolated three-month-old *Tetragastris* seedling was only twice as likely to survive the next year as a seedling in a dense clump. Not surprisingly, *Tetragastris panamensis* is much less discriminating than *Virola* in the dispersers it attracts (Howe, this volume). So far, *Tetragastris panamensis* appears to violate the predictions of Janzen and Connell as decidedly as *Virola surinamensis* conforms to them. Howe (1989) believed that roughly half the tree species on Barro Colorado depend, like *Virola*, on effective seed dispersal, while the other half, like *Tetragastris*, have sufficiently well-defended seedlings that they grow quite adequately near their parents.

Now, however, a disease is afflicting the seedlings of *Tetragastris*, a phenomenon that may explain why even this tree species troubles to reward animals for dispersing its seeds (G. S. Gilbert and D. de Steven, unpublished).

THE FOREST DYNAMICS PLOT AND TREE DIVERSITY

In 1975 Thorington et al. (this volume) established five permanent 1-hectare plots near the laboratory clearing on Barro Colorado Island, and in the same year K. Milton established three other such plots on the central plateau (Milton, Laca, and Demment, 1994). These plots have been used for analyses of tree diversity (Thorington et al., this volume) and forest dynamics (Putz and Milton, this volume; Milton, Laca, and Demment, 1994). Can we learn more from larger plots?

Hubbell and Foster (1983, 1986a, 1986b, 1986c, 1990) organized the mapping of a Forest Dynamics Plot 500 × 1000 m, mostly in mature forest, on the central plateau of Barro Colorado Island. Between 1980 and 1982 every freestanding woody stem ≥1 cm dbh on that plot was mapped, measured and identified. This plot was recensused in 1985 and 1990 to assess mortality and to record stems that had attained 1 cm dbh since the preceding census. The following discussion is based primarily on unpublished data on the 50-hectare plot provided me by S. Loo de Lao on behalf of R. Condit, S. P. Hubbell, and R. B. Foster.

Piperno (1990) surveyed the soils of the plot for remains of fire and for phytoliths (particles of silica formed by vegetation, some of which have distinctive shapes that allow identification to species, genus, or family). There was no agriculture on the plot during the past 2500 years, except perhaps on its only hectare (hectare 6,4) of young forest. People did live, at least seasonally, on the plot in pre-Columbian times, building dwellings and chipping flints. Even so, tracts of this plot have been covered continuously by mature forest over at least the past 2500 years. Considering the density of human settlement on the Pacific slopes of Panama before the coming of Columbus (Piperno et al., 1991), it is rather surprising that the forest included in Barro Colorado's Forest Dynamics Plot has been so little disrupted.

Structure and Dynamics on the 50-hectare Plot

How does the mortality rate of tropical trees depend on size? In the 1980–82 census, the diameters of some large trees with outthrust buttresses were judged by eye. In 1985 and 1990 girths of these trees were measured above the buttresses, revealing startling shrinkage between 1982 and 1985. One must assess the "true" distribution of trees over diameter classes to learn how mortality rate depends on tree size. Doing this for the 1982 census took some fancy footwork, which led to some erroneous inferences. Trees whose measured 1985 diameters were smaller than their estimated 1982 diameters have been assigned their 1985 diameters for 1982 as well. Hubbell and Foster (1990) apparently corrected 1982 diameters in this fashion for trees still living in 1985. Diameters of trees dying between 1982 and 1985, however, were not measured in 1985: how can one correct their 1982 diameters? Hubbell and Foster (1990) appear to have ignored this problem. They concluded that between 1982 and 1985 death rate increased markedly with size class for trees ≥20 cm dbh. As death rates for trees ≥20 cm dbh show no clear trend with (uncorrected) size, and as few trees with dbh ≥20 cm dbh are buttressed, I assume here that the ratio of survival to mortality in each size class is the same for corrected as for uncorrected data (Table 1).

The savage El Niño drought of 1983 increased mortality, especially among trees ≥20 cm dbh (Condit,

Table 1. **Numbers of trees that survived (L) and trees that died (D) in each size class from 1982 to 1985, raw and adjusted data**

Size class (dbh, cm)	Uncorrected		Corrected	
	L	D	L	D
10 to ≤20	11512	972	11490	967
20 to ≤30	3216	387	3302	396
30 to ≤40	1462	170	1560	180
40 to ≤50	796	117	858	126
50 to ≤60	487	53	490	53
60 to ≤70	292	39	262	35
70 to ≤80	208	23	155	17
80 to ≤90	143	16	87	10
90 to ≤100	93	5	50	3
≥100	274	33	155	19

Table 2. Mortality among different size classes of trees on Barro Colorado Island's 50-hectare Forest Dynamics Plot within multiple-year intervals during 1982–90

Size class (dbh, cm)	1982–85			1985–90			1990, N
	N	D	m	N	D	m	
1 to ≤10	214530	18142	2.66	221284	24894	2.27	223412
10 to ≤20	12457	967	2.38	13038	1288	1.97	13161
20 to ≤30	3698	396	3.36	3546	340	1.90	3594
30 to ≤40	1740	180	3.32	1785	190	2.09	1737
40 to ≤50	984	126	4.06	981	109	2.16	926
50 to ≤60	543	53	2.96	568	70	2.39	553
60 to ≤70	297	35	3.61	304	29	1.81	329
70 to ≤80	172	17	3.08	179	18	1.91	166
80 to ≤90	97	10	3.12	92	9	1.85	119
90 to ≤100	53	3	1.44	60	4	1.25	78
≥100	174	19	3.28	174	12	1.28	169

N is the number of live trees at the start; D is the number of trees that died within the time interval; and m is annual mortality rate, expressed as a percentage.

Hubbell, and Foster, 1995, 1996). Among three 1-hectare plots in or near the Barro Colorado 50-hectare plot, 37 of 519 trees ≥20 cm dbh in 1975 died by 1980, suggesting a death rate among plateau trees of 1.5% per year (Milton, Laca, and Demment, 1994). This mortality rate, however, is unrepresentative. Of the 7689 trees ≥20 cm dbh on the 50-hectare Forest Dynamics Plot in 1985, 781 died during the 5.38 years before the 1990 census (Table 2), suggesting a death rate of 2% per year. This appears to be the *normal* mortality rate for Barro Colorado: between 1985 and 1995, the annual death rate among trees of all diameters >10 cm on the 50-hectare plot has been 2%, just the same mortality as on the study plots at La Selva (Lieberman and Lieberman, 1994, p. 110). This mortality rate is the benchmark by which we should assess the effect of the El Niño drought in 1983. Of the 7758 stems ≥20 cm dbh on the 50-hectare plot in 1982, 839 died before the 1985 census, a mortality of 11.3% per 3.35 years. The normal death rate for the period was 6.7%, suggesting that the El Niño drought imposed an additional mortality of 4.6% on trees ≥20 cm dbh.

Even though the 1983 El Niño drought imposed a mortality of roughly 6% on the Forest Dynamics Plot's larger trees, the size composition of stems on the 50-hectare plot remained remarkably stable between 1982 and 1990 (Table 2), a phenomenon remarked upon by Condit, Hubbell, and Foster (1992a). Basal area per hectare also changed little during this period. Contrary to Leigh, Windsor, et al. (1990), basal area of trees ≥10 cm dbh on the 50-hectare plot increased from somewhat below 27.5 m² per hectare in 1982 to 28.1 m² per hectare in 1985 and 28.4 m² per hectare in 1990. Basal area on Barro Colorado's Forest Dynamics Plot is somewhat higher than on plots 1 and 2 of Lieberman and Lieberman (1994) at La Selva. On those plots, the density of trees ≥10 cm dbh is similar, but their basal area is 25.5 m² per hectare.

Putz and Milton (this volume) found far higher mortality among trees ≥20 cm dbh in young forest plots both on the plateau and near the laboratory clearing (about 2% per year) than in plots of old forest on the central plateau (about 1% per year). There has been no such conspicuous difference between mortality of trees ≥20 cm dbh on the Forest Dynamics Plot's 1 hectare of young forest (hectare 6,4), and that on the remaining 49 hectares of the plot (Table 3).

What Does the 50-hectare Plot Reveal about Tree Diversity?

Although the Forest Dynamics Plot has provided abundant data on forest structure, tree mortality, and the like, the focus of scientific research on this plot has been to discover which factors are involved in maintaining tree diversity (Condit, 1995).

Measuring Diversity To make sense of the data on tree diversity, it would help to find a measure of diversity that does not depend on sample size. On Barro Colorado, Fisher's α (Fisher et al., 1943) comes close to satisfying this requirement (Foster and Hubbell, 1990). Fisher's α first appeared as a parameter in the log series distribution (Fisher et al., 1943), according

Table 3. Mortality of trees ≥20 cm dbh in young forest and of those in mature forest on Barro Colorado Island's 50-hectare Forest Dynamics Plot within multiple-year intervals during 1982–90

Sample	1982–85		1985–90	
	N	D	N	D
Young forest (hectare 6,4)	185	24 (13.0%)	181	17 (9.4%)
Old forest (other 49 hectares)	7583	815 (10.7%)	7573	764 (10.1%)

N is the number of live trees at the start; D is the number of (and in parentheses, the percentage of) trees that died within the time interval.

to which the number of species with m individuals apiece in a sample, p_m, equals $\alpha x^m/m$, where x is an auxiliary parameter that depends on sample size. If the log series distribution applies to a given sample, the total number of individuals, N, in that sample is

$$N = \sum_{m=1}^{\infty} mp(m) = \sum_{m=1}^{\infty} \alpha x^m = \frac{\alpha x}{1-x},$$

while the number of species, S, in that sample is

$$S = \sum_{m=1}^{\infty} p(m) = \alpha \int (1 + x + x^2 + \ldots)\,dx$$

$$= \int \frac{\alpha\,dx}{1-x} = \alpha \ln \frac{1}{1-x}.$$

Even when the log series distribution does not apply, these equations can be solved numerically to find α for a sample of S species among N individuals. On the Forest Dynamics Plot, α is remarkably independent of plot size except for very small plots, usually being close to 35. Moreover, α does not depend notably on the lower size limit of the stems sampled (Table 4; see also Condit, Foster, et al., 1996).

Documenting Diversity Tree diversity on the 50-hectare Forest Dynamics Plot does not depend markedly on habitat, although it is a bit higher on slopes, where moisture is more readily available from the soil at the height of dry season (R. Condit, S. Loo de Lao, S. P. Hubbell, R. B. Foster, and E. G. Leigh, Jr., unpublished). Moreover, tree diversity on this plot appears representative of tree diversity on other parts of Barro Colorado Island (Table 5). The controls on diversity seem to act regionally, not locally.

Regional differences in tree diversity, however, can be quite substantial. As mentioned above, 1 hectare of old-growth forest in Maryland contains 16 species among 351 trees ≥10 cm dbh, for an α of 3.5 (Burnham et al., 1992), while tropical forests are far more diverse. Regional differences in diversity *within* the tropics are also substantial. About 80 km from Barro Colorado Island, at Nusugandi, 300 m above the sea on the ridge that forms the southern boundary of the Comarca de San Blas, 1 hectare of forest contained 191 species among 559 trees ≥10 cm dbh, for an α of 102.4 (Rutilio Paredes, unpublished).

Physiological Tradeoffs and Tree Diversity We have mentioned both the tradeoff between a tree's ability to grow rapidly when light is abundant and its ability to survive in the shade (Brokaw, 1987) and the similar tradeoff between the ability to exploit moist condi-

Table 4. Tree diversity in relation to stem diameter and plot size on Barro Colorado's 50-hectare Forest Dynamics Plot (1985 census)

Plot size (hectares)	Trees ≥ 1 cm dbh			Trees ≥ 10 cm dbh			Trees ≥ 20 cm dbh			Trees ≥ 30 cm dbh		
	N	S	α	N	S	α	N	S	α	N	S	α
50	244111	303	34.1	21238	229	35.9	7754	181	33.2	4118	146	29.5
25	122056	280	34.2	10619	208	36.7	3877	163	34.5	2059	128	30.1
6.25	30514	233	34.3	2655	163	38.3	969	116	34.5	515	84	28.5
1.00	4882	172	34.9	425	91	36.0	155	54	29.5	82	35	23.8
0.25	1221	118	32.4	106	45	30.3	39	23	25.8	0	0	—

N is the average number of stems per plot, S is the average number of species per plot, and α is Fisher's index of diversity. Data from Condit, Foster, et al. (1996).

LEIGH

Table 5. Tree diversity at different sites on Barro Colorado

Size class of trees sampled	Site	Plots sampled		N	S	α	Authority[1]
		Size (hectares)	Total number				
≥5 cm dbh	Lutz, near lab	0.22	1	198	68	36.6	R. Werth
	35 × 70 m from hectare 6,2 of FDP	0.245	1	256	74	34.9	Condit et al.
	FDP	1.0	50	1022	129	39.1	Condit et al.
≥10 cm dbh	Lutz, near lab	0.22	1	120	52	34.9	R. Werth
	35 × 70 m from hectare 6,2 of FDP	0.245	1	110	45	28.4	Condit et al.
	FDP	0.25	200	106	45	29.5	Condit et al.
	Plot in swamp of FDP	0.84	1	277	75	33.8	Condit et al.
	FDP	1.0	50	425	91	36.0	Condit et al.
≥20 cm dbh	Near lab	1.0	5	171	53	26.5	Thorington et al.
	Poacher's	1.0	4	145	55	32.3	S. J. Wright
	FDP	1.0	50	155	54	29.0	Condit et al.
	Plot in swamp of FDP	0.84	1	105	47	32.7	Condit et al.
≥30 cm dbh	Poacher's	1.0	4	82	39	29.3	S. J. Wright
	FDP	1.0	50	82	35	23.1	Condit et al.

FDP is the 50-hectare Forest Dynamics Plot. The number of trees (N) and the number of tree species (S) are expressed as per-plot averages if more than one plot was sampled. α is Fisher's index of diversity.

[1] All sources were personal communications except Thorington et al. (1982, this volume). "Condit et al." represents R. Condit, S. P. Hubbell, and R. B. Foster.

tions to the full and the ability to survive drought. On the Forest Dynamics Plot saplings of some species, such as *Cecropia insignis* (Moraceae), are concentrated in areas of low canopy, where fallen trees have recently opened light gaps, while saplings of a few species, such as *Ocotea whitei* (Lauraceae), are commonest where the canopy is tallest (Hubbell and Foster, 1986a, Figure 8). Some species, such as *Unonopsis pittieri* (Annonaceae), are largely restricted to steeper slopes (Hubbell and Foster, 1986a, Figure 4), where the soil is wetter at the height of the dry season (Becker, Rabenold, et al., 1988), while others, such as *Faramea occidentalis* (Rubiaceae), maintain denser populations on the drier plateau (Hubbell and Foster, 1986a, Figure 5). On the Forest Dynamics Plot populations of moisture-loving species, such as *Poulsenia armata* (Moraceae) and *Virola surinamensis* (Myristicaceae), which are most common on steeper slopes that are wetter during the dry season, have been declining during the last few years (Condit, Hubbell, and Foster, 1992a, 1996). This may be due to a 60-year decline in annual rainfall that reached a climax in the El Niño drought of 1983 (Windsor, 1990). Nonetheless, 26 of the 41 species represented on the 50-hectare plot by more than 1000 stems apiece in 1982 were distributed randomly with respect to canopy height, 18 were distributed randomly with respect to habitat type (slope, plateau, streamside, or seasonal swamp), and 14 were distributed at random with respect to both canopy height and habitat type (Hubbell and Foster, 1986a). What factor might control tree abundances strictly enough to override tradeoffs as strong as these?

We have assessed the effectiveness of these tradeoffs from analyses of spatial pattern. Does spatial pattern reflect tree dynamics? Welden et al. (1991) compared recruitment, growth, and survival of saplings between 1 and 4 cm dbh under canopy <10 m and canopy >10 m high, to learn whether Barro Colorado's tree diversity was maintained by specialization of saplings of different species to light gaps of different sizes. In all, 92 species that were not "poor performers" could be compared in all three respects. Of these, Welden et al. classified six as pioneers: these recruited more rapidly and grew faster under low canopy. They classified 79 as generalists, whose saplings grew slowly and survived well under both low and high canopy. Saplings of more than half of these generalist species grew faster, and more than one-third recruited faster, under low canopy; saplings of 13 of the 79 generalist species survived better under higher canopy. Most of the commonest species on the plot were generalists. Despite the crudeness of this test, with its binary distinction between low and high canopy, Welden et al. (1991) support Hubbell and Foster's (1986a) conclusion that preferences for gaps of different sizes accounts for very little of Barro Colorado's tree diversity. Once again, what factor can override tradeoffs as striking as that between growing fast in full sun and surviving in the shade?

Specialized Pests and Tree Diversity It is high time to remember Dobzhansky's (1950) dictum that biotic interactions are the most influential ones in the lives of tropical organisms. Indeed, as mentioned above, one of the main functions of data from the Forest Dynamics Plot has been to test the notion that pest pressure maintains tree diversity.

The first tests of the Janzen–Connell hypothesis using plot data (Hubbell and Foster, 1986a, 1987) were based on pattern. The most successful of these approaches was to test whether saplings of a given species were rarer near conspecific adults than farther away (Hubbell and Foster, 1987). Saplings of the plot's most common species of canopy tree, *Trichilia tuberculata* (Meliaceae)—which is also the plot's third most common stem ≥1 cm dbh—were indeed rarer near conspecific adults than in the plot as a whole. Saplings of the second most common species of canopy tree, *Alseis blackiana* (Rubiaceae), were also rarer near conspecific adults, but unlike *Trichilia* they tended to be rarer near most big trees. Saplings of *Tetragastris panamensis* (Burseraceae) were as common near conspecific adults as elsewhere, and saplings of the shade-tolerant canopy tree species *Quararibea asterolepis* (Bombacaceae) and *Poulsenia armata* (Moraceae) were more common near conspecific adults than elsewhere (Hubbell and Foster, 1987). *Trichilia tuberculata* is also the only canopy species for which the number of adults in 1 hectare shows a convincing negative correlation with the number of juveniles (Hubbell and Foster, 1986a).

Studies of dynamics on the 50-hectare plot tend to support these conclusions. Between 1982 and 1985 saplings of *Trichilia tuberculata* 1–4 cm in diameter grew more slowly and suffered higher mortality when their nearest neighbor ≥30 cm dbh was a conspecific. This was true even though the nearest big neighbor tended to be smaller and farther away when it was a conspecific than when it belonged to another species (Hubbell, Condit, and Foster, 1990). Moreover, between 1982 and 1985 half as many *Trichilia* per hectare recruited (attained 1 cm dbh) within 5 m of a *Trichilia* ≥30 cm dbh as in the plot as a whole. The more *Trichilia* stems ≥16 cm dbh within 10 m of a *Trichilia* sapling <8 cm dbh, and the closer they were, the higher the chance that this sapling would die between 1982 and 1985; small *Trichilia* saplings suffered most from the proximity of conspecific trees (Hubbell et al., 1990). Between 1982 and 1985 the number of *Trichilia tuberculata* declined on those hectares with the most adults and increased on hectares with the fewest adults, as if some density-dependent factor were preventing this species from taking over the plot (Hubbell et al., 1990).

As studies of pattern also suggested, saplings of *Quararibea asterolepis* grew equally well under the crowns of canopy *Quararibea* as under canopy trees of other species; their saplings grew faster the more conspecifics ≥16 cm dbh were within 10 m, and in those areas where no conspecifics ≥16 cm dbh were within 10 m, *Quararibea* recruited more rapidly the more conspecifics ≥16 cm dbh were between 10 and 50 m away (Hubbell et al., 1990). The *Quararibea* results seemed a bit at variance with the incidence of a striking insect outbreak that defoliated many *Quararibea* at the beginning of the rainy season in 1985 (Wong et al., 1990). Saplings bearing young leaves were more likely to be defoliated if they were nearer to defoliated adults ≥16 cm dbh. An adult *Quararibea* was more likely to be defoliated the larger the number of defoliated trees among the three nearest neighboring *Quararibea* ≥16 cm dbh. Finally, *Quararibea* on a given hectare were more likely to be heavily eaten if this was also the case on adjoining hectares (Wong et al., 1990). Proximity to conspecifics whose leaves were already too old for the caterpillars to eat, however, had no effect on a *Quararibea*'s chances of being defoliated.

Similarly, saplings of the plot's most common understory treelet, *Faramea occidentalis* (Rubiaceae)—the second most common stem ≥1 cm dbh on the Forest Dynamics Plot—are also distributed in accord with the predictions of Janzen and Connell (Condit, Hubbell, and Foster, 1994). Between 1982 and 1990 *Faramea* saplings 1–2 cm in diameter grew significantly more slowly and suffered significantly higher mortality if conspecific adults >4 cm dbh were within 2 m. *Faramea* saplings grew more slowly and suffered higher mortality where there were many adult neighbors within 30 or 60 m. Between 1982 and 1990, moreover, *Faramea* recruitment was lower where *Faramea* adults were more abundant. Apparently, seedlings and saplings <1 cm dbh suffered enough to reverse the consequences of the fact that where *Faramea* adults occur in the highest density, their seeds survive better under conspecific adults (Schupp, 1992). In the plot's second most common understory treelet, *Desmopsis panamensis,* recruitment was slower within 2 m of adults ≥4 cm dbh, but in contrast to *Faramea,* the proximity of adult conspecifics did not slow the growth or increase the mortality of *Desmopsis* saplings (Condit, Hubbell, and Foster, 1994).

Condit, Hubbell, and Foster (1992b) undertook a comprehensive test of the Janzen–Connell hypothesis. For each species *A* common enough to test, they compared the distribution of distances of *A* recruits with that of non-*A* recruits (recruits of species other than *A*) to the nearest *A* adult. If a significantly smaller proportion of *A* than of non-*A* recruits was within some distance, *x* meters (*x* ≤ 20 m), of the nearest *A* adult, the distribution of *A* recruits was called "repelled." If the ratio of *A* to non-*A* recruits peaked at an intermediate distance from the nearest *A* adult, and if there was no significant shortage of *A* recruits close to *A* adults, the distribution of *A* recruits was called "partially repelled." If a significantly higher proportion of *A* than of non-*A* recruits was within *x* meters (*x* ≤ 20 m) of the nearest *A* adult, the distribution of *A* recruits was called "attracted." All other distributions were said to show no pattern. Condit et al. (1992b) considered attracted and no-pattern distributions inconsistent with the Janzen–Connell hypothesis. If all trees produce equal numbers of recruits, regardless of their species or position on the plot, attracted or no-pattern distributions would not help different species to coexist. But this method suffers from a problem of scale: the tendency of juveniles to cluster around, and grow better near, adults may reflect restriction to favorable habitat types, within which pests might still keep them well spaced.

Between 1982 and 1985 only three of twenty-three canopy tree species, two of twenty-three midstory tree species, two of nineteen understory tree species (counting *Faramea occidentalis;* cf. Condit, Hubbell, and Foster, 1992b, p. 276), and zero of fifteen shrub species tested had repelled distributions. Five of these canopy species, four midstory species, six understory species, and twelve shrub species had attracted distributions. Ten canopy species, fifteen midstory species, eleven understory species, and two shrub species showed no pattern. Thus, as one passes from canopy trees down to shrubs, an increasing majority of the recruit distributions is inconsistent with the Janzen–Connell hypothesis (Condit et al., 1992b). Yet in the absence of species-specific pests, recruits of all species should have attracted distributions. Thus, even though the results of Condit et al. (1992b) apparently contradict the Janzen–Connell hypothesis, they testify to the widespread effectiveness of some factor, which might be species-specific pests, in spacing out a tree's recruits.

The verdict of the research conducted at Barro Colorado Island on the Janzen–Connell hypothesis is ambiguous. On the one hand, recruitment is lower, growth slower, and/or mortality higher for saplings near conspecific adults only in a minority of the species tested (Hubbell, Condit, and Foster, 1990; Condit, Hubbell, and Foster, 1992b, 1994). On the other hand, attracted distributions of recruits are relatively rare except among shrubs (Condit et al.,

1992b), suggesting that seedlings of most species are more susceptible to pests if they are near their parents, a phenomenon for which Barro Colorado provides many examples. Does the prevalence of such pest pressure lend significance to the fact that the plot's most common canopy tree (Hubbell et al., 1990), its most common midstory tree (*Hirtella triandra,* Chrysobalanaceae; Condit et al., 1992b), and its most common understory treelet all behave in accord with the Janzen–Connell hypothesis—as if the most common species reach a limit imposed by pest pressure? The plot's most common stem ≥1 cm dbh, *Hybanthus prunifolius,* warns us against too facile a conclusion: although this species occasionally suffers from severe insect outbreaks (Wolda and Foster, 1978), its seed dispersal is woefully inefficient, and it does not seem to behave in accord with Janzen and Connell's prediction.

DO SEASONAL RHYTHMS IN PLANTS CONTROL ANIMAL POPULATIONS?

Seasonal Food Shortages and Vertebrate Populations

A primary theme of this book is that the forest on Barro Colorado Island limits its population of vertebrate herbivores by seasonal shortages of fruit and new leaves. Leigh and Windsor (this volume) suggested that Barro Colorado's forest can protect itself from vertebrate herbivores without the help of predators, such as big cats. Terborgh (1988) questioned this thesis. He argued that Barro Colorado's lack of jaguars and pumas explains why agoutis, pacas, and coatis are so much more common there than in the Parque Manú of Amazonian Peru, which has similar climate, soil, and vegetation but a full complement of top predators. This surplus of agoutis, pacas, and coatis, he argued, is altering the species composition of tree regeneration and influencing the forest community in other ways. Further work on Barro Colorado has told us more about the role of seasonal food shortage in limiting herbivore populations.

Estimating Mammal Populations Smythe et al. (this volume) argued that at certain seasons, there were more terrestrial frugivores than the supply of falling fruit could support. This argument depends on accurate estimate of mammal populations.

Barro Colorado's mammals have been censused by walking along trails and recording each mammal seen and its distance from the observer when first sighted. The formula most often used for the population density of a species (King's method; Glanz, this volume) is $2NLR$, where N is the number of individuals of that species seen while walking L meters of trail and R is the average distance from the observer of these individuals when first sighted. This technique suggests that within 500 m of the laboratory clearing on Barro Colorado, where human use of the trails is heaviest, agouti densities are three times higher, squirrel densities four times higher, and paca densities seven times higher than at more distant locations. These differences are almost certainly an artifact of habituation to human activity (Wright, Gompper, and de Léon, 1994). The inference of Smythe et al. (this volume), based on live-trapping mammals in Lutz catchment, that too little fruit falls to feed that catchment's terrestrial frugivores, probably applies to the whole of Barro Colorado.

Moreover, estimates from such trail censuses of terrestrial mammal populations at other Neotropical sites are probably too low, because the animals there are not habituated by high levels of "benign" human activity (Wright, Gompper, and de Léon, 1994). More accurate counts would probably show that at Parque Manú in Peru, the observed supply of falling fruit (Terborgh, 1983) is also too low at certain seasons to feed the terrestrial frugivores. In addition, there are Neotropical sites with a full complement of big cats where pacas and agoutis are roughly as common as on Barro Colorado (Wright et al., 1994). Apparently, pumas and jaguars do not play a crucial role in limiting populations of terrestrial herbivores. This question is important, however, and merits closer attention.

Observed densities of primates and coati bands, however, were not higher close to Barro Colorado's laboratory clearing (Glanz, 1990; Wright et al., 1994).

The Season of Fruit Shortage as a Time of Hunger
Smythe et al. (this volume), Glanz et al. (this volume), Milton (this volume), and Worthington (this volume) presented a variety of evidence that the time of minimum fruit fall is a time of hunger for fruit-eating mammals and birds. More evidence for this proposition has since accumulated. Schupp (1990) found that in four successive years, seeds of the understory treelet *Faramea occidentalis* disappeared much more rapidly from the forest floor before the onset of the March–May fruiting peak than after fruit began falling abundantly.

Scheelea palms fruit from May to November or December (Wright, 1990). In young forest, where *Scheelea* are far more abundant, fruit fall peaks in June and declines steadily thereafter, with little sign of Foster's (1982a, this volume) September–October fruiting peak (Smythe, 1970). In 1990 fruit fall from *Scheelea* palms peaked in late July. From August through October, as the young forest's food shortage worsened, the proportion of freshly fallen *Scheelea* fruit that was al-

ready chewed by mammals (mostly squirrels and agoutis) steadily increased. Beginning in August Forget, Munoz, and Leigh (1994) placed marked, intact *Scheelea* seeds in the forest during three successive months. Of those seeds whose fate could be traced, more were eaten and fewer buried for later use as the young forest's fruit shortage worsened. Furthermore, the proportion of freshly fallen *Scheelea* fruit attacked by bruchid beetles steadily declined from mid-August through November, a phenomenon witnessed in a different year by Wright (1990). Presumably, these beetles cease laying eggs on *Scheelea* fruit in proportion to the increasing likelihood that they will die when mammals eat the fruit they are in (Forget et al., 1994). The season of animal hunger appears to occur so predictably that the bruchid beetles that prey upon *Scheelea* seeds have adjusted their egg-laying cycles in response to it.

White-faced monkeys, *Cebus capucinus*, however, react rather differently from most of Barro Colorado's other animals to the seasonal rhythms of fruit ripening (Mitchell, 1989). Mitchell's (1989) study focused primarily on *Cebus* in old forest, in the 50-hectare Forest Dynamics Plot. From mid-December through mid-August most fruits eaten by these *Cebus* were supplied by a few tall, large-crowned trees. Most of these fruits were large and difficult for young *Cebus* to handle. From mid-August through September, *Cebus* food was relatively more abundant. The monkeys ate fruits of intermediate size and handling difficulty. Again, however, much of this food was provided by relatively few large-crowned trees. From October through mid-December *Cebus* food was very abundant and scattered over a large number of small-crowned treelets and shrubs. These fruits were small, and easy even for baby monkeys to handle. The seasonal timing of *Cebus* births seemed adjusted so that infant monkeys were weaned in October, when shrubs and treelets whose crowns infant monkeys could easily reach bore plentiful fruit, which these infants could readily eat. Oddly, this season, which is so favorable for newly weaned *Cebus*, overlaps very largely with the season of greatest food scarcity for most of Barro Colorado's mammals.

Quantifying the Food Shortage Using monthly records of fruit fall from Smythe (1970), Smythe et al. (this volume) found that in November and December too little fruit fell to feed the terrestrial frugivores. Similarly, Worthington (this volume) compared the supply of fruit of types eaten by manakins (small fruit-eating birds) and found that late in the rainy season there was too little fruit to feed the manakins.

More recently, Handley and Leigh (1991) tried to quantify the seasonal shortage of fruit for *Artibeus ja-*

maicensis, the Jamaican fruit bat. Female bats of this species normally bear two young a year: one in February or March, which is weaned during the April–May fruiting peak, and one in July or August, which is weaned during the September–October fruiting peak. These bats appear to time their reproduction so as to wean their young when fruit is most abundant (D. E. Wilson et al., 1991).

How severe is the November–February fruit shortage for *Artibeus jamaicensis*? A guild of seven species of bats, whose two largest members are the 70-g *Artibeus lituratus* and the 50-g *Artibeus jamaicensis,* feed primarily on figs (Bonaccorso, 1979). Morrison (1978, 1980; Morrison and Hagen Morrison, 1981) found that when feeding on *Ficus insipida,* an *Artibeus jamaicensis* eats about seven 10-g figs per night, 19% of which is dry matter. An *Artibeus jamaicensis* thus eats 13 g dry weight of fruit per night, or 4.8 kg per year. As Barro Colorado has about two *Artibeus jamaicensis* per hectare (3000 in all; Leigh and Handley, 1991), these bats eat 9.6 kg dry weight of fruit, mostly figs, per hectare per year. Between November and March, when many *Artibeus literatus* migrate to Barro Colorado, *Artibeus jamaicensis* may account for a bit less than one-third of the weight of figs eaten by bats on Barro Colorado.

On Barro Colorado, howling monkeys also eat many figs. Barro Colorado has roughly 1300 howling monkeys (Milton, 1990). They eat 85 kg dry weight of food per hectare per year (Nagy and Milton [1979] calculated that if Barro Colorado had 1370 howlers, they would eat 90 kg dry weight of food per hectare). Of their food intake 60%, say 50 kg dry weight per hectare per year, is fruit (Hladik and Hladik, 1969). Judging by the proportion of their feeding time that howlers allot to fig trees (50% in young forest, 25% in old; Milton, 1980), howlers in young forest eat 25 kg dry weight of figs per hectare per year, while howlers in old forest eat about 13 kg. Since half the island is old forest (Foster and Brokaw, this volume), howlers probably average 19 kg dry weight of figs per hectare per year. Unlike bats, howlers eat unripe figs, so they get first crack at this resource. In November and December, when fruit of other kinds is scarce, bats and howling monkeys together may eat figs at an annual rate of 40 kg dry weight per hectare.

What is the island's fig production? From 1976 through 1979, the 49 *Ficus insipida* in the 25 hectares of young forest surrounding the laboratory clearing annually produced 34 full fig crops, averaging perhaps 40,000 7-g figs apiece; the 71 *Ficus yoponensis* in this area produced 64 full crops per year, averaging 40,000 3.5-g figs apiece (Handley and Leigh, 1991). If these figs are 19% dry matter, the *Ficus* in these 25 hectares of young forest produce 140 kg dry weight of

figs per hectare per year. Since *Ficus insipida* and *Ficus yoponensis* are uncommonly abundant near the laboratory clearing and almost absent from old forest, while strangler figs are more common in old forest (Handley and Leigh, 1991), Barro Colorado's fig production may average 80 kg dry weight per hectare per year for the island as a whole. In the season when fruit in general is most scarce, figs fruit at a normal rate, but the fruit they supply is probably insufficient to meet the extra demand from other arboreal frugivores. Does this circumstance explain why bats respond, not to a seasonal fig shortage that usually occurs in August and September (Handley, Gardner, and Wilson, 1991), but to the seasonal shortage of fruit in general?

Worthington (1990) compared food supply with the requirements of two small fruit-eating birds, the red-capped manakin, *Pipra mentalis,* and the golden-collared manakin, *Manacus vitellinus,* for the year following the one reported in this volume. From December 1978 through November 1980, Worthington (1990) censused birds of these two species on an 18-hectare island, Orchid Island, just off Barro Colorado. She recorded each instance she observed of a manakin eating fruit and noted the fruit's species. She then estimated the manakins' food requirements from measurements of their basal metabolism. She also evaluated the total fruit production per fortnight of a set of species of trees and shrubs on Orchid Island that provided 78% of these manakins' total fruit intake during this study's first year and 51% during the second. These birds also ate insects; censused fruits thus accounted for 71% of their total *food* intake during the first year and 44% during the second.

Numbers of manakins of these two species found on Orchid Island during successive half-years varied as follows:

Species	Dec. 1978 to May 1979	June–Dec. 1979	Apr.–June 1980	Aug.–Dec. 1980
Red-capped	46	70	49	142
Golden-collared	32	39	45	53

She assumed that the increase in counts of golden-collared manakins during her study reflected her improving ability to see them, and that the numbers of red-capped manakins counted during the first half of each year reflected a stable base population, while the extra individuals of the second half of each year reflected a seasonal influx of migrants. She accordingly calculated the basic food demands of Orchid Island's manakins as that of 47 red-capped manakins (2.6 per hectare) plus 55 golden-collared manakins (3.0 per hectare). In total, her manakins required the equivalent of 22.5 g dry weight of food per hectare per day, 316 g per fortnight.

Fruit production of censused shrubs exceeded 224 g dry weight per hectare per fortnight (71% of the food requirements of the resident manakins) from December 1978 through July 1979. It exceeded 139 g dry weight per hectare per fortnight (44% of their food requirement) from 20 December 1979 through 21 July 1980. In both species, male manakins courted females by displaying in leks only when, judging from the censused shrubs, Orchid Island was producing enough fruit to feed its manakins.

Did Worthington (1990) prove too much? When there is too little fruit for the resident manakins, what can the vagrants be living on? Worthington's figures may exaggerate the food shortage a bit. A smaller proportion of the fruit that manakins ate came from censused plants during the lean season: 63% of all feeding records from August through December were from censused shrubs, compared to 75% from January through July. Moreover, during the fat season, manakins derived much of their fruit from a few rich sources, while during the lean season they had to visit many more fruiting species to meet their needs. Let us measure fruit diet breadth, B, as $1/\Sigma_i x_i^2$, where x_i is the proportion of all fruit-eating records in which species i was eaten. For red-capped manakins, $B = 3.28$ in the fat season and 9.72 during the lean season. For golden-collared manakins, $B = 5.74$ in the fat season and 15.85 during the lean season. When birds are drawing their fruit from more and different sources, each of which is less conspicuous, might the observer's record of their diet be less comprehensive?

Nonetheless, just as a biologist trying to piece together support for research from a variety of minor sources is probably ill funded compared to a colleague with a few larger grants, so the very diversity of manakin diets from August through December suggest that the manakins are at least relatively short of food during this season. Moreover, dietary overlap between the two manakin species is somewhat lower during the second half-year, as if to reduce the likelihood that one species will competitively displace the other from Orchid Island during the lean season (see below). If x_i is the proportion of feeding records on species i among the fruit-eating records for red-capped manakins, and y_i is the same for golden-collareds, the dietary overlap between the species may be measured by the quantity $2\Sigma_i x_i y_i / [\Sigma_i (x_i^2 + y_i^2)]$ (Horn, 1966). This quantity is 0.73 during the fat season and 0.63 during the lean season. The difference is not large, but it is suggestive.

Dietary Overlap and Food Shortage Zaret and Rand (1971) observed that dietary overlap among stream fishes was lower during the season of food shortage than when food was abundant. Smythe (1978) remarked that when fruit is abundant, all of Barro Colorado's terrestrial frugivores share in the bounty, while during the season of fruit shortage, each species resorts to a different "fall-back strategy": agoutis live off buried seeds, pacas browse seedlings, coatis search the leaf litter for small animals, and so forth. Terborgh (1983, 1986a, 1986b) noticed that in the Manú, coexisting species of monkeys that eat fruit when it is abundant each resort to a different specialty when fruit is rare.

Species are more likely to coexist if each specializes to a different diet during the season of food shortage. Why, however, should animals specialize when food is scarce: is this not the time to eat everything one can? Rosenzweig and Abramsky (1986) have answered this question. They showed that, for a set of species that shared a common primary food preference but differed in their secondary preferences, niche overlap would be *less* when the food they all preferred was scarce. Snuffling out litter invertebrates, browsing seedlings, and living off buried seeds require very different characteristics, so it is not surprising that niche differentiation among Barro Colorado's terrestrial frugivores centers on their secondary food preferences.

Experiments on Food Limitations in Vertebrate Populations We have given various reasons for believing that populations of vertebrate herbivores on Barro Colorado Island are limited by seasonal shortage of fruit and new leaves. Nevertheless, much of the argument hinges on correlations. Now Gregory Adler, of the University of Wisconsin, Oshkosh, is devising experiments to test whether a population of vertebrate frugivores is limited by seasonal shortage of suitable food.

When the Chagres was dammed to form Gatun Lake, separating Barro Colorado from the surrounding mainland, many smaller islands were also formed (Leigh, Wright, et al., 1993). Islands of about 2 hectares had resident populations of spiny rats, *Proechimys semispinosus*, but no other resident mammals (Adler and Seamon, 1991). Different tree species were common on different islands, so the seasonal rhythm of fruit availability differed greatly from island to island. Adler (1994) has followed changes in the populations of spiny rats on eight 2-hectare islands since January 1991, live-trapping animals each month. If one sums the populations from all eight islands, the seasonal cycle thus obtained closely resembles the mainland cycle, but each island's annual population cycle is different, apparently in response to differences in timing of fruit availability (Adler, 1994). Trees on these islands have been censused and identified, and fruit fall on these islands is now being monitored, so that we can relate the differences in these seasonal population cycles more precisely to the rhythms of fruit fall on the different islands.

For his experimental test of the mechanisms of population regulation in *Proechimys*, Adler has added four more 2-hectare islands to his study. To assess the effect of lowering adult numbers on reproductive behavior of the remaining adults and the numbers of young that become big enough to trap, and the proportion of those young that reach adulthood, half the adult females were removed from one set of islands in June 1994 and half the adult males from another set of islands in June 1995. I await the outcome with interest.

Is Seed Predation by Mammals More Intense on Barro Colorado Than Elsewhere?

To compare the impact of mammals on *Dipteryx* regeneration at Barro Colorado and in the Manú, Terborgh and Wright (1994) placed *Dipteryx* seeds in fenced exclosures to exclude all nonclimbing mammals, "semipermeable" exclosures admitting only small rodents, and unprotected control plots. Predation on unprotected *Dipteryx* seeds and on *Dipteryx* seeds accessible only to small rodents was equally intense at both sites (Terborgh and Wright, 1994). Exclosures enhanced recruitment of plants of all kinds at Manú and Barro Colorado alike, but did not affect their survival (Terborgh and Wright, 1994). More such comparisons are needed.

Seasonal Rhythms and Insect Populations

Insects and the Seasonal Rhythm of Leaf Flush

On Barro Colorado, there are distinct seasonal rhythms in insect abundance and activity (Smythe, this volume; Wolda, this volume), even though insects are never as rare or inactive as during winter in the north temperate zone (Wolda, 1983). It is becoming clear that insects influence the timing of leaf flush. Leaf-eating insects (Coley, this volume), like leaf-eating vertebrates, prefer young leaves. Flushing leaves in synchrony, especially at the beginning of rainy season, before insect populations have had a chance to build up, reduces herbivory (Aide, 1991). Aide (1992) experimentally delayed the initial rainy-season leaf flush in some individuals of the understory shrub *Hybanthus prunifolius*, by laying plastic over the soil surrounding their stems before the rains started. The individuals thus treated flushed leaves only after the plastic was removed several weeks after the rains began, allowing rainwater to reach the soil around their roots. As predicted, these individuals flushed leaves later, out of synchrony with their conspecifics,

and their leaves were much more heavily eaten. Many understory shrubs reduce herbivory by flushing some leaves in the dry season, when insect populations are lower (Aide, 1988, 1993).

Seasonal Rhythms of Herbivorous Insects and Their Cues

Many insects appear at the beginning of the rainy season, when many trees are flushing new leaves (Leigh and Smythe, 1978; Wolda, this volume). Nonetheless, irrigating forest plots during the dry season has no more effect on seasonal changes in the abundance or species composition of the insect fauna (Wolda and Wright, 1992) than it does on the timing or abundance of flowers, fruit, and new leaves produced by the forest canopy trees (Wright and Cornejo, 1990a).

What cues do different insects use to time their seasonal rhythms? The tropical fungus beetle *Stenotarsus rotundus* (Endomychidae) diapauses in aggregations of tens of thousands on the trunks of palms for up to ten months of the year. These aggregations form in June. After aggregating, the diapausing beetles resorb their gonads and flight muscles (Wolda and Denlinger, 1984). These beetles fly off again just after the first heavy rains of April or May (Tanaka, Denlinger, and Wolda, 1987). To do so, they must begin regenerating their flight muscles well before the rainy season comes. How do they know when to begin? It turns out that in late February, increasing day length triggers the regeneration of their gonads and flight muscles; increased atmospheric humidity speeds this process (Tanaka, Denlinger, and Wolda, 1987, 1988).

Six species of cicada that emerge on the average starting date of rainy season emerge at much the same time each year, regardless of when that year's rains begin (Wolda, 1989a). If the nymphs were not underground, it would be logical to assume that they were responding to day length (photoperiod). Could they be responding to the impact of photoperiod on their host plants?

The seed-bugs *Jadera obscura* and *Jadera aeola* (Rhopalidae), which feed on seeds of the plant family Sapindaceae, aggregate on leaves of understory shrubs during the first half of Barro Colorado's dry season (December–February), when suitable food is not available (Wolda and Tanaka, 1987). They leave these aggregations in late February, apparently in response to the appearance of an abundance of mature seeds of *Thinouia* spp. and *Serjania* spp. (Sapindaceae) in the forest canopy (Wolda, 1988, p. 11). In March and April these bugs feed and reproduce in the forest canopy, dropping their eggs to the forest floor, where their nymphs also feed on seeds of the family Sapindaceae.

Adult *Jadera obscura* emerge in April and May. It is thought that they feed in the canopy or migrate off the island for the remainder of the rainy season, before aggregating for their early dry-season diapause. There are two morphs among the newly emerged adults of *Jadera aeola*. One is a long-winged morph that enters diapause immediately and delays reproduction until the following dry season (Tanaka, Denlinger, and Wolda, 1987). The other is a short-winged morph, whose individuals resorb flight muscles, reproduce immediately, producing long-winged offspring, and then die (Tanaka and Wolda, 1987). This dimorphism is related to the unpredictable onset of rainy season. In years when the sapindaceous seed crop is copious and the rains, which deny these seeds to the bugs by causing them to germinate or rot, come late, the short-winged morphs do well. If, however, the seed crop is scarce or the rains come early, the long-winged morphs have the advantage (Tanaka and Wolda, 1987). Are the short-winged morphs induced by local environmental conditions? They do not occur in all populations.

One of the strangest aspects of tropical insects is how little energy some expend during diapause. At the beginning of diapause, the fresh weight of a fungus beetle averages 17 mg, of which 5 mg is fat. These beetles lose 4 mg of fat apiece during their ten-month rest: they appear to have no other source of energy (Wolda and Denlinger, 1984). This fat expenditure represents a respiration of 0.09 ml O_2 per gram of beetle per hour (Wolda, 1989b)—an energy expenditure of 0.432 calorie (1.81 joules) per gram of beetle per hour (Vleck and Vleck, 1979). From September through February, when they lack gonads and flight muscles, these beetles consume 0.22 ml O_2 per gram of body weight per hour, an energy expenditure of 0.44 joule per gram of beetle per hour (Wolda, 1989b). Thus, at the height of their diapause, 200 kg of these beetles expend as much energy as a 6-kg howler monkey (Nagy and Milton, 1979) or a 25-watt lightbulb. Isolated beetles expend much more energy; diapausing *Stenotarsus* keep their energy expenditure so low by sticking together in aggregations (Tanaka, Wolda, and Denlinger, 1988).

Other insects appear to avoid the season of shortage by migrating elsewhere (Williams, 1958; Smith, this volume, 1992). Some attention has been devoted to the energetics of migration (De Vries and Dudley, 1990; Dudley and De Vries, 1990). Nevertheless, we still have no idea where the migrants go.

Seemingly Unregulated Populations

Herbivorous Insects   Continuing Smythe's (this volume) and Wolda's (this volume) monitoring of insect

catches at light traps, Wolda (1992) recorded the numbers of individuals of each species of Homoptera, Orthoptera, sphinx moth, and cockroach caught during 14 successive years in Barro Colorado's light traps. Populations of most species fluctuated markedly from year to year. In each of these four groups, species composition changed progressively over time: that is to say, the species compositions of the samples in two different years were less similar, the greater the time interval separating the two sample years. Moreover, 22% of the 518 species with a total catch of more than 25 individuals, and 7 of the 78 species with a total catch of more than 1000 individuals, showed a directional trend in their abundance over this 14-year period of more than 10% of their average abundance per year. That is to say, the regression of their abundance on time would show at least a 3.4-fold increase, or decrease, in their abundance over this 14-year interval (Wolda, 1992). How can one speak of population regulation (not to mention equilibrium population sizes) of these insects, in the face of such data as these?

An Insectivorous Lizard of the Forest Floor   On Barro Colorado, the population of the insectivorous lizard *Anolis limifrons* fluctuates as markedly as one of Wolda's insect populations. Andrews and Rand (this volume) tried to make sense of this variation. Their explanation has been much modified since. By now, Andrews (1991; also see Andrews, Rand, and Guerrero, 1983) has followed these fluctuations for 22 years in Lutz ravine and for shorter periods at other sites. When populations are higher, the proportion of juveniles is lower, and lizards of given length weigh less, suggesting that density-dependent factors influence the population's dynamics. Yet these factors seem unable to regulate this population. What drives these fluctuations?

From 1970 through 1980, lizard numbers were highest at the ends of years with short dry seasons—years when the sum of April's and the preceding December's rainfall was highest (Andrews and Rand, this volume). The 1970–84 time series suggested that numbers were lowest at the ends of years with the most rain from October through December, when rainy season peaks and ends (Andrews and Rand, 1990). The 1970–89 time series suggested that numbers were lower in years with more rain from May through July (Andrews, 1991). This seems like a textbook example warning about the dangers of trusting correlations.

Wright's (1991) watering experiment shed some light on this problem. *Anolis limifrons* were censused on irrigated and unwatered control plots from 1986 through 1988. Watering affected neither food supply nor adult survival. In the first half of 1986 watering enhanced the recruitment of juveniles, apparently by increasing survival among the eggs (Andrews, 1988), causing an *Anolis* population explosion on the watered plots in 1986 (Andrews and Wright, 1994). In 1987 and 1988 *Anolis* populations on the watered plots fell back toward the levels on unwatered ones, thanks to a sharp decrease in recruitment. Did sustained watering eventually cause egg-eating ants or egg-destroying pathogens to multiply? We do not know, but this experiment does suggest how we might make sense of *Anolis* population dynamics. Would closer study also make more sense of the fluctuations in Wolda's insect populations?

MUTUALISMS

When the first edition of this book was written, the importance of mutualisms—particularly those between plants and the animals that pollinated their flowers and dispersed their seeds—was recognized (Augspurger, this volume; Foster, 1982a, this volume; Howe, this volume). Nevertheless, mutualisms permeate tropical forest to a far greater extent than we realized at the time. In addition to their pollinators and seed dispersers, plants need root fungi, mycorrhizae, to help them extract nutrients from the soil (Janos, 1980, 1983; Alexander, 1989). Some plants need mammals to bury their seeds out of reach of insect pests (Smythe, 1989; Forget and Milleron, 1991). Others employ ants to defend their leaves and flowers against assorted herbivores (Schemske, 1980, 1982; Schupp and Feener, 1991). Caterpillars have perverted some ant–plant mutualisms by drinking the extrafloral nectar intended for the ants and producing secretions the ants prefer—thus using the plant's nectar, suitably transformed, to pay the ants to protect the caterpillars as they consume this plant's leaves (De Vries and Baker, 1989; De Vries, 1990, 1991a, 1991b, 1991c, 1992). We are now beginning to learn how important it is to understand the many and varied ways plant populations depend on animals, and the alternate habitats, foods, and other resources these needed animals require to complete their life cycles. Such knowledge is essential in order to design intelligent programs for preserving tropical diversity (Leigh and de Alba, 1992).

On Barro Colorado Island, mutualisms and their role in the ecological organization of tropical forest are receiving increasing attention. Herre's study of the mutualism between fig trees and their pollinating wasps began as an inquiry into how population subdivision affects selection on the sex ratio (Herre, 1985). Probing the natural history of this mutualism and analyzing how natural selection affects the relationships among its participants revealed how profoundly this mutualism has affected the biology of fig trees and the ecology of tropical forest (Herre, 1989; Patiño, Herre, and Tyree, 1994). Exploration in depth of the ramifications of this interaction has inspired new directions of research on Barro Colorado.

Pollination, Dispersal, and Genetic Diversity

Where there are more species, but the total number of individuals is fixed, there are necessarily fewer individuals per species. Thus tree species of tropical forest are rarer than those of less diverse temperate-zone forests. Do tropical tree species maintain levels of genetic diversity as high as those of their temperate-zone counterparts? If so, how is this accomplished?

The 136 nontropical species of trees and shrubs reviewed by Hamrick, Godt, and Sherman-Broyles (1992) were polymorphic at an average of 53.4% of the loci studied. Individual plants of these species were heterozygous at an average of 15.8% of their loci, while the average invertebrate was heterozygous at 10% of its loci, and the average vertebrate at 5.4% (Hamrick et al., 1992). Gymnosperms tend to be common where found (Regal, 1977), which permits their wind-carried pollen to achieve extensive outcrossing. Twenty species of coniferous tree were polymorphic at an average of 67.7% of the loci studied; individual trees of these species were heterozygous at an average of 20.7% of their loci (Hamrick and Loveless, 1989). The 102 species of gymnosperms reviewed by Hamrick et al. (1992) were polymorphic at 53.4% of their loci (the same figure as for their nontropical trees), and individual gymnospermous trees were heterozygous at 15.1% of their loci.

Hamrick and Loveless (1989) assessed genetic diversity among 16 species of tropical trees and shrubs common on Barro Colorado's 50-hectare Forest Dynamics Plot. In 1982 densities of adults of reproductive size ranged from 0.3 per hectare to 1200 per hectare, with a median of 8 adults per hectare. The three commonest species were the shrubs *Hybanthus prunifolius*, with 1200 adults per hectare; *Psychotria horizontalis*, with 129 adults per hectare; and *Sorocea affinis*, with 30 adults per hectare (S. P. Hubbell and R. B. Foster, unpublished data). These 16 species were polymorphic at an average of 60.9% of the loci studied; individual plants were heterozygous at 21.1% of their loci (Hamrick and Loveless, 1989). Nine of these sixteen species were trees that attained reproductive maturity at a stem diameter of 10 cm or more. On the 50-hectare plot, these trees were represented in 1982 by 0.3–12.7 adults per hectare, the median density being two adults of reproductive size per hectare (S. P. Hubbell and R. B. Foster, unpublished data). These nine tree species were polymorphic at an average of 60.1% of the loci studied; individual trees of these species were polymorphic at an average of 21.4% of the loci studied (Hamrick and Loveless, 1989). There was relatively little genetic variation among populations a few kilometers apart of these 16 species, as if long-distance pollen transfer or seed dispersal occurred frequently in these species (Hamrick and Loveless, 1989).

On Barro Colorado rarer species of trees and shrubs maintain lower levels of genetic diversity. Hamrick and Murawski (1991) assessed genetic diversity among 16 rare species of trees and shrubs, represented on Barro Colorado's 50-hectare plot in 1982 by between 0 and 0.3 stems of reproductive size per hectare (S. P. Hubbell and R. B. Foster, unpublished data), the median abundance being 0.07 adults per hectare. These species were polymorphic at an average of 41.8% of the loci studied, and individuals of these species were heterozygous at an average of 14.2% of their loci. Thirteen of these sixteen species were trees that attain reproductive maturity at a diameter of 10 cm or more. These tree species were polymorphic at an average of 46.3% of the loci studied, and individual trees of these species were heterozygous at an average of 15.8% of their loci. Genetic diversity is lower among these 16 rare species than among their 16 commoner counterparts. Nonetheless, these sparse tropical populations maintained levels of diversity comparable to those of woody perennials of the temperate zone; the average population of those woody perennials reviewed by Hamrick, Godt, and Sherman-Broyles (1992) is polymorphic at 49.3% of its loci, and the average individual within these populations is heterozygous at 14.8% of its loci (Hamrick et al., 1992).

How do populations of such rare plants maintain such high levels of polymorphism and heterozygosity? Hamrick and Loveless (1986) found no correlation among the nine tropical woody species they studied between the percentage of heterozygous loci among the individuals of a species and the (presumed) effectiveness of that species's seed dispersers, as measured by the distance its seeds are carried. Their failure to find a correlation may reflect limited sample size and/or failure to take into account the possibility that rarer species compensate for their rarity by attracting pollinators and dispersers that travel farther. In Hamrick, Godt, and Sherman-Broyles's (1992) analysis of 199 woody species, those whose seeds were dispersed in the guts of animals maintained the highest levels of polymorphism and diversity of any of their dispersal categories.

In the tropics the ratio of genetic variance among different populations of a plant species to genetic vari-ance within these populations is far lower for species with animal-dispersed seeds than for species whose seeds are dispersed by gravity or wind (Loveless, 1992, pp. 79–80). Moreover, the ratio of genetic variance among different populations on Barro Colorado to variance within populations appears lowest for those species with strong-flying pollinators and mobile seed dispersers. Hamrick and Loveless (1989) ranked 14 species in order of their presumed likelihood of having their genes carried far by pollinators or seed dispersers. Species to which they assigned higher prospects of long-distance gene flow had significantly lower ratios of among- to within-population variance. Hamrick and Loveless (1986) found no correlation between the ratio of among- to within-population genetic variance and the presumed effectiveness of seed dispersal among the nine tropical species they considered. This was because they assumed that the manakins and other understory birds that eat the fruits of the shrubs *Psychotria horizontalis, Sorocea affinis,* and *Swartzia simplex* carry seeds farther than the bats that disperse the fruits of the canopy trees *Quararibea asterolepis* and *Poulsenia armata.* The reverse is almost certainly true. Correcting their rankings of effectiveness of seed dispersal yields a significant correlation among those nine species between effectiveness of seed dispersal and homogeneity of the genetic composition of the species.

On Barro Colorado most plant species seem to have efficient pollinators, capable of carrying pollen to conspecifics some distance away. Seven of the nine species studied by Murawski and Hamrick (1991) are almost entirely outcrossed. In the tree species *Tachigali versicolor* and *Platypodium elegans,* a substantial proportion of seeds have pollen parents more than 500 m away.

The strangler fig *Ficus obtusifolia* (Nason et al., 1995) and its congeners have brought the effectiveness of pollination to new heights. Like every other fig species (Corner, 1940), *Ficus obtusifolia* has its own species of pollinating wasp. When a fig fruit ripens to the stage where it is essentially a hollow sphere lined on the inside by hundreds of flowers, one or more pollen-bearing female wasps enters the fruit and pollinates its female flowers: each pollinating wasp carries pollen from a single parent tree (indeed, a single parent fruit). By germinating the seeds from a fruit pollinated by a single wasp and subjecting the leaves of these seedlings to starch gel electrophoresis, the genotypes of both seed and pollen parent can be determined for this fruit's seeds. Twenty-eight figs, each pollinated by a single wasp, collected simultaneously from a single *Ficus obtusifolia,* were examined: these 28 wasps came from 22 different pollen-parent trees. The wasps pollinating 24 single-pollinator figs collected from the fruit crop of another *Ficus obtusifolia* were judged to have come from 13 different paternal trees. Mature forest on Barro Colorado has roughly one *Ficus obtusifolia* of fruit-bearing size per 7 hectares. A fig tree of this species releases wasps during not more than two five-day periods per year (Windsor, Morrison, et al., 1989). These wasps apparently do not eat after leaving their natal fig and die after about three days. Thus wasps are available from a given fig for not more than 16 days per year. If wasp release is equally likely at any time of year, which is not far from the truth (Windsor et al., 1989), wasps should be available, on average, from one tree per 160 hectares. If so, a *Ficus obtusifolia* ready for pollination is receiving wasps from thousands of hectares of forest. Barro Colorado appears to be too small to have supplied all, or even most, of the pollen parents for Nason, Herre, and Hamrick's two *Ficus obtusifolia* fig crops. Despite the rarity of *Ficus obtusifolia*, this species is polymorphic at 84.2% of its loci so far assessed (Hamrick and Murawski, 1991). This proportion is exceeded by only one of the thirty-three species on Barro Colorado so far assessed for genetic variation: *Alseis blackiana*, with nine reproductively mature adults per hectare, 89.3% of whose loci are polymorphic (Hamrick and Loveless, 1989).

The evolution of "directed pollination," by which plants induce animals to carry pollen from one conspecific to another, appears to be an event that was crucial to the diversification of angiosperms (Crepet, 1984). Figs seem to have developed the art of pollination to an unheard-of degree of refinement.

The Cost of Pollinators

How much does the Barro Colorado forest, taken as a whole, pay for its pollinators? Roubik (1993) estimated the energetic intake of bees in lowland forest in Panama; bees are this forest's principal pollinators, but there are many others, such as bats, hummingbirds, flies, and beetles.

Direct counts in nearby Barro Colorado and in nearby mainland forests (Roubik, 1993) suggest that lowland forest in Panama has six colonies of stingless bees per hectare, averaging 2000 foragers and 4000 other adults apiece; the average weight of these bees is 16 mg. Judging by the ratio of colony foragers to other bees seen flying about the forest, Roubik inferred that there were 8300 solitary bees per hectare, weighing an average of 32 mg apiece. Thus the forest supports 860 g wet weight (530 g dry weight) of bees per hectare.

These bees are supposed to eat their fresh weight in nectar each day—314 kg nectar per hectare per year. Roubik assumes that this nectar is 40% sucrose.

As the energy content of 1 g of sucrose is roughly that of 1 g of dried vegetable matter (Roubik, 1993), these bees eat 126 kg sucrose per hectare per year, the equivalent of 126 kg dry weight of vegetable matter. Stingless bee foragers also collect twice their weight in resin each day. Twelve thousand 16-mg foragers, collecting twice their weight in resin, collect 140 kg resin per hectare per year (Roubik, 1993). One gram of resin is said to have twice the energy content of 1 g sugar (or dry vegetable matter). Thus, if Roubik's assumptions about feeding rate and resin collection are correct, Barro Colorado's bees use the energetic equivalent of 400 kg vegetable dry matter per hectare per year (nearly half the forest fruit production; Leigh and Windsor, this volume). Curiously, only one-third of the cost of supporting these bees is paid by the forest's flowers. This work needs to be checked, followed up, and extended.

Figs and Fig Wasps

The Mutualism and Its Impact on the Forest As we have mentioned, each species of fig has its own species of pollinating wasp. A fig fruit, or syconium, is essentially a head of flowers turned outside in to form a bag or hollow sphere lined on the inside with flowers, which has a small hole at the top (Corner, 1940). As the fruit develops, one or more fertilized female pollinating wasps enter it, fertilizing the flowers and laying eggs on some of them (Corner, 1940; Herre, 1989). In most species, the figs in an individual tree's fruit crop become ready for pollination all at once (Janzen, 1979), and wasps flock to the tree from many miles around (Nason et al., 1995). Each wasp larva develops within a single seed (Herre, 1989). Some four to six weeks after the eggs are laid (Janzen, 1979; Herre, 1993), male adults eclose and mate, apparently at random, with the females in their own fruit. The fertilized females leave in search of other fruits to pollinate, whereupon their natal figs ripen, attracting a host of animals to eat them and disperse their seeds (Terborgh, 1986b; Herre, 1989).

Fig wasps are short-lived, and need to find fig fruits in want of pollinators fairly soon after they emerge (Janzen, 1979). To maintain their pollinators, at any time of year each of Barro Colorado's fig species has some trees with fruit ready for pollination, either on that island or nearby (Milton, Windsor, et al., 1982; Windsor, Morrison, et al., 1989; Milton, 1991). As a result, ripe fig fruit is also available on Barro Colorado throughout the year. This reliable source of food has attracted a guild of seven species of fruit-eating bats, mentioned above, that feed mostly on figs (Bonaccorso, 1979). This guild of fig-eating bats appears to provide a good example of niche differentiation along a single resource axis—in this case, fruit size. As predicted by May and MacArthur (1972) and May (1974), it appears that the average of the logarithms of fruit weights eaten by each bat species differs from that of its next smaller competitor by the standard deviation in the logarithms of weights of fruits eaten by a single species (Handley and Leigh, 1991).

On Barro Colorado mammals other than bats and howler monkeys prefer other fruits to figs, so fig trees that fruit when most other species of canopy tree do not should attract more dispersers (Milton, Windsor, et al., 1982). Fig fruiting there does seem to peak when other kinds of fruit are in short supply (Milton et al., 1982; Windsor, Morrison, et al., 1989). The size of this peak is presumably limited by competition for pollinating wasps released by trees fruiting before the peak. Thus, on Barro Colorado, as in the Parque Manú of Amazonian Peru (Terborgh, 1986a) and in the dipterocarp forest of Borneo (Leighton and Leighton, 1983), figs are a keystone resource in times of fruit shortage for vertebrate frugivores. Thus the mutualism between figs and their pollinating wasps has conferred an ecological importance on fig trees out of proportion to their abundance.

Lessons for Ecologists and Evolutionary Theorists

1. *Fig Wasps and Trait-group Selection.* Depending on the fig species, from one to six "foundress" wasps pollinate a fig fruit. These foundresses form a "trait-group" (D. S. Wilson, 1975) whose offspring mate among themselves. The females thus fertilized can be viewed as joining a common pool from which the next generation's trait-groups are drawn at random; each such group includes the pollinators of one fig fruit. What are the implications of the circumstance that the progeny of a single trait-group of fertilized wasps compete among themselves for mates, while the female wasps fertilized in this competition disperse far off, each to a different, new trait-group? To find out, let us consider a fig fruit as a retort in which entering mated females elaborate a new generation of mated females. Here, two levels of selection affect the sex ratio (ratio of males to females) among the offspring of these foundresses (Colwell, 1981). Selection within the fruit to increase the proportion of one's own genes among those the newly fertilized females carry off favors producing as many male as female young, because a successful sperm contributes as much to the genetics of future generations as a successful egg (Fisher, 1930; Charnov, 1982). Selection among different fruits to increase the number of fertilized females each fruit contributes to the pool from which the next generation of trait-groups is formed favors producing as high a proportion of females as

possible and only enough males to fertilize these females. Selection on these wasps is a prototype of selection on any organism whose reproductive output, like a tree's, is governed by the outcome of competition with a few fixed neighbors, but whose young disperse far beyond their parents' competitive reach (D. S. Wilson, 1980; Leigh, 1991, 1994). Thus, we will consider selection on the sex ratio of these wasps in some detail.

In fig species with smaller foundress numbers— that is to say, with fewer pollinating wasps entering each fruit—a higher proportion of these foundresses' offspring is female (Herre, 1985; also see Hamilton, 1967). A brief explanation for this runs as follows. In any species of fig wasp, the sex ratio of the offspring reflects a balance between selection within fruits for a 50:50 sex ratio and selection among fruits to produce as many females as possible. Changing foundress number changes the effectiveness of selection within, relative to that among, mating trait-groups. This is because selection requires genetic variance in order to effect change (Fisher, 1930). In fig fruits with only one foundress, there is no among-foundress genetic variance, so selection within fruits cannot oppose the selection among fruits for a higher proportion of female offspring. In fig species with one foundress per fruit, selection favors devoting as much of the foundresses' reproductive effort as possible to producing female young: there should be only enough males to fertilize these females. In species with N foundresses per fruit, variance among foundresses within a fruit averages $(N-1)/N$ times that in the population as a whole, while genetic variance among the sets of fertilized females released by different fruits is the variance in means of samples of size N, or $1/N$ times that in the population as a whole. Here, selection within fruits is $N-1$ times as effective as an equally strong selection among fruits. The larger the foundress number, N, the more preponderant the effect of selection within fruits, and the more closely the ratio of male to female offspring approaches unity. The fulfillment of this prediction is evidence that, at least among fig wasps, two-tier "trait-group selection" is real and not merely a theoretical construct.

2. *The Advantage of Effective Seed Dispersal.* From the fig's point of view, male wasps beyond the minimum necessary to fertilize the females (or to cut an exit hole for them; it could be argued that the fig tree does not care whether the wasps it sends out are fertilized or not, so long as they carry pollen to suitable destinations) is a waste of effort that could have been spent producing either more seeds or more pollen-carrying females. The decisive factor in wasp sex ratio, however, is foundress number. Thus, figs can influence wasp sex ratio only through the influence

they have on foundress number. Limiting foundress number might, however, limit the size of fig fruits, for fig species with larger fruits tend to have higher foundress numbers and, indeed, to need more foundresses to pollinate their flowers (Herre, 1989).

Large-fruited fig species have another disadvantage. It would take only a few degrees' increase in the midday air temperature to kill a fig fruit's wasps. Small figs—say, those 1 cm in diameter—are cooled sufficiently by the surrounding air to keep their wasps from overheating. Large figs must transpire water to keep their wasps from overheating (just as the transpiration of a whole rainforest keeps the forest from overheating). In bright sunlight, a fig 2.3 cm in diameter dissipates half its heat load by evaporative cooling. If large figs are painted with grease to prevent transpiration, they overheat and their wasps die, while painting small figs with grease has no such ill effect (Patiño, Herre, and Tyree, 1994). Thus, large-fruited fig trees must expend water to keep their fruits cool, as well as waste more energy on the production of male wasps.

Yet some fig species do have large fruits. Why? Large fig fruits attract bigger bats, which fly farther. It would appear that the advantage of more effective seed dispersal more than compensates for the disadvantages of making larger fruits. Closer study of this system may allow us to assess more accurately the importance of effective seed dispersal.

3. *Fig Wasps and the Evolution of Virulence in Parasites.* Furthermore, a fig fruit contains a rather complex community of interacting organisms, some of which have lessons for the evolutionary theorist (Herre, 1989, 1993). For example, each species of pollinating wasp appears to be parasitized by its own species of nematode, *Parasitodiplogaster* sp. Nematodes enter a female wasp when it is ready to leave its natal fig seed. The parasitized wasp carries its nematodes into the fig fruit it pollinates. The nematodes leave their wasps after feeding on their innards, mate with the other nematodes within their fruit, and lay eggs. The resulting young enter the next generation of female wasps when the latter are ready to leave their seeds (Poinar and Herre, 1991). Such nematodes apparently began parasitizing fig wasps before Africa separated from South America (Poinar and Herre, 1991). Since that time, they appear to have radiated in parallel with their host wasps.

Symbionts and mutualists as different as mitochondria (Margulis, 1981) and fig wasps (Wiebes, 1979) appear to have evolved from parasitic ancestors. Do hosts necessarily "tame" their parasites? Do parasites necessarily evolve to become more benign? The nematodes parasitic upon fig wasps provide a good opportunity to test this proposition (Herre, 1993). For each of 11 species of fig, Herre (1993) measured the effect of nematodes on their hosts by the ratio of the number of wasps hatching from a single-foundress fig fruit with nematodes to the number hatching from a nematode-free single-foundress fruit: the lower this ratio, the more virulent the relevant species of parasitic nematode.

Fig species most of whose fruits are pollinated by more than one wasp have pollinating wasps that are parasitized by more virulent nematodes. In a species where all fruits are single-foundress, the reproduction of the nematodes is utterly dependent upon the reproduction of the wasps that carry them. If their host's progeny do not reach other fig fruits to pollinate, the nematodes die too. On the other hand, the larger the number of foundress wasps per fig fruit, the more opportunity for nematodes to switch to a different wasp's progeny, and thus the less danger accrues from ruining their current host. Indeed, in fruits pollinated by more foundresses, a nematode derives relatively more advantage from increasing the proportion of its offspring among the nematodes carried from its fruit than from increasing the number or health of the wasps leaving its fruit. A three-tier (nematodes within a wasp, nematodes of all the wasps within a fruit, and nematodes in different fruits) analogue to the two-tier selection that governs the wasps' sex ratio (Herre et al., 1987, pp. 235–236) appears to govern the virulence of their parasitic nematodes. The average foundress number for a fig species thus governs the virulence of its wasps' nematodes (Herre, 1993). Since, as we have seen, there is no reason to believe that foundress number decreases over evolutionary time, there is no reason to believe that nematode virulence does either.

4. *Adaptation to Frequent and Infrequent Events.* Herre's study of sex ratios in fig wasps has yet another implication. Herre (1985) deduced a numerical prediction of a fig wasp's sex ratio as a function both of the average foundress number in its species and the foundress number in the particular fruit it enters. He correctly predicted the increase in proportion of males with increased actual foundress number. Comparing fruits with the same actual foundress number across different species, his qualitative prediction that those species with higher *average* foundress number would have a higher proportion of male offspring was correct. Nevertheless, Herre's quantitative predictions were often far off the mark. Wasps produced young in the most nearly correct sex ratio in those fruits whose foundress numbers were closest to the average for their species, and the wasp species with the most adjustable sex ratios were those that experienced the most variable foundress numbers (Herre, 1987). Wasps were most likely to produce young in in-

appropriate sex ratios when in fruits with a foundress number unusual for their species.

Herre's (1987) discovery is an aspect of a truth whose implications are too seldom considered. Organisms behave most adaptively under the conditions they experience most often. Does this observation have ecological correlates? For example, is there something special about an "intermediate" level of disturbance that allows the most species to coexist (cf. Connell, 1978)? Or is diversity highest under the most usual, the most prevalent, conditions (cf. Terborgh, 1973), where mutual adjustments between different species are most precise? Considering what circumstances allow the most species to be packed into a community raises another issue: do the factors that allow species to coexist reflect the most dominant problems in their members' lives? Ashton (1988, 1989) argued, with some reason (Appanah and Weinland, 1993), that dipterocarps coexist by virtue of different habitat preferences. In the Neotropics, however, specialist herbivores appear to be the primary factor allowing different species of tree to coexist (Janzen, 1970). Could this mean that, for some reason, Neotropical trees are more edible, so that herbivores play a larger role in their dynamics than in the dynamics of dipterocarps?

Mutualism and the Preservation of Tree Diversity

Animals do many things that help plant populations to persist. The survival or reproduction of some plants depends on certain animal activities. Fig trees cannot reproduce without the help of their pollinator wasps (Corner, 1940). It is hard to imagine how *Virola surinamensis* could persist on Barro Colorado without toucans to disperse its seeds away from their parents (Howe et al., 1985). Indeed, Emmons (1989) warned that a rainforest's diversity could be lost without cutting a single tree, if its larger mammals and birds were hunted to extinction. The disappearance of these animals would deprive many tree species of the pollinators and dispersers they need to reproduce.

Other animals help keep some relationships mutualistic. For example, fruiting trees attract predators (Handley and Morrison, 1991, p. 137), so frugivores take their fruit away to other, presumably safer, sites before eating it and dropping its seeds (Howe, 1979). If predators are hunted out, and if frugivores consequently lose their instinct to remove fruit elsewhere before eating it, *Virola surinamensis*, several species of fig, and other tree species that depend on fearful frugivores to disperse their seeds may die out as a result.

Vertebrates perform yet other services essential for the persistence of some species of plants. In central Panama the spiny palm *Astrocaryum standleyanum* can reproduce only if agoutis bury its seeds (Smythe, 1989), because bruchid beetles destroy unburied seeds. At first this discovery seemed to be a curious bit of natural history. Then Forget and Milleron (1991) discovered that, at least in one year, weevils destroyed seeds of *Virola surinamensis* left unburied by agoutis. Indeed, agoutis may turn out to be keystone animals for the preservation of tree diversity. On islets <1 hectare in area near Barro Colorado in Gatun Lake, tree diversity is far lower than on nearby mainland sites. These islets lack resident mammals (Adler and Seamon, 1991). A small group of tree species is spreading over these islands, of which the most conspicuously abundant are *Protium panamense* (Burseraceae), *Swartzia simplex* (Leguminosae), and the two palms *Scheelea zonensis* and *Oenocarpus mapora* (Leigh, Wright, et al., 1993). All four of these species have relatively large seeds; insects attack only those of *Scheelea*. If the bruchids that attack *Scheelea* seed behave the same way on these islets as on Barro Colorado, they do not infest seeds falling late in *Scheelea* fruiting season (Forget, Munoz, and Leigh, 1994). Thus, all these species drop some seeds that are safe from insect attack, and they can accordingly reproduce without agoutis to bury their seeds. Are these species replacing others that need agoutis to bury their seeds? If so, agoutis would appear to be key animals for preserving tree diversity.

Intelligent planning for conservation presupposes an understanding of the many ways in which populations of different plants depend on animals. We must also learn the other needs of these necessary animals. For example, the 70-g bat *Artibeus lituratus* is the principal disperser of the seeds of the canopy tree *Dipteryx panamensis* (Bonaccorso et al., 1980; Forget, 1993). Most *Artibeus lituratus* appear to leave Barro Colorado for more than half the year (Bonaccorso, 1979). Presumably, like many of the fruit-eating birds at La Selva (Loiselle and Blake, 1991), these bats migrate to other habitats, which must be preserved if the bats are to continue dispersing the seeds of Barro Colorado's *Dipteryx*. The plants and animals of tropical forest are linked by a multitude of interrelationships, many of which are among the most remarkable of natural history. If we are to preserve tropical diversity, we must learn enough about these interrelationships to avoid disrupting them.

LITERATURE CITED

Adler, G. H.
1994.   Tropical Forest Fragmentation and Isolation Promote Asynchrony among Populations of a Frugivorous Rodent. *Journal of Animal Ecology,* 63:903–911.

Adler, G. H., and J. O. Seamon
1991. Distribution and Abundance of a Tropical Rodent, the Spiny Rat, on Islands in Panama. *Journal of Tropical Ecology*, 7:349–360.

Aide, T. M.
1988. Herbivory as a Selective Agent on the Timing of Leaf Production in a Tropical Understory Community. *Nature*, 336:574–575.
1991. Synchronous Leaf Production and Herbivory in Juveniles of *Gustavia superba*. *Oecologia*, 88:511–514.
1992. Dry Season Leaf Production: An Escape from Herbivory. *Biotropica*, 24:532–537.
1993. Patterns of Leaf Development and Herbivory in a Tropical Understory Community. *Ecology*, 74:455–466.

Aide, T. M., and E. C. Londoño
1989. The Effects of Rapid Leaf Expansion on the Growth and Survivorship of a Lepidopteran Herbivore. *Oikos*, 55:66–70.

Alexander, I.
1989. Mycorrhizas in Tropical Forests. Pages 169–188 in *Mineral Nutrition in Tropical Forest and Savanna Ecosystems*, edited by J. Proctor. Oxford, U.K.: Blackwell Scientific Publications.

Andrews, R. M.
1988. Demographic Correlates of Variable Egg Survival for a Tropical Lizard. *Oecologia*, 76:376–382.
1991. Population Stability of a Tropical Lizard. *Ecology*, 72:1204–1217.

Andrews, R. M., and A. S. Rand
[1982] Seasonal Breeding and Long-term Population Fluctu-
1995. ations in the Lizard *Anolis limifrons*. Pages 405–412 in *The Ecology of a Tropical Forest*, edited by E. G. Leigh, Jr., et al. Washington, D.C.: Smithsonian Institution Press.
1990. Adición: Nuevas percepciones derivadas de la continuación de un estudio a largo plazo de la lagartija *Anolis limifrons*. Pages 477–479 in *Ecología de un bosque tropical: Ciclos estacionales y cambios de largo plazo*, edited by E. G. Leigh, Jr., A. S. Rand, and D. M. Windsor. Balboa, Panama: Smithsonian Tropical Research Institute.

Andrews, R. M., A. S. Rand, and S. Guerrero
1983. Seasonal and Spatial Variation in the Annual Cycle of a Tropical Lizard. Pages 441–454 in *Advances in Herpetology and Evolutionary Biology: Essays in Honor of Ernest E. Williams*, edited by A. G. J. Rhodin and K. Miyata. Cambridge: Harvard University Museum of Comparative Zoology.

Andrews, R. M., and S. J. Wright
1994. Long-term Population Fluctuations of a Tropical Lizard: A Test of Causality. Pages 267–285 in *Lizard Ecology: Historical and Experimental Perspectives*, edited by L. J. Vitt and E. R. Pianka. Princeton: Princeton University Press.

Appanah, S., and G. Weinland
1993. A Preliminary Analysis of the 50-hectare Pasoh Demography Plot: I. Dipterocarpaceae. *Forest Research Institute Malaysia Research Pamphlet*, 112:1–183.

Ashton, P. S.
1988. Dipterocarp Biology as a Window to the Understanding of Tropical Forest Structure. *Annual Review of Ecology and Systematics*, 19:347–370.

1989. Dipterocarp Reproductive Biology. Pages 219–240 in *Tropical Rain Forest Ecosystems: Biogeographical and Ecological Studies*, edited by H. Leith and M. J. A. Werger. Amsterdam: Elsevier.

Augspurger, C. K.
[1982] A Cue for Synchronous Flowering. Pages 133–150 in
1995. *The Ecology of a Tropical Forest*, edited by E. G. Leigh, Jr., et al. Washington, D.C.: Smithsonian Institution Press.
1983. Seed Dispersal of the Tropical Tree, *Platypodium elegans*, and the Escape of Its Seedlings from Fungal Pathogens. *Journal of Ecology*, 71:759–771.
1984. Seedling Survival of Tropical Tree Species: Interactions of Dispersal Distance, Light Gaps and Pathogens. *Ecology*, 65:1705–1712.

Augspurger, C. K., and C. K. Kelly
1984. Pathogen Mortality of Tropical Tree Seedlings: Experimental Studies of the Effects of Dispersal Distance, Seedling Density and Light Conditions. *Oecologia*, 61:211–217.

Basset, Y.
1992. Host Specificity of Arboreal and Free-living Insect Herbivores in Rain Forests. *Biological Journal of the Linnean Society*, 47:115–133.

Becker, P., L. W. Lee, E. D. Rothman, and W. D. Hamilton
1985. Seed Predation and the Coexistence of Tree Species: Hubbell's Model Revisited. *Oikos*, 44:382–390.

Becker, P., P. E. Rabenold, J. R. Idol, and A. P. Smith
1988. Water Potential Gradients for Gaps and Slopes in a Panamanian Tropical Moist Forest's Dry Season. *Journal of Tropical Ecology*, 4:173–184.

Bonaccorso, F. J.
1979. Foraging and Reproductive Ecology in a Panamanian Bat Community. *Bulletin of the Florida State Museum, Biological Sciences*, 24:359–408.

Bonaccorso, F. J., W. E. Glanz, and C. M. Sandford
1980. Feeding Assemblages of Mammals at Fruiting *Dipteryx panamensis* (Papilionaceae) Trees in Panama: Seed Predation, Dispersal and Parasitism. *Revista de biología tropical*, 28:61–72.

Brokaw, N. V. L.
[1982] Treefalls: Frequency, Timing, and Consequences.
1995. Pages 101–108 in *The Ecology of a Tropical Forest*, edited by E. G. Leigh, Jr., et al. Washington, D.C.: Smithsonian Institution Press.
1987. Gap-phase Regeneration of Three Pioneer Tree Species in a Tropical Forest. *Journal of Animal Ecology*, 75:9–19.

Brown, E. T., R. F. Stallard, M. C. Larsen, G. M. Raisbeck, and F. Yiou
1995. Denudation Rates Determined from the Accumulation of in situ–produced ^{10}Be in the Luquillo Experimental Forest, Puerto Rico. *Earth and Planetary Science Letters*, 129:193–202.

Burnham, R. J., S. L. Wing, and G. G. Parker
1992. The Reflection of Deciduous Forest Communities in Leaf Litter: Implications for Autochthonous Litter Assemblages from the Fossil Record. *Paleobiology*, 18:30–49.

Canny, M. J.
1995. A New Theory for the Ascent of Sap—Cohesion Supported by Tissue Pressure. *Annals of Botany,* 75:343–357.

Cavelier, J.
1989. Root Biomass Production and the Effect of Fertilization in Two Tropical Rain Forests. Ph.D. dissertation, Botany School, Cambridge University, Cambridge.

Charnov, E. L.
1982. *The Theory of Sex Allocation.* Princeton: Princeton University Press.

Cochard, H., F. W. Ewers, and M. T. Tyree
1994. Water Relations of a Tropical Vine-like Bamboo (*Rhipidocladum racemiflorum*): Root Pressures, Vulnerability to Cavitation and Seasonal Changes in Embolism. *Journal of Experimental Botany,* 45:1085–1089.

Cody, M. L.
1966. A General Theory of Clutch Size. *Evolution,* 20:174–184.

Coley, P. D.
[1982] Rates of Herbivory on Different Tropical Trees. Pages
1995. 123–132 in *The Ecology of a Tropical Forest,* edited by E. G. Leigh, Jr., et al. Washington, D.C.: Smithsonian Institution Press.
1987. Interspecific Variation in Plant Anti-herbivore Properties: The Role of Habitat Quality and Rate of Disturbance. *New Phytologist,* 106 (Supplement): 251–263.
1988. Effects of Plant Growth Rate and Leaf Lifetime on the Amount and Type of Anti-herbivore Defense. *Oecologia,* 74:531–536.

Coley, P. D., J. P. Bryant, and F. S. Chapin III
1985. Resource Availability and Plant Anti-herbivore Defense. *Science,* 230:895–899.

Colwell, R. K.
1981. Group Selection Is Implicated in the Evolution of Female-biassed Sex Ratios. *Nature,* 290:401–404.

Condit, R.
1995. Research in Large, Long-term Tropical Forest Plots. *Trends in Ecology and Evolution,* 10:18–22.

Condit, R., R. B. Foster, S. P. Hubbell, R. Sukumar, E. G. Leigh, Jr., N. Manokaran, and S. Loo de Lao
1996. Assessing Forest Diversity from Small Plots: Calibration Using Species–Individual Curves from 50 Ha Plots. In *Measuring and Monitoring Forest Biodiversity: The International Network of Biodiversity Plots,* edited by F. Dallmeier, in press. Washington, D.C.: Smithsonian Institution, Man and the Biosphere Program.

Condit, R., S. P. Hubbell, and R. B. Foster
1992a. Short-term Dynamics of a Neotropical Forest. *BioScience,* 42:822–828.
1992b. Recruitment near Conspecific Adults and the Maintenance of Tree and Shrub Diversity in a Neotropical Forest. *American Naturalist,* 140:261–286.
1994. Density Dependence in Two Understory Tree Species in a Neotropical Forest. *Ecology,* 75:671–680.
1995. Mortality Rates of 205 Neotropical Tree and Shrub Species and Their Responses to a Severe Drought. *Ecological Monographs,* 65:419–439.
1996. Changes in Tree Species Abundance in a Neotropical

Forest over Eight Years: Impact of Climate Change. *Journal of Tropical Ecology,* 12:231–256.

Connell, J. H.
1971. On the Role of Natural Enemies in Preventing Competitive Exclusion in Some Marine Animals and in Rain Forest Trees. Pages 298–312 in *Dynamics of Numbers in Populations,* edited by P. J. den Boer and G. R. Gradwell. Wageningen, Netherlands: Center for Agricultural Publishing and Documentation.
1978. Diversity in Tropical Rain Forests and Coral Reefs. *Science,* 199:1302–1310.

Cornejo, F. H., A. Varela, and S. J. Wright
1994. Tropical Forest Litter Decomposition under Seasonal Drought: Nutrient Release, Fungi and Bacteria. *Oikos,* 70:183–190.

Corner, E. J. H.
1940. *Wayside Trees of Malaya.* Singapore: Government Printer.

Crepet, W. L.
1984. Advanced (Constant) Insect Pollination Mechanisms: Pattern of Evolution and Implications vis-à-vis Angiosperm Diversity. *Annals of the Missouri Botanical Garden,* 71:607–630.

De Vries, P. J.
1990. Enhancement of Symbioses between Butterfly Caterpillars and Ants by Vibrational Communication. *Science,* 248:1104–1106.
1991a. Evolutionary and Ecological Patterns in Myrmecophilous Riodinid Butterflies. Pages 143–156 in *Ant–Plant Interactions,* edited by C. R. Huxley and D. F. Cutler. Oxford: Oxford University Press.
1991b. Mutualism between *Thisbe irenea* Butterflies and Ants, and the Role of Ant Ecology in the Evolution of Larval–Ant Associations. *Biological Journal of the Linnean Society,* 43:179–195.
1991c. Call Production by Myrmecophilous Riodinid and Lycaenid Butterfly Caterpillars (Lepidoptera): Morphological, Acoustical, Functional and Evolutionary Patterns. *American Museum Novitates,* 3025:1–23.
1992. Singing Caterpillars, Ants and Symbiosis. *Scientific American,* 267 (4): 76–82.

De Vries, P. J., and I. Baker
1989. Butterfly Exploitation of an Ant–Plant Mutualism: Adding Insult to Herbivory. *Journal of the New York Entomological Society,* 97:332–340.

De Vries, P. J., and R. Dudley
1990. Morphometrics, Airspeed, Thermoregulation, and Lipid Reserves of Migrating *Urania fulgens* (Uraniidae) Moths in Natural Free Flight. *Physiological Zoology,* 63:235–251.

Diaz, H. F., and G. N. Kiladis
1992. Atmospheric Teleconnections Associated with the Extreme Phase of the Southern Oscillation. Pages 7–28 in *El Niño: Historical and Paleoclimatic Aspects of the Southern Oscillation,* edited by H. F. Diaz and V. Markgraf. Cambridge: Cambridge University Press.

Dietrich, W. E., D. M. Windsor, and T. Dunne
[1982] Geology, Climate, and Hydrology of Barro Colorado
1995. Island. Pages 21–46 in *The Ecology of a Tropical Forest,* edited by E. G. Leigh, Jr., et al. Washington, D.C.: Smithsonian Institution Press.

Dobzhansky, T.
1950. Evolution in the Tropics. *American Scientist*, 38:209–221.

Dudley, R., and P. J. De Vries
1990. Flight Physiology of Migrating *Urania fulgens* (Uraniidae) Moths: Kinematics and Aerodynamics of Natural Free Flight. *Journal of Comparative Physiology*, Series A, 167:145–154.

Emmons, L. H.
1989. Tropical Rain Forests: Why They Have So Many Species and How We May Lose This Biodiversity without Cutting a Single Tree. *Orion Nature Quarterly*, 8 (3): 8–14.

Fisher, R. A.
1930. *The Genetical Theory of Natural Selection*. Oxford, U.K.: Clarendon Press.

Fisher, R. A., A. S. Corbet, and C. B. Williams
1943. The Relation between the Number of Species and the Number of Individuals in a Random Sample of an Animal Population. *Journal of Animal Ecology*, 12:42–58.

Forget, P.-M.
1993. Post-dispersal Predation and Scatterhoarding of *Dipteryx panamensis* (Papilionaceae) Seeds by Rodents in Panama. *Oecologia*, 94:255–261.

Forget, P.-M., and T. Milleron
1991. Evidence for Secondary Seed Dispersal by Rodents in Panama. *Oecologia*, 87:596–599.

Forget, P.-M., E. Munoz, and E. G. Leigh, Jr.
1994. Predation by Rodents and Bruchid Beetles on Seeds of *Scheelea* Palms on Barro Colorado Island, Panama. *Biotropica*, 26:420–426.

Foster, R. B.
[1982a] The Seasonal Rhythm of Fruitfall on Barro Colorado
1995. Island. Pages 151–172 in *The Ecology of a Tropical Forest*, edited by E. G. Leigh, Jr., et al. Washington, D.C.: Smithsonian Institution Press.
[1982b] Famine on Barro Colorado Island. Pages 201–212 in
1995. *The Ecology of a Tropical Forest*, edited by E. G. Leigh, Jr., et al. Washington, D.C.: Smithsonian Institution Press.

Foster, R. B., and N. V. L. Brokaw
[1982] Structure and History of the Vegetation of Barro Col-
1995. orado Island. Pages 67–81 in *The Ecology of a Tropical Forest*, edited by E. G. Leigh, Jr., et al. Washington, D.C.: Smithsonian Institution Press.

Foster, R. B., and S. P. Hubbell
1990. Estructura de la vegetación y composición de especies de un lote de cincuenta hectáreas en la Isla de Barro Colorado. Pages 141–151 in *Ecología de un bosque tropical: Ciclos estacionales y cambios de largo plazo*, edited by E. G. Leigh, Jr., A. S. Rand and D. M. Windsor. Balboa, Panama: Smithsonian Tropical Research Institute.

Gentry, A. H.
1988. Tree Species Richness of Upper Amazonian Forests. *Proceedings of the National Academy of Sciences, USA*, 85:156–159.

Gilbert, G. S., S. P. Hubbell, and R. B. Foster
1994. Density and Distance-to-Adult Effects of a Canker Disease in a Moist Tropical Forest. *Oecologia*, 98:100–108.

Glanz, W. E.
[1982] The Terrestrial Mammal Fauna of Barro Colorado
1995. Island: Censuses and Long-term Changes. Pages 455–468 in *The Ecology of a Tropical Forest*, edited by E. G. Leigh, Jr., et al. Washington, D.C.: Smithsonian Institution Press.
1990. Neotropical Mammal Densities: How Unusual Is the Community on Barro Colorado Island, Panama? Pages 287–313 in *Four Neotropical Rainforests*, edited by A. H. Gentry. New Haven: Yale University Press.

Glanz, W. E., R. W. Thorington, Jr., J. Giacalone-Madden, and L. R. Heaney
[1982] Seasonal Food Use and Demographic Trends in
1995. *Sciurus granatensis*. Pages 239–252 in *The Ecology of a Tropical Forest*, edited by E. G. Leigh, Jr., et al. Washington, D.C.: Smithsonian Institution Press.

Hamilton, W. D.
1967. Extraordinary Sex Ratios. *Science*, 156:477–487.

Hamrick, J. L, M. J. W. Godt, and S. L. Sherman-Broyles
1992. Factors Influencing Levels of Genetic Diversity in Woody Plant Species. *New Forests*, 6:95–124.

Hamrick, J. L., and M. D. Loveless
1986. The Influence of Seed Dispersal Mechanisms on the Genetic Structure of Plant Populations. Pages 211–223 in *Frugivores and Seed Dispersal*, edited by A. Estrada and T. H. Fleming. Dordrecht, Netherlands: W. Junk.
1989. The Genetical Structure of Tropical Tree Populations: Associations with Reproductive Biology. Pages 129–146 in *The Evolutionary Ecology of Plants*, edited by J. Bock and Y. B. Linhart. Boulder, Colo.: Westview Press.

Hamrick, J. L., and D. A. Murawski
1990. The Breeding Structure of Tropical Tree Populations. *Plant Species Biology*, 5:157–165.
1991. Levels of Allozyme Diversity in Populations of Uncommon Neotropical Tree Species. *Journal of Tropical Ecology*, 7:395–399.

Handley, C. O., Jr., A. L. Gardner, and D. E. Wilson
1991. Food Habits. Pages 141–146 in Demography and Natural History of the Common Fruit Bat, *Artibeus jamaicensis*, on Barro Colorado Island, Panamá, edited by C. O. Handley, Jr., D. E. Wilson, and A. L. Gardner. *Smithsonian Contributions to Zoology*, 511:1–173.

Handley, C. O., Jr., and E. G. Leigh, Jr.
1991. Diet and Food Supply. Pages 147–149 in Demography and Natural History of the Common Fruit Bat, *Artibeus jamaicensis*, on Barro Colorado Island, Panamá, edited by C. O. Handley, Jr., D. E. Wilson, and A. L. Gardner. *Smithsonian Contributions to Zoology*, 511:1–173.

Handley, C. O., Jr., and D. W. Morrison
1991. Foraging Behavior. Pages 137–140 in Demography and Natural History of the Common Fruit Bat, *Artibeus jamaicensis*, on Barro Colorado Island, Panamá, edited by C. O. Handley, Jr., D. E. Wilson, and A. L. Gardner. *Smithsonian Contributions to Zoology*, 511:1–173.

Handley, C. O., Jr., D. E. Wilson, and A. L. Gardner (eds.)
1991.   Demography and Natural History of the Common Fruit Bat, *Artibeus jamaicensis*, on Barro Colorado Island, Panamá. *Smithsonian Contributions to Zoology*, 511:1–173.

Hart, T. B, J. A. Hart, and P. G. Murphy
1989.   Monodominant and Species-rich Forests of the Humid Tropics: Causes for Their Co-occurrence. *American Naturalist*, 133:613–633.

Herre, E. A.
1985.   Sex Ratio Adjustment in Fig Wasps. *Science*, 228:896–898.
1987.   Optimality, Plasticity and Selective Regime in Fig Wasp Sex Ratios. *Nature*, 329:627–629.
1989.   Coevolution of Reproductive Characteristics in 12 Species of New World Figs and Their Pollinator Wasps. *Experientia*, 45:637–647.
1993.   Population Structure and the Evolution of Virulence in Nematode Parasites of Fig Wasps. *Science*, 259:1442–1445.

Herre, E. A., E. G. Leigh, Jr., and E. A. Fischer
1987.   Sex Allocation in Animals. Pages 219–244 in *The Evolution of Sex and Its Consequences*, edited by S. C. Stearns. Basel: Birkhäuser.

Hladik, A., and C. M. Hladik
1969.   Rapports trophiques entre végétation et primates dans la forêt de Barro Colorado (Panama). *La Terre et la vie*, 23:25–117.

Hobbie, S. E.
1992.   Effects of Plant Species on Nutrient Cycling. *Trends in Ecology and Evolution*, 10:336–339.

Horn, H. S.
1966.   Measurement of "Overlap" in Comparative Ecological Studies. *American Naturalist*, 100:419–424.

Howe, H. F.
1979.   Fear and Frugivory. *American Naturalist*, 114:925–931.
[1982]   Fruit Production and Animal Activity in Two Tropi-
1995.   cal Trees. Pages 189–199 in *The Ecology of a Tropical Forest*, edited by E. G. Leigh, Jr., et al. Washington, D.C.: Smithsonian Institution Press.
1989.   Scatter- and Clump-Dispersal and Seedling Demography: Hypothesis and Implications. *Oecologia*, 79:417–426.
1990.   Seed Dispersal by Birds and Mammals: Implications for Seedling Demography. Pages 191–218 in *Reproductive Ecology of Tropical Forest Plants*, edited by K. S. Bawa and M. Hadley. Park Ridge, N.J.: Parthenon Publishing.

Howe, H. F., E. W. Schupp, and L. C. Westley
1985.   Early Consequences of Seed Dispersal for a Neotropical Tree (*Virola surinamensis*). *Ecology*, 66:781–791.

Hubbell, S. P.
1979.   Tree Dispersion, Abundance, and Diversity in a Tropical Dry Forest. *Science*, 203:1299–1309.
1980.   Seed Predation and the Coexistence of Tree Species in Tropical Forests. *Oikos*, 35:214–229.

Hubbell, S. P., R. Condit, and R. B. Foster
1990.   Presence and Absence of Density Dependence in a Neotropical Tree Community. *Philosophical Transac-*
tions of the Royal Society of London, Series B, 330:269–281.

Hubbell, S. P., and R. B. Foster
1983.   Diversity of Canopy Trees in a Neotropical Forest and Implications for Conservation. Pages 25–41 in *Tropical Rain Forest: Ecology and Management*, edited by S. L. Sutton, T. C. Whitmore, and A. C. Chadwick. Oxford, U.K.: Blackwell Scientific Publications.
1986a.   Commonness and Rarity in a Neotropical Forest: Implications for Tropical Tree Conservation. Pages 205–231 in *Conservation Biology: The Science of Scarcity and Diversity*, edited by M. E. Soulé. Sunderland, Mass.: Sinauer Associates.
1986b.   Biology, Chance, and History and the Structure of Tropical Rain Forest Tree Communities. Pages 314–329 in *Community Ecology*, edited by J. Diamond and T. J. Case. New York: Harper and Row.
1986c.   Canopy Gaps and the Dynamics of a Neotropical Forest. Pages 77–96 in *Plant Ecology*, edited by M. J. Crawley. Oxford, U.K.: Blackwell Scientific Publications.
1987.   The Spatial Context of Regeneration in a Neotropical Forest. Pages 395–412 in *Colonization, Succession and Stability*, edited by A. J. Gray, M. J. Crawley, and P. J. Edwards. Oxford, U.K.: Blackwell Scientific Publications.
1990.   Structure, Dynamics, and Equilibrium Status of Old-growth Forest on Barro Colorado Island. Pages 522–541 in *Four Neotropical Rainforests*, edited by A. H. Gentry. New Haven: Yale University Press.

Janos, D. P.
1980.   Mycorrhizae Influence Tropical Succession. *Biotropica*, 12 (Supplement): 56–64.
1983.   Tropical Mycorrhizas, Nutrient Cycles and Plant Growth. Pages 327–345 in *Tropical Rain Forest: Ecology and Management*, edited by S. L. Sutton, T. C. Whitmore, and A. C. Chadwick. Oxford, U.K.: Blackwell Scientific Publications.

Janzen, D. H.
1970.   Herbivores and the Number of Tree Species in Tropical Forests. *American Naturalist*, 104:501–528.
1979.   How to Be a Fig. *Annual Review of Ecology and Systematics*, 10:13–51.

Johnsson, M. J., and R. F. Stallard
1989.   Physiographic Controls on the Composition of Sediments Derived from Volcanic and Sedimentary Terrains on Barro Colorado Island, Panama. *Journal of Sedimentary Petrology*, 59:768–781.

Keller, M., D. J. Jacob, S. C. Wofsy, and R. C. Harriss
1991.   Effects of Tropical Deforestation on Global and Regional Atmospheric Chemistry. *Climatic Change*, 19:139–158.

King, D. A.
1994.   Influence of Light Level on the Growth and Morphology of Saplings in a Panamanian Forest. *American Journal of Botany*, 81:948–957.

Kira, T.
1978.   Community Architecture and Organic Matter Dynamics in Tropical Lowland Rain Forest of Southeast Asia with Special Reference to Pasoh Forest, West Malaysia. Pages 561–590 in *Tropical Trees as Living Systems*,

edited by P. B. Tomlinson and M. H. Zimmermann. Cambridge: Cambridge University Press.

Kitajima, K.
1994.   Relative Importance of Photosynthetic Traits and Allocation Patterns as Correlates of Seedling Shade Tolerance of 13 Tropical Trees. *Oecologia*, 98:419–428.

Kursar, T. A.
1989.   Evaluation of Soil Respiration and Soil CO_2 Concentration in a Lowland Moist Forest in Panama. *Plant and Soil*, 113:21–29.

Kursar, T. A., and P. D. Coley
1991.   Nitrogen Content and Expansion Rate of Young Leaves of Rain Forest Species: Implications for Herbivory. *Biotropica*, 23:141–150.

1993.   Photosynthetic Induction Times in Shade-tolerant Species with Long- and Short-lived Leaves. *Oecologia*, 93:165–170.

Kursar, T. A., S. J. Wright, and R. Radulovich
1995.   The Effects of the Rainy Season and Irrigation on Soil Water and Oxygen in a Seasonal Forest in Panama. *Journal of Tropical Ecology*, 11:497–516.

Leigh, E. G., Jr.
[1982]
1995.   Introduction: Why Are There So Many Kinds of Tropical Trees? Pages 63–66 in *The Ecology of a Tropical Forest*, edited by E. G. Leigh, Jr., et al. Washington, D.C.: Smithsonian Institution Press.

1990.   Community Diversity and Environmental Stability: A Re-examination. *Trends in Ecology and Evolution*, 5:340–344.

1991.   Genes, Bees and Ecosystems: The Evolution of a Common Interest among Individuals. *Trends in Ecology and Evolution*, 6:257–262.

1994.   Do Insect Pests Promote Mutualism among Tropical Trees? *Journal of Ecology*, 82:677–680.

Leigh, E. G., Jr., and G. de Alba
1992.   Barro Colorado Island, Panamá, Basic Research, and Conservation. *George Wright Forum*, 9:32–45.

Leigh, E. G., Jr., and C. O. Handley, Jr.
1991.   Population Estimates. Pages 77–87 in Demography and Natural History of the Common Fruit Bat, *Artibeus jamaicensis*, on Barro Colorado Island, Panamá, edited by C. O. Handley, Jr., D. E. Wilson, and A. L. Gardner. *Smithsonian Contributions to Zoology*, 511:1–173.

Leigh, E. G., Jr., and N. Smythe
1978.   Leaf Production, Leaf Consumption, and the Regulation of Folivory on Barro Colorado Island. Pages 33–50 in *The Ecology of Arboreal Folivores*, edited by G. G. Montgomery. Washington, D.C.: Smithsonian Institution Press.

Leigh, E. G., Jr., and D. M. Windsor
[1982]
1995.   Forest Production and Regulation of Primary Consumers on Barro Colorado Island. Pages 111–122 in *The Ecology of a Tropical Forest*, edited by E. G. Leigh, Jr., et al. Washington, D.C.: Smithsonian Institution Press.

Leigh, E. G., Jr., D. M. Windsor, A. S. Rand, and R. B. Foster
1990.   The Impact of the "El Niño" Drought of 1982–83 on a Panamanian Semideciduous Forest. Pages 473–486 in *Global Ecological Consequences of the 1982–83 El Niño–*

Southern Oscillation, edited by P. W. Glynn. Amsterdam: Elsevier.

Leigh, E. G., Jr., and S. J. Wright
1990.   Barro Colorado Island and Tropical Biology. Pages 28–47 in *Four Neotropical Rainforests*, edited by A. H. Gentry. New Haven: Yale University Press.

Leigh, E. G., Jr., S. J. Wright, F. E. Putz, and E. A. Herre
1993.   The Decline of Tree Diversity on Newly Isolated Tropical Islands: A Test of a Null Hypothesis and Some Implications. *Evolutionary Ecology*, 7:76–102.

Leighton, M., and D. R. Leighton
1983.   Vertebrate Responses to Fruiting Seasonality within a Bornean Rain Forest. Pages 181–196 in *Tropical Rain Forest: Ecology and Management*, edited by S. L. Sutton, T. C. Whitmore, and A. C. Chadwick. Oxford, U.K.: Blackwell Scientific Publications.

Lieberman, M., and D. Lieberman
1994.   Patterns of Density and Dispersion of Forest Trees. Pages 106–119 in *La Selva: Ecology and Natural History of a Neotropical Rain Forest*, edited by L. McDade et al. Chicago: University of Chicago Press.

Loiselle, B. A., and J. G. Blake
1991.   Temporal Variation in Birds and Fruits along an Elevational Gradient in Costa Rica. *Ecology*, 72:180–193.

Loveless, M. D.
1992.   Isozyme Variation in Tropical Trees: Patterns of Genetic Organization. *New Forests* 6:67–94.

MacArthur, R. H.
1961.   Population Effects of Natural Selection. *American Naturalist*, 95:195–199.

Machado, J.-L., and M. T. Tyree
1994.   Patterns of Hydraulic Architecture and Water Relations of Two Tropical Canopy Trees with Contrasting Leaf Phenologies: *Ochroma pyramidale* and *Pseudobombax septenatum*. *Tree Physiology*, 14:219–240.

Margulis, L.
1981.   *Symbiosis in Cell Evolution*. San Francisco: W. H. Freeman.

May, R. M.
1974.   On the Theory of Niche Overlap. *Theoretical Population Biology*, 5:297–332.

May, R. M., and R. H. MacArthur
1972.   Niche Overlap as a Function of Environmental Variability. *Proceedings of the National Academy of Sciences, USA*, 69:1109–1113.

Milton, K.
1980.   *The Foraging Strategy of Howler Monkeys*. New York: Columbia University Press.

[1982]
1995.   Dietary Quality and Demographic Regulation in a Howler Monkey Population. Pages 273–289 in *The Ecology of a Tropical Forest*, edited by E. G. Leigh, Jr., et al. Washington, D.C.: Smithsonian Institution Press.

1990.   Annual Mortality Patterns of a Mammal Community in Central Panama. *Journal of Tropical Ecology*, 6:493–499.

1991.   Leaf Change and Fruit Production in Six Neotropical Moraceae Species. *Journal of Ecology*, 79:1–26.

Milton, K., E. A. Laca, and M. W. Demment
1994. Successional Patterns of Mortality and Growth of Large Trees in a Panamanian Lowland Forest. *Journal of Ecology*, 82:79–87.

Milton, K., D. M. Windsor, D. W. Morrison, and M. A. Estribi
1982. Fruiting Phenologies in Two Neotropical *Ficus* Species. *Ecology*, 63:752–762.

Mitchell, B. J.
1989. Resources, Group Behavior, and Infant Development in White-faced Capuchin Monkeys, *Cebus capucinus*. Ph.D. dissertation, Department of Zoology, University of California, Berkeley.

Morrison, D. W.
1978. Foraging Ecology and Energetics of the Frugivorous Bat, *Artibeus jamaicensis*. *Ecology*, 59:716–723.
1980. Efficiency of Food Utilization by Fruit Bats. *Oecologia*, 45:270–273.

Morrison, D. W., and S. Hagen Morrison
1981. Economics of Harem Maintenance by a Neotropical Bat. *Ecology* 62:864–866.

Mulkey, S. S., A. P. Smith, S. J. Wright, J. L. Machado, and R. Dudley
1992. Contrasting Leaf Phenotypes Control Seasonal Variation in Water Loss in a Tropical Forest Shrub. *Proceedings of the National Academy of Sciences, USA*, 89:9084–9088.

Murawski, D. A., and J. L. Hamrick
1991. The Effect of the Density of Flowering Individuals on the Mating Systems of Nine Tropical Tree Species. *Heredity*, 67:167–174.

Nagy, K., and K. Milton
1979. Energy Metabolism and Food Consumption by Wild Howler Monkeys *(Alouatta palliatta)*. *Ecology*, 60:475–480.

Nason, J. D., E. A. Herre, and J. L. Hamrick
1995. Paternity Analysis of the Breeding Structure of Strangler Fig Populations: Evidence for Substantial Long-distance Wasp Dispersal. *Journal of Biogeography*, in press.

Nortcliff, S., and J. B. Thornes
1989. Variations in Soil Nutrients in Relation to Soil Moisture Status in a Tropical Forested Ecosystem. Pages 43–54 in *Mineral Nutrients in Tropical Forest and Savanna Ecosystems*, edited by J. Proctor. Oxford, U.K.: Blackwell Scientific Publications.

Patiño, S., E. A. Herre, and M. T. Tyree
1994. Physiological Determinants of *Ficus* Fruit Temperature and Implications for Survival of Pollinator Wasp Species: Comparative Physiology through an Energy Budget Approach. *Oecologia*, 100:13–20.

Patiño, S., M. T. Tyree, and E. A. Herre
1995. Comparisons of Hydraulic Architecture of Woody Plants of Differing Phylogeny and Growth Form with Special Reference to Free-standing and Hemi-epiphytic *Ficus* Species from Panama. *New Phytologist*, 129:125–134.

Phillips, O. L., P. Hall, A. H. Gentry, S. A. Sawyer, and R. Vásquez
1994. Dynamics and Species Richness of Tropical Rain Forests. *Proceedings of the National Academy of Sciences, USA*, 91:2805–2809.

Piperno, D.
1990. Fitolitos, arquelogía y cambios prehistóricos de la vegetación en un lote de cincuenta hectáreas de la Isla de Barro Colorado. Pages 153–156 in *Ecología de un bosque tropical: Ciclos estacionales y cambios de largo plazo*, edited by E. G. Leigh, Jr., A. S. Rand, and D. M. Windsor. Balboa, Panama: Smithsonian Tropical Research Institute.

Piperno, D. R., M. B. Bush, and P. A. Colinvaux
1991. Paleoecological Perspectives on Human Adaptation in Central Panama. II. The Holocene. *Geoarchaeology*, 6:227–250.

Poinar, G. O., Jr., and E. A. Herre
1991. Speciation and Adaptive Radiation in the Fig Wasp Nematode, *Parasitodiplogaster* (Diplogasteridae: Rhabditida) in Panama. *Revue de nématologie*, 14:361–374.

Putz, F. E., and K. Milton
[1982] Tree Mortality Rates on Barro Colorado Island. Pages
1995. 95–100 in *The Ecology of a Tropical Forest*, edited by E. G. Leigh, Jr., et al. Washington, D.C.: Smithsonian Institution Press.

Quinn, W. H.
1992. A Study of Southern Oscillation–related Climatic Activity for A.D. 622–1990 Incorporating Nile River Flood Data. Pages 119–149 in *El Niño: Historical and Paleoclimatic Aspects of the Southern Oscillation*, edited by H. F. Diaz and V. Markgraf. Cambridge: Cambridge University Press.

Rand, A. S., and W. M. Rand
[1982] Variation in Rainfall on Barro Colorado Island. Pages
1995. 47–59 in *The Ecology of a Tropical Forest*, edited by E. G. Leigh, Jr., et al. Washington, D.C.: Smithsonian Institution Press.

Regal, P. J.
1977. Ecology and Evolution of Flowering Plant Dominance. *Science*, 196:622–629.

Reich, P. B., and R. Borchert
1982. Phenology and Ecophysiology of the Tropical Tree, *Tabebuia neochrysantha* (Bignoniaceae). *Ecology*, 63:294–299.
1984. Water Stress and Tree Phenology in a Tropical Dry Forest in the Lowlands of Costa Rica. *Journal of Ecology*, 72:61–74.

Rosenzweig, M. L., and Z. Abramsky
1986. Centrifugal Community Organization. *Oikos*, 46:339–348.

Roubik, D. W.
1993. Direct Costs of Forest Reproduction, Bee-cycling and the Efficiency of Pollination Modes. *Journal of Bioscience*, 18:537–552.

Schemske, D. W.
1980. The Evolutionary Significance of Extrafloral Nectar Production by *Costus woodsonii* (Zingiberaceae): An Experimental Analysis of Ant Protection. *Journal of Ecology*, 68:959–967.
1982. Ecological Correlates of a Neotropical Mutualism: Ant Assemblages at *Costus* Extrafloral Nectaries. *Ecology*, 63:932–941.

Schupp, E. W.
1990.   Annual Variation in Seedfall, Postdispersal Predation, and Recruitment of a Neotropical Tree. *Ecology*, 71:504–515.
1992.   The Janzen–Connell Model for Tropical Tree Diversity: Population Implications and the Importance of Spatial Scale. *American Naturalist*, 140:526–530.

Schupp, E. W., and D. H. Feener, Jr.
1991.   Phylogeny, Lifeform and Habitat Dependence of Ant-defended Plants in a Panamanian Forest. Pages 175–197 in *Ant–Plant Interactions*, edited by C. R. Huxley and D. F. Cutler. Oxford: Oxford University Press.

Sevenster, J. G., and J. J. M. van Alphen
1993a.   A Life History Trade-off in *Drosophila* Species and Community Structure in Variable Environments. *Journal of Animal Ecology*, 62:720–736.
1993b.   Coexistence in Stochastic Environments through a Life History Trade Off in *Drosophila*. Pages 155–172 in *Adaptation in Stochastic Environments*, edited by J. Yoshimura and C. W. Clark. Lecture Notes in Biomathematics, no. 98. Berlin: Springer.

Silver, W. L., F. N. Scatena, A. H. Johnson, T. G. Siccama, and M. J. Sanchez
1994.   Nutrient Availability in a Montane Wet Tropical Forest: Spatial Patterns and Methodological Considerations. *Plant and Soil*, 164:129–145.

Smith, N. G.
[1982]   Population Irruptions and Periodic Migrations in the
1995.   Day-flying Moth *Urania fulgens*. Pages 331–344 in *The Ecology of a Tropical Forest*, edited by E. G. Leigh, Jr., et al. Washington, D.C.: Smithsonian Institution Press.
1992.   Reproductive Behaviour and Ecology of *Urania* (Lepidoptera: Uraniidae) Moths and of Their Larval Food Plants, *Omphalea* spp. (Euphorbiaceae). Pages 576–593 in *Insects of Panama and Mesoamerica: Selected Studies*, edited by D. Quintero and A. Aiello. Oxford: Oxford University Press.

Smythe, N.
1970.   Relationships between Fruiting Seasons and Seed Dispersal Methods in a Neotropical Forest. *American Naturalist*, 104:25–35.
1978.   The Natural History of the Central American Agouti (*Dasyprocta punctata*). *Smithsonian Contributions to Zoology*, 257:1–52.
[1982]   The Seasonal Abundance of Night-flying Insects in a
1995.   Neotropical Forest. Pages 309–318 in *The Ecology of a Tropical Forest*, edited by E. G. Leigh, Jr., et al. Washington, D.C.: Smithsonian Institution Press.
1989.   Seed Survival in the Palm *Astrocaryum standleyanum*: Evidence for Dependence upon Its Seed Dispersers. *Biotropica*, 21:50–56.

Smythe, N., W. E. Glanz, and E. G. Leigh, Jr.
[1982]   Population Regulation in Some Terrestrial Frugivores.
1995.   Pages 227–238 in *The Ecology of a Tropical Forest*, edited by E. G. Leigh, Jr., et al. Washington, D.C.: Smithsonian Institution Press.

Sollins, P., F. Sancho M., R. Mata Ch., and R. L. Sanford, Jr.
1994.   Soils and Soil Process Research. Pages 34–53 in *La Selva: Ecology and Natural History of a Neotropical Rain Forest*, edited by L. McDade et al. Chicago: University of Chicago Press.

Sternberg, L. da S. L., S. S. Mulkey, and S. J. Wright
1989.   Ecological Interpretation of Leaf Carbon Isotope Ratios: Influence of Respired Carbon Dioxide. *Ecology*, 70:1317–1324.

Tanaka, S., D. L. Denlinger, and H. Wolda
1987.   Daylength and Humidity as Environmental Cues for Diapause Termination in a Tropical Beetle. *Physiological Entomology*, 12:213–224.
1988.   Seasonal Changes in the Photoperiodic Response Regulating Diapause in a Tropical Beetle, *Stenotarsus rotundatus*. *Journal of Insect Physiology*, 34:1135–1142.

Tanaka, S., and H. Wolda
1987.   Seasonal Wing Length Dimorphism in a Tropical Seed Bug: Ecological Significance of the Short-winged Form. *Oecologia*, 73:559–565.
1988.   Oviposition Behavior and Diel Rhythms of Flight and Reproduction in Two Species of Tropical Seed Bugs. *Proceedings of the Koninklijke Nederlandse Akademie van Wetenschappen*, Series C, 91:165–174.

Tanaka, S., H. Wolda, and D. L. Denlinger
1987.   Seasonality and Its Physiological Regulation in Three Neotropical Insect Taxa from Barro Colorado Island, Panama. *Insect Science and Its Application*, 8:507–514.
1988.   Group Size Affects the Metabolic Rate of a Tropical Beetle. *Physiological Entomology*, 13:239–241.

Terborgh, J.
1973.   On the Notion of Favorableness in Plant Ecology. *American Naturalist*, 107:481–501.
1983.   *Five New World Primates: A Study in Comparative Ecology*. Princeton: Princeton University Press.
1986a.   Community Aspects of Frugivory in Tropical Forests. Pages 371–384 in *Frugivores and Seed Dispersal*, edited by A. Estrada and T. H. Fleming. Dordrecht, Netherlands: W. Junk.
1986b.   Keystone Plant Resources in the Tropical Forest. Pages 330–344 in *Conservation Biology: The Science of Scarcity and Diversity*, edited by M. Soulé. Sunderland, Mass.: Sinauer Associates.
1988.   The Big Things That Run the World—A Sequel to E. O. Wilson. *Conservation Biology*, 2:402–403.

Terborgh, J., and S. J. Wright
1994.   Effects of Mammalian Herbivores on Plant Recruitment in Two Neotropical Forests. *Ecology*, 75:1829–1833.

Thorington, R. W., Jr., B. Tannenbaum, A. Tarak, and R. Rudran
[1982]   Distribution of Trees on Barro Colorado Island: A
1995.   Five-Hectare Sample. Pages 83–94 in *The Ecology of a Tropical Forest*, edited by E. G. Leigh, Jr., et al. Washington, D.C.: Smithsonian Institution Press.

Tilman, D., and S. Pacala
1993.   The Maintenance of Species Richness in Plant Communities. Pages 13–25 in *Species Diversity in Ecological Communities*, edited by R. E. Ricklefs and D. Schluter. Chicago: University of Chicago Press.

Tissue, D. T., and S. J. Wright
1995.   Effect of Seasonal Water Availability on Phenology and the Annual Shoot Carbohydrate Cycle of Tropical Forest Shrubs. *Functional Ecology* 9:518–527.

Tyree, M. T., D. A. Snyderman, T. R. Wilmot, and J.-L. Machado
1991.   Water Relations and Hydraulic Architecture of a

Tropical Tree *(Schefflera morototoni)*. *Plant Physiology,* 96:1105–1113.

Vleck, C. M., and D. Vleck
1979.   Metabolic Rate in Five Tropical Bird Species. *Condor,* 81:89–91.

Waring, R. H., and W. H. Schlesinger
1985.   *Forest Ecosystems: Concepts and Management.* Orlando, Fla.: Academic Press.

Welden, C. W., S. W. Hewett, S. P. Hubbell, and R. B. Foster
1991.   Sapling Survival, Growth and Recruitment: Relationship to Canopy Height in a Neotropical Forest. *Ecology,* 72:35–50.

Wiebes, J. T.
1979.   Co-evolution of Figs and Their Insect Pollinators. *Annual Review of Ecology and Systematics,* 10:1–12.

Williams, C. B.
1958.   *Insect Migration.* London: Collins.

Wilson, D. E., C. O. Handley, Jr., and A. L. Gardner
1991.   Reproduction on Barro Colorado Island. Pages 43–52 in Demography and Natural History of the Common Fruit Bat, *Artibeus jamaicensis,* on Barro Colorado Island, Panamá, edited by C. O. Handley, Jr., D. E. Wilson, and A. L. Gardner. *Smithsonian Contributions to Zoology,* 511:1–173.

Wilson, D. S.
1975.   A Theory of Group Selection. *Proceedings of the National Academy of Sciences, USA,* 72:143–146.
1980.   *The Natural Selection of Populations and Communities.* Menlo Park, Calif.: Benjamin/Cummings.

Windsor, D. M.
1990.   Climate and Moisture Availability in a Tropical Forest: Long-term Records from Barro Colorado Island, Panamá. *Smithsonian Contributions to the Earth Sciences,* 29:1–145.

Windsor, D. M., D. W. Morrison, M. A. Estribi, and B. de Leon
1989.   Phenology of Fruit and Leaf Production by "Strangler" Figs on Barro Colorado Island, Panamá. *Experientia,* 45:647–653.

Windsor, D. M., A. S. Rand, and W. M. Rand
1990.   Caracteristicas de la precipitación en la Isla de Barro Colorado. Pages 53–71 in *Ecología de un bosque tropical: Ciclos estacionales y cambios de largo plazo,* edited by E. G. Leigh, Jr., A. S. Rand, and D. M. Windsor. Balboa, Panama: Smithsonian Tropical Research Institute.

Wolda, H.
[1982]   Seasonality of Homoptera on Barro Colorado Island.
1995.   Pages 319–330 in *The Ecology of a Tropical Forest,* edited by E. G. Leigh, Jr., et al. Washington, D.C.: Smithsonian Institution Press.
1983.   Spatial and Temporal Variation in Abundance in Tropical Animals. Pages 93–105 in *Tropical Rain Forest: Ecology and Management,* edited by S. L. Sutton, T. C. Whitmore, and A. C. Chadwick. Oxford, U.K.: Blackwell Scientific.
1988.   Insect Seasonality: Why? *Annual Review of Ecology and Systematics,* 19:1–18.
1989a.   Seasonal Cues in Tropical Organisms. Rainfall? Not Necessarily! *Oecologia,* 80:437–442.
1989b.   Energy Requirements of Tropical Insects during an Adverse Season. Pages 1–9 in *Proceedings of the Nutritional Ecology of Insects and Environment Symposium.* Muzeffarhagar, India.
1992.   Trends in Abundance of Tropical Forest Insects. *Oecologia,* 89:47–52.

Wolda, H., and D. L. Denlinger
1984.   Diapause in a Large Aggregation of a Tropical Beetle. *Ecological Entomology,* 9:217–230.

Wolda, H., and R. Foster
1978.   *Zunacetha annulata* (Lepidoptera: Dioptidae): An Outbreak Insect in a Neotropical Forest. *Geo-Eco-Trop,* 2:443–454.

Wolda, H., and S. Tanaka
1987.   Dormancy and Aggregation in a Tropical Insect *Jadera obscura* (Hemiptera: Rhopalidae). *Proceedings of the Koninklijke Nederlandse Akademie van Wetenschappen,* Series C, 90:351–366.

Wolda, H., and S. J. Wright
1992.   Artificial Dry Season Rain and Its Effects on Tropical Insect Abundance and Seasonality. *Proceedings of the Koninklijke Nederlandse Akademie van Wetenschappen,* 95:535–548.

Wong, M., S. J. Wright, S. P. Hubbell, and R. B. Foster
1990.   The Spatial Pattern and Reproductive Consequences of Outbreak Defoliation in *Quararibea asterolepis,* a Tropical Tree. *Journal of Ecology,* 78:579–588.

Woodring, W. P.
1958.   Geology of Barro Colorado Island, Canal Zone. *Smithsonian Miscellaneous Collections,* 135 (3): 1–39.

Worthington, A.
[1982]   Population Sizes and Breeding Rhythms of Two Species of Manakins in Relation to Food Supply. Pages 213–225 in *The Ecology of a Tropical Forest,* edited by E. G. Leigh, Jr., et al. Washington, D.C.: Smithsonian Institution Press.
1990.   Comportamiento de forrajeo de dos especies de saltarines en respuesta a la escasez de frutos. Pages 285–304 in *Ecología de un bosque tropical: Ciclos estacionales y cambios de largo plazo,* edited by E. G. Leigh, Jr., A. S. Rand, and D. M. Windsor. Balboa, Panama: Smithsonian Tropical Research Institute.

Wright, S. J.
1990.   Cumulative Satiation of a Seed Predator over the Fruiting Season of Its Host. *Oikos,* 58:272–276.
1991.   Seasonal Drought and the Phenology of Understory Shrubs in a Tropical Moist Forest. *Ecology,* 72:1643–1657.

Wright, S. J., and F. H. Cornejo
1990a.   Seasonal Drought and the Timing of Flowering and Leaf Fall in a Neotropical Forest. Pages 49–61 in *Reproductive Ecology of Tropical Forest Plants,* edited by K. S. Bawa and M. Hadley. Park Ridge, N.J.: Parthenon Publishing.
1990b.   Seasonal Drought and Leaf Fall in a Neotropical Forest. *Ecology,* 71:1165–1175.

Wright, S. J., M. E. Gompper, and B. de León
1994.   Are Large Predators Keystone Species in Neotropical Forests? The Evidence from Barro Colorado Island. *Oikos,* 71:279–294.

Yavitt, J. B., and R. K. Wieder
1988.   Nitrogen, Phosphorus, and Sulfur Properties of Some Forest Soils on Barro Colorado Island, Panama. *Biotropica*, 20:2–10.

Yavitt, J. B., R. K. Wieder, and S. J. Wright
1993.   Soil Nutrient Dynamics in Response to Irrigation of a Panamanian Tropical Moist Forest. *Biogeochemistry*, 19:1–25.

Zaret, T. M., and A. S. Rand
1971.   Competition in Tropical Stream Fishes: Support for the Competitive Exclusion Principle. *Ecology*, 52:336–342.

Zimmermann, M. H.
1983.   *Xylem Structure and the Ascent of Sap*. Berlin: Springer.

Zimmermann, U., A. Haase, D. Langbein, and F. Meinzer
1993.   Mechanisms of Long-distance Water Transport in Plants: A Re-examination of Some Paradigms in the Light of New Evidence. *Philosophical Transactions of the Royal Society of London*, Series B, 341:19–31.

Zimmermann, U., F. C. Meinzer, R. Benkert, J. J. Zhu, H. Schneider, G. Goldstein, E. Kuchenbrod, and A. Haase
1994.   Xylem Water Transport: Is the Available Evidence Consistent with the Cohesion Theory? *Plant, Cell and Environment*, 17:1169–1181.

Zotz, G., M. T. Tyree, and H. Cochard
1994.   Hydraulic Architecture, Water Relations and Vulnerability to Cavitation of *Clusia uvitana* Pittier: A C_3-CAM Tropical Hemiepiphyte. *New Phytologist*, 127:287–295.

Zotz, G., and K. Winter
1993.   Short-term Photosynthesis Measurements Predict Leaf Carbon Balance in Tropical Rain-forest Canopy Plants. *Planta*, 191:409–412.
1994a.   Photosynthesis of a Tropical Canopy Tree, *Ceiba pentandra*, in a Lowland Forest in Panama. *Tree Physiology*, 14:1291–1301.
1994b.   A One-year Study on Carbon, Water and Nutrient Relationships in a Tropical C_3-CAM Hemiepiphyte, *Clusia uvitana* Pittier. *New Phytologist*, 127:45–60.
1994c.   Annual Carbon Balance and Nitrogen-Use Efficiency in Tropical C_3 and CAM Epiphytes. *New Phytologist*, 126:481–492.
1994d.   Predicting Annual Carbon Balance from Leaf Nitrogen. *Naturwissenschaften*, 81:449.

DATE DUE	
APR 1 5 2000	
GAYLORD	PRINTED IN U.S.A.